Transnational Law

Transnational Law

Cases and Problems in an Interconnected World

Alfred C. Aman, Jr.
Roscoe C. O'Byrne Professor of Law
Indiana University
Maurer School of Law

Carol J. Greenhouse
Arthur W. Marks '19 Professor of Anthropology
Princeton University

Carolina Academic Press
Durham, North Carolina

ISBN 978-1-42249-640-4
eISBN 978-1-63284-978-6
LCCN 2017939772

Carolina Academic Press, LLC
700 Kent Street
Durham, North Carolina 27701
Telephone (919) 489-7486
Fax (919) 493-5668
www.cap-press.com

Printed in the United States of America

Contents

Table of Cases

Preface

The term "transnational law" was coined in 1956 by Phillip Jessup, when he gave his Storrs Lectures at Yale Law School that title.[1] In those lectures, he claimed that transnational law includes "all law which regulates actions or events that transcend national frontiers. Both public and private international law are included, as are other rules which do not wholly fit into such standard categories." In the decades since Jessup's lectures, the term *transnational law* has become well established, even if its usage remains slippery—sometimes referring to practical questions such as jurisdiction and remedies, and sometimes to theoretical questions such as arise in relation to the disciplinarity of law, or the status of law as scientific knowledge, or the distinction between academic and political work.[2] In general, transnational law is taken to refer to the body or bodies of law that govern across jurisdictions, or in the gaps between them. This casebook takes its point of departure in the possibility that those apparent gaps may be fully inhabited. We approach our subject matter from a vantage point grounded in the various legal settings in which domestic legal institutions struggle with questions arising from the tensions between the inherently extraterritorial aspects of capitalism and the presumptively territorial commitments of national sovereignty.

Jessup's celebrated formulation serves us well, since—at least for our purposes—its key elements are in his references to *transcending national frontiers* and to the *partial fit* with standard legal categories. These phrases are related, in that they point to the relevance of domestic law as the main location of transnational law, and, correspondingly, to the ways transnational law flows through standard categories while also unsettling them. That is our approach in this volume: we focus on the relationship between domestic and transnational law, as that relationship is institutionally produced in treaties, agreements, codes, and judgments, and as it introduces both constraints and opportunities for those who would choreograph the movements of

1. Phillip Jessup, Transnational Law: Storrs Lectures on Jurisprudence (1956).

2. "The ambiguity of technical terms, legal concepts and principles coincides with the daily challenge to position oneself and one's work. This anxiety is particularly prevalent where academic research, writing and teaching is so intertwined with real politics. The open-endedness of categories such as labour law, economic law, social law, 'public' and 'private' law, allows us to lay bare and to make visible 'national traditions' of legal scholarship; in turn, these traditions are themselves intertwined, non-linear, disputed and contested." Peer C. Zumbansen, *Transnational Law* (Comparative Research in Law & Political Economy, Research Paper 09/2008) http://dx.doi.org/10.2139/ssrn.1105576.

people, goods, and capital investment. The traditional authority of the president in foreign affairs, for example, takes on new meaning—and significant new powers—in the context of a world economy now reliant on trade agreements and other such protocols. There are many such examples in the materials of the book; their common touchstone is uncertainty.

Accordingly, we delve into the shifting ground under issues of trade, territoriality, separation of powers, and related questions in the following chapters. For now, suffice it to say that our goal in this book is not a comprehensive account of transnational law. Such would entail a major review of the law of trade, banking and securities, family law, telecommunications, human rights, humanitarianism, immigration, and international law, as well as standard domestic law categories such as torts, business law, constitutional law, criminal law, property and administrative law—among other components of the standard law curriculum. While we intend this book to be useful to students, scholars and practitioners as a stand-alone resource, we would be well pleased to know that it is useful as a supplement to resources in these fields (including more technical and comprehensive accounts of transnational law principles, procedures, jurisdiction and litigation). We also hope that the book will be useful to social science scholars engaged with law.

It would be natural for readers to expect an account that follows the contours of the world economy. However, the seemingly borderless world of global capitalism is only one vector of contemporary transnationalism. Others inhere in highly territorialized or localized scenarios—since that is where people live, work, shop and vote, and that is where companies are located and corporations registered. Our approach emphasizes the tensions between globalism and localism as domestic law contends with problems that—as Jessup phrased the matter—transcend national frontiers. Our attention to the local aspects of transnational law also invites analytical resources beyond law. This is an interdisciplinary account, drawing especially on anthropologists' ethnographic accounts of law. Contrary to the stereotype of anthropology, ethnographic accounts of law do not deal mainly with custom or quaint localisms, but with the ways interpersonal relations and various forms of collective social life both shape and are shaped by their context in regional, national and transnational affairs. Ethnography is especially useful, then, as a resource for understanding both the diversity of human arrangements under common or uncommon constraints, and interrelationships among categories of law that, seen from above, might seem to be unrelated (e.g., kinship obligations and international investment—an example from Chapter 6).

Our book is arranged in three parts, after an introductory chapter that elaborates the scope and aims of the volume and explicates the key terms of its analysis. Part I ("Governance through treaties and international agreements") first takes up the law, politics, and social effects of multinational agreements on tariffs and climate change. Part II ("Rights and responsibilities offshore") takes up situations from the spheres of multinational corporations in which offshore investment creates complex webs of public-private interlegality with heavy consequences for workers. Part III

("Governance through government") considers the implications of transnational law for the relationship between judicial and arbitral regimes, and, in the U.S., in relation to questions of judicial review and separation of powers—culminating in a discussion of what we call the transnational executive.

In addition to emphasizing the book's selectivity in focusing on particular dilemmas of transnational law where its social and political effects are particularly evident, we should also note the book's periodization—for the most part—in the Clinton, Bush and Obama years. Divided government and impeachment during the Clinton years, followed by the intensive unilateralism of the Bush years and the obstructionist response to the Obama administration in the U.S. Congress, have made for a turbulent domestic front in relation to presidential power, "free trade," human rights, collective bargaining, and immigration. The case materials reflect that turbulence, as territoriality became increasingly politicized in terms of its potential for encoding unilateralism in the security context, and, more recently, restrictions on immigration, particularly across the southern border of the United States. Such rationales and codings are sometimes explicit (as in the case materials discussed in Part III) but not always; our commentary teases out these wider realms of significance as the Trump administration begins.

In sum, we hope that our interdisciplinary effort will be helpful to readers interested in law as a dimension of contemporary transnationalism. In each chapter, we offer critical and activist perspectives, as well as those of the relevant courts or other legal institutions—both to remind readers that law and markets remain indelibly interconnected, and that the character and consequences of those interconnections are not givens. A more equitable world is always possible.

Acknowledgments

We wish to thank students from the Indiana University Maurer School of Law who served as research assistants during the course of this project. Ryan Weiss '13 and Jillian Rountree '13 provided invaluable help in the early stages of this book. As the project neared completion, we benefitted from assistance in many forms from a superb team: Alexandra Muir '16, Drew Waldbeser '16, Michael Ruderman '16, Landyn Rookard '16, Alexander Avtgis '17, Brandon Dawson '17, Allison Gardner '17, Stephanie Goldkopf '18, Zena Braish '18 and Brad Schlotter '18. Each of these students contributed siginificantly to the completion of this book and we are very grateful for all of their help.

In addition, our very special thanks to Jane Leigh Decker, who took on the heavy responsibility of managing the permissions process. Her dedication and steady hand, as well as her judicious treatment of the many issues that arose, were indispensable to timely completion of the work. We are extremely grateful.

Professor Aman would like to express his gratitude to Professor Peer Zumbansen, for their many exchanges on the subject of transnational law, particularly in connection with their participation as co-conveners of an international and interdisciplinary Some Institutes of Advanced Study Summer Institute (SIASSI), initiated by Professor Zumbansen, on "Regulating the World Society: Law, Governance and the Quest for Global Justice." The Summer Institute was held under the joint aegis of the Institute for Advanced Study (Wissenschaftskolleg zu Berlin) and the National Humanities Center, in Berlin and Bloomington, Indiana (in 2011 and 2012, respectively).

A book of this kind is woven of many threads, and for each of us as co-authors, these tie back to years of conversations with colleagues and with students too numerous to mention by name. We are deeply grateful to our respective institutions—Indiana University Maurer School of Law and Princeton University—for many forms of material and intellectual support. We feel particularly fortunate to have had opportunities to hone our own ideas over the years in stimulating dialogue with undergraduates, graduate students and law students in our respective seminars at Indiana and Princeton. This book is for them.

We list below, with grateful acknowledgment, the authors and publishers who kindly granted us permission to excerpt their copyrighted work. In most cases, notes and references have been omitted from the excerpts (exceptions are noted in the main text). Credit lines below are grouped by chapter, and appear in alphabetical order *by author.* The format of each listing is as follows: copyright holder, followed by author's name and the source citation, supplemented where required or requested by the rights-holder with additional details. Specific citations for the excerpts themselves are included in the main text. Where requested or required by the rights-holder, additional details also accompany the excerpts in the main text:

Chapter 1

The Lawfare Institute: John Bellinger, *U.S. Delegation Asserts Article 16 of Convention Against Torture Applies Outside U.S. Territory in Certain Circumstances, but Law of Armed Conflict "Takes Precedence" in Situations of Armed Conflict*, LawFare Blog, November 12, 2014.

Nebraska Law Review: Harold Hongju Koh, *Transnational Legal Process*, 75 Nebraska Law Review 181 (1996)

Oxford University Press: Ole Jacob Sending and Iver B. Neumann, *Governance to Governmentality: Analyzing NGOs, States, and Power*, 50 International Studies Quarterly 651 (2006)

Stanford Journal of Civil Rights and Civil Liberties: Ayelet Shachar, *The Shifting Border of Immigration Regulation*, 3 Stanford Journal of Civil Rights and Civil Liberties 165, 166–69 (2007). Reprinted with the permission of the Stanford Journal of Civil Rights and Civil Liberties solely for this English-language edition.

Sage Publications: Mariana Valverde, *Jurisdiction and Scale: Legal "Technicalities" as Resources for Theory*, 18 Social and Legal Studies 139 (2009)

Chapter 2

Yale Law Journal: Alfred C. Aman, Jr., *The Earth as Eggshell Plaintiff*, 102 Yale Law Journal 2107 (1993)

Center for Climate and Energy Solutions: Daniel Bodansky, *Legal Options for U.S. Acceptance of a New Climate Change Agreement* (2015)

Climate Law: Daniel Cole, *From Global to Polycentric Climate Governance*, 2 Climate Law 295 (2011)

University of California-Irvine Law Review: Scott Cummings, *Preemptive Strike: Law in the Campaign for Clean Trucks*, 4 University of California-Irvine Law Review 939 (2014)

American Constitution Society for Law and Policy: Oona Hathaway, *The Case for Replacing Article II Treaties with Ex Post Congressional-Executive Agreements*, American Constitutional Society Issue Brief (2008)

Yale University Press: Douglas Kysar, Regulating from Nowhere. Yale University Press (2010)

Virginia Journal of International Law: Hari M. Osofsky, *Is Climate Change "International"? Litigation's Diagonal Regulatory Role*, 49 Virginia Journal of International Law 585 (2009)

Springer: Elinor Ostrom, *Nested Externalities and Polycentric Institutions: Must We Wait for Global Solutions to Climate Change Before Taking Actions at Other Scales?* 49 Journal of Economic Theory 353 (2012)

Chapter 3

Harvard Law Review Association: Bruce Ackerman and David Golove, *Is NAFTA Constitutional?* 108 Harvard Law Review 799 (1994/5)

John Wiley & Sons: Mark Aspinwall, *NAFTA-ization: Regoinalization and Domestic Politial Adjustment in the North American Economic Area,* 47 Journal of Common Market Studies 1 (2009)

Academy of Political Science: William P. Avery, *Domestic Interests in NAFTA Bargaining,* 113 Political Science Quarterly 283 (1998)

Hoover Institution Press: Michael J. Boskin, NAFTA at Twenty (2014)

Robert J. Carbaugh, *NAFTA and the U.S.-Mexico Trucking Dispute,* 4 International and Global Economic Studies 1 (2011)

University of Calgary Press: Stephen J. Randall and Herman W. Konrad, Introduction—NAFTA in Transition (1995)

Cambridge University Press: Saskia Sassen, The Mobility of Labor and Capital: A Study in International Investment and Labor Flow © 1988, Cambridge University Press. Reprinted with the permission of Cambridge University Press.

Taylor & Francis Publishers: Fernanda Somuano, *The Changing Structure of Mexican Politics* in Laura Randall, ed. The Changing Structure of Mexico, 2nd Edition. Routledge (2015)

Houston Journal of International Law: Marcia J. Staff and Christina W. Lewis, *Arbitration under NAFTA Chapter 11: Past, Present, and Future,* 25 Houston Journal of International Law 301 (2002)

Chapter 4

American Society of International Law: Jagdish Bhagwati, *Afterword: The Question of Linkage,* in Symposium: The Boundaries of the WTO (ed. José E. Alvarez) 96 American Journal of International Law 126 (2002)

Oxford University Press: Daniel Bodansky and Jessica C. Lawrence, *Trade and Environment* in The Oxford Handbook of International Trade Law (Daniel Bethlehem, Isabelle van Damme, Ronald McRae and Rodney Neufeld, eds.), 506 (2009). By permission of Oxford University Press.

North Carolina Journal of International Law and Commercial Regulation: Renee Chartres and Bryan Mercurio, *Afterword: A Call for an Agreement on Trade-Related Aspects of Labor,* 37 North Carolina Journal of International Law and Commercial Regulation 665 (2012)

Princeton University Press: Christina Davis, Why Adjudicate? (2012)

Jean Monnet Center—New York University: Robert Howse, *Human Rights in the WTO*, Jean Monnet Working Paper 12/02) (2002)

International Center for Trade and Sustainable Development (ICTSD): ICTSD, *WTO Members Comment on Indigenous Amicus Brief in Lumber Dispute*. 12 May 2002.

Council on Foreign Relations: Robert Z. Lawrence, *The United States and the WTO Dispute Settlement System*, Council on Foreign Relations No. 25 (March 2007), Copyright 2007 by the Council on Foreign Relations. Reprinted with permission.

Thomson Reuters: Robin Miller, *Effect of World Trade Organization (WTO) Decisions Upon United States*, 17 American Law Reports, Fed 2d 1 (2007)

Oxford University Press—Journals: Ernst-Ulrich Petersmann, *The WTO Constitution and Human Rights*, 3 Journal of International Economic Law 19 (2000)

Oxford University Press—Journals: Elizabeth Trujillo, *A Dialogical Approach to Trade and Environment*, 16 Journal of International Economic Law 535 (2013)

University of Kansas Law Review: Lori M. Wallach, *Accountable Governance in the Era of Globalization*, 50 University of Kansas Law Review 4 (2002)

Wolters Kluwer: Humberto Zúñiga Schroder, Harmonization, Equivalence and Mutual Recognition of Standards in WTO Law, © 2011. Reproduced with the permission of the publisher.

Chapter 5

Apple Inc.: Apple Supplier Code of Responsibility, 2016. Courtesy of Apple Inc.

Stanford Law and Policy Review: Harry Arthurs, *Extraterritoriality by Other Means: How Labor Law Sneaks Across Borders, Conquers Minds, and Controls Workplaces Abroad*, 21 Stanford Law and Policy Review 527 (2010)

Annual Reviews, Inc.: Kevin Davis, *Legal Indicators: The Power of Quantitative Measures in Law.* 10 Annual Review of Law and Social Science 37 (2014)

School of Advanced International Studies Review of International Affairs: Yukon Huang, *China's Conflict Between Economic and Political Liberalization*, 32 SAIS Review of International Affairs 51, at 52 (2012)

Electronics Industry Citizenship Coalition (EICC): EICC Code of Conduct (2016).

Cambridge University Press: Cesar Rodríguez-Garavito, *Nike's Law*, in Law and Globalization from Below (Boaventura de Sousa Santos and Cesar Rodríguez-Garavito, eds.), at 64 (2005)

Chapter 6

International Labor Rights Forum: Laborrights.org (1) *Stop Firestone Coalition Celebrates Victory as Liberian Supreme Court Decision Approves Union Election on Firestone Plantation*. December 21, 2007. (2) *Firestone Agricultural Workers Union of Liberia Awarded 2007 George Meany-Lane Kirkland Human Rights Award*. March 5, 2008.

Yale Law Journal: Harold Hongju Koh, *Transnational Public Law Litigation*, 100 Yale Law Journal 2347 (1991)

Chapter 7

Indiana University Press, Journals: Alfred C. Aman, Jr. *Globalization and the Privatization of Welfare Administration in Indiana*, 20 Indiana Journal of Global Legal Studies 377(2013), pp. 400–01, 409–412. ©. Reprinted with permission of Indiana University Press.

Fordham Urban Law Journal: Alfred C. Aman, Jr. & Carol J. Greenhouse, *Prison Privatization and Inmate Labor in the Global Economy: Reframing the Debate over Private Prisons*, 42 Fordham Urb. L. J. 355 (2014)

Stanford Journal of Complex Litigation: Theodore J. Boutrous, *Ten Lessons from the Chevron Ecuador Litigation: The Defense Perspective*, 1 Stanford Journal of Complex Litigation 219 (2013). Reprinted with the permission of the Stanford Journal of Complex Litigation solely for this English-language edition.

Indiana University Press, Journals: A. Claire Cutler, *Transformations in Statehood, the Investor-State Regime, and the New Constitutionalism*, Indiana Journal of Global Legal Studies 23:1 (2016), pg. 110–111. ©. Reprinted with permission of Indiana University Press

Stanford Journal of Complex Litigation: Michael B. Goldhaber, *The Rise of Arbitral Power over Domestic Courts*, 1 Stanford Journal of Complex Litigation 373 (2013). Reprinted with the permission of the Stanford Journal of Complex Litigation solely for this English-language edition.

Stanford Journal of Complex Litigation: Judith Kimerling, *Lessons from the Chevron Ecuador Litigation: Proposed Intervenors' Perspective*, 1 Stanford Journal of Complex Litigation 241 (2013). Reprinted with the permission of the Stanford Journal of Complex Litigation solely for this English-language edition.

Harvard University Press: Saskia Sassen, Expulsions: Brutality and Complexity in the Global Economy. Cambridge, Mass.: The Belknap Press of the Harvard University Press, Copyright © 2014 by the President and Fellows of Harvard College.

European Trade Union Institute (ETUI): Isabelle Schömann, *ISO 26000: The New Face of Corporate Social Responsibility?* ETUI Policy Brief 1-2012 (January, 2012)

Transnational Institute (TNI): TNI, Primer, February 2013.

Chapter 8

Indiana University Press, Journals: Hannah Buxbaum, *National Jurisdiction and Global Business Networks*, Indiana Journal of Global Legal Studies vol. 17 No. 1, pp. 168–173 © (2010). Reprinted with permission of Indiana University Press.

Oxford University Press—Journals: Martti Koskenniemi, *The Politics of International Law—20 Years Later*, 20 European Journal of International Law 7 (2009)

Bloomsbury Publishing: Martti Koskenniemi, The Politics of International Law. Hart Publishing (2011), used by permission of Bloomsbury Publishing Plc.

Cambridge University Press: Tonya L. Putnam, Courts without Borders: Domestic Sources of U.S. Extraterritoriality in the Regulatory Sphere, Cambridge University Press. Copyright © 2009 The IO Foundation. Reprinted with permission of Cambridge University Press.

Virginia Journal of International Law: Anne-Marie Slaughter, *Judicial Globalization*, 40 Virginia Journal of International Law 1103 (2000)

University of Chicago Press: Alan O. Sykes, *Transnational Forum Shopping as a Trade and Investment Issue*, 37 Journal of Legal Studies 339 (2008)

Chapter 9

Fordham Law Review: Jason A. Cade, *Enforcing Immigration Equity*, 84 Fordham Law Review 661 (2015)

Harvard Civil Rights—Civil Liberties Law Review: Harold Edgar and Benno C. Schmidt, Jr., *Curtiss-Wright Comes Home: Executive Power and National Security Secrecy*, 21 Harvard Civil Rights—Civil Liberties Law Review 349 (1986).

Harvard Law Review Association: Harvard Law Review, *Federal Courts—Standing—Sixth Circuit Denies Standing to Challenge Terrorist Surveillance Program—ACLU v. NSA, 493 F.3rd 644 (6th Cir. 2007)*, 121 Harvard Law Review 922 (2008)

California Law Review: Geoffrey Stone, *National Security v. Civil Liberties*, Reprinted from California Law Review—95 Cal. L. Rev. 2203 (2007) © 2007 by permission of the California Law Review, Inc.

Transnational Law

Chapter 1

Introduction

I. What and where is transnational law?

In this chapter, we introduce our discussion of transnational law with an overview of the book's thesis, scope and aims, as well as the main concepts underlying our approach. The problems addressed by transnational law are wide ranging. International trade, international security, human rights and the global environment—together with their problems of rule-making and norms, jurisdiction, implementation and enforcement, and so forth—are no doubt prominent for readers as they pick up this book. But these areas of transnational legal work do not operate in isolation from each other; their convergences, divergences, synergies, and contradictions must be central to any analysis—whether the analyst is a student, practitioner, or scholar. Referring to the international law field, Oren Perez takes this state of affairs as a point of departure for a reassessment of international law and its social effects:

> Modern international law seems to be in disarray. The classic doctrines of international law, with their focus on sovereignty, state consent, custom, and treaty, do not provide a satisfactory explanation for many of the practices and institutional structures that fill the global legal universe. The contemporary legal terrain seems to be characterized by overlapping jurisdictions, inconsistent doctrinal interpretations, and competing worldviews. But what are the social implications of the deepening fragmentation and increasing complexity of the global legal system?

Oren Perez, *Purity Lost: The Paradoxical Face of the New Transnational Legal Body*, 33 Brooklyn L.J. 3 (2007).

In the spirit of Perez's question, we focus on key zones of such activity—zones where established domains of domestic law are unsettled by their application to transnational legal problems, or where transnational law is revised as it is absorbed into domestic law. We should emphasize from the outset, however, that we make no *a priori* assumptions as to the extent to which transnational and national legal systems are or might eventually become integrated into some global system. This is for three reasons, spelled out further in the course of the book. First, the relationship between transnational and domestic law is first and foremost a political relationship, involving myriad stakeholders and positioning national governments squarely at the intersection of law and economy. So-called global capitalism relies on national states in the form of treaties, contracts, trade agreements, and other forms of legal coordination (e.g., in laws governing investment, labor, environment and human rights). Second, transnational law (which combines national, regional, international and global agreements and institutions) renders territoriality ambiguous in ways that significantly complicate any *a priori* assessment of what is internal or external to a national state. Third, transnational law is as likely to produce tensions as it is to somehow fill gaps in a presumptively global system. We refer to these various interrelated cross-currents and their inherent tensions as "interlegalities"—borrowing the term (which we discuss further below) from Boaventura de Sousa Santos as a reference to the dynamics of legal pluralism and their synergistic effects in terms of generating new problems for law, as well as new forms of authority, legitimacy, and political mobilization.[1]

Our selection of cases and problems is guided by our interest in the interlegal dynamics of contemporary transnational legal development, especially in the United States. Our book is organized around three main sources of transnational law in the United States—states, multinational corporations, and international organizations—and their principal vehicles of transnational governance. For our purposes, these are, respectively, treaties and agreements; supply chain contracts and industry codes and standards; and the voluntary norms and procedures associated with global governance institutions.

The book overall is organized by our thesis that contemporary transnational law is shaped by the politicization of tensions between the borderless aspirations of international trade and investment on the one hand and the territoriality of sovereign states on which civil rights, human rights, and rights of collective bargaining depend. Labor has become marginal and arguably more symbolic than real as a political force in the United States; however, labor and capital remain profoundly relevant to the organization of global capitalism as an economic, political and social fact. Indeed, the multiplicity of legal regimes (i.e., legal pluralism) inherent in transnational law is not its most salient feature. Rather, it is the relationship between them (including the possibility of disjunction) as lawyers, politicians and market actors jockey for maximum effect on behalf of their clients and constituents—and as people find new ways of speaking for themselves. Throughout the book, we attend to situations in which the multilateral effort to coordinate global markets through law is apparent. We also attend to situations in which such efforts run into resistance. The global economy presumes that all goods are available for market (including land, labor and natural resources), but as we shall see, this premise is not universally shared, and in each chapter, we include materials and discussion related dissent, resistance, or affirmatively different views of globalization's potential to benefit humankind. These differences are not entirely reducible to antagonistic relations of labor and capital, but *labor* today is global capitalism's primary social interface. As such, it is iconic of a wide range of affirmative forms of social security beyond (but still including) market forms. As such, then, labor (in both theory and

1. "Interlegality" is borrowed from Boaventura de Sousa Santos, *Law: A Map of Misreading—Toward a Postmodern Conception of Law*, 14 J. L. & Soc'y 279, 297–98 (1987).

practice) represents a distinct set of interests in relation to the governance of global capital. Given the prominence of stakeholder participation and territoriality questions in our attention to transnational governance, labor gives us a lens through which we may clarify contemporary forms of inclusion and exclusion as issues for transnational law around the world—related as it is to other forms of community, ownership and civic participation.

The prominence of the spheres of legal activity marking the global expansion of capital underscores their fundamental relevance to basic living conditions the world over—justifying the assessment that "social orders increasingly are legalized transnationally."[2] Reconceiving local social life as relevant to transnational legality is a reminder as to both the pervasive effects of law on the means of daily living (e.g., in contracts, working conditions, the availability of consumer goods and their prices, etc.). This point also reminds us as to the ethical burdens of law. The ethical aspects of law—even at its most technical—are hidden in plain sight. Examples in this book include such matters as labor migration, wage suppression, and displacement from the land as international trade and development go forward on a calculus of costs and benefits that makes these acceptable losses. While our account also recognizes the benefits of globalization, our analysis necessarily extends beyond the technicalities of doctrine and techniques of legal practice to questions of social context, social effects, and law reform. Our hope is that such an approach will provide lawyers and other readers with a deeper understanding of the rules already in place and the knowledge necessary to imagine change. Above all, our goal is to help readers of this book conceive of transnational law as a human relation, and to understand the difference this makes in a broader analysis of transnationalism and its futures.

A. Synergies and drivers of transnational law

The transnational private sector is now the preeminent site of standard setting, rule making, contracting, monitoring, and enforcement. The executive branch is the primary location for the agencies responsible for national security, immigration controls, the development of international agreements, and other relations with external sovereignties. We discuss these in Part I. The rise of corporate economic power and federal executive power are inseparable developments in our times, tending to transnationalize and extend the global reach of the United States through particular institutions—the multinational corporation and the executive branch, particularly administrative agencies in addition to the president. It also affects the functions of international organizations such as the World Trade Organization, tribunals associated with bilateral and multilateral trade agreements, and international courts.[3] These are issues in Part II. This in turn yields important intra-governmental effects:

2. Terence C. Halliday & Gregory Shaffer, Transnational Legal Orders 3 (Terence C. Halliday & Gregory Shaffer, eds., 2015).

3. Christina Davis, Why Adjudicate? (2012).

expanding the powers of executive departments and agencies mainly involved with transnational legal work; and exerting pressure on other branches of government—making the U.S. Supreme Court central to the management of intra-governmental tensions in certain respects. These dynamics are taken up in Part III. The book is cumulative overall. In sum, in the United States, the synergies of legal mobilization across the main spheres of transnational activity drive the distribution of legal authority. We give particular attention to international agreements (Part I), supplier codes and contracts as features of world trade (Part II), and the structure of legal authority within the federal government (Part III) as evidence of where and how transnational law and domestic legal authority are meshed.

The eight chapters that follow are organized around the three main problem areas mentioned above. Each of them involves critical dilemmas arising from the fact that global capitalism resides primarily in institutions located outside the state and capable of operating across boundaries (i.e., in corporations, supranational organizations, and private interactions). As we discuss at length in Chapter 7, the image of a borderless world associated with colloquial understandings of "globalization" is only one side of a more complex picture in which national sovereignties remain deeply relevant. We look to both sides of that picture, so that advocates, future advocates, and scholars can more readily anticipate potential areas of litigation, reform and theoretical revision. With regard to the social science implications of our analysis, we look to transnational law as a congeries of institutional and other social locations, together with their procedures, where enabling or disabling conditions for economic opportunity, political participation, employability, mobility and governance are worked out in relation to the competing demands of globalism (in relation to capitalism) and territoriality (in relation to sovereign states). In this sense, our analysis is informed in part by debates between realists and institutionalists in political science,[4] with their concerns for various forms of hard and soft power[5] and the inseparability of political economy and security.[6] But our account owes even more

4. Realists take national states as the key actors in world politics, looking to common interests and deterrence as the principal factors governing cooperation; institutionalists look to international organizations as the crucial arenas in which the conditions of cooperation may be achieved by equalizing access to information, minimizing uncertainty, and providing forums for dispute resolution. Robert O. Keohane & Lisa Martin, *The Promise of Institutionalist Theory,* 20 INT'L SECURITY 39, 40–41 (1995). *See also* ROBERT O. KEOHANE, AFTER HEGEMONY: COOPERATION AND DISCORD IN THE WORLD POLITICAL ECONOMY 12–13 (1984).

5. The phrase "hard power" refers to direct coercion (by force or by purchase); "soft power"—a term coined by Joseph Nye—refers to the work of diplomacy, persuasion, and forging common interests. JOSEPH S. NYE, JR., SOFT POWER: THE MEANS TO SUCCESS IN WORLD POLITICS (2004). Nye subsequently formulates "smart power" and "contextual intelligence" to refer to strategic combinations of hard and soft power. *See also* STEPHEN D. KRASNER, POWER, THE STATE, AND SOVEREIGNTY: ESSAYS ON INTERNATIONAL RELATIONS (2009).

6. On the inseparability of economy and security, see Keohane & Martin, *supra* note 5, at 41. As Robert Keohane has written: "International cooperation among the advanced industrialized countries since the end of World War II has probably been more extensive than international cooperation among major states during any period of comparable length in history. . . . Yet cooperation

to the insights of ethnographers whose intensively actor-centered methodologies contribute understandings of the ways globalization shapes and is shaped by social relationships — through their research on bureaucracy, democratic mobilization, rights-claiming, and resistance, among other contexts that confirm both the diversity and interconnectedness of contemporary forms of localism and globalism around the world.[7] Ethnography offers abundant resources for an effective "analytical eclecticism" in relation to transnational law that not only deepens understandings of how legality works through social arrangements, but also makes such understandings more available to grounded discussions of the principles and pragmatics of reform.[8]

B. Main themes

Overall, our thesis accounts for the three principle themes of this book, each of which runs through the work as a whole.

First, the driving synergies we identify in each chapter are not just legal in character— any more than trade is wholly economic or environmental issues are wholly natural. These are complex and dynamic situations, not so much *defined* by law as they are *made visible* in particular ways by law. Each of these key scenarios involves distinctive opportunities and constraints that reveal the different ways in which parties mobilize law *among other forms of authority and power*, within and across national borders. Thus, one theme in this book involves the complex dynamism of the interests and authorities involved in transnational law at these junctures, unsettling jurisdictions and endowing particular classes of non-legal actors with legalized authority and significance.

In this book, we will often refer to the *relationships* that converge in transnational law *situations*. There is no singular or set way in which these relationships are forged, and no singular structure to transnational law situations. Transnational problems usually do not fit neatly into any single framework or jurisdiction, legal or otherwise. Situations of parallel and multiple jurisdictions are dilemmas practicing lawyers

---

remains scarce relative to discord because the rapid growth of international economic interdependence since 1945, and the increasing involvement of governments in the operation of modern capitalist economies, have created more points of potential friction." KEOHANE, *supra* note 4, at 5.

7. For further reading on bureaucracy, see the symposium issue ("Bureaucracy") of Political and Legal Anthropology Review. *See* 34 POL. & LEGAL ANTHROPOLOGY REV. 1 (2011). For further reading on democracy promotion, see Susan Ellison, *Replicate, Facilitate, Disseminate: The Micropolitics of U.S. Democracy Promotion in Bolivia*, 38 POL. & LEGAL ANTHROPOLOGY REV. 318 (2015); Sian Lazar, *Of Autocracy and Democracy, or Discipline and Anarchy: When Organizational Structure Meets Political Ideology in Argentine Public Sector Trade Unions*, 38 POL. & LEGAL ANTHROPOLOGY REV. 279 (2015). For more on mobilizations of law in relation to the sovereignty claims of indigenous communities, see JOHN L. COMAROFF & JEAN COMAROFF, ETHNICITY, INC. (2009). These are examples from what is now a burgeoning literature in anthropology.

8. We borrow the term "analytical eclecticism" and its promise in relation to policy-relevant theorizing from Rudra Sil and Peter J. Katzenstein. *See* RUDRA SIL & PETER J. KATZENSTEIN, BEYOND PARADIGMS: ANALYTICAL ECLECTICISM IN THE STUDY OF WORLD POLITICS 1, 19 (2009).

face, and are themselves subjects of transnational law. Solutions to such problems may ignore, stretch, reify, or re-conceptualize the concepts of boundaries and the law that applies within them. The creation of transnational law, accordingly, does not follow a well-worn procedural path. The materials in the following chapters involve multiple legal sites and mechanisms, crisscrossed series of strategic improvisations, and innovative applications of conventional law doctrine.

Second, for these very reasons, transnational law should not be imagined as somehow offering a *bridge* between U.S. and foreign legal systems, or *between* international and domestic law. Transnational law has implications for the salience of geography in law, but it is not first and foremost geographic in its legal referentiality. It is shaped only selectively (and often strategically) in relation to territoriality and territorialized forms of sovereignty. Thus, the vagaries of territoriality offer another key theme throughout this book, as borders are selectively and simultaneously opened and closed, extended, or suspended, by various sorts of relationships, interests, and effects. Appreciating such vagaries is essential so as to avoid the commonplace error of equating territory with jurisdiction.

This aspect of our account departs from a commonplace assumption that law involves a series of discrete levels, as if on a ladder extending upward from local and national to the international and global. Our analysis is deliberately agnostic with respect to what is "up" or "down" in any given situation, since the question of a hierarchy of authorities is among those that transnational law (in our approach) keeps open. For our purposes, then, the idea of legal pluralism as a set of self-contained (autopoetic) legal orders "above," "below" and "within" state legal systems understates (and may even lead to misunderstanding) the complexity of contemporary legal pluralism.[9] Transnational law is "interlegal"—as we discuss extensively below.[10] For now, it is enough to understand that transnational law is not some sort of layering, diffusion or homogenization of some previously set legal form. It is not global or universal, in the colloquial sense of these terms. Transnational law is not everywhere, as if a general condition; nor is it nowhere, as if located in some empty space between national jurisdictions.

Transnational law involves diverse actors—stakeholders, citizens, non-state actors, businesses, and governmental bodies—drawn into cooperative or conflictual relations as their interests, and sometimes they themselves, cross national borders. It does not entail any inherent tendency toward homogenization or diversification, nor is it guaranteed that a transnational legal solution will always improve on a more localized one. Sometimes—indeed, often—a transnational legal solution *is* a local one (a possibility we shall consider later).

---

9. For a thoughtful example of legal pluralism in these terms, see Richard Nobles & David Schiff, *Using Systems Theory to Study Legal Pluralism: What Could Be Gained?*, 46 Law & Soc'y Rev. 265 (2012).

10. Santos, *supra*, note 1.

For all of these reasons and more, a categorical definition of *transnational law* is not possible, and those concerned with transnational law as advocates or analysts must be prepared to appreciate this complexity as an opening to new understandings and possibilities, not as an obstacle. Appreciating transnational law in this way is a resource for a creative analysis of other domains of law. Preparing students, practitioners, and scholars to appreciate transnational law in just this way is the purpose of this book.

Finally, third, being both legal and social in its genesis, transnational law is not a distinct and unified body of law, but rather exists as a highly eclectic archive of modifications on the rules and procedures of domestic and international law occasioned by the opportunities and dilemmas of living in an interconnected world. Transnational law is called into being as recombinations (sometimes novel recombinations) of mandates, authorities, powers, and accountabilities. To the extent that transnational law involves different *countries*, it does so in diverse ways—sometimes as sovereign relations, but also involving member states (in the U.S.), corporations, agencies, and even individual persons.

Our approach to the interdisciplinary aspects of the book is indebted to scholarship in the social sciences and humanities, particularly in conversations in the anthropology of law and politics, the Law & Society movement and, in particular, the New Legal Realism—all of which have significantly shaped the field of transnational law for the social sciences and sociolegal scholarship.[11] Each of these fields has generated extensive empirical, theoretical and methodological engagement in zones where transnational law is made, and made to matter in social life—and, conversely, showing how and where dilemmas of living yield demands on and for law. Our aim is to contribute to this rich scholarly literature along four main lines:

(1) We follow the path of new legal realists in attending to "dimensions of legality"[12] beyond law per se, in particular attending to the ways in which the means of transnational law become available to new participants with alternative ends—using law against law, to press for reform. As sociologist Peter Evans observes, noting the emergence of transnational social movements alongside global governance:

> Ideologically, neo-liberal globalization creates two kinds of opportunity. It imposes . . . risks on communities and families while refusing compensatory social protection, and it enthrones the normative value of democracy while being . . . incapable of implementing genuine democratic rule, most blatantly at the global level. Laid out as abstractions, the prerequisites for being able to seize these opportunities look stringent, but movements, both local and transnational, have long been building the experience necessary to address them. By intersecting across boundaries and levels, connecting issues and constituencies and generating innovative discourses of transformation, they are

11. These are professional associations and broad rubrics of scholarly literature. *See* https://politicalandlegalanthro.org; http://www.lawandsociety.org and http://www.newlegalrealism.org.

12. Sally Merry, *New Legal Realism and the Ethnography of Transnational Law*, 31 Law & Soc. Inquiry 975 (2006).

> developing practice that responds to the challenges. The structure and ideology of the "actually existing movement of movements" is creating a new basis for belief in a globally organized project of transformation that maximizes democratic political control and turns the equitable development of human capabilities and environmental stewardship into the most urgent priorities.

Peter Evans, *Is an Alternative Globalization Possible?*, 36 POL. & SOC'Y 271, 298 (2008). In other words, we regard the "dimensions of legality" as an issue internal to law, as well as external to it (e.g., in its implementation, enforcement, reception or response).[13]

(2) With regard to the New Legal Realist methodological innovations in the direction of "deterritorialized" ethnography,[14] we emphasize throughout the extent to which *territory* is itself highly unstable as a legal category in ways that have direct bearing on the civil rights and human rights of individuals. The deterritorialized "flows" of modern social life are well remarked by scholars;[15] we take these as givens. In this context, it is important to understand that geography alone does not settle questions of jurisdiction or scale.[16] We treat territoriality and scale as political, legal and social questions, rather than first and foremost as geographical ones.

(3) We share the law and society movement's characteristic "skeptic[ism] about the impact of formal law" on social life,[17] in the sense that law's efficacy cannot be assumed as a general matter. But we find that in specific sectors—such as affecting the status of migrants, detainees, and civilians in war zones, or of peasants and others living at or below subsistence level—such skepticism may be overstated. Law matters, not just as part of a larger context, but as contributing to the very meaning of context—particularly in relation to the dynamic interlegalities of transnational law.

(4) Relatedly, we share with New Legal Realists a view of the relevance of interdisciplinary scholarship, expressed by Gregory Shaffer in his claim that "comparative institutional analysis and new legal realism are complementary components of any policy-relevant analysis of law."[18] To this we would add the cautionary note that

---

13. On the cultural and subjective aspects of legal technique from within the sites of its production, see ANNELISE RILES, COLLATERAL KNOWLEDGE: LEGAL REASONING IN THE GLOBAL FINANCIAL MARKETS (2011).

14. See *Merry*, *supra* note 12.

15. In this context, the metaphor of flow is Arjun Appadurai's, as he finds "five dimensions of global cultural flow . . . : (a) ethnoscapes; (b) mediascapes; (c) technoscapes; (d) finanscapes; and (e) ideoscapes." Arjun Appadurai, *Disjuncture and Difference in the Global Cultural Economy*, 7 THEORY, CULTURE & SOC'Y 295 (1990).

16. *See* Santos, *supra* note 2, on the limits of "cartographic thinking"; also Valverde's elaboration of Santos's critique in her analysis of scale as a form of social distance. Mariana Valverde, *Jurisdiction and Scale: Legal "Technicalities" as Resources for Theory*, 18 SOC. & LEGAL STUD. 143–44 (2009). On jurisdiction, *see also* Justin B. Richland, *Jurisdiction: Grounding Law in Language*, 42 ANNUAL REV. ANTHROPOLOGY 209 (2013).

17. *See* Bryant Garth, *Introduction: Taking New Legal Realism to Transnational Issues and Institutions*, 31 LAW & SOC. INQUIRY 939 (2006).

18. Gregory Shaffer, *Comparative Institutional Analysis and a New Legal Realism*, 2013 WIS. L. REV. 609 (2013).

complementarity at the interpretive or analytical level does not imply that the stakes (or benefits) of transnational law are evenly or reciprocally distributed as a practical matter. We do not gainsay the benefits of globalization for some, for example, but we do not take those benefits as defining globalization.

In a variety of ways, as is perhaps already clear, an analysis of transnational law is integral not just to the contemporary profession and the demand for law, but also to the theoretical concerns of anthropology and adjacent disciplines with regard to the question of how access to law, and use of legal institutions, are related to both the form and substance of public life and personal experience. It lends itself to interdisciplinary and multidisciplinary study. Carrie Menkel-Meadow, a sociolegal scholar, connects the dynamic complexity of the "modern world of human activity" to the broad relevance of transnational law in legal education:

> This is the modern world of human activity, facilitated, regulated, sometimes thwarted, and often affected, by laws that "cross borders" in order to effectuate their purposes.... How these transfers actually occur may or may not conform to national, regional, or international rules and regulations. Lawyers of the twenty-first century must come to understand that, with respect to most of what we do or want to do, we are now in an interdependent world of manufacturing, distribution, consumption, and promotion of creative action, as well as, sometimes sadly, destructive sites of interaction. Even if national legal systems wanted to control and cabin all that happened within their points of impact (with varying degrees of legal liability). This recognition of our legally "migratory" society, or "globalization" as others controversially label it, requires some reorientation of conventional legal education.[19]

Professor Harold Koh, a former Legal Adviser to the State Department, also relates the relevance of transnational law to the law school curriculum specifically in terms of the dynamic interplay of domestic and transnational legalities:

> Perhaps the best operational definition of transnational law, using computer-age imagery, is: (1) law that is "downloaded" from international to domestic law: for example, an international law concept that is domesticated or internalized into municipal law, such as the international human rights norm against disappearance, now recognized as domestic law in most municipal systems; (2) law that is "uploaded, then downloaded": for example, a rule that originates in a domestic legal system, such as the guarantee of a free trial . . . which then becomes part of international law . . . and (3) law that is borrowed or "horizontally transplanted" from one national system to another: for example, the "unclean hands" doctrine, which migrated from the British law of equity to many other legal systems.

---

19. Carrie Menkel-Meadow, *Why and How to Study "Transnational" Law*, 1 U.C. IRVINE L. REV. 97, 99–100 (2011).

> Today, the concept of transnational law embraces a range of law school courses thought to be neither purely domestic nor purely international.... In... these legal areas, global standards have become fully recognized, integrated, and internalized into domestic legal systems.[20]

II. Key concepts

A. Legality and sociality

As noted in the previous section, this book focuses on three main areas of transnational law activity today: international treaties and agreements, multinational supply chain codes and contracts, and the relationship of global governance mechanisms to domestic federal authority. These domains of practice—superficially distinct—share broad conceptual and pragmatic commitments to globalization as *the future* of domestic law. In some contexts (such as environmental protection), that future is immediately evident in the treaty's stated purposes. In others, the future is implicit, as a putative or desired function of effective governance. Purpose (as intention) and function (as intended or unintended effects) are not the same, making *practice* a key concept. The human sciences have turned to *practice* as a reminder that the classic distinction between *theory* and *praxis* compels attention, and, even more importantly in our account, to highlight the ways in which theorizing itself is a practical activity. Practice always entails the possibility of alternative options, strategies and paradigms.[21] Throughout, we emphasize the ways in which transnational law is, in effect, a theory of power. In practice, as the relationship of territory and jurisdiction comes into question in diverse ways, law becomes inseparable from the organization of markets and market processes, and their social consequences.

We borrow the term *practice* from contemporary cultural theory because it allows us to acknowledge power effects without making *a priori* ascriptions of motivation or intent. In other words, thinking in terms of practice allows us to think laterally across interrelated developments in a flexible way, without exaggerating the coherence or orderliness of those developments, or presupposing their systemic or

---

20. Harold Hongju Koh, *Why Transnational Law Matters*, 24 PENN ST. INT'L L. REV. 745, 745–46 (2006).

21. Michel de Certeau, a principal contributor to practice theory in anthropology and cultural studies, introduces his seminal *The Practice of Everyday Life* with a statement of purpose calling for the study of "ways of operating" that would not only excavate background rules but also investigate the ways they structure strategic and tactical behavior in anything but neutral ways: "This goal will be achieved if everyday practices, 'ways of operating' or doing things, no longer appear as merely the obscure background of social activity, and if a body of theoretical questions, methods, categories and perspectives, by penetrating this obscurity, make it possible to articulate them." MICHEL DE CERTEAU, THE PRACTICE OF EVERYDAY OF LIFE (Steven Rendall trans., 1984). *Practice* in this sense challenges analysts to interrogate the very procedures (conventions, canons, various forms of professionalism and disciplinarity, etc.) by which so-called objective knowledge is distinguished from other forms of knowledge and valorized as such. *See* PIERRE BOURDIEU, OUTLINE OF A THEORY OF PRACTICE (Richard Nice trans., 1987).

hierarchical character. Transnational law is eclectic, episodic and in many ways unsettled; we do not treat it as an "order" unto itself.

By conceiving of transnational law through the lens of practice—whether as ideas committed to text or as physical activity—we can explore the chains of consequences (both intended and unintended) that *literally* make law transnational. Putting ideas such as free trade into practice generates new interests, some of which entail new demands for law, or new uses of law. For example, we do not distinguish between intended and unintended consequences in drawing the connection between NAFTA and the precariousness of employment in the industrial export zones of Mexico, or between supply chain agreements in the apparel industry and the safety conditions in factories—but we do include selections that speak to the efforts of workers and others to insist on accountability and improve those conditions through law.

Accordingly, we emphasize the legal contexts in which transnational law—understood as practice in the sense described above—is called upon to decide the relative value of people's lives and livelihoods relative to other interests (e.g., public interests or corporate interests). Sometimes such appeals to law are explicit (as in an award of damages or improved working conditions); at other times, the decision is made implicitly, as a ruling on standing or extraterritorial applicability of U.S. law. In law as in life, success, failure, serendipity, and mishap have many sources. The key point is that law's social character is not limited to inputs and outputs (assumptions and impacts), nor to the practice of law as such. Rather, it is pervasive in the practices that constitute law as a sphere of discursive and material activity (i.e., how the crafting of law's language and practical arrangements becomes a site of political, legal and social investment). Here we repeat once more that our usage of *practice* is a reference not just to behavior and speech, but also to the tacit assumptions that edit the field of options in particular ways.

The concrete situations we pursue in this book involve fundamental tensions between the globalization of capital, the demands of national security (in the military sense) and the politicization of economic regulation under domestic law. This is a broad horizon from which we select telling examples that highlight the diversity of powers practiced through and as transnational law. We approach transnational law as emergent from the politicization of such tensions—evident in partisan divides within and between the main political parties at local, state, and federal levels; in inter-branch conflicts within government; and in relationships between government and governance, particularly in the multinational corporate sphere. These are characteristic lines of tension as Congress wrestles with presidents over executive power; as labor is increasingly exposed to the pressures against collective bargaining; as migrants are caught up (and often caught out) in today's restructured labor force; as courts adjudicate competing interests in today's diverse arrangements where Congress fails to do so; and as the executive branch deploys authority acquired in one domain to other domains that are superficially distant (e.g., trade and war powers). These are just some examples of the interlegal tensions that form the skeleton of this book and drive the discussion.

B. Governance and government

As indicated at the outset of this chapter, power takes many forms, and scholars distinguish among these in ways that overall distinguish between laws produced by states and the other forms of regulation, norms-making, and compliance that either facilitate the efficacy of state law, or operate apart from it, or both. Our key distinction in this regard distinguishes between government and governance—reserving government for the specific governing practices of state institutions, and governance for non-state practices.

Governance is a term familiar to lawyers (especially from international law) and social scientists, as a term of art for institutional and social norms that produce and sustain law-like effects—i.e., not law, but necessary to law's functioning. In this sense, we may distinguish between government and governance. Transnational law involves both.

The idea of governance entails three principal implications. First, its usage tends to imply that coordinated exercises of authority involving diverse entities and associations are possible.

Second, such interlegalities as evoked by Professor Koh facilitate global governance to the extent that they mobilize normative resources beyond domestic law's regulatory capacity and efficacy. As Eve Darian-Smith notes: "Global governance refers to the political networks, institutions, mechanisms, and agencies required to solve problems that confront multiple states or regions, and it is needed when there are limited alternative enforcement mechanisms available. . . . Global governance seeks to include national governments, international organizations, as well as a wide range of non-state actors, NGOs, and various community agencies in formulating global directives, policies, regulation, and accountability."[22]

Third, usage of the term *governance* tends to imply that such interrelated functions are integral to or aligned with law, whether law's sources are domestic or international. While this implication is borne out by myriad studies of "law and society," it does not necessarily mean that governance institutions in some way provide an alternative to government as if equal to its effects by different means. We are skeptical of this position, since governance institutions that function in this way would necessarily rely—sooner or later—on legitimations of authority ultimately derived from state delegation or deference. Moreover, states govern *through* civil society entities, not merely *in tandem with* or *in the context* of society.

The following excerpts argue for an idea of governance that applies to transnational law while resisting the conventional binarisms of government and governance, state and society, or "hard law" and "soft law." Sending and Neumann contextualize the idea of governance in the scholarship of the late 20th century. They

22. Eve Darian-Smith, Laws and Societies in Global Contexts: Contemporary Approaches 52 (2013).

also introduce us to the idea of *governmentality*—government as a form of power that extends beyond governing agents—that relies on the work of Michel Foucault, a major theorist of contemporary forms of power. The idea of governmentality will be crucial to the next Part, on governance through states—i.e., on legal situations in which states participate as parties, and in which they rely on forms of authority and legitimacy that are not limited to government institutions as such.

Ole Jacob Sending & Iver B. Neumann, *Governance to Governmentality: Analyzing NGOs, States, and Power*

50 Int'l Stud. Q. 651 (2006)

Studies of global governance typically claim that the state has lost power to nonstate actors and that political authority is increasingly institutionalized in spheres not controlled by states. In this article, we challenge the core claims in the literature on global governance. Rather than focusing on the relative power of states and nonstate actors, we focus on the sociopolitical functions and processes of governance in their own right and seek to identify their rationality as practices of political rule. For this task, we use elements of the conception of power developed by Michel Foucault in his studies of "governmentality." In this perspective, the role of nonstate actors in shaping and carrying out global governance-functions is not an instance of transfer of power from the state to nonstate actors but rather an expression of a changing logic or rationality of government (defined as a type of power) by which civil society is redefined from a passive object of government to be acted upon into an entity that is both an object *and* a subject of government. . . . [T]he self-association and political will-formation characteristic of civil society and nonstate actors do not stand in opposition to the political power or the state, but is a most central feature of how power understood as government, operates in late modern society.

During the course of the 1990s, global governance emerged as a new and powerful research agenda. This literature has produced a wealth of insights about the changing roles and significance of sovereign states in the governing of global or transnational affairs. There are at least three key interrelated claims within this literature. The first is that government must be studied as a process, not as an institution. This analytical move is said to make it possible to analyze changes from hierarchical and sovereignty- based modes of governing to more horizontal, network-based modes of governing. The second is that various nonstate actors have become much more powerful in global politics, and that the state hence is less powerful than before. The third is that political authority is increasingly dislodged from the sovereign state and in the direction of transnational policy-networks and functionally specific "spheres of authority" (SOAs), where the state plays a strategic but not necessarily dominant role. The analytical power of studies of global governance is thus said to lie in its ability to move beyond state-centric analyses to include a focus on the processes of governance, to highlight the power of nonstate actors, and to identify and theorize about the changing forms and institutionalization of political authority.

In this article, we critically review these three claims. We argue, first, that while the literature on global governance highlights governance as a set of interrelated processes, it does not provide the analytical tools to study these processes. Second, studies of global governance have a zero-sum conception of power where an increase in the power and influence of nonstate actors is ipso facto defined as a simultaneous reduction in state power and authority. Third, studies of global governance perpetuate the very same analytical framework that they purport to transcend as their key findings—about the power of nonstate actors and the diffusion of political authority from the state to other actors—is parasitic upon an analytical framework tied to the triad between sovereignty, authority and legitimacy.

These three limitations invite the formulation of a different theoretical approach. An attempt to grasp the role of nonstate actors, and civil society organizations in particular, requires an approach that can theorize about the specific relations between state and nonstate actors and about the logic of the processes of governance. For example, different types of nonstate actors are often funded, actively encouraged and supported by states both to mobilize political constituencies, to confer legitimacy to policy-processes, to implement policies, and to monitor and evaluate them. While these dimensions of global governance are mentioned in the literature on global governance, they are not theorized with a view to understanding the mechanisms of power implied in them. To grasp the thinking and practice associated with these relations, and the power implied in them, we draw upon the concept of "governmentality" originally developed by Michel Foucault.

In the governmentality perspective, the role of nonstate actors in shaping and carrying out global governance-functions is not an instance of transfer of power from the state to nonstate actors. Rather, it is an expression of a changing logic or rationality of government (defined as a type of power) by which civil society is redefined from a passive object of government to be acted upon and into an entity that is both an object and a subject of government. We argue that the self-association and political will-formation characteristic of civil society and nonstate actors do not stand in opposition to the political power of the state, but is a most central feature of how power operates in late modern society. In short, we argue that new insights can be generated if we study the sociopolitical functions of governance in their own right and seek to identify their rationality as governmental practices. This perspective on power enables us to identify dimensions of global governance that are largely omitted in the extant literature, and makes it possible to challenge some of the core claims in this literature about the autonomy and power of civil society actors.

* * *

Governance as a Process

... [G]lobal governance is commonly defined as a process that involves both public and private actors, the activities of which are coordinated through both formal and informal rules and guidelines in such a way that a common or public goal is advanced. However, while studies of global governance define their object of inquiry as a set of processes, their ontology and concomitant analytical tools are not equipped to grasp the content of the processes of governance itself. Rather, studies of global governance typically focus on the changing roles and power of state and nonstate actors, and on resulting changes in the institutionalization of political authority.

* * *

Dualism: The Power of Nonstate Actors

The central empirical claim in studies of global governance is that nonstate actors have emerged as powerful actors in world politics, thus challenging the power and authority of sovereign states. The increased influence and power of actors representing "civil society" and its implications for the power and authority of the state are at the core of what global governance is all about. Underlying the claim about the increased power of nonstate actors in shaping and carrying out governance function is a conception of the relation between state and nonstate actors as a zero-sum game: as nonstate actors have become more powerful, states have by definition become less so. Some authors note, for example, that states can no longer "bypass the concerns of transnational actors" as these have "strengthened their bargaining position with significant moral, financial and knowledge resources."

It is typically argued that there is a "relocation of authority *from* public *to* quasi-public, and to private, agencies." According to Rosenau for example, "The weakening of states has not been followed by authority vacuums (. . .) so much as it has resulted in a vast growth in the number of spheres in which authority has moved." Against this background, he suggests that an "appropriate ontology will highlight the extent to which the erosion of state authority and the proliferation of NGOs has resulted in a disaggregation of the loci of governance." While studies of global governance excel in charting the diffusion and disaggregation of authority from the state to nonstate actors, they fail in exploring both the power at work in the actual practices through which governance takes place, as well as the more specific content or logic of the relations between state and nonstate actors. The extent to which nonstate actors are directly funded by and actively encouraged by states to be engaged in processes of global governance is thus inadequately addressed. . . .

Sovereignty and Authority

* * *

By tying the analysis of the processes of governance to a concern with authority, studies of global governance inadvertently perpetuate the very state-centric framework that they seek to transcend: the focus is negatively defined in relation to sovereignty, aimed at analyzing to which actors power and authority have flowed from the state. The more recent interest in how to render global governance more legitimate and accountable is a testament to this feature of studies of global governance. Here, the focus is on the effects of the fact (established by studies of global governance) that the practices and processes of governance do not correspond to the site of the institutionalization of political authority in the sovereign state. Addressing the "democratic deficit" and lack of accountability and legitimacy of global governance, these studies typically note that global civil society emerges as a substitute for a national "demos" to which global governance is or can be made accountable.

The literature on global governance does provide important insights. There are, however, clear limits to the central concepts that guide studies of global governance. Because of its commitment to power as sovereignty and the associated concern with the institutionalization of political authority, studies of global governance misread central aspects of the relations between state and nonstate actors when it asserts that nonstate actors' power and authority has increased while that of states have decreased. Studies of global governance are thus also unable to deliver on its claim that global governance should be studied as a process, inasmuch as its analytical tools favor theorizing about what actors "are" in terms of which actors have power and authority rather than about what these actors "do" as they engage in the processes of governing. . . .

Government and Sovereignty

To grasp the meaning and import of "government" as a form of power it is useful to contrast it with that of sovereignty. Foucault identifies a historically significant transformation occurring from the sixteenth century onwards in which what he terms the "art of government" emerged to form a practice that was separate and partly autonomous from the principle and practice of sovereignty. . . . Government is for Foucault . . . defined in terms of the "conduct of conducts," involving a range of techniques and practices, performed by different actors, aimed to shape, guide, and direct individuals' and groups' behavior and actions in particular directions. The central elements of government as a form of power are captured in the following distinction made [by Foucault] between the workings of sovereignty and the workings of government:

> with sovereignty the instrument that allowed it to achieve its aims that is to say, obedience to the laws—was the law itself: law and sovereignty were absolutely inseparable. . . . [W]ith government it is a question not of imposing law on men, but of disposing things; that is to say, of employing tactics rather than laws, and even of using laws themselves as tactics—to arrange things in such a way that, through a certain number of means, through a certain number of means, such and such ends may be achieved.

The concepts of "disposing things" and "employing tactics" are an essential feature of government as a form of power. In contrast to both sovereignty and discipline, which are the two other key modes of power theorized by Foucault, government takes the freedom and agency of those that are governed as both an end and means for governing.

Governmentality

Governmentality is an analytical concept aimed at grasping government as a form of power. . . .

A focus on governmentality implies at least three things. First, it is aimed at investigating the specific practices and techniques of governing as an empirical phenomenon, thus seeking to replace a focus on institutions (characteristic of studies focused on sovereignty) with a focus on practices. Second, it is aimed at identifying the "mentality" or rationality that characterizes the systematic thinking and knowledge that is integral to and renders possible different modes of governing. Third, it does not replace sovereignty or discipline—each of which represents distinct forms of power. As Mitchell Dean argues, "rather than displacing discipline or sovereignty, the in modern art of government recasts them within this concern for the population and its optimization (in terms of wealth, health, happiness, prosperity, efficiency), and the forms of knowledge and technical means appropriate to it." Sovereignty and discipline, then, are reconfigured in that, as Foucault puts it, the essential aspect of government is the "introduction of economy into political practice."

With respect to global governance, the perspective of governmentality offers a good optic for analyses. First, it explicitly builds on, and was originally developed as a tool for, studying the processes of governing. The concept of governmentality is aimed at investigating the practices of governing as an empirical phenomenon but also to identify the "mentality"—the rationality characteristic of the systematic thinking, reflection, and knowledge that is integral to different modes of governing. Second, it delivers a conception of the relation between the state and nonstate actors that places the focus of sovereignty within a more general concern for changes in the practices and rationality of governing.

The key point to recognize is that this analytical perspective focuses on how certain identities and action-orientations are defined as appropriate and normal and how relations of power are implicated in these processes. A focus on governmentality, therefore, seeks to analyze the "relation between individuals and the political order from the perspective of the *different processes whereby the former are objectified as certain kinds of subject through the ways they are targeted by political power*."

* * *

In this view, the ascendance of nonstate actors in shaping and carrying out global governance-functions is not an instance of transfer of power from the state to nonstate actors, or a matter of the changing sources of, or institutional locus for, authority. Rather, it is an expression of a *change* in governmentality by which civil society is redefined from a passive object of government to be acted upon and into an entity that is both an object *and* a subject of government.

* * *

Conclusion

* * *

We have found that civil society is increasingly defined as a field populated by political subjects whose autonomy, expertise and ability to responsibly channel political will-formation has become crucial to the tasks of governing. We have identified a governmental rationality where political power operates *through* rather than *on* civil society. Governing is performed *through* autonomous subjects, not *on* passive objects.

Like Neumann and Sending in their critique of a government/governance binary, Ralf Michaels cautions against a binary distinction between the categories *state* and *non-state*, to the extent that the rubric *non-state* implies the existence of a stable state—a "romantic idea" outmoded by contemporary governance practices:

> The state has long been the most important political myth to determine and constrain our political thinking. Yet non-state governance is, if anything, more, not less, mythical: an ideologically laden concept, a romantic idea. It looks attractive to those who oppose the state—free market proponents on the political right, advocates for local indigenous communities on the left. But from this perspective, the idea of non-state law and non-state governance appears rather antiquated . . . [and] non-state is the false perspective for these phenomena. Non-state governance is a mirage, a mere mirror image of the state—its opposite or its copy. . . . If we want to overcome our traditional focus on the state, we must overcome our focus on the non-state, too. Instead of the formal and artificial differentiation state/non-state, we should look for functional differentiations between different modes of governance.

Ralf Michaels, *The Mirage of Non-State Governance*, 2010 UTAH L. REV. 31 (2010). We share these reservations as to the risks in overstating binary categories. In this volume, we use the terms government, governance, state and non-state to differentiate between institutional locations and to remark on their interrelations. In particular, we use the term non-state as an umbrella rubric for agencies having governance functions without governmental status. Avant, Finnemore, and Sell propose "global governors" as a term that highlights the agency of diverse institutions, combining states and non-state organizations, without reifying them in structural terms: "Global governors are authorities who exercise power across borders for purposes of affecting policy. Governors thus create issues, set agendas, establish and implement rules or programs, and evaluate and/or adjudicate outcomes. . . . [We] focus on two types of relationships: relationships between governors and the governed, and relationships among governors, themselves."[24] We follow Avant, Finnemore, and Sell's emphasis on agency (i.e., the relevance of action on the part of the parties involved), so as to maximize the potential for cross-referencing transnational law and its many points of contact with other bodies of law and communities of stakeholders.

We focus especially on six main vehicles of transnational law, each one entailing its own circuits of agency and effect: treaties (including executive agreements and executive-congressional agreements), legislation, contracts, industrial codes and

---

24. DEBORAH D. AVANT, MARTHA FINNEMORE & SUSAN K. SELL, WHO GOVERNS THE GLOBE? 2 (Avant et al. eds., 2010).

standards, global voluntary rules and executive action. Each chapter remixes these registers of transnational law in a distinctive way. We also consider several different sorts of international institutions—the WTO, ISO, United Nations, and the International Commission for the Settlement of Investor Disputes among them—but the sheer number of international institutions in the world today precludes comprehensive coverage.

C. Plurality and interlegality

Transnational law is fascinating for legal professionals and social scientists precisely because of the propensity for transnational problems to proliferate novel lines of intra- and intergovernmental engagement. Transnational law may also promote novel interrelationships among persons (i.e., natural persons), businesses, corporations (such as business firms but also such corporate entities as cities), and state actors at home and abroad. Such dynamics may be cooperative or conflictual—or both, at different times. Above all, they involve many legal regimes simultaneously, as well as diverse social arrangements of a non-legal (but not necessarily illegal) nature. This proliferation and simultaneity of legal and social orders is endemic to contemporary conditions, as legal scholars Martti Koskenniemi and Paivi Leino suggest:

> [T]oday, domestic sovereignty has been tamed and split. . . . The crisis of domestic sovereignty is paralleled by the collapse of the image of the international world as a single, hierarchical structure at the top of which the United Nations governs a world of tamed sovereigns through public law and diplomacy. . . . The economy is, of course, global. But the "international" and "national" may no longer be usefully separated even as distinct realms of politics and government. Without attempting yet another sociology of globalisation, it may be accepted that political communities have become more heterogeneous, their boundaries much more porous, than assumed by the received images of sovereignty and the international order, and that the norms they express are fragmentary, discontinuous, often ad hoc and without definite hierarchical relationship.

Martti Koskenniemi & Paivi Leino, *Fragmentation of International Law? Postmodern Anxieties*, 15 LEIDEN J. INT'L L. 553, 556–58 (2002).

In this context, as noted at the outset, the idea of legal pluralism—a classic concept in sociolegal studies—holds renewed relevance. In sociolegal studies, *legal pluralism* classically refers variously to delegations of state authority and other means by which state power is decentralized to institutions of varying types, or to situations in which state institutions function formally or informally alongside non-state institutions. The term has been used both broadly (as a reference to the diversity of normative institutions and communities) and narrowly (as a reference to state delegations). In our view, legal pluralism loses meaning when it is used as a general or all-encompassing rubric, since competing regimes of legitimacy and authority may be involved. Moreover, due to the influence of classic anthropological studies of customary law on social science and social science approaches to law, legal pluralism and cultural pluralism are sometimes confused for one another, but it is important to maintain these situations as distinct (since a single institution may have a multicultural staff and constituency, and multiple institutions may be managed by a homogenous elite).

When the concept of legal pluralism is restricted to state delegation, deference and decentralization, it is referred to as a *state centric* conception of legal pluralism. Critics of this view point to other situations in which diverse legal institutions do not draw their authority from a common source; thus, for them, *legal pluralism* contrasts with *state centrism*. For these legal pluralists, the term refers to diverse legal institutions operating simultaneously in the same jurisdictional space. The analytical emphasis is on their normative and procedural differences and competitive conflicts of various kinds.[23] Our usage is more in line with the latter view, but we prefer to use the term *interlegality*—per Santos[24]—to capture the dynamic interrelations involved in legal pluralism, beyond the mere fact of pluralism. Some prefer the term *polycentricity* for such situations, where there are constellations of institutions involved in a coordinated way.

There are also other situations, in which there may be conflict—even sharp conflict—within a legal order, indeed, even within a single institution, without there being an implication of a pluralist or polycentric structure. In sum, legal difference does not automatically imply cultural difference, cultural difference does not imply community difference, and diversity automatically implies neither cooperation nor conflict. Legal pluralism—whether centralist or pluralist in conception—is not the division of some flat space, or reducible to questions of kind or degree; rather, it is a critical reminder that law is always plural in its makings and undertakings, and plural, too, in its social effects over time.[25]

In this regard, as already noted, we find especially suggestive the formulations of legal scholar Boaventura de Sousa Santos, who posits *legal pluralism* and *interlegality* as two characteristic features of "postmodern" law. For Santos, legal pluralism refers to "multiple networks of legal orders" and interlegality to the dynamic quality of their simultaneous mixings.[26] Legal pluralism, in other words, is a structural situation. Santos distinguishes it from interlegality—his term for the correspondingly dynamic aspect of that complex networked structure at work. Accordingly, he calls for an end to "cartographic" thinking in relation to law—an end, in other words, to imagining law as a concentric arrangement of territorialized jurisdictions ranging from small

23. John Griffiths, *What is Legal Pluralism?*, 24 J. Legal Pluralism & Unofficial L. 1 (1979); Halliday & Shaffer, *supra* note 2, at 26–28.

24. Santos, *supra* note 1.

25. Franz von Benda-Beckmann, *Who's Afraid of Legal Pluralism?* 47 J. Legal Pluralism & Unofficial L. 37 (1979).

26. Santos, *supra* note 1.

to large to global. All scales—from the smallest to the largest—are simultaneously accessible from any point.

Taking up Santos' critique of cartographic thinking and his notion of interlegality, sociologist Mariana Valverde goes farther, arguing not just that all scales are accessible as a matter of standpoint, but that legal institutions have their own scaling effects—such that local and global (for example) may be simultaneously relevant. Valverde's account differentiates between two main types of administrative regimes—risk management based on a policing model and rights-based citizenship based on a constitutional model. The former is global, extending outward as policing extends beyond local law enforcement to global security and management of risk in other settings altogether. The latter is local, a register of belonging. In this sense, a local encounter with the police is *simultaneously* local and global; its empirical location does not determine either its jurisdiction nor its analytical significance. She urges us to rethink the conventions that associate jurisdiction and scale with gradations of territorial extent and territorialized sovereignties. Instead, she argues, *jurisdiction* is itself a form of legal work entailing multiple scales and authorities:

> In the routine work of jurisdiction, territories and sovereigns tend to be seen as part of the same package, such that sorting out territories simultaneously sorts out governing authorities. Jurisdiction, however, distinguishes more than territories and authorities, more than the where and the who of governance. Jurisdiction also differentiates and organizes the "what" of governance—and, most importantly because of its relative invisibility, the "how" of governance. Thus, jurisdiction sorts the where, the who, the what, and the how of governance through a kind of chain reaction, whereby if one question (where, who) is decided, then the answers to the other questions seem to follow automatically. . . . [27]

In our view, Santos's concept of pluralism as interlegality, together with Valverde's reformulation of scale and jurisdiction, are useful starting points for a fresh approach to transnational law. Today, law's production and circulation cannot be contained by any singular legal entity or definite series of entities. In some ways, of course, this has always been true—once we accept that law is a social institution, and produced by men and women from their own social understandings, including some who are informed and disciplined by their professionalism. But in the passages quoted above, as in much writing about transnational law, there is an implicit periodization that connects transnational law to the challenges of our own times—a fundamental challenge, we submit, of reconciling the globalization of capital to ideals of social security that for two centuries have been claimed as the basic rationale for territorial national states. An understanding of transnational law is improved if—following the insights of Santos and Valverde—one does not take the national state as if it were law's natural jurisdiction. We presuppose neither the demise nor the

27. Valverde, *supra* note 16.

endurance of the national state as the starting point for our discussion of transnational law.

D. Territoriality and jurisdiction

Understanding the transnational aspects of law puts a premium on understanding the ways in which domestic and international law are interlinked through jurisdictions. *Jurisdiction* is a critical area of practice in the sense elucidated above.[28] Transnational jurisdictions are not consistently organized territorially; indeed, one and the same location can be both territorial and extraterritorial depending (for example) on the citizenship of individuals, or the ownership and management of a business firm. In questions of civil jurisdiction, domicile is not necessarily decisive. Additional considerations include contract terms, subject matter, the weight of relationships, instrumentalities and agencies, interests, stakes, individuals' exposure to harm, and even the timing of filings when multiple jurisdictions are involved.[29] These are complex legal issues. For our purposes at this juncture, we observe that the pluralism and interlegality of transnational law is such that global problems do not always require or allow global solutions. Scale, jurisdiction, and legal locations are constantly in play.[30]

As we track these complexities, we emphasize perspectives from domestic law, so readers can more readily appreciate how "acting locally" may mean "thinking transnationally." In fact, domestic law features prominently in most of the new relationships created by transnational law. The conventional picture of globalization is of a global structure to which domestic legal regimes must inevitably adapt—if they are relevant at all. But globalization is not a structure—it is a multi-stranded, polycentric process in real time. This means that it can be shaped, influenced, and changed from multiple locations and legal forums. In this sense, transnational law highlights all of the subjects taught in the usual law school curriculum, but interrelates them in new ways in light of emergent contexts of legal action in the current transnational situation.

Transnational law, then, does not begin in the inevitability of global markets but in the role of domestic law and politics that makes markets and states mutually interdependent—even if they are theoretically independent. Alfred Aman has called

---

28. Justin B. Richland, a lawyer and linguistic anthropologist, highlights the discursive aspects of jurisdiction, showing how jurisdiction is made in linguistic practice. Justin B. Richland, *Jurisdiction: Grounding Law in Language*, 42 Annual Rev. Anthropology 209 (2013).

29. For comprehensive discussion, see Joachim Zekoll, Michael G. Collins & George A. Rutherglen, Transnational Civil Litigation (2013).

30. For these same reasons, we should not presuppose that transnational law always supersedes domestic law in some top-down or hegemonic arrangement, as if "higher" than domestic law. *See* Halliday & Shaffer, *supra* note 2, at 478. (For this very reason, we differ with Halliday and Shaffer's exclusion of legal anthropology's usual subject matter as "a bridge too far" in the study of transnational law. *See id.* at 477.)

this interdependency the "domestic face of globalization."[31] The domestic face of globalization is perhaps most readily visible when government functions are outsourced to multinational firms operating domestically, such as privatized administrative services in government agencies, or privatized services in prisons, and so forth. Some such circumstances are discussed in Chapter 7. Additional examples include presidential fast-track authority in international trade agreements, discussed in Chapter 3. Sovereign states are also drawn into interdependent relations—albeit often of a highly asymmetrical nature—as multilateral agreements generate new relationships and interests that entail jurisdictional implications. Examples are discussed mainly in Chapters 4, 5 and 6.

Turning to territoriality, the following excerpt underscores its instability; the selection involves modern dilemmas of immigration regulation and citizenship. National territorial borders become problematic as new circumstances in the political economy of labor and trade render territoriality selectively indeterminate:

Ayelet Shachar, *The Shifting Border of Immigration Regulation*

3 Stan. J. C.R. & C.L. 165, 166–69 (2007)

A novice to the field of immigration might expect the legal boundaries of inclusion and exclusion to correlate with the "cartographic" borders of U.S. territory. The reality, however, is far more complicated. The firm borderlines drawn in the world atlas do not necessarily coincide with those adhered to, indeed created through, immigration law and policy. Instead, we increasingly witness a border that is in flux: at once more open and more closed than in the past. More important still for the purpose of our discussion, the location of the border is shifting—at times penetrating into the interior, in other circumstances extending beyond the edge of the territory. And in other contexts, these borders are reappearing, ever more robustly, as a physically refortified barrier, offering a sharp demarcation line between the U.S. and its neighbors to the South and the North.

While American immigration law is still largely informed by the doctrine of plenary power, which holds that "[a]dmission to the United States is a privilege granted by the sovereign" (as the Supreme Court asserted in *Knauff* more than fifty years ago), what has dramatically changed in recent years is the location of "our gates," which no longer stand at the country's territorial edges. Instead, the border itself has become a moving barrier, a legal construct that is not tightly fixed to territorial benchmarks. This *shifting border of immigration regulation*, as we might call it, is selectively utilized by national immigration regulators to regain control over their crucial realm of responsibility, to determine who to permit to enter, who to remove, and who to keep at bay.

---

31. Alfred C. Aman, Jr., The Democracy Deficit: Taming Globalization Through Law Reform (2004).

The crux of my argument is that the state's ability to flexibly redraw the border for immigration regulation purposes is a key component in the new policy-toolbox developed by the U.S. (and other leading immigrant-destination countries) to reassert control over their so-called "broken" borders in the age of increased international mobility and security risks. In contrast with the predictions of post-nationalists and others who have told us that the retreat of the regulatory state and the breaking down of borders is imminent, the domestic and comparative examples discussed here demonstrate how border controls are being "retooled and redesigned" by nation-states to better respond to changing needs and challenges in the current age of globalization.

This redesign has been accomplished by enforcing the sovereign prerogative to deny or permit access in a whole new way: by redrawing (indeed, redefining) the once fixed and static territorial border, transforming it into something more malleable and movable, which can be placed and replaced—by the words of law—in whatever location that best suits the goal of restricting access. By employing sophisticated legal maneuvers that establish this new multi-faceted border, the regulatory state is enhancing and expanding—rather than waning and losing (as many theorists have suggested) its immigration-enforcement authority to act against "unwanted intruders."

* * *

The classic Westphalian ideal of statehood places the border as a permanent and *static* barrier that stands at the frontier of a country's territory. This formidable border serves a crucial role in delimiting (externally) and binding (internally) a nation's territory, jurisdiction, and peoplehood, correlating with a notion of fixed "legal spatiality." For many years, this concept permeated immigration law and policy. Accordingly, it is at the border that agents of the state are permitted to exercise the utmost control over access, including the decision "to turn back from our gates any alien or class of aliens." Yet this resolves only part of the puzzle. The question that occupies us here is where precisely the border itself is to be found for immigration regulation purposes. It is here that the classic notion of the firmly planted territorial border simply does not correlate with the actual reality we find on the ground.

Neither, however, does the fashionable claim that borders are "disappearing" provide a satisfactory explanation to the phenomenon of the shifting border. In recent years, theorists of post-nationalism, trans-nationalism, and open-border admission policies have painted a picture of a new world order in which borders are blurred, global commerce and human mobility is on the rise, and international human rights instruments gain sway. As a corollary, those theorists have claimed that the old territorial border can no longer carry the weight of restricting access of non-citizens seeking to enter. Such developments, so goes the standard argument, eventually lead to a decline in the power of states to exercise exclusive authority over spatially bounded territories and their respective inhabitants. On this account, immigrants are seen as the vanguards in testing "the new world order"—their authorized (or more so, *un*authorized) movement across borders symbolizes the impossibility of enforcing strict immigration controls over access in an increasingly interdependent world.

While these arguments may appear persuasive on paper, in practice, immigration law's shifting borders have not necessarily correlated with the demise of regulatory authority over defining whom to include and whom to exclude. If anything, an opposite trend can be identified: the relaxing of the linkage between territory and authority has given greater latitude for national legislatures and regulatory agencies to develop new enforcement policies that manipulate the border—bleeding it into the interior or extending it beyond the territory's exterior—whenever such maneuvers are beneficial to deter access by irregular migrants deemed inadmissible or deportable.

Readers may already be well accustomed to the transborder nature of many forms of economic activity (including labor migration and resulting questions of citizenship such as pursued by Shachar, *supra*). As we have seen, trade and investment unsettle territoriality—even as immigration policy and national security may seem to fix borders in place. Sociologist Saskia Sassen suggests that borders generate migration. So, too, borders generate national security as a conceptual field that is in turn contingent on potentially contentious issues of jurisdiction, standing and applicability.[34] The following excerpt indicates territoriality as a subject of political debate within the government. "Global" capital and "global" security are anything but borderless. We offer a brief comment by former Legal Adviser John Bellinger on the recent shift in the U.S. position on the extraterritorial applicability of the Convention Against Torture:

John Bellinger, *U.S. Delegation Asserts Article 16 of Convention Against Torture Applies Outside U.S. Territory in Certain Circumstances, but Law of Armed Conflict "Takes Precedence" in Situations of Armed Conflict*

LawfareBlog.com (Nov. 12, 2014, 2:10 PM)[35]

As previewed by Charlie Savage in the *New York Times* this morning, the U.S. delegation appeared before the Committee Against Torture in Geneva today and announced a modest but important change in the U.S. Government position regarding extraterritorial application of Article 16 of the Convention Against Torture (which prohibits cruel, inhuman, and degrading treatment in "territory under U.S. jurisdiction"). At the same time, the U.S. delegation reaffirmed that U.S. military operations are governed by the laws of war, not the CAT, although the U.S. delegation carefully avoided using the fraught phrase *lex specialis*. As I explain below, however, this should not necessarily be viewed as a concern from a human rights perspective.

---

34. Saskia Sassen. The Mobility of Labor and Capital 33–37 (Cambridge University Press 1988).

35. For full text of the blog post, see http://www.lawfareblog.com/2014/11/u-s-delegation-asserts-article-16-of-convention-against-torture-applies-outside-u-s-territory-in-certain-circumstances-but-law-of-armed-conflict-takes-precedence-in-situations-of-armed-confli/.

In her opening statement, Acting Legal Adviser Mary McLeod stated that the obligations in Articles 2 and 16 of the CAT "extend to certain areas beyond the sovereign territory of the State Party, and more specifically to 'all places that the State Party controls as a governmental authority.'" She added that "We have determined that the United States currently exercises such control at the U.S. Naval Station at Guantanamo Bay, Cuba, and with respect to U.S. registered ships and aircraft."

This is a welcome clarification. As Harold Koh had noted in his memo on the CAT, former Legal Adviser Abe Sofaer and I had both taken the position that Article 16 of the CAT applies outside the territory of the United States in some circumstances. Harold quoted from a memorandum I had written to the Secretary of State in 2005 arguing that Article 16 should apply in Guantanamo. I would add that the newly stated U.S. position does not reverse what the U.S. delegation told the CAT committee in 2006. Then, the U.S. delegation did not state that Article 16 does not apply outside U.S. jurisdiction. Instead, the U.S. delegation told the CAT that "the U.S. does not accept that *de facto* control equates to territory under its jurisdiction." The U.S. Government position announced today that Article 16 applies to "all places that the State Party controls as governmental authority" appears to reaffirm that the U.S. continues to believe that *de facto* control does not trigger extraterritorial obligations under Article 16, but that *de jure* control will do so.

While acknowledging for the first time that Article 16 applies outside the United States in some circumstances, the U.S. delegation was careful to state that "the law of armed conflict is the controlling body of law with respect to the conduct of hostilities and the protection of war victims." A statement issued by the NSC spokesman today adds some additional gloss on this point: "Although the more specialized laws of war—which contain parallel categorical bans on torture and other inhumane treatment in situations of armed conflict—take precedence over the Convention where the two conflict, the laws of war do not generally displace the Convention's application." In other words, the U.S. Government has reaffirmed that the law of armed conflict, or international humanitarian law, is the lex specialis applicable to U.S. military operations. Although the U.S. was criticized (and I was personally pilloried) for stating this same position in 2006, this was a longstanding U.S. view. Indeed, as I noted in my Lawfare post last month [*The Convention Against Torture: Extraterritorial Application and Application to Military Operations*], Harold Koh had stated in his memorandum on the extraterritorial application of the ICCPR that "U.S. military operations in the conduct of the armed conflict with al Qaida (and associated forces) in Afghanistan and elsewhere are properly governed by relevant standards of international humanitarian law, not international human rights law."

The U.S. delegation also added today that "a time of war does not suspend operation of the Convention Against Torture, which continues to apply even when a State is engaged in armed conflict." This is clearly correct, and the U.S. delegation had made the same statement in 2006.

Finally, I should note that the continuing U.S. position that the law of armed conflict takes precedence over the CAT as applied to U.S. military operations should not necessarily be problematic from a human rights perspective. When it gave its consent to the CAT in 1994, the Senate (then with a Democratic majority) included a reservation that the cruel, inhuman, and degrading treatment prohibited by Article 16 was the same treatment already prohibited by the Fifth, Eighth, and Fourteenth Amendments of the Constitution. Thus, U.S. obligations under Article 16 are limited by U.S. domestic law. In contrast, U.S. obligations under Common Article 3 of the Geneva Conventions (which also prohibits cruel, humiliating, or degrading treatment, or outrages on the personal dignity) are subject to no such reservation.

So far, our discussion of key concepts unsettles usages of such terms as law and society, state and non-state, legal pluralism, and territoriality that readers may be more familiar with. Indeed, our purpose is, in part, to challenge assumptions that would render transnational law as *law dealing with foreign jurisdictions*, since—as we shall see by Part III—such a rendering would concede extensive powers to the president and executive branch, a scenario at the heart of globalization's democracy deficit. Retaining globalization's "domestic face" keeps local legal, political and social institutions in the picture. As we track the dynamics of transnational law within and across borders, we consider the strategic importance of such dynamics—expressed here as verticality and horizontality—as parties seek to supplement the authority of their position by invoking "higher" authorities or by stepping into a lateral arena subject to different (perhaps more favorable) rules. We turn next to the dynamics of verticality and horizontality.

E. Verticality and horizontality

This book is organized thematically around plurality and the dynamics of interlegality in the production, circulation and reformulation of transnational law. For heuristic purposes, we sometimes use verticality and horizontality as shorthand for channels of legal authority in specific situations. As we have already explained, we do not consider transnational law to be structured by levels in any settled way. Still, in particular circumstances, it is helpful to be able to point to the way legal authority moves—verticality referring to aggregations of state and supra-state authority, and horizontality referring to delegations to nonstate entities through outsourcing, contracting and deferral. Horizontality and verticality sometimes correspond to private sector governance and public sector government, but again, as explained above, there is no automatic parallel between horizontality and verticality and particular forms of governance, government or their hybrid forms.[32]

---

32. Lawyers use "public" as proxy for "state"; however, in other disciplines, public has other meanings—e.g., in the public interest. In anthropology, public refers broadly to political community (with no state implication). We follow lawyers' usage. Note that these are rubrics for heuristic purposes, not categorical definitions. It is well established that public and private, state and nonstate, cannot be neatly distinguished as empirical realities.

Verticality is organized through executive power and executive actions related to domestic, international and supranational lawmaking. Horizontality is organized through contracts, between government and the private sector, between corporations, or between other parties. Contracts are key to the thick interlegalities that make transnational law relevant to people's lives. In the following chapters, we examine the vertical and horizontal dimensions of state power together with their admixture under the conditions of transnational law. Vertical arrangements involving suprastate organizations spin off laterally—for example, as when nations agree to set up new international institutions. Horizontal arrangements involving state delegations to the private sector may spin off vertically, as when a contest between labor and business drives governmental action in particular directions. These are active dynamics, not settled structures. For further discussion, see Slaughter, Chapter 8, *infra*.

The following case study draws on a case that touches on each of the core concepts discussed in this section. As you read the case, consider what it shows with regard to governance, government, sovereignty, territoriality, jurisdiction, interlegality, executive power, and the complexities of verticality and horizontality.

III. Case Study: *Dames & Moore v. Regan*

Dames & Moore v. Regan

453 U.S. 654 (1981)

Rehnquist, J., delivered the opinion of the Court.

The questions presented by this case touch fundamentally upon the matter in which our Republic is to be governed. Throughout the nearly two centuries of our Nation's existence under the Constitution, this subject has generated considerable debate.

Our decision today will not dramatically alter this situation, for the Framers "did not make the judiciary the overseer of our government." [*Youngstown Sheet & Tube v. Sawyer*, 343 U.S. 579 (1952).] We are confined to a resolution of the dispute presented to us. That dispute involves various Executive Orders and regulations by which the President nullified attachments and liens on Iranian assets in the United States, directed that these assets be transferred to Iran, and suspended claims against Iran that may be presented to an International Claims Tribunal. This action was taken in an effort to comply with an Executive Agreement between the United States and Iran. We granted certiorari before judgment in this case, and set an expedited briefing and argument schedule, because lower courts had reached conflicting conclusions on the validity of the President's actions and, as the Solicitor General informed us, unless the Government acted by July 19, 1981, Iran could consider the United States to be in breach of the Executive Agreement.

Perhaps it is because it is so difficult to reconcile the foregoing definition of Art. III judicial power with the broad range of vitally important day-to-day questions regularly decided by Congress or the Executive, without either challenge or interference by the Judiciary, that the decisions of the Court in this area have been rare, episodic, and afford little precedential value for subsequent cases.

As we now turn to the factual and legal issues in this case, we freely confess that we are obviously deciding only one more episode in the never-ending tension between the President exercising the executive authority in a world that presents each day some new challenge with which he must deal and the Constitution under which we all live and which no one disputes embodies some sort of system of checks and balances.

I

On November 4, 1979, the American Embassy in Tehran was seized and our diplomatic personnel were captured and held hostage. In response to that crisis, President Carter, acting pursuant to the International Emergency Economic Powers Act, 91 Stat. 1626, 50 U.S.C. §§ 1701–1706 (1976 ed., Supp. III) (hereinafter IEEPA), declared a national emergency on November 14, 1979, and blocked the removal or transfer of "all property and interests in property of the Government of Iran, its instrumentalities and controlled entities and the Central Bank of Iran which are or become subject to the jurisdiction of the United States . . . ." Exec. Order No. 12170, 3 CFR 457 (1980), note following 50 U.S.C. § 1701 (1976 ed., Supp. III). President Carter authorized the Secretary of the Treasury to promulgate regulations carrying out the blocking order. On November 15, 1979, the Treasury Department's Office of Foreign Assets Control issued a regulation providing that "[u]nless licensed or authorized . . . any attachment, judgment, decree, lien, execution, garnishment, or other judicial process is null and void with respect to any property in which on or since [November 14, 1979,] there existed an interest of Iran." 31 CFR § 535.203(e) (1980). The regulations also made clear that any licenses or authorizations granted could be "amended, modified, or revoked at any time." § 535.805.

On November 26, 1979, the President granted a general license authorizing certain judicial proceedings against Iran but which did not allow the "entry of any judgment or of any decree or order of similar or analogous effect . . . ." § 535.504(a). On December 19, 1979, a clarifying regulation was issued stating that "the general authorization for judicial proceedings contained in § 535.504(a) includes pre-judgment attachment." § 535.418.

On December 19, 1979, petitioner Dames & Moore filed suit in the United States District Court for the Central District of California against the Government of Iran, the Atomic Energy Organization of Iran, and a number of Iranian banks. In its complaint, petitioner alleged that its wholly owned subsidiary, Dames & Moore International, S.R.L., was a party to a written contract with the Atomic Energy Organization, and that the subsidiary's entire interest in the contract had been assigned to petitioner. Under the contract, the subsidiary was to conduct site studies for a proposed nuclear power plant in Iran. As provided in the terms of the contract, the Atomic Energy Organization terminated the agreement for its own convenience on June 30, 1979. Petitioner contended, however, that it was owed $3,436,694.30 plus interest for services performed under the contract prior to the date of termination.[37] The District Court issued orders of attachment directed against property of the defendants, and the property of certain Iranian banks was then attached to secure any judgment that might be entered against them.

On January 20, 1981, the Americans held hostage were released by Iran pursuant to an Agreement entered into the day before and embodied in two Declarations of the Democratic and Popular Republic of Algeria. Declaration of the Government of the Democratic and Popular Republic of Algeria (App. to Pet. for Cert. 21–29), and Declaration of the Government of the Democratic and Popular Republic of Algeria Concerning the Settlement of Claims by the Government of the United States of America and the Government of the Islamic Republic of Iran (*id.*, at 30–35). The Agreement stated that "[i]t is the purpose of [the United States and Iran] . . . to terminate all litigation as between the Government of each party and the nationals of the other, and to bring about the settlement and termination of all such claims through binding arbitration." *Id.*, at 21–22. In furtherance of this goal, the Agreement called for the establishment of an Iran-United States Claims Tribunal which would arbitrate any claims not settled within six months. Awards of the Claims Tribunal are to be "final and binding" and "enforceable . . . in the courts of any nation in accordance with its laws." *Id.*, at 32. Under the Agreement, the United States is obligated "to terminate all legal proceedings in United States courts involving claims of United States persons and institutions against Iran and its state enterprises, to nullify all attachments and judgments obtained therein, to prohibit all further litigation based on such claims, and to bring about the termination of such claims through binding arbitration." *Id.*, at 22.

In addition, the United States must "act to bring about the transfer" by July 19, 1981, of all Iranian assets held in this country by American banks. *Id.*, at 24–25. One billion dollars of these assets will be deposited in a security account in the Bank of England, to the account of the Algerian Central Bank, and used to satisfy awards rendered against Iran by the Claims Tribunal. *Ibid.*

On January 19, 1981, President Carter issued a series of Executive Orders implementing the terms of the agreement. Exec. Orders Nos. 12276–12285, 46 Fed.Reg. 7913–7932. These Orders revoked all licenses permitting the exercise of "any right, power, or privilege" with regard to Iranian funds, securities, or deposits; "nullified" all non-Iranian interests in such assets acquired subsequent to the blocking order of November 14, 1979; and required those banks holding Iranian assets to

---

37. [Footnote 4 of opinion: The contract stated that any dispute incapable of resolution by agreement of the parties would be submitted to conciliation and that, if either party was unwilling to accept the results of conciliation, "the matter shall be decided finally by resort to the courts of Iran." Pet. for Cert. 7, n.2. In its complaint, which was based on breach of contract and related theories, petitioner alleged that it had sought a meeting with the Atomic Energy Organization for purposes of settling matters relating to the contract but that the Organization "has continually postponed [the] meeting and obviously does not intend that it take place." Complaint in *Dames & Moore v. Atomic Energy Organization of Iran*, No. CV 79-04918 LEW (Px) (CD Cal.), ¶ 27.]

transfer them "to the Federal Reserve Bank of New York, to be held or transferred as directed by the Secretary of the Treasury." Exec. Order No. 12279, 46 Fed.Reg. 7919.

On February 24, 1981, President Reagan issued an Executive Order in which he "ratified" the January 19th Executive Orders. Exec. Order No. 12294, 46 Fed.Reg. 14111. Moreover, he "suspended" all "claims which may be presented to the . . . Tribunal" and provided that such claims "shall have no legal effect in any action now pending in any court of the United States." *Ibid.* The suspension of any particular claim terminates if the Claims Tribunal determines that it has no jurisdiction over that claim; claims are discharged for all purposes when the Claims Tribunal either awards some recovery and that amount is paid, or determines that no recovery is due. *Ibid.*

Meanwhile, on January 27, 1981, petitioner moved for summary judgment in the District Court against the Government of Iran and the Atomic Energy Organization, but not against the Iranian banks. The District Court granted petitioner's motion and awarded petitioner the amount claimed under the contract plus interest. Thereafter, petitioner attempted to execute the judgment by obtaining writs of garnishment and execution in state court in the State of Washington, and a sheriff's sale of Iranian property in Washington was noticed to satisfy the judgment. However, by order of May 28, 1981, as amended by order of June 8, the District Court stayed execution of its judgment pending appeal by the Government of Iran and the Atomic Energy Organization. The District Court also ordered that all prejudgment attachments obtained against the Iranian defendants be vacated and that further proceedings against the bank defendants be stayed in light of the Executive Orders discussed above. App. to Pet. for Cert. 106–107.

On April 28, 1981, petitioner filed this action in the District Court for declaratory and injunctive relief against the United States and the Secretary of the Treasury, seeking to prevent enforcement of the Executive Orders and Treasury Department regulations implementing the Agreement with Iran. In its complaint, petitioner alleged that the actions of the President and the Secretary of the Treasury implementing the Agreement with Iran were beyond their statutory and constitutional powers and, in any event, were unconstitutional to the extent they adversely affect petitioner's final judgment against the Government of Iran and the Atomic Energy Organization, its execution of that judgment in the State of Washington, its prejudgment attachments, and its ability to continue to litigate against the Iranian banks. *Id.*, at 1–12. On May 28, 1981, the District Court denied petitioner's motion for a preliminary injunction and dismissed petitioner's complaint for failure to state a claim upon which relief could be granted. *Id.*, at 106–107. Prior to the District Court's ruling, the United States Courts of Appeals for the First and the District of Columbia Circuits upheld the President's authority to issue the Executive Orders and regulations challenged by petitioner. See *Chas. T. Main Int'l, Inc. v. Khuzestan Water & Power Authority*, 651 F.2d 800 (CA1 1981); *American Int'l Group, Inc. v. Islamic Republic of Iran*, 211 U.S.App.D.C. 468, 657 F.2d 430 (1981).

On June 3, 1981, petitioner filed a notice of appeal from the District Court's order, and the appeal was docketed in the United States Court of Appeals for the Ninth Circuit. On June 4, the Treasury Department amended its regulations to mandate "the transfer of bank deposits and certain other financial assets of Iran in the United States to the Federal Reserve Bank of New York by noon, June 19." App. to Pet. for Cert. 151–152. The District Court, however, entered an injunction pending appeal prohibiting the United States from requiring the transfer of Iranian property that is subject to "any writ of attachment, garnishment, judgment, levy, or other judicial lien" issued by any court in favor of petitioner. *Id.*, at 168. Arguing that this is a case of "imperative public importance," petitioner then sought a writ of certiorari before judgment. Pet. for Cert. 10. See 28 U.S.C. § 2101(e); this Court's Rule 18. Because the issues presented here are of great significance and demand prompt resolution, we granted the petition for the writ, adopted an expedited briefing schedule, and set the case for oral argument on June 24, 1981. 452 U.S. 932 (1981).

II

The parties and the lower courts, confronted with the instant questions, have all agreed that much relevant analysis is contained in *Youngstown Sheet & Tube Co. v. Sawyer*, 343 U.S. 579 (1952). Justice Black's opinion for the Court in that case, involving the validity of President Truman's effort to seize the country's steel mills in the wake of a nationwide strike, recognized that "[t]he President's power, if any, to issue the order must stem either from an act of Congress or from the Constitution itself." *Id.*, at 585, 72 S.Ct. at 864. Justice Jackson's concurring opinion elaborated in a general way the consequences of different types of interaction between the two democratic branches in assessing Presidential authority to act in any given case. When the President acts pursuant to an express or implied authorization from Congress, he exercises not only his powers but also those delegated by Congress. In such a case the executive action "would be supported by the strongest of presumptions and the widest latitude of judicial interpretation, and the burden of persuasion would rest heavily upon any who might attack it." *Id.*, at 637, 72 S.Ct., at 871. When the President acts in the absence of congressional authorization he may enter "a zone of twilight in which he and Congress may have concurrent authority, or in which its distribution is uncertain." *Ibid.* In such a case the analysis becomes more complicated, and the validity of the President's action, at least so far as separation-of-powers principles are concerned, hinges on a consideration of all the circumstances which might shed light on the views of the Legislative Branch toward such action, including "congressional inertia, indifference or quiescence." *Ibid.* Finally, when the President acts in contravention of the will of Congress, "his power is at its lowest ebb," and the Court can sustain his actions "only by disabling the Congress from acting upon the subject." *Id.*, at 637–638, 72 S.Ct., at 871–872.

Although we have in the past found and do today find Justice Jackson's classification of executive actions into three general categories analytically useful, we should be mindful of Justice Holmes' admonition, quoted by Justice Frankfurter in *Youngstown*, *supra*, at 597, 72 S.Ct., at 890 (concurring opinion), that "[t]he great ordinances of the Constitution do not establish and divide fields of black and white." *Springer v. Philippine Islands*, 277 U.S. 189, 209 (1928) (dissenting opinion). Justice Jackson himself recognized that his three categories represented "a somewhat over-simplified grouping," 343 U.S., at 635, and it is doubtless the case that executive action in any particular instance falls, not neatly in one of three pigeonholes, but rather at some point along a spectrum running from explicit congressional authorization to explicit congressional prohibition. This is particularly true as respects cases such as the one before us, involving responses to international crises the nature of which Congress can hardly have been expected to anticipate in any detail.

III

In nullifying post-November 14, 1979, attachments and directing those persons holding blocked Iranian funds and securities to transfer them to the Federal Reserve Bank of New York for ultimate transfer to Iran, President Carter cited five sources of express or inherent power. The Government, however, has principally relied on § 203 of the IEEPA, 91 Stat. 1626, 50 U.S.C. § 1702(a)(1) (1976 ed., Supp. III), as authorization for these actions. Section 1702(a)(1) provides in part:

> "At the times and to the extent specified in section 1701 of this title, the President may, under such regulations as he may prescribe, by means of instructions, licenses, or otherwise—
>
> "(A) investigate, regulate, or prohibit—
>
> "(i) any transactions in foreign exchange,
>
> "(ii) transfers of credit or payments between, by, through, or to any banking institution, to the extent that such transfers or payments involve any interest of any foreign country or a national thereof,
>
> "(iii) the importing or exporting of currency or securities, and
>
> "(B) investigate, regulate, direct and compel, nullify, void, prevent or prohibit, any acquisition, holding, withholding, use, transfer, withdrawal, transportation, importation or exportation of, or dealing in, or exercising any right, power, or privilege with respect to, or transactions involving, any property in which any foreign country or a national thereof has any interest;
>
> "by any person, or with respect to any property, subject to the jurisdiction of the United States."

The Government contends that the acts of "nullifying" the attachments and ordering the "transfer" of the frozen assets are specifically authorized by the plain language of the above statute. The two Courts of Appeals that have considered the issue agreed with this contention. In *Chas. T. Main Int'l, Inc. v. Khuzestan Water & Power Authority*, the Court of Appeals for the First Circuit explained:

> "The President relied on his IEEPA powers in November 1979, when he 'blocked' all Iranian assets in this country, and again in January 1981, when he 'nullified' interests acquired in blocked property, and ordered that property's transfer. The President's actions, in this regard, are in keeping with the language of IEEPA: initially he 'prevent[ed] and prohibit[ed]' 'transfers' of Iranian assets; later he 'direct[ed] and compel[led]' the 'transfer' and 'withdrawal' of the assets, 'nullify[ing]' certain 'rights' and 'privileges' acquired in them.
>
> "Main argues that IEEPA does not supply the President with power to override judicial remedies, such as attachments and injunctions, or to extinguish 'interests' in foreign assets held by United States citizens. But we can find no such limitation in IEEPA's terms. The language of IEEPA is sweeping and unqualified. It provides broadly that the President may void or nullify the 'exercising [by *any* person of] *any* right, power or privilege with respect to . . . any property in which any foreign country has any interest . . . .' 50 U.S.C. § 1702(a)(1)(B)." 651 F.2d, at 806–807 (emphasis in original).

Petitioner contends that we should ignore the plain language of this statute because an examination of its legislative history as well as the history of § 5(b) of the Trading With the Enemy Act (hereinafter TWEA), 40 Stat. 411, as amended, 50 U.S.C. App. § 5(b) (1976 ed. and Supp. III), from which the pertinent language of § 1702 is directly drawn, reveals that the statute was not intended to give the President such extensive power over the assets of a foreign state during times of national emergency. According to petitioner, once the President instituted the November 14, 1979, blocking order, § 1702 authorized him "only to continue the freeze or to discontinue controls." Brief for Petitioner 32.

We do not agree and refuse to read out of § 1702 all meaning to the words "transfer," "compel," or "nullify." Nothing in the legislative history of either § 1702 or § 5(b) of the TWEA requires such a result. To the contrary, we think both the legislative history and cases interpreting the TWEA fully sustain the broad authority of the Executive when acting under this congressional grant of power. See, *e.g., Orvis v. Brownell*, 345 U.S. 183 (1953). Although Congress intended to limit the President's emergency power in peacetime, we do not think the changes brought about by the enactment of the IEEPA in any way affected the authority of the President to take the specific actions taken here. We likewise note that by the time petitioner instituted this action, the President had already entered the freeze order. Petitioner proceeded against the blocked assets only after the Treasury Department had issued revocable licenses authorizing such proceedings and attachments. The Treasury Regulations provided that "unless licensed" any attachment is null and void, 31 CFR § 535.203(e) (1980), and all licenses "may be amended, modified, or revoked at any time." § 535.805. As such, the attachments obtained by petitioner were specifically made subordinate to further actions which the President might take under the IEEPA. Petitioner was on notice of the contingent nature of its interest in the frozen assets.

This Court has previously recognized that the congressional purpose in authorizing blocking orders is "to put control of foreign assets in the hands of the President. . . ." *Propper v. Clark*, 337 U.S. 472, 493 (1949). Such orders permit the President to maintain the foreign assets at his disposal for use in negotiating the resolution of a declared national emergency. The frozen assets serve as a "bargaining chip" to be used by the President when dealing with a hostile country. Accordingly, it is difficult to accept petitioner's argument because the practical effect of it is to allow individual claimants throughout the country to minimize or wholly eliminate this "bargaining chip" through attachments, garnishments, or similar encumbrances on property. Neither the purpose the statute was enacted to serve nor its plain language supports such a result.

Because the President's action in nullifying the attachments and ordering the transfer of the assets was taken pursuant to specific congressional authorization, it is "supported by the strongest of presumptions and the widest latitude of judicial interpretation, and the burden of persuasion would rest heavily upon any who might attack it." *Youngstown*, 343 U.S., at 637 (Jackson, J., concurring). Under the circumstances of this case, we cannot say that petitioner has sustained that heavy burden. A contrary ruling would mean that the Federal Government as a whole lacked the power exercised by the President, see *id.*, at 636–637 and that we are not prepared to say.

IV

Although we have concluded that the IEEPA constitutes specific congressional authorization to the President to nullify the attachments and order the transfer of Iranian assets, there remains the question of the President's authority to suspend claims pending in American courts. Such claims have, of course, an existence apart from the attachments which accompanied them. In terminating these claims through Executive Order No. 12294 the President purported to act under authority of both the IEEPA and 22 U.S.C. § 1732, the so-called "Hostage Act." 746 Fed.Reg. 14111 (1981).

We conclude that although the IEEPA authorized the nullification of the attachments, it cannot be read to authorize the suspension of the claims. The claims of American citizens against Iran are not in themselves transactions involving Iranian property or efforts to exercise any rights with respect to such property. An *in personam* lawsuit, although it might eventually be reduced to judgment and that judgment might be executed upon, is an effort to establish liability and fix damages and does not focus on any particular property within the jurisdiction. The terms of the IEEPA therefore do not authorize the President to suspend claims in American courts. . . .

The Hostage Act, passed in 1868, provides:

> "Whenever it is made known to the President that any citizen of the United States has been unjustly deprived of his liberty by or under the authority of any foreign government, it shall be the duty of the President forthwith to demand of that government the reasons of such imprisonment; and if it appears to be wrongful and in violation of the rights of American citizenship, the President shall forthwith demand the release of such citizen, and if

> the release so demanded is unreasonably delayed or refused, the President shall use such means, not amounting to acts of war, as he may think necessary and proper to obtain or effectuate the release; and all the facts and proceedings relative thereto shall as soon as practicable be communicated by the President to Congress." Rev.Stat. § 2001, 22 U.S.C. § 1732.

We are reluctant to conclude that this provision constitutes specific authorization to the President to suspend claims in American courts. Although the broad language of the Hostage Act suggests it may cover this case, there are several difficulties with such a view. The legislative history indicates that the Act was passed in response to a situation unlike the recent Iranian crisis. Congress in 1868 was concerned with the activity of certain countries refusing to recognize the citizenship of naturalized Americans traveling abroad, and repatriating such citizens against their will. See, *e.g.*, Cong. Globe, 40th Cong., 2d Sess., 4331 (1868) (Sen. Fessenden); *id.*, at 4354 (Sen. Conness); see also 22 U.S.C. § 1731. These countries were not interested in returning the citizens in exchange for any sort of ransom. This also explains the reference in the Act to imprisonment "in violation of the rights of American citizenship." Although the Iranian hostage-taking violated international law and common decency, the hostages were not seized out of any refusal to recognize their American citizenship—they were seized precisely *because of* their American citizenship....

Concluding that neither the IEEPA nor the Hostage Act constitutes specific authorization of the President's action suspending claims, however, is not to say that these statutory provisions are entirely irrelevant to the question of the validity of the President's action. We think both statutes highly relevant in the looser sense of indicating congressional acceptance of a broad scope for executive action in circumstances such as those presented in this case. As noted in Part III, *supra*, at 2982–2983, the IEEPA delegates broad authority to the President to act in times of national emergency with respect to property of a foreign country. The Hostage Act similarly indicates congressional willingness that the President have broad discretion when responding to the hostile acts of foreign sovereigns. As Senator Williams, draftsman of the language eventually enacted as the Hostage Act, put it:

> "If you propose any remedy at all, you must invest the Executive with some discretion, so that he may apply the remedy to a case as it may arise. As to England or France he might adopt one policy to relieve a citizen imprisoned by either one of those countries; as to the Barbory powers, he might adopt another policy; as to the islands of the ocean, another. With different countries that have different systems of government he might adopt different means." Cong. Globe, 40th Cong., 2d Sess., 4359 (1868).

Proponents of the bill recognized that it placed a "loose discretion" in the President's hands, *id.*, at 4238 (Sen. Stewart), but argued that "[s]omething must be intrusted to the Executive" and that "[t]he President ought to have the power to do what the exigencies of the case require to rescue [a] citizen from imprisonment." *Id.*, at 4233, 4357 (Sen. Williams). An original version of the Act, which authorized the President to suspend trade with a foreign country and even arrest citizens of that country in the United States in retaliation, was rejected because "there may be a great variety of cases arising where other and different means would be equally effective, and where the end desired could be accomplished without resorting to such dangerous and violent measures." *Id.*, at 4233 (Sen. Williams).

Although we have declined to conclude that the IEEPA or the Hostage Act directly authorizes the President's suspension of claims for the reasons noted, we cannot ignore the general tenor of Congress' legislation in this area in trying to determine whether the President is acting alone or at least with the acceptance of Congress. As we have noted, Congress cannot anticipate and legislate with regard to every possible action the President may find it necessary to take or every possible situation in which he might act. Such failure of Congress specifically to delegate authority does not, "especially . . . in the areas of foreign policy and national security," imply "congressional disapproval" of action taken by the Executive. *Haig v. Agee*, 453 U.S. 280, 291. On the contrary, the enactment of legislation closely related to the question of the President's authority in a particular case which evinces legislative intent to accord the President broad discretion may be considered to "invite" "measures on independent presidential responsibility," *Youngstown*, 343 U.S., at 637 (Jackson, J., concurring). At least this is so where there is no contrary indication of legislative intent and when, as here, there is a history of congressional acquiescence in conduct of the sort engaged in by the President. It is to that history which we now turn.

Not infrequently in affairs between nations, outstanding claims by nationals of one country against the government of another country are "sources of friction" between the two sovereigns. *United States v. Pink*, 315 U.S. 203, 225 (1942). To resolve these difficulties, nations have often entered into agreements settling the claims of their respective nationals. As one treatise writer puts it, international agreements settling claims by nationals of one state against the government of another "are established international practice reflecting traditional international theory." L. Henkin, Foreign Affairs and the Constitution 262 (1972). Consistent with that principle, the United States has repeatedly exercised its sovereign authority to settle the claims of its nationals against foreign countries. Though those settlements have sometimes been made by treaty, there has also been a longstanding practice of settling such claims by executive agreement without the advice and consent of the Senate. Under such agreements, the President has agreed to renounce or extinguish claims of United States nationals against foreign governments in return for lump-sum payments or the establishment of arbitration procedures. To be sure, many of these settlements were encouraged by the United States claimants themselves, since a claimant's only hope of obtaining any payment at all might lie in having his Government negotiate a diplomatic settlement on his behalf. But it is also undisputed that the "United States has sometimes disposed of the claims of its citizens without their consent, or even without consultation with them, usually without exclusive regard for their interests, as distinguished from those of the nation as a whole." . . . It is clear that the practice of settling claims continues today. Since 1952, the President has entered into at least

10 binding settlements with foreign nations, including an $80 million settlement with the People's Republic of China.

Crucial to our decision today is the conclusion that Congress has implicitly approved the practice of claim settlement by executive agreement. This is best demonstrated by Congress' enactment of the International Claims Settlement Act of 1949, 64 Stat. 13, as amended, 22 U.S.C. § 1621 *et seq.* (1976 ed. and Supp. IV). The Act had two purposes: (1) to allocate to United States nationals funds received in the course of an executive claims settlement with Yugoslavia, and (2) to provide a procedure whereby funds resulting from future settlements could be distributed. To achieve these ends Congress created the International Claims Commission, now the Foreign Claims Settlement Commission, and gave it jurisdiction to make final and binding decisions with respect to claims by United States nationals against settlement funds. 22 U.S.C. § 1623(a). By creating a procedure to implement future settlement agreements, Congress placed its stamp of approval on such agreements. Indeed, the legislative history of the Act observed that the United States was seeking settlements with countries other than Yugoslavia and that the bill contemplated settlements of a similar nature in the future. H.R.Rep. No. 770, 81st Cong., 1st Sess., 4, 8 (1949).

Over the years Congress has frequently amended the International Claims Settlement Act to provide for particular problems arising out of settlement agreements, thus demonstrating Congress' continuing acceptance of the President's claim settlement authority. With respect to the Executive Agreement with the People's Republic of China, for example, Congress established an allocation formula for distribution of the funds received pursuant to the Agreement. 22 U.S.C. § 1627(f) (1976 ed. and Supp. IV). As with legislation involving other executive agreements, Congress did not question the fact of the settlement or the power of the President to have concluded it. In 1976, Congress authorized the Foreign Claims Settlement Commission to adjudicate the merits of claims by United States nationals against East Germany, prior to any settlement with East Germany, so that the Executive would "be in a better position to negotiate an adequate settlement . . . of these claims." S.Rep. No. 94-1188, p. 2 (1976), U. S. Code Cong. & Admin. News, 1976, pp. 5582, 5583; 22 U.S.C. § 1644b. Similarly, Congress recently amended the International Claims Settlement Act to facilitate the settlement of claims against Vietnam. 22 U.S.C. §§ 1645, 1645a(5) (1976 ed., Supp. IV). The House Report stated that the purpose of the legislation was to establish an official inventory of losses of private United States property in Vietnam so that recovery could be achieved "through future direct Government-to-Government negotiation of private property claims." H.R.Rep. No. 96-915, pp. 2–3, U. S. Code Cong. & Admin. News, 1980, pp. 7328, 7329–7330. Finally, the legislative history of the IEEPA further reveals that Congress has accepted the authority of the Executive to enter into settlement agreements. Though the IEEPA was enacted to provide for some limitation on the President's emergency powers, Congress stressed that "[n]othing in this act is intended . . . to interfere with the authority of the President to [block assets], or to impede the settlement of claims of U. S. citizens against foreign countries." S.Rep. No. 95-466, p. 6 (1977), U. S. Code Cong. & Admin. News, 1977, pp. 4540, 4544; 50 U.S.C. § 1706(a)(1) (1976 ed., Supp. III).

In addition to congressional acquiescence in the President's power to settle claims, prior cases of this Court have also recognized that the President does have some measure of power to enter into executive agreements without obtaining the advice and consent of the Senate. In *United States v. Pink*, 315 U.S. 203 (1942), for example, the Court upheld the validity of the Litvinov Assignment, which was part of an Executive Agreement whereby the Soviet Union assigned to the United States amounts owed to it by American nationals so that outstanding claims of other American nationals could be paid. The Court explained that the resolution of such claims was integrally connected with normalizing United States' relations with a foreign state:

> "Power to remove such obstacles to full recognition as settlement of claims of our nationals . . . certainly is a modest implied power of the President. . . . No such obstacle can be placed in the way of rehabilitation of relations between this country and another nation, unless the historic conception of the powers and responsibilities . . . is to be drastically revised." *Id.*, at 229–230.

Similarly, Judge Learned Hand recognized:

> "The constitutional power of the President extends to the settlement of mutual claims between a foreign government and the United States, at least when it is an incident to the recognition of that government; and it would be unreasonable to circumscribe it to such controversies. The continued mutual amity between the nation and other powers again and again depends upon a satisfactory compromise of mutual claims; the necessary power to make such compromises has existed from the earliest times and been exercised by the foreign offices of all civilized nations." *Ozanic v. United States*, 188 F.2d 228, 231 (CA2 1951).

Petitioner raises two arguments in opposition to the proposition that Congress has acquiesced in this longstanding practice of claims settlement by executive agreement. First, it suggests that all pre-1952 settlement claims, and corresponding court cases such as *Pink*, should be discounted because of the evolution of the doctrine of sovereign immunity. Petitioner observes that prior to 1952 the United States adhered to the doctrine of absolute sovereign immunity, so that absent action by the Executive there simply would be no remedy for a United States national against a foreign government. When the United States in 1952 adopted a more restrictive notion of sovereign immunity, by means of the so-called "Tate" letter, it is petitioner's view that United States nationals no longer needed executive aid to settle claims and that, as a result, the President's authority to settle such claims in some sense "disappeared." Though petitioner's argument is not wholly without merit, it is refuted by the fact that since 1952 there have been at least 10 claims settlements by executive agreement. Thus, even if the pre-1952 cases should be disregarded, congressional acquiescence in settlement agreements since that time supports the President's power to act here.

Petitioner next asserts that Congress divested the President of the authority to settle claims when it enacted the Foreign Sovereign Immunities Act of 1976 (hereinafter FSIA), 28 U.S.C. §§ 1330, 1602 *et seq.* The FSIA granted personal and subject-matter jurisdiction in the federal district courts over commercial suits brought by claimants against those foreign states which have waived immunity. 28 U.S.C. § 1330. Prior to the enactment of the FSIA, a foreign government's immunity to suit was determined by the Executive Branch on a case-by-case basis. According to petitioner, the principal purpose of the FSIA was to depoliticize these commercial lawsuits by taking them out of the arena of foreign affairs—where the Executive Branch is subject to the pressures of foreign states seeking to avoid liability through a grant of immunity—and by placing them within the exclusive jurisdiction of the courts. Petitioner thus insists that the President, by suspending its claims, has circumscribed the jurisdiction of the United States courts in violation of Art. III of the Constitution.

We disagree. In the first place, we do not believe that the President has attempted to divest the federal courts of jurisdiction. Executive Order No. 12294 purports only to "suspend" the claims, not divest the federal court of "jurisdiction." . . . The President has exercised the power, acquiesced in by Congress, to settle claims and, as such, has simply effected a change in the substantive law governing the lawsuit.

In light of all of the foregoing—the inferences to be drawn from the character of the legislation Congress has enacted in the area, such as the IEEPA and the Hostage Act, and from the history of acquiescence in executive claims settlement—we conclude that the President was authorized to suspend pending claims pursuant to Executive Order No. 12294. As Justice Frankfurter pointed out in *Youngstown*, 343 U.S., at 610–611, 72 S.Ct., at 897–898, "a systematic, unbroken, executive practice, long pursued to the knowledge of the Congress and never before questioned . . . may be treated as a gloss on 'Executive Power' vested in the President by § 1 of Art. II." Past practice does not, by itself, create power, but "long-continued practice, known to and acquiesced in by Congress, would raise a presumption that the [action] had been [taken] in pursuance of its consent. . . ." *United States v. Midwest Oil Co.*, 236 U.S. 459, 474 (1915). See *Haig v. Agee*, 453 U.S., at 291, 292. Such practice is present here and such a presumption is also appropriate. In light of the fact that Congress may be considered to have consented to the President's action in suspending claims, we cannot say that action exceeded the President's powers.

Our conclusion is buttressed by the fact that the means chosen by the President to settle the claims of American nationals provided an alternative forum, the Claims Tribunal, which is capable of providing meaningful relief. The Solicitor General also suggests that the provision of the Claims Tribunal will actually *enhance* the opportunity for claimants to recover their claims, in that the Agreement removes a number of jurisdictional and procedural impediments faced by claimants in United States courts. Brief for Federal Respondents 13–14. Although being overly sanguine about the chances of United States claimants before the Claims Tribunal would require a degree of naiveté which should not be demanded even of judges, the Solicitor General's point cannot be discounted. Moreover, it is important to remember that we have already held that the President has the statutory authority to nullify attachments and to transfer the assets out of the country. The President's power to do so does not depend on his provision of a forum whereby claimants can recover on those claims. The fact that the President has provided such a forum here means that the claimants are receiving something in return for the suspension of their claims, namely, access to an international tribunal before which they may well recover something on their claims. Because there does appear to be a real "settlement" here, this case is more easily analogized to the more traditional claim settlement cases of the past.

Just as importantly, Congress has not disapproved of the action taken here. Though Congress has held hearings on the Iranian Agreement itself, Congress has not enacted legislation, or even passed a resolution, indicating its displeasure with the Agreement. Quite the contrary, the relevant Senate Committee has stated that the establishment of the Tribunal is "of vital importance to the United States." S.Rep.No.97-71, p. 5 (1981). We are thus clearly not confronted with a situation in which Congress has in some way resisted the exercise of Presidential authority.

Finally, we re-emphasize the narrowness of our decision. We do not decide that the President possesses plenary power to settle claims, even as against foreign governmental entities. As the Court of Appeals for the First Circuit stressed, "[t]he sheer magnitude of such a power, considered against the background of the diversity and complexity of modern international trade, cautions against any broader construction of authority than is necessary." *Chas T. Main Int'l, Inc. v. Khuzestan Water & Power Authority*, 651 F.2d, at 814. But where, as here, the settlement of claims has been determined to be a necessary incident to the resolution of a major foreign policy dispute between our country and another, and where, as here, we can conclude that Congress acquiesced in the President's action, we are not prepared to say that the President lacks the power to settle such claims.

V

We do not think it appropriate at the present time to address petitioner's contention that the suspension of claims, if authorized, would constitute a taking of property in violation of the Fifth Amendment to the United States Constitution in the absence of just compensation. However, this contention, and the possibility that the President's actions may effect a taking of petitioner's property, make ripe for adjudication the question whether petitioner will have a remedy at law in the Court of Claims under the Tucker Act, 28 U.S.C. § 1491 (1976 ed., Supp. III), in such an event.

It has been contended that the "treaty exception" to the jurisdiction of the Court of Claims, 28 U.S.C. § 1502, might preclude the Court of Claims from exercising jurisdiction over any takings claim the petitioner might bring. At oral argument, however, the Government conceded that § 1502 would not act as a bar to petitioner's action in the Court of Claims. Tr. of Oral Arg. 39–42, 47. We agree. See *United States v. Weld*, 127 U.S. 51 (1888); *United States v. Old Settlers*, 148 U.S. 427 (1893); *Hughes Aircraft Co. v. United States*, 534 F.2d 889, 209 Ct.Cl. 446 (1976). Accordingly, to the extent petitioner believes it has suffered an unconstitutional taking by the suspension of the claims, we see no jurisdictional obstacle to an appropriate action in the United States Court of Claims under the Tucker Act.

The judgment of the District Court is accordingly affirmed, and the mandate shall issue forthwith.

It is so ordered.

Notes and Questions

1. In his article, *Transnational Legal Process*, 75 NEB. L. REV. 181, 183–84 (1994), Professor Koh offers several defining factors with respect to transnational legal processes in general, and *Dames & Moore* specifically:

> Transnational legal process has four distinctive features. First, it is non-traditional: it breaks down two traditional dichotomies that have historically dominated the study of international law: between domestic and international, public and private. Second, it is nonstatist: the actors in this process are not just, or even primarily, nation-states, but include nonstate actors as well. Third, transnational legal process is dynamic, not static. Transnational law transforms, mutates, and percolates up and down, from the public to the private, from the domestic to the international level and back down again. Fourth and finally, it is normative.

How do these criteria apply to *Dames & Moore v. Regan*? Does the Iranian hostage crisis fit within the traditional categories of domestic or international law? In what ways was this process a dynamic one? Who were the actors in this case? What new law was created in the process?

2. The Executive Branch is responsible for conducting foreign affairs. As transnational legal disputes grow in frequency and complexity, private entities may increasingly turn to the executive for assistance in transnational legal disputes. How does this fit within existing ideas of executive power as outlined in Part II of the *Dames & Moore* opinion?

3. We will see in later chapters—particularly Chapters 3 and 9—that transnational law often involves the executive playing a role beyond its traditional responsibility to "take care that the laws be faithfully executed." U.S. CONST. art. II § 3. Such instances are by their very nature ones that compel rethinking about what may be long-settled frameworks for the exercise of executive power. In *Dames & Moore*, what does the Court say about the requirement that Congress delegate new authority for the executive prior to the action in question? Is the mere fact that Congress does not explicitly challenge executive power sufficient as evidence of their agreement that such a power exists? Citing *Haig v. Agee*, 453 U.S. 280 (1981), the Court apparently thinks so: "Congress cannot anticipate and legislate with regard to every possible action the President may find it necessary to take or every possible situation in which he might act. Such failure of Congress specifically to delegate authority does not, especially . . . in the areas of foreign policy and national security, imply congressional disapproval of action taken by the Executive." In light of this passage, can you imagine circumstances or action(s) by Congress that might lead the Court to a different conclusion?

4. An update: The Supreme Court upheld the creation of the Iran-United States Claims Tribunal, noting that it provided an alternative for Americans who were no longer able to litigate their claims in U.S. or Iranian courts. One of the last claims pending in this tribunal involved Iran's claim for $400 million paid for military equipment that was not received due to the intervening events of the revolution. Over time, that claim grew to $1.7 billion, reflecting accrued interest. Iran sought further compensation for damages in arbitration at the Hague. In 2016, the White House settled the case in the context of successful negotiations that ended Iran's nuclear arms program and a long period of international sanctions. Within a short time, payment was made, and three Americans then held in Iran were released. The timing of the arms agreement, payment of the settlement and the release of detainees became a source of controversy in the United States. "The White House described the settlement as a victory for taxpayers, arguing that the U.S. was likely to lose in arbitration under way at the Hague . . . and could have been liable for billions more if the process had dragged on. 'Iran will be returned its own funds, including appropriate interest, but much less than the amount that Iran sought,' President Obama said on Sunday. But the transaction is stirring a debate here over whether the funds were essentially a ransom paid to Iran's leadership." Jay Solomon, *U.S. Payment of $1.7 Billion to Iran Raises Questions of Ransom*, WALL STREET JOURNAL (Jan. 21, 2016), http://www.wsj.com/articles/u-s-payment-of-1-7-billion-to-iran-raises-questions-of-ransom-1453421778.

5. Do transnational problems necessitate solutions that are parallel in scale? Consider the analysis of Mariana Valverde in *Jurisdiction and Scale: Legal 'Technicalities' as Resources for Theory*, 18 SOC. & LEGAL STUDIES 139, 144 (2009).

> As is well known, jurisdiction often refers to territorial divides: California versus Oregon, France versus Europe, Russian polar waters versus international waters. In the routine work of jurisdiction, territories and sovereigns tend to be seen as part of the same package, such that sorting out territories simultaneously sorts out governing authorities. Jurisdiction, however, distinguishes more than territories and authorities, more than the where and the who of governance. Jurisdiction also differentiates and organizes the 'what' of governance—and, most importantly because of its relative invisibility, the 'how' of governance. Thus, jurisdiction sorts the where, the who, the what, and the how of governance through a kind of chain reaction, whereby if one question (where, who) is decided, then the answers to the other questions seem to follow automatically. . . .
>
> The way the game works is as follows. If a decision is made—by a court of appeal, by a legislature, or by an international body—that a certain entity, say, a supply of fish, is indeed located in a certain space (say, Canadian territorial waters rather than international waters) then the answers to the other key questions of governance will generally flow in a certain direction.

> There may be obstacles or struggles, say, as between an aboriginal group and a Canadian province, that make the workings of the jurisdictional machine less than smooth, but jurisdictional assemblages have a strong path dependence. If the fish are deemed to be Canadian, then the logic of 'natural resources' will certainly be deployed to govern them, but the political consequences of unemployment in East Coast fishing villages will also be taken into account: the 'who', then, ends up determining much of the 'how'.
>
> While disputes about 'who rules' are relatively common, especially in post-colonial settings and at the international level, legal challenges to the 'how' dimension are rarer—at least as direct challenges. In the earlier example, an animal rights group could perhaps try to claim that the fish in the sea are not 'a resource' but rather individual rights-bearers, a move that would draw on a completely different jurisdictional apparatus, but such a claim would be farfetched precisely because it directly targets the 'how'. An animal rights group seeking to change the 'how' is more likely to creatively use the jurisdictional machine that exists, arguing that fish are actually the property of aboriginal nations, for example—a move that would challenge one particular use of authority but would leave jurisdiction as such even stronger than before.

6. Dames & Moore ultimately had their claim before the Iran-United States Claim Tribunal dismissed for lack of jurisdiction. Could Valverde's approach of evaluating the "how" question of governance have provided an alternative series of arguments for Dames & Moore before the Supreme Court? How might such an argument have been presented by Dames & Moore?

IV. Discussion

In this Introduction, we have undertaken to present our thesis as to the interlegal complexities of transnational law. We have also introduced the main areas of transnationalism that inform our analysis. We have indicated several key implications that follow from our theme as to the relational and episodic aspects of transnational law, its embeddedness in forms of authority and power beyond those of the law, and its availability to multidisciplinary analysis. We introduced readers to our principal key concepts: legality and society, plurality and interlegality, territoriality and jurisdiction, and verticality and horizontality. *Dames & Moore* illustrates these elements of our approach—including the extent to which the primary element of private rule-making (the contract) today entails implications for executive power, and vice versa.

What remains is to explain the organization of the book itself, as a function of these conceptual elements, taken together. Since our interest is in advancing an understanding of transnational law as *practice*, the book is organized around the pragmatics of transnational legal work—concentrating on its main working vehicles. In Part I, we attend to treaties and international agreements. In Part II, we turn to supply chain contracts and industrial codes of conduct. In Part III, we reprise these elements by taking up specific forms of interlegality arising from global governance (ISO standards and guidance, voluntary rules of land tenure, privatization and arbitration) and the pressures these exert—directly and indirectly—on domestic courts and executive powers. The thematics introduced in this chapter reappear in various recombinations in all chapters. Throughout, in each chapter, we relate the issues in law to their human consequences on the ground, not merely as an exercise in tracking the circulation of law's power, but to highlight crucial sites of legal mobilization and contestation, as well as consequential exclusions, as transnational law develops amidst powers and authorities of other kinds.

Part One

Governance through Treaties and International Agreements

Chapter 2

Treaties and Agreements: The Global Environment

I. Introduction

Many people encountering the idea of transnational law for the first time imagine that it involves a sort of world government, or global law. In this chapter, we feature international treaties and agreements intended to govern chlorofluorocarbons (CFCs) and carbon emissions in the interest of averting the destruction of the ozone layer and mitigating the risks of climate change. We feature environmental protection for two reasons. First, the planetary aspect of environmental protection is the very essence of popular understandings of globalization—literally, the globe as a unitary whole. Some readers may remember the thrilling shock of those first photographs of Earth from space—round, beautiful, a jewel of green and blue, wrapped in white clouds. Second, and closer to the discussion in this chapter, in no other area of transnational law are the changing vectors of interlegality within the government itself so clear as in the environmental sector. Our examples in this chapter are the Montreal Protocol and the Paris Accords on Climate Change. Between the Montreal Protocol (a treaty approved by Congress) and the Paris Accords (brought forward as an executive agreement) are four decades of deepening political fracture over regulation, climate change, presidential authority and congressional obstruction.

Most transnational law is not global law in the way environmental treaties and agreements are. And as we shall see in the suite of materials in this chapter (ranging from global accords to municipal regulations), so-called global law has strong interlegal aspects, in both its making and implementation. Global governance involves coordinated exercises of power that can transcend states, regions, and municipalities and include state as well as non-state actors—while at the same time working through those state and non-state agencies, as Neumann and Sending and others suggest (see Chapter 1, *supra*). As Eve Darian-Smith notes: "Global governance refers to the political networks, institutions, mechanisms, and agencies required to solve problems that confront multiple states or regions, and it is needed when there are limited alternative enforcement mechanisms available."[1] In this chapter, we consider the ways states are drawn into governance relations through multinational treaties and

1. Eve Darian-Smith, Laws and Societies in Global Contexts: Contemporary Approaches 52 (2013).

agreements—reinforcing their vertical dimensions by expanding their horizontal reach to external sovereignties, often facilitated through non-state agencies and actors. That theme continues in the next two chapters, featuring the North American Free Trade Agreement (NAFTA) and the World Trade Organization (WTO), respectively.

All of the legal arrangements or proposals in these chapters represent what we might call traditional attempts to solve global or transnational problems—traditional in the sense that the scale of the perceived problem aligns with the scale of the legal solution devised. In the case of environmental problems such as ozone depletion or climate change which are truly global in nature, the traditional legal solution is a multilateral treaty or agreement—a kind of global legislation. Similarly, regional trade agreements such as NAFTA and the proposed TPP[2] draw on parties from a common region. But it would be misleading to conclude that such traditional approaches to parity of scale are automatically appropriate. For example, as we shall see later in this chapter, global problems sometimes invite creative local solutions. The processes involved in reaching such agreements involve multiple legal frameworks, institutions and actors, often interacting in new ways. Despite the state solution imposed in the form of a treaty, private actors play a significant role in crafting these outcomes and making them effective. Polycentric solutions can often be more effective than global ones, as we shall see as we analyze the intricate layerings of law, politics and markets.

Professor David Held captures some of these complexities as he highlights the diversity of the formal properties of global governance:

> Global governance today is a multilayered, multidimensional and multiactor system. It is multilayered in so far as the development and implementation of global policies involve a process of political coordination between suprastate, transnational, national and often substate agencies. It is multidimensional in so far as the engagement and configuration of agencies often differs from sector to sector and issue to issue.... Further, many of the agencies of, and participants in, the global governance complex are no longer purely intergovernmental bodies.... Accordingly global governance is a multiactor complex in which diverse agencies participate in the development of global public policy. Of course, this essentially pluralistic conception of global governance does not presume that all states or interests have an equal voice in, let alone an equal influence over, its agenda or programmes—not at all.[3]

Professor Darian-Smith takes up the asymmetry of governance powers as a compounding factor related to global inequalities of other kinds:

> [T]oday's global governance complex is unequivocally facilitating world inequalities and inequities .... Certainly all people, wherever they live, are

2. As this book goes to press, the Trump administration has withdrawn from the negotiations over the Trans-Pacific Partnership (TPP), but the agreement is still pending among the remaining partners.

3. David Held, Global Covenant: The Social Democratic Alternative to the Washington Consensus 79–84 (2004).

> potentially subject to exploitation, poverty, environmental disaster, and disease. As underscored by the 2011 Occupy movements, people living in the wealthiest countries are not buffered from the impact of global economic recession, high unemployment, labor exploitation, or environmental disasters caused by oil spills and tsunamis. That being said, the vast percentage of the world's populations — the hundreds of millions of people who live at or below poverty living in the global South — bear the brunt of power inequities in the international and global arena . . . . [4]

The diversity of governance forms through states, the legal and policy issues that arise, especially their human consequences, are the themes of this chapter. We will explore the relatively formal context of a multilateral treaty. We will first examine the creation of the Montreal Protocol on Ozone depletion, with careful attention being paid to how it was that ultimately 197 countries (including the European Union) participated and how it was that this treaty turned out to be such a success. It is often seen as a one-off solution resulting from a uniquely favorable combination of science, politics and economic interests that (in that viewpoint) would be virtually impossible to duplicate.

We appreciate the circumstances of the Montreal Protocol but we do not share this "perfect storm" analysis. There are aspects of the treaty that provide important blueprints for future efforts. We shall examine the 2015 Paris Accords in this light. As we look at the components of these processes and regulatory approaches — breaking them down, to see the legal, economic, and political relationships involved — we consider what might be transportable into other contexts. For example, as we shall see, one of the most important aspects of the Montreal Protocol's regulatory approach to phasing out CFCs was its regulatory certainty. The Montreal Protocol incorporated an approach that phased out offending chemicals and at the same time introduced strong market incentives to environmentally friendly substitutes.

In terms of the core concepts outlined in Chapter 1, we shall examine problems of scale through consideration of the local and polycentric approaches to environmental problems that have been proposed or tried alongside the global efforts reflected in Montreal and Paris. The questions of presidential power raised in this chapter surface again in Chapter 3 (on NAFTA) and throughout the chapters of Part III, culminating in Chapter 9 (on what we call the transnational executive). But the project of environmental protection also involves demands for law reform through local political processes; we touch on some of these in the discussion section at the end of the chapter. Appreciating the extent to which global, national and local efforts intersect in this context lays the groundwork understanding the relevance of sometimes intensely local accounts that we draw into the discussion of transnational interlegalities throughout the book.

---

4. Darian-Smith, *supra* note 1, at 53–54.

II. Multinational treaties and agreements

This section considers the global governance of environmental problems as developed by treaty—the traditional image of international law—as well as by executive agreement. In theory, the U.S. treaty process proceeds as follows: 1) various actors, who may include the president, NGOs, private citizens, and members of Congress, apply pressure to the Congress or to the president to pursue an international treaty; 2) Congress may authorize the pursuit of a treaty, based upon a set of guiding principles (as was the case with the Montreal Protocol), or the president may initiate the treaty of and by his own initiative; 3) following the treaty negotiations, the parties to the treaty sign the document, which conveys the implicit promise to seek ratification by the home countries' governments; and 4) the national governments ratify the treaty (in the United States, the Senate ratifies treaties),[5] thereby making the treaty provisions binding upon the respective domestic constituencies. In the United States, it is the Constitution's Supremacy Clause that makes lawfully enacted treaties domestically binding, assuming they are intended to be self-executing, or legislation to carry out their requirements is in place:

> This Constitution, and the Laws of the United States which shall be made in pursuance thereof; and all treaties made, or which shall be made, under the authority of the United States, shall be the supreme law of the land; and the judges in every state shall be bound thereby, anything in the constitution or laws of any state to the contrary notwithstanding.[6]

Accordingly, once the Senate has ratified a treaty, the executive branch and the courts enforce its provisions.

As we shall see, in reality, treaties and executive agreements (as well as congressional-executive agreements) are subject to radically different constraints as intra- and intergovernmental tensions pose interlegal dilemmas that must be addressed procedurally. The story this chapter tells is less concerned with the substance of international negotiations than with the interlegalities involved in processes of approval and implementation. The synergies discussed in the previous chapter are on display here. As you read the case studies, ask yourself what made it politically possible for the Montreal Protocol to be adopted in the United States, and how the politics, science, and substantive regulatory approaches involved contributed to making the treaty a reality. Later, turning to the Paris Accords, you will find a very different world and domestic political universe. The Paris Accords' success turned in large measure on the participation of the United States.[7] In that context, a strong emphasis on

---

5. U.S. Const. art. 2, §2, cl. 2 ("[The President] shall have Power, by and with the Advice and Consent of the Senate, to make Treaties, provided two thirds of the Senators present concur....").

6. U.S. Const. art. VI, §2.

7. Daniel Bodansky, Legal Options for U.S. Acceptance of a New Climate Change Agreement (2015), http://www.c2es.org/docUploads/legal-options-us-acceptance-new-climate-change-agreement.pdf ("Participation by the United States in the Paris outcome is, of course, not sufficient to assure success, but it is necessary.").

voluntarism was necessary to ensure that the Accords would be politically viable in the United States—where, meanwhile, climate change itself had become politically controversial with respect to the regulatory implications of climate science.

The Republican majority in the Senate, including some climate change skeptics, was explicit in demonstrating its lack of appetite to approve any climate change agreement—insisting that the Accords constituted a treaty within the meaning of Article II of the U.S. Constitution.[8] In November 2015, a group of 30 Republican senators introduced a "sense of Congress" resolution calling on "the Obama administration submit to the Senate any climate agreements 'whether deemed "legally binding" or not'—especially ones that includes [sic] targets or timetables."[9] The resolution also set up budget constraints pending Senate approval of such agreements.[10]

The congressional resolution implied that all such international agreements fall under the rubric of Article II treaties; however, Daniel Bodansky, writing prior to the Conference of Parties that produced the Paris Accords, identifies three potential bases for United States adoption without further senatorial or congressional approval. First, the president's "core foreign affairs powers" in the Constitution allow the president to communicate with foreign governments.[11] To the extent that the Paris Accords consist of reporting and review, they fall within the president's core constitutional authority.[12]

Second, the Senate advised and consented to the United States' membership in the United Nations Framework Convention on Climate Change in October, 1992. Where the agreement references an obligation "under the Convention," it is invoking the United States' existing obligations under the UNFCCC and thus may fall within the Senate's original advice and consent.[13]

Third, Bodanksy finds that the Clean Air Act may already provide the statutory framework needed to implement any obligation under the Paris Accords, obviating any need for further congressional approval. The Supreme Court's ruling in *Massachusetts v. EPA*, 549 U.S. 497 (2007), discussed *infra,* held that the Act authorizes the EPA to regulate carbon dioxide. Carbon dioxide does not respect territorial borders, so effective regulation of domestic emissions may *require* the executive to enter into international agreements. The Clean Air Act, section 115, addresses international air pollution and authorizes reciprocal federal action with other states to curb transnational pollution. The Global Climate Protection Act of 1987 further found that "the global nature of [the climate change] problem will require vigorous efforts to achieve

8. U.S. Const., art. II, § 2, cl. 2.

9. Karoun Demirjian & Steven Mufson, *Trick or Treaty? The Legal Question Hanging Over the Paris Climate Change Conference,* Wash. Post: Power Post (Nov. 30, 2015), https://www.washingtonpost.com/news/powerpost/wp/2015/11/30/trick-or-treaty-the-legal-question-hanging-over-the-paris-climate-change-conference/.

10. *Id.* (quoting S. Con. Res. 25, 114th Cong., Nov. 19, 2015 (introduced resolution)).

11. *Id.* at 14.

12. *Id.*

13. *Id.*

international cooperation aimed at minimizing and responding to adverse climate change."[14] The Paris Accords may thus fall within the ambit of existing statutory schemes to address domestic pollution, bolstered by the Supreme Court's broad interpretation of the EPA's statutory authority (as discussed in Section D, *infra*).

Professor Bodansky sets out well-established non-Article II bases for international agreements:

Daniel Bodansky, *Legal Options for U.S. Acceptance of a New Climate Change Agreement*

Center for Climate and Energy Solutions (2015)

Types of International Agreements under U.S. Law

Article II Treaties (consent by 2/3 of Senate)

Congressional-Executive Agreements (legislative approval by Congress)

- Ex post approval by statute
- Ex ante authorization by statute

Treaty-Executive Agreements (accepted by the President under a prior treaty)

- Presidential-Executive Agreements (accepted by the President)
- President has independent constitutional authority
- Agreement consistent with and can be implemented under existing U.S. law

[N]on-Article II procedures for entering into international agreements have several textual underpinnings. First, Article I, Section 10, implies that not all international agreements constitute "treaties," since states are precluded from entering into "treaties" with other countries, but are allowed to enter into "agreements" and "compacts" with congressional approval. Since Article II, by its terms, applies only to "treaties," it leaves open the procedure for approving other types of international agreements. Second, Article II does not state that its treaty-making procedure is exclusive. Third, the extensive powers granted by the Constitution to Congress and the president provide bases for agreement-making that are additional to the Article II procedure. For example, international agreements may be made by Congress in the exercise of its Article I power to regulate foreign commerce, and by the president in the exercise of his constitutional power to recognize foreign governments.

Historical practice and case law have firmly established the constitutionality of congressional-executive, treaty-executive, and presidential-executive agreements. The United States has adopted more than 18,000 treaties as "executive agreements," approximately 95 percent of all international agreements to which the United States is a party.[15]

---

14. Global Climate Protection Act of 1987, P.L. 100-204, Title XI, § 1102(5) (1987).

15. Bodansky, *supra* note 7, at 5–6.

The State Department has its own procedure for determining whether an international agreement is a treaty. Circular 175 (C-175), circulated in 1955 and currently published in the Department's Foreign Affairs Manual (FAM), guides the State Department's determination:

> **11 FAM 723.2-2(B) Agreements Pursuant to Legislation**
>
> The President may conclude an international agreement on the basis of existing legislation, or subject to legislation to be adopted by the Congress, or upon the failure of Congress to adopt a disapproving joint or concurrent resolution within designated time periods.
>
> **11 FAM 723.2-2(C) Agreements Pursuant to the Constitutional Authority of the President**
>
> The President may conclude an international agreement on any subject within his constitutional authority so long as the agreement is not inconsistent with legislation enacted by the Congress in the exercise of its constitutional authority. The constitutional sources of authority for the President to conclude international agreements include:
>
> (1) The President's authority as Chief Executive to represent the nation in foreign affairs;
>
> (2) The President's authority to receive ambassadors and other public ministers, and to recognize foreign governments;
>
> (3) The President's authority as "Commander-in-Chief"; and
>
> (4) The President's authority to "take care that the laws be faithfully executed."
>
> **11 FAM 723.3 Considerations for Selecting Among Constitutionally Authorized Procedures**
>
> In determining a question as to the procedure which should be followed for any particular international agreement, due consideration is given to the following factors along with those in 11 FAM 723.2:
>
> (1) The extent to which the agreement involves commitments or risks affecting the nation as a whole;
>
> (2) Whether the agreement is intended to affect state laws;
>
> (3) Whether the agreement can be given effect without the enactment of subsequent legislation by the Congress;
>
> (4) Past U.S. practice as to similar agreements;
>
> (5) The preference of the Congress as to a particular type of agreement;
>
> (6) The degree of formality desired for an agreement;
>
> (7) The proposed duration of the agreement, the need for prompt conclusion of an agreement, and the desirability of concluding a routine or short-term agreement; and

(8) The general international practice as to similar agreements.

> In determining whether any international agreement should be brought into force as a treaty or as an international agreement other than a treaty, the utmost care is to be exercised to avoid any invasion or compromise of the constitutional powers of the President, the Senate, and the Congress as a whole.[16]

These factors for determining whether an agreement is a treaty are not law but rather serve to guide executive discretion.[17]

In sum, the president and the State Department have the authority to decide whether to submit an international agreement to the Senate for approval as an Article II treaty to both houses for majority approval (either ex ante or ex post), or to act without further congressional action pursuant to existing statutory or constitutional authority.

Professor Oona Hathaway has proposed a number of reforms to streamline this process and increase the democratic legitimacy of international agreements, while still giving the president needed flexibility in establishing international agreements. For example, Hathaway suggests that the president and Congress should do away with Article II treaties in most situations in favor of ex post congressional-executive agreements.[18] Hathaway observes that in "areas most dominated by the Treaty Clause—human rights chief among them—agreements are much more vulnerable to being held hostage by a small number of extreme political actors, are more difficult to implement, and are easier for the president to unilaterally undo."[19] Submitting an international agreement to both houses, Hathaway argues, is more democratic, requiring a broader consensus of congresspersons while precluding "senators representing only about 8% of the country's population" from stifling the agreement.[20] Furthermore, such an agreement "creates a more reliable commitment on behalf of the United States than does a treaty because unlike a treaty it erases the line between domestic and international law"—i.e., the agreement *is both* domestic and international law, requiring no further action to become binding and enforceable. Finally, this process would stabilize agreements since a president would "likely ... find it more difficult to withdraw unilaterally from a congressional-executive agreement than an Article II treaty. This is because Congress can, as part of the legislation authorizing the agreement, commit the country to a certain course of action even in the absence of a formalized international commitment."[21]

16. Negotiation and Conclusion, 11 FAM 720, 732.2(B)–732.3 (2006).

17. Bodansky, *supra* note 7, at 8.

18. Oona A. Hathaway, The Case for Replacing Article II Treaties with Ex Post Congressional-Executive Agreements, American Constitution Society Issue Brief (2008), *available at* https://www.acslaw.org/files/Hathaway%20Issue%20Brief.pdf.

19. *Id.* at 3.

20. *Id.* at 5.

21. *Id.* at 14.

Hannah Chang suggests that the UNFCCC could provide ample authority for an agreement that, like the Paris Accords, obligates the United States to what she calls "MRV" responsibilities—measurement, reporting, and verification—when considered alongside the president's constitutional authority:

> The single commentator who has analyzed the authority to enter executive agreements pursuant to the UNNFCC has largely dismissed the UNFCCC because [it is] non-self-executing ... [and] the President may not "point to [the UNFCCC] as authority to implement new executive agreements on climate change under domestic law." The UNFCCC should not be dismissed so hastily, however. The authority the treaty lends to "enter into a new international obligation" can be relied on, together with the President's foreign affairs powers and his role as the sole organ of communications between the United States and the international community, as convincing legal authority to enter an executive agreement pursuant to UNFCCC obligations. As for execution, the domestic legislation under which the UNFCCC's MRV obligations have been implemented may well enable execution of other MRV agreements.[22]

Comparing the Montreal Protocol and the Paris Accords, we observe that the nature and the complexity of the regulatory problems differed, but the differences in the political contexts in which they were addressed were even more stark. The Montreal Protocol process benefitted from the perception of a broad public mandate for governmental action and the high public regard for science. A generation later, the Paris Accords process was burdened by the politicization of climate change science, as well as by deep tensions within the Congress and between the congressional majority and the executive branch. For the congressional majority, the Paris Accords were a form of economic regulation more certainly than they were science-based reform, making the Accords a further front in their long and entrenched anti-regulatory position. Anticipating such opposition, Secretary of State Kerry carried forward existing legislation (the Clean Air Act of 1970) as the authorization for the executive agreement embodied in the Accords, and incorporated a strong emphasis of voluntarism.

Let us now turn to the Montreal Protocol, returning to the Paris Accords in Section D.

A. Ozone depletion and the Montreal Protocol

The Montreal Protocol sought to reduce and ultimately eliminate ozone-depleting chemicals from global production and consumption. Ozone depletion presented global actors with a new and daunting set of challenges, to which they responded with a combination of innovation and traditional treaty procedures. As you read through the case study, consider the treaty process, especially the "matching" that occurred among international industrialists, scientists, and government agents.

---

22. Hannah Chang, *International Executive Agreements on Climate Change*, 35 Colum. J. Envtl. L. 337, 358–59 (2010).

1. Background Events

In 1974, a team of scientists published their hypothesis that certain forms of industrial pollutants, especially chlorofluorocarbons (CFCs), were actively destroying the Earth's ozone layer.[23] The ozone layer provides critical protection against the sun's ultraviolet radiation. Without an ozone layer, the unfiltered ultraviolet radiation would cause cancer, cataracts, and mutations in humans, animals, and plants. CFCs, however, were something of a wonder-chemical in the middle of the twentieth century. CFCs are stable, nonflammable, nontoxic to humans, and noncorrosive, which allowed them to be used in a variety of industrial and household applications, including refrigeration, air conditioning, propellants in spray canisters, and cleaners.[24] CFCs were also inexpensive, and by 1974, annual production of CFCs had reached 800,000 metric tons.[25]

Scientific research confirmed that CFCs have a costly downside: ozone depletion. Once CFCs enter the stratosphere, solar radiation slowly—over many decades—breaks down the CFC molecules.[26] As the CFCs disintegrate, they release large amounts of chlorine into the atmosphere, destroying ozone at a rate of tens of thousands of ozone atoms for every chlorine atom.[27] Since it takes many years for CFCs to disintegrate, scientists reasoned that immediate action was needed by the global community in order to stave off disaster. At the time, the science establishing the link between CFCs and what became known as the "ozone hole" (an area of depleted ozone concentrated over Antarctica) was new. Thirteen years later—1987—a group of nation-states, including the United States, signed the Montreal Protocol on Substances That Deplete the Ozone Layer (the Protocol).[28] The Protocol called for the gradual elimination of CFC and other chemical use by the signatory nations. Within nineteen months, sixty-two countries had ratified the Protocol,[29] and as of this writing, that number has increased to 197.[30] The Protocol marked the "first time that the world community committed itself to imposing controls on an important industrial sector *before* actual damages to human health and ecology were registered."[31]

---

23. *See* Richard Elliot Benedick, Ozone Diplomacy: New Directions in Safeguarding the Planet 9 (1991). Richard Elliot Benedick was the chief U.S. negotiator for the Montreal Protocol.

24. *Id.* at 10.

25. *Id.* at 11.

26. *Id.*

27. *Id.* at 10.

28. Montreal Protocol on Substances That Deplete the Ozone Layer (Sept. 16, 1987), https://treaties.un.org/doc/Publication/UNTS/Volume%201522/volume-1522-I-26369-English.pdf. *See also Evolution of the Montreal Protocol*, U.N. Envir. Programme, Ozone Secretariat, http://ozone.unep.org/en/handbook-montreal-protocol-substances-deplete-ozone-layer/27570.

29. Benedick, *supra* note 23, at 8.

30. *Status of Ratification*, U.N. Envir. Programme, Ozone Secretariat, http://www.unep.ch/ozone/Ratification_status/index.shtml.

31. Alfred C. Aman, Jr., Administrative Law in a Global Era 137 (1992) (internal quotation and citation omitted).

The process by which the Protocol came into being will be discussed in the following pages. As you read, consider the difference between internationalization, which involves state interests, and globalization, which concerns the broader, common interests of mankind, quite apart from territorial concerns. Did the global legislation that resulted in the Montreal Protocol reflect, at least to some extent, an alignment of the two concepts? Also, bear in mind other current "global" environmental issues, such as global warming and polluted oceans. Are these problems similar or dissimilar from the ozone issues discussed below? Furthermore, think of how nation-state governments, NGOs, and private individuals "matched" their respective authority and jurisdiction over various areas in order to create the Protocol.

Soon after the publication of the CFC hypothesis, the U.S. news media picked up on the story, and the resulting public outcry led to congressional action. After a series of hearings in 1974–1975, Congress passed the Toxic Substances Control Act of 1976, which banned the use of CFCs in aerosol propellants in nonessential applications.[32] The passage of the Act, however, was insufficient to stave off global ozone depletion. While the United States was a major producer of CFCs, many nations around the world—both industrialized and developing—also contributed to the problem. CFCs would continue to accumulate in the stratosphere and to destroy ozone so long as any nation continued to use them. It became apparent, therefore, that a transnational solution was needed to address this problem.

The United States was able to take an active role in the anti-CFC campaign in part because of the passage of the Clean Air Act of 1970.[33] The Act indicated that "the President through the Secretary of State and the Assistant Secretary of State for Oceans and International Environmental and Scientific Affairs, shall negotiate multilateral treaties for these [environmental] purposes."[34] Moreover,

> The consent of the Congress is hereby given to two or more States to negotiate and enter into agreements or compacts, not in conflict with any law or treaty of the United States, for (1) cooperative effort and mutual assistance for the prevention and control of air pollution and the enforcement of their respective laws relating thereto, and (2) the establishment of such agencies, joint or otherwise, as they may deem desirable for making effective such agreements or compacts. No such agreement or compact shall be binding or obligatory upon any State a party thereto unless and until it has been approved by Congress.[35]

Congress amended the Clean Air Act in 1977[36] to cover ozone depletion. The amended Act permitted the head of the Environmental Protection Agency (EPA) to regulate "any substance ... which in his judgment may reasonably be anticipated to

32. Benedick, *supra* note 23, at 24 (citing 15 U.S.C. § 2601).
33. 42 U.S.C. § 7456 (1970).
34. *Id.*
35. *Id.* § 7402(c).
36. 42 U.S.C. § 7456 (1970).

affect the stratosphere, especially ozone in the stratosphere, if such effect may reasonably be anticipated to endanger public health or welfare."[37]

Accordingly, American environmental negotiators carried with them the explicit authority to pursue multilateral treaties with foreign nations to solve the ozone riddle, well in advance of what became the Vienna Convention and Montreal Protocol (discussed *infra*). As the United States was the world's richest nation, as well as its largest CFC polluter, it was able to exert considerable influence over other nations regarding CFC regulation. The United States pursued this agenda through diplomatic conversations via its foreign embassies, scientific conferences, and meetings between industry leaders and U.S. officials.[38]

The global community began to address the ozone issue beginning in 1977, when the United Nations Environmental Programme (UNEP) organized a meeting that resulted in the adoption of a World Plan of Action on the Ozone Layer, as well as the creation of a Coordinating Committee to guide the international effort through its initial stages.[39] While the United States and UNEP had accepted the grave threat of ozone depletion, and had begun to combat this menace proactively, there remained resistance from European nations and their associated industrial constituents. Much hinged on CFC production economics: "Relative to gross national product, the value of the [European Community's] production of [CFCs] was over 50 percent higher than that of the United States . . . [and] the EC was the almost unchallenged supplier to the rest of the world . . . ."[40]

Unlike in Europe, the U.S. media and environmental NGOs actively lobbied for increased restrictions on CFC use, both domestically and internationally.[41] The U.S. State Department, recognizing the power of these groups, actively encouraged them to attempt to influence their European counterparts.[42] The U.S. scientific community also enjoyed persuasive authority vis-à-vis their European colleagues, due in part to its advanced aerospace institutions—NASA and NOAA—and well-funded research universities.

While U.S. scientists and diplomats were working on persuading their European counterparts to take action on CFC production, there was also intense transnational and domestic debate amongst industrialists. U.S. CFC producers, such as Du Pont, had initially balked at further CFC restrictions, as the industrial stakes were considerable. For example, the ban on the use of CFCs as aerosol propellants in nonessential applications had impacted nearly $3 billion in sales for producers of

---

37. Benedick, *supra* note 23, at 24 (note omitted).

38. *See id.* at 28–34.

39. Mark Weston Janis & John E. Noyes, International Law: Cases and Commentary 714 (4th ed. 2011).

40. Benedick, *supra* note 23, at 26.

41. *See id.* at 28.

42. *Id.*

CFC-utilizing goods.[43] But consumer pressure incrementally forced the industry to change its posture regarding regulation.[44] Domestic industry leaders in the U.S. watched anxiously as some states enacted CFC restrictions, thus creating a patchwork regulatory structure.[45] In a strange twist of fate, the CFC industry eventually came to favor a unifying federal regulatory structure for CFC production, in order to facilitate interstate trade. These same companies also became increasingly concerned over their public image regarding CFC production and consumption—again taking into account the significant clout of the U.S. media and consumer pressure.

Predictably, as the regulatory structure tightened in the United States, U.S. CFC producers pressed for similar restrictions to be placed upon their European competitors, citing the competitive advantage enjoyed by the unencumbered Europeans. This situation mirrored in some ways the child labor law struggles of the American Progressive Era: before Congress stepped in to regulate interstate child labor practices, employers in regulated states were at a competitive disadvantage compared with similar employers in unregulated areas. As business naturally gravitated towards cheaper, unregulated environs, the regulated industrialists became increasingly vocal in clamoring for an interstate standard. The same process began to unfold with CFC production, and by 1986, many influential U.S. business leaders had begun to realize that the risk of ozone depletion would not go away, and moreover, that production of CFCs had resumed an upward growth path. It became apparent to U.S. industry that the likelihood of an international treaty could no longer be discounted.[46]

U.S. industrialists duly formed the Alliance for Responsible CFC Policy, a group composed of 500 U.S. CFC producer and user companies, and which released a collective statement in support of international regulation of CFCs.[47] Some U.S. businesses "favor[ed] at least a freeze on CFC production and … others were prepared to accept substantial cuts—as long as adequate time was allowed for development of substitutes."[48]

Significant European opposition to international regulation remained, despite UNEP and U.S. political, scientific, and (gradually) industry pressure. This resistance stemmed from a variety of sources: distrust of U.S. business motives; doubts regarding the veracity of the scientific research; and unwillingness to submit to an international regulatory structure.

These circumstances began to change in 1985, especially after British scientists showed evidence of a massive Antarctic "ozone hole."[49] What was once an abstract

43. *Id.* at 24.
44. *Id.* at 30–31.
45. *Id.* at 31.
46. *Id.*
47. *Id.* at 32.
48. *Id.*
49. Benedick, *supra* note 23, at 214.

concept—ozone depletion as the effect of a complex chemical process—now had a visible face: a literal hole in the Earth's ozone shield against solar radiation. The image of a hole in the protective ozone layer, along with intense transnational communication, led in part to the adoption of the Vienna Convention on Substances that Deplete the Ozone Layer by twenty countries, along with the EC Commission, in 1985.[50] Although the Vienna Convention did not contain binding stipulations, it did lay out a general framework for what became the Montreal Protocol: "a framework convention/protocol approach to a regime regulating the environment . . . [that] sets general principles and establishes institutions and procedures that allow the later adoption of more specific requirements."[51]

The Vienna Convention stated that "the Parties shall take appropriate measures . . . to protect human health and the environment against adverse effects resulting or likely to result from human activities which modify or are likely to modify the ozone layer."[52] With these broad strokes of mutual understanding in place, the international negotiators turned their attention to forging a workable protocol.

2. Framing the Montreal Protocol

What eventually became the Montreal Protocol began with a series of workshops in Europe and the United States, coordinated by the UNEP. The UNEP invited all U.N. member governments to send both private and public-sector officials to the workshops, but there were no official national delegations.[53]

> These workshops established a framework for the difficult formal negotiations ahead. The process was characterized by breaking down the problems into smaller components, developing consensus by incremental stages, and, as important as any other factor, establishing a degree of rapport and mutual confidence among future participants in the diplomatic negotiations.[54]

The workshops received considerable media attention, and President Reagan gave his full support to the negotiators.[55] The formal Protocol conference began in September 1987, and the negotiators were confronted with a wide range of problems for implementing an effective ozone solution: what explicit guidelines would there be for reducing CFCs? How could developing countries continue to industrialize while limiting their ozone-depleting chemical use? What procedure should be employed to amend the Protocol in light of subsequent scientific developments? How would the Protocol be enforced? Could states withdraw from the treaty?

---

50. 26 I.L.M. 1529 (1987). *See also* BENEDICK *supra* note 23, at 44–45.

51. JANIS & NOYES, *supra* note 39, at 714.

52. VIENNA CONVENTION FOR THE PROTECTION OF THE OZONE LAYER art. 2 § 1 (Mar. 22, 1985, rev. 2002).

53. BENEDICK, *supra* note 23, at 47.

54. *Id.*

55. *Id.* at 67.

At its core, the Protocol directed the participating nations to freeze their consumption levels of certain CFCs at 1986 levels, and then to reduce their consumption by 50% over ten years.[56] Subsequent amendments to the Protocol expanded the list of targeted chemicals and called for further reductions in consumption.

Article 5 concerned developing countries, and sought to avoid hindering the industrial progression of these poorer nations while gradually substituting alternative, non-CFC-based technology into those nations' industrial infrastructures. The Protocol permitted developing nations to delay their compliance for ten years beyond the industrialized nations' deadline.[57] Meanwhile, richer nations were expected to provide financial and scientific assistance: "The Parties undertake to facilitate access to environmentally safe alternative substances and technology for Parties that are developing countries and assist them to make expeditious use of such alternatives."[58] Additionally: "The Parties undertake to facilitate bilaterally or multilaterally the provision of subsidies, aid, credits, guarantees or insurance programmes to Parties that are developing countries for the use of alternative technology and for substitute products."[59]

The 1990 amendments to the Protocol clarified the provision of aid to developing countries. There would be a Multilateral Fund for the developing nations, which would be funded by industrialized countries.[60] The fund would operate under the philosophical foundation that "States have common but differentiated responsibilities" regarding "global environmental degradation."[61] Developing nations would provide the Fund's Executive Committee with detailed outlines for reducing their consumption and production of ozone-depleting products. In return, the Fund would provide financial backing for the closure of CFC production facilities, industrial conversion, and technical assistance and training, in an effort at phasing out and replacing CFCs in the developing nations.[62] The industrialized nations ultimately pledged $2.7 billion between 1991 and 2010.[63] The Protocol drafters recognized that the treaty was merely the beginning of the campaign against ozone-depleting materials. The years ahead would require scientific research into the efficacy of the Protocol's original measures, as well as new explorations into methods to reduce CFC consumption. "This is a crucial feature of the protocol that helps renew the links between the participation by the signatories and the scientific discourse that first

56. MONTREAL PROTOCOL art. 2 §§2, 4. There was an intermediate step of a 20% reduction beginning in mid-1993. *Id.*

57. MONTREAL PROTOCOL art. 5 § 1.

58. MONTREAL PROTOCOL art. 5 §2.

59. MONTREAL PROTOCOL art. 5 §3.

60. *See About the Multilateral Fund: Overview*, Multilateral Fund for the Implementation of the Montreal Protocol, http://www.multilateralfund.org/aboutMLF/default.aspx.

61. *See* The Rio Declaration on Environment and Development (Rio Declaration), U.N. Conference on Environment and Development, Principle 7, June 14, 1992, 31 I.L.M. 874 (1992).

62. Rio Declaration, Principle 7.

63. *About the Multilateral Fund: Overview*, Multilateral Fund for the Implementation of the Montreal Protocol, http://www.multilateralfund.org/aboutMLF/default.aspx.

made agreement possible."[64] The Protocol, therefore, called for regular meetings of the participating nations, to review the implementation of the Protocol, establish new guidelines and procedures for reporting information, and augment the list of targeted chemicals.[65] Article 6, for instance, directs that

> [b]eginning in 1990, and at least every four years thereafter, the Parties shall assess the control measures provided for in Article 2 on the basis of available scientific, environmental, technical and economic information. At least one year before each assessment, the Parties shall convene appropriate panels of experts qualified in the fields mentioned and determine the composition and terms of reference of any such panels.[66]

If a party wishes to add a new chemical to the Protocol's list, it must obtain the ratification of two-thirds of the signatories, resulting in a formal amendment to the Protocol.[67] Moreover, such changes do not bind parties who do not ratify the amendment.[68]

The Protocol then turned to enforcement provisions, deploying an economic pressure mechanism to penalize states that had not signed the Protocol. Under Article 4 ("Control of Trade with Non-Parties"), "each Party shall ban the import of controlled substances from any State not party to this Protocol," and "no [developing nation] . . . may export any controlled substance to any State not party to this Protocol."[69] Other Article 4 provisions directed the signatory nations to "discourage" the sale of CFC production technology to non-party states, as well as to avoid providing financial aid to non-party states for such production capacity.[70] The effect of Article 4 was twofold: it prevented the Parties from circumventing the domestic CFC prohibitions through importing CFCs from non-signatory nations; and it applied economic leverage upon non-signatory nations to comply with Protocol provisions, even if the non-signatory nations did not formally ratify the Protocol. Accordingly, Section 8 of Article 4 allows Parties to import controlled substances from non-signatories "if that State is determined, by a meeting of the [Protocol signatories], to be in full compliance with [the Article 2 CFC control mechanisms], and has submitted data to that effect as specified in Article 7."[71]

Moreover, the Vienna Convention and the Montreal Protocol relied on two governmental entities to monitor and enforce the new ozone regime: national governments, which would ensure domestic compliance with the Protocol provisions, and a supranational agency, the Ozone Secretariat, which would coordinate the efforts of the various nation-states, as well as monitor compliance.

---

64. AMAN, *supra* note 31, at 147.
65. MONTREAL PROTOCOL art. 11.
66. MONTREAL PROTOCOL art. 6.
67. *See* AMAN, *supra* note 31, at 147.
68. *Id.*
69. MONTREAL PROTOCOL art. 4, §§ 1–2.
70. MONTREAL PROTOCOL art. 4, §§ 5–6.
71. MONTREAL PROTOCOL art 4, § 8.

Lastly, if any nation wished to withdraw from the Protocol, the drafters provided for such a course of action in Article 19:

> Any such Party may withdraw from this Protocol by giving written notification to the Depositary at any time after four years of assuming the obligations specified in paragraphs 1 to 4 of Article 2. Any such withdrawal shall take effect upon expiry of one year after the date of its receipt by the Depositary, or on such later date as may be specified in the notification of the withdrawal.[72]

Article 19's provisions therefore locked the Parties into at least a five-year commitment to the Protocol provisions, which the treaty drafters hoped would begin to yield improvements in the ozone layer. The participating nations signed the Protocol in September, 1987, and the United States ratified the treaty in 1988.[73]

3. Analysis of the Protocol Process

Traditionally, domestic and international institutions matched the scale of domestic and international problems. The institutions have a defined sphere of jurisdiction, which also facilitates interactions between domestic and foreign opposite governmental entities, in order to address international issues. The Nuclear Regulatory Commission, for instance, would naturally interact with the United Kingdom's Health and Safety Directorate to coordinate nuclear regulatory standards between the two nation-states.

Ozone depletion defied the established order of jurisdictional matching—a deficiency that the Montreal Protocol drafters sought to remedy. Ozone depletion would affect all nations adversely, and in this sense, the challenges of addressing ozone depletion's complexity and global reach far exceeded familiar institutional norms. For illustration, the U.S. EPA could limit ozone-depleting chemicals domestically with a positive effect on reducing total CFC consumption, but even eliminating all U.S. CFC production and consumption would not solve the global problem. Ozone depletion would continue to menace the United States unless a new coalition of global institutions pooled their respective jurisdictional sovereignties, in order to create a sufficiently far-reaching regulatory regime. The chosen vehicle for this matching was a multilateral treaty binding a group of nation-states to a core set of principles, regulations, and short- and long-term objectives.

Ozone depletion represented a global commons problem with a clearly defined source, but a less defined solution. The Montreal Protocol's negotiators confronted a problem affecting a resource that no one owned—the Earth's atmosphere—and that would negatively affect everyone, if destroyed.

> Solutions to such chronic pollution problems usually involve both regulation of the manufacturing processes within the countries involved and international determination of the relative contribution each country makes to

72. Montreal Protocol art. 19.

73. Benedick, *supra* note 23, at 115.

> the harm inflicted on other countries. Domestic regulatory reforms without international cooperation cannot cure this problem. The international component of a solution to [a problem such as ozone depletion or large-scale radioactive contamination] thus often comes in the form of bilateral or multilateral treaties. Such treaties are possible only when each of the countries involved determines that the international solution is worth the economic, and, perhaps, political costs necessary to deal with the issue domestically. The inability to solve the [international pollution] problem or even to ignore it effectively without engaging in international negotiation makes the entanglement of domestic policy and domestic politics with international policy and politics inevitable. Nevertheless, in terms of the political and legal questions they raise, the blurring of the distinction between international and domestic, and the scientific challenges involved, global-commons issues are even more complicated than transboundary issues in both scope and content. [74]

A primary reason for the Protocol's success was that the problem and solution that the Protocol sought to address were clear: 1) this precise phenomena; 2) caused by these specific chemicals; 3) with these demonstrated risks; 4) affecting all people; 5) could be remedied by these specific actions, with available substitutes; 6) over a specific timeline. The negotiators had a comprehensible, focused, and universally applicable problem before them. The ozone-depletion threat was truly global in terms of the scope of its potential consequences, as well as the contributing factors to the problem; indeed, the "external costs imposed by modern technology in an interconnected world [made] the boundaries between nations relatively meaningless . . . ."[75]

The Protocol process was remarkable because of its reliance on science for crafting a cogent argument before the international community. Recall that the ozone problem arose from a scientific publication in 1974, and within a mere two years, the U.S. Congress had passed legislation to curb domestic CFC use. Thirteen years after the publication of the ozone-depletion hypothesis, a binding multinational treaty regulating CFC consumption was signed. The participants of the Montreal Protocol came to the table from markedly divergent viewpoints—several represented constituencies that were heavily invested in the production and use of CFCs. Reliable scientific evidence helped to unify the international community: "The formation of a commonly accepted body of data and analyses and the narrowing of ranges of uncertainty were prerequisites to a political solution among negotiating parties initially far apart."[76]

> Science and the credibility of scientific discourse provided the central terms of [the Protocol's formation]. Science offered the possibility of an analysis of environmental problems that could be shared by all countries. It

74. Aman, *supra* note 31, at 134 (note omitted).

75. *Id.* at 133.

76. Benedick, *supra* note 23, at 204.

> facilitated a conception of the problem, a solution to it, and a language for discussing it that transcended a solely (and overtly) political view of the issues involved. . . . the language of science is not tied to any one state; the credibility of scientific claims of objectivity and universality created important substantive and symbolic aspects of the agreement.[77]

The Preamble to the Protocol reflects this ethos:

> The Parties to this Protocol,
>
> *Being* Parties to the Vienna Convention for the Protection of the Ozone Layer,
>
> *Mindful* of their obligation under that Convention to take appropriate measures to protect human health and the environment against adverse effects resulting or likely to result from human activities which modify or are likely to modify the ozone layer,
>
> *Recognizing* that world-wide emissions of certain substances can significantly deplete and otherwise modify the ozone layer in a manner that is likely to result in adverse effects on human health and the environment,
>
> *Conscious* of the potential climatic effects of emissions of these substances,
>
> *Aware* that measures taken to protect the ozone layer from depletion should be based on relevant scientific knowledge, taking into account technical and economic considerations,
>
> *Determined* to protect the ozone layer by taking precautionary measures to control equitably total global emissions of substances that deplete it, with the ultimate objective of their elimination on the basis of developments in scientific knowledge, taking into account technical and economic considerations,
>
> *Acknowledging* that special provision is required to meet the needs of developing countries for these substances,
>
> *Noting* the precautionary measures for controlling emissions of certain chlorofluorocarbons that have already been taken at national and regional levels,
>
> *Considering* the importance of promoting international co-operation in the research and development of science and technology relating to the control and reduction of emissions of substances that deplete the ozone layer, bearing in mind in particular the needs of developing countries [have adopted the Protocol].[78]

Government officials brought to the Protocol process the authoritative weight of their respective national governments, as well as accessible communication abilities through pre-established diplomatic channels. While scientists and industrial leaders often had to forge transnational relationships on an ad hoc basis as the Protocol

---

77. Aman, *supra* note 31, at 138.

78. Montreal Protocol Preamble.

process unfolded, government agents—diplomats and bureaucrats—had defined jurisdictional roles and boundaries before they were confronted with the ozone depletion crisis.

As previously noted, there was initial opposition by the CFC industry to accept the urgency of the ozone problem, and to make recommended changes to their industries. The Protocol succeeded in large part, however, because industry leaders were willing (albeit with a significant degree of cajoling from scientists, government officials, and the media[79]) to modify their industries, and to implement available substitutes to replace the harmful CFCs.

Industry leaders in the United States and abroad (Europe especially) carefully matched each other's actions in gradually "disarming" their industries of CFC production, and substituting ozone-friendlier substitutes. For example, in September 1988, the U.S. Alliance for Responsible CFC Policy announced that it was in favor of the CFC phase-out, and the United Kingdom's Imperial Chemicals Industries followed suit soon thereafter.[80] Industrialists in the Federal Republic of Germany, Japan, and other major industrial countries, seeing the path set forth by Britain and the United States, began to draw down their CFC use as well. This industrial cooperation strengthened the signatories' momentum going into the Protocol negotiations, and contributed to the relatively seamless implementation process that followed the signing of the Protocol.[81]

Notes and Questions

1. The drafters of the Protocol recognized that the Protocol was just the beginning of a solution to the ozone problem. Subsequent meetings and agreements would be needed to ensure a successful resolution of the issue. Accordingly, the Protocol was amended in 1990, 1992, 1997, and 1999.[82] While each amendment set has attracted fewer signatories (196 for the Montreal Protocol; 195 for the 1990 Amendments; 192 for the 1992 Amendments; 181 for the 1997 Amendments; and 165 for the 1999 Amendments),[83] the ozone regulatory system has been successful. The U.N. Department of Economic and Social Affairs notes:

> Protection of the ozone layer is a global success story. [Since the Protocol's ratification,] developed countries have virtually eliminated ozone-depleting substances, and the developing world is not far behind. Without these reductions, ozone depletion would have increased tenfold by 2050 compared to

---

79. Benedick, *supra* note 23, at 206.

80. *Id.* at 118.

81. *Id.*; *see also* Cass R. Sunstein, *Of Montreal and Kyoto: A Tale of Two Protocols* 31 Harv. Envtl. L. Rev. 1, 5 (2007).

82. *See* Janis, *supra* note 39, at 715.

83. *Id.* at 717.

> current levels, resulting in millions more cases of melanoma, other cancers and eye cataracts.[84]

Moreover, the U.S. EPA predicted that had the Protocol (or a similar treaty) not been implemented, there could have been more than 150 million new skin cancer cases in the United States for people who were alive or born by 2075, resulting in a predicted three million deaths. The UNEP currently forecasts that the Earth's ozone density will return to 1980 levels by the latter part of the twenty-first century.[85]

2. How did the Montreal Protocol treat the equitable differences existing between developed and developing nations? How is this relevant to some of today's pressing issues such as global warming? Consider the following in Alfred C. Aman, Jr., *The Earth as Eggshell Plaintiff*, 102 YALE L. REV. 2107, 2120 (1993):

> The Montreal Protocol and its amendments . . . do not disregard equity. In attempting to regulate CFC's and other ozone depleting materials, the agreement is among the first to recognize the need to treat less developed countries differently when it comes to formulating and enforcing global legislation. The 1990 London Amendments to the Montreal Protocol, for example, at least begin to address difficult problems, such as technology transfer and wealth disparities, inherent in making such agreements meaningful and possible for less developed countries to sign.
>
> The Montreal Protocol and its amendments are also technology-forcing pieces of global legislation. For example, the Montreal Protocol's rigid timetable for phasing out CFC's created a market for and thereby promoted the development of substitutes. Consider, for example, the case of CFC-113, widely used as a solvent in the manufacture of computer chips. During discussions on phasing out CFC's, manufacturers claimed that CFC-113 would be too costly to replace. Yet it was the first of the CFC's to disappear after researchers discovered an equally effective, inexpensive water and citrus-based solution. Though economics suggests firms minimize costs, the cheaper process was not discovered earlier.
>
> Inevitably, if it is to succeed, the global regulatory structure now developing will have to solve a variety of complex problems, including how developing countries can enjoy economic growth without adopting nineteenth or early twentieth-century approaches to industrialization. This is by far the greatest challenge, particularly given the enormous disparities of wealth around the world. Technology-forcing legislation can help promote new green technologies which then could be shared worldwide in some equitable

---

84. U.N. Dept. of Econ. and Soc. Aff., *The Millennium Development Goals Report 2006*, June 17, 2006, *available at* http://unstats.un.org/unsd/mdg/Resources/Static/Products/Progress2006/MDG Report2006.pdf.

85. U.N. Envir. Programme, *Environmental Effects of Ozone Depletion and Its Interactions with Climate Change*, xv (Dec. 2010), *available at* http://ozone.unep.org/Assessment_Panels/EEAP/eeap-report2010.pdf.

> manner. Intellectual property rights are held by private corporations, not by the countries doing the negotiations for the creation of new global legislative regimes. The end result is that it is difficult to facilitate the transfer of these new technologies without expropriation, from the point of view of the holders of these property rights, or a new form of economic colonialism, from the point of view of the less developed countries. These, however, are some of the regulatory problems for which solutions must be found. Simply going about our business on a domestic level as if we were not tied to the global demands of an unequal world is no longer possible in the new global era.

3. What role does information play in spurring regulatory innovation? Consider the following in Aman, *id.*, at 2121:

> ... [T]he Montreal Protocol has also helped develop a mechanism for the creation and dissemination of information. Such information, essential to enforcement, keeps everyone apprised of progress towards reducing CFC's in the atmosphere. This aspect of knowledge creation and dissemination is a key factor in the proposal for a Sustainable Development Commission made at the first Earth Summit held in Rio de Janeiro in June, 1992. The purpose of this Commission is to develop the information on emission levels of greenhouse gases to enable it to determine whether any progress is being made toward the agreed-upon goals of the framework convention. It is thus a new international information agency enabling nations to monitor progress on this important global issue—an environmental Amnesty International, but one that includes representatives from various nation-states, thus giving it a multinational and global imprimatur.

B. Domestic law: Implementing the Montreal Protocol

As the following case shows, the regulatory processes spawned by the adoption and implementation of the Montreal Protocol raised various legal issues concerning the treaty's domestic implementation in the United States. We are accustomed to delegating legislative power to administrative agencies, so long as that delegation is accompanied by legislative standards to guide the agencies' interpretations of the statutes involved. Federal administrative agencies usually consist of "Officers of the United States" appointed pursuant to Article II, Section 2 by the President with advice and consent of the Senate. Agencies are thus connected to the political process and the decision makers involved are political appointees. But what about committees established by treaties to whom power is delegated to conform the regulatory powers of the treaty to new and developing situations on the ground? The members of these regulatory committees are not officers of the United States (i.e., they are not appointed by the President with advice and consent of the Senate) nor are they necessarily citizens of the U.S. When U.S. domestic law delegates to an international body such as this, must the manner by which that power is transferred conform to the mandates of U.S. delegation doctrine? Put another way, when a body like this issues rules, are they binding? Do they constitute law?

Natural Resources Defense Council v. Environmental Protection Agency

464 F.3d 1 (D.C. Cir. 2006)

RANDOLPH, CIRCUIT JUDGE.

The United States and other countries entered into the Montreal Protocol on Substances that Deplete the Ozone Layer, Sept. 16, 1987, S. TREATY DOC. NO. 100-10, 1522 U.N.T.S. 29 ("Montreal Protocol"), a treaty in which the signatory nations agreed to reduce the use of certain substances, including methyl bromide that degrade the stratospheric ozone layer. The Environmental Protection Agency issued a rule implementing "critical use" exemptions from the treaty's general ban on production and consumption of methyl bromide. . . .

I.

In the mid-1970s, scientists discovered that certain man-made chemicals can destroy the layer of ozone gas in the stratosphere approximately ten to twenty-five miles above the Earth's surface. Stratospheric ozone absorbs ultraviolet radiation; as the ozone layer thins, less radiation is absorbed. Increased human exposure to ultraviolet radiation is linked to a range of ailments, including skin cancer and cataracts.

Amidst growing international concern about ozone depletion, the United States and twenty-four other nations entered into the Montreal Protocol. The Protocol requires signatory nations—which now number 189—to reduce and eliminate their production and use of ozone-depleting chemicals in accordance with agreed-upon timetables. Montreal Protocol arts. 2-2I. The Senate ratified the treaty in 1988, and Congress incorporated its terms into domestic law through the Clean Air Act Amendments of 1990 . . . . Since then, the United States has reduced its use of methyl bromide to less than 39% of its 1991 baseline.

In 1997, the Parties "adjusted" the Protocol to require developed-country Parties to cease "production" and "consumption" of methyl bromide by 2005. . . . In response, Congress amended the Clean Air Act to require EPA to "promulgate rules for reductions in, and terminate the production, importation, and consumption of, methyl bromide under a schedule that is in accordance with, but not more stringent than, the phaseout schedule of the Montreal Protocol Treaty as in effect on October 21, 1998." 42 U.S.C. § 7671c(h).

Methyl bromide is a naturally occurring gas produced by oceans, grass and forest fires, and volcanoes. . . . It is also man-made and used as a broad-spectrum pesticide. Methyl bromide is typically injected into soil as a fumigant before several types of crops are planted. The United States regulates methyl bromide as a "class I" ozone-depleting substance. Methyl bromide has an "ozone depletion potential" ("ODP") of 0.38–0.60. This puts it in the middle range of substances scheduled for elimination under the Protocol. It is not nearly as destructive as chlorofluorocarbons and most other class I substances, almost all of which were phased out in 2000. . . . On the other hand, it is significantly more destructive than "class II" substances, which are to be phased out in 2030.

In light of methyl bromide's wide use and the lack of comparable substitute pesticides, the Protocol allows exemptions from the general ban "to the extent that the Parties decide to permit the level of production or consumption that is necessary to satisfy uses agreed by them to be critical uses." . . . The Parties to the Protocol meet annually to "decide to permit the level of production or consumption that is necessary to satisfy uses agreed by them to be critical uses." . . . At one of these meetings the Parties set general guidelines for implementing the critical-use exemptions ("Decision IX/6"), and at another the Parties approved exemptions for 2005. The United States formally began the process of establishing its 2005 critical-use exemptions in May 2002, when EPA published a notice in the Federal Register seeking applications for 2005 and 2006 critical uses of methyl bromide and the amounts of new production and consumption needed to satisfy those uses. EPA teams composed of biologists and economists reviewed each application and decided which to include in the aggregate U.S. nomination to the Parties. The final U.S. nomination, submitted to the Montreal Protocol's administrative body (the "Ozone Secretariat") in February 2003, requested a total exemption of about ten-thousand metric tons of methyl bromide for sixteen different uses.

The process then moved to the international stage. The Parties reached agreement at their First Extraordinary Meeting in March 2004. They granted the United States critical uses in sixteen categories, amounting to 8,942 metric tons of methyl bromide. To satisfy these critical uses, the Parties authorized 7,659 metric tons of new production and consumption, with the remainder (1,283 metric tons) to be made up from existing stocks of methyl bromide. . . . (Mar. 27, 2004) ("Decision Ex.I/3").

With Decision Ex.I/3 in hand, EPA proposed rules to implement the critical-use exemption. . . . Many parties, including NRDC, submitted comments. The Final Rule, issued in December 2004, authorized new production and consumption up to the limit established in Decision Ex.I/3 . . . It also authorized the use of stocks as permitted by the decision, and permitted noncritical users to draw upon existing stocks . . . .

NRDC believes the Final Rule violated Decision IX/6 and Decision Ex.I/3 because EPA failed to disclose the full amount of existing stocks, failed to offset new production and consumption by the full amount of these stocks, and failed to reserve the stocks for critical uses, and because the total amount of methyl bromide critical use the Final Rule authorized is not the technically and economically feasible minimum. These claims depend upon the legal status of Decisions IX/6 and Ex.I/3.

II.

[The court here concludes that NRDC has standing to seek review of the EPA's regulation in this case.]

III.

On the merits, NRDC argues that "EPA's 2005 critical-use rule violates the express terms of the Montreal Protocol Parties' unanimous Decisions," and therefore is "not in accordance with law." ...

NRDC believes EPA's rule departs from these post-treaty agreements in three respects. First, the rule authorizes 7,659 metric tons of new production and consumption—the maximum agreed upon in Decision Ex.I/3—without offsetting this amount by existing stocks.... EPA declined to disclose the size of the total nationwide methyl bromide stockpile—an action NRDC claims is itself a violation of the Clean Air Act.... Still, the record suggests that the stockpile is at least as large as the United States' total critical-use allocation for 2005. Second, EPA's rule allows noncritical users to draw down existing stocks. NRDC claims that the "decisions" implicitly reserve the stocks for critical users only. Third, EPA approved 8,942 metric tons of critical uses—again the maximum agreed upon in Decision Ex.I/3—without considering anew whether this was the minimum amount feasible. EPA counters that it adhered to the agreed-upon critical-use and new production and consumption levels, and that the remainder of the decisions are "hortatory." ...

NRDC fashions the entirety of its argument around the proposition that the "decisions" under the Protocol are "law." This premise is flawed. The "decisions" of the Parties—post-ratification side agreements reached by consensus among 189 nations—are not "law" within the meaning of the Clean Air Act and are not enforceable in federal court.

The Clean Air Act authorizes EPA to "exempt the production, importation, and consumption of methyl bromide for critical uses" only "[t]o the extent consistent with the Montreal Protocol." ... The Protocol bans the production or consumption of methyl bromide after December 31, 2004, except "to the extent that the Parties decide to permit the level of production or consumption that is necessary to satisfy uses agreed by them to be critical uses." ... NRDC argues that because the Clean Air Act requires EPA to abide by the Protocol, and because the Protocol authorizes future agreements concerning the scope of the critical-use exemption, those future agreements must "define the scope of EPA's Clean Air Act authority." ...

NRDC's interpretation raises significant constitutional problems. If the "decisions" are "law"—enforceable in federal court like statutes or legislative rules—then Congress either has delegated lawmaking authority to an international body or authorized amendments to a treaty without presidential signature or Senate ratification, in violation of Article II of the Constitution. The Supreme Court has not determined whether decisions of an international body created by treaty are judicially enforceable. But there is a close analogy in this court. The United States is a party to a treaty establishing the International Court of Justice (ICJ). In *Committee of United States Citizens Living in Nicaragua v. Reagan*, 859 F.2d 929 (D.C.Cir.1988), we held that rulings of the ICJ do not provide "substantive legal standards for reviewing agency actions," . . . because the rulings, though authorized by the ratified treaty, were not themselves self-executing treaties.

* * *

Although *Committee of United States Citizens* is highly suggestive of the outcome in this case, several features of the Montreal Protocol "decisions" may distinguish them from ICJ "adjudications." For one thing, Congress implemented the Montreal Protocol with a direction to EPA to abide by its terms. . . . For another, Montreal Protocol "decisions" are not adjudications between parties; instead, they purport to set rules for implementing ongoing treaty commitments.

The legal status of "decisions" of this sort appears to be a question of first impression. A holding that the Parties' post-ratification side agreements were "law" would raise serious constitutional questions in light of the non-delegation doctrine, numerous constitutional procedural requirements for making law, and the separation of powers.

We need not confront the "serious likelihood that the statute will be held unconstitutional." . . . It is far more plausible to interpret the Clean Air Act and Montreal Protocol as creating an ongoing international political commitment rather than a delegation of lawmaking authority to annual meetings of the Parties.

* * *

Nowhere does the Protocol suggest that the Parties' post-ratification consensus agreements about how to implement the critical-use exemption are binding in domestic courts. The only pertinent language in Article 2H(5) states that the Parties will "decide to permit" production and consumption necessary to satisfy those uses that they "agree[]" to be critical uses. The Protocol is silent on any specific conditions accompanying the critical-use exemption. Post-ratification agreements setting these conditions are not the Protocol.

To illustrate, suppose the President signed and the Senate ratified a treaty with Germany and France to conserve fossil fuel. How this is to be accomplished the treaty does not specify. In a later meeting of representatives of the signatory countries at the United Nations, a consensus is reached to lower the speed limits on all major highways of the signatory nations to a maximum of 45 miles per hour. No one would say that United States law has thus been made.

EPA characterizes the decisions as "subsequent consensus agreements of the Parties that address the interpretation and application of the critical use provision . . . ." This may be so. Like any interpretive tool, however, the "decisions" are useful only to the extent they shed light on ambiguous terms in the Protocol. But the details of the critical-use exemption are not ambiguous. They are nonexistent. The "decisions" do not interpret treaty language. They fill in treaty gaps.

Article 2H(5) thus constitutes an "agreement to agree." The parties agree in the Protocol to reach an agreement concerning the types of uses for which new production and consumption will be permitted, and the amounts that will be permitted.

"Agreements to agree" are usually not enforceable in contract. . . . And the fruits of those agreements are enforceable only to the extent that they themselves are contracts. There is no doubt that the "decisions" are not treaties.

The Parties' post-ratification actions suggest their common understanding that the decisions are international political commitments rather than judicially enforceable domestic law. The Parties met to decide the 2006 critical-use exemptions well after EPA's rule went into effect. . . . Yet they did not invoke the Protocol's internal noncompliance procedure against the United States, see Montreal Protocol art. 8, nor did they admonish the United States to change its interpretation of the previous decisions. This course of dealing suggests that the Parties intended the side agreements to be enforceable as a political matter at the negotiating table.

Our holding in this case in no way diminishes the power of the Executive to enter into international agreements that constrain its own behavior within the confines of statutory and treaty law. The Executive has the power to implement ongoing collective endeavors with other countries. . . . Without congressional action, however, side agreements reached after a treaty has been ratified are not the law of the land; they are enforceable not through the federal courts, but through international negotiations . . . .

Because the post-ratification agreements of the parties are not "law," EPA's rule—even if inconsistent with those agreements—is not in violation of any domestic law within the meaning of the Clean Air Act, 42 U.S.C. § 7607(d) (9)(A), the petition for review is denied.

So ordered.

Notes and Questions

1. If the International Committee's decision is not law and it is not binding on a federal court, what is it? Can the executive nonetheless decide to follow the International Committee's recommendations in any event? Could it change its mind? Could a new administration decide to change the policy without fear of reprisal from the international community?

2. What would the constitutional arguments against delegating power to an international committee be? Do they turn on the fact that foreign bodies are neither appointed by the President with advice and consent of the Senate, nor are they a part of the executive branch of government? On the other hand, how significant were the changes being proposed here? Did they in any way alter the fundamentals of the treaty which had already been approved by the Senate?

3. How do you assess the decision to leave such decisions to the discretion of the executive branch? Could producers of methyl bromide challenge such executive decisions as unauthorized?

C. Comparing climate change with ozone depletion

As we shall see below, the collective action problems inherent in climate change issues were far more complex than those dealt with by the Montreal Protocol. This complexity did not prevent agreement, but it makes the Montreal Protocol and the Paris Accords difficult to compare. In its broad outlines, the 2015 Paris Accords incorporated some aspects of the Montreal Protocol regulatory approach, particularly in its use of regulation to create an incentive structure to develop new technologies—although it is too soon to know how companies devoted to soft energy like solar and wind power will respond. A comparison of the equitable principles in the Protocol and the Paris Accord is also instructive.

Exploring these and other questions begins at the domestic level. The case law that has developed around the Clean Air Act of 1970 as amended, and related statutes, has now been adapted to the global climate change issues—a prime example of how law can be effectively transnationalized, sometimes by Congress, but often by the interpretive powers of executive federal agencies themselves, assisted at times, as here, by the courts. The case below recounts some of the United States legal history with the difficult issue of climate change. It also—indirectly at least—points to the additional difficulties posed by the political and regulatory climate in the U.S. Congress. As noted above, the anticipation of congressional obstruction may well have contributed to framing the agreement as an executive order. Specifically, the likely inability to obtain two-thirds support in the Senate or a majority in both houses of Congress may have affected the way the U.S. approached the negotiation of the climate accords, and consequently, at least to some extent, the voluntary nature of the Accord. By contrast, the Montreal Protocol arose at a time when environmental issues were very much at the political forefront, and science was popularly viewed as authoritative. The same cannot be said for the current regulatory era.

As you review the case below, take note of the means by which domestic law is transnationalized. Why is standing in doubt here? How does the majority overcome the doubts? How do the majority and the dissent differ in the ways they respectively frame the problem of standing with respect to the global environment and, more importantly, whether global environmental problems can be remedied by one country alone?

Massachusetts v. Environmental Protection Agency

549 U.S. 497 (2007)

Justice Stevens delivered the opinion of the Court.

A well-documented rise in global temperatures has coincided with a significant increase in the concentration of carbon dioxide in the atmosphere. Respected scientists believe the two trends are related. For when carbon dioxide is released into the atmosphere, it acts like the ceiling of a greenhouse, trapping solar energy and retarding the escape of reflected heat. It is therefore a species—the most important species—of a "greenhouse gas."

Calling global warming "the most pressing environmental challenge of our time," a group of States, local governments, and private organizations alleged in a petition for certiorari that the Environmental Protection Agency (EPA) has abdicated its responsibility under the Clean Air Act to regulate the emissions of four greenhouse gases, including carbon dioxide. Specifically, petitioners asked us to answer two questions concerning the meaning of § 202(a)(1) of the Act: whether EPA has the statutory authority to regulate greenhouse gas emissions from new motor vehicles; and if so, whether its stated reasons for refusing to do so are consistent with the statute.

In response, EPA, supported by ten intervening States and six trade associations, correctly argued that we may not address those two questions unless at least one petitioner has standing to invoke our jurisdiction under Article III of the Constitution. Notwithstanding the serious character of that jurisdictional argument and the absence of any conflicting decisions construing § 202(a)(1), the unusual importance of the underlying issue persuaded us to grant the writ. 548 U.S. 903 (2006).

I

Section 202(a)(1) of the Clean Air Act, provides:

> "The [EPA] Administrator shall by regulation prescribe (and from time to time revise) in accordance with the provisions of this section, standards applicable to the emission of any air pollutant from any class or classes of new motor vehicles or new motor vehicle engines, which in his judgment cause, or contribute to, air pollution which may reasonably be anticipated to endanger public health or welfare . . . ."

The Act defines "air pollutant" to include "any air pollution agent or combination of such agents, including any physical, chemical, biological, radioactive . . . substance or matter which is emitted into or otherwise enters the ambient air." § 7602(g). "Welfare" is also defined broadly: among other things, it includes "effects on . . . weather . . . and climate." § 7602(h).

When Congress enacted these provisions, the study of climate change was in its infancy. In 1959, shortly after the U.S. Weather Bureau began monitoring atmospheric carbon dioxide levels, an observatory in Mauna Loa, Hawaii, recorded a mean level of 316 parts per million. This was well above the highest carbon dioxide concentration—no more than 300 parts per million—revealed in the 420,000-year-old ice-core record. By the time Congress drafted § 202(a)(1) in 1970, carbon dioxide levels had reached 325 parts per million.

In the late 1970's, the Federal Government began devoting serious attention to the possibility that carbon dioxide emissions associated with human activity could provoke climate change. In 1978, Congress enacted the National Climate Program Act, . . . which required the President to establish a program to "assist the Nation and the world to understand and respond to natural and man-induced climate processes and their implications." President Carter, in turn, asked the National Research Council, the working arm of the National Academy of Sciences, to investigate the subject. The Council's response was unequivocal: "If carbon dioxide continues to increase, the study group finds no reason to doubt that climate changes will result and no reason to believe that these changes will be negligible . . . . A wait-and-see policy may mean waiting until it is too late."

Congress next addressed the issue in 1987, when it enacted the Global Climate Protection Act . . . Finding that "manmade pollution—the release of carbon dioxide, chlorofluorocarbons, methane, and other trace gases into the atmosphere—may be producing a long-term and substantial increase in the average temperature on Earth," § 1102(1), 101 Stat. 1408, Congress directed EPA to propose to Congress a "coordinated national policy on global climate change," § 1103(b), and ordered the Secretary of State to work "through the channels of multilateral diplomacy" and coordinate diplomatic efforts to combat global warming, § 1103(c). Congress emphasized that "ongoing pollution and deforestation may be contributing now to an irreversible process" and that "[n]ecessary actions must be identified and implemented in time to protect the climate." § 1102(4).

Meanwhile, the scientific understanding of climate change progressed. In 1990, the Intergovernmental Panel on Climate Change (IPCC), a multinational scientific body organized under the auspices of the United Nations, published its first comprehensive report on the topic. Drawing on expert opinions from across the globe, the IPCC concluded that "emissions resulting from human activities are substantially increasing the atmospheric concentrations of . . . greenhouse gases [which] will enhance the greenhouse effect, resulting on average in an additional warming of the Earth's surface."

Responding to the IPCC report, the United Nations convened the "Earth Summit" in 1992 in Rio de Janeiro. The first President Bush attended and signed the United Nations Framework Convention on Climate Change (UNFCCC), a nonbinding agreement among 154 nations to reduce atmospheric concentrations of carbon dioxide and other greenhouse gases for the purpose of "prevent[ing] dangerous anthropogenic [i.e., human-induced] interference with the [Earth's] climate system." . . . The Senate unanimously ratified the treaty.

Some five years later—after the IPCC issued a second comprehensive report in 1995 concluding that "[t]he balance of evidence suggests there is a discernible human influence on global climate"—the UNFCCC signatories met in Kyoto, Japan, and adopted a protocol that assigned mandatory targets for industrialized nations to reduce greenhouse gas emissions. Because those targets did not apply to developing and heavily polluting nations such as China and India, the Senate unanimously passed a resolution expressing its sense that the United States should not enter into the Kyoto Protocol. . . . President Clinton did not submit the protocol to the Senate for ratification.

II

On October 20, 1999, a group of nineteen private organizations filed a rulemaking petition asking EPA to regulate "greenhouse gas emissions from new motor vehicles under § 202 of the Clean Air Act." Petitioners maintained that 1998 was the "warmest year on record"; that carbon dioxide, methane, nitrous oxide, and hydrofluorocarbons are "heat trapping greenhouse gases"; that greenhouse gas emissions have significantly accelerated climate change; and that the IPCC's 1995 report warned that "carbon dioxide remains the most important contributor to [manmade] forcing of climate change." The petition further alleged that climate change will have serious adverse effects on human health and the environment. As to EPA's statutory authority, the petition observed that the Agency itself had already confirmed that it had the power to regulate carbon dioxide. In 1998, Jonathan Z. Cannon, then EPA's general counsel, prepared a legal opinion concluding that "CO 2 emissions are within the scope of EPA's authority to regulate," even as he recognized that EPA had so far declined to exercise that authority. Cannon's successor, Gary S. Guzy, reiterated that opinion before a congressional committee just two weeks before the rulemaking petition was filed....

Fifteen months after the petition's submission, EPA requested public comment on "all the issues raised in [the] petition," adding a "particular" request for comments on "any scientific, technical, legal, economic or other aspect of these issues that may be relevant to EPA's consideration of this petition." EPA received more than 50,000 comments over the next five months.

Before the close of the comment period, the White House sought "assistance in identifying the areas in the science of climate change where there are the greatest certainties and uncertainties" from the National Research Council, asking for a response "as soon as possible." ... The result was a 2001 report titled Climate Change Science: An Analysis of Some Key Questions (NRC Report), which, drawing heavily on the 1995 IPCC report, concluded that "[g]reenhouse gases are accumulating in Earth's atmosphere as a result of human activities, causing surface air temperatures and subsurface ocean temperatures to rise. Temperatures are, in fact, rising."

On September 8, 2003, EPA entered an order denying the rulemaking petition. The Agency gave two reasons for its decision: (1) that contrary to the opinions of its former general counsels, the Clean Air Act does not authorize EPA to issue mandatory regulations to address global climate change; and (2) that even if the Agency had the authority to set greenhouse gas emission standards, it would be unwise to do so at this time.

In concluding that it lacked statutory authority over greenhouse gases, EPA observed that Congress "was well aware of the global climate change issue when it last comprehensively amended the [Clean Air Act] in 1990," yet it declined to adopt a proposed amendment establishing binding emissions limitations. Congress instead chose to authorize further investigation into climate change. EPA further reasoned that Congress' "specially tailored solutions to global atmospheric issues" ... —in particular, its 1990 enactment of a comprehensive scheme to regulate pollutants that depleted the ozone layer—counseled against reading the general authorization of § 202(a)(1) to confer regulatory authority over greenhouse gases . . . .

EPA reasoned that climate change had its own "political history": Congress designed the original Clean Air Act to address local air pollutants rather than a substance that "is fairly consistent in its concentration throughout the world's atmosphere," and addressed global climate change in other legislation. Because of this political history, and because imposing emission limitations on greenhouse gases would have even greater economic and political repercussions than regulating tobacco, EPA was persuaded that it lacked the power to do so. In essence, EPA concluded that climate change was so important that unless Congress spoke with exacting specificity, it could not have meant the Agency to address it.

Having reached that conclusion, EPA believed it followed that greenhouse gases cannot be "air pollutants" within the meaning of the Act. The Agency bolstered this conclusion by explaining that if carbon dioxide were an air pollutant, the only feasible method of reducing tailpipe emissions would be to improve fuel economy. But because Congress has already created detailed mandatory fuel economy standards subject to Department of Transportation (DOT) administration, the Agency concluded that EPA regulation would either conflict with those standards or be superfluous.

Even assuming that it had authority over greenhouse gases, EPA explained in detail why it would refuse to exercise that authority. The Agency began by recognizing that the concentration of greenhouse gases has dramatically increased as a result of human activities, and acknowledged the attendant increase in global surface air temperatures. EPA nevertheless gave controlling importance to the NRC Report's statement that a causal link between the two "'cannot be unequivocally established.'" Given that residual uncertainty, EPA concluded that regulating greenhouse gas emissions would be unwise.

The Agency furthermore characterized any EPA regulation of motor-vehicle emissions as a "piecemeal approach" to climate change, and stated that such regulation would conflict with the President's "comprehensive approach" to the problem. That approach involves additional support for technological innovation, the creation of nonregulatory programs to encourage voluntary private-sector reductions in greenhouse gas emissions, and further research on climate change—not actual regulation. According to EPA, unilateral EPA regulation of motor-vehicle greenhouse gas emissions might also hamper the President's ability to persuade key developing countries to reduce greenhouse gas emissions.

III

* * *

IV

[Here, the Court held that petitioners had standing, focusing on Massachusetts.

First, the Court noted two special circumstances weighing in favor of standing: (1) Congress specifically authorized the challenge to EPA action. (2) Massachusetts, as a sovereign state, has a *parens patriae* interest in representing its state citizens. States, in joining the Union, forfeit the ability to pursue its interests in many fora, including war and diplomacy. Thus, access to the courts is especially important for the states, and Massachusetts "is entitled to special solicitude in our standing analysis."

Second, the Court addressed the injury alleged. The Court determined that "[t]he harms associated with climate change are serious and well recognized." The Court rejected the argument that standing was improper because of the general applicability of risks associated with climate change. Massachusetts' allegations of losing coastal land due to sea levels rising was a sufficient "particularized injury in its capacity of landowner."

Third, the Court rejected the EPA's argument that the causal relationship between new motor vehicle emissions and global warming is too attenuated to warrant standing. "Incremental" steps toward solving a larger problem are cognizable, the Court held. Reviewing the evidence, the Court stated that the emissions "make a meaningful contribution to . . . global warming."

Finally, the Court determined that the remedy would redress Massachusetts' injury: "While it may be true that regulating motor-vehicle emissions will not by itself *reverse* global warming, it by no means follows that we lack jurisdiction to decide whether EPA has a duty to take steps to *slow* or *reduce* it." The Court rejected the argument that the remedy would have no impact due to other polluting countries: "A reduction in domestic emissions would slow the pace of global emissions increases, no matter what happens elsewhere."]

V

The scope of our review of the merits of the statutory issues is narrow. As we have repeated time and again, an agency has broad discretion to choose how best to marshal its limited resources and personnel to carry out its delegated responsibilities. . . . That discretion is at its height when the agency decides not to bring an enforcement action. Therefore, in *Heckler v. Chaney*, 470 U.S. 821 (1985), we held that an agency's refusal to initiate enforcement proceedings is not ordinarily subject to judicial review. Some debate remains, however, as to the rigor with which we review an agency's denial of a petition for rulemaking.

There are key differences between a denial of a petition for rulemaking and an agency's decision not to initiate an enforcement action. In contrast to nonenforcement decisions, agency refusals to initiate rulemaking "are less frequent, more apt to involve legal as opposed to factual analysis, and subject to special formalities, including a public explanation." They moreover arise out of denials of petitions for rulemaking which (at least in the circumstances here) the affected party had an undoubted procedural right to file in the first instance. Refusals to promulgate rules are thus susceptible to judicial review, though such review is "extremely limited" and "highly deferential." *National Customs Brokers & Forwarders Assn. of America, Inc. v. United States*, 883 F.2d 93, 96 (CADC 1989).

EPA concluded in its denial of the petition for rulemaking that it lacked authority under 42 U.S.C. § 7521(a)(1) to regulate new vehicle emissions because carbon dioxide is not an "air pollutant" as that term is defined in § 7602. In the alternative, it concluded that even if it possessed authority, it would decline to do so because regulation would conflict with other administration priorities. As discussed earlier, the Clean Air Act expressly permits review of such an action. § 7607(b)(1). We therefore "may reverse any such action found to be . . . arbitrary, capricious, an abuse of discretion, or otherwise not in accordance with law." § 7607(d)(9).

VI

On the merits, the first question is whether § 202(a)(1) of the Clean Air Act authorizes EPA to regulate greenhouse gas emissions from new motor vehicles in the event that it forms a "judgment" that such emissions contribute to climate change. We have little trouble concluding that it does. In relevant part, § 202(a)(1) provides that EPA "shall by regulation prescribe . . . standards applicable to the emission of any air pollutant from any class or classes of new motor vehicles or new motor vehicle engines, which in [the Administrator's] judgment cause, or contribute to, air pollution which may reasonably be anticipated to endanger public health or welfare." 42 U.S.C. § 7521(a)(1). Because EPA believes that Congress did not intend it to regulate substances that contribute to climate change, the agency maintains that carbon dioxide is not an "air pollutant" within the meaning of the provision.

The statutory text forecloses EPA's reading. The Clean Air Act's sweeping definition of "air pollutant" includes "*any* air pollution agent or combination of such agents, including *any* physical, chemical, . . . substance or matter which is emitted into or otherwise enters the ambient air . . ." § 7602(g) (emphasis added). On its face, the definition embraces all airborne compounds of whatever stripe, and underscores that intent through the repeated use of the word "any." Carbon dioxide, methane, nitrous oxide, and hydrofluorocarbons are without a doubt "physical [and] chemical . . . substance[s] which [are] emitted into . . . the ambient air." The statute is unambiguous . . . .

While the Congresses that drafted § 202(a)(1) might not have appreciated the possibility that burning fossil fuels could lead to global warming, they did understand that without regulatory flexibility, changing circumstances and scientific developments would soon render the Clean Air Act obsolete. The broad language of § 202(a)(1) reflects an intentional effort to confer the flexibility necessary to forestall such obsolescence. . . . Because greenhouse gases fit well within the Clean Air Act's capacious definition of "air pollutant," we hold that EPA has the statutory authority to regulate the emission of such gases from new motor vehicles.

VII

The alternative basis for EPA's decision—that even if it does have statutory authority to regulate greenhouse gases, it would be unwise to do so at this time—rests on reasoning divorced from the statutory text. While the statute does condition the exercise of EPA's authority on its formation of a "judgment," that judgment must relate to whether an air pollutant "cause[s], or contribute[s] to, air pollution which may reasonably be anticipated to endanger public health or welfare." Put another way, the use of the word "judgment" is not a roving license to ignore the statutory text. It is but a direction to exercise discretion within defined statutory limits....

In short, EPA has offered no reasoned explanation for its refusal to decide whether greenhouse gases cause or contribute to climate change. Its action was therefore "arbitrary, capricious, ... or otherwise not in accordance with law." 42 U.S.C. § 7607(d)(9)(A). We need not and do not reach the question whether on remand EPA must make an endangerment finding, or whether policy concerns can inform EPA's actions in the event that it makes such a finding. Cf. *Chevron U.S.A. Inc. v. Natural Resources Defense Council, Inc.*, 467 U.S., at 843–844. We hold only that EPA must ground its reasons for action or inaction in the statute.

VIII

The judgment of the Court of Appeals is reversed, and the case is remanded for further proceedings consistent with this opinion. It is so ordered.

CHIEF JUSTICE ROBERTS, with whom JUSTICE SCALIA, JUSTICE THOMAS, and JUSTICE ALITO join, dissenting.

Global warming may be a "crisis," even "the most pressing environmental problem of our time." Pet. for Cert. 26, 22. Indeed, it may ultimately affect nearly everyone on the planet in some potentially adverse way, and it may be that governments have done too little to address it. It is not a problem, however, that has escaped the attention of policymakers in the Executive and Legislative Branches of our Government, who continue to consider regulatory, legislative, and treaty based means of addressing global climate change.

Apparently dissatisfied with the pace of progress on this issue in the elected branches, petitioners have come to the courts claiming broad-ranging injury, and attempting to tie that injury to the Government's alleged failure to comply with a rather narrow statutory provision. I would reject these challenges as nonjusticiable. Such a conclusion involves no judgment on whether global warming exists, what causes it, or the extent of the problem. Nor does it render petitioners without recourse. This Court's standing jurisprudence simply recognizes that redress of grievances of the sort at issue here "is the function of Congress and the Chief Executive," not the federal courts. *Lujan v. Defenders of Wildlife*, 504 U.S. 555, 576 (1992). I would vacate the judgment below and remand for dismissal of the petitions for review....

II

. . . The very concept of global warming seems inconsistent with this particularization requirement. Global warming is a phenomenon "harmful to humanity at large," 415 F.3d, at 60 (Sentelle, J., dissenting in part and concurring in judgment), and the redress petitioners seek is focused no more on them than on the public generally—it is literally to change the atmosphere around the world.

If petitioners' particularized injury is loss of coastal land, it is also that injury that must be "actual or imminent, not conjectural or hypothetical," *Defenders of Wildlife, supra*, at 560 (internal quotation marks omitted), "real and immediate," *Los Angeles v. Lyons*, 461 U.S. 95, 102 (1983) (internal quotation marks omitted), and "certainly impending," *Whitmore v. Arkansas*, 495 U.S. 149, 158 (1990) (internal quotation marks omitted).

As to "actual" injury, the Court observes that "global sea levels rose somewhere between 10 and 20 centimeters over the 20th century as a result of global warming" and that "[t]hese rising seas have already begun to swallow Massachusetts' coastal land." *Ante*, at 19. But none of petitioners' declarations supports that connection. One declaration states that "a rise in sea level due to climate change is occurring on the coast of Massachusetts, in the metropolitan Boston area," but there is no elaboration. Petitioners' Standing Appendix in No. 03-1361, etc. (CADC), p. 196 (Stdg. App.). And the declarant goes on to identify a "significan[t]" non-global-warming cause of Boston's rising sea level: land subsidence. *Id.*, at 197; see also *id.*, at 216. Thus, aside from a single conclusory statement, there is nothing in petitioners' 43 standing declarations and accompanying exhibits to support an inference of actual loss of Massachusetts coastal land from 20th century global sea level increases. It is pure conjecture.

The Court's attempts to identify "imminent" or "certainly impending" loss of Massachusetts coastal land fares no better. See *ante*, at 19–20. One of petitioners' declarants predicts global warming will cause sea level to rise by 20 to 70 centimeters by the year 2100. Stdg. App. 216. Another uses a computer modeling program to map the Commonwealth's coastal land and its current elevation, and calculates that the high-end estimate of sea level rise would result in the loss of significant state-owned coastal land. *Id.*, at 179. But the computer modeling program has a conceded average error of about 30 centimeters and a maximum observed error of 70 centimeters. *Id.*, at 177–178. As an initial matter, if it is possible that the model underrepresents the elevation of coastal land to an extent equal to or in excess of the projected sea level rise, it is difficult to put much stock in the predicted loss of land. But even placing that problem to the side, accepting a century-long time horizon and a series of compounded estimates renders requirements of imminence and immediacy utterly toothless. See *Defenders of Wildlife, supra*, at 565, n. 2 (while the concept of " 'imminence' " in standing doctrine is "somewhat elastic," it can be "stretched beyond the breaking point"). "Allegations of possible future injury do not satisfy the requirements of Art. III. A threatened injury must be *certainly impending* to constitute injury in fact." *Whitmore, supra*, at 158 (internal quotation marks omitted; emphasis added).

III

Petitioners' reliance on Massachusetts's loss of coastal land as their injury in fact for standing purposes creates insurmountable problems for them with respect to causation and redressability.

Petitioners view the relationship between their injuries and EPA's failure to promulgate new motor vehicle greenhouse gas emission standards as simple and direct: Domestic motor vehicles emit carbon dioxide and other greenhouse gases. Worldwide emissions of greenhouse gases contribute to global warming and therefore also to petitioners' alleged injuries. Without the new vehicle standards, greenhouse gas emissions—and therefore global warming and its attendant harms—have been higher than they otherwise would have been; once EPA changes course, the trend will be reversed.

The Court ignores the complexities of global warming, and does so by now disregarding the "particularized" injury it relied on in step one, and using the dire nature of global warming itself as a bootstrap for finding causation and redressability. First, it is important to recognize the extent of the emissions at issue here. Because local greenhouse gas emissions disperse throughout the atmosphere and remain there for anywhere from 50 to 200 years, it is global emissions data that are relevant. See App. to Pet. for Cert. A-73. According to one of petitioners' declarations, domestic motor vehicles contribute about 6 percent of global carbon dioxide emissions and 4 percent of global greenhouse gas emissions. Stdg. App. 232. The amount of global emissions at issue here is smaller still; § 202(a)(1) of the Clean Air Act covers only new motor vehicles and new motor vehicle engines, so petitioners' desired emission standards might reduce only a fraction of 4 percent of global emissions.

This gets us only to the relevant greenhouse gas emissions; linking them to global warming and ultimately to petitioners' alleged injuries next requires consideration of further complexities. In light of the bit-part domestic new motor vehicle greenhouse gas emissions have played in what petitioners describe as a 150-year global phenomenon, and the myriad additional factors bearing on petitioners' alleged injury—the loss of Massachusetts coastal land—the connection is far too speculative to establish causation.

IV

Redressability is even more problematic. To the tenuous link between petitioners' alleged injury and the indeterminate fractional domestic emissions at issue here, add the fact that petitioners cannot meaningfully predict what will come of the 80 percent of global greenhouse gas emissions that originate outside the United States. As the Court acknowledges, "developing countries such as China and India are poised to increase greenhouse gas emissions substantially over the next century," *ante*, at 23, so the domestic emissions at issue here may become an increasingly marginal portion of global emissions, and any decreases produced by petitioners' desired standards are likely to be overwhelmed many times over by emissions increases elsewhere in the world.

Petitioners offer declarations attempting to address this uncertainty, contending that "[i]f the U.S. takes steps to reduce motor vehicle emissions, other countries are very likely to take similar actions regarding their own motor vehicles using technology developed in response to the U.S. program." Stdg. App. 220; see also *id.*, at 311–312. In other words, do not worry that other countries will contribute far more to global warming than will U.S. automobile emissions; someone is bound to invent something, and places like the People's Republic of China or India will surely require use of the new technology, regardless of cost. The Court previously has explained that when the existence of an element of standing "depends on the unfettered choices made by independent actors not before the courts and whose exercise of broad and legitimate discretion the courts cannot presume either to control or to predict," a party must present facts supporting an assertion that the actor will proceed in such a manner. *Defenders of Wildlife*, 504 U.S., at 562 (quoting *ASARCO Inc. v. Kadish*, 490 U.S. 605, 615 (1989) (opinion of Kennedy, J.); internal quotation marks omitted). The declarations' conclusory (not to say fanciful) statements do not even come close.

[E]ven if regulation does reduce emissions—to some indeterminate degree, given events elsewhere in the world—the Court never explains why that makes it likely that the injury in fact—the loss of land—will be redressed.

V

Petitioners' difficulty in demonstrating causation and redressability is not surprising given the evident mismatch between the source of their alleged injury—catastrophic global warming—and the narrow subject matter of the Clean Air Act provision at issue in this suit. The mismatch suggests that petitioners' true goal for this litigation may be more symbolic than anything else. The constitutional role of the courts, however, is to decide concrete cases—not to serve as a convenient forum for policy debates.

Justice Scalia, with whom The Chief Justice, Justice Thomas, and Justice Alito join, dissenting.

... The Court's alarm over global warming may or may not be justified, but it ought not distort the outcome of this litigation. This is a straightforward administrative-law case, in which Congress has passed a malleable statute giving broad discretion, not to us but to an executive agency. No matter how important the underlying policy issues at stake, this Court has no business substituting its own desired outcome for the reasoned judgment of the responsible agency.

Notes and Questions

1. Douglas A. Kysar contrasts the dissent's skepticism with the United States' leadership in the Montreal Protocol:

> Chief Justice Roberts dismissed out of hand this vision of a socialized international policy space, sharply rejecting the challengers' argument that unilateral action by the United States on climate change might inspire other states to take similar steps. In essence, Roberts sought to enshrine into legal

> standing doctrine the rational-choice-theory approach to international relations. . . . To Roberts, the possibility that domestic U.S. steps toward greenhouse gas emissions abatement would alter the international policy arena seemed simply unimaginable, a skepticism that ignored the earlier example of ozone-depleting substances in which American leadership had encouraged precisely that effect.
>
> The chief justice's restrictive views on redressability in the global environmental context deserve serious scrutiny: If the test for standing were made to depend so heavily on consequentialist efficacy in this manner, even domestic environmental laws would not fare well, for many of the goals of those laws face serious disruption from extraterritorial action.[86]

How do traditional notions of state sovereignty and autonomy pose barriers to addressing global problems that transcend political borders? How can we effect change in spite of these barriers? How would you describe the dissenting Justices' conception of territory that seems to underlie their views?

2. After this decision, the EPA issued an "endangerment finding" that stated that carbon dioxide and other greenhouse gases may cause danger to human health or welfare. It then issued several rules pertaining to climate change. One such rule was the "Tailpipe Rule," limiting greenhouse gas emissions in vehicles. Another rule requires major stationary sources to obtain permits, though the EPA determined that the sheer number of such sources would create an administrative burden and it thus postponed permitting requirements for smaller sources under the "Timing and Tailoring Rule." In *Coalition for Responsible Regulation, Inc. v. EPA*, 684 F.3d 102 (D.C. Cir. 2012), a group of states and industry groups challenged these measures. Specifically, the petitioners challenged the endangerment finding on the basis that scientific evidence was lacking and the Tailpipe Rule on the basis that the EPA failed to consider the costs associated with such a rule. The court held that it lacked jurisdiction to determine the Timing and Tailoring Rules challenge (due to petitioners' failure to show injury), and it held that the EPA's endangerment finding and Tailpipe Rule were not arbitrary or capricious.

3. The Clean Air Act (CAA) was passed in 1970. Can it carry the full weight of this kind of regulation? Why is the United States relying on a statute passed in the 1970s rather than a new statute dealing directly with problems of climate change today?

4. How do the problems to be solved by a climate change agreement differ from those we have just studied dealing with ozone depletion? Consider the following from Daniel H. Cole, *From Global to Polycentric Climate Governance*, 2 Climate L. 395, 398–400 (2011):

---

86. Douglas A. Kysar, Regulating From Nowhere: Environmental Law and the Search for Objectivity 145 (2010).

Depletion of the stratospheric ozone layer presented the international community with a very different kind of global public-good problem. Simply put, the problem stemmed from anthropogenic emissions of ozone depleting substances (ODSs)—primarily chemical refrigerants—emitted from millions of discrete sources throughout the world, but primarily from developed countries, where refrigeration and air conditioning are more prevalent. ODSs depleted the stratospheric ozone layer that protects the earth and its inhabitants from harmful ultraviolet radiation. Because ODSs were produced in several countries and every country emitted ODSs, a single country could not resolve the problem on its own. The problem was, however, successfully resolved through global collective action. The 1987 Montreal Protocol on Substances that Deplete the Ozone Layer, and other documents comprising the "Ozone Accords," phased out of production and use the most harmful ozone depleting substances (ODSs), several of which are also harmful greenhouse gases.

The fact that relatively few parties had significant commercial interests at stake in the ozone negotiations made it a relatively simple global problem to resolve. Climate change, by contrast, presents a far more difficult collective-action problem for several reasons (presented here in brief): (1) the costs and benefits of climate change (or climate change mitigation) are expected to be distributed differentially around the world, creating (comparatively at least) winners and losers; (2) the goal of climate stabilization conflicts with the countervailing need to meet rising global energy demand, which is a major concern for all developed and developing countries; (3) low-carbon energy technologies that might ameliorate conflicts between the twin goals of reducing carbon emissions and increasing energy supplies are not yet "available" as substitutes for fossil fuels, and will certainly not supplant fossil fuels for at least the next couple of decades; and (4), in large part because of (3), climate change mitigation lacks the kind of substantial corporate/commercial support DuPont supplied to the Ozone Accords. These reasons go a long way toward explaining the various flaws and weaknesses in the Kyoto Protocol and related global climate change agreements.

Consider Nobel Prize winner Elinor Ostrom's view that global problems may not need global solutions:

Elinor Ostrom, *Nested Externalities and Polycentric Institutions: Must We Wait For Global Solutions to Climate Change Before Taking Actions at Other Scales?*

49 ECON. THEORY 353, 353–69 (2012)

1. Introduction

The Fourth Assessment Report of the Intergovernmental Panel on Climate Change (2007) and the Stern Report both stress the need to recognize the impact of human actions on the global environment. Even though there is now a relatively high level of agreement among scientists about the danger that humans are facing related to the uncorrected negative externalities of greenhouse gas emissions, little agreement exists about what should and could be done. Further, agreement among citizens concerning the seriousness of global warming is falling. In the March 2010 Gallup Poll on the Environment, 48% of those surveyed responded that the seriousness of global warming was generally exaggerated—a 13% increase as contrasted with poll results in 2008.

The Kyoto Protocol to the United Nations Framework Convention on Climate Change is an international environmental treaty created and signed at the Conference of the Parties of the UNFCC in Kyoto in 1997. More than 180 countries have now ratified the protocol, but the United States has not. Considerable disagreements exist even among the major states that have signed regarding how large a reduction in emissions should be imposed. Major debates exist over a number of issues related to achieving efficient and equitable mechanisms at a global level. One issue relates to who is responsible for the current and immediate future levels of CO2 in the atmosphere. In other words, who should bear the primary burden of paying for solutions? Other debates address whether taxes or quotas are the best instrument for achieving abatement. Similar scholarly concerns have also been raised regarding claims that Payments for Ecosystem Services (PES) can increase carbon sequestration while at the same time enhancing species conservation on the same landscape.

Given the failure to reach agreement at the international level on efficient, fair, and enforceable reductions of greenhouse gas emissions, continuing to wait without investing in efforts at multiple scales may defeat the possibilities of significant abatements and mitigations in enough time to prevent tragic disasters. We need to make a scholarly investment in a more appropriate theory of global change that offers a better explanation of micro-level incentives and outcomes as well as being a foundation for more effective public policies. This paper represents an effort to posit a theory of nested externalities at multiple scales to provide a better foundation for analyzing the multiple scales involved in reducing the threat of climate change. Another goal is to balance the arguments made in the policy literature that a global solution is the only way to cope with climate change. "Global solutions" negotiated at a global level—if not backed up by a variety of efforts at national, regional, and local levels—are not guaranteed to work effectively.

The problem of averting massive climate change is a global "public good." Millions of actors affect the global atmosphere and they all benefit from reduced greenhouse gas emissions. The problem is they benefit whether or not they pay any of the costs since beneficiaries cannot be excluded.

Trying to solve the problem of providing a public good is a classic collective-action dilemma. It is probably the largest dilemma the world has ever knowingly faced. Many analysts call for an institutional solution at the global level.

Given the widespread presumption that any collective-action problem that has global effects must be "solved" entirely at the global level, several theoretical questions need to be addressed as analysts undertake the next round of research on climate change. They include:

1. How may polycentric institutions improve exclusive reliance on a global approach to cope up with global climate issues?
2. Are multiple, nested externalities produced by decisions made at less than a global scale?
3. What types of actions are being taken at less-than-global scale to reduce greenhouse gas emissions?
4. Are large-scale governments usually better equipped to cope with collective-action problems that have outcomes that are large scale themselves?
5. If multiple governments and other organizations work to reduce energy consumption and greenhouse gas emissions, does that only produce leakage, chaotic systems, and potentially counterproductive processes?

* * *

2. A polycentric approach

Let us briefly review the origin of the term "polycentricity." During the 1950s, massive academic criticism was leveled at metropolitan areas across the United States and Europe due to the large number of small-, medium-, and large-scale governmental units operating at the same time. Scholars thought this was chaotic. Ostrom et al. wrote a classic article in (1961) entitled "The Organization of Government in Metropolitan Areas: A Theoretical Inquiry." The authors reasoned that a simple dichotomy between "the" market and "the" government was not a good scientific approach to the study of public economies. Further, "the" market is not a single unit. It is composed of many small-, medium-, and large-scale firms. The expected efficiency of a market disappears if it were consolidated into a monopoly. There is no reason to presume that a monopoly government is more efficient than a system of governmental units at multiple scales.

Economic theory teaches us about the dangers of allocating all capabilities to a single unit even though one cannot apply all lessons derived from the analysis of market economies to the public sector. Ostrom referred to a polycentric system as "one where many elements are capable of making mutual adjustments for ordering their relationships with one another within a general system of rules where each element acts with independence of other elements." A polycentric system exists when multiple public and private organizations at multiple scales jointly affect collective benefits and costs. The early theoretical work on polycentricity stimulated intensive research on the governance of one of the major public goods for urban areas—that of providing public safety—and is a foundation for the theory presented herein.

Readers of this article may ask: What is the relevance of polycentric systems for the analysis of global public goods? The initial relevance of the polycentric approach is the parallel between the earlier theoretical presumption that only the largest scale was relevant for the provision and production of public goods for metropolitan areas, and the contemporary presumption that only the global scale is relevant for policies related to climate change. Extensive empirical research found that while large-scale units were an essential part of effective governance of metropolitan areas, small- and medium-scale units were also necessary components (Parks and Ostrom 1999). An important lesson is that relying entirely on international efforts to solve global climate problems needs to be rethought.

* * *

4. What efforts to reduce greenhouse gas emissions now occur at less than a global scale?

It is not possible to list the large number of projects going on across the world at multiple scales. What I will do is focus on some of the projects that have been organized at a local level as part of the Clean Development Mechanism of the Kyoto Protocol, at the level of a state government in the United States, at a regional level, and discuss some of the efforts in Europe to substantially reduce emissions. Schreurs (2008) and Hoffman and Eidelman (2009) have identified a large number of experiments at multiple levels that reflect action by diverse governance arrangements to take climate change seriously and take actions to reduce the threat.

* * *

4.1 Local-level projects and alliances to reduce local-level externalities

* * *

Multiple cities have started to initiate a variety of "green" initiatives that are prominently displayed on their home pages on the Web. The city of Toronto, for example, has established an "environmental portal" that announces more than a dozen current city policies, related publications, and meetings that are focused on climate change. The city has supported a number of renewable energy projects including major investments averaging around $100,000 each for building rooftop gardens, solar photovoltaic panels on houses, and solar water-heating systems. The city also funds smaller projects to support neighborhood efforts to enhance the forested areas of local parks, local gardens, and for organizations at the local level that are working with communities to hold planning meetings to discuss better bicycle paths and other activities that can be undertaken at a small, neighborhood scale.

Large-city mayors are also banding together to discuss actions to reduce carbon emissions that can be taken locally but if taken jointly, can have a much bigger effect. In October 2005, 18 large cities sent representatives to London to examine actions that could be taken at a municipal level to reexamine various urban policies that could be revised including their own purchasing policies and ways of encouraging more investment in climate-friendly technologies in their cities. The C40 Large Cities Climate Summit occurred in May 2007 for the exchange of information about many policies adopted to reduce emissions and the announcement of a $5 billion global Energy Efficiency Building Retrofit Program by the Clinton Climate Initiative.

* * *

7. Conclusion

Given that the recognition of the danger of climate change among citizens and public officials is still relatively recent, and that major debates about potential solutions are continuing, one cannot expect a global solution to be constructed in the near future. Building a global regime is a necessity, but building a polycentric system starts the process of reducing greenhouses gas emissions and acts as a spur to national and international regimes to get their act together!

Recognizing the potential of building more effective ways of reducing energy use at multiple scales is thus an important step forward. Further, an important strategy for reducing CO2 in the atmosphere is developing more effective policies for protecting ecosystem services—particularly those related to carbon sequestration. Developing effective and adaptive programs, however, requires selecting appropriate areas, developing plans for leaving some areas untouched, and for making major investments in the flora and fauna as well as the technological infrastructure of other areas. This requires substantial investment in scientific modeling and use of geographic information systems combined with in-depth knowledge of the biophysical settings to map ecological systems over time. The models, however, need to be developed at multiple scales so that relevant decision-making units can address what policies can be adopted to improve carbon sequestration that fits the ecology at that particular scale.

Building a strong commitment to finding ways of reducing individual emissions is an important element for coping with climate change. Building such a commitment can be more effectively undertaken in small- to medium-scale governance units that are linked together through information networks and monitoring at all levels. Global policies are indeed necessary but they are not sufficient.

Notes and Questions

1. To what extent do you think the Paris Accords summarized below improve the prospects for dealing with global climate change? Specifically, does the global regulatory dimension of the Accords contribute to their effectiveness? Do these Accords obviate the bottom-up approaches such as described by Ostrom above, or do they remain relevant?

2. How did this global agreement come into existence? Is it likely to be more effective than the Kyoto Protocol that preceded it? As you read the discussion below, notice the voluntary nature of the Accords. This made it possible to gain the support of 197 countries at the close of the negotiations. What do you see as trade-offs, if any?

D. The Paris Accords of 2015

Gathering in Paris just weeks after the city was rocked by terror attacks, French President François Hollande greeted delegates with resilient words:

> I'm not choosing between the fight against terrorism and the fight against global warming. These are two global challenges we must overcome. We must leave our children more than a world free of terrorism. We owe them a

> planet protected from disasters. . . . Essentially, what is at stake at this climate conference is peace.[87]

After twelve days of negotiations among high-level politicians,[88] the Conference of the Parties of the United Nations Framework Convention on Climate Change produced a framework to halt the "global average temperature to well below 2 °C above pre-industrial levels and to pursue efforts to limit the temperature increase to 1.5 °C above pre-industrial levels, recognizing that this would significantly reduce the risks and impacts of climate change."[89]

This framework, embodied in a short, eleven-page, twenty-nine-article Annex to the longer United Nations Adoption Proposal, represents myriad compromises between developed and developing countries; flexibility and commitment; pragmatism and aspiration. While perhaps unsatisfactory to those hoping for an immediate "decarbonization of global economies,"[90] the Paris Agreement represents the most serious efforts yet among the 195 country-parties to curtail greenhouse gas emissions. Here, we address several of its most critical features, including the parties' commitments, the Agreement's approach to voluntariness, the enforcement mechanism, and the Agreement's treatment of equity.

1. Goals

To what has the Conference of the Parties agreed? Article 2 outlines the Agreement's objectives:

Article 2

1. This Agreement, in enhancing the implementation of the Convention, including its objective, aims to strengthen the global response to the threat of climate change, in the context of sustainable development and efforts to eradicate poverty, including by:
   (a) Holding the increase in the global average temperature to well below 2 °C above pre-industrial levels and to pursue efforts to limit the temperature increase to 1.5 °C above pre-industrial levels, recognizing that this would significantly reduce the risks and impacts of climate change;
   (b) Increasing the ability to adapt to the adverse impacts of climate change and foster climate resilience and low greenhouse gas emissions development, in a manner that does not threaten food production;

---

87. Roger-Mark De Souza & Meaghan Parker, *An Empty Table? Food-Climate-Conflict Connections in Paris*, WILSON CENTER (Dec. 21, 2015), https://www.wilsoncenter.org/article/empty-table-food-climate-conflict-connections-paris.

88. *See* Ruth Greenspan Bell, *The Climate Community Turns to Pragmatism, Mostly*, WILSON CENTER (Dec. 18, 2015), https://www.wilsoncenter.org/article/the-climate-community-turns-to-pragmatism-mostly ("[T]he United States sent its A team to the negotiations. . . . It is believed that President Obama remained engaged behind the scenes, calling world leaders when necessary.").

89. Art. 2 ¶ 1(a).

90. Maxine Burkett, *Small Island States and the Paris Agreement*, WILSON CENTER (Dec. 21, 2015) https://www.wilsoncenter.org/article/small-island-states-and-the-paris-agreement.

(c) Making finance flows consistent with a pathway towards low greenhouse gas emissions and climate-resilient development.

2. This Agreement will be implemented to reflect equity and the principle of common but differentiated responsibilities and respective capabilities, in the light of different national circumstances.

These goals are primarily implemented through

- concrete and transparent promises to reduce anthropogenic emissions and increase removals by sinks of greenhouse gasses;[91]
- concrete and transparent promises to increase funding to developing countries to mitigate and adapt;[92] and
- concrete and transparent reporting mechanisms on each country's performance of its promised biological and monetary contribution.[93]

In the following sections, we discuss the precise nature of the parties' commitments and how they contribute to the Agreement's broad acceptance.

2. *Voluntary Approach*

As one commentator observed, "First, and most important, participation [in the Agreement] is comprehensive."[94] But why, and especially in stark contrast to Kyoto, is this so? The answer, in part, is that the Agreement relies upon state-driven solutions to solving the collective action problem.[95] Consider, for example, the tenor of Articles 3 and 4, which outline some of the general goals of the Agreement:

Article 3

As nationally determined contributions to the global response to climate change, all Parties are to undertake and communicate ambitious efforts . . . with the view to achieving the purpose of this Agreement as set out in Article 2. The efforts of all Parties will represent a progression over time, while recognizing the need to support developing country Parties for the effective implementation of this Agreement.

Article 4

1. In order to achieve the long-term temperature goal set out in Article 2, Parties aim to reach global peaking of greenhouse gas emissions as soon as possible, recognizing that peaking will take longer for developing country Parties, and to undertake rapid reductions thereafter in accordance with best available

---

91. *See* Article 4, ¶ 2 ("Parties aim . . . to undertake rapid reductions thereafter in accordance with best available science, so as to achieve a balance between anthropogenic emissions by sources and removals by sinks of greenhouse gases . . . .").

92. *See* Article 9, ¶ 5 & discussion, *infra*.

93. *See id.*; Article 3 & discussion, *infra*.

94. Jeffrey Frankel, *A Fair, Efficient, and Feasible Climate Agreement*, Project Syndicate (Dec. 17, 2015) https://www.project-syndicate.org/commentary/paris-climate-agreement-four-strengths-by-jeffrey-frankel-2015-12.

95. *See id.*; Bell, *supra* note 88.

science, so as to achieve a balance between anthropogenic emissions by sources and removals by sinks of greenhouse gases in the second half of this century, on the basis of equity, and in the context of sustainable development and efforts to eradicate poverty.

2. Each Party shall prepare, communicate and maintain successive nationally determined contributions that it intends to achieve. Parties shall pursue domestic mitigation measures with the aim of achieving the objectives of such contributions. . . .

Many of the specific obligations and goals of the parties are also couched in state-centric terms. Paragraph 5 of Article 7, which deals with adaptation to the risks posed by climate change,[96] states:

> Parties acknowledge that adaptation action should follow a *country-driven*, gender-responsive, participatory and fully transparent approach, taking into consideration vulnerable groups, communities and ecosystems, and should be based on and guided by the best available science and, as appropriate, traditional knowledge, knowledge of indigenous peoples and local knowledge systems, with a view to integrating adaptation into relevant socioeconomic and environmental policies and actions . . . .[97]

Article 9, paragraph 4 provides that funding provided to developing countries to deal with adaptation and mitigation should "tak[e] into account country-driven strategies."

The goals of Article 2, discussed in the previous Section, are therefore made concrete by clear, quantified, and publicly-available commitments by party countries. For example, 186 of the 196 parties to the Agreement submitted "Intended Nationally Determined Contributions," which are published on the UN website and outline each country's particular commitments to reducing greenhouse gas emissions, prior to the end of the Paris talks.[98]

Financial support for developing countries' efforts must be similarly concrete and transparent, as Article 9 makes clear:

Article 9

1. Developed country Parties shall provide financial resources to assist developing country Parties with respect to both mitigation and adaptation in continuation of their existing obligations under the Convention.

2. Other Parties are encouraged to provide or continue to provide such support voluntarily.

---

96. Roger-Mark De Souza, *A New Era for Climate Diplomacy*, WILSON CENTER (Dec. 21, 2015), https://www.wilsoncenter.org/article/new-era-for-climate-diplomacy.

97. Emphasis added.

98. Robert Stavins, *Thanks to Paris, We Have a Foundation for Meaningful Climate Progress*, THE CONVERSATION: COP21 BLOG (Dec. 17, 2015, 10:38 AM), https://theconversation.com/thanks-to-paris-we-have-a-foundation-for-meaningful-climate-progress-52525; *see* Article 3, *supra*; Adoption of the Paris Agreement ¶¶ 12–22.

3. As part of a global effort, developed country Parties should continue to take the lead in mobilizing climate finance from a wide variety of sources, instruments and channels, noting the significant role of public funds, through a variety of actions, including supporting country-driven strategies, and taking into account the needs and priorities of developing country Parties. Such mobilization of climate finance should represent a progression beyond previous efforts.
4. The provision of scaled-up financial resources should aim to achieve a balance between adaptation and mitigation, taking into account country-driven strategies, and the priorities and needs of developing country Parties, especially those that are particularly vulnerable to the adverse effects of climate change and have significant capacity constraints, such as the least developed countries and small island developing States, considering the need for public and grant-based resources for adaptation.
5. Developed country Parties *shall biennially communicate indicative quantitative and qualitative information* related to paragraphs 1 and 3 of this Article, as applicable, including, as available, projected levels of public financial resources to be provided to developing country Parties.[99] Other Parties providing resources are encouraged to communicate biennially such information on a voluntary basis. . . .

In the supporting decision text, the parties agreed to "set a new collective quantified goal [of funds to aid developing countries] from a floor of USD 100 billion per year" prior to 2025.[100] But each country's commitments to greenhouse gas reductions and financial contributions are just that—they are commitments. The voluntarism written into the Accords made agreement possible for many countries, including the United States. The voluntary nature of the financial and policy commitments undoubtedly saved the Agreement, even as activists continue to push for more. As was widely reported in the press at the time, the proposed substitution of "shall" for "should" to describe detailed financial obligations in a part of the draft nearly upended the agreement, with Secretary Kerry warning, "We cannot do this."[101]

The opposition of the Republican majority in the U.S. Congress made the Accords' voluntarism politically expedient within the United States. Well aware of this reality, U.S. negotiators, including Secretary of State John Kerry, moved immediately to repair the text where "should" was over-written by a misplaced "shall" that crept into the text after all, as the final Accords were read at the end of the Conference:

> According to that "final" version, whereas "developing" country Parties "*should* continue enhancing their mitigation efforts, and are encouraged to move over time towards economy-wide emission reduction or limitation targets in the light of different national circumstances", the *developed* country

99. Emphasis added.
100. Adoption of the Paris Agreement, ¶ 54.
101. Burkett, *supra* note 90.

> Parties—including the United States—"***shall*** continue taking the lead by undertaking economy-wide absolute emission reduction targets."
>
> The word "shall" apparently had been added at the last minute—reportedly a mistake made by "fatigued" staffers. It was only a tiny, one-word change . . . yet it was a scrivener's error the United States could not live with.[102]

Without legally binding commitments to provide a certain amount of funds (for example), the United States may be able to navigate around the Article II requirement that treaties be ratified by a two-thirds majority of the Senate.[103]

3. *Enforcement*

The word "enforcement" does not appear in either the Agreement or Adoption. Instead, as alluded to in the previous section, the substantial reporting requirements provide a built-in enforcement mechanism: The "naming and shaming" of the parties who fail to comply, or who fail to put forth substantial efforts relative to other countries. To wit, all country commitments are published online. Financial commitments must be reassessed biennially.[104] Nationally determined contributions to greenhouse gas reductions are required to be reestablished every five years.[105]

Reports on national greenhouse gas emissions must use recognized methodology, as Article 4, paragraphs 13 and 14, and Article 15 make clear:

Article 4

13. Parties shall account for their nationally determined contributions. In accounting for anthropogenic emissions and removals corresponding to their nationally determined contributions, Parties shall promote environmental integrity, transparency, accuracy, completeness, comparability and consistency, and ensure the avoidance of double counting, in accordance with guidance adopted by the Conference of the Parties serving as the meeting of the Parties to the Paris Agreement.
14. In the context of their nationally determined contributions, when recognizing and implementing mitigation actions with respect to anthropogenic emissions and removals, Parties should take into account, as appropriate, existing methods and guidance under the Convention, in the light of the provisions of paragraph 13 of this Article.

Article 15

1. A mechanism to facilitate implementation of and promote compliance with the provisions of this Agreement is hereby established.

---

102. Marty Lederman, *The Constitutionally Critical, Last-Minute Correction to the Paris Climate Change Accord*, Balkinization (Dec. 13, 2015), http://balkin.blogspot.com/2015/12/the-last-minute-correction-to-paris.html.

103. U.S. Const., art. II, § 2, cl. 2.

104. Article 9, ¶ 5.

105. Article 4, ¶ 9.

2. The mechanism referred to in paragraph 1 of this Article shall consist of a committee that shall be expert-based and facilitative in nature and function in a manner that is transparent, non-adversarial and non-punitive. . . .

Furthermore, Article 14 provides for global accountability with the "global stocktake," a means and procedure to assess the success of the entire regime:

Article 14

1. The Conference of the Parties serving as the meeting of the Parties to the Paris Agreement shall periodically take stock of the implementation of this Agreement to assess the collective progress towards achieving the purpose of this Agreement and its long-term goals (referred to as the "global stocktake"). It shall do so in a comprehensive and facilitative manner, considering mitigation, adaptation and the means of implementation and support, and in the light of equity and the best available science.
2. The Conference of the Parties serving as the meeting of the Parties to the Paris Agreement shall undertake its first global stocktake in 2023 and every five years thereafter unless otherwise decided by the Conference of the Parties serving as the meeting of the Parties to the Paris Agreement.
3. The outcome of the global stocktake shall inform Parties in updating and enhancing, in a nationally determined manner, their actions and support in accordance with the relevant provisions of this Agreement, as well as in enhancing international cooperation for climate action.

4. Equity

Where, among all of the voluntary commitments of the developed nations, does equity come into play? After all, as we just explained, financial and mitigation commitments are not enforceable by any party. The small island developing states arrived at Paris with three principal demands:

> [F]irst, make the Warsaw International Mechanism (WIM) on Loss and Damage into a permanent mechanism (otherwise the WIM might have ended at COP22 in December 2016). Second, elevate the issue of displacement and migration to one of nine action areas under the agreed work program of the WIM. They called for it to be under a separate "facility" that recognizes the importance of needing to deal with displacement and migration due to climate change which, if not dealt with, could potentially exacerbate existing problems of displacement and migration. Third, recognize some form of finance for irrecoverable loss and damage, possibly through innovative financing channels.[106]

---

106. Saleemul Huq, *Not Fully Lost and Damaged: How Loss and Damage Fared in the Paris Agreement*, Wilson Center (Dec. 22, 2015), https://www.wilsoncenter.org/article/not-fully-lost-and-damaged-how-loss-and-damage-fared-the-paris-agreement.

While their demands were certainly not met in full, developing nations received several concessions, including an admission from the "rich countries" of "their moral responsibility to help small island states, for example, cope with 'loss and damages' from sea-level rise."[107] This is embodied in Article 8:

Article 8

1. Parties recognize the importance of averting, minimizing and addressing loss and damage associated with the adverse effects of climate change, including extreme weather events and slow onset events, and the role of sustainable development in reducing the risk of loss and damage.
2. The Warsaw International Mechanism for Loss and Damage associated with Climate Change Impacts shall be subject to the authority and guidance of the Conference of the Parties serving as the meeting of the Parties to the Paris Agreement and may be enhanced and strengthened, as determined by the Conference of the Parties serving as the meeting of the Parties to the Paris Agreement.
3. Parties should enhance understanding, action and support, including through the Warsaw International Mechanism, as appropriate, on a cooperative and facilitative basis with respect to loss and damage associated with the adverse effects of climate change.
4. Accordingly, areas of cooperation and facilitation to enhance understanding, action and support may include:
   (a) Early warning systems;
   (b) Emergency preparedness;
   (c) Slow onset events;
   (d) Events that may involve irreversible and permanent loss and damage;
   (e) Comprehensive risk assessment and management;
   (f) Risk insurance facilities, climate risk pooling and other insurance solutions;
   (g) Non-economic losses;
   (h) Resilience of communities, livelihoods and ecosystems.
5. The Warsaw International Mechanism shall collaborate with existing bodies and expert groups . . . .

The accompanying decision reaffirms that "Article 8 of the Agreement does not involve or provide a basis for any liability or compensation."[108] As Secretary of State John Kerry bluntly stated, "We're not against [loss and damage]. We're in favor of framing it in a way that doesn't create a legal remedy because Congress will never buy into an agreement that has something like that. . . . [T]he impact of it would be

107. Frankel, *supra* note 94.
108. Adoption of the Paris Agreement, ¶ 52.

to kill the deal."[109] Furthermore, developing countries failed to get a binding financial commitment into the Agreement, with an aspirational goal instead reflected in the nonbinding decision.

As Professor Jeffrey Frankel reflects,

> This was a reasonable outcome in a difficult situation. Rich countries can't deny that their past emissions have inflicted harm on the world. In a domestic legal system, an entity whose land was, say, flooded would have a claim to compensation from the entity that had caused the damage. But sovereign countries are not operating in such a system. The $100 billion in finance has always seemed problematic. The developing countries fear that the rich countries won't deliver the money, at least not cash; and they are right. The rich countries fear that such "reparations" would disappear into the pockets of local elites; and they, too, are right. So it is better not to make promises.[110]

Notes and Questions

1. How does this agreement compare to the Montreal Protocol in terms of regulatory rigor? In terms of equity? In terms of incentives for the development of new, green technologies?

2. Assuming this agreement is implemented only by executive agreement—that is, without congressional approval—is it likely to survive a court challenge?

3. Whether the Clean Air Act can authorize the president's actions in Paris has become substantially more uncertain recently with the Supreme Court's unprecedented stay of the EPA's Carbon Pollution Emission Guidelines for Existing Stationary Sources: Electric Utility Generating Units[111] pending review in the D.C. Circuit.[112] Part of President Obama's highly-touted "Clean Power Plan," the EPA's final rule established carbon dioxide emission guidelines for "electric generating units"—fossil-fueled power plants. Somewhat analogous to the Paris Accords' state-focused approach, the stayed EPA rule requires states to submit compliance plans to reach the EPA's carbon emissions goals. To do so, the states are encouraged, for example, to implement and expand cap-and-trade measures, develop interstate approaches, and develop their own "emissions reduction trajectories" to meet the rule's interim targets. Ultimately, the rule requires (or at least required prior to the Supreme Court action) states to submit compliance plans by September 2016, with a two-year extension available. Interim reduction deadlines begin in 2022 with full compliance with the reduction standards required in 2030.

---

109. Huq, *supra* note 105.

110. Frankel, *supra* note 94. For a brief note on the political and economic challenges Korea might face in complying with the Paris agreement, see, for example Byung-Woon Lyou, *The 2015 Paris Climate Agreement*, 9 NE. ASIAN L. REV. 249 (2015).

111. 40 C.F.R. Pt. 60, 80 Fed. Reg. 64,662 (October 23, 2015).

112. *E.g.* Chamber of Comm. v. EPA, No. 15A787, 2016 WL 502658 (Feb. 9, 2016) (mem.) (5–4 decision) (one of five identical orders granting stay).

A stay requires that the applicant demonstrate "(1) a reasonable probability that four Justices would vote to grant certiorari; (2) a significant possibility that the Court would reverse the judgment below; and (3) a likelihood of irreparable harm, assuming the correctness of the applicant's position, if the judgment is not stayed."[113] The 29 states challenging the EPA rule argued that they were already expending resources to comply with the rule's obligations, even though they were not compulsory until 2022. Utilities groups argued that coal companies were facing financial hardship and bankruptcy. The eighteen states and environmental groups opposing the stay emphasized the irreversible impact of climate change and increasing incidence of extreme weather events. The coal industry's challenges, they argued, were the result of increased market competition from renewable sources and natural gas, not the impending regulations.[114]

By a five-to-four split, the Supreme Court determined without opinion that the challengers to the EPA rule met their burden. In doing so, the Court, for the very first time, stayed a regulation prior to review by a federal appeals court.[115] While the case awaits expedited review in the D.C. Circuit, the stay may delay the implementation of the rule until after the conclusion of Obama administration, if it is upheld. Given the executive's likely reliance upon the Clean Air Act to regulate and reduce greenhouse gas emissions, the ultimate result could have enormous implications for the success of the Paris Accords.

For a detailed analysis of precisely how the Clean Air Act might operate to reduce greenhouse gas emissions, see the recent report released by Michael Burger et al., *Legal Pathways to Reducing Greenhouse Gas Emissions Under Section 115 of the Clean Air Act* (2016).[116]

4. Hannah Chang suggests that other statutes, too, may already provide legal grounds for the types of "measurement, reporting, and verification" obligations raised by the Paris Accords. Chang cites a variety of statutes, including the Foreign Relations Authorization Act of 1979, which directs the president to "assess and initiate appropriate international scientific and technological activities which are based upon domestic scientific and technological activities of the United States Government";[117] the International Development and Food Assistance Act of 1977, which provides that "the President is authorized to furnish assistance . . . for developing and strengthening the capacity of developing countries to protect and manage their environment and natural resources";[118] and the Endangered Species Act, which instructs the

113. Packwood v. Sen. Select Comm. on Ethics, 510 U.S. 1319 (1994) (citations omitted).

114. Adam Liptak & Coral Davenport, *Justices Deal Blow to Obama Effort on Emissions*, N.Y. Times (Feb. 10, 2016) at A1, http://www.nytimes.com/2016/02/10/us/politics/supreme-court-blocks-obama-epa-coal-emissions-regulations.html.

115. *Id.*

116. Available at https://web.law.columbia.edu/sites/default/files/microsites/climate-change/legal_pathways_to_reducing_ghg_emissions_under_section_115_of_the_caa.pdf.

117. 22 U.S.C. § 2656c(a)(b).

118. 22 U.S.C. § 2151p(b).

Secretary of State to "encourage foreign countries to provide for the conservation of fish or wildlife and plants" and "the entering into of bilateral or multilateral agreements with foreign countries to provide for such conservation,"[119] among others.[120]

5. Justice Jackson's famous concurrence in *Youngstown Sheet & Tube Co. v. Sawyer* set out a framework, widely embraced to this day by academics and courts, for assessing the independent power of the executive.

> 1. When the President acts pursuant to an express or implied authorization of Congress, his authority is at its maximum, for it includes all that he possesses in his own right plus all that Congress can delegate. In these circumstances, and in these only, may he be said (for what it may be worth), to personify the federal sovereignty. If his act is held unconstitutional under these circumstances, it usually means that the Federal Government as an undivided whole lacks power. A seizure executed by the President pursuant to an Act of Congress would be supported by the strongest of presumptions and the widest latitude of judicial interpretation, and the burden of persuasion would rest heavily upon any who might attack it.
>
> 2. When the President acts in absence of either a congressional grant or denial of authority, he can only rely upon his own independent powers, but there is a zone of twilight in which he and Congress may have concurrent authority, or in which its distribution is uncertain. Therefore, congressional inertia, indifference or quiescence may sometimes, at least as a practical matter, enable, if not invite, measures on independent presidential responsibility. In this area, any actual test of power is likely to depend on the imperatives of events and contemporary imponderables rather than on abstract theories of law.
>
> 3. When the President takes measures incompatible with the expressed or implied will of Congress, his power is at its lowest ebb, for then he can rely only upon his own constitutional powers minus any constitutional powers of Congress over the matter. Courts can sustain exclusive Presidential control in such a case only be disabling the Congress from acting upon the subject. Presidential claim to a power at once so conclusive and preclusive must be scrutinized with caution, for what is at stake is the equilibrium established by our constitutional system.[121]

Given the potential bases for the president's authority under extant law, into which *Youngstown* category do the obligations imposed by the Paris Accords fall? Does it depend upon the level of generality with which we define these obligations? Chang provided many citations to statutes that allow for the president to engage in activities

---

119. 16 U.S.C. § 1537(b)(1)-(2).

120. Chang, *supra* note 22, at 365–70.

121. Youngstown Sheet & Tube Co. v. Sawyer, 343 U.S. 579, 635–38 (1952) (Jackson, J., concurring).

to promote international cooperation to address environmental concerns, and the president has constitutional authority to act as the sole voice for the United States. Does it matter that no statute speaks specifically to the precise reporting under the Accords if the Accords impose no further binding substantive obligations? Should it matter?

6. In the face of broad and indeterminate congressional grants of authority to the president, Oona Hathaway proposes an "Administrative Procedure Act for international law." Such a system would further several ends:

> Bringing agreements that are regulatory in nature into this new administrative system would serve to make them both more effective and more legitimate—for example, by making them available to Congress and the public before, rather than after, they become law. The process would offer greater openness, more public participation, and better transparency. Agreements would be eligible for this administrative track if they were authorized under an express delegation of authority to the President by Congress in prior legislation, or if they fall within the President's own constitutional powers.
>
> All other agreements would be subject to a heightened legislative approval process. . . . In addition, I propose an expanded "fast track" process that would permit streamlined congressional approval of agreements. By making the process of obtaining congressional approval less cumbersome, the expansion of existing fast track procedures would make it more attractive for the President to submit international agreements for the approval of both houses of Congress.[122]

The "fast track" process would simply require a change of congressional rules to require prompt debate of any international agreement submitted to Congress and circumvent the often-politicized committee procedures. Such a process would provide incentives for the president to actually seek congressional approval (because the president would know that it would be given immediate consideration) while also encourage the president to be thoughtful about invoking the procedure (because it could be amended by legislative rule).[123]

What do you think of Hathaway's proposals? Do they strike an appropriate balance? Might they appease the worries of some who believe that the president is unduly constrained by congressional politicking and the worries of others who believe that the president possesses excessive unilateral authority?

7. Does the essentially voluntary approach set forth in the Accords foster local legislation and the kinds of initiatives discussed by Ostrom above?

8. One obstacle to law reform is preemption doctrine, an area of law that was "[o]nce an arcane backwater of constitutional jurisprudence loved almost

---

122. Oona A. Hathaway, *Presidential Power Over International Law: Restoring the Balance*, 119 YALE L.J. 140, 148 (2009).

123. *Id.* at 263–66.

exclusively by law professors."[124] It "has become the focus of the country's most contentious political issues."[125] Underlying preemption doctrine is the straightforward proposition that states may not undermine the authority of Congress, in areas of the law where Congress is permitted to legislate. While the principle is well established, its application to specific circumstances often leads to intense debate over the gray zones where Congress has not been explicit as to its intent.[126]

Is it necessary to modify fundamental legal doctrines governing preemption, for example, if we are to ensure our domestic legal system has the flexibility necessary for experimentation?

III. Local approaches to global problems

Paris represents a great breakthrough after decades of struggle by state leaders to address global warming. Transnational horizontal networks of cities, nongovernmental organizations, scientists, and activists have long endeavored to contribute to the effort, and will likely continue to do so under the Paris framework. For example, in 2005 the mayor of London organized a group of 18 "megacities," now known as C40, to confront the challenges posed by climate change. Since 2005, the group has exploded to include 83 affiliated large cities, making up 25 percent of the global GDP and representing one-twelfth of the world's population.[127] Other international city networks open to smaller cities have diverse origins, including the Cities for Climate Protection, another global city network; the Climate Alliance, a bottom-up network of European cities; and Energie-Cités, stemming from an EU-funded project.[128]

Over 950 NGOs across 110 countries have banded together to form the Climate Action Network.[129] In 1950, scholars and scientists formed the World Meteorological Organization, which became a U.N. special agency after formation. The Future Earth project links the social and natural sciences by networking organizations such as the International Social Science Council, the International Council for Science, and UNESCO, to name just a few.[130] The group "350" takes full advantage of the modern internet to connect over 200 local, grassroots groups of activists to resources,

---

124. Jamelle C. Sharpe, *Legislating Preemption*, 53 Wm. & Mary L. Rev. 163, 166 (2011).

125. *Id.*

126. Jamelle C. Sharpe, *Toward (a) Faithful Agency in the Supreme Court's Preemption Jurisprudence*, 18 Geo. Mason L. Rev. 367, 380 (2011). *See also* Mary J. Davis, *Unmasking the Presumption in Favor of Preemption*, 53 S.C. L. Rev. 967 (2002) (suggesting that the Court is favorable to preemption).

127. *C40 Cities*, http://www.c40.org/cities.

128. Kristine Kern & Gotelind Alber, *Governing Climate Change in Cities: Modes of Urban Climate Governance in Multi-level Systems*, *in* Competitive Cities and Climate Change 171, 184 (2008), http://www1.oecd.org/gov/regional-policy/50594939.pdf.

129. *About CAN*, Climate Action Network International, http://www.climatenetwork.org/about/about-can.

130. *Who We Are*, http://www.futureearth.org/who-we-are.

information, and each other.[131] 350 receives support from numerous NGOs and conservationist groups.

While lacking the global reach of a top-down approach or the ability to impose regulations as such, these networks have unique benefits of their own. Devani Adams identifies five such benefits: First, and particularly for networks of city leaders, "transnational networks provide an alternative forum for policymakers to discuss issues of concern without the pressures or rigidity of traditional lawmaking."[132] Second, horizontal networks provide a direct channel for policymakers, NGOs, and social and climate scientists to exchange information. They "eliminate the traditional filter that applies to the top-down approach and they equalize information-sharing between entities not traditionally thought of as equals."[133] Third, horizontal networks simply help to create more institutions to fight climate change by, for example, providing resources and expertise. Fourth, transnational networks "educate individuals, communities, and nations" and provide forums for productive deliberations.[134] Finally, fifth, transnational networks can act immediately, without waiting for the often glacial pace of formal activity.

Kern and Alber agree that horizontal networks have a critical role to play in addressing climate change and highlight several further strengths:

> [Horizontal networks] can provide [policy] guidelines, like the U.S. Mayors Climate Protection Agreement, particularly if the federal government does not provide such documents. Furthermore, national and transnational city networks can commit their members to GHG emission goals, stimulate actions to reach these goals and monitor progress; they can even set up benchmarking systems to assess their progress.[135]

Kern and Alber observe that "national and transnational city networks consist mainly of pioneering cities."[136] They suggest that

> city networks can try to counterbalance the gap between pioneers and laggards by setting tiered standards that attract members with varying levels of performance and ambition. The role of city networks, in particular their function in motivating cities and supporting capacity-building in the area of climate change policy, is crucial and should be rewarded by recognition and reliable funding from national governments or international agencies."[137]

131. *See How We Work*, 350, http://350.org/how/.

132. Devani G. Adams, *Why We Cannot Wait: Transnational Networks as a Viable Solution to Climate Change Policy*, 13 Santa Clara J. Int'l L. 307, 329 (2015).

133. *Id.* at 330.

134. *Id.*

135. Kern & Alber, *supra* note 128, at 189.

136. *Id.*

137. *Id.* at 190.

The following case highlights one city's efforts to contribute positively to the mitigation of climate change.

Metropolitan Taxicab Board of Trade v. City of New York

633 F. Supp. 2d 83 (S.D.N.Y. 2009)

Paul A. Crotty, District Judge:

This case involves a dispute between New York City taxicab fleet owners and the City's Taxicab & Limousine Commission ("TLC"), relating to new TLC regulations that promote the purchase of hybrid taxicabs by reducing the rates at which taxicab owners may lease their vehicles to taxi drivers—thus reducing the owners' overall profit—if the vehicle does not have a hybrid or clean-diesel engine. The questions in this case are whether the TLC's new rules are a mandate to taxicab owners to purchase only hybrid or clean-diesel vehicles, and whether such a mandate is preempted by federal law.

The history of this case is relevant: on October 31, 2008, the Court preliminarily enjoined New York City's requirement that all new taxicabs meet a specific miles-per-gallon ("mpg") rating. The mpg regulation required taxicab owners in New York City to purchase vehicles with hybrid or clean-diesel engines, or wheelchair-accessible vehicles. The Court found that the federal Energy Policy and Conservation Act ("EPCA") preempted the local imposition of mpg standards. The City immediately announced it would pursue an alternative strategy. Mayor Bloomberg stated that, "The courts are not the only way we can reach our goal of a cleaner fleet of taxi cabs. Greening the taxi fleet is a major priority, and we are going to use every mechanism at our disposal to make New York a cleaner, healthier city."

The City pursued a regulatory framework that would encourage taxicab fleet owners to buy hybrid taxicabs in increasing numbers and discourage them from purchasing long bodied, conventionally powered taxicabs, which the City had approved for use in 2001. Under the City's new rules, if an owner purchases a taxicab with a hybrid or clean-diesel engine (hereinafter, "hybrid"), the rate at which the vehicle can be leased to a driver for a 12-hour shift is increased by $3. By contrast, if an owner leases out a non-hybrid, nonwheelchair accessible vehicle (i.e. a Crown Victoria), the maximum lease rate an owner may charge a driver is reduced by $4 immediately, $8 in May 2010, and $12 in May 2011. The new rules substantially reduce profits for the owner who continues to choose non-hybrid taxicabs, and Plaintiffs challenge the disincentive aspect of the new regulations.

DISCUSSION

I. Preliminary Injunction Standard

a. Are the Lease Cap Rules a Mandate?

i. Legal Precedent

There are no controlling cases that deal with whether the Lease Cap Rules are a mandate, and, if so, whether the Rules are preempted. Both parties cite to cases involving the Employee Retirement Income Security Act of 1974 ("ERISA"), in which the Supreme Court and lower courts have addressed the issue of preemption where a state law, while seemingly presenting choices, essentially mandates an outcome that is preempted by federal law.

ii. Application to the Facts

The Lease Cap Rules at issue control the maximum lease rates which taxicab owners may charge. They allow a higher rate for hybrids and much lower rates for Crown Victorias. While silent on mileage and emission standards, the Rules were expressly adopted to encourage the purchase of hybrid vehicles which meet the City's mileage goals and desired emission standards.

The Court must look to the effect of the Lease Cap Rules on Fleet Owners to determine if they are a de facto mandate to purchase hybrid vehicles. Plaintiffs bear the burden to persuade the Court that the Rules constitute a mandate "by a clear showing." *Mazurek v. Armstrong*, 520 U.S. 968, 972 (1997) (citation omitted). While *Travelers Insurance*, *Dillingham Construction*, *Fielder*, and *Suffolk County* describe how a court should analyze the interplay between an effective mandate and preemption, they provide little guidance on how a court should determine whether specified economic incentives actually create a mandate. For this reason the Court asked the parties to present expert evidence on the effect of the Lease Cap Rules.

In his written declaration of May 18, 2009, and at the May 20, 2009 evidentiary hearing, Plaintiffs' expert economist, Dr. Levinsohn, estimated the expected impact of the Lease Cap Rules on Fleet Owners by using financial data supplied by the Plaintiffs.

If the lease cap rates had remained unchanged, Dr. Levinsohn estimated that Fleet Owners using Crown Victorias made approximately $8,500 per year in profits, while those using hybrids earned only $5,100 in profits, meaning that hybrid profit was $3,400 less per vehicle per year.

The City states that DOVs [individuals who own vehicles but lease medallions] account for approximately 7,000 taxicabs, more than 50% of all cabs. Non-affiliation owners account for 3,000 taxicabs. In the 16-month period from January 2008 to April 2009, vehicles purchased by DOVs were split 55% Crown Victoria and 40% hybrid or clean diesel. Vehicles purchased by non-affiliation owners during that time were 47% Crown Victoria and 47% hybrid or clean diesel. Fleet Owners purchased 70% Crown Victorias and 28% hybrid or clean diesel.

The City argues that since DOVs and non-affiliation owners—the parties with a greater economic incentive to purchase hybrids due to high gas prices—continued to purchase Crown Victorias even after the economic incentive to purchase hybrids existed, it proves that taxi owners will still choose to buy Crown Victorias even when confronted by a substantial economic incentive not to do so. This argument is a surmise because the existing buying pattern does not reflect the $12 per-shift disincentive the City adopted for the express policy purpose of putting more hybrid taxicabs on the street.

Based on the foregoing evidence from the testimony at the hearing and the written declarations of the parties, there is one clear conclusion to be drawn from the Lease Cap Rules, the manner in which they were adopted, and the methodology of the new regulatory architecture. The Lease Cap Rules' purpose is to incentivize the purchase of hybrids, while at the same time provide a very meaningful disincentive to the continuing use of conventionally powered vehicles. The combined effect of the lease cap changes, and even the disincentive alone, constitutes an offer which cannot, in practical effect, be refused.

Looking at all the evidence, it is clear to the Court that the Lease Cap Rules do not present viable options for Fleet Owners and instead operate as an effective mandate to switch to hybrid vehicles. Having decided that the Lease Cap Rules constitute a mandate, the Court turns to the issue of preemption.

b. Preemption Under the EPCA

Preemption claims turn on Congress' intent, so the Court must review Congress' goals in enacting the EPCA and the relevant text of the provision in question....

Congress enacted the EPCA to address the energy crisis resulting from the 1973 Mideast oil embargo.

The EPCA contains an express preemption clause:

> When an average fuel economy standard prescribed under this chapter ... is in effect, a State or political subdivision of a State *may not adopt or enforce a law or regulation related to fuel economy standards or average fuel economy standards* for automobiles covered by an average fuel economy standard under this chapter.

49 U.S.C. § 32919(a) (emphasis added). This language is quite clear: "Congress's undoubted intent was to make the setting of fuel economy standards exclusively a federal concern." *Green Mountain* [*Chrysler Plymouth Dodge Jeep v. Crombie*], 508 F.Supp.2d at 354.

The City acknowledges that the prior 25/30 Rules are preempted under the EPCA because they "related to fuel economy standards." Defendants now argue that the Lease Cap Rules, even if they are a mandate, are not preempted under the EPCA because they simply designate hybrid vehicles as required taxicabs and do not require vehicles with a certain mpg rating. The City argues that the term "related to" should be construed narrowly, so that a de facto requirement to purchase hybrid taxicabs does not "relate to" fuel economy standards under 49 U.S.C. § 32919(a).

A constricted interpretation of the term "related to" is not appropriate. The Supreme Court just recently referred to that term as "expansive." In *Travelers Indemnity Co. v. Bailey*,—U.S.—, 129 S.Ct. 2195 (2009), a case dealing with the enforceability of a Bankruptcy Court order enjoining related state court lawsuits, the Supreme Court stated unequivocally that "[i]n a statute, '[t]he phrase "in relation to" is expansive.'" 508 U.S. 223, 237. Although the Court noted that at some point the term "relate to" loses any meaning because " 'everything is related to everything else,' " *id.* (quoting [*California Division of Labor Standards Enforcement v.*] *Dillingham Construction*, 519 U.S. at 335), the Court found that the state claims at issue "clearly" related to the Bankruptcy Court's injunction and so there was no need to "stake out the ultimate bounds" of the connection. *Id.*

In this case, while it is true that the Lease Cap Rules do not require a specific mpg rating, the effect of the rules is to force taxicab owners to meet an mpg threshold determined by the mileage rating of the TLC's approved hybrid or clean diesel vehicles. All of the TLC-approved hybrids or clean diesel vehicles are rated 25 mpg or higher. These are the same vehicles that the TLC approved under the preempted 25/30 Rules.

The City's purpose in enacting the Lease Cap Rules also sheds light on the issue of preemption. While consideration of the purpose of the local regulation is not the end-all to the Court's preemption review, that does not mean it should be ignored. It is fair to consider purpose in conjunction with the law's effects. Here, one of the City's stated purposes in enacting the Lease Cap Rules was to allow taxi owners who choose "a fuel efficient" vehicle to realize a greater lease income than owners who choose "a less efficient vehicle." The City's discussion of "efficient" vehicles relates to how many miles per gallon a vehicle travels. Indeed, the exact amount of the disincentive is based on a calculation of miles per gallon. . . . Focusing on the effect and purpose of the Lease Cap Rules, it is clear that the rules "relate to" fuel economy standards, as contemplated in 49 U.S.C. § 32919(a), the EPCA preemption clause. The 25/30 Rules specifically referred to mpg standards, but creative drafting and the absence of specific reference to mileage do not make the effect—or the purpose—of the Lease Cap Rules any different than the prior preempted regulations. The Lease Cap Rules effectively mandate the use of taxicabs with a certain mpg rating. The express language of the EPCA preemption clause and the clear message from the White House that the federal government is active within the preempted field of fuel economy standards lead to one conclusion: fuel economy standards are a federal matter and the EPCA preempts local laws, such as the Lease Cap Rules, that infringe upon the federal prerogative.

Further, the City cannot argue that the Lease Cap Rules do not "relate to" fuel economy standards because the rules burden only a small percentage of taxicab owners and only insignificantly affect the EPCA's objectives. As discussed in the previous litigation in this case, the Supreme Court foreclosed such an argument in Engine Manufacturers. The Court found that the aggregate effect of allowing every state or political subdivision to enact seemingly harmless rules would create an "end result [that] would undo Congress's carefully calibrated regulatory scheme." *Engine Manufacturers* [*Association v. South Coast Air Quality*], 541 U.S. at 255.

The purpose and effect of the Lease Cap Rules is to force Fleet Owners to purchase taxicabs with a certain mpg rating. Reading the language of the EPCA preemption statute, 49 U.S.C. § 32919(a), it is clear that the Plaintiffs are likely to succeed in showing that the Lease Cap Rules are "related to" fuel economy standards and are preempted under the Supremacy Clause.

c. Preemption Under the CAA

The Clean Air Act empowers the Environmental Protection Agency ("EPA") to promulgate regulations necessary to prevent deterioration of air quality. 42 U.S.C. § 7601(a); *Central Valley* [*Chrysler-Jeep, Inc. v. Goldstene*], 529 F.Supp.2d at 1156. Part of the EPA's mandate under the CAA is to set standards relating to emissions from new vehicles. 42 U.S.C. § 7521(a)(1); *Motor & Equip. Mfrs. Ass'n v. Nichols*, 142 F.3d 449, 452 (D.C.Cir.1998) ("Subchapter II of the [CAA] vests in the federal government the almost exclusive responsibility for establishing automobile emission standards for new cars."). The CAA contains a preemption provision at § 209(a):

> No State or any political subdivision thereof shall adopt or attempt to enforce *any standard relating to the control of emissions from new motor vehicles or new motor vehicle engines* . . . No State shall require certification, inspection, or any other approval relating to the control of emissions from any new motor vehicle or new motor vehicle engine as condition precedent to the initial retail sale, titling . . . or registration of such motor vehicle, motor vehicle engine, or equipment.

42 U.S.C. § 7543(a) (emphasis added).

Congress preempted states—and their political subdivisions—from creating their own emissions standards for new vehicles because Congress was concerned about the possibility of 50 different standards applying to one vehicle that so easily moves across state lines.

The question for the Court is whether the Lease Cap Rules, which effectively mandate the purchase of hybrid taxicabs, relate to the control of emissions. In the prior litigation the Court found that the 25/30 Rules did not relate to emissions standards because those rules specifically targeted fuel economy but were silent as to emissions. This case is different. One of the stated purposes of the Lease Cap Rules is to "create incentives for taxicab owners to buy cleaner vehicles." Additionally, the rules reduce the maximum lease cap for "owners of less clean taxicabs." While the enjoined 25/30 Rules specifically did not target emissions, it is clear that one purpose of the Lease Cap Rules is to affect taxicab emissions by mandating the purchase of "cleaner vehicles."

In *American Automobile Manufacturers Association v. Cahill*, the Second Circuit discussed a New York law requiring that a percentage of cars sold be "zero emission vehicles," or "ZEVs." 152 F.3d at 197. The court looked at the regulation's purpose and effect, and found that even though the ZEV requirement did not impose a precise limit on emissions levels, the sales regulation was preempted because it had the purpose of "effect[ing] a general reduction in emissions" and was "in the nature of a command having a direct effect on the level of emissions." *Id.* at 200.

The case here is not unlike *American Automobile Manufacturers Association*. The Lease Cap Rules have a purpose of reducing emissions from taxicabs. The Court has already found that the rules are effectively a mandate requiring the purchase of hybrid taxicabs. Similar to what the Second Circuit reasoned when looking at the ZEV sales requirement, a requirement to purchase hybrid taxicabs is also a command that would directly affect the level of emissions. This is certainly the City's goal in enacting the Lease Cap Rules, and reducing emissions would be its result. Section 209(a), the CAA preemption provision, specifically reserves emissions regulation for new vehicles to the federal government. As discussed earlier, even though the effect of the Lease Cap Rules on nationwide regulation and vehicle production will be minor, the aggregate effect of permitting such local regulation would create an "end result [that] would undo Congress's carefully calibrated regulatory scheme." *Engine Mfrs.*, 541 U.S. at 255, 124 S.Ct. 1756.

Engine Manufacturers is instructive in another aspect. The Court there held that the CAA preempted local rules requiring fleet operators to use "alternative-fuel vehicles" or vehicles that met certain emission specifications. *Id.* at 259, 124 S.Ct. 1756. With almost no discussion, the Court assumed that regulations requiring "alternative-fuel vehicles" related to the control of emissions under the CAA's preemption statute. *Id.* at 249–52, 124 S.Ct. 1756. The Supreme Court in *Engine Manufacturers* did not need testimony from scientific experts to explain the connection between "alternative-fuel vehicles" and emissions regulation. Neither does his Court need further testimony to understand the close relation between hybrid vehicles and emissions.

The Lease Cap Rules effectively force Fleet Owners to purchase hybrid taxicabs, and the purpose and effect of the rules is to reduce emissions.13 CAA § 209(a) preempts New York City from enacting regulations related to emissions control, and the Plaintiffs have demonstrated a likelihood of success in proving such preemption.

CONCLUSION

For the reasons previously stated, the Court finds that the Lease Cap Rules area de facto mandate upon the Plaintiffs to purchase hybrid vehicles. The Court further finds that the Plaintiffs have demonstrated irreparable harm and a likelihood of success in showing that such a mandate is preempted by the EPCA and the CAA. The Lease Cap Rules relate to fuel economy and emissions regulation, which are substantially federal concerns. Accordingly, the Plaintiffs' motion for a preliminary injunction is GRANTED.

SO ORDERED.

Notes and Questions

1. Compare the above case to California's attempts to decrease its transportation emissions. Also consider why California and the intervening states would want to be able to develop their own more stringent emissions standards.

> The road to California's dispute with the EPA began in July 2002, with the passage of AB 1493, which requires the California Air Resources Board (CARB) to promulgate vehicle emissions regulations that maximize greenhouse gas emissions reductions. 142 CARB created such regulations in 2004, and pursuant to Section 209(b) of the Clean Air Act, petitioned the EPA in 2005 for a waiver of preemption for these standards. Although all of California's previous waiver requests had been granted at least in part through a deferential review process, EPA Administrator Stephen Johnson denied California's waiver request in December 2007, with a formal denial following in March 2008.
>
> In January 2008, California—with eighteen other states ultimately moving to intervene in support—petitioned the Court of Appeals for the Ninth Circuit to overturn the waiver denial. California also petitioned the District Court for the Northern District of California to obtain records regarding the denial decision. Simultaneously, on the congressional front, seventeen senators—including then-Senator Obama—cosponsored a bill introduced by California Senator Barbara Boxer to overturn the decision, with similar legislation soon following in the House of Representatives.
>
> The federal government has yet to promulgate motor vehicle GHG emissions regulations that go as far as those of California. As a result, emissions are higher than they would have been if California and the other states had been allowed to go forward. Even if the waiver ultimately is granted in some form or the federal government passes more stringent regulations, each of which appears likely to occur under the Obama administration, the period from the 2005 waiver request until that point will be one of greater emissions than it could have been.[138]

2. Now compare these stories with the case of San Bernardino County, discussed here:

> On March 13, 2007, San Bernardino's Board of Supervisors approved an update of its General Plan and certified its accompanying Final Environmental Impact Report (FEIR). The updated General Plan—which adopts goals and policies that will underlie future land use, growth, and transportation—projects a sixty-four percent increase in population from 2000 to 2020. It notes in conjunction with the projection that "[c]onstant, and relatively high increases in population growth in the past, have resulted in urban development and increased demand for available land."
>
> The General Plan does not include the phrases "climate change," "global warming," or "greenhouse gas emissions." The accompanying FEIR does address climate change, however, but uses scientific uncertainty together

138. Hari M. Osofsky, *Is Climate Change "International"? Litigation's Diagonal Regulatory Role*, 49 Va. J. Int'l L. 585 (2009) (footnotes omitted).

with oblique scalar arguments to explain its lack of plans for specific steps on climate change emissions or impacts. For example, it acknowledges the California Global Warming Solutions Act of 2006 as creating a statewide regulatory program, but explains that "[i]t is not yet clear how, or if, these future regulations would affect local governments or how they might influence local land use planning decisions." Similarly, after noting comments indicating that the Environmental Impact Assessment must include "quantified analysis of greenhouse gas emissions" and "specify mitigation measures," it declines to provide these specifics on the ground that the California Air Resources Board has not yet given the County enough guidance. Although these arguments take the form of standard objections to action without regulatory guidance, they are being used to avoid any specific steps on emissions reduction.

The Center for Biological Diversity, Sierra Club, and San Bernardino Valley Audubon Society—NGOs that interact with a range of local, state, national, and international actors—filed a Petition for Writ of Mandate under the CEQA on April 11, 2007, which asked the superior court to provide a range of injunctive relief. The petition claims that the County of San Bernardino failed to disclose and analyze adequately the project's impacts, to analyze adequately mitigation measures and alternatives, to support its Statement of Overriding Considerations with substantial evidence, to recirculate the Environmental Impact Report (EIR), to respond adequately to comments, and to provide an adequate description of the existing environment. Two days later, the Attorney General of California filed a CEQA suit requesting similar relief, with a single cause of action: failure to comply with the CEQA and prejudicial abuse of discretion.

On August 21, 2007, the State and County entered into a settlement agreement that represents a significant compromise. The County agreed to amend its General Plan to add a policy of emissions reduction and a call for the adoption of a Greenhouse Gas Emissions Reduction Plan. That plan will include an extensive inventory of sources and emissions and also reduction targets. In addition, the County agreed to conduct an environmental review of both the amendments and the reduction plan. The agreement includes a timeline, however, that allows the County to keep its current plan in place as it prepares these replacement plans and inventories. The Attorney General also agreed to assist the County to obtain funding for its emissions reduction efforts.

Since then, the County has been taking steps to implement the settlement agreement, including hiring a consultant to develop its emissions reduction plan. The plan includes bringing emissions down to 1990 levels and adopting mitigation measures to achieve that target. Moreover, after the County agreed to some additional environmental protection measures, the non-governmental petitioners agreed to drop their CEQA action.[139]

3. The article continues with reflections on the relevance of adjudication to issues of scale and horizontality/verticality:

> As . . . scalar contests play out in the judicial branch, the vertical, horizontal, and diagonal pressure they create may impact policy dialogues at international and local levels—as well as those at every level in between—and encourage greater diagonal integration. For example, as noted previously, San Bernardino County likely would not have agreed to these steps without these petitions, and California continues to push all of its counties aggressively to regulate their greenhouse gas emissions.
>
> However, litigation is not the only type of diagonal mechanism available. Regulatory arrangements—whether cooperative or conflictual—can have simultaneous horizontal and vertical elements without the involvement of courts. But comparatively few of the current U.S. regulatory approaches formally have this diagonal quality. Many instances exist of horizontal cooperation in which states or cities, sometimes even across international borders, form a coalition. Some of these initiatives have a vertical dimension in the sense that they create a larger-scale entity; for example, California is collaborating with six other U.S. states and three Canadian provinces on a Western Climate Initiative. Even with this somewhat diagonal quality, though, their primary character is horizontal because the main dynamics are among entities at the same regulatory level.
>
> Similarly, a wide array of predominantly vertical efforts exist, some of which take the form of traditional top-down efforts to foster smaller scale activity. For example, towards the end of President Bill Clinton's administration, the EPA offered states funding to develop climate regulation plans. This instance has horizontal dimensions, in that the EPA made the offer to multiple states, but it is predominantly vertical. Here, the states are not behaving as a coalition, but rather are being individually incentivized by the EPA; the top-down quality of the action reduces the horizontal dimension.
>
> Vertical efforts can also be bottom-up, such as when a state requests federal action or a city requests state action. The California waiver case, if it did not have the horizontal elements of multiple states and branches, exemplifies this variation. The key question regarding whether an effort is vertical is not the direction of vertical movement, then, but its dominance. As with the primarily horizontal efforts, vertical ones show little simultaneous activity across the other axis. The efforts are multiscalar but without strong activity across individual levels.

139. Hari M. Osofsky, *Is Climate Change "International"? Litigation's Diagonal Regulatory Role*, 49 Va. J. Int'l L. 585 (2009) (footnotes omitted).

> The transnational legal process and geographic network theory approaches, from which the Article's diagonal model draws, both suggest that informal diagonals likely arise regardless of whether or not they are formally structured. As a range of actors interact with and restructure sociolegal spaces across scales, this process moves across horizontals and verticals in multiple directions. Because many entities that are not formally part of structured initiatives interact with these actors, even efforts that are neither horizontal nor vertical in their formal conception often interact across both axes.... A snapshot of current efforts, even with their limited formal diagonal quality, thus would show an ever-evolving array of vertical, horizontal, and diagonal interactions."

Hari M. Osofsky, *Is Climate Change "International"? Litigation's Diagonal Regulatory Role*, 49 VA. J. INT'L L. 585 (2009).

4. *American Trucking Associations, Inc. v. City of Los Angeles.* The "epic" fight between labor and environmentalists on one side and industry on the other over Los Angeles's "Clean Trucks Program" required no fewer than three separate trips to the Ninth Circuit, capped off by a unanimous Supreme Court opinion in 2013.[140]

As Professor Scott L. Cummings describes in rich detail in his article *Preemptive Strike: Law in the Campaign for Clean Trucks*, the seeds for the struggle were planted in 2006 when the "Los Angeles Alliance for a New Economy—known as LAANE—organized the Coalition for Clean and Safe Ports with key labor, community, and environmental allies, particularly the International Brotherhood of Teamsters and the Natural Resources Defense Council."[141]

> This campaign emerged as a fight over air quality, but developed as a struggle over the conditions of short-haul truckers [who delivered cargo to the port, and] whose precarious economic status as independent contractors[142] contributed to poorly maintained trucks that were a key cause of air pollution....
>
> The campaign rested on an innovative legal hook: the port, as a publicly owned and operated entity, had the power to define the terms of entry for trucking companies through concession agreements—essentially private contracts permitting trucks onto port property. The campaign therefore hinged on how these agreements treated truckers and what types of standards the agreements set. Labor and environmental activists formed a coalition with residents of low-income communities adjacent to the port. Together, they sought to make new law that would convert truckers into employees of

---

140. Scott L. Cummings, *Preemptive Strike: Law in the Campaign for Clean Trucks*, 4 UC IRVINE L. REV. 939, 940 (2014).

141. *Id.* 943.

142. Cummings writes elsewhere that the "effective wage rate" for independent contractor truckers is less than ten dollars per hour. Scott L. Cummings, *The L.A. Ports Strike*, ONLABOR (Sept. 1, 2013), http://onlabor.org/2013/09/01/the-l-a-ports-strike/.

> their companies (thus enabling unionization), while requiring the gradual upgrading of trucks to reduce pollution.[143]
>
> The program, passed by the Los Angeles Board of Harbor Commissioners and approved by city council, conditioned the concession agreements on two basic requirements: first, that trucking companies (with port financial subsidies) agree to gradually convert their fleets to low-emissions vehicles and that they agree to convert all of their drivers to employees. [The second of these became known as the "employee-driver provision."] Under this new program, the environmental movement would achieve one of its long-standing goals—"greening" the port—while the Teamsters could pursue unionization of the newly converted employees. It was a win-win designed to address the structural economic problem contributing to port pollution: low-paid independent contractors did not have the resources to maintain and upgrade their trucks to current environmental standards. The port was thus where old, dirty diesel trucks went to die. The Clean Trucks Program would take maintenance out of the drivers' hands, making the companies internalize the costs, thus creating a sustainable foundation for clean trucking over time. A compelling concept, brilliantly executed.[144]

By specifically targeting an area of law with special city interests—law governing the port that the city operated—the coalition sought "to minimize ex ante legal risk and ultimately defended it—with mixed results—against a federal preemption challenge."[145] In particular, the American Trucking Associations argued that the Clean Trucks Plan was preempted by the Federal Aviation Administration Authorization Act (FAAA Act), which was enacted in:

> 1994 to prevent States from undermining federal deregulation of interstate trucking. The FAAA Act provides as a "general rule" that "a State [or] political subdivision of a State . . . may not enact or enforce a law, regulation, or other provision having the force and effect of law related to a price, route, or service of any motor carrier . . . with respect to the transportation of property."[146]

The Ninth Circuit explained its preemption analysis under the FAAA Act thusly:

> First, we must consider whether the provision "relate[s] to a price, route, or service of a motor carrier." If the answer is no, the provision does not fall within the preemptive scope of § 14501(c)(1). If the answer is yes, we must consider whether the provision "has the force and effect of law"—that is, whether the provision was enacted pursuant to the State's regulation of the

143. *Id.* 940–41.

144. Cummings, *supra* note 140.

145. Cummings, *supra* note 140, at 941.

146. American Trucking Ass'ns, Inc. v. City of Los Angeles, 660 F.3d 384, 395 (9th Cir. 2011) (citations omitted) (quoting 49 U.S.C. § 14501(c)(1)), *rev'd in part* 133 S. Ct. 2096 (2013).

> market, rather than the State's participation in the market in a proprietary capacity. 49 U.S.C. § 14501(c)(1).[147]

This second inquiry, whether the provision "has the force and effect of law," provides what is known as the market participant doctrine. The court took aim at the employee-driver provision requiring carriers to convert all independent operators to employee drivers:

> The FAAA Act preempts only State regulation, and not actions a State takes as a market participant. In applying the market participant doctrine, we undertake a single inquiry: whether the challenged program constitutes direct State participation in the market.[148]
>
> * * *
>
> We conclude that the employee driver provision seeks to impact third party behavior unrelated to the performance of the concessionaire's obligations to the Port. One of the Port's primary motives in adopting the employee driver provision was to increase stability in Port drayage by ensuring that drivers were paid higher wages. As a facilities provider, the Port has an interest in continued provision of drayage services, but it may not obtain that stability by unilaterally inserting itself into the contractual relationship between motor carriers and drivers. The Port, unlike the governmental entities in Boston Harbor or Johnson, does not pay driver salaries or subsidize benefits, so has no connection with drayage drivers justifying interference with the drivers' employment relationships.
>
> The Port argues that it subsidized approximately 35% of the drayage trucks operating at the Port, and believes that employee-drivers will better protect that investment. But the concession agreements bind all licensed motor carriers operating at the Port, not merely those who drive Port-subsidized trucks. Accordingly, even assuming that the Port's investment in drayage trucks entitles it to control the employment status of the drivers of subsidized trucks, the employee-driver provision still seeks to impact behavior beyond the scope of the obligations imposed by the subsidies.
>
> We recognize that a facilities provider in the Port's position has a proprietary interest in ministration. We also recognize that the employee-driver provision furthers this interest, because it permits the Port to hold accountable a smaller number of licensed motor carriers, rather than having to monitor a large number of independent owner-operators. Nevertheless, under the circumstances, this is insufficient to outweigh the Port's avowed desire to impact wages not subsidized by the State. The employee-driver provision is tantamount to regulation and thus does not fall under the market participant exception.[149]

---

147. *Id.* (citations omitted).
148. *Id.* at 397 (citations omitted).
149. *Id.* at 408 (citations omitted).

This result, however, left in place the requirement that port trucking companies replace their fleet with low-emissions trucks. The Supreme Court further gutted some of the minor requirements of the Clean Trucks Plan,[150] though:

> [t]he one silver lining of the Court's decision was that it did not touch the underlying doctrinal basis for local government efforts to intervene in labor issues through the market participant exception to federal preemption. But that was likely cold comfort to all of those who had worked so hard to get the Clean Truck Program passed in the first instance.
>
> It was also cold comfort to the truckers themselves, who now find themselves in a new box: obliged to acquire and maintain new, more expensive low-emission trucks (that part of the program was not enjoined), yet still in the degraded economic position of independent contractors. The campaign thus succeeded in producing a "green fleet" at the port—Los Angeles now boasts one of the cleanest ports in the world. Yet the truckers, despite the labor movement's monumental effort, still may have to bear the costs.[151]

Much like the principal *Taxicab* case, *ATA v. Los Angeles* involved local government trying to come up with a local solution to a global problem. Furthermore, as Professor Cummings eloquently describes, the challenged program was the result of careful collaboration among many local stakeholders. The entire community was sick and weary of the substantial pollution produced by the high-traffic port and developed a solution.

Did Congress really intend to foreclose these types of locally driven, narrowly crafted solutions with the broad language of the statute ("may not enact or enforce a law, regulation, or other provision . . . related to a price, route, or service of any motor carrier")? *Should* Congress be able to preempt local laws in such broad terms, or should it be required to be more explicit so as to limit any "collateral" or unintended consequences of its statute? Can you think of any way that the coalition could try to maintain the environmental benefits of its plan while mitigating its impact on the truckers? Among other strategies, the coalition supporting the Clean Trucks Plan after their shortcomings in the courts began a widespread campaign of misclassification litigation, arguing generally that the truckers who were treated as independent contractors were actually employees under federal law.[152]

5. As discussed above, the lack of commitment among the developing countries—particularly China—was a key sticking point that turned public favor in the United States against the Kyoto Protocol. In a development that surprised some observers, the Obama administration announced that China has agreed to implement a

150. *See* American Trucking Associations, Inc. v. City of Los Angeles., 133 S. Ct. 2096 (2013) (unanimous decision).

151. Cummings, *supra* note 140.

152. Cummings, *supra* note 140, at 1130–41.

cap-and-trade system beginning in 2017.[153] China's decision is in part the result of pressure from urban residents.[154]

6. What is a cap-and-trade system? As Professor Robert Stavins describes, a cap-and-trade system provides economic incentives to reduce emissions as much and as efficiently as possible:

> A cap-and-trade system limits the aggregate emissions of a group of regulated sources by creating a limited number of tradable emission allowances and requiring each firm to surrender a quantity of allowances equal to its own emissions. . . . [T]he need to surrender valuable allowances to cover any emissions and the opportunity to trade those allowances create a price signal for emissions. . . . Overall, a cap-and-trade system provides certainty regarding emissions from regulated sources because aggregate emissions from all regulated entities cannot exceed the total number of allowances.
>
> A well-designed cap-and-trade system will minimize the costs of achieving any given emissions target. Firms have flexibility regarding precisely how much they emit, but because they must surrender an allowance for each ton of emissions, they will undertake all emission reductions that are less costly than the market price of an allowance. Through trading, this allowance price adjusts until aggregate emissions are brought down to the level of the cap. Firms' ability to trade emission allowances creates a market in which allowances migrate toward their highest-valued use, protecting those emissions that are the most costly to reduce. Conversely, as a result of trading, the emission reductions undertaken to meet the cap are those that are least costly to achieve.[155]

Domestic action on the environment has consequences far beyond any one country's borders. A cap-and-trade system in the United States would clearly result in a reduction of domestically-produced emissions. However, Daniel Cole argues that such a system should also cause a global reduction of emissions:

> [N]ational and sub-national policies, if adopted by key actors, could have a substantial positive impact on international climate regimes. A very interesting recent working paper by Geoffrey Heal and Howard Kunreuther employs Thomas Schelling's tipping model to show that a small set of countries, by adopting climate control measures, could "make it in the interests of all others to do likewise." For example, Heal and Kunreuther find that "China and the EU between them have been instrumental in making carbon-free energy considerably less expensive, suggesting that they could

153. Julie Hirschfield Davis & Coral Davenport, *U.S. Says China Will Announce Cap-and-Trade Emissions Plan*, N.Y. Times (Sept. 25, 2015), at A1.

154. Scott Centrowski, *China's Pollution Crisis Has Political Blowback*, Fortune (Dec. 23, 2015), available at: http://fortune.com/2015/12/23/china-air-pollution-beijing-smog/.

155. Robert N. Stavins, *A Meaningful U.S. Cap-and-Trade System to Address Climate Change*, 32 Harv. Envtl. L. Rev. 293, 298–99 (2008).

> be part of a tipping set, or even form one." In a similar vein, as argued in this paper, if the US adopted a cap-and-trade regime similar in structure, scale, and scope to the EU ETS, the resulting market would predominate and possibly displace the Kyoto mechanisms.[156]

7. As Cass Sunstein has pointed out, the Montreal Protocol succeeded in part because its implementation increased the costs of using CFCs to the point where they were more expensive than environmentally-friendly alternatives.[157] The global guarantee that CFCs would not resurface as an option provided incentives to develop new environmentally-friendly replacement materials. Could this same incentivizing effect be accomplished with carbon? Compare the complexities of incentive-based models for greenhouse gases and carbon.

8. Not everyone is on board with market-based solutions to global warming, however. Pope Francis entered the debate with criticisms of cap-and-trade systems in his recent encyclical:

> The strategy of buying and selling "carbon credits" can lead to a new form of speculation which would not help reduce the emission of polluting gases worldwide. This system seems to provide a quick and easy solution under the guise of a certain commitment to the environment, but in no way does it allow for the radical change which present circumstances require. Rather, it may simply become a ploy which permits maintaining the excessive consumption of some countries and sectors.[158]

Economist William Nordhaus responded to the Pope's criticism by distinguishing between markets and market distortions:

> The idealized world of Adam Smith ignores two major shortcomings of a realistic market economy. The first is the presence of market failures, such as monopoly or unregulated pollution, that distort market decisions and outcomes, and the second is inequality of opportunities and income....
>
> Unfortunately, *Laudato Si'* does not recognize the fact that environmental problems are caused by market distortions rather than by markets per se....
>
> Permits for emissions are traded like other financial assets, and indeed they are often highly volatile.... [T]hey are volatile because future economic conditions (such as electricity demand or natural gas prices) are uncertain.[159]

---

156. Daniel H. Cole, *From Global to Polycentric Climate Governance*, 2 Climate Law 395, 412 (2011).

157. Cass R. Sunstein, *Of Montreal and Kyoto: A Tale of Two Protocols* 31 Harv. Envtl. L. Rev. 1 (2007).

158. Pope Francis, *Encyclical Letter:* Laudato Si' *of the Holy Father Francis on Care For Our Common Home* ¶ 171, http://w2.vatican.va/content/francesco/en/encyclicals/documents/papa-francesco_20150524_enciclica-laudato-si.html.

159. William D. Nordhaus, *The Pope & the Market*, N.Y. Rev. Books (October 8, 2015), available at http://www.nybooks.com/articles/archives/2015/oct/08/pope-and-market/#fnr-5.

9. A carbon tax is another market-based solution that incentivizes cleaner energy solutions by raising the cost of pollution. Congress has proposed such a tax several times, with each falling far short of enactment.[160] These proposals have included a tax on fuels, tailored to the carbon content of each fuel type;[161] a tax of fifty dollars per ton of carbon dioxide emitted by power plants;[162] and an excise tax of thirty cents per megawatt of power on fossil fuel-burning power plants.[163]

Professor Roberta Mann argues that a carbon tax is preferable to a cap-and-trade system for four reasons: "simplicity, transparency, efficiency, and certainty (of cost)."[164] Taxing carbon is no different than any other tax; it requires a determination of the pollutant to be taxed, the tax rate, and the measurement standards.[165] As Mann notes, "[T]here already exists a large and effective government for the collection of taxes."[166] Cap-and-trade systems, by comparison, can be enormously complex, requiring at minimum a determination of the size of the cap, the allocation of allowances, and a regulatory infrastructure to create and maintain the market.[167] These problems make cap-and-trade systems less efficient at reducing pollution and more subject to manipulation by regulated entities:

> The complexity allows affected industries to jockey for advantage and exemptions without the general public understanding what is going on.... This may be viewed as a political advantage—if consumers don't understand that some industries are getting off without paying their fair share, it is unlikely that consumers will raise objections. Political compromises can then be made among the industries without fear of public uproar. In short, a cap-and-trade system provides cover for the government's decision as to who "wins" and who "loses." ... Of course, a federal cap-and-trade program could be structured to provide public benefits, a level playing field, and fairness and cost containment for all industries and consumers. The odds are just overwhelmingly against that result.[168]

By contrast, Mann states that a carbon tax—if properly focused on the goal of reducing carbon emissions—would be simple and transparent, and would leave no room for finagling over the critical minutiae of a cap-and-trade system.[169] Achieving such a tax would be no easy feat, as Mann realizes. Perhaps the biggest problem is in the name: it is a tax, and American politicians are notoriously averse to endorsing a

---

160. Roberta Mann, *Waiting to Exhale?: Global Warming and Tax Policy*, 51 Am. U. L. Rev. 1135, 1212 (2002).

161. *Id.* at 1212 & n.549 (citing H.R. 1086, 102d Cong. (1991); H.R. 804, 103d Cong. (1993)).

162. *Id.* at 1212 & n.550 (citing S. 2636, 105th Cong. § 9 (1999)).

163. *Id.* at 1212 & n.552 (citing S. 1131, 107th Cong. § 7 (2001)).

164. Roberta F. Mann, *The Case for the Carbon Tax*, 39 Envtl. L. Rep. News & Analysis 10118, 10122 (2009).

165. *Id.* at 10120.

166. *Id.*

167. *Id.*

168. *Id.* at 10123.

169. *Id.* at 10124.

new tax of any type.[170] Mann points out the irony in this situation: a cap-and-trade system, just like a carbon tax, will certainly increase energy costs to consumers.[171] However, if Mann is correct that a carbon tax would lower pollution more quickly and at less cost, then a carbon tax may actually succeed at a lower cost to taxpayers.[172]

IV. Discussion: Climate politics

This chapter has explored international agreements in the form of global environmental treaties and agreements. The interlegalities of such agreements are evident both in the processes of reaching agreement and in ratification processes that anticipate legislative opposition in the countries involved. In this regard, the differences between the Montreal Protocol and the Paris Accords are suggestive of the very different political climates that prevailed in the United States in their respective eras. Moreover, in the years between the Montreal Protocol and the Paris Accords, there has been significant scientific mobilization (through the United Nations Environmental Program and the Intergovernmental Panel on Climate Change, for example).[173]

The transnational complexities of such agreements can be read alongside more localized experiences with climate change. In many parts of the world, recent changes in climate conditions compromise the sustainability of rural farmers' operations, particularly as new extremes in temperature fluctuation, as well as new hydrological conditions, affect their viability.[174] Anthropologists Kristine Skarbo and Kristin VanderMolen detail such issues in the Andes (and by extension to other mountainous regions in the subtropics), emphasizing the immediacy of the climate crisis in local communities and the corresponding political pressures on government officials to reform and guarantee water rights. [175] But while rural villagers have particular vulnerabilities, they are not passive victims. Anthropologist David Hughes cautions against "the victim slot" as a conceptual barrier to more constructive

---

170. *Id.* at 10125–26.

171. *Id.*

172. *See id.*

173. The United Nations Environmental Programme (UNEP) supports the United Nations Framework Convention on Climate Change; http://www.unep.org. The Intergovernmental Panel on Climate Change (ICPP) was created in 1988 by UNEP and the World Meteorological Organization (WMO); its membership consists of 195 countries that are members of either the UN or WMO, https://www.ipcc.ch/.

174. On one such development scheme in Indonesia and its unintended (negative) consequences, see Tania Murray Li, The Will to Improve: Governmentality, Development and the Practice of Politics (2007). *See also* Susan A. Crate, *Gone the Bull of Winter? Grapping wth the Cultural Implications of Anthropologists' Role(s) in Global Climate Change*, 49 Current Anthropology 569 (2008) (on the limits of adaptability to climate change among indigenous communities in the Arctic region).

175. Kristin Skarbo & Kristin VanderMolen, *Irrigation Access and Vulnerability to Climate-Induced Hydrological Change in the Andes*, 36 Culture, Agriculture, Food & Envt. 28 (2014).

engagement.[176] More generally, the complexities of "renewable energy transitions" that are now a feature of "climate politics" lead anthropologist Cymene Howe to observe that "the reality of increased global energy consumption and its concomitant climatological effect has meant that local practices are now universal concerns."[177]

This is but a brief note on a large topic. In terms of the issues that interest us in this book overall, the interlegalities of "climate politics" as seen from local ground quickly blur the lines between local government and governance of the environment, and just as quickly, challenge assumptions as to the relative powers of public (state) actors and private non-state actors in the energy sector. Arun Agrawal has introduced the term "environmentality" to convey the ways in which the specific properties of natural resources entail different problems and projects of governance.[178] Such "technologies of government" blur the distinction between a natural substance (oil, for example), the social conditions of its extraction and refinement, and the political economy of its production and global sale. For example, referring to the situation in the Niger River delta region of Nigeria, Michael Watts examines the properties of oil that that make it "governable" through modes of chieftainship, ethnic minorities and the national state, each with their own (but compounding) tensions and conflicts—concluding that "oil is the theatre of conflict within which Nigerian politics is currently being played out."[179] (We return to oil politics in Chapter 7, as we take up the *Chevron* case.) After Kyoto, the commodification of carbon creates a new market that has also begun to interest anthropologists as a new form of global currency that flattens other registers of social value.[180]

This is the context in which we now turn to transnational trade agreements that functionally rework not only the interrelationships of the ratifying countries, but also domestic political alignments.

---

176. David McDermott Hughes, *Climate Change and the Victim Slot: From Oil to Innocence*, 115 Am. Anthropolgist 570, 570 (2013).

177. Cymene Howe, *Latin America in the Anthropocene: Energy Transitions and Climate Change Mitigations*, 20 J. Latin Am. & Caribbean Anthropology 231, 232 (2015).

178. Arun Agrawal, Environmentality: Technologies of Government and the Making of Subjects (2005).

179. Michael Watts, *Resource Curse? Governmentality, Oil, and Power in the Niger Delta, Nigeria*, 9 Geopolitics 50, 52, 54 (2004). *See also* Timothy Mitchell, Carbon Democracy: Politics and Power in the Age of Oil (2011).

180. In particular, see Steffen Dalsgaard, *The Commensurability of Carbon: Making Value and Money of Climate Change*, 3 J. Ethnographic Theory 80 (2013).

Chapter 3

Regional Trade Agreements: The North American Free Trade Agreement

I. Internationalism and free trade

Intergovernmental agreements on tariff reduction have proliferated around the world since the 1980s. They are *international* in a sense quite different from the internationalism of the Montreal Protocol and the Paris Accords. Tariff reduction agreements entail dense ongoing relations that reach deeply into each country's legal, political, and social life. In practice, such agreements inhabit intricate networks of interests that are highly diverse in character, dynamic in their relations, and—potentially—deeply relevant to specific communities, firms, and even individuals. Such agreements are bound up in formal and informal relations involving diverse institutional actors from the public and private sectors, highly dispersed centers of rule-making and monitoring, diverse sources of legality and agents of law enforcement, and a vast array of intended and unintended social, political, and economic arrangements. Paradoxically, transnational tariff-reduction agreements—though aimed at cross-border investment and trade—add significantly to the stakes in maintaining national boundaries conceived in territorial terms. This is the case not just because free trade continues to meet opposition among protectionists, but also because free trade involves the restructuring of relations between national and local governments, state and non-state agencies, and differently positioned stakeholders who operate under their own national legal systems. In this chapter, we emphasize this paradoxical connection between transnational trade agreements and the entrenchment of territoriality.

Our focus is the North American Free Trade Agreement (NAFTA). NAFTA is important in its own right in any account of transnational law. But it is also a productive case study—illuminating dilemmas in the dual development of democracy and capital growth, as well as the tight threads by which government and governance, legality and illegality, and globalism and localism may be bound together in the forms of transnationalism chartered by such agreements. To think of NAFTA only as a trilateral agreement is to radically understate the extent of such interconnections. Our discussion emphasizes the debates leading up to NAFTA, the terms of the Agreement (particularly its dispute resolution provisions) and some of its main effects in terms of new interests and stakeholders in the United States, Mexico, and Canada. We draw extensively on concepts developed in Chapters 1 and 2 with regard to the distinctions and connections between government and governance, sovereignty and territory, and legal pluralism and interlegality.

II. The North American Free Trade Agreement: Background

A. Legalities and socialities

NAFTA created a free trade zone affecting most but not all market sectors across Canada, Mexico, and the United States. It was preceded by the Canada-United States Free Trade Agreement of 1989 and liberalization reforms in Mexico under the Salinas administration beginning in 1988. NAFTA was signed by Presidents Salinas and Bush and Prime Minister Mulroney at a ceremony in San Antonio, Texas, on October 7, 1992. At the time of its implementation, NAFTA created the largest free trade zone in the world. Although the implementation agreement gained Congressional approval after Bill Clinton took office in 1993, opposition to NAFTA in Congress did not come to an end with the passage of that bill.

In this background section, we emphasize the differences among the three signatories in terms of the domestic interests that led to the agreement, debates internal to each country, and the social effects of NAFTA over time. Our purpose in emphasizing the differences among the parties is to underscore the extent to which transnational law is built of multiple constituencies and legalities. Transnational law does not erase or homogenize such differences. Rather, in the trade context discussed in this chapter, it establishes new forms of governance through its alignment of government and the transnational private sector.

The years before and after NAFTA's passage saw numerous bilateral and U.S./regional free trade bills in Congress, and intense partisan debate over the potential trade-offs of the agreement in terms of risks to U.S. jobs and border environments. Ultimately, HR 3450 (The North American Free Trade Agreement Implementation Act) passed both chambers by a vote of 234–200 in the House of Representatives, and 60–38 in the Senate.[1] It became U.S. law on December 8, 1993, taking effect on January 1, 1994, as Public Law 103-182. Between 1995 and 2014, there were at least eight bills, resolutions, or concurrent resolutions introduced in the House of Representatives calling for a renegotiation, withdrawal, or notice of withdrawal from NAFTA.[2] Additional legislative activity focused on particular products, powers, and perceived risks (notably in terms of U.S. job loss, environmental risks, and truck safety).

---

1. North American Free Trade Agreement Implementation Act, H.R. 3450, 103d Cong. (1993) (enacted).

2. Congressional legislative tracking can be found at http://www.thomas.gov. The bills and resolutions referred to in the main text include: H.R. 499, 104th Cong. (1995); H.R. Con. Res. 224, 108th Cong. (2004); H.R. Con. Res. 186, 109th Cong. (2005); H.R. 1087, 110th Cong. (2007); H.R. Con. Res. 22, 110th Cong. (2008); H.R. 4759, 111th Cong. (2010); H.R. 29, 112th Cong. (2011); H.R. 156, 113th Cong. (2013). None of these bills, resolutions, or concurrent resolutions became law.

Organized labor in the United States generally opposed NAFTA, and the Clinton administration's emphasis on environmental protection in the border region may be understood in part as an attempt to conciliate domestic interests in terms other than jobs. In Mexico, controversies also involve labor and the environment, but even more fundamentally, contested powers as between local authority and the national state, and threats to peasant and indigenous farming. In Canada, job loss and deterioration of agriculture have also been sources of controversy. We discuss these and related issues further below. It is very much to the point of our analysis that there can be no single standpoint from which to narrate the history, impact, or future of NAFTA. NAFTA continues to be adjusted in response to legal, legislative, and diplomatic challenges surrounding these and other issues. The impact of NAFTA on labor north and south of the U.S./Mexico border is part of a larger story—the historical relationship of labor migration and economic restructuring associated with the globalization of capitalism in the U.S., Europe, and their respective peripheries over the centuries comprising the industrial era.[3] This makes specific impacts of NAFTA difficult to assess, since the agreement punctuated ongoing developments in transnational law, rather than initiating something altogether new.[4]

The following excerpt, written shortly after NAFTA's implemention, captures the dynamic context of controversy involved in its creation. As you read this excerpt, track the different stakeholders, interests, and political contexts among the three signatory countries.

Stephen J. Randall & Herman W. Konrad, *Introduction*,

in NAFTA IN TRANSITION 1–5

(Stephen J. Randall & Herman W. Konrad eds. 1995)

In 1989, Canada and the United States concluded a bilateral free trade agreement (FTA), following one of the most intense political debates in Canadian history over relations with the United States and the nature of the Canadian political economy. The

---

3. *See* Jane Collins, *Deterritorialization and Workplace Culture*, 29 AM. ETHNOLOGIST 151 (2002) (comparing the situations of U.S. and Mexican textile workers with respect to the deterioration of workplace protections supporting effective claims-making).

4. For example, U.S. labor unions were already under significant pressure. UNIONS IN TRANSITION: ENTERING THE SECOND CENTURY (Seymour Martin Lipset, ed., Institute for Contemporary Studies Press 1986). In Mexico, earlier liberalization reforms by the Salinas administration had already had significant impact on key sectors. Shannon Speed, *New Directions in Mexico Research: The Calderón Era*, 13 NORTH AM. DIALOGUE 4, 5 (2010). Salinas' reforms withdrew state supports from the dairy industry, resulting in sagging prices and deterioration of smaller and middle-sized farms, favoring large farming enterprises. James H. McDonald, *NAFTA and the Milking of Dairy Farming in Central Mexico*, 15 CULTURE & AGRIC. 13 (1995). For a comparison of NAFTA with the U.S.-Canada Free Trade Agreement (FTA), see Alan Rugman, *A Canadian Perspective on NAFTA*, 36 INT'L EXECUTIVE 33 (1994). And for a further comparison of NAFTA, FTA, and WTO with regard to the Canadian food sector, see Karl Meilke & Erna van Duren, *The North American Free Trade Agreement and the Canadian Agri-Food Sector*, 44 CANADIAN J. AGRIC. ECON. 19 (1996).

Canadian federal election of 1988, in which the FTA featured as the single most important issue, and the subsequent conclusion of the agreement have not ended that debate.

The vitality of the issue derived from several factors. The first was the continuing evolution of Canada-United States economic, political, and cultural relations. A second factor was the discontent fostered by the international economic recession in 1990–92, and the widespread impression in Canada that the high loss of jobs in industrial Canada to the United States and Mexico was a result of the FTA. A third factor was the high current level of political conflict in Canada over a wide range of issues, from the FTA to federal-provincial relations, the constitutional crisis, and the controversial economic policies of the Conservative government.

With the Salinas turnabout, in favour of a Mexico-United States FTA, and Canada's entry into the negotiations, resulting in the NAFTA agreement inked by Brian Mulroney, Carlos Salinas, and George Bush in Texas in late 1992, the free trade debate took on new dimensions. Opposition parties in all three countries—the Canadian Liberal Party led by Jean Chrétien, the Mexican Party of the Democratic Revolution (PRD) under Cuauhtémoc Cardenas, and the U.S. Democratic Party led by Bill Clinton provided political platforms for intensive scrutiny and debate. Clinton, once elected, became a staunch advocate of NAFTA provided that side-agreements were negotiated on labour and environmental issues. The rich and eccentric H. Ross Perot, with Republican (for example, Robert Torricelli) and Democratic (the AFL-CIO) bedfellows, campaigned vigorously against it. For this "unholy" alliance, which included a broad spectrum of concerned U.S. citizens, NAFTA represented massive job losses, environmental degradation, and an attack on the "American Dream." Buttressed by Big Business, a lot of arm twisting, and the hastily negotiated side-agreements, the Clinton forces won sufficient congressional votes to allow the mandated 1 January 1994 NAFTA start-up date to become a reality.

Jean Chrétien, having decimated the governing Conservatives and routed the New Democrats in the 1993 elections, made the traditional Liberal Party adjustments to expediency. Now comfortably again in power, the Canadian Liberals were free to adopt policies previously opposed while in opposition. Faced with the realities of the economic agendas of Canada's new political alignment—the western-based Reform Party and the separatist Bloc Québecois, both pro-NAFTA—Chrétien has become a national and hemisphere sponsor of not only North American but also hemisphere free trade. He has led significant trade delegations to Mexico and South America and, at the Hemisphere heads-of-state meetings in Miami (December 1994), was actively lobbying for Chile's entry into NAFTA. Meanwhile, in Canada, the Canadian Labour Congress and the Canadian Auto Workers have led the critique of bilateral and trilateral free trade, insisting that the agenda is to exploit Mexico's cheap labour at the expense of Canadian labour and investment in Canada.

In Mexico, with the all-powerful PRI party behind him and most of the public media onside, Carlos Salinas's economic and constitutional adjustments to meet his neoliberal economic agenda and its free trade implications were easily implemented. His acquiescent Congress and Senate, despite strident opposition from the PRD, quickly approved presidential initiatives. Ratification of the NAFTA, requiring only Senate approval, took place almost immediately after the bill's passage in the United States. Mexicans were led to believe, and the majority appeared ready to believe, that a brighter, more prosperous future would be forthcoming with Mexico as a formal economic partner with its richer U.S. and Canadian neighbours. The business at hand now, in late 1993, was the forthcoming national elections for which Salinas unveiled Luis Donaldo Colosio as the PRI standardbearer. Like the earlier López Portillo forecast of Mexico needing to think in terms of coming to terms with the management of prosperity, based on projected petroleum revenues, the Salinas forecast was framed in terms of Mexico moving from third to first world status.

Unforeseen events shattered both optimistic forecasts. The 1982 collapse of oil prices unraveled the López Portillo vision of the future, plunging Mexico into a decade of belt-tightening economic adjustments. For Salinas, the shot that undermined his first world future came from marginalized, mostly indigenous and economically depressed Chiapas in the form of the masked Zapatista Army of National Liberation (EZLN). Led by the charismatic *subcomandante,* Marcos, who claimed only to be the voice of the General Command of the Clandestine Revolutionary Indigenous Committee (CCRI), this jungle-trained group of insurgents declared war on the Mexican Federal Army. The declaration, symbolized by the armed occupation of San Cristobal de las Casas, in the first hour of 1 January 1994, was purposely timed to coincide with the official start-up of NAFTA. It, claimed the rebels, represented the death-knell of Mexico's rural indigenous peasantry. Echoing the rallying call of revolutionary Mexico's Emiliano Zapata, whose ideals they identified with, the EZLN demanded "Work, Land, Housing, Food, Health, Education, Democracy, Liberty, Peace, Independence, and Justice" (*trabajo, tierra, techo, pan, salud, educación, democracia, libertad, paz, independencia, y justicia*). The immediate response of the national and international media, and the Mexican army, quickly focused attention on the "other face" of Salinas's Mexican "miracle"—the lag between social/political/economic progress, and economic and constitutional restructuring—for Mexico's rural and urban underclasses.

Although shaken, the Salinas agenda was not derailed by the upstart EZLN, more skilled in attracting media attention than military actions. This attention, and increased scrutiny by the NAFTA partners, resulted in electoral reforms and uneven foreign investment in Mexico. The March 23rd assassination of the PRI presidential candidate and the failure to reach a negotiated settlement with the Zapatistas heightened national tensions, increased international concerns regarding Mexican stability and the outcome of the August 21st national elections, and stimulated the flight of capital—both national and foreign speculative—but did not alter the PRI tradition of an almost clean sweep, or *carro completo,* in election results. Salinas's hastily designated Colosio substitute, Ernesto Zedillo, backed by official and unofficial financing, the organizing skills of the PRI conservative wing (known as the "dinosaurs"), and a flood of funds channeled to rural sectors through government programs (*Procampo* and *Pronasol*), brought out unprecedented numbers of voters on August 21st.

For the first time in Mexico's history its election run-up and voting was accompanied by a presidential candidates' televised national debate, numerous polls, international observers, and exit polls. Despite vigorous campaigning, large crowds in public meetings but little media exposure, Cuauhtémoc Cardenas' anti-NAFTA forces suffered a resounding defeat. The pro-NAFTA conservative National Action Party (PAN) replaced the PRD as the main opposition party. The PRI, in sharp contrast to the 1988 disputed electoral results, this time appeared to be firmly in control, following an election internationally recognized as the cleanest in Mexican memory. Salinas's restructuring program, under Zedillo, would continue, with sighs of relief coming from Washington and Ottawa. North America's future, as the world's largest free-trade block, appeared to be moving in the right direction. The assassination of José Francisco Ruis Massieu, designated leader of the PRI-dominated Chamber of Deputies, in October 1994, raised questions about political stability but not about economic directions. Salinas finished his six-year term inaugurating countless public and private economic projects, including many foreign-financed business ventures looking to take advantage of Mexican opportunities under NAFTA. Attention now turned to the optimistic forecasts of the Zedillo term of office (1994–2000) and its impact. The Zapatista "problem" had been overtaken by voter confidence in continuity under a political party in power since 1929.

Yet no sooner was Zedillo installed as president (1 December 1994), with an administration replete with Salinas hold-overs, than the wheels began to fall off the restructured Mexico, built to meet the challenges of the future. The Zapatista revoking of the military truce which had held up for most of the year, and the draining of Mexico's financial reserves by anxious Mexicans and nervous investors, quickly resulted in a run on, and collapse of, the Mexican peso. Jaime Serra Puche, under Salinas Mexico's NAFTA negotiator, and now finance minister, was forced to resign in disgrace. Public anger directed at Salinas and his cabinet, for not having made earlier adjustments which might have avoided the economic collapse, resulted in public and opposition parties' calling for a public accounting and judicial penalties against the former president. Zedillo was forced to turn to foreign banks and the International Monetary Fund for a financial bail-out in an attempt to halt the run on Mexican currency which was having a ripple effect (*efecto tequila*) on all hemisphere financial institutions. Mexico, within a matter of a few months, according to national and international commentators, had been transformed from the "model third world economy" on the road to prosperity to a "basket-case." By March 1995, President Zedillo had been forced to make a series of cabinet changes, issue a stream of economic stabilization plans, and accept externally-conditioned financial rescue packages. Carlos Salinas, like Luís Echevarria (in 1977) and José López Portillo (in 1983), was forced to leave Mexico after the arrest of his brother Raul as the intellectual co-author of the Ruis Massieu assassination. Mexico, once again, faced the trauma of the belt-tightening hard times and an uncertain economic future.

By the beginning of spring 1995 the political and economic face of North America was less optimistic. The Mexican peso had crashed, the U.S. dollar had sagged, and the Canadian dollar had slipped badly in comparison with the currencies of North America's competing economies in Japan and Europe. The architects of the FTA and NAFTA (Mulroney, Reagan/Bush, Salinas) and their trade negotiators had been replaced by new national leaders faced by new domestic challenges. The Republican, Gingrich-led nationalism (Contract with America) in the United States, and the Quebec separatism and Western provincial opposition in Canada, has forced a more inward-looking emphasis by the northern NAFTA partners, while Mexico's economic and political turmoil provides even less scope for grand continental or hemisphere plans. The national governments, having given birth to a treaty framework for free trade, accompanied by increased privatization of state enterprises, appear ready to rely upon the private sector to bring forth the promised results. All three countries officially promote NAFTA and its eventual extension to include all the countries of the hemisphere despite the emergence of contradictory initiatives by special interest groups.

Whether the rest of the 1990s has as many unpredicted economic and political surprises as the first 15 months of the post-NAFTA era . . . remains to be seen. Whether the private sector is able to take advantage of the now-established framework for continental economic integration, to bring forth projected results, also remains to be seen.

Twenty years later, the Hoover Institution convened a conference at which the trade representatives involved in the creation of NAFTA reminisced about the negotiations.[5] They tell a different story about the same events; their conversation is a vivid reminder that international agreements begin as interpersonal agreements, in this case among chief executives and their representatives.

NAFTA: From Conception to Creation

in NAFTA AT 20 (Michael J. Boskin ed. 2014)

The chief negotiators—Michael H. Wilson for Canada, Jaime Serra Puche for Mexico, and Carla A. Hills for the United States—reflect on the lengthy negotiations and political complications, interrupted by brief moments of drama, that culminated in the signing and ratification of the North American Free Trade Agreement.

Michael H. Wilson: Let me put a little bit of historical context on all of this. Free trade with the United States had been a subject of discussion for probably a hundred years, on and off. We had another election, 1911, that was fought on free trade. The Liberals proposed it, Conservatives strongly opposed it, and the Conservatives won

5. The twentieth anniversary of NAFTA generated extensive analysis and commentary in the three countries among scholars, interest groups and in the media on the agreement's social and economic effects. *See* Julián Aguilar, *Twenty Years Later, NAFTA Remains a Source of Tension*, N.Y. TIMES (December 7, 2012), http://www.nytimes.com/2012/12/07/us/twenty-years-later-nafta-remains-a-source-of-tension.html.

and that put the whole idea to bed for a long time because it was seen as a bit of a third rail.

We did take the first step in 1965 with the Auto Pact, a very important trade agreement between the US and Canada. It was particularly important for Canada because it allowed us to modernize our sector. What happened out of that was about 90 percent of what we produced was sold in the United States, and about 90 percent of what we consumed was bought from the United States. So it was the first sign of real integration, and the start of the so called North American Supply Chain.

Then in the years leading up to the (Prime Minister Brian) Mulroney election in 1984, there was some talk of broadening from the Auto Pact and moving into other sectors. But it quickly became apparent that we would be taking the low-hanging fruit off the table and taking away the leverage that we would need to get a broader agreement on the much tougher issues that would become part of the overall agreement. The issue was not on the table at all in the 1984 election. The Liberal government had formed the Macdonald Commission, led by Don Macdonald, who is the foreign minister of everything in the Liberal government. He came up with a phrase which became the real talking point. He said that he thought that Canada should take a leap of faith and consider a free trade agreement with the United States.

Mulroney quickly grabbed this, and shortly after that we had the so-called Shamrock Summit in Quebec City with President Reagan and Prime Minister Mulroney agreeing to study the possibility of a free trade agreement between the two countries.

Throughout this period, President Reagan stood back from it. He did not want to be seen as being the aggressor taking the initiative. He very rightly thought that if he did that, it would attract a lot of negative attention in Canada, and he would become the focal point. He thought it would be better to have Mulroney take the initiative and the idea be seen as more of a Canadian idea, rather than something that the United States was imposing upon us.

But the underlying fear was that a free trade agreement with a country ten times the size of Canada both in terms of GDP and population would inevitably lead, directly or indirectly, to a significant erosion of our sovereignty. But in face of all of this, Mulroney, in September 1985, announced that he would propose a negotiation with the United States. President Reagan responded positively and enthusiastically.

Mulroney, though, in his announcement, was very careful to set out some of the things that he felt were the essence of Canada and would not be the subject of negotiation: our national sovereignty, our social policies, our cultural policies, the capacity to address regional disparities, our distinct linguistic character. These were the things that he focused on, understanding that these would become very significant in the concerns expressed by people opposed to the agreement.

But apart from that, he wanted the broadest package possible on the table. Inevitably, the cry went out right after that Mulroney was proposing to sell out Canada and that was something that carried through right into the subsequent election.

The key drivers in the negotiation were clear. We wanted to get access to a market ten times our size, our number one trading partner. We wanted to have access to the United States market because that would allow us to rationalize away from a very fragmented economy into an economy that was more integrated with this great big economy to our south, and allow us to specialize and focus on our areas of strength. These were very strong considerations.

Let me give you an example. I remember talking to a CEO of one of our large companies, and I said, "What would free trade do for you?" He said, "about a third of our business would be gone. Absolutely, we could not compete. Two-thirds would be OK."

I said, "One-third is quite a big piece of your company. How can you do this?" He said, "Well, that part of the company is not going to go anywhere. Our future lies in those two-thirds, and we have to see ourselves capable of rationalizing between what we should put in the United States and what we should put in Canada. A free trade agreement would give us that direction to allow us to make those investment decisions."

An agreement was also needed to reduce trade disputes, and this became the key sticking point in the negotiation with the United States. We had seen a period leading up to this when we would be subject to trade disputes with the United States, molded largely by congressional pressure. What we felt was that, if we were going to go into an agreement with a country ten times our size, we had to have a dispute settlement mechanism where disputes would be settled by impartial bodies that would be based on the facts, rather than simply driven by politics.

The dialogue that we had within Canada during this period leading up to the final agreement was a very broad dialogue. We had ITAC (International Trade Advisory Committee) and SAGIT (Sectoral Advisory Group on International Trade). These were the principle consultative bodies and were very important in the advice that the negotiators would receive. The political debate itself was on economic issues, social policy implications, and the national interest, the national sovereignty, things like that.

These were the sorts of debates that we had, and they centered on those issues that Mulroney identified in his earlier announcement. But to that, we added water. People were terrified that we would have water directed out of the Great Lakes into other parts of the United States, or that we would be forced to redirect waters in western Canada so that they would be largely serving the interests of the United States. Agriculture became very important and there were also fears that we would have a managed foreign exchange agreement with the United States, which naturally would accrue to the favor of the United States rather than Canada.

Key issues were dairy and poultry, wine, textiles and clothing, soft-wood lumber (which did not become part of the agreement, but continued to be a narrative between the two countries). Rules of origin were an important part of that as well.

We had a deadline, which was October 3, 1987, and that was because of the Fast Track authority, where we had an up-or-down vote in the United States.

Periodically, during those last two days, Baker would leave the room. And partway through, he told me that he went to speak to Dan Rostenkowski and Sam Gibbons, the two senior Democrats on trade agreements from their position on the House Ways and Means Committee. That was very important in giving him the confidence to be able to accept this or reject that. I was on a platform with Jim about a year ago and I reminded Jim that he was doing this and he smiled. I said, "In today's environment in the United States Congress, would you be able to do that?" And he said, "No, I couldn't."

Fast forward now to 6:30 on the night of October 3. We had five-and-a-half hours to the deadline, and we reached a deadlock on the dispute settlement agreement. We broke. A few of us got on the phone with the prime minister, we told him where it all was, and we said we do not think he can accept this. He agreed. He said, "You'd better go and speak to Baker and tell him that we will put it to bed. But let's try and do it in the right way. I'd like to speak to the president to put it to bed as nicely as possible."

I went to see Baker. He agreed, and he said, "Well, let's give it another try" In addition—I didn't realize it at the time—Mulroney was not able to get through to the president. But he picked up the phone and called Baker and said, "How are you going to explain to your people that you can get a nuclear arms agreement with your worst enemy, the USSR, and you can't get a god damned free trade agreement with your best friends, the Canadians?" That, I think, was a significant factor in getting us over the top, because we did get the dispute settlement mechanism, and everything moved nicely from there.

Conservatives were obviously in favor, and both the opposition parties were opposed . . . . It got to be very bitter.

There are some quotes that will give you a sense that the future of the country was at stake, according to the national newspapers in Canada. "We said we are going to build a nation." The Liberals said, "You sold us out. You destroyed a 120-year-old dream called Canada. You are surrendering one by one our levers of economic independence." "Made in Ottawa, not in Washington." "It is bad for everyone. It has to be rejected."

We won the election. We were in third place with two weeks to go, and Mulroney was told to be a statesman. Just talk about the importance of it to the country and be a statesman. Well, we were in third place, two weeks to go, and he said, "To hell with being a statesman, we've got to fight for this thing." He just took his jacket off, very passionate, saying how important this was, that it was essential for the country to have, and we won a very strong majority We got 171 seats in a 284-seat House. So it was a very prominent victory.

After that, things settled down, and by the time the discussion of NAFTA came, there was a pretty good acceptance of free trade. The Liberals had opposed the free trade agreement with the United States when they won the election of November 1993; but within days, they reversed their position on trade.

Carla A. Hills: Let me talk about some of the challenges and opportunities that the North American Free Trade Agreement produced. I have to give credit to Jaime Serra, who raised the subject, not of the NAFTA, but of a bilateral agreement between the United States and Mexico, in Davos in January 1990. As we met in Davos, the US economy was not in robust circumstances. It is a fact that when the economy is down, that stokes economic nationalism. We had been through a battle with Canada over our free trade agreement with it, which almost brought the Mulroney government down.

I brought home from Davos the idea of a free trade agreement with Mexico to the president. I thought it was a good idea. I supported the notion that we expand free trade to all of North America. The president was receptive. We had extensive internal discussions with some yeas and some nays in the administration. But during the months of February and March 1990, we got primary support within the White House and among my cabinet colleagues.

However, some pointed out, are we really taking on more than we can do? We are negotiating the Uruguay Round (of the General Agreement on Tariffs and Trade), which is our top priority, and now we are talking about adding a major bilateral agreement. But in enumerating the many challenges, I would say the number one challenge was to secure Fast Track legislation prior to beginning negotiations. (Mexican) President Salinas made it very clear to President Bush that he wanted the same Fast Track procedures governing the bilateral agreement as Canada and Israel had had with the United States.

Once we decided that we wanted to have a negotiation with Mexico, we had to go to work not only on the content of the negotiation but also on persuading members of Congress that this was a worthy negotiation deserving of Fast Track procedures. And we met a lot of headwind, no question about it. We worked with the two chairs of the relevant committees—Senator Lloyd Bentsen, chair of the Senate Finance Committee, and Congressman Dan Rostenkowski, chair of the Ways and Means Committee—and all members of those committees, since they had primary jurisdiction over trade.

We were facing election in 1992, so we knew that two years out, some of these members were going to be facing even more headwinds at home if we reached an agreement. So we activated our presidential advisory groups in the United States. We had about nineteen presidential advisory groups on trade, and we got businesses activated to explain the merits of an agreement with Mexico. I personally met with all 535 members of Congress and tried to talk to each of them and, more importantly, to listen to what their concerns were. And even when their concerns were wildly off base economically, I would say, "You know, Congressman, that's truly an interesting idea that never occurred to me, and I won't forget it."

By the time we got to August 1990, the two presidents were able to sign a joint agreement that they were thinking positively about a bilateral agreement. They could not officially say they were going to move forward because that would have triggered the Fast Track process. The next day, Jaime and I issued a report that said a bilateral agreement was a good idea, and our recommendation to our presidents was to move forward.

It was just about that time that we got a call from Canada Michael Wilson's predecessor, John Crosbie, a wonderful man from Newfoundland, called me and said, "Carla, what about Canada? We want to join." I said, "John, you just went through an election that almost brought the government down. You don't want to join." He said, "Yes, I do. I do not wish to be left out." Then, of course, Mulroney called Bush, and there was a discussion on how do we deal with this. We did not want to offend our very best friend on our northern border, but we did want to move forward. And so we decided, Jaime Serra and I, to invite John Crosbie to dinner in New York, where we had a robust discussion about whether Canada could stand the heat, and the subjects that we would cover in a trilateral trade agreement.

At the end of the dinner, we decided to issue a press release that said the three governments were going to move forward to negotiate a trilateral agreement, but if one of the governments decided to pull out anywhere along the line, the other two would move forward. We did not mention Canada, but we wanted to make clear that the negotiation was going to go forward—bilaterally or trilaterally.

President Bush moved forward and asked for the Fast Track to run until June 1, 1993, which got us over the November 1992 election. The request included Canada, but it did give Congress another opportunity to block the negotiations.

It was about a week later that House Majority Leader Richard Gephardt sent us a ten-page, single-spaced letter outlining his numerous objections and concerns about the agreement. The letter covered labor, environment, autos, agriculture, jobs. You name it—it was on the list. Both Chairmen Rostenkowski and Bentsen had sent earlier letters that were more manageable, but we had to get the Gephardt letter answered and talk about how we were going to deal with the politics going forward. We intensified our meetings with Congress. I think it was extremely important to the success of this trilateral negotiation that we spent so much time with Congress. It was necessary to keep them apprised, particularly those who were going to be forceful supporters. We had numerous executive sessions, which were not publicized, with the Ways and Means and the Finance committees.

Finally, June 1, 1991, arrived. The sixty legislative days had passed, giving us Fast Track authority to negotiate an agreement with both Mexico and Canada. The official negotiation started on June 12, 1991. The next challenge occurred as we tried to negotiate the agreement and to keep the parties who were concerned about the negotiation apprised. We spoke at the Governor's Conference in Seattle. We took eleven members of Congress and twenty-six members of the Private Sector Advisory Group on Trade down to Mexico City to meet with President Salinas. We had hundreds of meetings with various interest groups. I personally spoke to the textile manufacturing association. I got booed, but I said, "You know, we will have a long transition, and this is something that you will benefit from in the long run." To negotiate acceptance, not great support, was to talk about the transition. This was not going to hit tomorrow where the businesses couldn't adapt, but we would deal with these issues, and similarly so, of course, would Mexico.

The tough issues were on autos. We were pushing very hard for 65 percent of NAFTA content, duty drawbacks, the opening of services, particularly including banking and insurance, the limiting of screening of investments, which Canada also did. That is, if you wanted to have a merger or an acquisition, it could be screened, which we felt was very contrary to the free market system. But by August 1992, fourteen months to the day that we began the negotiations, we shook hands in agreement. It was the first comprehensive free trade agreement that had been negotiated between developed and developing countries. It achieved broader and deeper market openings than any prior trade agreement. It opened markets by eliminating tariffs on all industrial goods, guaranteeing unrestricted access of agricultural trade between the United States and Mexico. (Canada did not participate in the agricultural market opening.)

It opened a broad range of services, including financial services, and created national treatment for cross-border service providers. It provided high standards to protect patents, trademarks, copyrights, trade secrets, and it was the first trade agreement to do that anywhere in the world. It also prohibited barriers such as local content and import substitution, which were heavily prevalent in the economies that we were negotiating with.

The final challenge was to move the agreement to signature by the heads of the three governments. The Fast Track legislation set forth rules governing when the president could sign the agreement. After we shook hands in August 1992, President Bush lost the election in November. A number of steps were required before he could sign the agreement and leave it to his successor to obtain congressional approval. He could not get it approved by Congress, because of the Fast Track timing rules. Under the legislation, the US Private Sector Advisory Groups, each of them, I think there were nineteen, had to prepare a report for the Congress and for the public on the merits of each of the sections of the agreement. In addition, an overall report on the merits of the agreement was required from the president's Private Sector Advisory Group on trade. It took some time for them to prepare those reports. It was not until the reports were available to Congress—and that meant all of them—that the president could give Congress his notice of intent to sign, and he could not sign until ninety days after giving the notice, which he did give. In December 1992, the president was able, with the expiration of that ninety-day period, to sign the NAFTA. At that point we left it to our successors to get the agreement approved, and they did a magnificent job, in our opinion.

And just to mention the opportunities: one of the great opportunities, of course, was working with great people like Michael Wilson and John Crosbie in Canada and Jaime Serra in Mexico, and we have all become fast friends. Twenty years later, we are even better friends than we were around the conference table.

Jaime Serra Puche: I am going to try to avoid repetition, but I will try to clarify certain things. First, the economic rationale for Mexico: it was not just that Salinas and I woke up one morning in Davos and said, "Oh, let's have a free trade agreement."

Mexico had been a highly protectionist economy for five or six decades. Mexico joined GATT in 1986, forty years after it was created. So it took us forty years to understand that we had to belong to GATT. We had introduced huge distortions in our trade, in relative prices, and we were not competitive. So, when we came into power, we said we have to further liberalize, and we put together a project that was partly a stabilization program, partly a competitiveness-oriented or export-oriented program. We announced it at the beginning of the six-year term. We thought that it would be really welcomed by the rest of the world, but when we went to Davos a few months later, we were facing lukewarm reactions. They said, "These guys have a long way to go." The wall in Berlin had just fallen, so people were looking at the Eastern European countries. At the end of one evening, very late at night, Salinas came to my room and said, "We have to do something. We are not on the map for foreign direct investment. Why don't we start thinking about this idea of trade with the US?" I said, "I have this meeting with Carla tomorrow morning to discuss the textile quotas (our trade was then conducted separately in many sectors, each with specific quotas). I can at least ask my deputy to talk to her deputy and I can talk to her about this." So that's what we did. So that's when I presented the idea to Carla of a Mexico-US free trade agreement. Let me go back to the economic rationale. There were three economic rationales for that decision.

First, as I have said, Mexico was not on the world map for direct investment and we needed foreign investment badly, because we did not generate enough domestic savings to support growth.

Second, we were the number one user of the Generalized System of Preferences (GSP) with the US, which means, for example, that we could export up to 100,000 microphones to the US, paying no tariff. But that system says that if we export 100,000 plus one, you lose the preference for the whole 100,000 microphones every year. So we had a perverse situation in Mexico. Plants that were exporting would close in October because they did not want to lose the preference and they did not want to accumulate inventories. Many plants that were exporting refrigerators or TVs were closing in October instead of keeping up production in order to avoid these costs.

And the third issue we had was that we had to negotiate, annually or biannually, the quotas for the central agreement. So, exporters could say, "Well, how good are these negotiations going to be this year? As I don't know how the negotiations will go this year, I better not invest more." Even when we had reached a good level of exports, we were stuck because of these distortions. Having an agreement with NAFTA was an opportunity to consolidate all the discounts of the GSP and to eliminate all the sectoral agreements. And that actually resulted in a huge incentive for our exporting system.

So the economic rationale was: let's do NAFTA because we need to be on the world map for foreign investment and to get rid of the distortions of the GSP and sectoral agreements. And this will give an impulse to our exporters and manufacturers to grow dramatically into the US market.

After the Davos meeting, several things happened. There was no way we would have gone into that negotiation without Fast Track. I am extremely surprised that the Trans-Pacific Partnership (TPP) countries are negotiating without Fast Track authority. The Fast Track authority is more important for the other negotiating countries than for the US, and that has to be understood properly. Thus, Fast Track was very important for Mexico, probably more important than it was for the US government. We participated for the first time in the lobbying effort. Fast Track (now Trade Promotion Authority) has nothing to do with timing; it has to do with an up-or-down vote, without amendment.

I was preparing for our first ministerial meeting, and I received a phone call from the Canadian ambassador in Mexico, David Winfield. Three or four months before this, Salinas, Mulroney, and I had a conversation, and I told Prime Minister Mulroney that it would be wonderful to have a trilateral agreement. The rationale for Mexico was to not be alone against the elephant. But Mulroney told us, "No way, we just had our election. It was very close, and the FTA was in the center of the debate. But we will give you all sorts of advice."

Then, with three weeks to go to our first meeting, the Canadian ambassador called me and said they want to be on the table. And I said, "But three months ago, your prime minister told us he didn't want to get involved in that anymore." He said, "Things have changed, we want to be there."

There is another issue which is very relevant: the politics changed dramatically in the US when Bush lost the election, Clinton won the election. During the campaign the position of the Clinton team was not very in favor of a NAFTA agreement. Politically they had a very complicated situation. The negotiation under Bush was a complicated negotiation but, in a way, it was simple because we had an agreement on where we wanted to get to. We knew that we wanted a free trade agreement with no tariffs, with no obstacles to trade, with investment chapters, with intellectual property, with dispute settlement. So a good chunk of the negotiation was how to get there, the transition period. Among other things, the Canadians stayed out of agriculture, we stayed out of energy, and the Americans kept maritime transportation. Except for a few things like that, there was a clear understanding of what we wanted to achieve.

For the second part of the negotiation, under Clinton, the politics around the trade agreement were different. That is where the contributions by Mickey Kantor, Bill Daley, and Ron Brown came in. Our perception was that the side agreements on the environment and labor were a new element of protectionism facing Mexican products. It took us almost a year to negotiate the two side agreements, compared to thirteen or fourteen months to negotiate the main text. If I remember properly, we proposed that the side agreement would incorporate labor and the environment, but the premise of that negotiation would be: "Let's not change the text that is already signed and agreed upon." Fortunately, the Clinton administration, under Mickey's leadership, agreed with that. That was a huge step that facilitated the negotiation, because if we had reopened the text that we had approved a few months before, it would have been a very complicated negotiation, possibly the end of the whole process. I remember at one point when Mickey told me that the agreement was not going to fly with his friend Dick Gephardt. I told Mickey, "Listen. This is such a big issue in Mexico that if it fails, we have to agree on how to announce it, because we are going to have anti-US demonstrations in Mexico. And probably we will actually push for some demonstrations to do some face-saving." We weren't as elegant as you guys when Mulroney talked to Baker. But we did not have to go through that radical scenario. I think it worked out nicely.

B. Transnational law: Domestic effects

The success of the trilateral process of executive negotiation that created NAFTA should not be conflated with the politics of its reception and implementation. This is arguably always the case in international agreements, as the horizontal (*inter*national) and vertical (*intra*national) negotiations unfold separately, even if synergistically.[6] In the case of NAFTA, at every stage of its development, popular opinion opposed the agreement in all three countries, and—as the trade representatives quoted in the previous excerpt indicate—this posed challenges for the negotiators and the national leaders they represented. [7] One analyst characterized the NAFTA

6. Putnam's influential thesis refers to this aspect of international agreement as a "two-level bargaining game." Robert D. Putnam, *Diplomacy and Domestic Politics: The Logic of Two-Level Games*, 42 Int'l Org. 427 (1988).

7. In the United States, popular support has been consistently low, only very recently surpassing a plurality. *See* Siobhan Hughes, *Americans Warming Up to Free Trade—WSJ/NBC Poll*, Wall Street J. (May 4, 2015, 6:34 PM), http://blogs.wsj.com/washwire/2015/05/04/americans-warming-to-free-trade-wsjnbc-poll/; *see also NAFTA Update*, Public Perspective, Nov./Dec. 1993, at 76, http://ropercenter.cornell.edu/public-perspective/ppscan/51/51076.pdf (showing U.S. opinion regarding NAFTA was divided more strongly by education, income and union status than by political party affiliation); William P. Avery, *Domestic Interests in NAFTA Bargaining*, 113 Pol. Sci. Q. 281, 281–82 (1998) (focusing on the debate within the United States, where the strongest opposition involved concerns about the implications of an agreement with Mexico; the U.S.-Canada side of the agreement was less controversial). U.S. opposition reflected concerns about agricultural protections, job losses to Mexico, and environmental vulnerability in the border region. *Id.* at 282.

Mexicans also voiced concerns over the environmental effects of NAFTA, not only in the industrial areas near the border, but also in terms of potential losses of sustainable practices as traditional agriculture gives way to large agri-businesses, and new issues of water insecurity develop as water is diverted to large agri-businesses involved in the export market to the United States. On sustainability and other environmental concerns in Mexico, see Scott Whiteford, et al., *Mexican Environmental Issues and the North American Free Trade Agreement*, Culture & Agric., March 1992, at 7. On water inequality in the export farming regions, see Christian Zlolniski, *Water Flowing North Of The Border: Export Agriculture and Water Politics in a Rural Community in Baja California*, 26 Cultural Anthropology 565 (2011). On Mexico's "overwhelming" popular opposition, see Ann E. Kingsolver, *Stories of Accountability: NAFTA and the Contested Bottom Line*, 5 North Am. Dialogue 6, 7 (2002).

negotiation and ratification processes as subject to "the push and pull of powerful and often contradictory political pressures so intense that agreement on the various trade issues was nearly impossible."[8] The politics of NAFTA promotion deployed conventionalized narratives with regard to various "win/win/win" scenarios with respect to job creation, market integration, capital growth and democratization.[9] Some of these scenarios rested on dubious generalizing assumptions about the ways markets and governments work. For example, the "conventional wisdom" regarding U.S. imports of Mexican grain and meat exaggerated Mexico's share of the agricultural import market in the United States, and NAFTA proponents oversold the prospective benefits of dismantling Canada's agricultural marketing boards.[10] More fundamentally, a stereotyped assessment of Mexico as a corrupt and "childlike" state served both sides in the U.S. debate—as a basis for opposition as well as support, especially for those proponents who subscribed to the "double transition thesis," associating free trade with democratization.[11] More broadly still, the debates over NAFTA contributed to the internationalization of legal studies and social science, advancing scholars' awareness of various forms of transnationalism as ground for new research and theoretical stocktaking.[12]

The Canadian Assembly of First Nations passed two resolutions opposing NAFTA on grounds of its failure to acknowledge indigenous interests in natural resources, including water. Megan Davis, *Identity, Power, and Rights: The State, International Institutions, and Indigenous Peoples in Canada*, *in* THE POLITICS OF RESOURCE EXTRACTION: INDIGENOUS PEOPLES, MULTINATIONAL CORPORATIONS, AND THE STATE 230, 245 (Suzana Sawyer & Edmund Terence Gomez eds. 2012); *see also* D.B. Smith, *Economies at Risk if NAFTA Ignores Native Rights*, 11 WINDSPEAKER 1 (1993), http://www.ammsa.com/node/19214.

8. Avery, *supra* note 7, at 281.

9. President Salinas used the formulation "win/win/win" in his commencement address to the MIT graduating class of 1993, while NAFTA was still being debated in the U.S. Congress. Deborah A. Levinson, *Vest, Salinas Challenge Grads*, THE TECH, June 23, 1993, at 1, http://tech.mit.edu/V113/PDF/V113-N29.pdf.

10. On Mexican agricultural imports, see Annette Higby, *The North American Free Trade Agreement and U.S. Agriculture*, CULTURE & AGRIC., March 1992, at 2. On Canadian grain, see Terry Pugh, *Free Trade Creates Difficulties for Canadian Family Farmers*, CULTURE & AGRIC., March 1992, at 4, 5.

11. On national character stereotypes of Mexico, see Amy Skonieczny, *Constructing NAFTA: Myth, Representation, and the Discursive Construction of U.S. Foreign Policy*, 45 INT'L STUD. Q. 433 (2001), and Suzanne Simon, *Framing the Nation: Law and the Cultivation of National Character Stereotypes in the NAFTA Debate and Beyond*, 30 POL. & LEGAL ANTHROPOLOGY REV. 22 (2007). On the "double transition thesis," see Miguel Angel Centeno, *Between Rocky Democracies and Hard Markets: Dilemmas of the Double Transition*, 20 ANN. REV. SOC. 125 (1994); Pablo Calderón Martínez, *Internationalisation as a Democratic Tool: Revisiting Mexico's Double Transition*, 33 BULL. LATIN AM. RES. 174 (2014).

12. With specific reference to NAFTA, see Centeno, *supra* note 11, at 141 (discussing the need for new field-based research); Sally Merry, *Anthropology and International Law*, 35 ANN. REV. ANTHROPOLOGY 99 (2006); Tamara Kay, *Legal Transnationalism: The Relationship between Transnational Social Movement Building and International Law*, 36 LAW & SOC. INQUIRY 419 (2011); David Schneiderman, *Investment Rules and the New Constitutionalism*, 25 LAW & SOC. INQUIRY 757 (2000); David M. Trubek et al., *Transnationalism in the Regulation of Labor Relations: International Regimes and Transnational Advocacy Networks*, 25 LAW & SOC. INQUIRY 1187 (2000).

But the concerns of NAFTA's critics did not always fit the conventional story line of the "double transition thesis" about the benefits of opening up markets to international investment and competition. The debate sharpened the "cultural and conceptual divide" between labor and environmental protections on the one hand, and profitability on the other; in this context, "many national leaders have come to see themselves as more accountable to transnational entities . . . than to their own publics" and "accountability" became a potent keyword.[13] As trade liberalization in Mexico, Latin America, and elsewhere has brought about conditions in which peasant agriculture (and therefore peasant communities) can no longer survive, agriculture is increasingly given over to large-scale corporate farming, and conversion to demand-driven markets specializing in the export of "sumptuary" products (such as fruits and vegetables that are off-season for northern consumers).[14] In Mexico, it is not surprising, then, that opposition to liberalization was not limited to NAFTA per se, but extended far into the infrastructure of state/local authority as it had been developing since the early 1980s.[15] As anthropologist Rebecca Galemba has observed from her research site at the Mexican-Guatemalan border, the national discourse of "free trade" has been taken up by local authorities and individual entrepreneurs: "Creating an alternative local moral and political economy, border residents' practices challenge both the state's right to control the economy and the hegemonic structures that define what it means to work in the *free* trade era."[16]

The liberalization for Mexico's agricultural sector displaced peasant and indigenous communities from farming, resulting in losses of social integration as precarity drove individuals from the land, to seek employment elsewhere in Mexico and in the United States. Liberalization also created conditions that favored the development of

---

13. Kingsolver, *supra* note 7, at 6.

14. On the effects of liberalization on agriculture (including sumptuary markets) in Latin America and worldwide, see Flavia Echánove & Cristina Steffen, *Coping with Trade Liberalization: The Case of Mexican Grain Producers*, Culture & Agric., September 2003, at 1. In Mexico and Guatemala, see Shannon Speed et al., *Remapping Gender, Justice, and Rights in the Indigenous Americas: Toward a Comparative Analysis and Collaborative Methodology*, 14 J. Latin Am. & Caribbean Anthropology 300 (2009).

15. Kingsolver, *supra* note 7, at 7; June Nash, *Mexico Turns South for its Future*, 6 North Am. Dialogue 6 (2003). On local authorities' participation in their own version of the "free market," see Rebecca B. Galemba, *"Corn is Food, Not Contraband": The Right to "free trade" at the Mexico-Guatemala Border*, 39 Am. Ethnologist 716 (2012); Rebecca B. Galemba, *Taking Contraband Seriously: Practicing "Legitimate Work" at the Mexico-Guatemala Border*, 22 Anthropology Work Rev. 3 (2012).

16. Galemba, *Practicing "Legitimate Work," supra* note 15, at 9 (footnote omitted). On the complex opportunities and vulnerabilities in the post-NAFTA landscape at the most local levels, see anthropologist Kedron Thomas's ethnographic accounts of the blurring of licit and illicit activity among small-scale indigenous garment entrepreneurs in Guatemala, as they confront larger transnational garment firms: Kedron Thomas, *Brand "Piracy" and Postwar Statecraft in Guatemala*, 28 Cultural Anthropology 144 (2013); Kendron Thomas, *Corporations and Community in Highland Guatemala*. 37 Pol. & Legal Anthropology Rev. 231 (2014); Kedron Thomas, *Structural Adjustment, Spatial Imaginaries, and "Piracy" in Guatemala's Apparel Industry*, 30 Anthropology Work Rev. 1 (2009).

export-market factories, or *maquiladoras*. Maquiladoras preceded NAFTA, but NAFTA allowed Mexico to consolidate its reliance on maquiladoras as the engine of its "export-led development strategy," particularly along the northern border and in the central western region of the country.[17] Maquiladoras—mainly assembly plants for electronics and apparel for U.S. (and, increasingly, East Asian) firms—account for Mexico's main non-oil exports. Their products represent one half of all exports, and 55–60 percent of all of Mexico's manufacturing exports.[18] Maquiladoras are highly vulnerable to fluctuating demand from the United States, and recently, transnational firms have begun to leverage their comparative advantage in Mexico by building plants in rural areas, on ejido land (i.e., communal property, formerly farmed).[19]

Maquiladora workers are predominantly women—"cheap labor" is female labor. Electronics assembly draws younger educated urban women; apparel assembly draws uneducated older women, often single mothers, who have been displaced from their homes elsewhere in Mexico.[20] Today, maquiladoras are also manufacturing and assembling auto parts, with no gains in wages for this more complex employment.[21] Working and living conditions—particularly in the northern border region—are notoriously dangerous. Reports of health disparities arising from working conditions in the plants, and living conditions adjacent to the plants, abound, leading one analyst to observe that "the Mexican state has mediated the relationship between global processes of competition and local contexts of violence by transferring the costs of insecurity and restructuring onto maquila workers through downward pressures on wages and benefits."[22] Labor unions have made a positive difference in some locales, pressing for social services and coming forward to block plant relocations.[23] As Professor Fernández-Kelly observes—as the first anthropologist

---

17. Rafael Tamayo-Flores, *NAFTA-Driven Changes in the Regional Pattern of Economic Growth in Mexico: Profile and Determinants*, *in* CHANGING STRUCTURE OF MEXICO: POLITICAL, SOCIAL, AND ECONOMIC PROSPECTS 119 (Laura Randall ed. 2006).

18. On exports, see Tamayo-Flores, *supra* note 17, at 130–31. On emergence of East Asian firms, see Tamayo-Flores, *supra* note 17, at 133. The East Asian presence in maquiladoras has contributed to a reversal of job losses from Mexican maquiladoras to Chinese assembly plants in the early 2000s.

19. Tamayo-Flores, *supra* note 17, at 134–35.

20. MARÍA PATRICIA FERNÁNDEZ-KELLY, FOR WE ARE SOLD, I AND MY PEOPLE: WOMEN AND INDUSTRY ON MEXICO'S FRONTIER 3–4 (1984).

21. Hepzibah Muñoz Martinez, *The Double Burden on Maquila Workers: Violence and Crisis in Northern Mexico* (June 15, 2010), http://www.global-labour-university.org/fileadmin/GLU_conference_2010/papers/26._The_Double_Burden_on_Maquila_Workers_Violence_and_Crisis_in_Northern_Mexico.pdf.

22. *Id.*; *see also* Stephanie Navarro, *Inside Mexico's Maquiladoras: Manufacturing Health Disparities*, http://med.stanford.edu/schoolhealtheval/files/StephanieNavarro_HumBio122MFinal.pdf. On violence in the northern border region, see Gilberto Rosa, *Policing Life and Thickening Delinquency at the New Frontier*, 16 J. LATIN AM. & CARIBBEAN ANTHROPOLOGY 24 (2011). On working conditions, see KATHRYN KOPINAK, DESERT CAPITALISM: MAQUILADORAS IN NORTH AMERICA'S WESTERN INDUSTRIAL CORRIDOR (1996).

23. Muñoz Martinez, *supra* note 21.

to study maquiladoras—international capitalism is a social arrangement that must be understood from the levels of household and community.[24]

C. NAFTA: Government and governance

In Mexico, NAFTA's effects are heterogeneous by region, sector, and product. And although NAFTA has contributed to a dispersal of entrepreneurial energy to cities outside of Mexico City, the trend shows increasing regional disparities (wealthier regions becoming wealthier, and poorer regions becoming poorer).[25] A "new governance nexus" has formed, adjoining interlegalities with the transnational private sector, while simultaneously putting distance between national and local interests—generating new centers and peripheries, new political actors and networks of influence, and a fragmented political space in which NGOs are prevalent.[26] The following excerpt details the role of an important network of NGOs in relation to NAFTA and the development of the World Social Forum (a "global south" counter-globalization movement):

Fernanda Somuano, *Nongovernmental Organizations and the Changing Structure of Mexican Politics*,

in Changing Structure of Mexico 489–500 (Laura Randall ed., 2d ed. 2006)

The impact that NGOs have had upon national and international environmental policies can be analyzed, for example, through their participations in the Global Forum in Rio de Janeiro in 1992, which provided an important and well-publicized opportunity to present the views of various representatives of civil society. As well, the NGOs' presence in the Mexican Action Network Against Free Trade (Red Mexicana de Acción Frente al Libre Comcercio, RMALC) allowed the introduction of the environmental agreements among Mexico, Canada, and the United States. This last

---

24. Fernández-Kelly, *supra* note 20, at 3.

25. Tamayo-Flores, *supra* note 17, at 136.

26. On new centers, see Arthur D. Murphy et al., *The Urban System in the Central Valleys of Oaxaca*. 2 Econ. Anthropology 84, 90 (2015), and Tamayo-Flores, *supra* note 17, at 122. On political transformation of Mexico (growth of NGOs), see Fernanda Somuano, *Nongovernmental Organizations and the Changing Structure of Mexican Politics, in* Changing Structure of Mexico 489–500 (Laura Randall ed., 2d ed. 2006), excerpted below. On the "rescaling" of Mexican governance, see Mildred Warner & Jennifer Gerbasi, *Rescaling and Reforming the State Under NAFTA: Implications for Subnational Authority*, 28 Int'l J. Urb. & Regional Res. 858 (2004). Among the new interlegalities, ethnographers point to the recent resurgence of indigenous law: "The decentralization of justice systems resulted in state recognition and even promotion of so called indigenous law, including the creation of state-funded indigenous courts. This was a response to long-standing indigenous demands for legal and political recognition. In many cases, these legal forums have been established with limited jurisdictional attributes extended to indigenous authorities. Nonetheless, these new official spaces have permitted a renovation of indigenous justice practices and the ways in which particular customs and traditions (themselves in a constant process of re-elaboration) are incorporated as legitimate dimensions of legal procedures." Speed et al., *supra* note 14 (footnotes omitted).

case may serve as an illustration of the main strategies used by these organizations in advancing their goals.

RMALC was formally constituted in April 1991. Although it is not an environmental network, one of RMALC's main wings includes environmental activists and their organizations, and one of its key concerns was the environmental impact on Mexico of the North American Free Trade Agreement (NAFTA). RMALC's concern about NAFTA was based both on negative experience of Canadian workers with the earlier U.S.-Canada free trade agreement, and on the fact that the Mexican government had already begun free trade negotiations with the United States. Many Mexican NGOs and social organizations saw the need to open debate in their country and to improve existing information channels with their North American counterparts.

Besides that, the stated goals of RMALC were: to call for national debate and the public participation in the free trade agreement (FTA); to spread information anmount social organizations about economic integration and its potential costs; to open a permanent space for civil society to reflect on alternative development and to express its opinions and demands; to analyze the impact of free trade on specific sectors; and to define common strategies to influence public opinion and demand of government minimum guarantees that the FTA would not damage the rights or sovereignty of the Mexican people.

In March 1992, three prominent Mexican intellectuals revealed a draft of the FTA (the "Dallas draft," named for the ministry-level trade negotiations in that city), which had been "filtered" to them through the Canada Action Network (CAN). RMALC brought the document to the Mexican Congress and to the attention of the public, analyizing its contents by early April and publicizing its reasons for judging NAFTA to be unfavorable to Mexico (Umlas 1996). The network's most important activity, outside of fomenting regular, informal contact among its Mexican members and its counterparts in the Americas, was its organization or co-sponsorship, with U.S. and Canadian networks, of tri-national and international conferences parallel to official strategies, as several of the conferences were planned and undertaken simultaneously and in the same city as official ministerial negotiations of NAFTA.

RMALC rejected NAFTA because of its lack of consultation with society and lack of public information, and for damage it would do to Mexico's "capacity for self-determination," as well as to particular Mexican sectors. In the medium and long term, RMALC's strategy included the building of a "continental social pact" that was to extend the tri-national solidarity of networks formed around free trade to the rest of the continent. RMALC made extensive use of these ties in Canada, the United States, and Latin America to enable it both to secure documents and data and to help increase the circle of debate about free trade and development throughout the Americas.

With regard to relations with the Mexican government, RMALC also pursued a specific strategy that consisted in recognizing the need to seek a relationship with the state and to influence political parties. In May 1994, RMALC and several

Mexican environmental NGOs and networks called a metting to discuss the composition and functions of the National Consultative Committee, which was provided for in the environmental sidebar agreement of NAFTA, and which in theory would enable citizens to bring environmental complaints to the North American Commission on Environment Cooperation (NACEC), also created in 1994 as part of the environmental sidebar.

After the passage of NAFTA, in addition to its work with environmental organizations to influence NACEC proceedings, RMALC began to monitor NAFTA's effects on environment, labor, and other indicators, and continued to call for the treaty's renegotiation. Moreover, the network formed new goals since NAFTA became a reality. These goals included sharing lessons of RMALC's NAFTA experience with other networks in the region, building more systematic tri-national movement, and strengthening efforts to modify international trade regulations.

Despite a decline in participation in the network since 1994 (because of the natural discouragement due to the passage of NAFTA); the scarcity of resources; the lack of outreach in the Mexican provinces; and the network's inability, due to the lack of funds, to capitalize on its relations with groups abroad, RMALC provides interesting lessons. It has lasted well beyond the passage of NAFTA. It joined many diverse groups, sectors, and themes, and can be seen as an example of an important mulisectoral space for debate, and a provider of information and communication linkages. So, while RMALC could not prevent the passage of NAFTA, it definitely modified the government's agenda on environmental issues and became an actor that government could not easily ignore.

In Canada, the political, legal, economic and social response to NAFTA—as a proposal and as fact—was foreshadowed by the politics of the Canada-US Free Trade Agreement in 1988, which had been intensely fought out and politically, to some extent, settled.[27] Prime Minister Mulroney's election (on a conservative majority in only two of Canada's ten provinces—Alberta and Quebec) was evidence of a coalition between large corporate interests and Quebec nationalists.[28] He moved quickly to shift the FTA into a foreign policy frame, and it was on this ground that NAFTA—after Mulroney announced his retirement from politics—was approved in 1993. The Liberals won the October 1993 elections in part on the pledge to renegotiate NAFTA, but then approved the agreement "almost without revision" when

27. Commentators observe that Canadians' current concerns with regional trade agreements are more focused on pending agreements with the European Union and Asian countries. There is little ethnography to provide details of the Canadian and U.S. responses to NAFTA, or specific effects attributable to NAFTA. *See supra* note 7.

28. Erin Weir, *Canada's Free Trade Agreement with the USA and Mexico: The Exaggeration of North American Trade*, *in* International Trade and Neoliberal Globalism: Towards Re-Peripheralisation in Australia, Canada and Mexico? 88–104, 90 (Paul Bowles et al. eds., 2008).

they came to power.[29] The debate over NAFTA was inseparable from other tensions over sovereignty internal to Canada, particularly between francophone and anglophone communities in Quebec and elsewhere in Canada. Quebec nationalists supported NAFTA in part because they saw its transnationalism (i.e., as a pluralist arrangement of "concurrent sovereignties") as preferable to the integrationist federalism espoused by those who saw in NAFTA the end of Canadian culture and sovereignty. Indeed, the debate over NAFTA in Canada was in certain respects a debate over the relationship of culture, sovereignty, and economy—and the mutually contingent limits of pluralism across Canadian life.[30] Trade with the United States was already important in Canada's economic integration, in particular as between Quebec and the rest of Canada—an "external dependent unity."[31]

The prior effects of liberalization make NAFTA's effects impossible to assess, and—as in the United States—post-NAFTA opinion remains divided. The general consensus among proponents of NAFTA seems to be that the agreement has delivered economic growth, perhaps especially in agriculture; however, critics point to intra-sectoral differences as evidence that businesses involved in export markets are driving down firms that serve a more traditional domestic clientele.[32] First Nations have been consistently opposed to NAFTA since its inception, due to the parties' failure to recognize indigenous rights in natural resources and water; First Nations have brought complaints to the NAFTA secretariat as well as to the WTO.[33] As in the case of Mexico—and, as we shall see, also the United States—the internationalism of NAFTA in each case remains deeply and distinctively enmeshed in the specificities of the national experience and their political, cultural, and economic expression.

D. Government: Verticality—Governance: Horizontality?

So far, we have been emphasizing the separate experiences of the three signatories in relation to NAFTA. Those differences highlight the significance of the ways in which NAFTA set up conditions for political and legal adjustments resulting in particular forms of integration across the three countries. As you read the following excerpt, consider how this transnational agreement simultaneously lengthened the

---

29. *Id.* at 91–92.

30. The discussion of Canadian debates in these terms is based on the analysis of Guy Lachapelle, *Quebec Under Free Trade: Making Policy in North America*, *in* QUEBEC UNDER FREE TRADE 3–24 (Guy Lachapelle ed., 1995).

31. *Id.* at 14–15. *See also* Anne-Marie Cotter, *Quebec in North America: Historical and Socio-Political Dimensions*, *in supra* note 30, at 25–48; Gilles Duruflé & Benoît Tétrault, *The Impact of the Free Trade Agreement on Bilateral Trade between Quebec and the United States*, *in* QUEBEC UNDER FREE TRADE 137–74 (Guy Lachapelle ed., 1995).

32. Duruflé and Tétrault, *supra* note 31, make this point specifically with regard to Quebec.

33. On legal activity by First Nations peoples, see Jack D. Forbes, *A Native American Perspective on NAFTA*, CULTURAL SURVIVAL Q. (1993), http://www.culturalsurvival.org/publications/cultural-survival-quarterly/canada/native-american-perspective-nafta. On NAFTA and WTO litigation in the *Softwood Lumber* case (USA-CDA-2002-2904_03), see Davis, *supra* note 7, at 245.

vertical axis *within* the three countries, and tightened the horizontal axis *across* their respective governments. What accounts for that paradoxical effect? What does that double effect tell us about the relationship of government to transnational governance?

Mark Aspinwall, *NAFTA-ization: Regionalization and Domestic Political Adjustment in the North American Economic Area*,

47 J. Common Mkt. Stud. 1, 7–8, 11, 17, 21 (2009)

Mexican legal and administrative adjustment was more profound [than in USA]. NAFTA-induced changes occurred in Mexican policy on telecommunications, intellectual property rights, automotive sector, competition, monetary policy, inward investment and others. For example, legislative changes were made to allow more liberalization in the auto sector—all three member states created uniform regulations 'regarding the interpretation, application and administration of the rules of origin that they would then entrench in each system of national law [. . .]. NAFTA caused a direct change to the legal and administrative orders affecting auto manufacturing.' Mexico agreed to phase out its 'auto decrees', which included restrictions on imports and foreign ownership of auto producers, as well as domestic content requirements. Likewise, in a 1992 law on anti-trust, Mexico created the Comisión Federal de Competencia. The approaches to property rights, land ownership and the legal framework on competition and corruption all were transformed, according to one observer.

NAFTA resulted in wholesale legal changes to the Mexican trade regime, because it did not have laws on anti-dumping or countervailing duties. It amended its Foreign Trade Law regarding administrative procedures and made adjustments to allow access to information and widen participation in dispute settlement. It also reformed its 1994 Federal Act of Administrative Procedures in 2000 with four main objectives: to increase transparency in drafting regulations, promote public participation, increase legal certainty regarding enforcement and provide that benefits outweigh costs of regulation. In December 1993 Mexico passed a Foreign Investment Law that removed most of the existing restrictions on inward investment. This change was prompted by NAFTA. Thirteen sectors remained shielded from foreign investment, including oil, energy, mining, telecoms and transport. The 1993 law was amended in December 1996 to permit greater foreign investment in communication and transport sectors, and again in September 1998 to streamline administrative procedures. These adaptations were not accidental but were directly the result of the NAFTA agreement.

Yet while institutional adjustment is light, officials from numerous agencies on both sides of the border state that NAFTA has produced a denser network of departmental contacts between US and Mexican agencies. There has been an evolution in the relationship, more conversations about a broader range of issues and a recognition that 'we're all in this together' (*vis-à-vis* competition with Asia and Europe). According to a USTR [U.S. Trade Representative] official, NAFTA 'has made an enormous difference' to contacts with Mexico. Cross-border contacts are very frequent between lower-ranking officials. The discourse has changed as well. Mexico became a promoter of, and believer in, free trade. Incentives have increased to harmonize standards and minimize differences. The member states have initiated a dialogue over BSE,[34] for example, because of the highly developed and integrated nature of meat markets. The same is true of intellectual property rights. Prior to NAFTA, Mexico did not talk about piracy and intellectual property rights issues.

However, there are some important differences between CLC and CEC,[35] reflecting the higher political sensitivity associated with labour issues and the deep reluctance to permit any supranational authority to emerge. The labour side agreement is about enforcing national law, not harmonizing law. The CEC has the authority to collect facts and information, and convene dispute panels, while the CLC does not have these powers (although it does produce reports on the North American labour market). Public submissions on labour matters get resolved with ministerial negotiations and are channelled through national governments. No expert panels are convened by the CLC, which is not part of the public information process. There is no interaction with the public or with interest groups. The CLC must communicate with National Administrative Offices to get information, and communications tend to be on routine administrative issues only. The CLC plays a limited role in forming relationships with NGOs, and there is no direct official contact. Staff must get permission for meetings and get approval for their research. The level of funding for the CLC is lower than for the CEC—about $2.1 million per year from the three governments, whereas the CEC receives about $9 million.

However, despite the nationalistic and intergovernmental approach, NAFTA has brought some important changes. First, according to a well-placed official in the US Labor Department, there is greater collaboration with Mexico and Canada than ever before on this issue, and without the side agreement there would not be this level of interaction. The creation of the CLC and National Administrative Offices brought structures which helped institutionalize co-operation, including information sharing, expertise, meetings, seminars and outreach/education. Moreover, the US government has tended to look more legalistically at Mexico following NAFTA to determine whether they are meeting their legal agreements.

At the same time, there are national, sectoral and institutional variations in the level of political adjustment. National variability denotes far higher pressure to adjust in Mexico than the US. This is not simply because of the power of the US as a hegemonic force *vis-à-vis* Mexico but also the latter's decision that it needed to open its economy and reform its political structures. Adjustment depended on the level of development. There are also sectoral variations. Oil in Mexico and shipping in the US were excluded for example, and some sectors faced only partial liberalizing pressures. In affected sectors with exposure to international competition, patterns of interest demands and bureaucratic activity with counterparts from other member

34. Authors' note: Bovine Spongiform Encephalopathy, known colloquially as "mad cow disease."

35. Authors' note: Commission for Environmental Cooperation (CEC); Commission for Labor Cooperation (CLC).

states have increased. NAFTA therefore has both a territorial/regional component (in its trinational policies and institutions) and a functional component (in its uneven application to economic sectors).

Variations in institutional capacity also affect political adjustment. Both countries' Congresses contain sovereignty-conscious nationalist anti-NAFTA opinion, and so efforts have been made to bypass them. Where they can be bypassed, national executives are more able to achieve adaptation (as on SPP [Security and Prosperity Partnership] issues for example). Executive agreements not requiring legislative approval have been pursued as a more effective way of achieving change.

The importance of the discussion in this chapter so far has been to highlight the range of interests, legal institutions, and law in which NAFTA developed in Canada, Mexico and the United States. We have emphasized the Mexican "case" because it highlights the extent to which the transnational agreement intensified political tensions across various levels of government (especially local and national) in key sectors affected by the agreement.[36] (Indeed, the Mexican "case" is not just one, but many, as NAFTA's context and effects have been highly heterogeneous.) Still, by contrast with the situation in Mexico, one can readily see that the political, social, and economic space of the United States was relatively well suited to NAFTA, in that most of the U.S. population was already living in relative isolation in suburbs, already mobile in relation to job opportunities, and not involved in communal forms of social action such as collective bargaining and local political activity. In the strong "private enterprise culture" of the United States, union membership was on the decline and collective bargaining was pervasively under attack.[37]

As we return to the United States for the rest of this chapter, it is important to recognize the specific conditions that accounted for the political success of the agreement. We turn now to those conditions and the legal process by which NAFTA became law in the United States.

III. Free trade, Congress and executive power

A. Fast track power and NAFTA

As our discussion of NAFTA continues, it is important to understand just how NAFTA came to be. As we will see in the following section, NAFTA was passed pursuant to the President's "fast track authority." Having a basic understanding of fast

---

36. Centeno, *supra* note 11, at 129–131.

37. The characterization of the USA as a "private enterprise culture" is offered by Stephen McBride as a contrast with Canada's public services culture: Stephen McBride, *State Formation and Class Formation within the Global Context: The Political Economy of Canadian Development in a Long-Run Perspectve*, *in* International Trade and Neoliberal Globalism: Towards Re-Peripheralisation in Australia, Canada and Mexico? 75 (Paul Bowles et al. eds., 2008).

track authority is integral to the analysis needed for this next section in our exploration of NAFTA.

Ian F. Fergusson, Cong. Res. Serv., Trade Promotion Authority (TPA) and the Role of Congress in Trade Policy (2015)[38]

For more than 30 years, Congress has granted the President TPA/fast track authority, agreeing to consider trade agreement implementing legislation expeditiously and to vote on it without amendment, provided the President meets certain statutory negotiating objectives and consultation requirements, and the implementing bill contains the necessary and limited qualifying provisions. TPA strikes a delicate balance by clarifying how Congress chooses to exercise its constitutional authority over a particular aspect of trade policy, while presumably giving the President additional negotiating leverage by effectively assuring U.S. trade partners that a final agreement will be given timely and unamended consideration by Congress. Earlier incarnations of TPA, although controversial, were adopted with substantial bipartisan majorities. Over time, however, trade negotiations have become more complex. Congress also has insisted on tighter oversight and consultation requirements, and the trade debate has become more partisan in nature, making congressional renewal of TPA more controversial. The expiration of TPA raises the central questions of whether, when, and in what form TPA renewal might take.

A Brief History of TPA

TPA is the product of many decades of debate, cooperation, and compromise between Congress and the executive branch. At its foundation lie the respective constitutional powers granted to Congress and the President, as well as the pragmatic realization that a certain cooperative flexibility is needed if the United States is to negotiate reciprocal trade agreements credibly. The evolution of TPA to date shows, among other things, that the congressional-executive partnership on trade policymaking can be strengthened or strained as it adjusts to evolving political and economic conditions, as well as shifting priorities of the two branches.

The U.S. Constitution and Foreign Trade

The U.S. Constitution assigns express authority over the regulation of foreign trade to Congress. Article I, Section 8, gives Congress the power to "regulate commerce with foreign nations . . ." and to ". . . lay and collect taxes, duties, imposts, and excises . . . ." In contrast, the Constitution assigns no specific responsibility for trade to the President. Under Article II, however, the President has exclusive authority to negotiate treaties and international agreements and exercises broad authority over the conduct of the nation's foreign affairs. Both legislative and executive authorities come into play in the development and execution of U.S. trade agreements.

38. Available at http://www.fas.org/sgp/crs/misc/RL33743.pdf.

The Evolution of the Congressional-Executive Partnership

For roughly the first 150 years of the United States, Congress exercised its authority over foreign trade by setting tariff rates on all imported products. The tariff was the main trade policy instrument and primary source of federal revenue. Early congressional trade debates pitted Members from northern manufacturing regions, who benefitted from protectionist tariffs, against those from largely southern commodity exporting regions, who advocated low tariffs. During this period, the President's primary role in setting trade policy was to use his foreign affairs authority to negotiate, bring into force, and implement (with the advice and consent of the Senate) general bilateral treaties of friendship, commerce, and navigation. These treaties "included a U.S. commitment to most-favored-nation (MFN) treatment" or nondiscrimination in the application of tariffs for all treaty partners.

Two legislative events occurred in the 1930s that radically changed the shape and conduct of U.S. trade policy. The first was the "Smoot-Hawley" Tariff Act of 1930 (P.L. 71-361), which set prohibitively high tariff rates in response to U.S. producers seeking protection at the outset of the Great Depression. The act led to retaliatory tariffs by major U.S. trade partners, which severely restricted trade and contributed to the deep and prolonged effects of the depression. The damaging effects of Smoot-Hawley prompted the second major trade legislative event in the 1930s. Congress, with the guidance and encouragement of Secretary of State Cordell Hull, himself a former Senator, developed and enacted the Reciprocal Trade Agreements Act of 1934. The RTAA authorized the President to enter into reciprocal trade agreements that reduced tariffs within pre-approved levels. The tariffs were applied on an MFN basis. Under the RTAA, Congress authorized the President to implement the new tariffs by proclamation without additional legislation. The RTAA is important for several reasons:

- For the first time, Congress expressly delegated to the President an expanded trade agreements authority to reduce tariffs within congressionally predefined ranges. In so doing, some argued, Congress aimed to lessen the political pressure from special interests it often faced.
- The Smoot-Hawley Tariff Act was the last general tariff legislation passed by Congress. While still on the books, the Smoot-Hawley tariffs are now only applied to imports from those few countries, namely Cuba and North Korea, not receiving MFN status, now referred to as normal trade relations status (NTR) in U.S. trade laws.
- While delegating tariff-cutting authority, Congress did not surrender broader trade authority and insured legislatively against executive branch overreach by subjecting the trade agreements authority to a limited time period, making such authority subject to periodic review and renewal. Congress renewed presidential reciprocal trade agreements authority for tariff reductions 11 times until 1962 through trade agreement extension acts (see Appendix A [omitted]). General tariff levels declined and their significance as a trade barrier diminished.

> In addition, with the establishment of the General Agreement on Tariffs and Trade (GATT) in 1947, the major forum for trade negotiations shifted from bilateral to multilateral negotiations, and trade negotiations were eventually expanded beyond tariffs.

Under the Trade Expansion Act of 1962, Congress granted the President authority for five years to enter into agreements that negotiated the reduction or elimination of tariffs. The act also expanded Congress's role in the negotiating process by requiring the President to submit for congressional review a copy of each concluded agreement and a presidential statement explaining why the agreement was necessary. It allowed the President to conclude the GATT Kennedy Round (1963–1967), the last round in which tariff reduction was the primary focus of trade negotiations.

Creation of "Fast Track Trade Negotiating Authority"

The results of the Kennedy Round made evident that changes in nontariff barrier rules would increasingly dominate the agenda of future multilateral trade agreements, which would also require changes in U.S. law if the United States were to adhere to them. Concern over presidential encroachment on its legislative authority prompted Congress to seek a legislative remedy. The tariff modification authority in the Trade Expansion Act of 1962 expired on July 1, 1967, but Congress did not renew the authority for seven years as it debated legislative options. The Nixon Administration sought new authority to negotiate the Tokyo Round in the GATT, which Congress granted in the Trade Act of 1974 (P.L. 93-618). As before, the act provided the President with the authority to enter into trade agreements that reduced or eliminated tariffs within certain predefined parameters. To address the critical issue of agreements that required changes in U.S. law beyond tariff modifications, the act stipulated that nontariff barrier agreements entered into under this statute could only enter into force if Congress passed implementing legislation. Some in Congress, however, argued that subjecting implementing legislation to ordinary congressional debate and amendment procedures would defeat a major purpose for delegating trade agreements authority to the President in the first place—to reduce the special interest pressures inherent in trade policymaking. Many Members also recognized an important potential problem: that U.S. trading partners would be reluctant to negotiate agreements that would be subject to unlimited congressional debate and amendment.

As a solution, Congress agreed that each chamber would suspend its ordinary legislative procedures and give trade agreements expedited treatment. The relevant committees would be given limited time to consider implementing bills. Once they reached the floor, the implementing bills would be subject to time-limited debate and no amendments. In exchange, Congress required the executive branch to consult with relevant committees during the negotiations and to notify Congress 90 calendar days before signing an agreement. The act also provided for the accreditation of 10 Members of Congress as advisers to the U.S. delegation of negotiators.

With the trade "negotiating" authority and the "fast track" provisions of the Trade Act of 1974, the United States concluded the Tokyo Round of the GATT (1973–1979).

As expected, this round resulted in a number of agreements on NTBs, such as government procurement practices, product standards, customs regulations, and rules for administering antidumping and countervailing duty procedures. The resulting Trade Agreements Act of 1979 was the first trade implementing bill passed by Congress under the expanded trade agreements authority and expedited procedures.

Subsequent Renewals of Trade Agreements Authority

The expedited legislative procedures have not changed since first enacted in 1974. These provisions are ensconced in Sections 151–154 of the Trade Act of 1974, as amended, and are not subject to sunset provisions. The ability to use them, however, is subject to time limits, and Congress has revised them over the years.

The Bipartisan Trade Promotion Authority Act (BTPA) of 2002

In 2001, President George W. Bush requested a renewal of fast track authority. It was renamed in the legislation "trade promotion authority (TPA)," in part to counter what many viewed as a negative connotation associated with the term fast-track. The renewed authority is contained in the Bipartisan Trade Promotion Authority Act (BTPA) of 2002, which was enacted as Title XXI of The Trade Act of 2002.

The structure of TPA was consistent with previous trade agreements authority. It included new language for labor and environmental provisions, defining them as "principal negotiating objectives." TPA did not mandate the inclusion of minimal enforceable labor standards in trade agreements, one reason labor groups and many Members of Congress opposed it. The act also created a new mechanism for congressional consultation, the Congressional Oversight Group (COG), to operate in addition to the congressional trade advisors that were appointed under previous versions.

B. Negotiating NAFTA

As noted above, the public debate over NAFTA was driven by cross-currents that posed tough navigational challenges for the negotiators. In the following excerpt, William Avery tracks those currents, and their relevance to the "fast-track" debate (explained above) that was essential to the passage of the agreement.

William P. Avery, *Domestic Interests in NAFTA Bargaining*,

113 Pol. Sci. Q. 281, 283–91 (1998)*

The Market-Opening Coalition

In the early stages, attitudes toward the agreement were mixed within the Bush administration. The National Security Council and Department of State were strong backers, but U.S. Trade Representative Carla Hills feared NAFTA might interfere with negotiations in the Uruguay Round of the General Agreement of Tariffs and Trade

* Reprinted by permission from *Political Science Quarterly*, 113 (Summer 1998): 283–292. Original notes are indicated by bracketed numerals.

(GATT). Hills eventually concluded that the NAFTA negotiations might actually strengthen the U.S. hand in the GATT talk, where U.S. negotiating positions had experienced some rough sledding. In the end, the major players on trade in the Bush administration formed a solid bloc of NAFTA support.

Outside the Bush administration, support for the agreement was strongest among American business leaders. A survey conducted just after the agreement was signed showed that 72 percent of business executives supported NAFTA.[39] A broad coalition of business leaders joined the administration in promoting the agreement, led by the U.S. Chamber of Commerce, congres sional supporters (largely Republicans), a variety of agricultural groups, and even some environmentalists. The market-opening calition actually had formed a year earlier during the battle over congressional approval for the extension of fast-track authority for NAFTA. Such authority in a trade agreement requires Congress to consider the treaty in an up or down vote, without amendment, and within a specific period of time. Defeat on fast-track probably would have doomed the negotiations even before they got underway. Thus, for supporters of a free trade agreement, the fast-track vote in effect became a referendum on the agreement itself.

In recognition of the importance of the fast-track vote, "corporate America assembled a virtual lobbying Who's Who, including corporate chiefs from American Express Co., Eastman Kodak Co., Procter & Gamble Co. and many other blue-chip concerns."[40] Business supporters formed an umbrella organization called the Coalition for Trade Expansion that included more than 500 corporations and lobbyists. Five key business trade associations were represented in this coalition: the Business Roundtable, U.S. Chamber of Commerce, Emergency Committee for American Trade, National Association of Manufacturers, and National Foreign Trade Council.[41]

Much of the supportive infrastructure for NAFTA was provided by an extensive private-sector advisory system, first mandated by Congress in the Trade Act of 1974. The purpose of the advisory system was to facilitate consultation between the executive and domestic interests in shaping trade policy and to provide a base of support for the policies formulated. Coordinated by the Office of the U.S. Trade Representative (USTR), approximately 1,000 advisers are involved in a system that is similar to Stephen Cohen's description of U.S. trade policy making as a "multilayered pyramid of lobbying activity."[42]

At the top of the pyramid is the Advisory Committee for Trade Policy and Negotiations. The ACTPN has forty-four members, mostly top business leaders, representing

39. [4] "Survey Finds NAFTA Favored by 72% of U.S. Executives," *Journal of Commerce*, 24 September 1992, 12A.

40. [5] Jill Abramson, "U.S.-Mexico Trade Pact Is Pitting Vast Armies of Capitol Hill Lobbyists against Each Other," *Wall Street Journal*, 25 April 1991.

41. [6] *Ibid.*

42. [7] Stephen D. Cohen, *The Making of United States International Economic Policy: Principles, Problems, and Proposals for Reform*, 4th ed. (Westport, CT: Praeger, 1994), 125.

a cross-section of America's major economic sectors. The second level has seven committees that provide sector-specific advice from industry, agriculture, labor, and so on. A third level includes the numerous technical and sectoral advisory committees that provide the detailed information needed to assess the likely impact of trade policy on specific sectors. Although the USTR need not follow their recommendations, the committees must be informed of all "significant departures," and their views are communicated to Congress.

Altogether, this advisory system submitted thirty-seven reports on NAFTA. The report of the most senior panel, the Advisory Committee for Trade Policy and Negotiations, strongly endorsed NAFTA, with only the labor representatives dissenting. James Robinson III, chair of the panel and head of American Express, said the trade agreement would "enhance the international competitiveness of U.S. companies."[43] He praised the Bush administration for working closely with the private sector in the NAFTA negotiations, noting that nearly 1,000 meetings had been held with trade negotiators and government officials.[44] In Congress, a bipartisan coalition formed in both chambers to provide majority backing for fast-track authority. Although predominantly Republican, key members of the Democratic leadership also voted for the extension. In the House of Representatives, Speaker Thomas Foley (D-WA), Majority Leader Richard Gephardt (D-MO), and Ways and Means Committee Chair Dan Rostenkowski (D-IL) all supported fast-track. Gephardt, whose support for NAFTA was never very firm, later defected on final ratification. Strong support in the Senate came from Majority Leader George Mitchell (D-ME) and Finance Committee Chair Lloyd Bentsen (D-TX). The House vote was 231–192, with only ninety-one Democrats voting in the majority. On the Senate side, twenty-three Democrats joined thirty-six Republicans in a 59–36 vote to defeat a resolution to deny fast-track authority.[45]

Support for NAFTA among agricultural groups was mixed throughout the negotiations, reflecting the great diversity of interests in American agriculture. Perhaps nowhere was this diversity more evident than in the Agricultural Policy Advisory Committee (APAC), one of the sector-specific advisory committees within the president's private sector advisory system. APAC played an important role in the negotiations, largely because of the broad range of farm interests and groups it represented. It served as a forum where farms groups could express their views on the agricultural issues that emerged in the negotiations.[46] And while APAC could never speak with one voice on all issues, reflecting as it does the fragmented nature of American agricultural interests, it did provide a significant base of support for the agreement. In its report to the USTR, APAC concluded that "the proposed NAFTA agreement

43. [8] Japan Economic Institute, "Participation of the Private Sector in U.S. Trade Policymaking: The North American Free Trade Agreement as Case Study," *J EI Report* 39A (16 October 1992): 4.

44. [9] *Ibid.*

45. [10] Guy Gugliotta, "House Vote Backs Bush on Trade," *Washington Post,* 24 May 1991.

46. [11] W.A. Boutwell, president of the National Council of Farmer Cooperatives, interview with author, 4 February 1993.

provides long term net export growth opportunities for U.S. agriculture and is in the economic interest of the United States."[47] Recognizing that all trade agreements have winners and losers, APAC acknowledged that its objective of export growth opportunities could not be achieved for every commodity.

Grain producers were among NAFTA's strongest agricultural supporters for simple and straightforward reasons. In virtually every grain commodity, American farmers already had a commanding lead in trade with Mexico. Lowering trade barriers was expected to produce even more opportunities for grain exports. Wesley Peterson claims that NAFTA may lead to increased U.S. grain exports "even if . . . markets are only partially liberalized."[48] According to the *Wall Street Journal,* U.S. corn exports to Mexico "could easily double under free trade."[49] It is no surprise that two of the staunchest members of the market-opening coalition were the National Corn Growers Association and the U.S. Feed Grains Council.

One of America's largest farm organizations, the American Farm Bureau Federation, invested considerable time and effort in support of the agreement. The bureau commissioned a four-volume study of NAFTA's impact on various agricultural sectors[50] and sponsored four study missions to Mexico by about twenty representatives of their state organizations. The conclusion reached was that American agriculture "had less to fear than some people thought."[51] The bureau became an active supporter of fast-track authority and ratification, even organizing a coalition of supportive groups to lobby Congress.

A key decision by the bureau early in the negotiations was to oppose all exemptions in the accord. Farm Bureau officials wanted to avoid what had happened in the free trade agreement with Canada, where large product groups (dairy, peanuts, cotton, sugar, and sweeteners, known as Section 22 products) were excluded from free trade provisions. They argued that if the United States tried to exempt such products, for example, as fresh fruits and vegetables, Mexico would almost certainly protect corn. The bureau opposed all exemptions in order to gain access to Mexico's grain markets. As a spokesman for the bureau told this writer, "We wouldn't have much of an agreement, if we allowed the exceptions."[52]

---

47. [12] Agricultural Policy Advisory Committee (APAC), "Report of the Agricultural Policy Advisory Committee Regarding the North American Free Trade Agreement," unpublished document, n.d.

48. [13] E. Wesley F. Peterson, "The Implications of a Free Trade Agreement with Mexico for U.S. Grain and Oilseed Exports" in American Farm Bureau Federation, *NAFTA: Effects on Agriculture,* vol. 3 (Park Ridge, IL: American Farm Bureau Research Foundation, 1991), 27.

49. [14] Bob Davis, "U.S., Mexico on Verge of Agreement on Crops, Computers in Trade Talks," *Wall Street Journal,* 17 July 1992, A2. Trade in corn, which is probably Mexico's most politically sensitive commodity, would gradually become duty free over a fifteen-year period, as Mexican licenses are removed and U.S. export quotas expanded.

50. [15] See American Farm Bureau Federation, *NAFTA: Effects on Agriculture,* 4 vols.

51. [16] Paul A. Drazek, director of governmental relations, American Farm Bureau Federation, interview with author, 3 February 1993.

52. [17] *Ibid.*

The market-opening coalition included two more sources of support that warrant mention: the American consumer (or public opinion) and some environmental groups. Most public opinion polls revealed fairly broad support for free trade with Mexico, although that support slipped some as the recession tightened in 1992 and opponents became more vocal.[53] Favorable public opinion probably created some space within which congressional support could be built in the crucial battle for fast-track authority and later in the vote on the agreement itself.

As for the environmental groups, many opposed the treaty, but some did not. America's largest environmental group, the National Wildlife Federation, voiced qualified support early on for fast-tracking the agreement. In fact, as a member of one of the seven sector advisory groups (investment), the federation worked closely with the Bush administration to ensure the agreement would have adequate environmental safeguards.

The federation and other environmental groups were concerned about Mexico's existing environmental problems, especially in Mexico City and along the U.S.-Mexico border. The *New York Times* described the air in Mexico City as "an unequaled collection of atmospheric poisons."[54] Along the border, rapid and unplanned industrial development spurred by Mexico's expanding *maquiladora* program has produced contaminated water, careless and improper toxic waste disposal, and extensive degradation of air quality.[55] Environmentalists feared the free trade agreement would accelerate investment and production along the border and in Mexico City, exacerbating an already serious problem. Concern also was expressed about Mexico's lax enforcement of its environmental laws. It was argued that firms would move south to avoid tougher laws and enforcement in the United States and Canada.

President George Bush sought to assuage these concerns early on by promising to address environmental issues directly in the treaty itself and in cooperative bilateral agreements. In the end, six environmental groups, representing about seven million members, became part of the market-opening coalition. Joining the National Wildlife Federation were the Natural Resources Defense Council, World Wildlife Fund, National Audubon Society, Environmental Defense Fund, and Conservation International.[56]

The Status Quo Coalition

Opposition to the agreement formed early and strong. Organized under the name Citizen Trade Campaign, the status quo coalition included more than sixty

53. [18] "US, Canada, Mexico Reach North American Trade Agreement," *Facts on File,* 13 August 1992, 582.

54. [19] Mark Uhlig, "Mexico City's Toxic Residue Worsens Already Filthy Air," 12 May 1991, 1.

55. [20] Mexico's *maquiladora* program was set up in the 1960s to improve the nation's export performance. The program provides government incentives for assembly-oriented manufacturing plants that export most or all of the production. For instance, the plants are permitted to import components duty-free if the products are then exported. *Maquiladoras* were required to locate along the border with the United States.

56. [21] Keith Schneider, "Environment Groups Are Split on Support for Free-Trade Pact," *New York Times,* 16 September 1993.

organizations representing labor unions, environmental and consumer advocacy groups, some segments of agriculture, Jesse Jackson's Rainbow Coalition, and some religious and civic groups. The coalition claimed to represent more than 45 million people in all fifty states, with operations in thirty-eight states, including field staff in twenty-five states.[57] Led by organized labor, in particular the AFL-CIO, opponents began lobbying Congress against fast-track as early as autumn 1990, long before the pro-NAFTA coalition began its push. Arguments against the agreement ranged from loss of American jobs to concern about the reappearance of screwworm infestation in cattle.

By far the strongest opposition to NAFTA came from U.S. labor unions. The AFL-CIO disputed White House claims that free trade would create 44,000 to 150,000 new American jobs, charging that "tens of thousands" of jobs would flow to low-wage Mexico.[58] Economists for the labor-supported Economic Policy Institute claimed that because of increased investment in Mexico, "550,000 fewer high-paying jobs will be created in the United States with the trade pact than without it during the next 10 years."[59] At one point, the institute issued a report claiming "that 7.4 million manufacturing jobs currently located in the United States are *vulnerable* to relocation to Mexico. . . ."[60] A top AFL-CIO official called the agreement "a bad deal for American workers, consumers, and the long-term health of the American economy."[61]

Although not directly linked to the Citizens Trade Campaign, Ross Perot and his organization, United We Stand America, echoed many of the arguments put forward by organized labor. In a book co-written with Pat Choate in 1993, Perot criticized the agreement because among other things he believed American jobs would be lost to Mexico partly because of large differentials in wages. In a published debate between Choate and Deputy U.S. Trade Representative Rufus Yerxa, Choate cited figures showing Mexican workers earning one-seventh the wages of American workers. Choate also said that "by Mexico's own estimates, investors gain $15,000 or more per U.S. job that is shifted to Mexico." Choate concluded that "for U.S. companies undecided about moving to Mexico, NAFTA removes the remaining impediments and doubts."[62]

In addition to fears of job losses, labor leaders also charged that NAFTA did not protect worker rights and workplace standards in Mexico. They insisted that the

57. [22] Citizens Trade Campaign, "An Introduction to the Citizens Trade Campaign," Washington, DC, Mimeographed.

58. [23] Peter Truell and Eduardo Lachica, "Administration Gets Tough on Trade as Congress Gets Set to Vote on Extending Negotiating Power," *Wall Street Journal*, 29 April 1991.

59. [24] Stuart Auerbach, "Accord's Losers, Winners," *Washington Post*, 13 August 1992.

60. [25] T. Lee, "Jobs Vulnerable to Relocation Due to NAFTA: A State-by-State Breakdown," *Economic Policy Institute* (23 October 1992): 3.

61. [26] Stuart Auerbach, "US, Canada and Mexico Agree to Form Trade Bloc," *Washington Post*, 13 A ugust 1992.

62. [27] Rufus Yerxa and Pat Choate, "The Great NAFTA Debate," *Washington Post*, 3 October 1993.

agreement allow for trade sanctions should Mexico fail to respect workers' rights to organize and bargain collectively. Labor also demanded that sanctions be permitted to force "the establishment of strong workplace health and safety standards, appropriate minimum wage structures, the elimination of child labor, a prohibition on forced labor, and guarantees of nondiscrimination in employment."[63] Among other labor demands was "a prohibition on transferring work or workers across borders in the event of a labor dispute, and a prohibition on trade while a labor dispute is in progress."[64]

Many of the major environmental groups in the United States opposed the agreement on grounds that most Mexican environmental laws are weak or non-existent and not vigorously enforced. Such groups as the Sierra Club and Greenpeace pointed out that, for example, Mexico has no standards regulating emissions from paint coatings and solvents, while tough rules in California require cutting solvents by 93 percent in 1996.[65]

Such differences in environmental standards, they contend, would greatly accelerate job flight from U.S. companies under free trade. A spokesman for Friends of the Earth, responding to the Bush administration's claim that tougher Mexican environmental standards will follow economic growth, said: "The president's plan is flawed. What he is saying is that Mexico's environment will get better only as they get rich. . . . The president is throwing a party and hoping you collect enough at the door to buy a vacuum cleaner."[66]

Advocacy groups such as Ralph Nader's Public Citizen and the Child Labor Coalition also opposed the agreement. In fact, Public Citizen was one of the most active leaders of the status quo coalition. Nader's opposition was based largely on environmental concerns. He claimed that the trade pact would force the United States to abandon its own laws protecting health and the environment. He warned that American "laws on pesticide residues in food, contaminated food, and disposal of hazardous waste" would be victimized by free trade with Mexico.[67] Lori Wallach, a staff attorney for Public Citizen, raised another objection to the agreement in congressional testimony on NAFTA. She argued against the treaty because "rules are set and disputes are settled in an entirely anti-democratic fashion by unelected, unaccountable trade bureaucrats lobbied heavily by industry interests."[68] The Child Labor Coalition expressed concerns about exploitation of child labor under poorly enforced laws in Mexico.

---

63. [28] AFL-CIO, *NAFTA Action Source Book* (Washington, DC: AFL-CIO Task Force on Trade, n.d.), 3.

64. [29] *Ibid.*, 5.

65. [30] John Dillin, "Mexico's Pollution Threatens Free Trade," *Christian Science Monitor*, 13 May 1991.

66. [31] *Ibid.*

67. [32] "Review & Outlook," *Wall Street Journal*, 29 April 1991.

68. [33] U.S. House of Representatives, *North American Free Trade Agreement: American Jobs and Environmental Protection*, Hearing before the Subcommittee on International Economic Policy and Trade, Committee on Foreign Affairs, 102nd Congress, 1st sess., 9 December 1991, 39.

Agricultural groups in the status quo coalition tended to be linked to specific commodities. Among those most opposed were sugar, dairy, cotton, and peanut producers. In the agreement with Canada, they won a hard-fought battle for exemption from liberalization. In NAFTA, however, they will be subjected to gradual market-opening requirements that over some years will completely liberalize trade with Mexico in these products. Even though peanut and sugar producers are given the longest transition time (fifteen years), their opposition to the accord remained strong. Peanut growers even threatened an expensive television campaign to warn U.S. consumers of "danger" from imported peanuts.[69]

U.S. sugar producers long have been shielded from foreign competition under a GATT arrangement that permits only a small quota of sugar to be imported. The result is that American sugar producers receive 21 cents per pound for a commodity that sells on the world market for less than half that price. The U.S. sugar quota is currently at 1.5 million tons, which makes up the difference between domestic annual production and demand. Early in the negotiations, Mexico, also a net importer of sugar, sought to acquire all of this quota. Opponents of this proposal argued that since Mexican sugar production does not even cover domestic demand, Mexico would merely import cheap Cuban sugar to meet domestic demand and export its crop to the United States and reap huge profits. A spokesman for the National Farmers Union accused Mexico of already "going through the paperwork to be an exporter [of sugar]."[70]

American farmers most threatened by trade liberalization were fresh fruit and vegetable growers. The old system of complementary tariffs imposed duties on Mexican imports during the U.S. harvest season that dropped off to little or nothing for the rest of the year, thus protecting American growers from head-to-head competition with cheaper Mexican fruit and vegetables. NAFTA eventually uproots this protective tariff arrangement. For this reason, Florida farmers, especially those who grow oranges for juice concentrate, fiercely opposed the trade agreement, insisting that all winter fruit and vegetables be exempted. They provide more than half the nation's supply of winter produce crops, but share a growing season with Mexico. Dan Gunter, head of the Department of Citrus for the State of Florida, said: "if Mexico is given duty-free entry into the U.S., Florida orange juice will be but a memory. "[71]

California's produce growers shared many of the Florida growers' concerns. California accounts for about 90 percent of U.S. processed tomatoes, but could be damaged by imports from Mexico, where farm laborers are paid only about $4 per day. The California Tomato Growers Association claimed that Mexico already places tomatoes in the U.S. market at prices far below what American growers can match. Other similarly situated products are broccoli, cucumbers, table grapes,

69. [34] "NAFTA Watch," *Business Latin America,* 7 September 1992, 316.

70. [35] Scott Pendleton, "NAFTA Will Benefit US Agriculture in the Long Run," *Christian Science Monitor,* 13 August 1992.

71. [36] Scott Armstrong and Daniel D. Wood, "US Farmers Wary of Trade Pact with Mexicans," *Christian Science Monitor,* 28 May 1991.

and peppers.[72] Data reported by the American Farm Bureau Federation suggest this may be true. After trade barriers between Mexico and the United States began to fall in the mid-1980s, Mexican vegetable exports to the United States increased substantially.[73] Fearing this trend would grow, California tomato growers pressed for a transition period of more than twenty years, including "snap-back" protection.[74]

Avocado growers in California also mounted stiff opposition to the trade pact. The issue for them was not loss of tariff protection, but loss of a total ban on avocado imports from Mexico dating back to 1914. The ban existed because U.S. growers had claimed that Mexican avocados were infested with seed weevils and other pests that could destroy the entire American avocado industry. Mexico disputed this and countered that U.S. growers were merely protecting their market from a more competitively priced product. Lifting the ban would mean about $100 million in Mexican avocado exports to the United States and that the American consumer would see an immediate and dramatic drop in price.

During NAFTA negotiations, California avocado farmers insisted on retaining the ban, saying that no transition period was slow enough for them.[75] Agricultural opponents to free trade with Mexico had two important allies: a majority of congressional Democrats and the National Farmers Union, an organization representing about two million family farmers. The Farmers Union also provides a fairly solid base of electoral support for the Democratic party and its candidates among farm constituencies. Although some prominent Democrats gave qualified support for the agreement, most Democrats in the House and Senate did not. They sided with the objections raised by labor and other opponents of the agreement. In general, the Democratic party is not as likely to extend unqualified support to free trade as a matter of economic principle as is the Republican party. Moreover, Democrats were reluctant to go against unified labor opposition to NAFTA, because labor forms an important part of their financial and electoral support. During the congressional debate over fast-track, the Democratic National Committee (DNC) issued a formal statement opposing the agreement.[76]

The Farmers Union was an eager participant in the status quo coalition, although a spokesman was reluctant to characterize its position as protectionist. In an interview with this writer, the Union's chief Washington lobbyist rarely mentioned direct economic objections to agricultural provisions of the NAFTA. Instead, repeated references were made to the familiar arguments advanced by labor and environmental

72. [36] *Ibid.*, 2.

73. [38] American Farm Bureau Federation, *NAFTA*, vol. 4, 28.

74. [39] "Snapback" was designed as a special safeguard provision to protect against the damaging effects of import surges. When duty-free imports of certain products rise above pre-established trigger levels, the previous tariffs on those products could be reimposed by the importing country.

75. [40] Juanita Darling, "Fearing a Bitter Harvest," *Los Angeles Times*, 16 March 1992.

76. [41] Ronald Brownstein and Karen Tumulty, "Mexico Free-Trade Pact Faces Hard Sell in Congress," *Los Angeles Times*, 6 April 1991.

groups.[77] One analyst suggested that "since the arguments in favor of an agreement are compelling, opponents are casting about for noneconomic arguments to torpedo (the agreement)."[78] Whether this was the case with the Farmers Union is not clear, although it would appear far easier to base one's objection on protection of American health, jobs, and the environment than on more narrowly defined self interests.

The configuration of preferences and coalitions at the domestic level (Level II) divided along distinct lines, separating those who favored market opening and those who did not. As Putnam's analysis anticipated, the most significant disagreement among Level II constituencies was over whether the trade agreement with Mexico was better than no agreement at all. A spokesman for the Farm Bureau put it in precisely those terms: "NAFTA may not be perfect, but it is much better than no agreement at all."[79] Others took the opposite position. For them, the agreement suffered "fatal flaws" and was worse than no agreement.[80]

Putnam sees negotiators at Level I using such preference divisions to strengthen their hands in the negotiations. By constantly "looking over their shoulder" at Level II opponents, negotiators may try to squeeze additional concessions from the other side.[81] He cautions, however, that the effect of such Level II divisions may be reduction of the prospects for reaching a Level I agreement. If either side in the negotiations comes to doubt the ability of the other to deliver on promises made, it can undermine potential for agreement. "Credibility," Putnam argues," (and thus the ability to strike deals) at Level I is enhanced by a negotiator's (demonstrated) ability to 'deliver' at Level II."[82]

IV. Territoriality and jurisdiction

A. NAFTA in the idiom of national security

Upon NAFTA's passage, the U.S. press credited the new president, Bill Clinton, with legislative finesse. Significantly, President Clinton's speech celebrating NAFTA's passage leaned heavily on the idiom of national security—comparing NAFTA to the creation of NATO in the aftermath of the second world war. As we shall see later in this chapter, the link to national security was no mere metaphor; it was an assertion of the constitutionality of NAFTA.

The following excerpt is drawn from the concluding paragraphs of President Clinton's comments at the signing ceremony on December 8, 1993—a sweeping statement linking globalization (as free trade) to national security and national

77. [42] Michael V. Dunn, vice president for legislative services, National Farmers Union, interview with author, 4 February 1993.

78. [43] M.D. Baer, "Salinas's Achilles' Heel," *Christian Science Monitor,* 5 December 1990.

79. [44] Drazek interview with author.

80. [45] Dunn interview with author.

81. [46] Putnam, "Diplomacy and Domestic Politics," 444.

82. [47] *Ibid.*, 439.

competitiveness. Note the evocations of military security in his rhetoric, in the reference to world wars, NATO and, especially at the close, to a U.S. victory.

Bill Clinton, President of the United States, Remarks on the Signing of NAFTA (December 8, 1993)[83]

Today we have the chance to do what our parents did before us. We have the opportunity to remake the world. For this new era, our national security we now know will be determined as much by our ability to pull down foreign trade barriers as by our ability to breach distant ramparts. Once again, we are leading. And in so doing, we are rediscovering a fundamental truth about ourselves: When we lead, we build security, we build prosperity for our own people.

We've learned this lesson the hard way. Twice before in this century, we have been forced to define our role in the world. After World War I we turned inward, building walls of protectionism around our Nation. The result was a Great Depression and ultimately another horrible World War. After the Second World War, we took a different course: We reached outward. Gifted leaders of both political parties built a new order based on collective security and expanded trade. They created a foundation of stability and created in the process the conditions which led to the explosion of the great American middle class, one of the true economic miracles in the whole history of civilization. Their statecraft stands to this day: the IMF and the World Bank, GATT, and NATO.

In this very auditorium in 1949, President Harry Truman signed one of the charter documents of this golden era of American leadership, the North Atlantic Treaty that created NATO. "In this pact we hope to create a shield against aggression and the fear of aggression," told his audience, "a bulwark which will permit us to get on with the real business of Government and society, the business of achieving a fuller and happier life for our citizens."

Now, the institutions built by Truman and Acheson, by Marshall and Vandenberg, have accomplished their task. The cold war is over. The grim certitude of the contest with communism has been replaced by the exuberant uncertainty of international economic competition. And the great question of this day is how to ensure security for our people at a time when change is the only constant.

Make no mistake, the global economy with all of its promise and perils is now the central fact of life for hard-working Americans. It has enriched the lives of millions of Americans. But for too many those same winds of change have worn away at [the] basis of their security. For two decades, most people have worked harder for less. Seemingly secure jobs have been lost. And while America once again is the most productive nation on Earth, this productivity itself holds the seeds of further insecurity. After all, productivity means the same people can produce more or, very often, that fewer people can produce more. This is the world we face.

---

83. Available at http://millercenter.org/president/speeches/speech-3927.

We cannot stop global change. We cannot repeal the international economic competition that is everywhere. We can only harness the energy to our benefit. Now we must recognize that the only way for a wealthy nation to grow richer is to export, to simply find new customers for the products and services it makes. That, my fellow Americans, is the decision the Congress made when they voted to ratify NAFTA.

I am gratified with the work that Congress has done this year, bringing the deficit down and keeping interest rates down, getting housing starts and new jobs going upward. But we know that over the long run, our ability to have our internal economic policies work for the benefit of our people requires us to have external economic policies that permit productivity to find expression not simply in higher incomes for our businesses but in more jobs and higher incomes for our people.

That means more customers. There is no other way, not for the United States or for Europe or for Japan or for any other wealthy nation in the world. That is why I am gratified that we had such a good meeting after the NAFTA vote in the House with the Asian-Pacific leaders in Washington.

I am gratified that, as Vice President Gore and Chief of Staff Mack McLarty announced 2 weeks ago when they met with President Salinas, next year the nations of this hemisphere will gather in an economic summit that will plan how to extend the benefits of trade to the emerging market democracies of all the Americas.

And now I am pleased that we have the opportunity to secure the biggest breakthrough of all. Negotiators from 112 nations are seeking to conclude negotiations on a new round of the General Agreement on Tariffs and Trade; a historic world, de trade pact, one that would spur a global economic boon, is now within our grasp. Let me be clear. We cannot, nor should we, settle for a bad GATT agreement. But we will not flag in our efforts to secure a good one in these closing days. We are prepared to make our contributions to the success of this negotiation, but we insist that other nations do their part as well. We must not squander this opportunity. I call on all the nations of the world to seize this moment and close the deal on a strong GATT agreement within the next week. I say to everyone, even to our negotiators: Don't rest. Don't sleep. Close the deal. I told Mickey Kantor the other day that we rewarded his laborious effort on NAFTA with a vacation at the GATT talks. [Laughter]

My fellow Americans, bit by bit all these things are creating the conditions of a sustained global expansion. As significant as they are, our goals must be more ambitious. The United States must seek nothing less than a new trading system that benefits all nations through robust commerce but that protects our middle class and gives other nations a chance to grow one, that lifts workers and the environment up without dragging people down, that seeks to ensure that our policies reflect our values.

Our agenda must, therefore, be far reaching. We are determining that dynamic trade cannot lead to environmental despoliation. We will seek new institutional arrangements to ensure that trade leaves the world cleaner than before. We will press for workers in all countries to secure rights that we now take for granted, to organize and earn a decent living. We will insist that expanded trade be fair to our businesses and to our regions. No country should use cartels, subsidies, or rules of entry to keep our products off its shelves. And we must see to it that our citizens have the personal security to confidently participate in this new era. Every worker must receive the education and training he or she needs to reap the rewards of international competition rather than to bear its burdens.

Next year, our administration will propose comprehensive legislation to transform our unemployment system into a reemployment and job retraining system for the 21st century. And above all, I say to you we must seek to reconstruct the broad-based political coalition for expanded trade. For decades, working men and women and their representatives supported policies that brought us prosperity and security. That was because we recognized that expanded trade benefited all of us but that we have an obligation to protect those workers who do bear the brunt of competition by giving them a chance to be retrained and to go on to a new and different and, ultimately, more secure and more rewarding way of work. In recent years, this social contract has been sundered. It cannot continue.

When I affix my signature to the NAFTA legislation a few moments from now, I do so with this pledge: To the men and women of our country who were afraid of these changes and found in their opposition to NAFTA an expression of that fear—what I thought was a wrong expression and what I know was a wrong expression but nonetheless represented legitimate fears—the gains from this agreement will be your gains, too.

I ask those who opposed NAFTA to work with us to guarantee that the labor and side agreements are enforced, and I call on all of us who believe in NAFTA to join with me to urge the Congress to create the world's best worker training and retraining system. We owe it to the business community as well as to the working men and women of this country. It means greater productivity, lower unemployment, greater worker efficiency, and higher wages and greater security for our people. We have to do that.

We seek a new and more open global trading system not for its own sake but for our own sake. Good jobs, rewarding careers, broadened horizons for the middle class Americans can only be secured by expanding exports and global growth. For too long our step has been unsteady as the ground has shifted beneath our feet. Today, as I sign the North American Free Trade Agreement into law and call for further progress on GATT, I believe we have found our footing. And I ask all of you to be steady, to recognize that there is no turning back from the world of today and tomorrow. We must face the challenges, embrace them with confidence, deal with the problems honestly and openly, and make this world work for all of us. America is where it should be, in the lead, setting the pace, showing the confidence that all of us need to face tomorrow. We are ready to compete, and we can win.

Thank you very much.

B. Institutionalizing the link between tariff-reduction agreements and national security

The interrelation of international trade and national security has been a feature of modern international trade law since the inception of GATT:

> [N]ational security and international trade law are closely linked, and this link has existed ever since the birth of modern international trade law in 1947. The link between these two arenas is contained in the General Agreement on Tariffs and Trade ("GATT").
>
> Article XXI of GATT establishes a broad framework for imposing international trade measures for national security purposes. Since GATT was enacted in 1947, countries have occasionally implemented trade sanctions, sometimes invoking Article XXI as a justification for such action. During the Reagan, Bush, and Clinton Administrations, the United States has relied on Article XXI to support the unilateral enactment of highly controversial sanctions legislation. The rationale behind such legislation is "national security. . . ."[84]

Bill Clinton's successor, George W. Bush, made the connections between military security and economic security the linchpin of his national security strategy, explicitly coupling trade agreements with military alliances in the context of the international security crisis following the terrorist attacks on the New York and Washington, D.C., on September 11, 2001. Note the coupling of international trade and national security in President Bush's announcement of the National Security Strategy of 2002, excerpted here:

George W. Bush, President of the United States, Introduction to the Announcement of National Security Strategy 2002

The great struggles of the twentieth century between liberty and totalitarianism ended with a decisive victory for the forces of freedom—and a single sustainable model for national success: freedom, democracy, and free enterprise. In the twenty-first century, only nations that share a commitment to protecting basic human rights and guaranteeing political and economic freedom will be able to unleash the potential of their people and assure their future prosperity. People everywhere want to be able to speak freely; choose who will govern them; worship as they please; educate their children—male and female; own property; and enjoy the benefits of their labor. These values of freedom are right and true for every person, in every society—and the duty of protecting these values against their enemies is the common calling of freedom-loving people across the globe and across the ages.

Today, the United States enjoys a position of unparalleled military strength and great economic and political influence. In keeping with our heritage and principles, we do not use our strength to press for unilateral advantage. We seek instead to create a balance of power that favors human freedom: conditions in which all nations and all societies can choose for themselves the rewards and challenges of political and economic liberty. In a world that is safe, people will be able to make their own lives

84. Raj Bhala, *National Security and International Trade Law: What the GATT Says and What the United States Does*, 19 U. Pa. J. Int'l Econ. L. 263, 264–265 (1998).

better. We will defend the peace by fighting terrorists and tyrants. We will preserve the peace by building good relations among the great powers. We will extend the peace by encouraging free and open societies on every continent.

Defending our Nation against its enemies is the first and fundamental commitment of the Federal Government. Today, that task has changed dramatically. Enemies in the past needed great armies and great industrial capabilities to endanger America. Now, shadowy networks of individuals can bring great chaos and suffering to our shores for less than it costs to purchase a single tank. Terrorists are organized to penetrate open societies and to turn the power of modern technologies against us. To defeat this threat we must make use of every tool in our arsenal.

As we defend the peace, we will also take advantage of an historic opportunity to preserve the peace. Today, the international community has the best chance since the rise of the nation-state in the seventeenth century to build a world where great powers compete in peace instead of continually prepare for war. Today, the world's great powers find ourselves on the same side—united by common dangers of terrorist violence and chaos. The United States will build on these common interests to promote global security.We are also increasingly united by common values. Russia is in the midst of a hopeful transition, reaching for its democratic future and a partner in the war on terror. Chinese leaders are discovering that economic freedom is the only source of national wealth. In time, they will find that social and political freedom is the only source of national greatness. America will encourage the advancement of democracy and economic openness in both nations, because these are the best foundations for domestic stability and international order.We will strongly resist aggression from other great powers—even as we welcome their peaceful pursuit of prosperity, trade, and cultural advancement.

Finally, the United States will use this moment of opportunity to extend the benefits of freedom across the globe.We will actively work to bring the hope of democracy, development, free markets, and free trade to every corner of the world. The events of September 11, 2001, taught us that weak states, like Afghanistan, can pose as great a danger to our national interests as strong states. Poverty does not make poor people into terrorists and murderers. Yet poverty, weak institutions, and corruption can make weak states vulnerable to terrorist networks and drug cartels within their borders.

The United States will stand beside any nation determined to build a better future by seeking the rewards of liberty for its people. Free trade and free markets have proven their ability to lift whole societies out of poverty—so the United States will work with individual nations, entire regions, and the entire global trading community to build a world that trades in freedom and therefore grows in prosperity. The United States will deliver greater development assistance through the New Millennium Challenge Account to nations that govern justly, invest in their people, and encourage economic freedom.We will also continue to lead the world in efforts to reduce the terrible toll of HIV/AIDS and other infectious diseases.

In building a balance of power that favors freedom, the United States is guided by the conviction that all nations have important responsibilities. Nations that enjoy freedom must actively fight terror. Nations that depend on international stability must help prevent the spread of weapons of mass destruction. Nations that seek international aid must govern themselves wisely, so that aid is well spent. For freedom to thrive, accountability must be expected and required.

We are also guided by the conviction that no nation can build a safer, better world alone. Alliances and multilateral institutions can multiply the strength of freedom-loving nations. The United States is committed to lasting institutions like the United Nations, the World Trade Organization, the Organization of American States, and NATO as well as other long-standing alliances. Coalitions of the willing can augment these permanent institutions. In all cases, international obligations are to be taken seriously. They are not to be undertaken symbolically to rally support for an ideal without furthering its attainment.

Freedom is the non-negotiable demand of human dignity; the birthright of every person—in every civilization. Throughout history, freedom has been threatened by war and terror; it has been challenged by the clashing wills of powerful states and the evil designs of tyrants; and it has been tested by widespread poverty and disease. Today, humanity holds in its hands the opportunity to further freedom's triumph over all these foes. The United States welcomes our responsibility to lead in this great mission.

George W. Bush
THE WHITE HOUSE,
September 17, 2002

Here, a further excerpt from the National Security Strategy text shows how the policy explicitly connects free markets, free trade, and military security:

Ignite a New Era of Global Economic Growth through Free Markets and Free Trade[85]

A strong world economy enhances our national security by advancing prosperity and freedom in the rest of the world. Economic growth supported by free trade and free markets creates new jobs and higher incomes. It allows people to lift their lives out of poverty, spurs economic and legal reform, and the fight against corruption, and it reinforces the habits of liberty.

We will promote economic growth and economic freedom beyond America's shores. All governments are responsible for creating their own economic policies and responding to their own economic challenges. We will use our economic engagement

85. National Security Strategy of 2002, section VI, http://georgewbush-whitehouse.archives.gov/nsc/nss/2002/nss6.html.

with other countries to underscore the benefits of policies that generate higher productivity and sustained economic growth, including:

- pro-growth legal and regulatory policies to encourage business investment, innovation, and entrepreneurial activity;
- tax policies—particularly lower marginal tax rates—that improve incentives for work and investment;
- rule of law and intolerance of corruption so that people are confident that they will be able to enjoy the fruits of their economic endeavors;
- strong financial systems that allow capital to be put to its most efficient use;
- sound fiscal policies to support business activity;
- investments in health and education that improve the well-being and skills of the labor force and population as a whole; and
- free trade that provides new avenues for growth and fosters the diffusion of technologies and ideas that increase productivity and opportunity.

The lessons of history are clear: market economies, not command-and-control economies with the heavy hand of government, are the best way to promote prosperity and reduce poverty. Policies that further strengthen market incentives and market institutions are relevant for all economies—industrialized countries, emerging markets, and the developing world.

A return to strong economic growth in Europe and Japan is vital to U.S. national security interests. We want our allies to have strong economies for their own sake, for the sake of the global economy, and for the sake of global security. European efforts to remove structural barriers in their economies are particularly important in this regard, as are Japan's efforts to end deflation and address the problems of non-performing loans in the Japanese banking system. We will continue to use our regular consultations with Japan and our European partners—including through the Group of Seven (G-7)—to discuss policies they are adopting to promote growth in their economies and support higher global economic growth.

Improving stability in emerging markets is also key to global economic growth. International flows of investment capital are needed to expand the productive potential of these economies. These flows allow emerging markets and developing countries to make the investments that raise living standards and reduce poverty. Our long-term objective should be a world in which all countries have investment-grade credit ratings that allow them access to international capital markets and to invest in their future.

We are committed to policies that will help emerging markets achieve access to larger capital flows at lower cost. To this end, we will continue to pursue reforms aimed at reducing uncertainty in financial markets. We will work actively with other countries, the International Monetary Fund (IMF), and the private sector to implement the G-7 Action Plan negotiated earlier this year for preventing financial crises and more effectively resolving them when they occur.

The best way to deal with financial crises is to prevent them from occurring, and we have encouraged the IMF to improve its efforts doing so. We will continue to work with the IMF to streamline the policy conditions for its lending and to focus its lending strategy on achieving economic growth through sound fiscal and monetary policy, exchange rate policy, and financial sector policy.

The concept of "free trade" arose as a moral principle even before it became a pillar of economics. If you can make something that others value, you should be able to sell it to them. If others make something that you value, you should be able to buy it. This is real freedom, the freedom for a person—or a nation—to make a living. To promote free trade, the Unites States has developed a comprehensive strategy:

- *Seize the global initiative.* The new global trade negotiations we helped launch at Doha in November 2001 will have an ambitious agenda, especially in agriculture, manufacturing, and services, targeted for completion in 2005. The United States has led the way in completing the accession of China and a democratic Taiwan to the World Trade Organization. We will assist Russia's preparations to join the WTO.
- *Press regional initiatives.* The United States and other democracies in the Western Hemisphere have agreed to create the Free Trade Area of the Americas, targeted for completion in 2005. This year the United States will advocate market-access negotiations with its partners, targeted on agriculture, industrial goods, services, investment, and government procurement. We will also offer more opportunity to the poorest continent, Africa, starting with full use of the preferences allowed in the African Growth and Opportunity Act, and leading to free trade.
- *Move ahead with bilateral free trade agreements.* Building on the free trade agreement with Jordan enacted in 2001, the Administration will work this year to complete free trade agreements with Chile and Singapore. Our aim is to achieve free trade agreements with a mix of developed and developing countries in all regions of the world. Initially, Central America, Southern Africa, Morocco, and Australia will be our principal focal points.
- *Renew the executive-congressional partnership.* Every administration's trade strategy depends on a productive partnership with Congress. After a gap of 8 years, the Administration reestablished majority support in the Congress for trade liberalization by passing Trade Promotion Authority and the other market opening measures for developing countries in the Trade Act of 2002. This Administration will work with Congress to enact new bilateral, regional, and global trade agreements that will be concluded under the recently passed Trade Promotion Authority.
- *Promote the connection between trade and development.* Trade policies can help developing countries strengthen property rights, competition, the rule of law, investment, the spread of knowledge, open societies, the efficient allocation of resources, and regional integration—all leading to growth, opportunity, and confidence in developing countries. The United States is implementing The

Africa Growth and Opportunity Act to provide market-access for nearly all goods produced in the 35 countries of sub-Saharan Africa. We will make more use of this act and its equivalent for the Caribbean Basin and continue to work with multilateral and regional institutions to help poorer countries take advantage of these opportunities. Beyond market access, the most important area where trade intersects with poverty is in public health. We will ensure that the WTO intellectual property rules are flexible enough to allow developing nations to gain access to critical medicines for extraordinary dangers like HIV/AIDS, tuberculosis, and malaria.

- *Enforce trade agreements and laws against unfair practices.* Commerce depends on the rule of law; international trade depends on enforceable agreements. Our top priorities are to resolve ongoing disputes with the European Union, Canada, and Mexico and to make a global effort to address new technology, science, and health regulations that needlessly impede farm exports and improved agriculture. Laws against unfair trade practices are often abused, but the international community must be able to address genuine concerns about government subsidies and dumping. International industrial espionage which undermines fair competition must be detected and deterred.
- *Help domestic industries and workers adjust.* There is a sound statutory framework for these transitional safeguards which we have used in the agricultural sector and which we are using this year to help the American steel industry. The benefits of free trade depend upon the enforcement of fair trading practices. These safeguards help ensure that the benefits of free trade do not come at the expense of American workers. Trade adjustment assistance will help workers adapt to the change and dynamism of open markets.
- *Protect the environment and workers.* The United States must foster economic growth in ways that will provide a better life along with widening prosperity. We will incorporate labor and environmental concerns into U.S. trade negotiations, creating a healthy "network" between multilateral environmental agreements with the WTO, and use the International Labor Organization, trade preference programs, and trade talks to improve working conditions in conjunction with freer trade.
- *Enhance energy security.* We will strengthen our own energy security and the shared prosperity of the global economy by working with our allies, trading partners, and energy producers to expand the sources and types of global energy supplied, especially in the Western Hemisphere, Africa, Central Asia, and the Caspian region. We will also continue to work with our partners to develop cleaner and more energy efficient technologies.

Economic growth should be accompanied by global efforts to stabilize greenhouse gas concentrations associated with this growth, containing them at a level that prevents dangerous human interference with the global climate. Our overall objective is to reduce America's greenhouse gas emissions relative to the size of our economy, cutting such emissions per unit of economic activity by 18 percent over the next 10 years, by the year 2012. Our strategies for attaining this goal will be to:

- remain committed to the basic U.N. Framework Convention for international cooperation;
- obtain agreements with key industries to cut emissions of some of the most potent greenhouse gases and give transferable credits to companies that can show real cuts;
- develop improved standards for measuring and registering emission reductions;
- promote renewable energy production and clean coal technology, as well as nuclear power—which produces no greenhouse gas emissions, while also improving fuel economy for U.S. cars and trucks;
- increase spending on research and new conservation technologies, to a total of $4.5 billion—the largest sum being spent on climate change by any country in the world and a $700 million increase over last year's budget; and
- assist developing countries, especially the major greenhouse gas emitters such as China and India, so that they will have the tools and resources to join this effort and be able to grow along a cleaner and better path.

V. Was NAFTA constitutional?

Despite the United States' contention that "NAFTA is consistent not only with the Constitution but also with the decisions of the Supreme Court and the manner in which trade agreements of this kind have been implemented in this country for almost a century,"[86] the constitutionality of NAFTA remains a subject of debate. As Ackerman and Golove indicate in the following excerpt, *Dames & Moore v. Regan* was central to the formulation of executive power that allowed NAFTA to pass a constitutional test. In *Dames & Moore*, discussed in Chapter 1, we find executive power articulated in relation to what began as a straightforward business contract. When transnational law situations are linked vertically, executive power is inherently in play. Executive power—and in particular, the power of the president—is central to the interconnections between global trade and what has come to be called the war on terrorism.

In this excerpt, we see how transnational law emerges from the politicization of tensions between global economy, military security and domestic law—and how these tensions converge on issues of executive power. We consider the transnational aspects of executive power in Chapter 9. Appreciating the ways in which executive power integrates jurisdictions is critical to understanding transnational law, but so is the extent to which novel circumstances call on the architects of such agreements

86. Evelyn Iritani, *Court Rejects Challenge to Constitutionality of NAFTA*, L.A. Times (July 24, 1999), http://articles.latimes.com/1999/jul/24/business/fi-59072.

to improvise as they apply established principles to new situations. This is the theme of Professors Ackerman and Golove's consideration of the constitutional ambiguities that may arise in such contexts, specifically with reference to NAFTA:

Bruce Ackerman & David Golove, *Is NAFTA Constitutional?*

108 Harv. L. Rev. 799, 802–803, 804, 925–929 (1995).

The opponents [to NAFTA] were grimly determined to gain victory at all costs. They could well have mustered the thirty-four Senators needed to defeat NAFTA if it had been treated as a treaty rather than a congressional-executive agreement. And yet the obvious questions were left unasked. How did Americans come to the point where they undertake the most solemn international obligations through a procedure in which the House of Representatives joins the Senate, and simple majorities in both Houses serve to commit the nation? Is this alternative to treaty-making constitutionally legitimate? The real mystery, then, is not merely whether NAFTA is constitutional, but how and why we have gotten to the point where the foundational questions have become unaskable.

It was not always so. During the first 150 years in the life of the Republic, NAFTA would never have slipped by without fierce controversy. We begin with an exploration of this earlier constitutional world, now entirely obscured from view. We then turn to the transformation accomplished during the Roosevelt years. The climax came with the Second World War. As Allied armies swept through Europe, Americans recalled the disastrous denouement of the First World War. The Senate's rejection of the Treaty of Versailles had become a symbol of failure in the original constitutional design. The Senate's prerogative was now linked with an isolationism that was out of step with American public opinion.

The question was how this mobilized consensus would express itself in constitutional law. The movement went down two tracks. In May of 1945, two thirds of the House of Representatives approved a constitutional amendment requiring all treaties to be approved by majorities in both Houses rather than by two thirds of the Senate. But this movement was short-circuited by an informal process, which yielded the modern congressional-executive agreement. During and after the War, the President won the constitutional authority to substitute the agreement of both Houses for the traditional advice and consent of the Senate. It is this historical triumph that laid the foundation for NAFTA.

But not without a further step, taken a generation later. The Trade Act of 1974 made a comprehensive effort to restructure the modern two-House procedure to suit the needs of economic diplomacy. This framework has proved remarkably successful—to the point where it is now taken for granted by all foreign-trade professionals. This professional consensus accounts for the constitutional silence surrounding NAFTA. After two decades, it was only natural to negotiate NAFTA through the two-House procedure that had been perfected in a series of sweeping trade agreements.

The construction of a new framework for trade in 1974, however, could not have occurred without the constitutional breakthrough won by the internationalist generation who fought the Second World War. Without this earlier transformation, NAFTA would have been processed as a treaty—and condemned to defeat by thirty-four isolationist Senators.

The intentions of the Framers have been redeemed—so long as we recognize that the relevant Framers were the Americans who fought the Second World War and not those who fought the Revolution. These Americans were determined to avoid the tragic mistake of the Versailles Treaty—in which the United States turned its back on the world just as its ideals seemed to have triumphed. In the aftermath of the Cold War, the Versailles dilemma is once again upon us. The victory of American ideals in 1989 has provoked a renewed debate between isolationists and internationalists on the need for further engagement in the new world order. Like Versailles, NAFTA became a symbol of new-fangled internationalist entanglements that threaten to compromise our "sovereignty." Only this time, the contest was not conducted on a playing field that gives isolationists a decisive advantage. The Founders' "antidemocratic" and "outmoded" decision to privilege "one third plus one" of the Senate no longer monopolizes our constitutional vision. It remains available as an option but is no longer a requirement.

This does not mean that internationalists are destined to sustain the political momentum they gained during the Cold War era. But as NAFTA suggests, rules of the game do make a difference, and sometimes a large one, in the evolution of politics. If the Senate had rejected the North American Free Trade Treaty, this defeat would have jeopardized prospects for American involvement in the World Trade Organization. It also would have changed the face of American politics: rather than retreating from public view, Ross Perot might have been catapulted by his triumphant leadership in the NAFTA struggle to the center of the stage of presidential politics. These sorts of things can add up.

Though NAFTA glided through both Houses without constitutional debate, opponents of the next great initiative—the World Trade Organization—challenged the constitutionality of the Clinton Administration's decision to commit the nation through the two-House procedure. It may only be a matter of time before the Supreme Court gets into the act: what should it say?

This is precisely the approach suggested by the modern case closest to our problem. *Dames & Moore v. Reagan* involved President Carter's deal with the Iranian government securing the release of Americans held hostage in Teheran. As part of his executive agreement, the President reached a settlement that deprived creditors of their claims in American courts, transferring them to an international tribunal in The Hague. When they sued, the Court supported the President, but in an opinion marked by great caution. Rather than speaking expansively about *Curtiss-Wright,* then-Justice Rehnquist relied heavily on Justice Jackson's famous concurring opinion in the *Steel Seizure Case.* Speaking for the Court, Justice Rehnquist agreed with Jackson that the key variable in assessing the constitutionality of presidential action is the character of congressional support. Thus, even though Presidents had traditionally been conceded broad powers in settling international claims without any congressional or senatorial participation, Justice Rehnquist did not approve Carter's executive agreement on that ground alone. Instead, he carefully examined the quality of congressional support for the President's actions and conditioned the Court's approval on his positive assessment. While the Court could not find express statutory authorization for all aspects of the President's decision, it upheld his agreement only after concluding that Congress had "acquiesced in the President's action." Given the tenor of its opinion, the Court would have been delighted to find that both Houses of Congress had supported the President's decision with the majorities provided in the cases of NAFTA and the WTO.

Given its hesitations about *Curtiss-Wright,* the Court's embrace of a Marshallian reading of Article I should be seen as part of the solution, rather than part of the problem. By establishing a framework for foreign policy-making, statutes like the Trade Act of 1974 help avoid situations in which the President may otherwise be tempted to abuse his (uncertain) unilateral authority in foreign affairs. Rather than calling congressional power into question, a constructive Court opinion should encourage Congress and the President to build on the successes of NAFTA and the WTO and to construct new framework statutes in other fields of foreign policy. Only effective frameworks will discourage Presidents, and their underlings, from supposing that the Constitution grants the executive branch a vast prerogative for unilateral foreign adventurism.

But in the final analysis, there is more at stake than the avoidance of difficult constitutional questions. By affirming the Marshallian view of Article I, the Court would be endorsing the considered judgment of the generation that fought the Second World War. These men and women supposed that they had decisively resolved the question of constitutional interpretation that the critics of the WTO seek to revive. Though the Americans who fought the war and won the peace are now rapidly leaving the political stage, there is no reason to forget their enduring contribution to our constitutional tradition.

In the next case, we will view the constitutionality of NAFTA through another lens: the Treaty Clause of the Constitution. The Treaty Clause, found in Article II, Section 2, Clause 2 of the Constitution, states that the President shall have power, by and with the advice of the Senate, to make treaties provided two thirds of the Senate concur. Was NAFTA's ratification unconstitutional? No, says the Eleventh Circuit. Nonetheless, the issues discussed in the case offer substance for a robust discussion on NAFTA's constitutionality. As you read the case, think about the potential for tension between a nation's constitution and the international agreements to which it may agree. It is such tensions that necessitate a transnational analysis.

Made in the USA Foundation v. United States

242 F.3d 1300 (11th Cir. 2001)

FLETCHER, CIRCUIT JUDGE:

This case presents complex issues of first impression in this circuit in the realm of constitutional interpretation—namely, whether certain kinds of international commercial agreements are "treaties," as that term is employed in Article II, Section 2 of the United States Constitution; and if so, whether the Treaty Clause represents the sole means of enacting such agreements into law. The appellants, comprised of national and local labor organizations as well as a nonprofit group that promotes the purchase of American-made products, urge that the North American Free Trade Agreement (commonly referred to as "NAFTA") be declared unconstitutionally void, as it was never approved by a two-thirds supermajority of the United States Senate pursuant to the constitutionally-mandated procedures governing treaty ratification. The Government, on the other hand, invokes the political question doctrine and also claims that this court lacks jurisdiction due to the appellants' lack of standing. In addition, the Government argues on the merits that NAFTA's enactment did not require Senate ratification as a "treaty." The parties' respective arguments thus require us to engage constitutional issues of unusual breadth, complexity and import.

In a remarkably learned and thorough opinion, the district court granted the Government's motion for summary judgment. *Made in the USA Foundation v. United States,* 56 F.Supp.2d 1226 (N.D.Ala.1999). The court found that Article III standing requirements had been met for most of the original appellants and that the case did not present a nonjusticiable political question, thus electing to reach the merits of the case. Ultimately, however, the court held that even assuming NAFTA constitutes a full-fledged "treaty," the Treaty Clause does not constitute the exclusive means of enacting international commercial agreements, given Congress's plenary powers to regulate foreign commerce under Art. I, § 8, and the President's inherent authority under Article II to manage our nation's foreign affairs. Accordingly, the district court held that NAFTA's passage in 1993 by simple majorities of both houses of Congress was constitutionally sound.

We agree with the district court that the appellants have standing in this matter, and affirm the principle, as enunciated by the U.S. Supreme Court, that certain international agreements may well require Senate ratification as treaties through the constitutionally-mandated procedures of Art. II, § 2. *See, e.g., Holden v. Joy,* 84 U.S. (17 Wall.) 211, 242–43 (1872); *Missouri v. Holland,* 252 U.S. 416, 433, (1920). We nonetheless decline to reach the merits of this particular case, finding that with respect to international commercial agreements such as NAFTA, the question of just what constitutes a "treaty" requiring Senate ratification presents a nonjusticiable political question. Accordingly, we dismiss the appeal and remand with instructions to dismiss the action and vacate the decision of the district court. *See Goldwater v. Carter,* 444 U.S. 996, 1005 (1979); *United States v. Munsingwear, Inc.,* 340 U.S. 36, 39–40 (1950).

I. Introduction and Background

The United States, Mexico and Canada entered negotiations in 1990 to create a "free trade zone" on the North American continent through the phased elimination or reduction of both tariff and non-tariff barriers to trade. Following extensive negotiations, the North American Free Trade Agreement was completed and signed by the leaders of the three countries on December 17, 1992. Through the passage of the NAFTA Implementation Act ("Implementation Act") on December 8, 1993, Congress approved NAFTA and provided for a series of domestic laws to effectuate and enforce NAFTA's provisions.

Neither NAFTA nor the Implementation Act were subjected to the ratification procedures outlined in the Treaty Clause. Summoning primarily historical arguments, the appellants contend that this failure to go through the Art. II, § 2 procedures contravenes the original understanding of the Framers and therefore renders NAFTA and the Implementation Act unconstitutional.

Remarkably, although perhaps not altogether surprisingly, the United States Supreme Court has never in our nation's history seen fit to address the question of what exactly constitutes and distinguishes "treaties," as that term is used in Art. II, § 2, from "alliances," "confederations," "compacts," or "agreements," as those terms are employed in Art. I, § 10. Accordingly, the Court has never decided what sorts of international agreements, if any, might require Senate ratification pursuant to the procedures outlined in Art. II, § 2. Indeed, as will be discussed below, the only extended pronouncement of the Court's Treaty Clause jurisprudence can be found in *Goldwater v. Carter*—a case in which the Court effectively refused to require President Carter to submit the abrogation of a mutual defense treaty with Taiwan for Senate ratification, but failed to garner a majority of the Court behind a single rationale. In light of the Constitution's silence on the meaning of the word "treaty," as well as the relative dearth of Supreme Court jurisprudence in this area, the question of NAFTA's constitutionality has generated significant debate amongst prominent legal scholars.

II. Standing

[The court finds that the plaintiffs have standing.]

III. Political Question

We now turn to the Government's second jurisdictional argument. According to the Government, because the text of the Constitution fails to define what is meant by a "treaty" or to dictate the proper procedure for approving international commercial agreements, and because the Constitution has clearly granted the political branches an enormous amount of authority in the areas of foreign affairs and commerce, the choice of what procedure to use for a given agreement is committed to the discretion and expertise of the Legislative and Executive Branches by virtue of the political question doctrine. We substantially agree with the Government's contentions that this case does not present the type of question that can be properly addressed by the judiciary, given our belief that Supreme Court precedent and historical practice confirm the wisdom of maintaining the practice of judicial nonintervention into such matters. Drawing heavily from (then Associate) Justice Rehnquist's plurality opinion in *Goldwater v. Carter,* 444 U.S. 996 (1979)—as noted earlier, the only extended exposition of the Supreme Court's Treaty Clause jurisprudence—we conclude that this case presents a nonjusticiable political question.

The political question doctrine emerges out of Article III's case or controversy requirement and has its roots in separation of powers concerns. *Baker v. Carr,* 369 U.S. 186, 210 (1962). In *Baker,* the Supreme Court enumerated six criteria that courts should consider in determining whether a case is nonjusticiable:

> Prominent on the surface of any case held to involve a political question is found (1) a textually demonstrable constitutional commitment of the issue to a coordinate political department; or (2) a lack of judicially discoverable and manageable standards for resolving it; or (3) the impossibility of deciding without an initial policy determination of a kind clearly for nonjudicial discretion; or (4) the impossibility of a court's undertaking independent resolution without expressing lack of the respect due coordinate branches of government; or (5) an unusual need for unquestioning adherence to a political decision already made; or (6) the potentiality of embarrassment from multifarious pronouncements by various departments on one question.

369 U.S. at 217. Significantly, any one of the above-listed characteristics may be sufficient to preclude judicial review. *Id.*

In *Goldwater,* Justice Powell's concurrence suggested that the *Baker* analysis could be condensed into a three-question inquiry:

(i) Does the issue involve resolution of questions committed by the text of the Constitution to a coordinate branch of government?

(ii) Would resolution of the question demand that a court move beyond areas of judicial expertise?

(iii) Do prudential considerations counsel against judicial intervention?

444 U.S. at 998. Inasmuch as it incorporates the *Baker* criteria without abridging them, we find Justice Powell's analytical framework to be useful and proceed to apply each of these inquiries to the present case.

A. Constitutional Textual Commitment to Coordinate Branches

The term "treaties" appears four times in the text of the Constitution. The Treaty Clause, U.S. Const. Art. II, § 2, cl. 2, states that the President "shall have Power, by and with the Advice and Consent of the Senate, to make Treaties, provided two-thirds of the Senators present concur." The Compacts Clause, U.S. Const. Art. I, § 10, cl. 3, delineates the power of the states to deal with foreign powers, completely prohibiting the states from making "treaties" with foreign nations, but permitting states to enter into "agreements or compacts" with foreign powers with the consent of Congress. The Cases-and-Controversies Clause, U.S. Const. Art. III, § 2, states, in pertinent part, that "the judicial power shall extend to all cases, in law and equity, arising under this Constitution, the laws of the United States, and treaties made ...." And finally, the Supremacy Clause, U.S. Const. Art. Art. VI, cl. 2, states that "[t]his Constitution, and the laws of the United States which shall be made in pursuance thereof; and all treaties made, or which shall be made, under the authority of the United States, shall be the supreme law of the land." However, as noted earlier, the text of the Constitution does not (1) define the term "treaties"; (2) delineate the difference between treaties and other types of international agreements; (3) mandate that treaties are the exclusive means by which the federal government may make agreements with foreign powers; or (4) state that the Treaty Clause procedure is the only manner in which a treaty may be enacted. *See also Holmes v. Jennison,* 39 U.S. (14 Pet.) 540, 569 (acknowledging that the Treaty Clause is worded in "general terms, without any description of the objects intended to be embraced by it").

The Constitution confers a vast amount of power upon the political branches of the federal government in the area of foreign policy—particularly foreign commerce. The breadth of the President's inherent powers in foreign affairs arises from his role as Chief Executive, U.S. Const. Art. II, § 1, cl. 1, and as Commander in Chief, U.S. Const. Art. III, § 2, cl. 1. In addition to his power to "make Treaties" with the advice and consent of two-thirds of the Senators present, the President's authority in foreign affairs is further bolstered by his power to "appoint Ambassadors . . . and Consuls," U.S. Const. Art. II, § 2, cl. 2, and "to receive Ambassadors and other public Ministers," U.S. Const. Art. II, § 3. Meanwhile, Congress's enumerated powers in the realm of external affairs include its power "to declare war," U.S. Const., Art. I, § 8, cl. 11; "to raise and support armies," U.S. Const., Art. I, § 8, cl. 12; "to provide and maintain a navy," U.S. Const., Art. I, § 8, cl. 13; and the Senate's advice-and-consent role in the treaty-making process. Most significantly, the Constitution also confers on the entire Congress (and not just the Senate) authority "to regulate commerce with foreign nations," U.S. Const. Art. I, § 8, cl. 3—an express textual commitment that is directly relevant to international commercial agreements such as NAFTA.

The Supreme Court has repeatedly recognized that the President is the nation's "guiding organ in the conduct of our foreign affairs," in whom the Constitution vests "vast powers in relation to the outside world." *Ludecke v. Watkins,* 335 U.S. 160, 173 (1948); *see also Department of Navy v. Egan,* 484 U.S. 518, 529 (1988) ("recogniz[ing] 'the generally accepted view that foreign policy [i]s the province and responsibility of the Executive'" (citation omitted)). With respect to NAFTA, it is especially important to note that the Supreme Court has long since recognized the power of the political branches to conclude international "agreements that do not constitute treaties in the constitutional sense." *Curtiss-Wright,* 299 U.S. at 318.

The appellants concede, as they must, that the Constitution affords the political branches substantial authority over foreign affairs and commerce. The appellants also concede that the Supreme Court has recognized the constitutional validity of the longstanding practice of enacting international agreements which do not amount to full-fledged treaties. *See Curtiss-Wright,* 299 U.S. at 318; *see also* Ackerman and Golove, *supra,* at 858; Tribe, *supra,* at 1269 ("The authority to make international agreements that do not rise to the level of treaties has long been recognized as [an] inherent executive power [of the President].”). Nonetheless, the appellants argue that what is at issue here is not the authority of a branch of government over a certain subject matter, but whether that branch “has chosen a constitutionally permissible means of implementing that power.” *I.N.S. v. Chadha*, 462 U.S. 919, 940–41 (1983). This contention leads us to the second *Goldwater/Baker* inquiry: whether the resolution of this issue would require this court to move beyond recognized areas of judicial expertise.

B. Judicial Expertise

Under *Baker*, the second criterion by which we evaluate the justiciability of this case is whether or not there exist judicially manageable standards for determining when a given international commercial agreement must be approved pursuant to the Art. II, § 2 procedures. *Baker*, 369 U.S. at 217. The Government contends that such a decision would require this court to consider areas beyond its judicial expertise. We agree.

While the nature of the issue presented in *Goldwater* differs somewhat from the present case, we nonetheless find the disposition in *Goldwater* instructive, if not controlling, for our purposes, in that the Supreme Court declined to act because the constitutional provision at issue does not provide an identifiable textual limit on the authority granted by the Constitution. Indeed, just as the Treaty Clause fails to outline the Senate's role in the abrogation of treaties, we find that the Treaty Clause also fails to outline the circumstances, if any, under which its procedures must be adhered to when approving international commercial agreements.

Significantly, the appellants themselves fail to offer, either in their briefs or at argument, a workable definition of what constitutes a “treaty.” Indeed, the appellants decline to supply any analytical framework whatsoever by which courts can distinguish international agreements which require Senate ratification from those that do not. Rather, the appellants offer up the nebulous argument that “major and significant” agreements require Art. II, § 2 ratification, without defining how courts should go about making such distinctions. According to the appellants, it is neither possible nor necessary to define the meaning of a “treaty” to decide this case, so long as we find that if any commercial agreement qualifies as a treaty requiring Senate ratification, NAFTA surely does. We disagree, given that under *Baker* and *Goldwater*, the ascertainment of judicially manageable standards is essential before we may rule that this court even has jurisdiction to reach the merits of the case.

C. Prudential Considerations

Finally, under the *Goldwater/Baker* criteria, we find that a number of prudential factors are relevant to the resolution of this case, including: (1) the necessity of federal uniformity; (2) the potential effect of an adverse judicial decision on the nation's economy and foreign relations; and (3) the respect courts should pay to coordinate branches of the federal government. *See Goldwater*, 444 U.S. at 998 (Powell, J., concurring); *Baker*, 369 U.S. at 217.

As the Supreme Court stated in *Coleman v. Miller*, 307 U.S. 433, 454–55 (1930), “In determining whether a question falls within [the political question] category, the appropriateness under our system of government of attributing finality to the action of the political departments and also the lack of satisfactory criteria for a judicial determination are dominant considerations." In *Baker,* the Court recognized the special importance of our nation speaking with one voice in the field of foreign affairs. *Baker,* 369 U.S. at 211. The Court has further observed that "federal uniformity is essential" in the area of foreign commerce, *Japan Line, Ltd. v. County of Los Angeles,* 441 U.S. 434, 448 (1979), and that "the Federal Government must speak with one voice when regulating commercial relations with foreign governments." *Michelin Tire Corp. v. Commissioner,* 423 U.S. 276, 285 (1976).

A judicial declaration invalidating NAFTA at this stage would clearly risk "the potentiality of embarrassment from multifarious pronouncements by various departments on one question." *Baker,* 369 U.S. at 217. Although the appellants argue that these considerations are irrelevant to an assessment of the constitutionality of the treaty-making procedures, we believe in this case that a challenge to the procedures used to enact NAFTA is inextricably bound to its substantive provisions, inasmuch as a judicial declaration invalidating NAFTA would be aimed at forcing the withdrawal of U.S. participation in the agreement, with serious repercussions for our nation's external relations with Mexico and Canada.

A judicial order contradicting the actions of the President and Congress could also have a profoundly negative effect on this nation's economy and its ability to deal with other foreign powers. Significantly, granting the appellants' requested relief in this case would not only affect the validity of NAFTA, but would potentially undermine every other major international commercial agreement made over the past half-century. *See* Ackerman and Golove, *supra,* at 925 n. 519 (questioning, in light of the ongoing dispute between the Senate and the President over the meaning of Article 46 of the as-yet-unratified Vienna Convention of the Law of Treaties, that "[i]f the [Supreme] Court were to strike down the modern constitutional practice, what would be the status of all the unconstitutional agreements that have been negotiated over the last half-century?").

Finally, a review by this court of the process by which the President and Congress enter into international agreements would run the risk of intruding upon the respect due coordinate branches of government. As Justice Powell concluded in his concurrence in *Goldwater,* "Prudential considerations persuade me that a dispute between Congress and the President is not ready for judicial review unless and until each branch has taken action asserting its constitutional authority." *Goldwater,* 444 U.S. at 996 (Powell, J., concurring). Similarly, Justice Rehnquist's concurrence admonished that "[t]he Judicial Branch should not decide issues affecting the allocation of power between the President and Congress until the political branches reach an impasse." *Id.* at 1005 n. 1. Since no such impasse has been reached with respect to NAFTA, we believe this requires greater deference on the part of the Judiciary to the decisions of coordinate branches of government. In this regard, we note that no member of the Senate itself has asserted that body's sole prerogative to ratify NAFTA (or, for that matter, other international commercial agreements) by a two-thirds supermajority. In light of the Senate's apparent acquiescence in the procedures used to approve NAFTA, we believe this further counsels against judicial intervention in the present case.

IV. Conclusion

We therefore conclude that this case presents a nonjusticiable political question, thereby depriving the court of Article III jurisdiction in this matter.

In dismissing this case as a political question, we do not mean to suggest that the terms of the Treaty Clause effectively allow the political branches to exercise unfettered discretion in determining whether to subject a particular international agreement to the rigors of that Clause's procedural requirements; to state as much would be tantamount to rendering the terms of Art. II, § 2, cl. 2 a dead letter. Indeed, as the Court stated in *Missouri v. Holland,* 252 U.S. 416, 433 (1920), "[i]t is obvious that there may be matters of the sharpest exigency for the national well being that an act of Congress could not deal with but that a treaty followed by such an act could." We only conclude that in the context of international commercial agreements such as NAFTA—given the added factor of Congress's constitutionally-enumerated power to regulate commerce with foreign nations, as well as the lack of judicially manageable standards to determine when an agreement is significant enough to qualify as a "treaty"—the issue of what kinds of agreements require Senate ratification pursuant to the Art. II, § 2 procedures presents a nonjusticiable political question.

Accordingly, we DISMISS the appeal and REMAND with instructions to dismiss the action and vacate the decision of the district court. *See Goldwater,* 444 U.S. at 1005; *United States v. Munsingwear, Inc.,* 340 U.S. 36 (1950).

Notes and Questions

1. Unlike the District Court below, the Eleventh Circuit failed to reach the merits of this case. Are you persuaded that this was the best outcome? Does the court suggest that *all* congressional-executive agreements may be constitutional? If not, does it provide any guidance as to where the line should be drawn? The U.S. Supreme Court denied cert. shortly thereafter, thus leaving the issue unresolved. 534 U.S. 1039 (2001).

2. In a comment published shortly after the Eleventh Circuit decision, tellingly titled "11th Circuit Declines to Rewrite 20th Century World History" (75 Florida Bar Journal 1, 2001), Alan S. Lederman finds the court "understandably reluctant to issue a decision that could conceivably be interpreted as requiring that the U.S. withdraw from the International Monetary Fund, World Bank, World Trade Organiation, and NAFTA, close the Saint Lawrence Seaway, renege on up to 90 percent of its other international legal obligations, and ease enforcement of thousands of federal implementing statutes."[87]

---

87. Alan S. Lederman, *11th Circuit Declines to Rewrite 20th Century World History*, 75 FLA. B.J. 1, 5 (2001).

3. Disputes occurring under NAFTA fall into four general categories:

> The first results from ambiguities in the agreement itself, which have led to disputes over the interpretation of the agreement. Other trade disputes have emerged or intensified with the deepening of trade and increased integration of regional agricultural markets. With open borders, domestic polices that influence production, prices or trade have more direct spillover effects into agricultural markets in other NAFTA countries and may lead to trade frictions. Third, an increasing number of disputes are related to sanitary and phytosanitary issues; these disputes are particularly complicated due to the presence of three different regulatory frameworks managing disease and pests within the region. A fourth source of trade disputes is the increased competitive pressure under free regional trade that has led some industries to seek protection through trade actions.[88]

NAFTA created dispute resolution mechanisms in Chapters 11, 14, 19, and 20 of the agreement. Chapter 11 sets up procedures for investment disputes. Chapter 14 deals with disputes involving financial services. Chapter 19 addresses allegations of unfair trade actions—it "establishes a mechanism to provide an alternative to judicial review by domestic courts of final determinations in antidumping and countervailing duty cases, with review by independent binational panels." [89] Chapter 20 provides for disputes among the signatories over the interpretation or application of NAFTA's text. Specifically, it calls for consultation between parties, conciliation before an arbitration panel (the "Free Trade Commission") and implementation of an arbitral report. [90]

4. The relationship of NAFTA tribunals to Article III courts is varied and, to the extent that the tribunals are seen as a bypass of Article III courts, have been controversial. NAFTA procedures allow recourse to an ad hoc "Extraordinary Challenge Committee" composed of judges or former judges from NAFTA countries. [91] Is Chapter 11's exclusion of Article III judges in this context constitutional? Constitutional challenges to NAFTA tribunals remain unresolved by the courts. [92] For example, in *Fair Lumber Imps., Executive Comm. v. United States*, 471 F.3d 1329 (D.C. Cir. 1997) (per curiam), the question of NAFTA tribunals' constitutionality

---

88. Mary Burfisher, Terry Norman & Renée Schwartz, *NAFTA Trade Dispute Resolution: What are the Mechanisms?*, *in* Trade Liberalization Under NAFTA: Report Card on Agriculture 132 (R.M.A. Loyns et al. eds., 2000), http://www.farmfoundation.org/news/articlefiles/877-burfisher.pdf.

89. *Overview of the Dispute Settlement Provisions*, NAFTA Secretariat, http://www.nafta-sec-alena.org/Home/Dispute-Settlement/Overview-of-the-Dispute-Settlement-Provisions#Chapter11.

90. For detailed analysis of Chapter 20, see David A. Gantz, *Dispute Settlement Under the NAFTA and the WTO: Choice of Forum Opportunities and Risks for the NAFTA Parties*, 14 Am. U. Int'l L. Rev. 1025, 1030.

91. Patricia Isela Hansen, *Judicialization and Globalization in the North American Free Trade Agreement*, 38 Tex. Int'l LJ. 489, 494 (2003).

92. *See* Eugene Kontorovich, *The Constitutionality of International Courts: The Forgotten Precedent of Slave-Trade Tribunals*, 158 U. Pa. L. Rev. 39 (2010).

was never reached, as the court ruled that a U.S.-Canadian settlement agreement precluded review of a panel ruling. Similarly, in *American Coal for Competitive Trade v. Clinton*, 128 F.3d 761 (D.C. Cir. 1997), NAFTA tribunals' constitutionality was never considered. The court dismissed the suit for lack of standing where the petitioner "failed to establish the requisite causal connection between its alleged injury and the [Tribunal] system."

5. Professor Sergio Puig distinguishes Article III courts from NAFTA tribunals, arguing that constitutional courts (i.e., the branch of governments tasked with final constitutional oversight) are typically separate and distinct from the ordinary judiciary.[93] Puig explains that "Constitutional courts are considered fundamental to the political stability of their respective nations because they are, to a large extent, responsible for the social acceptance of the Constitutional and fundamental autochthonous norms and address the tensions between complex political structures and interest. Constitutional courts are by definition political. On the other hand, [chapter 11] tribunals arguably help to 'de-politicize' investment disputes by allowing individuals or corporations to proceed directly against a State in an international forum."[94] Puig concludes that "investor-State arbitration allow[s] states to increase economic policy stability for the sake of promoting foreign direct investment."[95] And, "because [chapter 11 tribunals] are founded upon international law,"[96] those tribunals' remedies may differ from those normally available in local court. (We discuss investor-state disputes further in Chapter 7, *infra.*)

6. Professor Susan Karamanian also supports the constitutionality of the tribunals, but (in contrast to Professor Puig) is critical of the idea that the tribunals are definitively outside of the judicial structure. Referencing critics of the constutionality of the tribunals, she characterizes as an "exaggeration" the view that they necessarily "circumvent" state and federal high courts.[97] Among the exaggerations, in her account, is the idea that the tribunals are "supranational courts that operate beyond the judicial regime established under the U.S. Constitution." In this connection, Professor Karamanian points to the involvement of the U.S. in creating NAFTA, "champion[ing]" the tribunals since their inception. Further, the fact that the U.S. President negotiated NAFTA's tribunals along with other NAFTA chapters in coordination with the U.S. Congress suggests that these "supranational" arguments are misplaced.[98]

93. Sergio Puig, *Investor-State Tribunals and Constitutional Courts: The Mexican Sweeteners Saga*, 2 Mexican L. Rev. 199 (2013).

94. *Id.*

95. *Id.*

96. *Id.*

97. Susan L. Karamanian, *Dispute Settlement Under NAFTA Chapter 11, in* The Sword and the Scales: The United States and International Courts and Tribunals 407 (Cesare P.R. Romano ed. 2009).

98. *Id.*

VI. NAFTA and the environment: *Department of Transportation v. Public Citizen*

As noted earlier, congressional approval of NAFTA's implementation did not bring opposition to an end, even within the Congress itself. The side agreement on environmental protection was essential to the implementation bill's passage. With the passage of that bill, environmental concerns continued, in particular focusing on cross-border trucking into the United States as a source of air pollution, particularly along the southern border. But even with the passage of NAFTA in 1993 and its implementation in 1994, the border between the U.S. and Mexico remained effectively closed to the international flow of trucks.

As economist Robert Carbaugh summarizes the situation:

> Despite the advantages of NAFTA, the United States refused to comply with NAFTA's regulations providing an open border policy in ground transportation of goods across the U.S.-Mexican border. Mexico's dissatisfaction regarding this issue resulted in its submission of the dispute to the NAFTA resolution panel in the year 2000. Also, Canada intervened in the conflict on behalf of Mexico, maintaining that NAFTA required the equal treatment of foreign and domestic truckers. However, the United States justified its position on the grounds of safety of trucks and drivers.[99]

In the case discussed in this section, domestic law—the Bus Regulatory Reform Act of 1982—was claimed by petitioners to provide a statutory basis for their efforts to restrict cross-border traffic into the United States. The statute imposed a moratorium on the granting of authority to Mexican and Canadian motor carriers to operate in the United States beyond a limited zone along the respective borders. The moratorium with respect to Canada was lifted that same year, giving U.S. carriers access to Canadian markets; but the restrictions on Mexican-domiciled trucks and regular-route buses remained. They could operate only in border commercial zones, generally three to twenty miles past a U.S. municipality's corporate limits. Beyond that limit, Mexican trucks had to offload their cargo onto American trailers. When American truckers crossed the border into Mexico, they were required to do the reverse. In other words, an international shipment traveling from Mexico to the United States or vice versa demanded at least two drivers and two trailers to perform a single freight movement.

The dispute concerning the opening of the U.S.-Mexican border to international trucking in this case grew out of a series of legislative and agency actions taken in the U.S. involving the deregulation of transportation generally. In 1978, the Federal Government had deregulated the airline industry and eventually abolished the Civil Aeronautics Board, the regulatory body in involved in that industry's

99. Robert J. Carbaugh, *NAFTA and the U.S.-Mexico Trucking Dispute*, 4 J. Int'l & Global Econ. Stud. 1, 4–5 (2011).

regulation. The deregulation of interstate trucking began in earnest in 1980 and culminated with the abolition of the Interstate Commerce Commission in 1994. Intrastate trucking was also deregulated in 1994. But even with the passage of NAFTA in 1993 and its implementation in 1994, trucking at the border between the U.S. and Mexico remained regulated, effectively closed to the international flow of trucks.

In March, 2002, the Federal Motor Carrier Safety Administration (FMCSA) proposed three regulations to allow Mexican trucks to operate beyond the commercial zones, setting safety-monitoring procedures for all Mexican-domiciled carriers operating anywhere in the United States. Before these rules were issued, an FMCSA assessment found that they would have no significant negative environmental impact. The agency therefore concluded that a full Environmental Impact Statement was not necessary. It then issued a finding of no significant impact, followed by the interim final rules. On November 27, 2002, President Bush modified the 1982 moratorium to clear the way for expanded truck and bus operations. At that point, Public Citizen, a public interest group, sued to require a NEPA statement from the FMCSA. That is the focus of the case below. Our purpose in examining the case is its demonstration of how interlegalities set up by the development of transnational law create new spaces for domestic legal mobilization.

Department of Transp. v. Public Citizen

541 U.S. 752 (2004)

Justice Thomas delivered the opinion of the Court.

In this case, we confront the question whether the National Environmental Policy Act of 1969 (NEPA), and the Clean Air Act (CAA), require the Federal Motor Carrier Safety Administration (FMCSA) to evaluate the environmental effects of cross-border operations of Mexican-domiciled motor carriers, where FMCSA's promulgation of certain regulations would allow such cross-border operations to occur. Because FMCSA lacks discretion to prevent these cross border operations, we conclude that these statutes impose no such requirement on FMCSA.

I

B

We now turn to the factual and procedural background of this case. Before 1982, motor carriers domiciled in Canada and Mexico could obtain certification to operate within the United States from the Interstate Commerce Commission (ICC). In 1982, Congress, concerned about discriminatory treatment of United States motor carriers in Mexico and Canada, enacted a 2-year moratorium on new grants of operating authority. Congress authorized the President to extend the moratorium beyond the 2-year period if Canada or Mexico continued to interfere with United States motor carriers, and also authorized the President to lift or modify the moratorium if he determined that doing so was in the national interest. Although the moratorium on Canadian motor carriers was quickly lifted, the moratorium on Mexican motor carriers remained, and was extended by the President.

In December 1992, the leaders of Mexico, Canada, and the United States signed the North American Free Trade Agreement (NAFTA), 32 I.L.M. 605 (1993). As part of NAFTA, the United States agreed to phase out the moratorium and permit Mexican motor carriers to obtain operating authority within the United States' interior by January 2000. On NAFTA's effective date (January 1, 1994), the President began to lift the trade moratorium by allowing the licensing of Mexican carriers to provide some bus services in the United States. The President, however, did not continue to ease the moratorium on the timetable specified by NAFTA, as concerns about the adequacy of Mexico's regulation of motor carrier safety remained.

The Government of Mexico challenged the United States' implementation of NAFTA's motor carrier provisions under NAFTA's dispute-resolution process, and in February 2001, an international arbitration panel determined that the United States' "blanket refusal" of Mexican motor carrier applications breached the United States' obligations under NAFTA. Shortly thereafter, the President made clear his intention to lift the moratorium on Mexican motor carrier certification following the preparation of new regulations governing grants of operating authority to Mexican motor carriers.

In May 2001, FMCSA published for comment proposed rules concerning safety regulation of Mexican motor carriers. One rule (the Application Rule) addressed the establishment of a new application form for Mexican motor carriers that seek authorization to operate within the United States. Another rule (the Safety Monitoring Rule) addressed the establishment of a safety-inspection regime for all Mexican motor carriers that would receive operating authority under the Application Rule.

In December 2001, Congress enacted the Department of Transportation and Related Agencies Appropriations Act. Section 350 of this Act, provided that no funds appropriated under the Act could be obligated or expended to review or to process any application by a Mexican motor carrier for authority to operate in the interior of the United States until FMCSA implemented specific application and safety-monitoring requirements for Mexican carriers. Some of these requirements went beyond those proposed by FMCSA in the Application and Safety Monitoring Rules. Congress extended the § 350 conditions to appropriations for Fiscal Years 2003 and 2004.

In January 2002, acting pursuant to NEPA's mandates, FMCSA issued a programmatic EA for the proposed Application and Safety Monitoring Rules. FMCSA's EA evaluated the environmental impact associated with three separate scenarios: where the President did not lift the moratorium; where the President did but where (contrary to what was legally possible) FMCSA did not issue any new regulations; and the Proposed Action Alternative, where the President would modify the moratorium and where FMCSA would adopt the proposed regulations. The EA considered the environmental impact in the categories of traffic and congestion, public safety and health, air quality, noise, socioeconomic factors, and environmental Justice. Vital to the EA's analysis, however, was the assumption that there would be no change in trade volume between the United States and Mexico due to the issuance of the regulations. FMCSA did note that § 350's restrictions made it impossible for Mexican motor carriers to operate in the interior of the United States before FMCSA's issuance of the regulations. But, FMCSA determined that "this and any other associated effects in trade characteristics would be the result of the modification of the moratorium" by the President, not a result of FMCSA's implementation of the proposed safety regulations. Because FMCSA concluded that the entry of the Mexican trucks was not an "effect" of its regulations, it did not consider any environmental impact that might be caused by the increased presence of Mexican trucks within the United States.

The particular environmental effects on which the EA focused, then, were those likely to arise from the increase in the number of roadside inspections of Mexican trucks and buses due to the proposed regulations. The EA concluded that these effects (such as a slight increase in emissions, noise from the trucks, and possible danger to passing motorists) were minor and could be addressed and avoided in the inspections process itself. The EA also noted that the increase of inspection-related emissions would be at least partially offset by the fact that the safety requirements would reduce the number of Mexican trucks operating in the United States. Due to these calculations, the EA concluded that the issuance of the proposed regulations would have no significant impact on the environment, and hence FMCSA, on the same day as it released the EA, issued a FONSI.

On March 19, 2002, FMCSA issued the two interim rules, delaying their effective date until May 3, 2002, to allow public comment on provisions that FMCSA added to satisfy the requirements of § 350. In the regulatory preambles, FMCSA relied on its EA and its FONSI to demonstrate compliance with NEPA. FMCSA also addressed the CAA in the preambles, determining that it did not need to perform a "conformity review" of the proposed regulations under 42 U.S.C. § 7506(c)(1) because the increase in emissions from these regulations would fall below the Environmental Protection Agency's (EPA's) threshold levels needed to trigger such a review.

In November 2002, the President lifted the moratorium on qualified Mexican motor carriers. Before this action, however, respondents filed petitions for judicial review of the Application and Safety Monitoring Rules, arguing that the rules were promulgated in violation of NEPA and the CAA. The Court of Appeals agreed with respondents, granted the petitions, and set aside the rules.

The Court of Appeals concluded that the EA was deficient because it failed to give adequate consideration to the overall environmental impact of lifting the moratorium on the cross-border operation of Mexican motor carriers. According to the Court of Appeals, FMCSA was required to consider the environmental effects of the entry of Mexican trucks because "the President's rescission of the moratorium was 'reasonably foreseeable' at the time the EA was prepared and the decision not to prepare an EIS was made." Due to this perceived deficiency, the Court of Appeals remanded the case for preparation of a full EIS.

The Court of Appeals also directed FMCSA to prepare a full CAA conformity determination for the challenged regulations. It concluded that FMCSA's determination that emissions attributable to the challenged rules would be below the threshold levels was not reliable because the agency's CAA determination reflected the "illusory distinction between the effects of the regulations themselves and the effects of the presidential rescission of the moratorium on Mexican truck entry."

We granted certiorari, and now reverse.

II

An agency's decision not to prepare an EIS can be set aside only upon a showing that it was "arbitrary, capricious, an abuse of discretion, or otherwise not in accordance with law." 5 U.S.C. § 706(2)(A). Here, FMCSA based its FONSI upon the analysis contained within its EA; respondents argue that the issuance of the FONSI was arbitrary and capricious because the EA's analysis was flawed. In particular, respondents criticize the EA's failure to take into account the various environmental effects caused by the increase in cross-border operations of Mexican motor carriers.

Under NEPA, an agency is required to provide an EIS only if it will be undertaking a "major Federal actio[n]," which "significantly affect[s] the quality of the human environment." Under applicable CEQ regulations, "[m]ajor Federal action" is defined to "includ[e] actions with effects that may be major and which are potentially subject to Federal control and responsibility." "Effects" is defined to "include: (a) Direct effects, which are caused by the action and occur at the same time and place," and "(b) Indirect effects, which are caused by the action and are later in time or farther removed in distance, but are still reasonably foreseeable." Thus, the relevant question is whether the increase in cross-border operations of Mexican motor carriers, with the correlative release of emissions by Mexican trucks, is an "effect" of FMCSA's issuance of the Application and Safety Monitoring Rules; if not, FMCSA's failure to address these effects in its EA did not violate NEPA, and so FMCSA's issuance of a FONSI cannot be arbitrary and capricious.

A

To answer this question, we begin by explaining what this case does not involve. What is not properly before us, despite respondents' argument to the contrary, is any challenge to the EA due to its failure properly to consider possible alternatives to the proposed action (i.e., the issuance of the challenged rules) that would mitigate the environmental impact of the authorization of cross-border operations by Mexican motor carriers. Persons challenging an agency's compliance with NEPA must "structure their participation so that it . . . alerts the agency to the [parties'] position and contentions," in order to allow the agency to give the issue meaningful consideration. None of the respondents identified in their comments any rulemaking alternatives beyond those evaluated in the EA, and none urged FMCSA to consider alternatives. Because respondents did not raise these particular objections to the EA, FMCSA was not given the opportunity to examine any proposed alternatives to determine if they were reasonably available. Respondents have therefore forfeited any objection to the EA on the ground that it failed adequately to discuss potential alternatives to the proposed action.

Admittedly, the agency bears the primary responsibility to ensure that it complies with NEPA, and an E.A's or an EIS' flaws might be so obvious that there is no need for a commentator to point them out specifically in order to preserve its ability to challenge a proposed action. But that situation is not before us. With respect to FMCSA's ability to mitigate, respondents can argue only that FMCSA could regulate emissions from Mexican trucks indirectly, through making the safety-registration process more onerous or by removing older, more polluting trucks through more effective enforcement of motor carrier safety standards. But respondents fail to identify any evidence that shows that any effect from these possible actions would be significant, or even noticeable, for air-quality purposes. The connection between enforcement of motor carrier safety and the environmental harms alleged in this case is also tenuous at best. Nor is it clear that FMC SA could, consistent with its limited statutory mandates, reasonably impose on Mexican carriers standards beyond those already required in its proposed regulations.

B

With this point aside, respondents have only one complaint with respect to the EA: It did not take into account the environmental effects of increased cross-border operations of Mexican motor carriers. Respondents' argument that FMCSA was required to consider these effects is simple. Under § 350, FMCSA is barred from expending any funds to process or review any applications by Mexican motor carriers until FMCSA implemented a variety of specific application and safety monitoring requirements for Mexican carriers. This expenditure bar makes it impossible for any Mexican motor carrier to receive authorization to operate within the United States until FMCSA issued the regulations challenged here. The promulgation of the regulations, the argument goes, would "caus[e]" the entry of Mexican trucks (and hence also cause any emissions such trucks would produce), and the entry of the trucks is "reasonably foreseeable." Thus, the argument concludes, under the relevant CEQ regulations, FMCSA must take these emissions into account in its EA when evaluating whether to produce an EIS.

Respondents' argument, however, overlooks a critical feature of this case: FMCSA has no ability to countermand the President's lifting of the moratorium or otherwise categorically to exclude Mexican motor carriers from operating within the United States. To be sure, § 350 did restrict the ability of FMCSA to authorize cross-border operations of Mexican motor carriers, but Congress did not otherwise modify FMCSA's statutory mandates. In particular, FMCSA remains subject to the mandate of 49 U.S.C. § 13902(a)(l), that FMCSA "shall register a person to provide transportation ... as a motor carrier if [it] finds that the person is willing and able to comply with" the safety and financial responsibility requirements established by the Department of Transportation. Under FMCSA's entirely reasonable reading of this provision, it must certify any motor carrier that can show that it is willing and able to comply with the various substantive requirements for safety and financial responsibility contained in DOT regulations; only the moratorium prevented it from doing so for Mexican motor carriers before 2001. Thus, upon the lifting of the moratorium, if FMCSA refused to authorize a Mexican motor carrier for cross-border services, where the Mexican motor carrier was willing and able to comply With the various substantive safety and financial responsibilities rules, it would violate § 13902(a)(1).

If it were truly impossible for FMCSA to comply with both § 350 and § 13902(a)(1), then we would be presented with an irreconcilable conflict of laws. As the later enacted provision, § 350 would quite possibly win out. But FMCSA can easily satisfy both mandates: It can issue the application and safety inspection rules required by § 350, and start processing applications by Mexican motor carriers and authorize those that satisfy § 13902(a)(1)'s conditions. Without a conflict, then, FMCSA must comply with all of its statutory mandates.

Respondents must rest, then, on a particularly unyielding variation of "but for" causation, where an agency's action is considered a cause of an environmental effect even when the agency has no authority to prevent the effect. However, a "but for" causal relationship is insufficient to make an agency responsible for a particular effect under NEPA and the relevant regulations. As this Court held in *Metropolitan Edison Co. v. People Against Nuclear Energy*, 460 U.S. 766, 774 (1983), NEPA requires "a reasonably close causal relationship" between the environmental effect and the alleged cause. The Court analogized this requirement to the "familiar doctrine of proximate cause from tort law." In particular, "courts must look to the underlying policies or legislative intent in order to draw a manageable line between those causal changes that may make an actor responsible for an effect and those that do not."

Also, inherent in NEPA and its implementing regulations is a "rule of reason," which ensures that agencies determine whether and to what extent to prepare an EIS based on the usefulness of any new potential information to the decision-making process. Where the preparation of an EIS would serve "no purpose" in light of NEPA's regulatory scheme as a whole, no rule of reason worthy of that title would require an agency to prepare an EIS.

In these circumstances, the underlying policies behind NEPA and Congress' intent, as informed by the "rule of reason," make clear that the causal connection between FMCSA's issuance of the proposed regulations and the entry of the Mexican trucks is insufficient to make FMCSA responsible under NEPA to consider the environmental effects of the entry. The NEPA EIS requirement serves two purposes. First, "[i]t ensures that the agency, in reaching its decision, will have available, and will carefully consider, detailed information concerning significant environmental impacts." Second, it "guarantees that the relevant information will be made available to the larger audience that may also play a role in both the decision-making process and the implementation of that decision." Requiring FMCSA to consider the environmental effects of the entry of Mexican trucks would fulfill neither of these statutory purposes. Since FMCSA has no ability categorically to prevent the cross-border operations of Mexican motor carriers, the environmental impact of the cross-border operations would have no effect on FMCSA's decision-making FMCSA simply lacks the power to act on whatever information might be contained in the EIS.

Similarly, the informational purpose is not served. The "informational role" of an EIS is to "giv[e] the public the assurance that the agency 'has indeed considered environmental concerns in its decision-making process,' and, perhaps more significantly, provid[e] a springboard for public comment" in the agency decision-making process itself. The purpose here is to ensure that the "larger audience" can provide input as necessary to the agency making the relevant decisions. But here, the "larger audience" can have no impact on FMCSA's decision-making, since, as just noted, FMCSA simply could not act on whatever input this "larger audience" could provide.

It would not, therefore, satisfy NEPA's "rule of reason" to require an agency to prepare a full EIS due to the environmental impact of an action it could not refuse to perform. Put another way, the legally relevant cause of the entry of the Mexican trucks is not FMCSA's action, but instead the actions of the President in lifting the moratorium and those of Congress in granting the President this authority while simultaneously limiting FMCSA's discretion.

Consideration of the CEQ's "cumulative impact" regulation does not change this analysis. An agency is required to evaluate the "[c]umulative impact" of its action, which is defined as "the impact on the environment which results from the incremental impact of the action when added to other past, present, and reasonably foreseeable future actions regardless of what agency (Federal or non-Federal) or person undertakes such other actions." The "cumulative impact" regulation required FMCSA to consider the "incremental impact" of the safety rules themselves, in the context of the President's lifting of the moratorium and other relevant circumstances. But this is exactly what FMCSA did in its EA. FMCSA appropriately and reasonably examined the incremental impact of its safety rules assuming the President's modification of the moratorium (and, hence, assuming the increase in cross-border operations of Mexican motor carriers). The "cumulative impact" regulation does not require FMCSA to treat the lifting of the moratorium itself, or consequences from the lifting of the moratorium, as an effect of its promulgation of its Application and Safety Monitoring Rules.

C

We hold that where an agency has no ability to prevent a certain effect due to its limited statutory authority over the relevant actions, the agency cannot be considered a legally relevant "cause" of the effect. Hence, under NEPA and the implementing CEQ regulations, the agency need not consider these effects in its EA when determining whether its action is a "major Federal action." Because the President, not FMCSA, could authorize (or not authorize) cross-border operations from Mexican motor carriers, and because FMCSA has no discretion to prevent the entry of Mexican trucks, its EA did not need to consider the environmental effects arising from the entry.

IV

FMCSA did not violate NEPA or the relevant CEQ regulations when it did not consider the environmental effect of the increase in cross-border operations of Mexican motor carriers in its EA. Nor did FMCSA act improperly by not performing, pursuant to the CAA and relevant regulations, a full conformity review analysis for its proposed regulations. We therefore reject respondents' challenge to the procedures used in promulgating these regulations. Accordingly, the judgment of the Court of Appeals is reversed, and the case is remanded for further proceedings consistent with this opinion.

It is so ordered.

Notes and Questions

1. Why does the Court conclude the NEPA was not applicable? What was the basis of this conclusion—pre-existing U.S. law or NAFTA? Both?

2. How does the *Public Citizen* Court's holding that the FMCSA did not need to consider NEPA affect the status of U.S. environmental law relative to NAFTA? Is U.S. environmental law strengthened or weakened by NAFTA?

3. The passage of NAFTA did not settle the question of its implementation, particularly along the southern border. In the following excerpt, Robert Carbaugh details Congressional efforts to tighten the border against Mexican trucking:

> From 2001 to 2006, Congress passed several pieces of legislation that made NAFTA's cross-border provision unachievable.
>
> In response to the termination of the [Bush-era] pilot program, the Mexican government in March, 2009 increased tariffs on 89 products, with a value of $2.4 billion, that were imported from the United States. Calibrated to make U.S. products uncompetitive in Mexico's market, the tariffs ranged from 10 to 45 percent and covered a variety of products that included paper, home appliances, vegetables, fruit, Christmas trees, suntan lotion, and other consumer goods. Among the states hit hardest by Mexico's tariffs were California, Oregon, and Washington, which exported these products to Mexico.
>
> To add to political pressure, in August, 2010 the Mexican government announced a new list of retaliatory tariffs on imports from the United States.
>
> In March 2011, President Obama and President Felipe Calderon of Mexico unveiled a deal to resolve the dispute that kept Mexican trucks off American roads and resulted in billions of dollars in tariffs on U.S. exports to Mexico. Under the plan, in exchange for giving Mexican trucks access to U.S. roadways, the Mexican government will eliminate its $2.6 billion in tariffs targeted at 99 products. The first half of the tariffs will be removed after both governments sign the agreement. The remaining tariffs will be eliminated after the first Mexican truck is certified under a series of new standards, including English-language, drug, and safety tests, which are monitored by the U.S. Department of Transportation. The proposed project will not be a pilot program but an initial stage that will include several thousand trucks and eventually bring as many vehicles as needed into the United States.

> The proposed requirements for Mexican trucks are more stringent than those previously established in NAFTA and somewhat tougher than those currently in force for American truckers. For example, Mexican trucks will have to carry electronic recorders to ensure that they make only cargo trips across the border and to track compliance with U.S. hours-of-service laws. This means that Mexican trucks will be prohibited from hauling freight between destinations within the United States.
>
> However, the Teamsters Union and certain trucking companies oppose the deal, saying it sacrifices American jobs when unemployment is high so that big business can save money partly by hiring cheaper drivers.[100]

4. The situation continued to unfold with the following developments:

After bilateral negotiations, the Obama Administration announced a new pilot program to allow long-haul Mexican trucks into the United States in April 2011. The first Mexican truck with long-haul operating authority crossed the border in October 2011.

> As of December 2013, there were 14 Mexico-domiciled carriers with active long-haul operating authority in the pilot program; 9 of these had been granted permanent operating authority, and 5 had provisional operating authority, although just 2 Mexican carriers accounted for most of the border crossing activity. Two additional carriers were in the process of applying for long-haul operating authority. The 14 approved carriers have used about 45 trucks to make nearly 10,000 border crossings since October 2011. To put this number in context, on average about 14,000 trucks cross the border from Mexico each day.[101]

5. The Bush and Obama programs differ in various ways, including the requirement (under the Obama program) that Mexican trucks carry recorders to track drivers' time on the road, and their whereabouts within U.S. territory. These are ostensibly safety measures put in place to address environmental concerns. But note how technology allows the environmental protection to morph into surveillance of truckers' movements—a concern related to U.S. controversies over immigration policy (discussed further in Section VI, below):

> Under the Bush program, Mexican trucks did not undergo a "full inspection" (as defined in regulation), but were "checked" to see whether the carrier had passed a pre-authority safety audit (by displaying a special decal) and whether the driver had a valid license and was proficient in English. The Obama Administration's pilot requires, during an initial period of at least three months, full inspections of all participating long-haul Mexican

100. Carbaugh, *supra* note 99, at 8.

101. John Frittelli, *Status of Mexican Trucks in the United States: Frequently Asked Questions* 1 (Cong. Res. Serv. 2014).

trucks when they arrive at the border. The Bush program anticipated the installation of global positioning system (GPS) devices on Mexican trucks to monitor their travel in the United States. The Obama pilot incorporates not only GPS devices but also electronic onboard recorders (EOBRs) to enforce driver hours-of-service limits and to track the trucks' movements inside the United States. The Bush program, limited to 100 carriers, would have used crash data to determine the safety of Mexican long-haul trucks. The Obama plan has no limit on the number of Mexican carriers and uses roadside inspection data rather than crash data to determine the safety of Mexican trucks.[102]

VII. Renewing the borders after NAFTA

NAFTA's suspension of tariffs allowed for an acceleration of trade across the northern and southern borders of the United States, but the potential for U.S. job loss remained a concern (as subsequent legislative initiatives in Congress indicate). After NAFTA's implementation in 1994, the Clinton administration worked with a bipartisan coalition in Congress to reform immigration—to criminalize visa overstays, bar unregistered immigrants from receiving health and welfare benefits, and, in particular, to harden the southern border. While political support for restricting immigration is by no means new in the United States, NAFTA highlights a logic by which economic relations are severed from non-economic considerations of social welfare, as the trilateral agreement facilitates transnational markets but blocks social concerns at the border. At the time, due to NAFTA and other factors, Mexican migration to the United States was rising, compounding some Americans' concerns with job loss. As free trade expanded under NAFTA, immigration into the United States became subject to new controls under the Illegal Immigration Reform and Immigrant Responsibility Act (IIRAIRA) of 1996 (Pub. L. 104-208). In that same year, the Clinton administration passed welfare reform legislation that ended key federal entitlements, mandating block grants to be administered by the separate states. [103]

The following excerpt from Saskia Sassen's analysis of labor migration in relation to global capitalism—written before NAFTA's passage—anticipates some of the effects of liberalization on labor migration from Mexico into the United States, as well as something of the politicization of migrant labor such that immigrants in the labor force have second-class status.

---

102. *Id.* at 2–3.

103. Personal Responsibility and Work Opportunity Reconciliation Act of 1996 (PRWORA). Pub.L. 104-193, 110 Stat. 2105.

Saskia Sassen, The Mobility of Labor and Capital

31, 33–34, 36–37 (1988)

International labor migrations did not evolve as an important labor-supply system until the consolidation phase of the world capitalist economy. The earlier phases of capitalist penetration and incorporation of new regions into a single world economy under European hegemony had generated different types of labor-supply systems. The most important types relied on (1) forced movements of people from one area of the periphery to another, and (2) the subjugation of indigenous and hitherto autonomous populations and their forced transformation into laborers through such means as slavery, *mita*, peonage, *encomienda*, and tribal contract labor. (Some of these persist today in areas not completely transformed by the generalization of market relations.)

* * * *

The incorporation of most areas of the world into the capitalist system resulted in the disintegration or subordination of non-capitalist forms of subsistence [references omitted]. Although in colonial areas this disintegration was less thorough than in Western Europe, it was sufficient to move large masses of people into the labor market. Here we find the conditions for the creation of a supply of potential migrant workers. . . .

The generalization of capitalist relations and the corresponding transformation of land into a commodity gave a "voluntary" quality to the resulting migrations. [Note omitted.] This was in contrast to the forced population transfers of the earlier stage. The disintegration of autonomous modes of subsistence resulted in the creation of labor reserves willing to be mobilized into the labor market. There was no longer a need for the direct, physical subjugation and mobilization of workers. The new social structure accomplished this by robbing them of their means of subsistence. This process was not fully completed until the twentieth century. [Note omitted.]

The consolidation of a world system through the subordination of large areas of the world in the form of a periphery also brought about a shift in the flow of labor. Henceforth, the major international labor flows originated in the less-developed countries and went to satisfy the labor needs of the industrializing countries. The flow was no longer from one colonial area to another, as was the case in the earlier phase of penetration and colonization. After the early phase of forced-labor mobilization, the reserves from which immigrant labor was drawn expanded gradually to encompass more and more parts of the world. The major Western European countries first imported labor from their immediate peripheries: Irish went to England; Poles to Germany; Italians and Belgians to France [references omitted]. Then this periphery was expanded to include all of Eastern and Southern Europe—the main sources of labor for Western Europe and eventually the United States. As these reserves were exhausted or their flows interrupted due to wars, China, Mexico, and North Africa emerged as important labor suppliers. In the last two decades, the Caribbean Basin and a growing number of countries in South America, Africa, and Asia have become major labor suppliers.

An important new pattern of labor flows has been added since the 1960s to the continuing flow from developing countries to developed countries. [Note omitted.] The export of jobs from the developed countries to the developing countries in the form of export processing zones, has brought about new domestic and international labor flows *within* the developing countries. Without the development of the new industrial zones, some of these internal migrations would not have occurred. . . .

The shift from mobilization of forced-labor and colonizing migrations to international labor migrations reflects the complex internal differentiation of the world system. The consolidation of the world economic system has paralleled the strengthening of the nation-state as the basic political unit. Since the late nineteenth century, the state has regulated the entry and exit of labor.

* * * *

At first glance, the strengthening of states and the concomitant enforcement of borders seems to counter the needs of a consolidated world economy for massive international labor migrations. In fact, national boundaries do not act as barriers so much as mechanisms reproducing the system through the international division of labor. The capitalist world economy consists of a multiplicity of political units, the nation-states. This ensures that no single political regime can gain full control over the world economy. . . . National boundaries are one way of facilitating international specialization and higher returns on accumulated capital, including human capital. Both are central tendencies in capitalist development.

The enforcement of national borders contributes to the existence of a large number of countries in the form of a periphery and the designation of its workers as a labor reserve for global capital. Border enforcement is a mechanism facilitating the extraction of cheap labor by assigning criminal status to a segment of the working class—illegal immigrants. Foreign workers undermine a nation's working class when the state renders foreigners socially and politically powerless. At the same time, border enforcement meets the demands of organized labor in the labor-receiving country insofar as it presumes to protect native workers. Yet *selective* enforcement of policies can circumvent general border policies and protect the interests of economic sectors relying on immigrant labor. This points out the contradictory role of the state in the accumulation process, especially evident in the consolidation of the liberal state [references omitted].

While the generalization of the labor market emerging from the consolidation of the world capitalist economy creates the conditions for international migrations as a world-level labor-supply system, the strengthening of the nation-state creates the conditions for immigrant labor as a distinct category of a nation's labor supply. That is to say, immigrant labor is not just any labor. It is a component in the labor supply with a distinct role in the labor process characterized by: (1) the institutional differentiation of the processes of labor-force reproduction and maintenance; and (2) a particular form of powerlessness, associated with formal or attributed foreign status, that meets the requirements of types of work organization based on direct rather than structural control over the workforce.

VIII. NAFTA and labor

As we have seen, the political debate over NAFTA pitted business and labor interests against each other in all three countries. In the previous section, Saskia Sassen's analysis of the relationship of international trade to labor migration underscores the extent to which labor's concerns with job loss were accommodated (and in some contexts demanded) in the form of restrictions on immigration. But competition for jobs in the homeland were not the only concern; the market for "comparative advantage" was also an issue, and NAFTA's labor provisions set some common standards. In this section, we will consider the labor provisions of NAFTA. NAFTA's labor standards come in the form of a supplemental labor pact called the North American Agreement on Labor Cooperation (NAALC). Negotiated in 1994 by the United States, Canada, and Mexico, NAALC's main objective is "to improve working conditions and living standards in the United States, Mexico, and Canada as NAFTA continue[d] to promote increased trade and closer economic ties among the three countries."[104] The Agreement established National Administrative Offices in each country to implement the agreement and to serve as points of contact between the governments.

As we will see, the labor accord of NAFTA imposed obligations on the United States, Canada, and Mexico to apply international labor principles domestically. In this sense, NAFTA created a transnational labor regime: one that created reciprocal obligations for each country's domestic law systems to adhere to decidedly international labor principles. Consider how these international principles—born in the 1980s from the Generalized System of Preferences' labor provisions—highlight NAFTA's commitment to fair labor standards, as discussed in the following excerpt by Professor Lance Compa.

Lance Compa, *From Chile to Vietnam: International Labour Law and Workers' Rights in International Trade*, *in* Critical Legal Perspectives on Global Governance 143, 150–152 (Gráinne De Búrca et al. eds. 2014)

Negotiated in 1993 by Canada, Mexico, and the United States, the North American Free Trade Agreement's supplemental labour pact, the North American Agreement on Labour Cooperation (NAALC), sets forth eleven 'Labour Principles' that the three signatory countries commit themselves to promote:

1) freedom of association and protection of the right to organize
2) the right to bargain collectively
3) the right to strike
4) forced labour
5) child labour
6) minimum wage, hours of work and other labour standards

104. U.S. Dep't Labor, http://www.dol.gov/ilab/trade/agreements/naalc.htm (last visited July 16, 2016).

7) non-discrimination
8) equal pay for equal work
9) occupational safety and health
10) workers' compensation
11) migrant worker protection.

As with the GSP articulation of 'internationally recognized worker rights', the NAALC's labour principles are not based on ILO standards. This time, rather than US congress declaring international 'rights,' the three NAFTA governments declared a set of 'principles' without reference to ILO standards, except for certain phraseological parallels. They pledged to effectively enforce their *national* labour laws in these 11 subject areas.

With this last, the NAALC introduced what has become a constant among labour provisions in trade agreements: the obligation nto effectively enforce national labour laws rather than to directly incorporate and apply international norms. Unlike much commercial law, labour law is tightly bound to national traditions and cultures of labour-management relations. Labour law reflects the compromise struck over a long period of class struggles within national boundaries.

Governments are loath to yield sovereignty over labour law in the way they might yield sovereignty over intellectual property or investment law. The early versions of labour clauses in trade agreements could not immediately jump to supranational standards and supranational enforcement. Effective enforcement of national law is a reasonable starting point, especially since much national labour law is favourable to workers and unions.

The NAALC principles ranged well beyond the later ILO 'core labour standards' of 1998. The ILO's 'core' addresses organizing and bargaining rights, forced labour, child labour, and discrimination. The NAALC included all these, as well as the 'acceptable conditions' in the GSP clause (wages, hours, health and safety, workers' compensation for workplace injury, and illness and migrant workers' rights).

The NAALC's ample subject matter jurisdiction created opportunities for advocacy not offered in other trade-labour systems. As recently as May 2012, a coalition of US and Mexican trade unions and lawyers' groups filed a complaint with the Mexican labour department against anti-immigrant legislation in Alabama and other US states. They argued, in an imaginative lawyerly fashion, that these state-level anti-immigrant laws made it impossible for the US to effectively enforce its labour laws in workplaces with migrant workers. No other trade agreement's labour chapter contemplates complaints over migrant workers' rights.

The NAALC's complaint procedures reflect a mostly soft-law system with investigations, public hearings, research and written reports, government-to-government consultations, independent evaluations, non-binding recommendations and similar measures. But a hard-law edge can be applied for three labor principles: those covering minimum wage, child labour and occupational safety and health. An independent arbitral panel is empowered to fine an offending government for a 'persistent pattern' of failure to effectively enforce domestic labour law. If the fine is not paid, the panel can apply trade sanctions on the firm, industry, or sector where workers' rights violations occurred.

For advocates willing to put it to the test, the NAALC has emerged as a viable arena for creative transnational action. With its unusual 'cross-border' complaint mechanism, the Agreement provided an opportunity for workers, trade unions and their allies in the US, Mexico and Canada to work together precisely to defend workers' rights against abused by corporations and governments.

The 40 cases filed since 1994 involved transnational coalitions of unions and allied human rights and community groups who found in the NAALC's mechanism new opportunities to develop relationships and joint action. Advocates demanded investigations, public hearings and government consultations on workers' rights violations. With the NAALC, they had space to strategise in a sustained fashion, gathering evidence for drafting a complaint, crafting its elements, setting priorities, defining demands, launching media campaigns, meeting with government officials to see the agenda for a hearing and to press them for thorough reviews and follow-up, preparing to testify in public hearings, engaging technical experts to buttress a case with scientific elements (a health and safety case, for example), influencing the composition of independent experts' panels and the terms of reference of their investigation, and other concrete tasks.

To take just one example of many: two US-based human rights groups, Human Rights Watch and the International Labor Rights Forum, along with the Mexican National Association of Democratic Lawyers (ANAD), filed a complaint with the National Administrative Office of the United States (NAO) in May 1997 alleging 'a pattern of wide-spread, state-tolerated sex discrimination against prospective and actual female workers in the *maquiladora* [supply-chain assembly factories] sector along the Mexico-US border.' The submission alleged a common practice of requiring pregnancy testing of all female job applicants and denying employment to those whose test results are positive. The complaint also said that employers pressure employees who become pregnant to leave their jobs.

The groups submitting the complaint argued that the practice by employers and the failure of the labour authorities to combat it—sometimes by omission, sometimes by overt support for the employers' discriminatory policy—violates Mexico's obligations under the NAALC. The US labour department accepted the case and held public hearings in cities along the Mexico-US border. Related complaints and demonstrations by workers and support groups on both sides of the bordered created a media firestorm. Several US companies in the *maquiladora* zones announced theyh would halt pregnancy testing, and the Mexican federal government prohibited pregnancy testing of women applying for employment in federal ministries.

The NAALC case gave new credibility and weight to women's rights advocates in Mexico. In Shareen Hertel's words: 'The creating of the NAFTA side accord presented activities with a new political opportunity . . . . Submission 9701 put pregnancy testing on the map internationally, and Mexican activists used that international attention to pressure their government for domestic reforms.'

The new instruments and institutions of international labour rights advocacy reflected in the NAALC were flawed. But the created spaces, terrains, platforms and other metaphorical *loci* where advocates could unite across frontiers to promote new norms, mobilise actors, call to account governments and corporations, disseminate research findings, launch media campaigns, educate each other and the public, challenge traditional notions of sovereignty, and give legitimacy to their cause by invoking human rights and labour rights principles. In summary, advocates redefined debates and discourse by breaking up old frameworks and shaping new ones.

As in the GSP process, lawyers played a driving role in NAALC complaints and case processing. Labour and human rights attorneys in the three NAALC partners created an enduring network that meets on a regular basis to review cases and make strategic choices for new ones.

Washington apples case

For an example of how NAALC has influenced cross-border policy, we turn to Mexican NAO Case Number 9802, or the "Washington State Apples Case."

The case involved more than 50,000 Mexican laborers, who worked in the apple orchards and processing plants of Washington state—the most prolific apple-growing region in the United States. Laborers' efforts to form trade unions, arrange collective bargaining, ensure job health and safety protection, and prevent workplace discrimination were repudiated by employers. In response, the laborers joined forces with the Teamsters Union and the United Farm Workers to work toward submitting a NAALC case on the issues they faced. The Teamsters Union and United Farm Workers were joined by numerous farmworker advocacy groups and human rights organizations, and a formal complaint was drafted. The background of the case involved complex cross-border mobilizations of farm workers:

> The two US unions were each trying to organize apple workers, one in the orchards and one in the processing plants. They wanted to avoid employers' countercharges that they were out to destroy apple workers' jobs. On the Mexican side, the independent union allies in the Unión Nacional de Trabajadores (UNT), the Frente Auténtico del Trabajo (FAT), the Frente Democrático de Campesinos (FDC) and other groups working with their US counterparts were sensitive to government and official union accusations that they were "puppets" of protectionist US unions. At the same time, from an inside-Mexico competitive standpoint, they wanted to be seen as front-line defenders of migrant workers in the United States, ahead of the official unions and ahead of the PRI government.[105]

---

105. Lance Compa, *NAFTA's Labor Side Agreement and International Labour Solidarity*, *in* Place, Space and the New Labour Internationalisms 159 (Peter Waterman & Jane Wills, eds. 2001).

The complaint filed with the Mexican NAO resulted in a ministerial order in May, 2000:

Ministerial Agreement Mexican NAO Case Nos. 9801 (*Solec*), 9802 (*Washington Apples*), and 9803 (*DeCoster Egg Farm*) (May 18, 2000)

Joint Declaration

The Department of Labor of the United States of America and the Department of Labor and Social Welfare of Mexico, in accordance with the provisions of the North American Agreement on Labor Cooperation (NAALC), and in order to address matters raised by submissions MX 9801, MX 9802, and MX 9803, agreed to carry out ministerial consultations in a spirit of cooperation and complete respect for the sovereignty of each country regarding labor law and practice on the principles of freedom of association and protection of the right to organize, the right to bargain collectively, minimum employment standards, elimination of employment discrimination, prevention of occupational injuries and illnesses, compensation in cases of occupational injuries and illnesses, and protection of migrant workers.

Acknowledging the commitment of our Governments under the NAALC to ensure the effective enforcement and promotion of our labor laws and regulations;

Recognizing that the NAALC has led to greater levels of cooperation on labor matters between our two countries and pledging to continue and enhance that cooperative spirit;

Understanding that an integral part of the Agreement is a commitment to review public submissions and engage in cooperative consultations on labor matters;

Reaffirming our commitment to the Agreement's eleven labor principles;

Recognizing the need to devote adequate resources for the inspection of workplaces, continued effective and speedy enforcement of safety and health laws and regulations, and promotion of and education about safe and healthy work place practices, as well as to ensure that persons with a legally recognized interest under the law in a particular matter have access to administrative and judicial proceedings for the impartial enforcement of labor laws; and

In conformity with the principles of the NAALC and in efforts to strengthen our commitment under that Agreement to cooperate on labor issues of mutual concern and promote the rights of migrant workers, and in order to promote the principles of freedom of association and the protection of the right to organize, the right to bargain collectively, minimum employment standards, elimination of employment discrimination, prevention of occupational injuries and illnesses, compensation in cases of occupational injuries and illnesses, and protection of migrant workers, the U.S. Department of Labor and the Mexican Department of Labor and Social Welfare agree to the following:

Action Plan

The U.S. Department of Labor and the Mexican Department of Labor and Social Welfare agree to work individually through our Departments and other governmental agencies, and jointly and cooperatively through our respective National Administrative Offices (NAOs), to address the specific concerns and the broad labor rights raised by submissions MX 9801, MX 9802, and MX 9803. We agree to cooperate to assure respect for freedom of association and the protection of the right to organize, which would benefit workers throughout North America. We agree to seek safe and healthy working environments for all workers and the enforcement of minimum employment standards. We agree to work together to eliminate employment discrimination and assure that migrant workers are accorded full protection under the laws.

A follow-up to the conference on agricultural migrant labor in North America will be held. The conference examined the legal, social, and economic issues facing agricultural migrant workers and their families. Participants included representatives of government, labor organizations, business, and non-governmental organizations. As a follow-up to the Conference, officials of the Governments of the United States and Mexico will meet to further exchange information with respect to the role of federal and state agencies in the protection and promotion of the rights of migrant workers in the United States and to explore potential avenues of cooperation regarding the protection of migrant workers. This information exchange will include the participation of labor department officials, Mexican Consular officials who have responsibility of aiding Mexican migrant workers abroad, and representatives of the Office for the Legal Defense of Workers (PROFEDET).

The U.S. Department of Labor will host a government-to-government session in Washington, D.C. to provide Mexican government officials information about the application of U.S. law focusing on the issues raised in submissions MX 9801, MX 9802, and MX 9803. Topics of discussion will include union organizing and bargaining rights, elimination of employment discrimination, minimum conditions of employment, including inspection programs and systems for determining violations of employment conditions for migrant workers, occupational safety and health, including inspection of migrant worker camps and overall working conditions in the agricultural sector, and protection of migrant workers' rights. Participants will include officials from the U.S. Occupational Safety and Health Administration, the U.S. Employment Standards Administration/Wage and Hour Division, the Office of the Solicitor of the Department of Labor, the Equal Employment Opportunity Commission, the National Labor Relations Board and officials from the Mexican Department of Labor and Social Welfare and Mexican consular officials in the United States.

The U.S. Department of Labor will conduct a public forum in the state of Maine where government officials will address migrant agricultural occupational issues and respond to questions of workers, employers, and their representatives. Such a forum will address freedom of association and protection of the right to organize, the right to bargain collectively, minimum employment standards, elimination of employment discrimination, prevention of occupational injuries and illnesses, compensation in cases of occupational injuries and illnesses, and protection of migrant workers, including presentation of compliance information, discussion of employment practices to ensure compliance with applicable U.S. laws and explanation of workers rights, and information on how to file complaints.

The Secretariat will produce a trilingual guide describing law and procedures covering labor rights and protections granted to migrant workers in the United States, Mexico, and Canada. The guide will be made available to workers, individuals, businesses, and organizations.

The U.S. Department of Labor and the Mexican Department of Labor and Social Welfare will continue cooperative consultations and exchange of information at the NAO level on these issues during the implementation of this declaration; and, at the end of the prescribed term, review the activities and commitments made pursuant to this Joint Declaration.

The NAOs shall develop a work plan for carrying out the programs called for under this declaration within 90 days. The program called for under this declaration should be completed within 15 months of the date of its signing.

The U.S. Department of Labor and the Mexican Department of Labor and Social Welfare will make available public information shared under the activities conducted pursuant to this Joint Declaration.

Notes and Questions

1. How does the ministerial agreement presented above affect the ability of labor to organize in the United States and Mexico?

2. Many Americans worry that NAFTA sends "American jobs" south, to Mexico. Meanwhile, proponents argue that NAFTA generates jobs and reduces income inequality between Mexican, Canadian and U.S. workers. Moreover, beyond jobs per se, as we have seen in this Chapter, NAFTA has also been the context of various forms of cross-border cooperation, as well as new forms of tension. An overall assessment remains controversial and open to debate. More than twenty years later, how should analysts assess NAFTA's impact on the working conditions and living standards in its member nations? Consider the following excerpt from the Congressional Research Service:

> Estimating the economic impact of trade agreements is a daunting task due to a lack of data and important theoretical and practical matters associated with generating results from economic models. In addition, such estimates provide an incomplete accounting of the total economic effects of trade agreements. Numerous studies suggest that NAFTA achieved many of the intended trade and economic benefits. Other studies suggest that NAFTA has come at a cost to U.S. workers. This has been in keeping with what most economists maintain, that trade liberalization promotes overall economic

> growth among trading partners, but that there are both winners and losers from adjustments. Not all changes in trade and investment patterns within North America since 1994 can be attributed to NAFTA because trade has also been affected by a number of factors. The sharp devaluation of the peso at the end of the 1990s and the associated recession in Mexico had considerable effects on trade, as did the rapid growth of the U.S. economy during most of the 1990s and, more recently, the economic slowdown caused by the 2008 financial crisis. Trade related job gains and losses since NAFTA may have accelerated trends that were ongoing prior to NAFTA and may not be totally attributable to the trade agreement.[106]

The Council on Foreign Relations further elucidates the actual effect of NAFTA on labor and—while acknowledging that it "is difficult to quantify NAFTA's effect very precisely, given the complexities involved in assigning direct causality between NAFTA's implementation and economic shifts"—concludes:

> Measuring the impact of a specific trade deal on a country's labor market is not a straightforward exercise, and analysts disagree on how to gauge NAFTA's effects. The USTR claims a broadly positive influence, citing figures that show an increase in overall U.S. employment of 24 percent since NAFTA's inception, as well as declining unemployment rates over the same period. In addition, the USTR cites data showing that inflation-adjusted U.S. wages rose 19.3 percent between 1993 and 2007, as compared to only 11 percent in the fourteen years prior.
>
> Many economists agree that NAFTA has had some positive impact on overall U.S. employment. But most also agree that gains have been accompanied by some painful side effects.... The Economic Policy Institute, a left-leaning research organization, says in a policy paper on NAFTA that the deal's trade agenda has served to widen U.S. trade deficits and has indirectly pushed some U.S. workers into lower-paying jobs. But most economists say it's a stretch to blame these shifts on NAFTA.[107]

IX. Discussion: Governance through states

In this chapter, we have presented a preliminary tour of the vertical dimension of transnational law, i.e., legal aspects of the global economy in its diverse relations to domestic social security and national security. We have examined selections from a thick interlegality organized on one hand around the core concepts of state sovereignty and its embodiment in various exercises of executive power, and on the other, in an array of domestic social and political communities differing in their capacity

106. M. Angeles Villarreal & Ian F. Fergusson, Cong. Res. Serv., The North American Free Trade Agreement (NAFTA) 9–10 (2015), http://www.fas.org/sgp/crs/row/R42965.pdf.

107. Lee H. Teslik, Council on Foreign Rel., NAFTA's Economic Impact (2008).

to mobilize as interest groups. The readings show that executive power may lead in the creation intergovernmental agreements to "free trade" by eliminating tariffs, and that the constitutionality of such exercises of power relies on the territorial expression of state sovereignty. Thus, free trade (as set up by NAFTA) does not eliminate national borders; on the contrary, in the United States, NAFTA is inseparable from the Clinton-era reforms of immigration and the George W. Bush conception of national security. We have also marked locations where law is available to domestic interests that are not prone to de-territorialization (especially in environmental protection). It is important to note the extent to which environmentalism and national security vie as proxies for global and domestic interests in relation to the trade issue—a prime example of what we mean by referring to territory as a political relation.

The overall relevance of these issues to the rest of the book is five-fold:

First and foremost, they demonstrate that *transnational law* refers not just to interlegalities that cross sovereign state borders, but also to the instability of the relationship between sovereignty and territoriality within the government—and the corresponding scope for political tensions at those very junctures.

Second, they demonstrate that executive power is central to the labile quality of territory in relation to U.S. sovereignty. Congress and the courts may be primarily reactive in terms of constitutional separation of powers issues, but this does not mean that the executive has free rein in negotiating international trade agreements.[108] Organized labor is actively marginalized in the contexts discussed in this chapter.

Third, they demonstrate that the state/territory relation is the focus of intensive political contestation and mobilization, in which localized (or localize-able) interests function as strategic checks on globalization through executive power, and vice versa. In this context, the global economy, social security and national security are *political* concepts as well as *legal* ones.

Fourth, for the reasons listed above (1–3), we have formulated *transnational law* as dynamic interlegalities shaped (and prone to further reshaping) by the *domestic* politicization of tensions between the global economy, social security and national security—not by actors in the international arena alone. While a full demonstration of the historical and legal development of transnational law is beyond the scope of this book, the point remains that history is relevant, particularly in underscoring the importance of legal locations less directly related to the regulation or deregulation of markets. Contemporary forms of transnational law are shaped not only by global capitalism, but also by the ways in which globalization, social security and

108. For example, tensions between the president and Congress with respect to trade may be expressed legislatively in terms of lower autonomy for executive agents. Davis analyzes this and other expressions of political pressures on executives by legislatures under various conditions (e.g., divided government and selective industry pressures). Christina Davis, Why Adjudicate: Enforcing Trade Rules in the WTO 45, 54, 61 (2012).

national security are mutually implicated with the result that an emphasis on any one unsettles the others.

Accordingly, transnational law is profoundly relevant to the basic conditions of living: employability and employment, wages, and pricing, as well as fundamental aspects of democratic life through political representation through government and associations. These are themes for the next chapter, as we turn to multinational firms and transnational governance by code and contract.

Chapter 4

The World Trade Organization and the Interlegalities of Globalization

I. From regionalization to globalization: Legality and sociality

The previous chapter on NAFTA emphasizes crucial qualifications of the idea of regionalization as implemented by that transnational agreement, as both the production and implementation of NAFTA show the ongoing relevance of distinct interests and impacts (intended and unintended) at all levels—among the negotiating parties and pervasively throughout the social, political and economic fields of the three countries and beyond. Attending to interlegalities (such as in our discussion of NAFTA and throughout this volume) draws attention to many ways in which legal agreements on *any* scale may yield effects on *every* scale. In this chapter, we turn to the WTO from an interlegal perspective.

As preface to that discussion, we recap the interlegalities in the previous chapter. The three signatories—represented by their chief executives and their trade representatives—had significantly different motivations, risks, and stakes in entering into negotiations and seeing them through to ratification. NAFTA was an intergovernmental agreement at the *national* level, and the unit of analysis for any understanding of subsequent adjustments should therefore also be understood as involving national governing bodies and agencies—not "countries" as wholes. The politics of NAFTA in the three countries set up different political consequences, but in all three countries, those consequences lengthened the vertical axis connecting the national government to local government, and more generally between government and governance. In economic terms, NAFTA had different consequences in the three countries, but in all three, sharpened the differences between large and small firms, and between firms with transnational markets and only local markets. In all three countries, again in different ways, NAFTA contributed to a reformulation of the relationship between sovereignty and territory—in the United States with respect to migration and national security, in Canada with respect to the Quebec question and the status of First Nations polities, and in Mexico with regard to new laws allowing Foreign Direct Investment. The discussion overall emphasized the extent to which regional agreements such as NAFTA both advance established interests and introduce new ones between countries as well as within them—in the process, creating the means and ends of new political organizations and mobilizations. In this sense, NAFTA and other such agreements should be understood as transformative, and not merely additive; they are at once stabilizing and destabilizing, depending on the sectors, actors, and communities involved. We carry these observations forward into the discussion of the WTO—an important institution in itself, but, in our volume, serving as our main case study of a global legal project.

The diversity of the dynamics surrounding NAFTA and (as we shall see) the WTO points to the relevance of domestic politics of law and the social dimensions of politics, law, and economy—not just as passive local effects, but also as sources of opportunity and constraint for national executives in their transnational dealings, particularly in democratic or democratizing regimes.[1] The dynamic complexity of domestic social and political economies of law thus adds an important dimension to one's understanding of the global system overall, specifically in relation to what political scientist Daniel Drezner refers to as the problem of "coordination outcomes" (i.e., capacity to align interests and procedures) as a function of countries' capacity to achieve a "great power concert":

> Structural theories lack the capacity to explain variation in coordination outcomes . . . . [T]he great powers—defined here as governments that oversee large internal markets—remain the primary actors writing the rules that regulate the global economy. The key variable affecting global regulatory outcomes is the distribution of interests among the great powers. A great power concert is a necessary and sufficient condition for effective global governance over any transnational issue. Without such a concert, government attempts at regulatory coordination will be incomplete, and nonstate attempts will prove to be a poor substitute.[2]

The distribution of interests within countries is integral to the capacity of national leaders to coordinate interests across countries. In this sense, the previous chapter also helps us understand why, as Professor Drezner observes in relation to the global regulatory system overall, "globalization increases the reward for policy coordination but has a negligible impact on the adjustment costs of coordination."[3] Adjustment costs are domestic, and depending on how the rewards of policy coordination are distributed domestically, rewards and costs may refer to distinct stakeholders. Thus,

---

1. On the correlation between participation in international organizations and democratization, see Jon C. Pevehouse, *Democracy from the Outside-In? International Organizations and Democratization*, 56 INT'L ORG. 515 (2002); Edward D. Mansfield & Jon C. Pevehouse, *Democratization and International Organizations*, 60 INT'L ORG. 137 (2006). *See also* Susan Aaronson & M. Rodwan Abouharb, *Unexpected Bedfellows: The GATT, the WTO and* Some *Democratic Rights*, 55 INT'L STUD. Q. 379 (2011).

2. DANIEL DREZNER, ALL POLITICS IS GLOBAL: EXPLAINING INTERNATIONAL REGULATORY REGIMES. 5 (2007).

3. *Id.*

any proposition linking preference formation and negotiation outcomes between domestic and international spheres is subject to a host of contingent complications.[4]

As we have already seen, that interlegal space is not empty. It is fully inhabited and increasingly a space of political cross-pressures and innovative mobilizations from the right and left. "Globalization" and "neoliberalism" currently feature prominently in the critical agendas of activists in national political parties around the world as well as in social movements, such as the indigenous and peasant movements we shall consider later in this chapter. Thus, the discussion in the previous chapter remains relevant as we turn our transnational lens to focus on the global regulatory system through cases and problems related to the World Trade Organization (WTO).

The WTO has more impact, involving more countries, with more effect, than any other international organization in the world.[5] But its impact should not be misunderstood as the automatically homogenizing effect of a global institution. On the contrary, the WTO functions interlegally—its trade rules driving myriad vectors of compliance, voluntary alignment, tangible and intangible incentives, and wide-ranging local effects. Alongside the WTO are hundreds of regional trade agreements (RTAs) and thousands of bilateral investment treaties (BITs) governing foreign direct investment, as well as unilateral projects of tariff reduction as offshoring replaces import substitution in some developing countries.[6] The very effort to effectuate global trade rules generates heterogeneity in practice as the liberalization encounters resistance, contradictions, exceptions, and unexpected situations—including "failures, flops, and false dawns."[7] A recent assessment finds the WTO "widely regarded as suffering from a deep malaise."[8] The WTO and the very idea of global liberalization are ideas subject to diverse understandings and applications.[9]

As the WTO has matured as an institution, the idea of *trade* as a system of exchange disembedded from other relationships has had to confront various challenges in the form of environmental, labor, and human rights questions. The idea of globalization has itself been challenged, sometimes sharply, by scholars and advocates—challenges

---

4. *See id.* at 6 ("Domestic factors account for preference formation, but not the outcomes of international bargaining.").

5. Gregory Shaffer, *How the World Trade Organization shapes regulatory governance*, 9 REG. & GOVERNANCE 1, 1 (2015).

6. A 2016 WTO report finds 635 notifications of RTAs, of which 267 are in force. *Regional Trade Agreement Gateway*, WORLD TRADE ORG., https://www.wto.org/english/tratop_e/region_e/regfac_e.htm. BITs number in the thousands, with new agreements signed on the average of over one hundred per year since the 1990s. Zachary Elkins, Andrew T. Guzman & Beth Simmons, *Competing for Capital: The Diffusion of Bilateral Investment Treaties, 1960–2000*, 60 INT'L ORG. 811, 814 (2006). On unilateral tariff reductions, see Richard Baldwin, *The World Trade Organization and the Future of Multilateralism*, 30 J. ECON. PERSP. 95, 108 (2016).

7. Baldwin, *supra* note 6, at 95.

8. *Id.*

9. David Singh Grewal & Jedediah Purdy, *Introduction: Law and Neoliberalism*, 77 L. CONTEMP. PROB. 1 (2015).

that involve conflicting assessments of the efficacy of the WTO.[10] The interlegal mobilization of globalization and various inflections of counterglobalization through the WTO are the themes in this chapter. A more comprehensive discussion would extend to the recent proliferation of regional trade agreements and bilateral investment treaties through which much of world trade now operates.[11] These are further evidence that the WTO functions amidst (and to some extent drives) proliferating interlegalities. For the most part these transnational arrangements are beyond the scope of our undertaking, except for their relevance to our discussion of arbitration in Chapter 7, *infra*.

As we turn from the internal complexities of NAFTA's regional system to the global aspirations of the WTO, the complications we considered in Chapter 3 remain relevant to rule-making, accession, complaints, and compliance.[12] This fact underscores the point made at the outset (in Chapter 1) that "the global" is not a structure consisting of nested levels of regulation, but rather of episodically interconnected institutions and investments (both literal and figurative), together with their dynamic pervasive effects.[13] Understanding such relations—or at least understanding their relevance—informs both the theory and pragmatics of international organizations. For example, John Ruggie's influential theory of "embedded liberalism" in post-war international regimes implicitly offers a broad opening for ethnographic analysis in his emphasis on

10. Materials related to challenges involving various issues involving the markets for comparative advantage in relation to the environment, labor and human rights are presented later in the chapter. For examples of conflicting assessments, compare these perspectives from scholars: "Contemporary power shifts have had a profoundly disruptive and destabilizing effect on the ability of the WTO to function and fulfill its intended role in the institutional project of neoliberal globalization. . . . The reason, I argue, is that these power shifts have exacerbated systemic contradictions in the American-led liberal world order." Kristen Hopewell, Breaking the WTO: How Emerging Powers Disrupted the Neoliberal Project 24 (2016). "Citizens are right to insist on greater transparency and openness of international trade policy-making processes: governments that are not held accountable for their policy failures may have little incentive to protect liberal trade. . . . WTO advocates should help democracy advocates to understand that transnational trade is no less beneficial than domestic trade, just as WTO guarantees of freedom and nondiscrimination are no less important than domestic freedoms and legal equality at home." Ernst-Ulrich Petersmann, *The WTO Constitution and Human Rights*, 3 J. Int'l Econ. L. 19, 25 (2000).

11. In contrast to trade and tariffs, there are no multilateral trading rules for foreign direct investment (FDI): "Direct investments in developing countries are overwhelmingly governed by bilateral investment treaties (BITs). BITs are agreements establishing the terms and conditions for private investment by nationals and companies of one country in the jurisdiction of another." Elkins, Guzman & Simmons, *supra* note 6, at 812.

12. On the benefits of accession as related to the accession process (long or short, with or without liberalization), see Todd L. Allee & Jamie E. Scalera, *The divergent effects of joining international organizations: Trade gains and the rigors of WTO accession*, 66 Int'l Org. 243 (2012). On compliance, see Beth A. Simmons, *Compliance With International Agreements*, 1 Ann. Rev. Pol. Sci. 75 (1998) (drawing on the proliferation of international organizations to challenge the assumption that sovereignty interests work against international agreements).

13. Gregory Shaffer, *How the World Trade Organization Shapes Regulatory Governance*, 9 Reg. & Governance 1, 4 (2015).

the potential disjunction between economic relations and social relations of a more intersubjective (i.e., interpersonal) kind.[14]

The regulatory environment—on any scale, large or small—is by definition a social environment, and even such fundamental features of a regulatory system as rules, dispute settlement, and enforcement cannot by themselves account for compliance or other co-alignments of an even more diffuse nature. As Chayes and Chayes suggest with respect to compliance, these basic features of the regulatory landscape (precisely because they *are* basic) are best thought of as heuristics—ideas to think with, rather than comparative empirical rubrics.[15] This is not an isolated point with regard to transnational law or international organizations. The dynamic interrelation of regulation and social life is foundational to modern law and to the significance of law as a subject for the social sciences and humanities. The "world system" makes such dynamics visible through the characteristic forms of contest they entail.[16] Thus, in this chapter, after a brief discussion of the WTO as a regulatory institution, we turn to its dispute settlement mechanisms and related forms of contestation—including contestation against the WTO itself.

The discussion in the previous chapter remains relevant as we turn our focus to the World Trade Organization (WTO). As with NAFTA, the fact of the WTO's global reach leads us to considerations of the diversity of factors that sustain its formal and informal powers and influence.

A. What is the WTO? Government and governance

What is the WTO? Robert Howse and Joanna Langille offer a useful capsule description:

> The WTO is a multilateral organization governing trade among nations, based upon obligations its member states undertake through a series of multilateral and plurilateral treaty instruments. The purpose of the WTO is "the substantial reduction of tariffs and other barriers to trade and . . . the elimination of discriminatory treatment in international trade relations." More controversially, the WTO has become a vehicle for limiting regulatory diversity in some areas of policy that are thought to affect the real value of the market access created by the removal of direct barriers to trade. The WTO has a complex legal regime regulating international trade, and countries that are members of the WTO must abide by these rules. If they do not,

14. John Gerard Ruggie, *International Regimes, Transactions, and Change: Embedded Liberalism in the Postwar Economic Order*, 36 INT'L ORG. 379 (1982).

15. Abram Chayes & Antonia Handler Chayes, *On Compliance*, 47 INT'L ORG. 175 (1993). *See also* Shaffer, *supra* note 5, at 1.

16. IMMANUEL WALLERSTEIN, WORLD-SYSTEMS ANALYSIS: AN INTRODUCTION (2007). For an influential formulation of world system theory as an ethnographic project, see George Marcus, *Ethnography in/of the World System: The Emergence of Multi-Sited Ethnography*, 24 ANN. REV. ANTHROPOLOGY 95 (1995).

> they can be brought before the WTO's dispute settlement process by other member states.[17]

In its own words, WTO activities consist of:

> Negotiating the reduction or elimination of obstacles to trade (import tariffs, other barriers to trade) and agree on rules governing the conduct of international trade (e.g. antidumping, subsidies, product standards, etc.); administering and monitoring the application of the WTO's agreed rules for trade in goods, trade in services, and trade-related intellectual property rights; monitoring and reviewing the trade policies of [its] members, as well as ensuring transparency of regional and bilateral trade agreements; settling disputes among [its] members regarding the interpretation and application of the agreements; building capacity of developing country government officials in international trade matters; assisting the process of accession of some 30 countries who are not yet members of the organization; conducting economic research and collecting and disseminating trade data in support of the WTO's other main activities; explaining to and educating the public about the WTO, its mission and its activities.[18]

The WTO was established on January 1, 1995, after many years of negotiation. In fact, while WTO was born directly out of a round of negotiations called the "Uruguay Round"—a series of negotiations spanning from 1986–1994—the organization actually originated from a conference held at the end of World War II called the Bretton Woods Conference.[19] The United States did not support Bretton Woods' proposed International Trade Organization. Nevertheless, Bretton Woods did catalyze the United States Congress to give the president the authority to negotiate a future treaty by extending the 1934 Reciprocal Trade Agreements Act, directly leading to the establishment of 1947's General Agreement on Tariffs and Trade (GATT).

GATT came into force on January 1, 1948, with the purpose of creating a "substantial reduction of tariffs and other trade barriers and the elimination of [trade] preferences, on a reciprocal and mutually advantageous basis."[20] GATT was originally composed of twenty-three founding members that did not provide for a formal trade institution, but rather for a Secretariat with "limited institution apparatus" that was headquartered in Geneva to administer the initiatives and resolve issues among GATT members.[21] While not a formal international organization, GATT

---

17. Robert Howse & Joanna Langille, *Permitting Pluralism: The* Seal Products *Dispute and Why the WTO Should Accept Trade Restrictions Justified by Noninstrumental Moral Values*, 37 Yale J. Int'l L. 367 (2012) (notes omitted).

18. *Overview*, World Trade Organization, https://www.wto.org/english/thewto_e/whatis_e/wto_dg_stat_e.htm.

19. Meredith A. Crowley, *An Introduction to the WTO and GATT*, 27 Econ. Perspectives 42 (2003).

20. General Agreement on Tariffs and Trade, Oct. 30 1947, 61 Stat. A-11, 55 U.N.T.S. 194 (hereinafter GATT).

21. Crowley, *supra* note 19.

functioned *de facto* as an organization that would conduct a series of trade negotiations; these led to the legalization of dispute settlement under the WTO.[22] As political scientist Christina Davis explains, comparing GATT to WTO:

Christina L. Davis, *Why Adjudicate? Enforcing Trade Rules in the WTO*

7–9 (2012)

The General Agreement on Tariffs and Trade (GATT) began as a provisional agreement in 1947 with informal consultations to resolve disputes, but within less than a decade practice had evolved to rely upon an appointed panel of experts who issued independent rulings on formal legal complaints about noncompliance. Although commonly referred to as *dispute settlement,* this is simply "a nice sort of nonadversarial, nonthreatening, look-at-the-positive-side phrase for what most people would call a lawsuit" according to Hudec. The ability of the defendant to block the establishment of the panel or adoption of a ruling limited the enforcement capacity of states under GATT, but its dispute procedures were nonetheless invoked in over two hundred cases, and states generally complied with rulings. Dispute settlement became more legalistic when the World Trade Organization (WTO) replaced the GATT procedures with a reformed dispute settlement understanding that ended the de facto veto right of defendants and added a standing Appellate Body of judges to review panel decisions. Now a highly legalized dispute settlement process enforces regulations over a wide range of economic policies for a membership of more than 150 states. Since its establishment in 1995, states have addressed over four hundred trade disputes within the WTO dispute settlement process. The issues before the court have ranged from the labeling of sardines the amount of subsidies received by Boeing and Airbus.

The WTO dispute settlement system is a technical legal process. The initial complaint consists of a request for consultations stating the legal basis for the complaint by one or more member government against a specific trade policy measure taken by another member government. All complaints are public information and become part of the official record of WTO disputes. Consultations take place as confidential negotiations in Geneva between the two parties. If settlement is not reached the Dispute Settlement Body will approve the request from the complainant for a panel, which is composed of three or five independent experts chosen in consultation with complainant and defendant. The panel process then requires written submissions from both parties to the panel. These submissions are complex legal arguments about the interpretation of WTO law and the facts related to the trade impact of the policy. The three meetings of the panel include opening and closing statements from

22. GATT members sought to formalize GATT at 1986's Uruguay Round, held in Punta del Este, Uruguay. The Uruguay Round—the eighth round of GATT negotiations—spanned over seven years, included 123 countries, and concluded in Marrakesh in 1994 with the formal adoption of the WTO. Today, there are 162 member countries in the WTO.

the two parties and any third parties with interest in the case, and response to questions from the panel. The process can be ended through mutual agreement at any stage. In the case of an appeal of the panel ruling, both sides again present new submissions to the Appellate Body before a final ruling is issued on the case. A small number of cases continue with further proceedings to evaluate compliance and arbitrate an amount for authorized sanctions. Panel and Appellate Body rulings are detailed legal documents that are typically hundreds of pages of length.

The trade regime relies on decentralized enforcement in which states bring forward claims. In contrast with domestic legal systems, there is no central public prosecutor. Some treaty organizations, such as the International Atomic Energy Agency in the Non-proliferation Treaty regime, provide centralized monitoring to coordinate enforcement actions. Although the Trade Policy Review Mechanism of the WTO provides information on member policies, it has not been used as a means to reveal noncompliance. The WTO Secretariat explicitly remains neutral on member inquiries about compliance questions, and the reviews all too infrequent to represent an alarm system alerting members about noncompliance. Only panels and the Appellate Body render judgments on compliance, and these are in response to member complaints. While strategic action by the court as an agent is possible in the ruling phase, the court cannot solicit or refuse to hear a case. This institutional design means states remain the central actor for enforcement because only states have the authority to enforce the agreement through filing a complaint under the dispute settlement provisions of the agreement. As a result, enforcement will be only as great as the willingness and capacity of states to monitor and challenge the trade barriers of their trade partners.[23]

B. The powers of the WTO

In her analysis of WTO adjudication, Professor Davis emphasizes the synergies between the legalization of international trade and the domestic politicization of trade law, noting that more democratic countries tend to be more active litigants than less democratic countries. Her account points to the relevance of democratic debate—and the impasses in such debates—over protectionism and free trade, and, correspondingly, to the importance of the WTO as a mechanism that effectively eases the pressure to resolve such disputes wholly internally. Her analysis underscores the wide range of local actors, interests, and strategies involved in what is conventionally (and simplistically) called the global governance of trade. She sets forth the main lines of her argument in the following excerpt, drawn from the introduction to her book on the WTO:

23. Christina Davis, Why Adjudicate? Enforcing Trade Rules in the WTO (2012) at 7–8 (section heading and notes omitted).

Christina L. Davis, Why Adjudicate? Enforcing Trade Rules in the WTO

1–2 (2012)

Why do states turn to international courts to resolve their disputes? Liberal protesters on the streets condemn international organizations as servants of corporate interests, while conservative skeptics of international law reject intervention into state decision making by international bureaucrats. Governments of both large and small states have reason to avoid courts. Powerful states like the United States and EU have tools for leverage in bilateral negotiations. Whether offering side payments or threatening unilateral sanctions, they can influence the behavior of smaller states without need for a third party. At the same time, small developing countries fear legalization will merely introduce another tool where they lack capacity and cannot defend their interests. It is not as if filing a lawsuit mobilizes a police force. For all of their "court like" appearance, international courts are fundamentally different from domestic courts because they lack the authority to impose their rulings in an anarchic international system. Moreover, using courts is costly. Hiring lawyers, preparing formal briefs, and taking a dispute into the public arena cost time and money and also risk injuring diplomatic relations. Nonetheless, we observe a clear trend toward legalization as more areas of international affairs are regulated by international law, and the number and authority of international courts have grown. States are increasingly turning to courts to solve disputes.

They do so in order to achieve better outcomes. The choice of adjudication represents a shift in process—not abdication of sovereignty. Governments negotiate international rules and decide when and how to enforce them. Often states retain gatekeeper status over which legal complaints are filed. They have discretion over whether to comply with rulings issued against them by international judges. Governments give up some control when they enter formal dispute settlement and open themselves to third-party involvement, but this sacrifice of autonomy comes as a deliberate choice.

Understanding the decision to use legal enforcement is critical for evaluating how international institutions shape state behavior. The effectiveness of any legal system depends upon the actions of the police, prosecutor, and judge. One must consider the interaction of law with the probability of enforcement. Given the same set of legal commitments and punishment standard, challenges to every small infraction push the system toward strict compliance while imperfect enforcement induces weak compliance. In the absence of a central prosecutor or police force, most international regimes depend upon member states to monitor the policies of other states and to challenge specific violations. What are the incentives for states to take on this enforcement role?

This book argues that states use international adjudication in order to manage domestic political pressure and pursue international cooperation. The decision to invoke international law in a dispute does not proceed automatically on merits of the case alone. While the stakes in the outcome and legal standard for each case are important factors in the decision to enforce rules, these are not the only criteria. One must recognize the intensely political nature of filing a lawsuit against another country. Addressing a dispute in a legal venue raises new costs for the state in terms of legal preparation, diplomatic relations, and risk of precedent that could affect a wider range of issues. Some actors may prefer negotiations that allow flexibility in terms of when and how to resolve the dispute between two states without formal procedures, third parties, and publicity. As a result, many cases that could be taken to court are instead negotiated. Those states with domestic constraints on executive autonomy, however, will find it hard to accept negotiated compromises. In democracies, and especially those democracies with sharp partisan divisions and institutional checks and balances in the structure of government, the executive faces demands from the legislature to demonstrate its effort to enforce the agreements ratified by the legislature. The executive here includes the president or prime minister and the bureaucracy. Domestic constraints that encourage visible accountability limit the flexibility for an executive to reach informal compromises. Engaging in political theater by initiating legal action against a foreign government proves to be an effective strategy not only for dealing with foreign governments but also for managing domestic pressure. Willingness to bear the costs of going to court signals that the government gives priority to enforcement. As a result, incentives to use courts arise from their usefulness as a political tool and not only from their role to interpret the law and allocate punishment.

This book will test the implications of political demand for adjudication in analysis of when and how states have used adjudication to resolve trade disputes. I develop a theory about domestic constraints to explain why democratic states are more likely to file legal complaints against trade barriers and select their cases based on the political influence of the affected industry. Checks on executive autonomy in the domestic institutional framework encourage the. government to be responsive to industry interests. Choosing adjudication as a trade strategy allows the government to visibly demonstrate enforcement actions to its domestic audience and signal strong resolve to a trade partner. Adjudication functions as a response to domestic pressure that promotes settlement of trade disputes by providing information about preferences.

The question of how states maintain cooperation in anarchy without centralized enforcement has been a major theme in international relations scholarship. Leading theories account for why states agree to a rule framework. Powerful states have incentives to provide public goods that benefit systemic stability and have the capacity to supply centralized enforcement. In the face of market failures that could prevent cooperation, states establish institutions that lower transaction costs. Distributional conditions along with the externalities of the issue influence how these institutions are designed to balance the interests of states. Legalization, defined in terms of the obligation for compliance, precision of rules, and delegation to third-party dispute settlement, represents one dimension of variation in the form of international institutions.

High levels of legalization that include delegation to third-party dispute settlement are evident across security, human rights, and economic issue areas. War crimes have been challenged by international tribunals since the Nuremberg Trials and more recently by the International Criminal Court. The International Court of Justice has a varied set of cases including territorial disputes and claims regarding .mistreatment of foreign nationals. The UN Convention on the Law of the Sea refers disputes that cannot be resolved amicably to the International Tribunal for the Law of the Seas. The European Human Rights Convention established a court that has a large docket of cases brought by individuals against their own governments. Regional integration has deepened as economic regulations for a common market are enforced by courts: the European Court of Justice is the most prominent regional court, but many other regional communities including the Andean Pact and Mercosur in Latin America and the Common Market of Eastern and Southern Africa have courts that hear cases related to economic disputes among member states. Bilateral investment treaties provide for dispute settlement by third parties such as the International Court of Arbitration or International Centre for Settlement of Investment Disputes. Finally, trade, as the area that is the subject of this book, offers an example of legalization with hundreds of trade disputes addressed in a formal dispute settlement process by members of the General Agreement on Tariffs and Trade (GATT) and now the World Trade Organization (WTO).

The legalization of international affairs has attracted growing attention, but there is a need to explain why states use courts. Research has primarily focused on when states comply with their commitments. Less attention has been given to how other states respond to violations. When the harm from cheating and benefits of cooperation are shared broadly across states, enforcement represents a public good where each state may seek to free ride on actions of others rather than "play the role of policeman". One of the main functions of international institutions is to provide information about compliance in order to increase the reputational costs of noncompliance. Yet many regimes rely upon decentralized enforcement. The states that challenge violations play an important role in establishing regime effectiveness because their actions trigger the material and reputational mechanisms for compliance in the institution.

Litigation also serves domestic purposes. Democratization and legalization have grown as two parallel trends in international politics. The increase in the number of democratic states since 1970 has been accompanied by an increase in the use of international courts across a range of policy areas from human rights to trade and investment. The close connection between democracy and judicial institutions within a state is widely recognized. More recently it has become evident that democratic states also show an affinity for the use of courts to resolve international disputes. The advanced industrial democracies have taken the leading role in the establishment of international courts. Democratic regime type increases the likelihood that a pair of states will seek legal dispute settlement of a territorial dispute. In the area of trade adjudication, research has highlighted the positive relationship between democracy and trade complaints in both the GATT and WTO periods. Indeed, during the first decade of WTO adjudication, authoritarian governments brought only ten disputes. The democratic preference for legalized dispute settlement is one dimension of a broader complementarity between democracy and multilateralism highlighted in several recent studies.[24]

II. WTO and harmonization of standards

As discussed above, the elimination of trade barriers is a key goal of the WTO. A major trade barrier recognized during the Uruguay Round was the system of many domestic and regional standards governing various industries, goods, and services. Increasingly over the course of the twentieth and twenty-first centuries, standards—both international and domestic—have proliferated across domains of production, fostering trade as well as networks of communication and other forms of exchange.[25]

In WTO law, there are two major agreements that govern harmonization: the Sanitary and Phytosanitary Measures (SPS) and Technical Barriers to Trade (TBT) Agreements. Both agreements contain provisions for harmonization of standards, as well as articles addressing other tools for attaining predictability and uniformity of standards. Not surprisingly, the effects of harmonization processes can also sharpen differences both between countries and within them—further evidence of the extent to which domestic and international spheres run on separate but overlapping circuits of interest, communication, and consequences.

A. Introduction to harmonization

The harmonization of standards in WTO law is a multilevel process that combines formal procedures and informal incentives:

Humberto Zúñiga Schroder, Harmonization, Equivalence and Mutual Recognition of Standards in WTO Law (pp. 21–23, 2011)

(Reproduced with the permission of the publisher © 2011; with original notes)

[S]tandards play an important role in protecting human health and safety and in allowing compatibility of products and processes. However, standards can also disrupt trade; for example, when they are used for anticompetitive purposes such as the protection of national industries, and also when they 'force' local manufacturers to incur expensive adaptations of their products in order to comply with the rules and standards of their major trading partners. That is the reason for which the GATT and subsequent the WTO have developed a thorough legal regime on standards, to provide solutions to such problems. One of the tools provided by such a regime is

24. Davis, *id.* at 1–3 (notes omitted).

25. For a history of international standards, see Kristina Tamm Hallstrom, Organizing International Standardization: ISO and the IASC in Quest of Authority (2004).

the so-called 'harmonization,' or the use of the same standards by different parties at the moment of exchanging goods.

Harmonization is a policy tool of the WTO legal system, regional trade agreements, and national legislation. Within the multilateral trading system, this instrument can be found in Articles 3 SPS and 2.4–2.6 TBT, which generally speaking, encourage the adoption of international standards issued by certain standardizing bodies. These Articles have been subject to analysis in two important WTO cases, namely *EC-Hormones*[26] and *EC-Sardines*, for SPS measures and TBT technical regulations respectively. However, the analysis carried out in these cases has not been without criticism, most of which has focused on whether the panels and Appellate Body (AB) have indeed clarified all the potential legal loopholes in these provisions.

* * *

Harmonization can be broadly defined, as Mayeda's words, 'as the process of making different regulations, principles, domestic laws and government policies substantially or effectively the same or similar.'[27] Applying such a definition to the present study, harmonization can be understood as the process by which different countries adopt the same—or *substantially the same*—standards, the phrase 'substantially the same' being emphasized because harmonization can be achieved either by the adoption of every element of the standard used as a basis of comparison or by the adoption of only its most important elements.

Harmonization can be accomplished at different levels, depending on the body with which national regulators decide to harmonize. For example, international harmonization involves the alignment of national standards with those issued by international standardizing bodies such as Codex or ISO, whereas regional harmonization entails the adoption of standards by regional bodies like CEN [(the European Committee for Standardization)]. . . . Similarly, harmonization can be achieved through the adoption of standards of another country, or even via the alignment of national standards with those set by specialized standardizing bodies such as ASME or ASTM International, *consortia* and private companies such as Microsoft or IBM.

Harmonization in the WTO realm is basically circumscribed to the international level. Such is the importance of this process in the multilateral trading system, that both the SPS and TBT Agreements have implemented a 'presumption of consistency' derived from the use of international standards which does not exist for, say, regional or *consortia* standards. . . . Evidently, if a standard reconciles the different needs and technological requirements of different countries (developed and developing equally), and if it is developed by an organization that prioritizes scientific and technological evidence (like most international standardizing bodies), then the logical consequence is that the majority of economic actors will be willing to accept a product manufactured under its specifications. That is why the use of international standards

26. Discussed *infra* at II.C [not part of this excerpt].

27. Graham Mayeda, *Developing Disharmony? The SPS and TBT Agreements and the Impact of Harmonization on Developing Countries*, 7 J. Int'l Econ. L. 737, 740 (2004).

is encouraged not only by the WTO, but also by regional standardizing bodies, trade blocs and regional free trade agreements, regional forums, and multilateral and bilateral free trade agreements, among others.

The harmonization of standards across borders may deliver significant impact on domestic law, but in ways that cannot themselves be standardized. Interdisciplinary scholarship on the WTO yields abundant evidence of regional, country, and community effects. Suffice it to say that transnational law by itself does not produce homogeneity, even when it fosters intergovernmental coordination. As we have already seen (and will continue to see throughout this book), law sometimes drives new forms of heterogeneity. Law is a "site that operates both for the reduction of social complexity and the increase of social complexity."[28] Under some circumstances, harmonization represents a race to the bottom, to the extent that international standardizing bodies are influenced by private entities to loosen restrictions. Under TBT and SPS, for example, domestic governments are empowered to set their own standards at levels that "achieve legitimate policy objectives, such as the protection of human health and safety, or protection of the environment." When the government's determination of a legitimate policy objective is significantly at odds with the international standard, it is prone to a challenge at the WTO in the form of a complaint charging discriminatory trade practices or disguised protectionism.[29] Under other circumstances, however, harmonization supports domestic standard-setting.[30]

The case study below, the *EC-Hormones* case, is the flagship example of the enforcement of international standards in favor of domestic standards.

1. Case Study: The Beef Hormone Dispute

Lori M. Wallach, *Accountable Governance in the Era of Globalization: The WTO, NAFTA, and International Harmonization of Standards*

50 U. Kan. L. Rev. 823 (2002)

WTO Enforces International Standards in the Beef Hormone Case

Since 1988, the EU has banned the sale of beef from cattle treated with artificial growth hormones. The EU ban applies in a non-discriminatory fashion to both

---

28. Boaventura de Sousa Santos & Flavia Carlet, *The Movement of Landless Rural Farmers in Brazil and Their Struggles for Access to Law and Justice*, *in* Marginalized Communities and Access to Justice 60–82 (Yash Ghai & Jill Cottrell eds., Abingdon: Routledge 2007).

29. *Standards and Safety: Technical Regulations and Standards*, World Trade Org., https://www.wto.org/english/thewto_e/whatis_e/tif_e/agrm4_e.htm#TRS.

30. On the embeddedness of social interests in the international system, see James A. Caporaso & Sidney Tarrow, *Polanyi in Brussels: Supranational Institutions and the Transnational Embedding of Markets*, 63 Int'l Org. 593 (2009).

domestic and foreign beef producers. Exposure to the artificial hormones themselves have been linked to cancer and premature pubescence in girls, although the risk to humans of artificial hormone residues in the meat they consume is uncertain.

On the basis of the known risks of direct exposure and the public's demand for a ban on meat from cattle treated with artificial hormones, the EU adopted a "zero risk" standard. Rather than trying to assess a tolerable amount of an indeterminable risk or waiting for negative human health effects to accrue over time, the EU chose to eliminate public exposure to the risk altogether. The EU made this policy choice after prolonged and effective consumer campaigns in numerous EU countries.

The U.S. beef and biotechnology industries have long opposed this EU policy, and in 1996 the U.S. challenged the EU ban in the WTO. In 1997, a WTO dispute panel ruled that the EU ban was illegal under the WTO's food rules, contained in the SPS Agreement, in part because the EU ban was not based on international standards. At that time, Codex rules allowed use of the artificial hormones and set residue levels for five of the six hormones at issue.

A key argument centered around the meaning of the term "based on international standards," a requirement in the SPS Agreement. The dispute panel ruled that "based on" meant "complied with," which essentially meant that all domestic standards had to be the same as international standards. Since the EU ban covered five hormones for which Codex had set maximum residue levels, the dispute panel ruled that the EU measures were not "based on" international standards. And since the EU measures were not based on international standards, under WTO rules they would be considered illegal trade barriers unless the EU could bear the burden of proving that its measures met a long set of tests set forth in the WTO text, including that the ban was "scientifically justified."

The dispute panel ruled: "Since in this dispute we have already found that there exist international standards and that the EC measures at issue are not based on these standards, we find that the burden of justifying the measures in dispute under Article 3.3 . . . rests on the European Communities." Article 3.3 of the SPS Agreement requires domestic standards that provide more consumer protection than international standards, among other conditions, to be based on a scientific risk assessment. The dispute panel concluded that the EU had not done a proper risk assessment and ruled the ban on hormones an illegal barrier to trade.

The EU appealed this decision to the WTO Appellate Body. Although the Appellate Body softened the harsh tone of the language in the dispute panel's opinion, it still upheld the panel's final decision and ordered the EU to allow importing U.S. artificial hormone-treated beef by May 13, 1999.

However, the EU refused to import the hormone-treated beef and commissioned the EU Scientific Committee on Veterinary Matters Related to Public Health to study the health effects of the hormones. The United States petitioned the WTO dispute panel for permission to impose sanctions on $202 million of EU exports, but the panel lowered that figure to $116.8 million.

The EU scientific committee found that one of the six artificial growth hormones used by U.S. cattlemen, 17 beta oestradiol, may cause cancer. The EC then issued a statement declaring, "[t]he Commission agreed that there can no longer be any question of lifting the ban on hormone-treated beef since the risk assessment has identified risks to health caused by hormones."

The Aftermath

Following the developments presented by Lori Wallach, the EU continued to claim that its ban was in compliance with WTO obligations, because the hormones had been linked to adverse effects on human health and safety. The dispute continued, as summarized by Renee Johnson and Charles Hanrahan:

> **2003:** The EU issued a new directive with a permanent ban on the one hormone with established health risks and provisional bans on the other five hormones, pending further scientific evidence.
>
> **2004–05:** The EU requests that U.S. and Canadian trade sanctions be lifted, in light of the EU's findings regarding the health and safety risks of the hormones in dispute. A WTO Panel holds a public meeting and commences work on the dispute.
>
> **2006–07:** The WTO Panel continues work, citing the complexity of the issues for its delay.
>
> **2008:** The WTO Panel issues its report, stating that the EU had not presented sufficient data to support its import ban, but that the U.S. and Canada had improperly imposed trade sanctions. Later that year, the Appellate Body ruled that the U.S. and Canada could continue to impose their trade sanctions against the EU, but that the EU could continue to ban imports of hormone-treated beef from the U.S. and Canada. This ruling meant that the EU was not in violation of WTO by imposing its ban, thus granting broader discretion for domestic food safety regulations.
>
> **2009:** The U.S. announces planned increases to its trade sanctions against the EU. However, by the end of the year, a Memorandum of Understanding is signed between the parties, including the suspension of many of the retaliatory tariffs and the expansion of the market for beef not treated with certain hormones. This MOU was renewed in 2013.[31]

Notes and Questions

1. When domestic regulations are more strict than those of a trade partner or the international trade community, can the party avoid compliance with the more restrictive standards?

---

31. Renee Johnson & Charles Hanrahan, *The U.S.-EU Beef Hormone Dispute*, Congressional Research Service (2010).

2. The standards for use of hormones in the meat industry are set by the Codex Alimentarius. What is the Codex? Here is Wallach's description:

> Codex Alimentarius is Latin for "food law." The Codex in Rome is one of the international standard-setting bodies recognized by both NAFTA and the WTO for setting global food standards. It was established as a voluntary standard-setting body in 1962 by the World Health Organization and the U.N. Food and Agriculture Organization primarily to facilitate international trade of food and agriculture products. Codex's initial mission was to boost trade by helping developing countries set food-related standards. Soon, numerous agribusiness, chemical, and food companies sought a role at Codex. Codex is officially comprised of government representatives, with active and formal assistance from official industry advisors, who serve as actual members on country delegations.
>
> Food industry giants, such as Hershey Foods, Nestle U.S.A., Kraft, General Foods, Coca Cola, and Pepsi, and trade groups, such as the Grocery Manufacturers of America and the National Food Processors Association, regularly attend international Codex meetings as part of the official U.S. delegation. These industries also have a central role in developing the U.S. positions taken to such meetings, including providing scientific data and scientists. A 1993 study showed that over four-fifths of the nongovernmental participants on all delegations to Codex committees represented industry, while only one percent represented public interest organizations.
>
> Until it was empowered by both NAFTA and the WTO as the presumptively-legal international food standard body, Codex published only voluntary standards for the hygienic and nutritional quality of food, food additives, pesticide residues, contaminants, labeling, and methods of analysis and sampling. Despite its important new duties, Codex's mission is still to promote food trade. Codex has no public health mandate to which it must conform its decisions. It even lacks power to compel production of data from industry for standard-setting.
>
> Codex holds meetings which are closed to the general public. Draft Codex standards are not made public until well into the process. . . .
>
> A significant number of Codex standards are weaker than food standards in the United States, which by law must be established using public health considerations. . . . Given that some of Codex's standards are lower than U.S. norms and that they now are empowered through NAFTA and the WTO, downward harmonization of U.S. food standards is a clear possibility. Alternatively, another country may simply challenge higher U.S. food standards using NAFTA or the WTO's dispute settlement process. To avoid such WTO challenges, for example, Japan preemptively lowered over 1500 of its domestic pesticide

standards which provided greater public health protections than Codex standards.[32]

Given that the Codex is the "presumptively-legal international food standard body," should it employ democratic tools such as open meetings, input from citizens, publication of documents, and more? How can an individual government ever retain sovereignty over its domestic regulations, when international bodies like the Codex have presumptive control over food standards?

3. When a dispute arises regarding a party's potential violation of an international standard, another party can bring a dispute before a WTO Panel. Between 1995 and 2016, 51 disputes had been brought under the TBT Agreement and 43 had been brought under the SPS Agreement.[33] How should we evaluate these case loads? What do they reveal with respect to WTO as a global regulatory body? Consider these questions as you read the next section on Dispute Resolution.

B. Other tools for international standards: Equivalence and mutual recognition

There are other methods for transnational standard-setting in addition to harmonization. Mutual recognition and equivalence are two frequently employed tools, and some have proposed that such transnational cooperation, including harmonization, could serve as an effective form of global governance.[34]

Mutual recognition is "an understanding among two or more states under which each recognizes the adequacy of the other's regulation or supervision of an activity or institution as a substitute for its own."[35] As such, it is an example of extraterritoriality; however, rather than the traditional unilateral extraterritoriality in which one state enforces its laws upon parties that are physically located in other jurisdictions, mutual recognition is more cooperative, as participating states recognize one another's standards or rules reciprocally. Mutual recognition is a collaboration between regulators and lawmakers across borders that aimed at dividing control between the "home states" and "host states." The EU has established mutual recognition as a core component of its regional governance and a long-standing principle of EU law.[36] In many ways, the exercise of mutual recognition in the EU—in areas as diverse as regulation of chemicals, licensing of professional services, and

32. Lori M. Wallach, *Accountable Governance in the Era of Globalization: The WTO, NAFTA, and International Harmonization of Standards*, 50 U. Kan. L. Rev. 823, 836 (2002).

33. There were 169 adopted decisions in WTO dispute settlement as of February 2014. Shaffer, *supra* note 5, at 1.

34. Kalypso Nicolaidis & Gregory Shaffer, *Transnational Mutual Recognition Regimes: Governance Without Global Government*, 68 Law & Contemp. Probs. 263, 263–64 (2005).

35. Pierre-Hugues Verdier, *Mutual Recognition in International Finance*, 52 Harv. Int'l L.J. 55, 63 (2011).

36. Christine Janssens, The Principle of Mutual Recognition in EU Law 2 (2013).

movement of goods—has provided ample guidance for other regional and bilateral networks to develop their own systems.

Equivalence is a principle similar to mutual recognition. However, unlike mutual recognition—which does not require the regulatory environments in the various states to be substantially similar—equivalence is a process by which one government, through an assessment process, unilaterally determines that another's regulation or supervision of an activity or institution is equivalent, and therefore adequate for the level of protection desired by the government.

III. WTO—Dispute resolution

A. The Dispute Settlement Understanding (DSU) Agreement

The WTO's ability to settle disputes is a "central pillar"[37] of the multilateral trading system. The WTO's dispute settlement system was established by the Dispute Settlement Understanding (DSU), an agreement negotiated as part of the Uruguay Round of 1995. Under that agreement, WTO members are permitted to resolve conflicts through the WTO's director general by agreeing to arbitration or invoking the formal dispute settlement mechanism.[38] The goal of the WTO's dispute settlement procedure is to make the trading system more "secure and reliable"; the system seeks to accomplish this goal by articulating "clearly-defined rules," within the bounds of pre-established timetables.[39] As Section 7 of the DSU states:

> The aim of the dispute settlement mechanism is to secure a positive solution to a dispute. A solution mutually acceptable to the parties to a dispute and consistent with the covered agreements is clearly to be preferred. In the absence of a mutually agreed solution, the first objective of the dispute settlement mechanism is usually to secure the withdrawal of the measures concerned if these are found to be inconsistent with the provisions of any of the covered agreements. The provision of compensation should be resorted to only if the immediate withdrawal of the measure is impracticable and as a temporary measure pending the withdrawal of the measure which is inconsistent with a covered agreement. The last resort which this Understanding provides to the Member invoking the dispute settlement procedures is the possibility of suspending the application of concessions or other obligations under the covered agreements on a discriminatory basis vis-à-vis the other Member, subject to authorization by the DSB of such measures.

---

37. Settling Disputes, 55 *available at:* https://www.wto.org/english/thewto_e/whatis_e/tif_e/utw_chap3_e.pdf.

38. Robert Z. Lawrence, The United States and the WTO Dispute Settlement System, 7 (Council on Foreign Relations, 2007).

39. *Id.*

Accordingly, this section addresses the formal dispute settlement mechanism at the WTO. We shall consider the scope of the mechanism, its procedures, and some of its strategic implications for individual member states.[40]

B. Processes and procedures

According to the WTO, the dispute settlement system is "essentially about broken promises." The process is usually invoked when one WTO country "adopts a trade policy measure or takes some action that one or more fellow-WTO member considers to be breaking the WTO agreements, or to be a failure to live up to obligations."[41] Settlement of the disputes themselves is the responsibility of a council called the "Dispute Settlement Body" ("DSB"), a group that consists of each WTO member. Authority is vested in the DSB to create "panels" to hear cases. These panels—like NAFTA Tribunals—consist of experts charged with considering the case. In the words of the WTO:

> Panels are like tribunals. But unlike in a normal tribunal, the panellists are usually chosen in consultation with the countries in dispute. Only if the two sides cannot agree does the WTO director-general appoint them. Panels consist of three (possibly five) experts from different countries who examine the evidence and decide who is right and who is wrong. The panel's report is passed to the Dispute Settlement Body, which can only reject the report by consensus. Panellists for each case can be chosen from a permanent list of well-qualified candidates, or from elsewhere. They serve in their individual capacities. They cannot receive instructions from any government.[42]

Once the panel has made a decision, the DSB monitors the implementation of the panel's rulings and recommendations and maintains the power to authorize punishment when a member does not comply with a panel's ruling. It is important to note that a panel's decision serves only as a recommendation to the DSB. The DSB, then, makes an official ruling. Practically speaking, it is difficult for the DSB to overturn a decision from the panel; however, a panel's decision can be rejected by a consensus of the members of the DSB.

As noted above, the WTO is not world government so much as it represents an interlegal complex, giving us another way of emphasizing the extent to which cooperation and compliance involve multiple legal, political and social regimes of different scales, and not merely a structural relation of parts and wholes. Legal scholar Gregory Shaffer emphasizes the importance of understanding the differences between

---

40. For an analysis of dilemmas of legitimacy in interlegal settings such as the WTO, and in particular, the legitimation of authority in WTO dispute settlement, see Joseph Conti, *Legitimacy Chains: Legitimation of Compliance with International Courts Across Social Fields*, 50 L. & Soc'y Rev. 154 (2016).

41. *Id.*

42. Settling Disputes, 56 *available at:* https://www.wto.org/english/thewto_e/whatis_e/tif_e/utw_chap3_e.pdf.

the WTO's first and second order compliance processes—first order being the dynamic development of WTO jurisprudence; second order being compliance following dispute settlement.[43] The thickly interlegal aspect of the WTO also helps account for the disparate uses and effects of WTO adjudication, as noted by Professor Davis (*supra*) and explained in the following excerpt:

Robert Z. Lawrence, *The United States and the WTO Dispute Settlement System*

Council on Foreign Relations No. 25, Pp. 7–12 (March 2007)

THE DISPUTE SETTLEMENT SYSTEM

According to the Dispute Settlement Understanding (DSU), the agreement establishing the dispute settlement system that was negotiated as part of the Uruguay Round of 1995, WTO members may seek to resolve conflicts through the good offices of the organization's director-general or by agreeing to arbitration; they may also invoke the formal dispute settlement mechanism. To pursue this last option, the parties in the dispute are first required to engage in consultation. If these consultations are unsatisfactory, a complainant can, within sixty days, request the establishment of a panel of three members to hear the case. The panel issues an interim report and then a final one. If it finds that a member has failed to comply, and that member does not appeal, the body can make a recommendation as to how the member could come into compliance. If it is impractical to comply immediately, the member is given "a reasonable period of time in which to do so." The finding can also be appealed to a second panel of three members of a permanent seven-person Appellate Body (AB), which operates like the supreme court of the organization.

If the member loses the appeal and fails to act within a reasonable period of time, the rules call for the parties to negotiate compensation, "pending full implementation." "Compensation" is generally understood to require the defendant to provide additional concessions, typically in the form of reducing other trade barriers of interest to the plaintiff. Compensation is, however, "voluntary"—and rare. If after twenty days, compensation cannot be agreed upon, the complainant may request authorization to suspend equivalent concessions. In particular, "the level of the suspension of concession . . . shall be equivalent to the level of nullification and impairment." When, for example, the WTO found that the EU had cost the United States $116.8 million worth of exports by illegally banning hormone-fed beef, the United States was authorized to impose punitive tariffs on $116.8 million worth of EU exports. Arbitration, to be completed within sixty days, may be sought on the level of suspension, the procedures, and the principles of retaliation.

The dispute settlement system has generally been successful in helping members resolve disputes and in obtaining compliance where violations have been found. Many

43. Shaffer, *supra* note 5, at 1–2.

cases have been settled in the consultation stage. While there are delays, particularly when legislative action is required, and a few cases in which compliance has been lacking, the evidence suggests that by and large the United States and other countries eventually come into compliance. Nations appear to comply less because of retaliation, which has rarely been used, but rather because they believe it is in their interest to do so. This is because on balance they benefit from the rules and care about their reputations in a system in which there are ongoing negotiations. They also care about their relationships with significant trading partners.

The system has been used extensively by the United States, but the United States has not dominated it.

* * *

Although the very least developed countries do experience difficulties in using the system, there is evidence that it is being widely used by both developed and developing countries in rough proportion to their shares in world trade. Between 1995 and 2000, for example, high-income countries filed 70.2 percent of disputes, while developing countries represented 29.8 percent of submitted cases. In the next five years (2001–2006), by contrast, developing countries filed a majority of the cases brought (52.1 percent). While these numbers reflect mainly developing countries with large export shares, such as India and Brazil, there are also cases of small developing countries that have leveraged the system effectively to challenge large trading partners. Another noticeable development is the increase in South-South disputes. All in all, recent trends attest to developing countries' increased knowledge of and confidence in the WTO dispute resolution process.

Several features of the system merit emphasis. First, the WTO itself does not conduct investigations and instigate proceedings. Although the WTO does review its members' trade policies, there is no central policing mechanism—enforcement is carried out entirely as a result of member initiatives. While the respondents cannot block the case from going forward, the claimant may withdraw the case at any time, even if the defendant has not come into compliance.

Second, the operation of the system reflects the nature of the WTO as an intergovernmental organization. Although private counsel can be employed to make arguments, and amicus briefs by nongovernmental entities have been allowed on occasion, only governments have standing to bring cases. There is no private right of action. Violations of the agreements may have damaged private parties, but they have no recourse on their own and must operate through their governments. Similarly, retaliation is undertaken against the defendant country, and it could inflict damage on the incomes of exporting firms that had nothing to do with the infraction and whose only error was being located in the defending country—a reason why some believe that only compensation should be allowed.

Third, the DSU does not ordain a common law system with binding precedents. Technically, there is no stare decisis. Each panel ruling is thus in principle unique—only the members themselves can adopt rules that "add to or diminish the rights and obligations" in the agreement. In practice, however, precedents are actually given great weight, and panel and Appellate Body reports refer frequently and deferentially in many footnotes to the reasoning contained in other reports. The Appellate Body plays a particularly important oversight role in disciplining judgments and ensuring their consistency. Thus, de facto, the DSU has established something approaching a commonlaw system.

Fourth, WTO rulings are not automatically implemented. In practice, even if not technically in law, members have discretion as to whether they will comply; they may refuse even though this may mean breaking the agreement and perhaps facing retaliation against their exports. De jure such retaliation is meant to be temporary and is not a substitute for compliance. But de facto retaliation can become the permanent outcome of a dispute. This means that the retaliation system may operate as a safety valve.

Fifth, there is no attempt to compensate the winner for damages incurred during the period of noncompliance, a practice that stands in contrast to contract cases in common-law legal systems. This has the advantage of not generating further disputes over the size and payment of such damages. But the downside is that parties expecting to lose have an incentive to delay the process as long as possible. Parties also may engage in rule-breaking behavior in the knowledge that the most that they will have to do is come into compliance at a later date.

In sum, the WTO dispute settlement mechanism is a distinctive form of arbitration combined with a variation of judicial review. The parties are required to submit to the process if one party launches a complaint. An arbitration panel investigates and reaches conclusions based on rules previously negotiated by the members. The resulting rulings are binding on the parties. Failure to comply or provide compensation can result in the suspension of concessions. The rulings are also subject to appeal. However, the WTO system remains weaker than the arbitration processes common in domestic legal systems for four major reasons: Enforcement is not automatic, precedents are not strictly binding, standing of all injured parties is not assured—only governments bring cases—and remedies are limited.

C. WTO dispute settlement—Combining politics and law

While the dispute settlement mechanisms of the WTO are available to all member states, their use is uneven. As noted above, in her study of WTO adjudication, Christina Davis finds that disputes are filed primarily by democratic countries; the United States is the leading complainant.[44] Her analysis shows that it is in democratic countries—notably the United States—that the accountability of the

44. Davis, *supra* note 23 at 9. *See also* Joseph A. Conti, *The Good Case: Decisions to Litigate at the World Trade Organization*, 42 L. & Soc'y Rev. 145 (2008); Joseph Conti, *Learning to Dispute: Repeat Participation, Expertise, and Reputation at the World Trade Organization*, 35 L. & Soc. Inquiry 625 (2010) (Conti's findings suggest that litigation rewards repeat players).

president, the effects of partisan political contests, and pressures from the private sector (industries and large corporations) combine in ways that make the WTO useful, in both practical and symbolic terms. In practical terms, the WTO provides a route to dispute settlement that is predictably less "costly" than a trade war—that is, less costly economically and diplomatically. In symbolic terms, the WTO provides an opening through what may otherwise be an impasse between an executive who seeks broad negotiating powers and a legislature inclined to protectionism or more enforcement, or both. The interests of executives, legislatures, and industries in compliance and enforcement may not be the same, and may even be antithetical (stretching the line between diplomatic and economic interests, for example).[45] In such instances, filing the complaint (costly in itself) may be sufficient. But the global expansion of trade agreements and the strategic importance of the WTO's dispute settlement system makes the WTO a critical and integral part of larger trends toward "legalization" in international affairs.[46] As Professor Davis observes: "Democratization and legalization have grown as two parallel trends in international politics. The increase in the number of democratic states since 1970 has been accompanied by an increase in the use of international courts across a range of policy areas from human rights to trade and investment.... [It] has become evident that democratic states... show an affinity for the use of courts to resolve international disputes."[47] With regard to the WTO in particular, the "gatekeeping" role of states in the legal process means that "the choice of adjudication represents a shift in process—not abdication of sovereignty."[48]

D. Are WTO tribunal decisions binding on the United States?

The political complexities and various forms of power associated with the legal aspects of WTO adjudication and compliance make the status of WTO tribunal decisions an interesting question, in theory and in practice.

There are two schools of thought regarding the domestic status of WTO rulings and the domestic status of international legal norms, generally. Jeffrey L. Dunoff explains:

> On the one side, a group of self-styled "internationalists" urge domestic courts to view themselves as part of a "global community" of courts, to engage in a process of transnational judicial dialogue and cross-fertilization, and to give direct effect to international legal norms. A competing group of "revisionists" counters that the international and domestic legal orders can and should be sharply distinguished. They argue that international norms do not and should not be directly effective domestically, and that

45. Davis, *supra* note 23, at 27, 28, 39.

46. *Id.* at 1.

47. *Id.* at 1.

48. *Id.* at 1.

> the political branches, rather than the courts, should determine the domestic status of international legal obligations.[49]

Professor Dunoff explains that U.S. domestic courts have created three lines of decisions regarding the effect of the WTO on domestic law: in the first line of decisions—the dominant line—the court outright denies the effect of WTO law on domestic matters; in the second line of decisions, the court uses WTO law as persuasive authority in reaching conclusions in domestic matters; and in the third line of cases, the court gives effect to WTO law on domestic matters.

The court's decision in the following case is illustrative of the dominant line of reasoning that denies effecting WTO law and decisions in domestic courts. Before reading the case, a general, albeit cursory, understanding of "antidumping law" is necessary. Professor Dunoff explains it this way:

> A product is considered as being dumped if it is introduced to the commerce of another country at less than its normal value. WTO law permits states to offset the price advantage that dumped goods enjoy through special tariffs known as antidumping duties. To do so, investigating authorities in the importing state must establish the dumping margin by calculating the difference between the normal value of the goods—usually the price on the exporter's home market—and the export price. In making this calculation, WTO rules require domestic authorities to conduct a fair comparison between the two prices.[50]

With that rudimentary understanding of antidumping laws in mind, consider the court's holding in *Timken Co. v. United States*, below.

Timken Co. v. United States

354 F.3d 1334 (Fed. Cir. 2004)

Prost, Circuit Judge.

Koyo Seiko Co., Ltd. and Koyo Corporation of U.S.A. (collectively, "Koyo") appeal the decision of the United States Court of International Trade in *Timken Co. v. United States,* 240 F.Supp.2d 1228 (CIT 2002), holding that the United States Department of Commerce ("Commerce") properly "zeroed" any negative dumping margins in calculating the weighted-average dumping margin applied to imports of Koyo's tapered roller bearings ("TRBs") from Japan. The Timken Company ("Timken") cross appeals arguing that Commerce, in calculating Koyo's constructed export price ("CEP"), improperly applied the adverse-facts-available rate to the entered value rather than the sales value of Koyo's TRBs. Because we agree with the Court of International Trade that Commerce properly resolved both issues, we affirm.

---

49. Jeffrey L. Dunoff, *Less Than Zero: The Effects of Giving Domestic Effect to WTO Law*, 6 Loy. U. Int'l L. Rev. 279, 281 (2008).

50. *Id.* at 286.

I

Commerce issues antidumping duty orders for imported merchandise that is sold in the United States below its fair value and materially injures or threatens to injure a domestic industry. *See* 19 U.S.C. § 1673e (2000); 19 U.S.C. § 1673d. Specifically, Commerce determines the antidumping duties by first calculating the "dumping margin," which is "the amount by which the normal value exceeds the export price or constructed export price of the subject merchandise." *Id.* § 1677(35)(A); *see also Koyo Seiko Co. v. United States,* 258 F.3d 1340, 1342 (Fed.Cir.2001). Commerce uses a CEP if, "before or after the time of importation, the first sale to an unaffiliated person is made by (or for the account of) the producer or exporter or by a seller in the United States who is affiliated with the producer or exporter." *Uruguay Round Agreements Act, Statement of Administrative Action,* H.R. Doc. No. 103-826, at 822 (1994), *reprinted in* 1994 U.S.C.C.A.N. 4040 ("*SAA*"). Various adjustments may be made to CEP, including reduction by "the cost of any further manufacture or assembly" in the United States.

After calculating the dumping margins on the individual U.S. transactions subject to review, Commerce calculates the weighted-average dumping margin "by dividing the aggregate dumping margins determined for a specific exporter or producer by the aggregate . . . constructed export prices of such exporter or producer." *Id.* § 1677(35)(B); *see also Koyo Seiko,* 258 F.3d at 1342–43. When calculating the weighted-average dumping margin, Commerce treats transactions that generate "negative" dumping margins (i.e., a dumping margin with a value less than zero) as if they were zero. This practice is referred to as "zeroing." Finally, Commerce uses this weighted-average dumping margin to calculate the duties owed on an entry-by-entry basis. 19 U.S.C. § 1675(a)(2).

In this case Commerce initiated an administrative review of alleged sales of TRBs from Japan at less than fair value during the period of October 1, 1998, through September 30, 1999. *Initiation of Antidumping and Countervailing Duty Administrative Reviews,* 64 Fed. Reg. 67,846 (Dec. 3, 1999). Based on its review, Commerce calculated preliminary dumping margins of 17.94% on TRBs greater than four inches in diameter and 14.86% on TRBs less than four inches in diameter. [Authorities omitted] Koyo exported both types of merchandise and thus became potentially liable for antidumping duties. *Id.* Both Koyo and Timken subsequently filed case and rebuttal briefs, with Koyo questioning, *inter alia,* Commerce's zeroing practice, and Timken questioning, *inter alia,* Commerce's application of the adverse-facts-available rate to the entered value rather than sales value of Koyo's TRBs. . . .

II . . .

A . . .

We conclude Commerce based its zeroing practice on a reasonable interpretation of the statute. First, while the statutory definitions do not unambiguously preclude the existence of negative dumping margins, they do at a minimum allow for Commerce's construction. Basically, one number "exceeds" another if it is "greater than" the other, meaning it falls to the right of it on the number line. Here, because Commerce's zeroing practice is a reasonable interpretation of the statutory language, we do not question it in light of other reasonable possibilities.

Second, Commerce's methodology for calculating dumping margins makes practical sense. Commerce calculates dumping duties on an entry-by-entry basis. 19 U.S.C. § 1675(a)(2). Its practice of zeroing negative dumping margins comports with this approach. . . .

Third, we note that the Court of International Trade has specifically addressed Commerce's zeroing practice and found it reasonable and in accordance with the law. . . .

We turn now to Koyo's argument that Commerce unreasonably interpreted § 1677(35) to allow for zeroing, beginning with a review of the WTO's *EC-Bed Linen* report upon which Koyo so heavily relies. *EC-Bed Linen* dealt with a trade dispute between the European Community ("EC") and India. *EC-Bed Linen,* WT/DS141/AB/R ¶ 1. The EC, in investigating and levying duties on the importation of bed sheets from India, engaged in the practice of zeroing negative-margin transactions. India brought an action at the WTO, claiming that the EC practice of zeroing violated Article 2.4.2 of the ADA. The WTO Appellate Body evaluated the EC's practice in light of both this article and Article 2.4, which states that one must make a "fair comparison" between the EP or CEP and the normal value when calculating dumping margins. It took the "fair comparison" language to mean that *all* transactions must be accounted for, whether creating positive or negative dumping margins. Thus, because it was unfair to exclude negative-margin transactions, the WTO Appellate Body concluded that the EC practice of zeroing during an antidumping investigation was impermissible under the ADA.

In light of the decision in *EC-Bed Linen,* Koyo asks us to interpret the "fair comparison" language in the U.S. antidumping statute in a manner consistent with U.S. international obligations, thereby adopting the holding in *EC-Bed Linen* and finding Commerce's zeroing practice an unreasonable statutory interpretation. The crux of its argument hinges on the *Charming Betsy* canon of claim construction, according to which courts should interpret U.S. law, whenever possible, in a manner consistent with U.S. international obligations. *Murray v. Charming Betsy,* 6 U.S. (2 Cranch) 64, 118, 2 L.Ed. 208 (1804); *see also Fed.-Mogul Corp. v. United States,* 63 F.3d 1572, 1581 (Fed.Cir.1995) (noting that trade laws are not exempt from the *Charming Betsy* principle); *Luigi Bormioli Corp. v. United States,* 304 F.3d 1362, 1368 (Fed.Cir.2002) ("[T]he statute must be interpreted to be consistent with [international] obligations, absent contrary indications in the statutory language or its legislative history."). Koyo secondarily relies on its claim that the EC and United States have functionally identical practices that demand similar treatment. Because Commerce has the authority to bring its practice into conformity with U.S. international obligations, Koyo contends, we should find that it was unreasonable for Commerce to continue interpreting the antidumping statute in a non-conforming manner by allowing zeroing.

Koyo's reliance on the "fair comparison" language is misplaced. . . .

Further, even assuming that the "fair comparison" language in § 1677b(a) did not limit the analysis to calculating normal value using the statutorily-prescribed adjustments, we would nonetheless find Commerce's continued practice of zeroing reasonable in light of *EC-Bed Linen.* As Koyo acknowledges, the decision is not binding on the United States, much less this court. While Koyo relies on *EC-Bed Linen* for its persuasive value in an effort to convince us of the unreasonableness of Commerce's zeroing practice, we do not find it sufficiently persuasive to find Commerce's practice unreasonable. In light of the fact that Commerce's "longstanding and consistent administrative interpretation is entitled to considerable weight," *Zenith,* 437 U.S. at 450, 98 S.Ct. 2441, we refuse to overturn the zeroing practice based on *EC-Bed Linen.*

Finally, we disagree with Koyo's assertion that the Court of International Trade erroneously distinguished *EC-Bed Linen.* As discussed above, the court distinguished *EC-Bed Linen* for two reasons: (1) it did not involve the United States, and (2) it dealt with an antidumping investigation as opposed to an administrative review of dumping. We agree with the Court of International Trade and find the absence of the United States as a party to be an important distinction.

As to the difference between an investigation and an administrative review, Koyo contends that the distinction is irrelevant—Article 2.4.2 and Article 9.3.1, dealing with investigations and administrative reviews respectively, should be read together. In addition, Koyo argues, the "fair comparison" requirements of § 1677b(a) do not differ depending on the nature of the action. We disagree and find that the Court of International Trade properly distinguished the current case over *EC-Bed Linen.*

Because we find Commerce's zeroing practice to be a reasonable interpretation of the statute, even in light of the decision in *EC—Bed Linen,* we do not address the government's or Timken's arguments that this court is statutorily precluded from reconciling the two under 19 U.S.C § 3533. . . .

* * *

CONCLUSION

For the foregoing reasons, we affirm the Court of International Trade's conclusion that Commerce's final results are supported by substantial evidence and otherwise in accordance with law.

AFFIRMED.

Notes and Questions

1. *Timken Co.* is representative of decisions in which a domestic court resists the priority of an international ruling. For a more recent case espousing a similar notion of WTO law vis-à-vis domestic law, see *Corus Staal v. Dep't of Commerce,* 395 F.3d

1343, 1348 (Fed. Cir. 2005), in which the court was resolute in confirming that WTO decisions are "not binding on the United States."

2. Compare the courts' reasoning in *Timken Co.* and *Cours Staal* to the holdings in the cases below (excerpted from Robin Miller's *Effect of World Trade Organization Decisions Upon United States*, 17 A.L.R. Fed 2d. 1 (2007)):

1. *Allegheny Ludlum Corp. v. U.S.*, 367 F.3d 1339, 26 Int'l Trade Re. (BNA) 1105 (Fed. Cir. 2004) (holding that a decision of the WTO's Appellate Body was one factor supporting a lower court's ruling and that a federal statute should be interpreted to be consistent with the international obligations of the United States, absent contrary indications in the statutory language or its legislative history).

2. *Acciai Speciali Terni S.p.A. v. U.S.*, 350 F. Supp. 2d 1254, 27 Int'l Trade Re. (BNA) 1017 (Ct. Int'l Trade 2004) (stating that, while neither the World Trade Organization's legal texts nor its Appellate Body and panel reports have direct applicability under United States law, the reasoning in those materials can be useful for clarifying federal statutory provisions).

3. *Usinor, Beautor, Haironville, Sollac Atlantique, Sollace Lorraine v. U.S.*, 342 F. Supp. 2d 1267, 26 Int'l Trade Re. (BNA) 1874 (Ct. Int'l Trade 2004) (rejecting the assertion that there is absolutely no need to look to either World Trade Organization agreements or WTO decisions; stating that a court's opinions may be informed by WTO documents; understanding fully that WTO agreements are not self-executing and that WTO panel and Appellate Body decisions are not stare decisis in United States courts; declaring that such authority, as well as treatises, law review articles, and commentaries—indeed, any unforeclosed source of valuable analysis—are matters a court can examine for persuasive rationale.)

3. Imagine you are a judge sitting on a domestic court. You are drafting an opinion to decide a case in which the laws of the United States and the WTO would reach different results: which line of reasoning would you use to reach your decision? Why?

IV. WTO, the environment and labor

From its earliest days, the WTO has drawn debate over the relationship between global trade and social standards, as noted by economist Kym Anderson: "Many in developing countries perceive the entwining of these social issues with trade policy as a threat to both their sovereignty and their economies, while significant groups in richer countries consider it unfair, ecologically unsound, and even immoral to trade with countries adopting much lower social standards than theirs."[51] The role of the

51. Kym Anderson, *Environmental and Labor Standards: What Role for the WTO?*, *in* THE WTO AS AN INTERNATIONAL ORGANIZATION 231, 231. (Anne O. Krueger, ed. 1998).

WTO in relation to social standards remains keenly controversial. In this section, we touch on the main elements of the controversies in relation to the environment and labor, as these come before the WTO.

A. The environment

The WTO identifies itself as committed to environmental "protection and preservation" (see note 53, *infra*); however, the trading rules preclude protectionist measures put in place to serve environmentalist ends:

> Sustainable development and protection and preservation of the environment are fundamental goals of the WTO. They are enshrined in the Marrakesh Agreement, which established the WTO, and complement the WTO's objective to reduce trade barriers and eliminate discriminatory treatment in international trade relations. While there is no specific agreement dealing with the environment, under WTO rules members can adopt trade-related measures aimed at protecting the environment provided a number of conditions to avoid the misuse of such measures for protectionist ends are fulfilled.[52]

This is the very issue in a dispute known as "Shrimp/Turtle"—a case involving the U.S. and five Asian countries (led by India) that came before the WTO when the U.S. sought to ban shrimp imports from countries that were not subject to the same environmental requirements that compelled U.S. shrimpers to protect sea turtles. Chris Wold and David Fullilove consider *Shrimp/Turtle* to offer the quintessence of the debate between WTO proponents and opponents:

> The *Shrimp/Turtle* dispute symbolizes the controversy between proponents and opponents of the World Trade Organization (WTO). Supporters of the WTO downplay the significance of the *Shrimp/Turtle* decision by claiming that the Appellate Body ruled only that the United States failed to *apply* its ban on shrimp imports in a nondiscriminatory way. In contrast, critics of the WTO often cite *Shrimp/Turtle* as proof that the WTO completely ignores the environment to promote liberalized trade. Both views are only partially correct. In truth, the Appellate Body interpreted the rules of the General Agreement on Trade and Tariffs (GATT) very narrowly. While the Appellate Body found that the United States applied its ban on shrimp imports discriminatorily, it also imposed interpretative hurdles that make it virtually impossible for a WTO Member to impose trade measures to protect the environment or natural resources.[53]

---

52. *Trade and Environment*, World Trade Org., https://www.wto.org/english/tratop_e/envir_e/envir_e.htm.

53. Chris Wold & Glenn Fullilove, *Turtle Briefing—Analysis of the WTO Appellate Body's Decision in Shrimp/Turtle*, Int'l Envtl. L. Proj., (Feb. 24, 2000), https://law.lclark.edu/clinics/international_environmental_law_project/our_work/trade_and_environment/turtle_briefing.php.

In its announcement of the decision in *Shrimp/Turtle* (Case 58), the WTO apparently felt a need to defend the ruling with an explanation of its environmental jurisdiction:

> In reaching these conclusions, we wish to underscore what we have *not* decided in this appeal. We have *not* decided that the protection and preservation of the environment is of no significance to the Members of the WTO. Clearly, it is. We have *not* decided that the sovereign nations that are Members of the WTO cannot adopt effective measures to protect endangered species, such as sea turtles. Clearly, they can and should. And we have *not* decided that sovereign states should not act together bilaterally, plurilaterally or multilaterally, either within the WTO or in other international fora, to protect endangered species or to otherwise protect the environment. Clearly, they should and do.[54]

As you read this section, consider the complexities facing the WTO and various parties as they press for protection and preservation of the environment—or resist it. Some of the complexities include wealth inequalities across countries, different policy priorities, and the ambiguity of environmental protection in relation to specific environmental problems as well as trade barriers. Today, RTAs and BITs contain environmental provisions, offering some scope for specificity as trading partnerships develop their own terms on these issues.

1. Shrimp/Turtle

The WTO's environmental authority is at issue in the *Shrimp/Turtle* case, described in the following excerpt, by Professor Trujillo. Her analysis focuses on Article XX of the GATT, on exceptions—in this case, specifically involving conservation of non-renewable natural resources. To read the full opinion, see Report of the Appellate Body on U.S. Import Prohibition of Certain Shrimp and Shrimp Products, Oct. 12, 1998, 38 I.L.M. 118 (1999).

Elizabeth Trujillo, *A Dialogical Approach to Trade and Environment*

16 J. Int'l Econ. L. 535 (2013)

In 1998, India, Pakistan, Malaysia, and Thailand initiated a WTO complaint alleging that the U.S. regulation requiring that all shrimpers, foreign and domestic, exporting shrimp to the United States use a "turtle excluder device" (TED) according to U.S. agency standards. The concern was that the purse-seine nets used to fish shrimp would accidentally catch sea turtles, an endangered species both under the CITES and the U.S. Endangered Species Act of 1973.

54. *Environment—Disputes 8. India (etc.) versus U.S.: "Shrimp-Turtle,"* World Trade Org., https://www.wto.org/english/tratop_e/envir_e/edis08_e.htm.

In order to better protect the turtles under these circumstances, the U.S. required the use of the TED devices, which had been shown to provide an escape route for turtles without drowning. The U.S. had begun international agreements with other nations to protect the turtles. However, India, Pakistan, Malaysia, and Thailand had not entered into such an agreement with the United States.

The WTO panel found the U.S. restriction to be a violation of GATT 1994 Article XI:1 violation and not justifiable under Article XX. The Panel decision focused on whether the domestic regulatory measure may affect the multilateral system in significant ways, particularly with respect to market access. The United States appealed and the Appellate Body, though agreeing that there was a violation, provided a small glimpse of hope for environmentalists in finding that Section 609[55] was indeed within the scope of Article XX. The Appellate Body emphasized that in adjudicating a domestic environmental regulation, it was important for panels to consider the manner in which the violation is applied. It recognized that nations had the sovereign right to regulate the environment; however, it faulted the United States for having done so unilaterally and without pursuing a multilateral forum. However, it also clarified that unlike the Panel's conclusion, the legal analysis under Article XX does not require a look into whether a domestic regulation undermines the multilateral trading system; rather, the crucial issue is whether it poses an "unjustifiable discrimination between countries." The Appellate Body determined this measure as unjustifiable and arbitrary under the *chapeau* of Article XX, the gatekeeper for possible Article XX exceptions.Without imposing a duty on nations to negotiate multilaterally, the Appellate Body once again brought domestic environmental regulations within its jurisdictional domain, and was cautious of unilateral solutions, while encouraging negotiated solutions.

Unlike the *US-Tuna Reports*, *Shrimp-Turtle* was decided under the WTO dispute settlement body and the panel and Appellate Body reports were adopted. However, like *US-Tuna I*, in *Shrimp-Turtle*, the U.S. cited a multilateral environmental agreement to provide strength to its argument that in fact Section 609 was compliant because it protected an endangered species as noted in this international environmental agreement. Though neither the Panel nor the Appellate Body provided guidance as to the relevance of CITES to the understanding of what constitutes an "exhaustible natural resource" under Article XX(g), once again through the adjudicatory process, the Parties were able to raise the argument that in fact a MEA[56] is relevant to trade jurisprudence. The Appellate Body also referred to environmental treaties and resolutions such as UNCLOS and Agenda 21 and considered the Resolution on Assistance to Developing Countries. Though the WTO still has not clarified the relationship of MEA's or international resolutions to the WTO Covered

55. Authors' note: Section 609 of Public Law 101-162 is an amendment to the Endangered Species Act, enabling the United States to protect sea turtles from incidental mortality during shrimp harvesting.

56. Authors' note: Multilateral Environmental Agreement.

Agreements or to the trade regime, these strategic legal arguments on the part of the Parties and the willingness of the WTO DSB to entertain these arguments highlights the dialogical qualities of the adjudicatory capacity of the WTO when it comes to trade and the environment. This has contributed enhanced cross-fertilization between the two camps.

Furthermore, *Shrimp-Turtle* also recognized that exhaustible resources under Article XX(g) are not limited to non-living natural resources; that " 'exhaustible' and 'renewable' natural resources are [not] mutually exclusive and that they are 'suspectible of depletion, exhaustion and extinction, frequently because of human activities.' " This recognition further highlights the role of the WTO adjudicatory process in cross-fertilizing trade regulation with that of the preservation of natural resources. The DSB here opened a door that has yet to be further unhinged when it stated that the words of Article XX(g) needed to be read "by a treaty interpreter in the light of contemporary concerns of the community of nations about the protection and conservation of the environment."

Though disturbing to environmentalists, these early environment and trade disputes allowed the WTO DSB to better identify the role of Article XX with respect to the trade and environment relationship. Though not fully understood at the time, *US-Shrimp* changed the way Appellate Bodies would deal with the compliance of environmental measures to the trade regime, recognizing that trade treaty interpretations had to be in light of environmental concerns.

Notes and Questions

1. *Shrimp/Turtle* was hailed by some observers as a long-term success for environmentalists due to the Appellate Body's willingness to consider environmental concerns. However, some countries—especially those in the global south—have continued to object that environmental regulations will be unfairly discriminatory to developing countries. Some scholars are not convinced that this preference for environmental protection must continue:

> The apparent "greening" of world trade rules achieved in the *Shrimp-Turtle* cases should not be regarded as an irreversible process. Just as the Appellate Body sought in that dispute to meet the expectations of many WTO members that environmental considerations be given a more prominent place in international trade law, it is entirely possible that future decision-makers may be more sympathetic to the views of some WTO members from the global south that the WTO regime should not privilege environmental interests at the expense of trade-led developmental policies.

Tim Stephens, International Courts and Environmental Protection 342 (2009). Is the WTO in a position to balance the interests of developed and developing countries with respect to a priority on environmental protection?

2. Most recently, the very nature of trade agreements has fundamentally shifted in the direction of regional trade agreements (RTAs) and bilateral investment

treaties (BITs). These agreements have their own specific provisions dealing with the environment and labor. More importantly, as Richard Baldwin argues in *The World Trade Organization and the Future of Multilaternalism*, 30 J. Econ. Persp. 95, 96 (2016):

> The rules and procedures of the WTO were designed for a global economy in which made-here-sold-there goods moved across national borders. But the rapid rising of offshoring from high technology nations to low-wage nations has created a new type of international commerce. In essence the flows of goods, services, investment, training, and know-how that used to move inside or between advanced-nation factories have now become part of international commerce.... The trade rules that matter are less about tariffs and more about protection of investments and intellectual property, along with legal and regulatory steps to assure that the two-way flows of goods, services, investment, and people will not be impeded.

3. The debate about the role of environmental regulations in international trade law has not been resolved. However, as domestic regulations and multilateral environmental agreements develop, the complex relationship between trade and the environment has evolved. Consider this 2009 excerpt from *The Oxford Handbook of International Trade Law*:

> As the linkages between trade and environment have moved to the centre of the scholarly map, a number of debates have crystallized regarding the scope and purpose of the international trade regime and its relationship to domestic and international environmental protection. Should trade agreements be self-contained, or should they incorporate environmental principles or consider other (environmental) agreements—for example, in the context of dispute settlement? Conversely, should national governments be free to impose trade restrictions in furtherance of their environmental goals, either individually or through multilateral environmental agreements? More generally, should the international community privilege free trade or environmental protection when conflicts between the two arise?
>
> In recent years, the trade and environmental communities have had a partial rapprochement, as each has become more sensitive to the other. However, a significant number of questions about the compatibility of environmental measures with trade rules remain unanswered. The task of reconciling the fundamental goals of free trade and environmental protection remains very much a work in progress.[57]

4. Legal scholars Mark Wu and James Saltzman, in *The Next Generation of Trade and Environmental Conflicts: The Rise of Green Industrial Policies*, 108 Nw. U.L. Rev. 401 (2014), update the *Shrimp/Turtle* dispute with their assessment

---

57. Daniel Bodansky & Jessica C. Lawrence, *Trade and Environment*, Oxford Handbook Int'l Trade L., Jan 2009.

of the recent rise of conflicts involving environmental protection before the WTO. The rise in a distinctive class of disputes—what they call "Next Generation" disputes—in 2012 and since follows a period of quiescence after *Shrimp/Turtle*'s resolution in 1998:

> The recent cases . . . are driven by the rapid rise of green industrial policies—the application of traditional industrial policy instruments to spur the development of renewable energy and environmentally friendly industries. Indeed, the policies underlying the recent disputes have more in common with recent industrial policy measures . . . than they do with the import measures on tuna and shrimp in the environmental disputes of the recent past[58]
>
> . . . Next Generation conflicts significantly raise the stakes for a trade war and will dominate the trade and environment discourse for the coming decade . . . . [T]hey force a profound reevaluation of our assumptions about trade and environment disputes . . . . [59]

Their conclusion points to important issues of legal pluralism arising at the intersection of trade rules and climate change agreements—the accomplishment of the Paris Accords still ahead as their article went to press.[60] In your view, how might the Paris Accords factor into the future of trade (including trade sanctions)? And conversely, can trade rules and the WTO dispute resolution process advance the goals of the Paris Accords?

B. WTO and labor

Scholars and activists debate the role of the WTO in relation to labor standards. Critics of the WTO have many of the same concerns regarding labor standards as they do with the environmental standards—based on the assumption that prioritizing free trade over labor protections will undermine domestic efforts at labor regulation, potentially risking human rights violations to maximize comparative advantage and profitability.

This dilemma—how to reduce the tensions between the projects of domestic protection of labor rights and advancing international trade—points in specific ways to the interlegalities of global trade. Rather than just a struggle between domestic and international law, there is a dynamic interplay between local, national, regional, and international labor standards. For example, developing countries tend to view the issue as an economic one. Strong domestic labor laws, much like strong

---

58. Mark Wu & James Salzman, *The Next Generation of Trade and Environment Conflicts: The Rise of Green Industrial Policy*, 108 Nw. U. L. Rev. 401, 404 (2014).

59. *Id.* at 405.

60. "[T]he rules shaping the race toward a renewable energy future have become an important part of the global climate regime. How these rules are determined will play an important role in charting the path toward a sustainable future." Wu & Saltzman, *supra* note 58, at 474.

environmental laws, may be used to mask a state's protectionist goals, with the result that developing countries are kept out of trade opportunities due to the potentially prohibitive costs of labor laws. Meanwhile, developed countries are often facing fierce domestic pressure from public interest groups to strengthen labor laws, both within that country's borders and abroad. The larger context involves the consistency—or lack thereof—between the International Labour Organization's standards and WTO agreements.

Labor standards in the era of the WTO are framed within the historical context of NAFTA, as discussed above, as well as the ILO and the myriad state-level human rights and labor laws. These issues are central to Chapters 5 and 6, *infra*.

1. The ILO core standards in global, regional and bilateral trade

The WTO is for the most part silent on the issue of labor standards.[61] The WTO provides the following statement:

> We renew our commitment to the observance of internationally recognized core labour standards. The International Labour Organization (ILO) is the competent body to set and deal with these standards, and we affirm our support for its work in promoting them. We believe that economic growth and development fostered by increased trade and further trade liberalization contribute to the promotion of these standards. We reject the use of labour standards for protectionist purposes, and agree that the comparative advantage of countries, particularly low-wage developing countries, must in no way be put into question. In this regard, we note that the WTO and ILO Secretariats will continue their existing collaboration.[62]

The ILO's four core standards include freedom of association, no forced labor, no child labor, and no discrimination at work (including gender discrimination). Beyond these standards, the ILO also relies on eight core labor conventions drafted and ratified since 1930. These standards are more often included in regional trade agreements and supplementary side agreements than they are in WTO agreements. Although the inclusion of labor standards might seem to indicate a trend towards a cohesive global labor system, that is not the case. A 2014 study by the ILO concluded that global mechanisms are needed to ensure collaboration and synergy among the many trade agreements. That study is excerpted here:

61. On labor mobility provisions, see Laura Dawson, *Labour mobility and the WTO: The limits of GATS Mode 4*, 51 Int'l Migration 1 (2013).

62. *Labour standards: consensus, coherence and controversy*, World Trade Org., https://www.wto.org/english/thewto_e/whatis_e/tif_e/bey5_e.htm.

Jordi Agustí-Panareda, Franz Christian Ebert & Desirée LeClercq, *Labour Provisions in Free Trade Agreements: Fostering their Consistency with the ILO Standards System*

International Labour Office, pp. 5–6, March 2014

International labour standards are becoming increasingly common in economic trade instruments.... The most significant and perhaps most controversial development in this regard is the insertion of labour provisions into trade agreements. While previous attempts to insert labour provisions (also referred to as the "social clause") into the multilateral trade framework of the World Trade Organization (WTO) have thus far not been successful, bilateral and regional trade agreements containing these labour provisions have proliferated with great speed over the past two decades. This proliferation has resulted in decentralized labour standards systems with increasing implications in the realm of international trade.

These increasing implications raise a question concerning the compatibility between decentralized labour systems and the global labour system of the International Labour Organization (ILO).... The impact may largely depend on mechanisms established within the decentralized system to foster consistency, promote positive synergies and avoid prejudicial interference.

2. Linking labor and trade

Debate continues over the inclusion of labor standards in global, regional, and bilateral trade agreements. Although (as noted above) the WTO itself is silent on labor standards, most regional agreements do include labor provisions, and many developed countries have called for labor standards to be incorporated in WTO agreements. This strategy—the linkage of labor standards with trade sanctions as an effort to ensure fair labor practices—has strong supporters as well as opponents. Consider this debate through the following excerpts.

a. Arguments Against Labor-Trade Linkage

Jagdish Bhagwati, *Afterword: The Question of Linkage Symposium: The Boundaries of the WTO,* José E. Alvarez, ed.

96 Am. J. Int'l L. 126, 130–132 (2002)

Can we make a strong case that labor standards must be encompassed by the WTO or trade treaties? I do not think so.

The arguments for linkage here can be subdivided into two sets: the "egoistical" (i.e., self-serving) ones and the "altruistic" (i.e., others-oriented) ones.

Take the former. The unions naturally feel threatened by competition from the low-wage, low-standards poor countries. They fear that it will reduce the real wages of unskilled workers, especially those that are their members; they also worry that their own labor standards, won by hard and glorious struggle over decades of organization and agitation, will be reduced by a "race to the bottom." But the empirical evidence does not corroborate these fears, widely prevalent as they often are.

Much empirical work has shown that, at worst, the adverse effect of trade with poor countries on the wages in the rich countries is small. My own work strongly suggests that trade may even have moderated the decline in real wages that would have occurred from unskilled-labor-saving technical change. The recent and influential empirical work of Robert Feenstra and Gordon Hanson, which models and estimates the effect on earnings of American unskilled workers from the outsourcing of labor-intensive inputs to the developing countries over two decades also does likewise: the effect is mildly favorable, and definitely not adverse.

Equally, there seems to be practically no empirical evidence of a race to the bottom in terms of our own labor standards. Daniel Drezner, who has written an entire book on the subject, confirms this conclusion: the rhetoric of globalization is used by both its enemies and its friends to create the mythology of such a race to the bottom. Indeed, even in the textile industry, many of whose firms have gone abroad to poor countries, sweatshops have not broken out in the rich countries as a result. The sweatshops of New York result from the influx of illegal immigrants and our attempts at curbing it, which drive these unfortunates into second-class underdog status where exploitation is easier. Blame must also be assigned to abysmally low levels of enforcement. Similarly, the astonishingly appalling record of the United States on protecting the workers' basic right to unionize, and the declining long-run trend in union membership, has little to do with globalization and much to do with the draconian antilabor legislation that goes back over half a century.

What about the altruistic grounds for pushing labor standards into trade treaties and institutions? … Here, too, the argument is far from compelling. Let me mention just two problems with, say, a social clause at the WTO that would link market access rights to the fulfillment of certain labor standards or rights.

First, trade sanctions can flag problems; they are not good at flogging them. Typically, when used, they also generate resentment and resistance. Thus, last November, when I interviewed the leaders of Indian trade unions, with a membership exceeding seven million, they opposed the social clause stoutly because they feared it would lead to protection that would harm them. The left-leaning among them had a special response: we did not get rid of the CIA to be run by the AFL-CIO!

The proponents of trade sanctions also deride the approach of moral suasion, saying it lacks teeth. My riposte is that God gave us not just teeth but also a tongue. A good tongue-lashing today, with the ubiquity of CNN and civil society groups, can be very effective.

In fact, if one looks at the International Programme for the Eradication of Child Labor of the International Labour Organization (ILO), it works very well since it does the heavy lifting necessary to make a dent on child labor. By contrast, trade sanctions, or their threat, have been not just unproductive, but also counterproductive. In

Bangladesh, the threat to exports when the Harkin bill on banning products using child labor was being considered in the U.S. Congress led to the discharge of female children in textiles, who were often forced instead into prostitution by destitute parents.

Besides, trade sanctions apply only to trade. But only 5 percent of the output of child labor in the world is exported, so that trade sanctions are not even a properly targeted policy. This point is also demonstrated by the sanctioned prohibition of imports of products made with prison labor in the original GATT. Can anyone seriously maintain that this proscription makes any sense today, when prisons in countries such as the United States typically engage inmates in work, nearly all of whose output is sold commercially at home? To eliminate prison labor, it would have to be reached at source, not through negligible exports.

This example also shows that these types of questions are too complex to be dealt with at the GATT or the WTO. Thus, today, we *want* prisoners to work. We just do not want gulag conditions. Besides, with privatization, many prisoners are working in effect without minimum wages and under conditions of forced labor: how do we address that situation? The WTO is hardly the place to discuss these questions meaningfully; the ILO is.

In fact, I would stress that the WTO does not begin to qualify to be the institution to manage the complex issues raised by "core labor standards" concepts such as the right to unionize and the absence of gender discrimination. Take just the latter. Even if we were to take merely the question of equal pay within its vast scope, such equality can be defined in different ways. Is it just payment of identical wages for equal merit when both women and men work for the American Society of International Law? Or is it also equal pay across different sectors for equal qualifications as determined, for instance, by a pay commission in several countries? Or do we raise questions of metapreferences and ask why women gravitate toward lower-paying occupations and what we need to do about it in terms of gender identity formation, values formation, role-playing, and so forth. Does anyone expect that all this can be sorted out at the WTO? Our distinguished congressmen, the trade aficionados such as Charles Rangel of New York, Robert Matsui of California, and Sander Levin of Michigan, appear to believe incorrectly that only the far-right Republicans and ideological free traders among the economists oppose the inclusion of such "core" standards into the WTO under a social clause. But they do not have a realistic comprehension of what they are asking for; and their demands seem to me to be inadequately thought through.

b. Arguments For Labor-Trade Linkage

Renee Chartres and Bryan Mercurio, *A Call for an Agreement on Trade-Related Aspects of Labor: Why and How the WTO Should Play a Role in Upholding Core Labor Standards*

37 N.C.J. Int'l L. & Com. Reg. 665, 665–70, 672–75, 681–83, 686–687, 691–693 (2012)

I. Introduction

Despite repeated proclamations that "the International Labor Organization is the competent body to set and deal with . . . [labor] standards," the World Trade Organization ("WTO") nevertheless regularly finds itself subjected to pressure to build labor standards into its legal architecture. The climax in the efforts to directly link labor standards and the international trading regime came in 1999 at the WTO Ministerial Meeting in Seattle, when the United States, European Communities ("EC"), and Canada all submitted proposals on labor standards and trade, and nearly 50,000 protesters gathered to demand, inter alia, a fairer trading system that upholds at least internationally recognized minimum labor standards. Yet, developing countries vehemently opposed the idea that trading rights could be conditional on compliance with labor standards, ensuring that even the most innocuous proposals dealing with the trade-labor linkage were stillborn. Continued resistance from developing countries, coupled with the Bush administration's refusal to promote the issue at the subsequent WTO negotiating round (the so-called "Doha Development Agenda" or "Doha Round"), meant that the trade-labor question has since been moved off the agenda for the WTO.

Despite being ignored in the current Doha Round, the issue of whether labor standards should be incorporated into the WTO continues to evoke heated discussion at the domestic, regional, and international levels and features prominently in academic and non-governmental organization ("NGO") discourse. More importantly, while the WTO's Dispute Settlement Body ("DSB") has not been asked to determine whether unilateral trade restrictions on goods produced in violation of labor standards are consistent with the General Agreement on Tariffs and Trade ("GATT") or any other WTO covered agreement, it has repeatedly been called upon to identify some of the contours of the relationship between trade and non-trade issues. To date, the DSB has not been asked to determine whether conditioning preferential market access through Generalized System of Preferences ("GSP") schemes on compliance with certain labor standards is consistent with the WTO's Enabling Clause. It is, however, likely that a WTO dispute on one or more of these issues will arise, and the inevitable arguments in support of interpreting trade and economic rules in conformity with human rights obligations will require discussion, analysis, and interpretation.

Given the uncertainty surrounding the consistency of unilateral trade restrictions for goods produced in violation of labor standards under the GATT, along with the rapid increase in labor standards and provisions appearing in GSPs and recently concluded bilateral and regional free trade agreements ("FTAs"), the time is ripe to review the trade-labor link and to consider what, if any, role the WTO should play in upholding labor standards without jeopardizing its key objectives of enhancing trade liberalization and eliminating discrimination in international trade relations.

* * *

II. Do Labor Standards Belong in the WTO?

Critics, such as Jagdish Bhagwati, argue that labor standards have no place in the WTO because it is an organization that exists primarily to promote mutually beneficial, non-coercive trade through reciprocal and mutually advantageous arrangements aimed at reducing barriers to trade. Under this view, the incorporation of labor standards for the purpose of upholding certain rights within a Member State is not a concern of the WTO, which has as its key objective the furtherance of Member rights regarding market access to other Members by upholding mutually agreed upon tariff rates and other concessions.

Bhagwati's view that the WTO's role is limited to regulating "pure" trade issues for the purposes of trade liberalization ignores that the GATT and WTO, as well as human rights treaties and organizations, were created for the purpose of increasing human welfare, and for the considerable evolution of the aims, objectives, and roles of the international trading regime, starting from the establishment of the GATT in 1947. For example, the preamble to the WTO Agreement cites "sustainable development" as an objective to be balanced against economic objectives. To most, human rights would be considered an element of "sustainable development" and thus implicitly included within the scope of the WTO. More directly, the WTO has expanded its coverage beyond "border measures," such as import tariffs, to include other policies which might affect trade—for instance, domestic policies concerning government regulation of investment, product and health standards, agricultural policy, and government procurement. The primary purpose of regulation on such topics has little, if anything, to do with trade, but instead concerns the fact that regulation in these areas could affect foreign producers and trade more generally. Furthermore, the Agreement on Trade-Related Intellectual Property Rights ("TRIPS Agreement") offers a cogent example of obligations imposed on wholly domestic activities, where such activities may affect international trade. Despite its name, the TRIPS Agreement sets minimum standards and requirements on a range of issues which, until now, were considered purely domestic considerations (ranging from the term of protection for a patent to the availability of judicial review and the criminal sanctions for certain infringements).

It is therefore a gross overstatement—and, in fact, simply incorrect—to state that the WTO has an inherent institutional difficulty imposing obligations that could be viewed as wholly internal. Of course, the WTO cannot incorporate every area or subject matter which merely may have an effect on trade and traders; there must be some criteria upon which to assess the suitability of incorporation.... The following four criteria would need to be satisfied in order for one to consider incorporation of [Core Labor Standards (CLS)] into the WTO framework: (1) CLS must be "trade-related"; (2) protection of CLS would positively affect international trade flows; (3) CLS are not sufficiently protected and enforced; and (4) CLS would need to be viewed as inherently deserving of protection. Even if one is not convinced that satisfying the above four criteria is justification for incorporating CLS into the WTO, there are several textual-based arguments from the GATT which favor such incorporation. . . .

A. Core Labor Standards Deserve Protection

1. Core Labor Standards Are "Trade-Related"

The fact that labor directly affects market share and activity is relatively uncontroversial. Labor is by nature an "intrinsic part of the production process that culminates in the manufacture of goods and services for trade." Simply stated, the conditions under which a product is manufactured or produced impact the quantity and cost of the product in the world market. As such, it seems only natural that labor standards should be viewed as an indispensable part of the effective trade in goods . . . .

2. Protection of Core Labor Standards Would Positively Affect International Trade Flows

The incorporation of [intellectual property rights (IPRs)] into the WTO framework indicates that governments are willing to allow for the regulation of internal activity if such regulation has the net effect of expanding the volume of world trade and, in so doing, increasing the security and predictability of markets. Yet, developing country governments, industry associations, certain economists, and some developing country NGOs often argue that the inclusion of CLS into the WTO would not expand trade volumes, but would rather operate as disguised protectionism to undermine developing countries' comparative advantage in cheap labor vis-à-vis developed countries. Thus, it is claimed that allowing Members to impose restrictive measures on products manufactured in contravention of CLS would have the net effect of reducing world trade—a result that is irreconcilable with the WTO's objective to further promote trade-liberalization and the expansion of trade.

Some commentators pursue this trajectory even further and argue that the imposition of CLS is philosophically incompatible with the WTO's goal of removing barriers to trade. Under this logic, the imposition of CLS on Members implies that a "fixing" of standards between countries, incompatible with market principles as regulatory policy, is a matter of comparative advantage. In other words, some argue that the imposition of artificial international standards into the domestic regulatory structure interferes with the market and thus impedes efficiency and stifles competition.

Before responding to these arguments, it is useful to briefly return to the four CLS in the ILO Declaration: (1) Freedom of association and the effective recognition of the right to collective bargaining; (2) the elimination of all forms of forced and compulsory labor; (3) the effective elimination of child labor; and (4) the elimination of discrimination in respect of employment and occupation. Critically, these rights do not encompass a "fair minimum wage" or compliance with occupational health and safety measures. It is generally accepted that low wages are a legitimate comparative advantage in international trade and that developing countries should not be denied that advantage; thus, rather than seeking to "equalize" the comparative advantage related to labor standards, the CLS concern practices that are not determined or fixed by market mechanisms—the absence of regulations actually denies workers comparable rights to use the freedom they otherwise would have to enable them to seek out better conditions of employment. Therefore, in denying the workers the freedom to seek out better working conditions, the absence of worker rights actually forecloses any possibility of a "natural market correction." In this sense, far from being incompatible with market philosophy, the decision not to enforce CLS in a domestic market is itself an interference with the free market . . . .

3. Core Labor Standards Suffer from Significant Under-Enforcement

Similar to the pre-TRIPS situation with regards to IPRs, CLS suffer from significant under-enforcement, with the existing international agency—that is, the ILO—seemingly impotent to enforce standards and curb widespread violations.

Despite being the body responsible for the protection of CLS, the ILO's enforcement record to date has proven to be consistently inadequate. This is not due to lack of effort; the ILO has adopted 188 binding conventions and approximately 200 non-binding resolutions since its creation in 1919. While it is difficult to pinpoint the precise reasons for the lack of enforcement, several impediments can be identified. One such impediment is that the ILO suffers from a disparate, and sometimes rather low, rate of ratification of its treaties (including by leading developed countries such as the United States). This, in turn, creates a "patchwork of inconsistent legal obligations" and serves as a major impediment to the global enforcement of labor standards. Moreover, a number of ILO conventions are ratified but not implemented.

Another impediment is that while in theory the ILO Constitution authorizes sanctions in the event of non-compliance, in practice the organization prefers to adopt a "soft" approach to the enforcement of its norms, relying on public identification, embarrassment and shaming, and technical assistance to promote compliance. The ILO does not even do this very well, as the ILO's "special list" of transgressions of CLS garners little international publicity and even less government attention; in fact, the list has not produced any substantial improvements in compliance with CLS . . . .

4. Core Labor Standards are Inherently Deserving of Protection

The fact that CLS are human rights is uncontroversial; no Member State voted against the ILO Declaration when it was put forth at the 86th Session of the General Conference of the ILO in June, 1998. The ILO Declaration itself acknowledges CLS have a special status within the international labor law hierarchy in that the CLS are imposed upon ILO Members by virtue of them simply being Members of the organization. Thus, Member States that have not ratified the relevant conventions are nevertheless bound to promote and realize the basic principles concerning the four CLS. Regardless of this requirement, all of the respective seven Conventions dealing with the standards currently enjoy almost universal acceptance, with the highest rate of ratification among all ILO conventions. The four principles are also broadly articulated in the Universal Declaration of Human Rights ("UDHR"), the International Covenant on Civil and Political Rights ("ICCPR"), the International Covenant on Economic, Social and Cultural Rights ("ICESCR"), and a number of other key human rights conventions, which signify the commitment of Members to protect workers on a much wider scale than that proposed by the CLS.

With such a high ratification rate and widespread endorsement within the broader international human rights system, the CLS do not simply constitute rights that belong to workers, but rather constitute rights that belong to individuals as human beings. Thus, child labor is prohibited not because the labor is cheaper than adult labor, but rather because the growth and development of children should not be undermined through labor; the operative principle is that children should be shielded from the burdens of labor, and concerns regarding the rate of pay a child receives are irrelevant by comparison. Similarly, forced labor is prohibited not because it creates an economic distortion, but rather because it denies workers their freedom. While prohibition of discrimination reaches beyond wage costs to protect workers' equal right to work and the right to equal treatment as part of the human right to be treated equally, freedom of association serves broader political and social goals than merely permitting unionization.

Given the above, any comparative advantage gained by non-compliance with these standards is not an advantage that should be shielded or trumped by liberalized trade. This is not a controversial statement; in fact, the vast majority of countries agree with such an edict. It is, therefore, extremely rare (if not completely unheard of) for a trade representative to publicly state that their country's comparative advantage is in child labor and the prohibition of unionization.

Notes and Questions

1. Consider how the issues of trade sanctions that promote environmental protection and labor rights affect developed and developing countries differently—as well as different economic sectors within countries, depending on their integration into regional and global markets.

2. Think about the strict environmental and labor standards that are included in global, regional, and bilateral trade agreements. Consider the potential "democracy deficit" in harmonization. Professor Aman writes:

"Still another kind of democracy deficit derives from the fact that the democratic processes used to conform domestic law to an international ruling may, in reality, be substantially less than those used to create these rules or laws in the first place. For example, pursuant to treaties negotiated within or judicial decisions rendered by the World Trade Organization (WTO), domestic law must often change to harmonize with these outcomes. The processes used appear to be democratic, but the outcome of these processes, given the prior commitments made in the treaties involved, means the outcomes usually are a foregone conclusion. The same processes used to promulgate a rule or pass a statute are employed to rescind the rule or amend the law, but the fait accompli nature of the processes used means, in reality, that the same is less. They have a rubberstamp quality to them."[63]

3. Many argue that free trade agreements exacerbate poor working conditions, such as sweatshops. How can trade partners ensure that labor conditions respect human rights while also respecting their partners' sovereignty?

4. If principles of environmental justice and labor rights are not articulated in trade agreements, what are alternative means of their advancement?

V. Counter-globalization movements

The WTO has inspired significant political opposition, mainly targeting its global project of trade liberalization. Major opposition has developed among indigenous and peasant organizations around the world. It also developed among middle class communities whose livelihoods have been rendered precarious by austerity measures put in place after the global financial crisis of 2008, and, earlier, by pressures on employment, wages and benefits.

A. Alter-globalizations: The World Social Forum, Occupy and other counter-movements

Understanding the dynamic complexity of globalization, seen as political and social effects at ground level, is essential to appreciating the diverse political topography of the oppositional movements against globalization that exists today. Myriad non-governmental organizations and social movements have developed in reaction to the expanded legalization of the mechanisms of transnational capitalism and their institutional forums—including the WTO, multinational corporations, the World Economic Forum, meetings of the economic powers (such as the G-8), and other transnational institutions such as the International Monetary Fund and the World Bank.[64] In search of alternative (or "alter") globalization(s), "the rise of the global left" [65] has developed around values of inclusive participation, "depolarized pluralities" of political and

63. Alfred C. Aman, Jr., The Democracy Deficit: Taming Globalization Through Law Reform, 4 (2004).

64. Legal sociologist Boaventura de Sousa Santos points specifically to the Zapatista insurgency in Chiapas, Mexico, in 1994, in response to the implementation of NAFTA and the protests at the WTO ministerial meeting in Seattle, in 1999. *See* Boaventura de Sousa Santos, *The World Social Forum and the Global Left*, 36 Pol. & Soc'y 247, 249 (2008).

65. Boaventura de Sousa Santos, The Rise of the Global Left: The World Social Forum and Beyond (2008).

social groups engaged in constructive opposition to the top-down powers of neoliberal capitalism associated with globalization, and a continual process of sharing experiences and ideas informing concrete proposals for reform.[66]

1. The World Social Forum

Emblematic of the alter-globalization movement is the World Social Forum, a broadly networked coalition of non-governmental organizations and civil society organizations that has met annually since 2001, usually in parallel with the meeting of the World Economic Forum in Davos, Switzerland. Its purposes are to provide a forum for groups excluded from the negotiations that produce transnational law in the more usual sense, and to articulate a critique of neoliberal globalization so as to expose its exclusions and failures, proposing an open-ended reform agenda, and keeping alive the idea that "another world is possible" (the motto of the World Social Forum).[67] It is not opposed to globalization as such, but to the fusion of state and corporate power that has been among the practical effects of neoliberalism—liberalizing for those who can participate in its benefits, but damaging for others, as their needs are costed out (sometimes to zero or less).

As such, the World Social Forum is a thriving "agora" (to borrow another of its terms), drawing tens of thousands to its annual meetings. It has also given rise to a substantial theoretical literature as scholars have taken up its challenges to the idea of global governance and considered in its place a multi-centered network of organizations (many of them transnational) committed to participatory democracy and social justice.[68] The Charter of Principles (excerpted below) commits the forum to a global participatory process:

World Social Forum Charter of Principles

* * *

1. The World Social Forum is an open meeting place for reflective thinking, democratic debate of ideas, formulation of proposals, free exchange of experiences and

---

66. "Depolarized pluralities" refers to the fluidity of collaborating groups and their emphasis on constructive participation. Santos, *supra* note 65, at 260. *See also* Boaventura De Sousa Santos & Cesar Rodríguez-Garavito, *Law, Politics, and the Subaltern in Counterhegemonic Globalization*, *in* LAW AND GLOBALIZATION FROM BELOW: TOWARDS A COSMOPOLITAN LEGALITY 1 (Boaventura de Sousa Santos & Cesar Rodríguez-Garavito, eds., 2005); Boaventura de Sousa Santos, *Beyond Neoliberal Governance: The World Social Forum as Subaltern Cosmopolitan Politics and Legality*, *in* LAW AND GLOBALIZATION FROM BELOW: TOWARDS A COSMOPOLITAN LEGALITY 29 (Boaventura De Sousa Santos & Cesar Rodríguez-Garavito, eds., 2005); Boaventura de Sousa Santos, *Globalizations*, 23 THEORY, CULTURE & SOC'Y 393 (2006).

67. *See* WORLD SOCIAL FORUM, https://fsm2016.org/en/ (last visited Oct. 6, 2016).

68. For synthetic reviews of such scholarship, foregrounding the critical relevance of perspectives on globalization from the "global south," see JEAN COMAROFF & JOHN COMAROFF, THEORY FROM THE SOUTH: OR, HOW EURO-AMERICA IS EVOLVING TOWARD AFRICA (2016); Santos & Rodríguez-Garavito, *supra* note 66; Robert Howse, *The End of the Globalization Debate: A Review Essay*, 121 HARV. L. REV. 1528 (2008).

interlinking for effective action, by groups and movements of civil society that are opposed to neoliberalism and to domination of the world by capital and any form of imperialism, and are committed to building a planetary society directed towards fruitful relationships among Humankind and between it and the Earth.

2. The World Social Forum at Porto Alegre was an event localized in time and place. From now on, in the certainty proclaimed at Porto Alegre that "another world is possible", it becomes a permanent process of seeking and building alternatives, which cannot be reduced to the events supporting it.

3. The World Social Forum is a world process. All the meetings that are held as part of this process have an international dimension.

4. The alternatives proposed at the World Social Forum stand in opposition to a process of globalization commanded by the large multinational corporations and by the governments and international institutions at the service of those corporations interests, with the complicity of national governments. They are designed to ensure that globalization in solidarity will prevail as a new stage in world history. This will respect universal human rights, and those of all citizens—men and women—of all nations and the environment and will rest on democratic international systems and institutions at the service of social justice, equality and the sovereignty of peoples.

5. The World Social Forum brings together and interlinks only organizations and movements of civil society from all the countries in the world, but it does not intend to be a body representing world civil society.

6. The meetings of the World Social Forum do not deliberate on behalf of the World Social Forum as a body. No-one, therefore, will be authorized, on behalf of any of the editions of the Forum, to express positions claiming to be those of all its participants. . . . It thus does not constitute a locus of power to be disputed by the participants in its meetings, nor does it intend to constitute the only option for interrelation and action by the organizations and movements that participate in it.

7. Nonetheless, organizations or groups of organizations that participate in the Forums meetings must be assured the right, during such meetings, to deliberate on declarations or actions they may decide on, whether singly or in coordination with other participants.

* * *

10. The World Social Forum is opposed to all totalitarian and reductionist views of economy, development and history and to the use of violence as a means of social control by the State. It upholds respect for Human Rights, the practices of real democracy, participatory democracy, peaceful relations, in equality and solidarity, among people, ethnicities, genders and peoples, and condemns all forms of domination and all subjection of one person by another.

11. As a forum for debate, the World Social Forum is a movement of ideas that prompts reflection, and the transparent circulation of the results of that reflection,

on the mechanisms and instruments of domination by capital, on means and actions to resist and overcome that domination, and on the alternatives proposed to solve the problems of exclusion and social inequality that the process of capitalist globalization with its racist, sexist and environmentally destructive dimensions is creating internationally and within countries.

12. As a framework for the exchange of experiences, the World Social Forum encourages understanding and mutual recognition among its participant organizations and movements, and places special value on the exchange among them, particularly on all that society is building to centre economic activity and political action on meeting the needs of people and respecting nature, in the present and for future generations.

13. As a context for interrelations, the World Social Forum seeks to strengthen and create new national and international links among organizations and movements of society, that—in both public and private life—will increase the capacity for nonviolent social resistance to the process of dehumanization the world is undergoing and to the violence used by the State, and reinforce the humanizing measures being taken by the action of these movements and organizations.

14. The World Social Forum is a process that encourages its participant organizations and movements to situate their actions, from the local level to the national level and seeking active participation in international contexts, as issues of planetary citizenship, and to introduce onto the global agenda the change-inducing practices that they are experimenting in building a new world in solidarity.

Approved and adopted in São Paulo, on April 9, 2001, by the organizations that make up the World Social Forum Organizing Committee, approved with modifications by the World Social Forum International Council on June 10, 2001.[69]

2. Experiments in democratizing globalization

As is clear from the Charter of Principles, the World Social Forum is conceived as an arena for the production and circulation of knowledge—principles perhaps familiar to any academic (whether student or scholar), given the extent to which disciplines and academic departments are constituted primarily around the value of open debate as integral to the production of new knowledge. The inherent value of sharing ideas, experiences, and interrelations finds expression in decentralization—a democratization of knowledge that is integral to the value of knowledge itself.[70] The connection between inclusive participation and organizational decentralization is at once an affirmation of personal experience as legitimate social knowledge, irreducible to representative forms beyond self-expression, and a theoretical challenge to

69. World Social Froum Charter of Principles, https://fsm2016.org/en/sinformer/a-propos-du-forum-social-mondial/ (last visited Oct. 6, 2016).

70. *See, e.g.*, Sonia E. Alvárez, Arturo Arias & Charles R. Hale, *Re-visioning Latin American Studies*, Cultural Anthropology 225, 227–229 (2011) (on the democratization and decentralization of Latin American Studies).

those who think of modern law and society as stable systems subject to consistent modes of thinking that give priority to doctrine over personal considerations.[71]

The Occupy movement—prominent in the urban landscapes of the United States and Europe in 2011 and 2012—was a strong response to the perceived anti-democratic aspects of globalization, understood as the top-down neoliberalization of global capitalism. Iconic of the movement was protesters' encampments in key locations associated with corporate capital (in New York City, for example, the site was Zuccotti Park, opposite the New York Stock Exchange building). So, too, were their modes of direct communication—for example, the "People's Mic" (hand signals that spread among the participants, allowing for general participation beyond the roster of speakers at large group meetings).[72] These registers of presence were the essence of Occupy's demonstration experiment in direct democracy—i.e., resisting the representative democratic forms conventional of liberal democracy (by which a few speak for the many) in the interest of fostering public engagement and a robust new politics.[73] Anthropologist David Nugent notes the "sense of rupture" and "independence of social form" that pervaded the encampments, some protesters claiming for themselves a new form of personhood pre-attuned ("prefigured") to the overhaul of global capitalism.[74] Occupy—while clear in its critique of elitism ("We are the 99 percent" was among its slogans)—was less about policy than recognition, or, as political scientist Sidney Tarrow calls it, a "we are here" movement.[75] In his analysis from the midst of events in 2011, Tarrow aligns Occupy Wall Street with New Deal populism and the women's movement of the 1970s—transformative by virtue of making visible entrenched exclusions—and concludes: "[O]ne thing is certain: we are hearing a wake-up call to a complacent corporate sector and its Washington enablers, signaling that there is a new force demanding change at the grassroots of American society."[76] This analysis proved to be prescient in relation to the current political scene as we write this book, as a "new force" takes shape as nationalist anti-globalization movements in the United Kingdom (forcing an exit from the European Union) and in the United States (under the banner of Donald Trump's election to the U.S. presidency).

---

71. Most influentially in this regard, classic sociological theorist Max Weber associates a mode of thinking he refers to as "bureaucratic rationality" with modern forms of power. MAX WEBER, ECONOMY AND SOCIETY VOL. 2, 956–1005 (Guenther Roth and Claus Wittich eds., Ephraim Fischoff et al. trans., University of California Press 1978) (1922).

72. Chris Garces, *People's Mic and "Leaderful" Charisma*, CULTURAL ANTHROPOLOGY (Feb. 14, 2013), https://culanth.org/fieldsights/65-people-s-mic-and-leaderful-charisma.

73. Jeffrey S. Juris, *Reflections on #Occupy Everywhere: Social Media, Public Space, and Emerging Logics of Aggregation*, 39 AM. ETHNOLOGIST 259 (2012) (describing Occupy objectives and practices); David Nugent, *Commentary: Democracy, Temporalities of Capitalism, and Dilemmas of Inclusion in Occupy Movements*, 39 AM. ETHNOLOGIST 280, 283 (2012).

74. On rupture, independence, and personhood, see Nugent, *supra* note 74, at 281.

75. Sidney Tarrow, *Why Occupy Wall Street is not the Tea Party of the Left: The United States' Long History of Protest*, FOREIGN AFFAIRS, (Oct. 10, 2011), https://www.foreignaffairs.com/articles/north-america/2011-10-10/why-occupy-wall-street-not-tea-party-left.

76. *Id.*

B. Indigenous and peasant movements against the WTO

In contrast to alter-globalization movements aimed at political participation such as World Social Forum and (in its very different terms) Occupy, indigenous and peasant movements draw attention to the interlegalities of the trading economy itself. Anthropological accounts of the impact of WTO rulings on peasant agriculture point to the highly disparate effects of trade liberalization in relation to agricultural products, given that elimination of protective tariffs leads to higher domestic prices, compromising access to food and other forms of market viability for farmers who serve only local markets.[77] Marc Edelman's analysis of 21st century peasant movements underscores the extent of transnational peasant mobilizations against the WTO's trade rules and consequent pressures against small farmers.[78] The alter-globalization movement around food sovereignty—i.e., withholding from WTO jurisdiction food that is produced and consumed within national territory—unites myriad organizations in various forms of protest against the WTO, the World Bank/IMF and the G8/G20.[79]

Anti-globalization activism is "a movement of movements"[80] with congresses (sometimes in parallel with the WTO's ministerial meetings, as noted above), statements of principles, and transnational agreements of their own—a major grassroots response to the WTO and other trade liberalization projects.[81] As a leading example, recent mobilizations of indigenous peoples underscore the extent to which the very concept of a "borderless world" challenges community rights to land, natural resources and self-determination. The WTO's ninth ministerial meeting (WTO MC9) in Bali was the occasion of a major gathering of indigenous organizations, resulting in a declaration of grievances and demands addressed to the WTO Director General:

---

77. On peasant mobilizations against the WTO, see Marc Edelman, *Bringing the Moral Economy Back In . . . to the Study of 21st Century Transnational Peasant Movements*, 107 Am. Anthropologist 331 (2005); *see also* Mark Moberg, *Certification and Neoliberal Governance: Moral Economies of Fair Trade in the Eastern Caribbean*, 116 Am. Anthropologist 8. (2014). An unusual anthropological project involved a team of ethnographers participating in a seminar with the director general of the WTO in Geneva—of mutual interest for them as ethnographers, and for the director general in his "hope that the attention of 'économie-anthropologie' [economic anthropology] to the effects of consumption, trade, and markets on human life and well-being might help renovate terms and concepts for a more sophisticated critical understanding of the limits of market capitalism." The authors go on to note that "he offered an account of emergent changes in the idea of what is valuable and how value can be negotiated in the context of trade . . . [commenting that] global trade talks can no longer be only about reducing barriers but must include governance in a broad sense that encompasses environmental, health, and other concerns that call for solidarity about values in terms other than exchange." Hadi N. Deeb & George E. Marcus, *In the Green Room: An Experiment in Ethnographic Method at the WTO*, 34 Pol. & Legal Anthropology Rev. 51 (2011).

78. Edelman, *supra* note 77.

79. Maeckelbergh's reference to alter-globalization includes, but is not limited to, the food sovereignty movement. Marianne Maeckelbergh, *Learning from Conflict: Innovative Approaches to Democratic Decision Making in the Alterglobalization Movement*, 21 Transforming Anthropology 27(2013); *see also* Edelman, *supra* note 77.

80. This phrase is apparently in general circulation as a rubric for the global justice movement. *See, e.g.*, Maeckelberg, *supra* note 79.

81. Among them is the World Social Forum, discussed *supra*.

DECLARATION
The World Trade Organization (WTO) and Indigenous Peoples: Resisting Globalization, Asserting Self-Determination[82]

We, the Indigenous Peoples of Mother Earth gathered here in Bali, Indonesia on 2–6 December 2013, organizing our own workshop and various events parallel to the World Trade Organization Ninth Ministerial Meeting (WTO MC9), hereby agreed to resist neoliberal globalization and assert our right to Self-Determination.

* * *

The WTO is the primary instrument of neoliberal globalization to further economic globalization especially in international trade. It aims to build a unitary system of trade relations of countries around the world governed by various agreements. WTO's catchphrases of "borderless world", "leveling the playing field" and "free market democracies", involves the removal of restrictions or so-called trade barriers that hinder greater corporate profit. While the WTO binds the Least Developed Countries (LDCs) to implement the neoliberal policies on trade of goods and services, the few capitalist countries on the other hand, protect their economies from these "free market" policies. Several WTO Ministerials, such as the Doha Development Round in 2001, collapsed due to continuing disagreements over subsidies on agricultural products, market access, and special safeguard mechanisms, and massive Peoples' protests. In its 9th Ministerial Conference, the WTO will make decisions on any of the multilateral trade related agreements such as the Agreement on Agriculture (AoA), Trade Related Aspects of Intellectual Property Rights (TRIPS), Trade Related Investment Measures (TRIMS), and General Agreement on Trade in Services (GATS), and forge new multilateral agreements. The proposed agreement for the MC9 called the Bali Package will push for greater liberalization in agriculture, acceleration of LDCs in the WTO, and expedite trade facilitation through restructuring of GATT articles on imports-exports and trade costs. The Bali Package, along with post-Bali issues on International Technology Agreement (ITA) and Trade in Services Agreement (TISA), are labeled by developed countries as the solution to the stalled Doha Round to pursue intensified trade liberalization.

Indigenous Peoples, especially future generations, will be extremely affected by these decisions and agreements. For over six decades now, since colonization, neoliberal policies have intensified the sufferings of the Indigenous Peoples. Our lands, territories and natural resources have been exploited by unsustainable

82. See the declaration of principles: *Indigenous Peoples and the World Trade Organization: Resisting Globalization, Asserting Self-Determination*, World Trade Org., (Dec. 6, 2013), https://www.wto.org/english/thewto_e/minist_e/mc9_e/indigenous_peoples_declaration.pdf (presented to the Director General of the WTO following a world congress of regional indigenous organizations in tandem with the WTO ministerial conference in Bali, December 3–6, 2013). The Bali workshop was preceded by indigenous people's declarations in 1999, at MC 3 in Seattle (http://wrm.org.uy/oldsite/actors/WTO/IPdecl.html) and, in 2005, at MC 5 in Cancun (http://www.ipcb.org/resolutions/htmls/cancun.html).

development projects, such as mono-cultural chemically intensive plantations, extractive industries such as mining, oil drilling, hydro projects and other environmentally destructive "renewable" energy projects. Trade and investment liberalization have resulted in development aggression and plunder of our territories. We have been displaced from our Indigenous lands and territories. Our Indigenous knowledge, values and spirituality have been bastardized. And our rights to self-determination, to our own governance and own self-determined development have been violated. While defending our inherent and collective rights, we continue to suffer from militarization and State terrorism, including extrajudicial killings, enforced disappearance, assassination, arbitrary arrests, imprisonment, criminalization of community resistance, harassment and vilification as "terrorists." All of this has happened for the sake of globalization, and is bound to worsen as the WTO imposes more agreements and policies.

Our experiences show that the removal of tariffs and quantitative restrictions on import goods has led to the influx of foreign products in domestic markets. The AoA has unleashed agricultural liberalisation and imposed the importation of agricultural crops even if locally produced. It has forced many developing countries to favor transnational agricultural companies like Monsanto and compelled impoverished Indigenous Peoples to use high yielding varieties (HYV) seeds without being informed of the negative effects. The AoA pushes for commercial agricultural production, replacing traditional plant varieties with genetically altered species marketed by agriculture companies, and chemical-laden foods. The AoA eliminates the ability of Indigenous Peoples to produce culturally appropriate and sufficient food. Such trading system is detrimental to Indigenous Peoples' food security, health and sustainability. It forces dependency to the capitalist market and weakens Indigenous Peoples' ability to self-determined development and food sovereignty. The WTO demands reduction of subsidies on price support, while capitalist countries refuse to apply this in their own economies. This has damaged livelihoods resulting in bankruptcy of farmers including Indigenous Peoples, as they are unable to compete with subsidized and cheaper imports from abroad. States worsen this situation by failing to protect Indigenous Peoples' sources of livelihood and food, land and resources.

Through our harmonious relations with nature as part of our spirituality, culture and beliefs, we maintain knowledge and practice of Indigenous medicines from medicinal plants and animals. We, however, are denied rights and control over our Indigenous medicines when these are taken over by big corporations as their intellectual property rights under WTO. Big pharmaceutical corporations race for patents to gain exclusive control for the production, marketing, distribution and sales of products derived from indigenous knowledge and practice. We are also alarmed that the WTO allows the patenting of life forms including extraction of genetic information under its TRIPS. These capitalist monsters treat Indigenous Peoples as valuable and vulnerable targets for medical research and experiments.

Trade agreements on services have further marginalized and impoverished us, with very limited access to basic social and health services, a situation worsened by government neglect and discrimination. Our right to quality and affordable education and health is further violated by GATS which allows foreign corporations to own and operate educational and health institutions leading to profit-oriented and corporate owned services that are available only to the few who have the means to pay. Education is designed to meet the needs and interests of the multinational corporations and the advanced capitalist countries above the social values and needs of Indigenous communities and national development of poor countries. As a result, the youth and the next generations' futures are bleak and the survival of our Indigenous knowledge is in peril.

Globalisation has even destroyed our biological and cultural diversity, ecosystems, values and traditional knowledge that constitute our existence as humans and as Indigenous Peoples. It is the culprit of the climate crisis, which exacerbates the historical, political, and economic marginalisation of Indigenous Peoples. It puts Indigenous Peoples in a very vulnerable situation, notwithstanding the fact that Indigenous Peoples have contributed the least to the climate crisis.

* * *

As we conclude our workshop and events parallel to the WTO MC9, we state the following demands to the World Trade Organisation, the States and Corporations:

We demand for focus on new economies based on the principles of living in harmony with nature and governed by the absolute limits and boundaries of ecological sustainability, the carrying capacities of Mother Earth, and in recognition of the Universal Declaration on the Rights of Mother Earth.

We demand for a stop to the capitalism of nature. All economic frameworks and trade regimes that privatise and financialise the functions of nature through green economy initiatives must be halted. Mother Earth is the source of life which needs to be protected, not a resource to be exploited and commodified as a natural capital. We call for the halt of allpolicies controlling the reproductive capacity of Mother Earth through market-based mechanisms that allow for the quantification and commodification of the natural processes of Mother Earth being branded as ecosystem services.

We demand for the respect of Indigenous Peoples' collective rights, such as but not limited to their traditional lands, territories, resources, free prior informed consent (FPIC), self-determination, culture and identity, and traditional management systems as enshrined in the UNDRIP and other international standards in negotiations and agreements. All trade agreements on investments, programs and projects affecting our lands, territories, communities, culture and identity without our FPIC must be immediately revoked and cancelled.

We demand for the repeal of all trade agreements affecting us without our meaningful, full and effective participation and FPIC. Likewise, we demand for Indigenous Peoples' full and active participation in decision-making processes and discourses on trade and other matters affecting us at all levels. Our right to FPIC is fundamental, and thus we continue to assert that this must be respected. Nothing About Us, Without Us!

We demand for the full recognition of Indigenous Peoples' inherent and inalienable right to self-determination and permanent sovereignty over our lands, territories, resources, air, ice, oceans, waters, mountains and forests.

We demand an end to the militarization of our communities, for States and corporations to be held accountable on human rights violations, and ensured justice to the victims and their families and communities who have experienced such atrocities.

Likewise, States should provide concrete support, such as appropriate technologies and funds, to help us develop for ourselves our own self-determined and sustainable development models ad methods.

Stop the theft and patenting of our traditional seeds, medicines, traditional knowledge, and our identity. Stop the commodification of our sacred culture for megatourism projects and other big businesses.

Stop the criminalization of community resistance and end the culture of impunity. Pull out State armed forces in Indigenous territories, and uphold the responsibility to provide basic social services to Indigenous communities.

Affirmed this 3rd day of December 2013, in Bali, Indonesia.

[Signatories omitted]

C. Indigenous peoples as third parties before the WTO

To date, only one indigenous organization has been a party in a case before the WTO. The Interior Alliance, a coalition of Canadian First Nations, filed an amicus curiae brief in the U.S.-Canada "soft lumber" dispute (DS 257 "*Soft Lumber IV*"). The case was settled by mutual agreement of the parties (without reference to Interior Alliance) in 2006.[83] The following excerpt summarizes the case and the procedural issues the Interior Alliance's participation entailed at the WTO:

WTO Members comment on indigenous amicus brief in lumber dispute

16 May 2002[84]

Last week, Canada, the US, the EU, Japan and India submitted comments to the WTO Panel regarding the "amicus curiae" brief submitted by the Canadian First Nations group Interior Alliance in relation to the ongoing US-Canadian dispute over

83. Dispute Settlement, *United States—Final Countervailing Duty Determination with respect to certain Softwood Lumber from Canada*, Dispute DS257, https://www.wto.org/english/tratop_e/dispu_e/cases_e/ds257_e.htm.

84. *WTO Members Comment on Indigenous Amicus Brief in Lumber Dispute*, Int'l Centre for Trade & Sustainable Development (May 16, 2002), http://www.ictsd.org/bridges-news/biores/news/wto-members-comment-on-indigenous-amicus-brief-in-lumber-dispute (internal notes omitted).

softwood lumber. In related news, the Canadian province British Columbia has developed a new forest management code, which would lead to a competitive market-based forest industry in British Columbia.

A brief history of the softwood lumber dispute

The Canada-US lumber dispute has been going on for almost 20 years, during which time US softwood lumber producers have repeatedly alleged that the stumpage fees—a tax on each harvested tree—levied by Canada's provincial governments are below market value and therefore constitute a subsidy to Canadian lumber producers. The US furthermore alleges that Canada allows its industry to illegally "dump" lumber in the US at artificially low prices. As a result, the US Department of Commerce on 9 August 2001 imposed preliminary countervailing duties amounting to 19.3 percent. On 2 May, US International Trade Commission (ITC) ruled that US industry "is threatened with material injury" by subsidised softwood lumber imported from Canada and sold in the US "at less than fair value", allowing the US Department of Commerce to issue countervailing duties averaging 27 percent on imports of softwood lumber products from Canada. However, the ITC ruled that the interim preliminary duty, which the US Department of Commerce had imposed in August last year, was not justified.

Following a Canadian request filed on 25 October in which Canada alleges that the 9 August interim duty violates a series of provisions in the WTO Agreement on Subsidies and Countervailing Measures (SCM) and in the GATT, a WTO panel was set up on 5 December 2001 to resolve the dispute. The panel is expected to report by 30 August this year. Canada has furthermore requested a binding panel to be established under the North American Free Trade Agreement (NAFTA) to review the US' countervailing duty determination. A final panel report is expected by 31 December 2002. Canada supplies about one third of the US market for construction lumber, with 75 percent of lumber produced in British Columbia and Quebec.

WTO Members comment on amicus brief

In the brief submitted by the Interior Alliance, the group backs the US claim that Canadian lumber is heavily subsidised. However, the group goes further, alleging that the non-recognition of Aboriginal land rights constitutes a subsidy under international trade law. That is, the group argues that the Canadian government's refusal to redistribute part of the revenue collected from the forest exploitation to indigenous peoples allows Canadian forest companies to sell their timber under market value and thereby provides a subsidy in addition to the artificially low stumpage rates. In its submission, the group calls on the WTO Panel to "maintain the present trade remedies necessary to restore fair competition and ensure that fundamental conditions for fair trade such as environmental protection and the recognition of indigenous rights, especially Aboriginal Title, be respected and met by the Canadian government and Canadian forest companies in the future."

In an unprecedented move, the Panel ruling in the softwood lumber dispute had asked state parties involved in the dispute to comment on the brief. As trade sources pointed out, the comments submitted by WTO Members showed that the governments did not want to get involved in a domestic matter, in this case disagreements between indigenous people and the Canadian government, but preferred the WTO Panel to decide on the legal matters of the dispute. However, Member positions varied in relation to the importance they gave to the issues raised in the amicus brief. One trade source stated that the Panel should consider the argument raised in the paper, namely whether the non-recognition of Aboriginal land rights constitutes a subsidy under international trade law, by looking at the legal issue of whether the Canadian Indians under Canadian civil law have property rights to the timber in question. In contrast, countries that have consistently opposed "amicus briefs" in the past are unlikely to comment on the brief at all, according to a developing country source. Similar to previous WTO cases were "amicus curiae" briefs were accepted, some countries disagreed with the Panel's decision to accept the brief.

The comments by the Member States are confidential until the Panel report is released, and none of those involved has made an official statements at this stage.

Amicus briefs at the WTO

While WTO panels are not obliged to take into account "amicus curiae" briefs, i.e. unsolicited submissions by non-parties of the dispute at issue, they can do so if they consider it appropriate. The acceptance of "amicus curiae" briefs has been a point of intense debate at the WTO and Member States' positions differ widely on this matter. The issue has recently received renewed attention after the EC filed a submission on 13 March to the improvement of the DSU (TN/DS/W/1), which also included regulations of "amicus curiae" briefs submissions, stating that panels should be encouraged to seek information from competent international organisations. India, in response to the EU paper submitted a communication on 7 May, which reflected India's general opposition to Panels or Appellate Bodies considering submissions by third parties (TN/DS/W/5). One of India's main arguments is that it would disadvantage developing country Members in disputes with developed countries, as very few entities from developing countries are in a position to make submissions.

The (de)regulation of Canadian forests

On 1 May the government of British Columbia (BC) presented a new code for the management of forests. The new forest requirements would be "science based" and "result oriented", and companies would have leeway to decide on how to meet the required environmental standards and management practices. The Sierra Club of BC, an environmental NGO, criticised the new code for deregulating forest management, selling out publicly-owned forests to forest corporations and further stirring the trade dispute with the US. According to the BC Coalition for Sustainable Forest Solutions—a broad coalition of citizens, First Nations, labour and environmental organisations—, increasing the rights of forest corporations over publicly-owned forests without acknowledging the rights of other interest groups would lead to more opportunities for subsidies and the selling of timber under market value and would thus further the trade dispute between Canada and the US. The new code should instead promote significant tenure reforms, encourage companies to support local economy, as well as obtain fair market value for the public timer from BC. This would then also help to settle the current lumber dispute with the US as timber from BC would then again achieve fair market prices, it is argued. The government of British Columbia is seeking inputs on the new code from the public and experts on "gaps and issues of high risk" until autumn 2002 when the legislation will be introduced with the code coming into effect in spring 2003.

D. Political mobilizations for social protection

The preceding discussion points to the potential availability of what sociologist Peter Evans (in the following excerpt) refers to as "a repertoire of tools" for alternative globalization projects:

> Neo-liberalism has . . . used the tools provided by generic globalization to construct a global system of domination. But generic globalization and the specific system of domination that made use of it in the late-twentieth century are not symbiotic in the long run. Generic globalization can also be seen as a repertoire of tools and resources potentially available to a range of political projects, including progressive ones. Seeing this new repertoire of tools and resources as something that can be appropriated by alternative projects is fundamental to the idea of counter-hegemonic globalization.
>
> A counter-hegemonic globalization perspective looks at the effects of globalization on the vitality of national movements for social protection from precisely the opposite perspective as structural pessimism. It does not deny that neo-liberal globalization constrains national state apparatuses and makes it more difficult for social protection movements to rely on responses from national governments. But it points to the simultaneous expansion of possibilities for trumping national constraints by organizing at the global level. If movements for social protection can exploit the repertoire of technological tools and the social, cultural, and organizational resources provided by generic globalization, [a countermovement for social protection] does not have to be flummoxed by the increased importance of organizing on a global scale . . . . [O]ptimism rests on the proposition that generic globalization (and neo-liberal globalization) has changed the world in ways that enable contemporary movements for social protection to organize globally in a way that they could not 100 years ago.[85]

Local experiments in participatory government have drawn the attention of anthropologists interested in the theoretical and practical implications of alter-globalization movements. For example, recent studies of the participatory

85. Peter Evans, *Is an Alternative Globalization Possible?*, 36 Pol. & Soc'y 271, 275 (2008).

budgeting process in Brazil suggest that participation yields contingent forms of interest, opportunity, and investment, resulting in new avenues of inclusion (especially for those who belong to civil society organizations) and new forms of exclusion for those who do not.[86] These findings underscore the dynamic diversity of the politics of law in the interlegal spaces generated by the tensions between local, national, and transnational powers.

VI. WTO and human rights

The effect of protest to issue a "wake-up call" takes us to a core issue in current debates surrounding the WTO and its role in relation to human rights. The WTO's silence on human rights leaves room for critics who see WTO rules as rendering human rights secondary to the goal of facilitating world trade. The question of the availability of WTO law—now or in the future—to settlement of disputes involving human rights violations for now remains an open one. One influential perspective is that of Gabrielle Marceau, a legal counselor to the WTO Secretariat, who argues that notwithstanding the limitations of the WTO rules and remedies (which are limited to economic law), the WTO is obligated under almost all circumstances to interpret the rules in a way that is consistent with international law, including human rights law.[87]

Beyond WTO jurisprudence per se, some advocates see positive potential for the functions of WTO rules in relation to advancing human rights, arguing that the rules facilitate conditions under which the benefits of trade might be more robust and more widely felt. For example, Robert D. Anderson (a former legal adviser to the GATT) and Hannu Wager propose that "[a] key requirement in facilitating the more efficient functioning of international markets for the welfare of all participiants is the progressive removal, over time, of barriers that prevent or make more difficult beneficial exchanges between producers and consumers located in different countries. This is a core aspect of the WTO's mission."[88] Citing Ernst-Ulrich

86. Brian Wampler, *Entering the State: Civil Society Activism and Participatory Governance in Brazil*, 60 Pol. Stud. 341 (2012) (on the effective mobilization of alliances across civil society organizations); Benjamin Junge, *NGOs as Shadow Pseudopublics: Grassroots Community Leaders' Perceptions of Change and Continuity in Porto Alegre, Brazil*, 39 Am. Ethnologist 407 (2012) (on the rising importance of NGOs and civil society organizations, and, in that context, an increasingly market-oriented ethos); Ana Paula Pimentel Walker, *The Conflation of Participatory Budgeting and Public-Private Partnerships in Porto Alegre, Brazil: The Construction of a Working-Class Mall for Street Hawkers*, 2 Econ. Anthropology 165 (2015) (on the emergence of class investments in an increasingly profit-oriented urban development agenda).

87. Gabrielle Marceau, *WTO Dispute Settlement and Human Rights*, 13 Eur. J. Int'l L. 753 (2002). *Cf.* Sarah Joseph, *Blame It on the WTO?: A Human Rights Critique*, Oxford Scholarship Online (Sept. 2011), http://www.oxfordscholarship.com/view/10.1093/acprof:oso/9780199565894.001.0001/acprof-9780199565894.

88. Robert D. Anderson & Hannu Wager, *Human Rights, Development, and the WTO: The Cases of Intellectual Property and Competition Policy*, 9 J. Int'l Econ. L. 707 (2006).

Petersman (see below) favorably, they suggest that the WTO should be considered a *forum* for debate and deliberation rather than a *framework* of fixed rules.[89] In Chapters 5, 6, and 7, readers will find accounts of stakeholder groups who are neither producers nor consumers, nor involved in cross-border marketing—leading us to observe that the temporality of reform envisioned by those who look to improvements "over time" may under some circumstances mask steep exclusions that are barriers to more general benefits. Thus, there are significant stakes in what may at first glance appear to be a purely theoretical question of the relationship between law and legal consciousness (i.e., ideas about law's purposes and functions) as drivers of positive social change. Such questions are at the heart of debates about the WTO and human rights—illustrated by the following excerpts by two leading legal scholars.

A. Free trade and other freedoms

In the following excerpt, legal scholar Ernst-Ulrich Petersmann responds to such arguments with proposals for stronger WTO provisions for human rights protections in the future:

Ernst-Ulrich Petersmann, *From 'Negative' to 'Positive' Integration in the WTO: Time for 'Mainstreaming Human Rights' into WTO Law?*

37 Common Market Law Review 1363 (2000), 1374–5, 1377

Since the inception of GATT 1947, GATT and WTO diplomats have conspicuously avoided any references to human rights law. This was no problem under GATT 1947 because "negative integration" under the old GATT rules raised less constitutional concerns than "positive integration" through WTO Rounds. The diplomatic preferences may also reflect the limited expertise of trade diplomats and the economic interests (e.g. of export industries) in avoiding a politicization of trade relations. The proposals by economists for de-linking human rights and other social issues from trade, and their objections against including "social" and "human rights clauses" into WTO law, likewise tend to be based on narrow utilitarian fears of protectionist abuses and the economic "inefficiency" of trade sanctions. However, just as Sherlock Holmes asked why the dog didn't bark, citizens in the 139 WTO member countries have reason to ask why WTO diplomats ignore human rights law, and why WTO Rounds focus so one-sidedly on producer interests (e.g. in WTO antidumping rules) to the detriment of consumer interests and the human rights of all citizens. The moral and legal entitlement of human beings to inalienable human rights, and to correlative duties of governments, has become a universally recognized part of modem general international law and UN law. The 1993 Vienna Declaration affirms "that all human rights derive from the dignity and worth inherent in the human person, and that

89. *Id.*

the human person is the central subject of human rights and fundamental freedoms, and consequently should be the principal beneficiary and should participate actively in the realization of these rights and freedoms." Section 1.5 of the Vienna Declaration emphasizes the "duty of States, regardless of their political, economic and cultural systems, to promote and protect all human rights and fundamental freedoms." Yet, the political compromise text of the Vienna Declaration leaves open whether this "duty of States" to "promote and protect all human rights and fundamental freedoms" should be construed in conformity with the categorical imperative of Kantian philosophy as an obligation to maximize the equal freedoms of the citizens, including their freedom of trade and their individual capacity to make effective use of freedom. From this Kantian ethical perspective, the guarantees of freedom and non-discrimination in WTO law serve human rights functions by enabling individuals to enhance their personal autonomy and welfare through peaceful cooperation across frontiers. The indivisibility of human rights is recognized in numerous worldwide and regional treaties and offers additional reasons for integrating human rights law into liberal trade law. Article 5 of the 1989 Lom6 Convention between the EC, the 15 EC Member States and 71 ACP developing countries offers an example for such a legal integration of economic and legal freedoms: "The rights in question are all human rights, the various categories thereof being indivisible and inter-related, each having its own legitimacy: non-discriminatory treatment; fundamental human rights; civil and political human rights; economic, social and cultural rights" (Art. 5(2)). For historical and political reasons, national constitutions and international treaties often do not address the "indivisibility" of civil, political and economic freedoms and human rights, nor their different "functions" (e.g. as defensive rights against governmental limitations of individual freedom, rights to participate in the exercise of government powers, rights to benefit from the governmental supply of public goods, or as constitutive principles for the determination of the "public interest" to be pursued by governments). Yet, the globalization of production, trade and economic markets cannot remain effective without a corresponding globalization of legal and institutional guarantees of individual freedom, non-discrimination, rule of law, access to courts and democratic government. As freedom from hunger and economic welfare are preconditions for the enjoyment of many other human rights, the WTO guarantees of economic liberties and of welfare-increasing cooperation across frontiers serve important human rights functions.[90]

* * *

The time has come to recognize that human rights law offers WTO rules moral, constitutional and democratic legitimacy that may be more important for the parliamentary ratification of future WTO Agreements than the traditional economic and utilitarian justifications. Future WTO negotiations on competition, investment, environmental and social rules will focus on nondiscriminatory national and

90. Ernst-Ulrich Petersmann, *From 'Negative' to 'Positive' Integration in the WTO: Time for 'Mainstreaming Human Rights' into WTO Law?* 37 COMMON MARKET L. REV. 1363, 1374–75 (2000).

international rules that can protect and extend the freedom and property rights of domestic citizens in obvious and direct ways. The traditional disregard in WTO law of human rights is becoming as outdated as the persistent disregard in international human rights instruments for economic liberty and freedom of trade as preconditions for individual welfare. Trade liberalization in the WTO should no longer be exclusively based on utilitarian objectives of "welfare maximization" but also on the human rights objectives of extending individual freedom (e.g. freedom from tariff and non-tariff trade barriers), non discrimination, and rule of law subject to judicial review by national courts and international adjudication.[91]

B. Free trade and political trade-offs

Responding to related arguments by Petersmann, legal scholar Robert Howse takes issue with Petersmann's optimism as to the inherent compatability of trading rules with human rights:

Robert Howse, *Human Rights in the WTO: Whose Rights, What Humanity? Comment on Petersmann*

Jean Monnet Working Paper 12/02, New York University Law School (2002)

It is impossible to disagree with many of Petersmann's propositions, stated at the high level of abstraction that characterizes much of this text. After the failure of communism in the Soviet Bloc, and of neo-Marxist development models in the third world, there are few who would disagree with Petersmann that the full realization of human rights is incompatible with ruthless suppression of market freedoms. Yet a moment's reflection on phenomena such as conflict diamonds and sex tourism suffices to remind us that the markets and trade are entwined with some of the most horrific human rights abuses, and on a massive scale. It is true that democracy and democratization have been linked to the project of a Free Trade Agreement of the Americas (and rightly so), but it is also true that the neo-liberal economic policy prescriptions presupposed by some (albeit not all) aspects of that project have contributed to social and political instability in some Latin American countries, threatening the gains of democratization. Nor is the European experience, on which Petersmann relies heavily, as straightforward as he presents it. Europe began with the European Coal and Steel Community (ECSC), not a free market project, but a dirigiste one, premised on the gains to social and political stability of industrial planning at the European level; and the early failure to transform the ECSC into a constitutional European project resulted in two tracks, a human rights track represented by the European Convention on Human Rights and the European Court of Human Rights, as well as a common market track, the latter entailing not only the protection of market freedoms but also supranational economic regulation, underpinned by institutions of governance. It is true, and indeed worthy of recollection,

91. *Id.* at 1377.

that free trade and human rights are both the intellectual progeny of the Enlightenment, represented by Petersmann through the figure of Immanuel Kant. But Kant, at least, was open-eyed; he saw the connection of the commercial spirit of his age not only with democratic republicanism but also with horrific imperialistic violence.

In sum, the relation of market freedom, or free trade, to human rights is in almost all situations a complex one, which cannot be well grasped by thinking in general terms about 'synergies', nor in terms of linear or teleological progression from economic integration to human rights-based constitutionalism. In order, therefore, to engage with Petersmann's project for the 'integration' of human rights and international economic law into a constitutional order, we have to pass to the specifics, and to be ever mindful of the context, the times in which we live, and in the name of *whom* and *what* the discourses of human rights, free trade, and constitutionalism are being invoked. God, or the devil, is in the details.

* * *

Ironically, when Petersmann goes on in his essay to discuss democracy, he himself points to a reason of principle why WTO dispute settlement tribunals should show some deference to domestic regulations, which is valid even where those regulations cannot be proven to be 'necessary' for the protection of human rights.

* * *

Yet Petersmann is too sharp a thinker to simply leave it at that. One reason why Petersmann's thought on these matters may be more consistent than it first seems is the influence that the example of the jurisprudence of the European Court of Justice has on his way of understanding the issues. Petersmann sees the Court as understanding the freedoms (free movement of goods, services, capital and people) in the Treaty of Rome as fundamental human rights; and he also sees the Court as sensitive to social justice and the democratic choices of member states. He might argue that a human rights approach to WTO rules does suggest a stricter legal test for limits to WTO obligations, but a stricter test *applied with a human rights sensibility* would actually result in more not less appropriate deference to domestic regulations.

Perhaps then we should support those aspects of Petersmann's project that suggest the desirability of building a human rights sensibility within the WTO. But what *kind* of human rights sensibility? Petersmann's reference to the 'integration' of different bodies of human rights law, or different rights, tends to obscure the fact that an emphasis on market freedoms as fundamental human rights reflects one *particular* kind of rights sensibility. There is a set of very basic political and normative struggles surrounding the entrenchment of the free market outlook into human rights law that have not, contrary to Petersmann, been exhausted by the Cold War. One only has to look at the controversy surrounding the expropriation provisions of the NAFTA investment Chapter, where individual investors have standing to sue governments, including for some kinds of regulatory changes that fundamentally affect the value of their property.

Given these controversies, it would appear to be in Petersmann's favour that he advocates greater democratic participation in the WTO as a corollary to the building of a human rights sensibility into the Organization. His idea of democracy, however, seems to focus on the creation of WTO advisory committees, of parliamentarians and NGOs. But it is an open question whether such ideas will ultimately not simply cabin or constrain democratic deliberation, through formalizing an understanding of which stakeholders have a legitimate place at the table; if democracy is about real power and real influence in shaping outcomes, these proposals risk being placebos. Periodic meetings of such committees are no substitute for an ongoing and inclusive process of engagement of civil society and political actors with the activities of the WTO.[92]

VII. Discussion

A full discussion of human rights law, even in just the specific connection with the WTO, would entail at least a volume by itself. We do not pretend that the discussion in this section has been comprehensive, given the extent to which the human rights issues in world trade do not present themselves as a generality. Rather, they emerge in specific contexts that make for an uneven canvas—as intellectual property rights (e.g., of pharmaceutical patents) and labor rights (e.g., in industrial or plantation settings, as in the following chapters) differ significantly in their legal infrastructures and social and political implications. We have concentrated on the aspects of the debate that respond most directly to the challenges of the alter-globalization movements, i.e., acknowledgment of the limits of world trade agreements to achieve non-economic ends, the limited availability of WTO law to address human rights violations, and the importance of public participation to the legitimacy (and ultimately, the efficacy) of the WTO.

A fuller discussion would review the history of human rights as a field of law with its own institutions, together with a history of the universalist/relativist debate associated with human rights in the social sciences (notably anthropology). The history of human rights law is relatively short, and emerged (according to historian Samuel Moyn) seemingly out of nowhere, as a "last utopia—one that became powerful and prominent because other visions imploded."[93] In the context of this volume, it is relevant to question human rights and world trade as parallel developments.

92. Robert Howse, *Human Rights in the WTO: Whose Rights? Whose Humanity?* (New York School of Law Jean Monnet Working Paper No. 12/02, 2002).

93. Samuel Moyn, The Last Utopia: Human Rights in History 4 (2010).

More to the point of our analysis, however, is the way the debate over human rights and the WTO informs an alternative to the stale universalist/relativist debate by showing how human rights conceived as *global* today articulate a demand for law consistent with the aspirations of other forms of globalism (e.g., corporate investment and transnational activists) but that in no way precludes (and may even encourage) local demands for law.[94] The fact of diversity in the field of human rights should not be viewed as a contradiction or a difference to be relativized any more than the simultaneous and mutual relevance of transnational and local markets (such as have been discussed in relation to NAFTA and the WTO) should be dismissed as an effect of scale or as some remainder in the emergence of a global order defined by the principles of free trade.

Our focus on the WTO and, for the most part throughout this volume, on issues arising from the liberalization of trade and corporate investment, reflects not only key areas of transnational law but also—precisely because of the dynamic interlegalities they entail—the visibility of their complex social entanglements and effects. Moreover, they show vividly—in the words of legal scholar David Schneiderman—"the central role of states both in binding governments and citizens to transnational legal strictures and in the unique legal capacity of states to undo those constraints. The state . . . has the jurisdiction to both knit and to unravel technologies of contemporary global governance."[95] These are the themes of the next chapters.

---

94. On the integral relation of human rights audits to global capitalism, see SALLY ENGLE MERRY, THE SEDUCTIONS OF QUANTIFICATION: MEASURING HUMAN RIGHTS, GENDER VIOLENCE, AND SEX TRAFFICKING (2016). On the deceptions of universalism and relativism in human rights prosecutions, see KAMARI CLARKE, FICTIONS OF JUSTICE: THE INTERNATIONAL CRIMINAL COURT AND THE CHALLENGE OF LEGAL PLURALISM IN SUB-SAHARAN AFRICA (2009); RICHARD WILSON, WRITING HISTORY IN INTERNATIONAL CRIMINAL TRIALS (2011).

95. DAVID SCHNEIDERMAN, RESISTING ECONOMIC GLOBALIZATION: CRITICAL THEORY AND INTERNATIONAL INVESTMENT LAW 159 (2016).

Part Two

Rights and Responsibilities Offshore

Chapter 5

Interlegalities of Offshore Supply Chains

I. Corporations move offshore

So far, we have been exploring the legal infrastructures by which regional and global partnerships form. Trading partnerships enable U.S. offshore corporate development, issues that form the context for the present chapter and Chapter 6. For reasons of length, they are divided into separate chapters, but in important respects they form a unit, and we introduce them together here. In this chapter and the next, we consider three main forms of interlegality: the development of supply chain codes of conduct; their relation to both industrial and domestic legal standards; and the relevance of labor organization and territoriality to the effectiveness of these forms of legality. When U.S. corporations move offshore, certain forms of regulation (such as workers' rights and rights of collective bargaining) are also "offshored." To convey something of the range of such situations in this chapter, we juxtapose high- and low-end manufacturing scenarios—contrasting Apple's assembly plants in China with the brand apparel industry's factory enterprises in Bangladesh, and contrasting both of these with a different arrangement involving agricultural labor. The variety of combinations of multinational corporations, voluntary codes, alignments of public and private rule-making and the relevance of organized labor comprise one thick connecting thread across this chapter. The other connecting thread involves labor markets, as each case study involves a distinct permutation of labor, labor markets and the mobility of people, goods and capital.

Labor is prominent throughout both chapters. Supplier codes of responsibility—this chapter's theme—are predominantly for the purpose of protecting workers from unsafe and exploitive working conditions, and these protections take various forms (sometimes relying on external monitoring, sometimes on internal complaints, for example). Whatever form such protections may take, labor relations in the context of multinational firms unsettle borders by creating new transnational interests and, to some extent, new identities as workers. Legal scholar Harry Arthurs clarifies ways in which labor relations illuminate fundamental instabilities of the borders between national legal systems:

Harry Arthurs, *Extraterritoriality by Other Means: How Labor Law Sneaks Across Borders, Conquers Minds, and Controls Workplaces Abroad*

21 Stan. L & Pol'y Rev. 527 (2010)

Introduction

Labor lawyers generally believe that each country's labor law, for better or worse, expresses its fundamental values and reflects its historic experience; that states can neither import nor export labor law because of the unique characteristics of each country's legal and industrial relations systems; and that the doctrine of extraterritoriality shields each state's labor law from the intrusion of others, thus ensuring that each can pursue its social and economic development in the manner it thinks best. While labor lawyers who hold these views are genuinely respectful of national sovereignty, some also chafe under its restrictions. They believe that the extraterritoriality doctrine unduly limits the capacity of a state to protect the labor rights of its own citizens while they are employed abroad. They are also concerned that a state cannot punish the businesses it has incorporated for engaging in exploitative labor practices when operating in foreign countries, thereby harming workers in those countries as well as undercutting labor standards at home.

This Article challenges this state-centered description of labor law and impoverished view of extraterritoriality. It suggests that transnational flows of technology and capital, goods and services, and ideas and information have brought in their wake changes in political economy and social relations that have transformed regimes of public and workplace governance in all countries. It proposes that the extraterritoriality doctrine operates, if at all, only in the formal sense of not allowing one state to overtly project its law into the territory of another. But extraterritoriality does little to prevent the rules governing employment relations in one country from taking root elsewhere, from shaping foreign labor market norms, institutions, and practices, and from being reproduced, in their original or mutant forms, in foreign systems of labor law. The result is the extraterritorial projection "by other means" of labor law and policy—a form of extraterritoriality that has the potential to enhance as well as undermine labor standards in global enterprises.

This challenge, in turn, rests on two premises.

The first is that all workplaces tend to generate their own law. The "law of the workplace" thus comprises not only state labor law but also (and more importantly) formal contractual understandings; workplace customs explicitly acted on and implicitly accepted as binding by workers and managers; and low-visibility behavioral norms embedded in operating manuals, daily routines, and workplace cultures. The law of the workplace has long been understood by industrial relations practitioners and socio-legal scholars to exist apart from—and sometimes in contravention of—state law. Indeed, given the unwillingness or incapacity of states to regulate the labor practices of transnational corporations, such corporations are relatively free to develop their own normative regimes. The law of the workplace is therefore not unduly influenced by national legal systems, though for their own reasons corporations may choose whether and to what extent they will comply with the local law of the countries in which they operate. Consequently, to describe labor law as operating extraterritorially is only to identify one more way (amongst many) in which it departs from the formal state-centered paradigm of law to which most jurists subscribe.

The second premise is that "labor" is not a discrete domain of law and policy. While a central preoccupation of labor law is indeed to regulate the balance of power between workers and employers, many of the factors that actually determine that balance are not conventionally perceived to be "labor" related. Trade and taxation, homeland security and health insurance, and insolvency and immigration laws and policies (to name but a few) have profound effects on labor markets in general, and therefore on particular economic sectors, enterprises, and workplaces. The result is that in many advanced economies—especially those where global corporations originate and dominate—labor law and policy become an incidental by-product, an externality, of other political preoccupations. The bargaining power of unions, the enforcement of labor standards legislation, and the provision of employment opportunities for excluded minorities are often determined in a practical sense by public policies whose primary purpose is to encourage or discourage consumption, pacify or punish particular political constituencies, or realign relations with foreign trading partners. Nor, given the declining political influence and bargaining strength of unions in most advanced economies, can workers count on recouping at the workplace level losses sustained in debates at the political level. And, of course, the situation of workers in most developing economies is even worse: they are not citizens of the metropolitan countries where important decisions are made that affect their jobs, are often denied a voice even in the political system of their own country, and seldom wield much power at the workplace level.

Thus, the "extraterritoriality" debate is not merely over the extent to which states have the right to project their labor laws beyond their territorial borders or, for that matter, to exempt foreign corporations from their labor laws. It is more fundamentally a debate over the multiple sources and meanings of "law," the permeable boundaries of "labor" as a policy domain, and the effects of globalization on these two difficult issues.

In *Doe I v. Wal-Mart Stores, Inc.*, 572 F.3d 677 (9th Cir. 2009) (discussed *infra*), the Ninth Circuit ruled that domestic law may not "sneak across borders"; however, Congress has, in some instances, enacted extraterritorial regulations affecting supply chains. Such regulation confronts challenges noted by Galit Sarfaty in her analysis of global supply chain responsibility codes:

> Domestic regulations on supply chains pose a unique compliance challenge to companies because these laws operate extraterritorially. Multinational companies are more than just regulated entities; they now also serve as regulators themselves, imposing standards on their third-party suppliers in

> other countries. Thus, regulation about outsourcing is itself being outsourced to companies, which are responsible for ensuring compliance by the firms within their multi-tiered supply chains. . . . Scholars have focused on the outsourcing of regulation to non-governmental organizations (NGOs), auditors, and other third parties that take on standard-setting, implementation, and enforcement functions traditionally occupied by regulatory agencies. Yet supply chain regulation exemplifies a distinct model of outsourcing that dilutes the host state's governing authority.
>
> While outsourcing regulation to companies is a means by which states can indirectly regulate firms in other countries, this practice raises accountability concerns when private actors are performing functions that are fundamentally public. Like other forms of public-private governance, there are risks to public values when private actors perform functions conventionally reserved for government agencies. Supply chain laws pose a greater risk to accountability given that the regulated entities themselves are sometimes ill-equipped to monitor and enforce compliance by third parties.[1]

Sarfaty illustrates these difficulties with an analysis of section 1502 of the Dodd-Frank Act, which seeks to limit exploitation of conflict minerals and indirectly inhibit financing of conflicts in the Democratic Republic of the Congo.[2] Section 1502 requires publicly traded companies to report to the SEC when it uses minerals sourced from central Africa. This report must include a description of the "due diligence measures," set by international standards, the company employed to determine whether the minerals directly or indirectly benefited combatants in the region.[3]

Sarfaty evaluates the effectiveness of companies' section 1502 due diligence measures by considering five factors: use of long-term supply chain recordkeeping; incorporation of supply chain policy and diligence process into supply contracts; surveying and following up with suppliers; a stated policy of risk mitigation, including termination of supply contracts if necessary; and direct encouragement of suppliers to become certified as conflict-free suppliers.[4]

Sarfaty finds that only seven percent of the 967 reporting companies exhibited "strong due diligence," which she defines as including at least four of the above factors. Through a series of ethnographic interviews with NGOs, law firms, industry groups and consultants, Sarfaty identifies three factors that help explain this poor compliance: (1) the infancy of international supply chain due diligence norms; (2) proliferation of certification and sourcing standards that are evolving and

---

1. Galit A. Sarfaty, *Shining Light on Global Supply Chains*, 56 HARV. INT'L L.J. 419, 421–22 (2015). For a somewhat more optimistic view of the efficacy of transnational private ordering in relation to labor standards, see Michael Vandenbergh, *The New Wal-Mart Effect: The Role of Private Contracting in Global Governance*, 54 UCLA L. REV. 913 (2007).

2. Sarfaty, *supra* note 1, at 422.

3. *Id.*

4. *Id.* at 441–44.

sometimes competing; and (3) poor local security and governance, which makes mapping of mineral supply chains difficult.[5] Rectifying these problems will require stronger local governance structures and improved corporate "culture of compliance," where an interdisciplinary team is established not only to implement supply chain management, but also to educate the larger organization about its maintenance.[6]

Our case studies in this chapter illustrate the governance mechanisms by contract that operate across interlegal junctures—that is, as the organization of production moves across multiple legal and normative registers. The first case study involves Apple and its relationship with a major Chinese supplier, the Foxconn Technology Group (Hon Hai Precision Industry, Co. Ltd.). As was widely reported in the press at the time, Apple and other major electronics firms have faced a variety of labor problems involving Foxconn in recent years, including worker suicides, a fatal accident, and worker protests. The second case study also garnered extensive media attention—involving the brand apparel industry in Bangladesh, site of two tragic accidents in which over a thousand workers died, most of them young women. (The third case, presented in Chapter 6, involves the Firestone rubber plantation in Liberia, where Liberian workers filed suit in the United States to seek relief from human rights abuses.) We punctuate the discussions of Apple and Bangladesh with *Wal-Mart*, in which the Ninth Circuit ruled that responsibility may not jump links in the supply chain (so to speak). The case from Liberia discussed in Chapter 6 was eventually resolved through a court-backed labor action in Liberia, after U.S. courts ruled against the plaintiffs' Alien Tort Statute claim. U.S. courts have shown their reluctance to make themselves available to human rights and other suits by workers seeking relief from conditions of offshore manufacturing and extraction. But this does not mean that firms can afford to be cavalier about their operations, since pressures by consumers, NGOs and organized labor may be significant.[7]

While similar in certain respects, the case studies also show significant differences relevant to our analysis. The Apple-Foxconn situation draws attention to the intergovernmental arrangements that make offshore contracts possible, and to the relevance of the host country's involvement in providing legal supports for such contracts and compliance with their terms—even when such compliance is designed as voluntary. The readymade garment (RMG) industry situation draws attention to the efficacy of collective corporate action relative to single-company supply chain codes and standards of responsibility. As we turn to the case study from Liberia, involving the Firestone Corporation and plantation workers who complained of human rights abuses, the discussion follows braided strands of transnationalism in the form of litigation and labor organization on both sides of the Atlantic. To anticipate what follows, supply chain contracts contribute significantly to the interlegalities affecting the

5. *Id.* at 448.

6. *Id.* at 461.

7. On CSR as risk management, see Mia Mahmudur Rahim, *Improving Social Responsibility in RMG with a New Governance Approach*, 138 J. Bus. Ethics 1 (2013).

lives of workers and their families; however, as all three case studies show, such contracts are most effective in contexts where industry and national legal systems are well aligned, and beyond this, where organized labor is involved.[8] We introduce the three case studies with a discussion of corporate social responsibility.

II. Self-Regulation: The legal authority of corporate social responsibility codes

In his analysis of private voluntary governance in the environmental sector, legal scholar Michael Vandenbergh finds not only new actors, but also a shift in power from public to private entities as private firms perform public functions:

> A new form of governance is emerging that achieves traditionally public ends through private contracting. . . . Nongovernmental organizations (NGOs), rather than lobbying national and international governmental bodies to generate public requirements, are using consumer pressure to demand that corporations engage in this form of private regulation. . . . [T]he resulting networks of private contracts form an integral part of the emerging global environmental governance regime.
>
> In the last decade, domestic and international law scholars have begun to shift from the traditional focus on states and governments to a focus on public-private collaborative governance and postsovereign public-private hybrids. The common feature of this work is the understanding that government acts in various forms of collaboration with private parties. Nevertheless, government remains central to the enterprise.[9]

Our focus in this chapter is on interlegalities involving corporations, workers and governments under the broad rubric of corporate social responsibility.

Corporate Social Responsibility (CSR) codes have developed as a way for corporations to define specific accountabilities of their suppliers. Monitoring is a challenge, and the organization of a firm may be so vast and complex that effective monitoring is virtually impossible. Effective monitoring ultimately depends on a supportive consumer response, as well as on domestic law. This latter point is often lost, to the extent that government and governance are conventionally imagined to be alternatives rather than mutually necessary (as discussed by Neumann and Sending, Chapter 1, *supra*). Reflecting on the impact of WTO dispute settlement mechanisms on public-private partnerships, Gregory Shaffer finds that the international trading system is increasingly "legalized", and that "the blurring of the public

---

8. On the social impacts and implications of supply chain contracts in the context of urbanism, see Saskia Sassen, *Global Inter-City Networks and Commodity Chains: Any Intersections?*, 10 Global Networks 1 (2010).

9. Vandenbergh, *supra* note 1, at 914.

and the private spurs the growth of international economic law."[10] In general, he writes, "at the international level, the impact of law is nowhere more clear than in the realm of trade."[11] Indeed, the case studies in this chapter show in detail the integral relation—an interlegal relation—of private contracts and law. Company standards may look very much like law. While perhaps appearing aspirational, CSR standards have gained legitimacy as a basis for external audits, enforcement and other accountability mechanisms.

CSR first emerged in the 1970s—an expression of corporate autonomy based on what have come to be known among scholars as an "internalist" account of the self-regulating capacity of corporations.[12] Early approaches were premised on the idea that corporations could regulate themselves without the involvement of external regulators. By the 1990s, responding to critiques of corporate power, CSR shifted to a compliance discourse, relying at least in part on sociolegal studies of corporate communities in the more general (non-business) sense, and the self-regulating functions of semi-autonomous groups.[13] In the context of debates over regulation at that time, such theories seemed to provide rationales for de-regulation, yet without taking an *anti*-regulatory position. Two decades on, contemporary scholarship is developing in a different context, in which neoliberalism[14] is the prevailing norm, consumers demand accountability, and CSR is well established as a set of core principles and practices central to global governance.[15] Reviewing the field's development in recent decades, legal sociologist Ronen Shamir notes the prominence of CSR today as a corporate philosophy (emphasizing "moral commitments to the general welfare"[16]), a set of business practices, and a source of "new types of legality":

> CSR is a phenomenon whereby commercial entities deploy social and environmental policies that go beyond their formal legal duties and potentially beyond their goal of maximizing profits for shareholders. This phenomenon is marked by the creation of multiple private and selfregulatory tools (sometimes referred to as soft law instruments) involving complex interactions among commercial entities, state agencies, nongovernmental organizations (NGOs), and other private authorities. In this respect, CSR is at once a field

10. Gregory Shaffer, Defending Interests: Public Private Partnerships in WTO Litigation, 3, 9 (Brookings Institution Press 2003).

11. *Id.* at 2.

12. Alwyn Lim & Kiyoteru Tsutsui, *The Social Regulation of the Economy in the Global Economy*, *in* Corporate Social Responsibility in a Globalizing World 1, 3 (Tsutsui & Lim eds., 2015); Ronen Shamir, *Capitalism, Governance, and Authority: The Case of Corporate Social Responsibility*, 6 Ann. Rev. Law & Soc. Sci. 531 (2010).

13. Shamir, *supra* note 12, at 538. For a history of CSR movements and their theoretical premises, see Lim & Tsutsui, *supra* note 12.

14. David Singh Grewal & Jedediah Purdy, *Introduction: Law and Neoliberalism*, 77 Law & Contemp. Probs. 1, 1 (2015).

15. Shamir, *supra* note 12.

16. Shamir, *supra* note 12, at 537.

> of action that presumably exists outside law and a terrain constitutive of new types of legality.[17]

Critical of the internalist approach, sociologists Alwyn Lim and Kiyoteru Tsutsui advance the thesis that CSR has become a "core component of the social regulation of the economy":[18] "We posit that external pressures exerted by trade and investment relations, government actions, social movement activism, and taken-for-granted models of appropriate organizational behavior work at both global and national levels to push corporations to engage in, co-opt, or react against CSR activities."[19]

CSR "compliance audits" have become a service industry, as governance institutions have promulgated guidelines for fair pay, safe working conditions, respect for the human rights of workers and environmental protection. Many companies now offer such services, including performance assessment, certification, verification, and training. Assessments include specialized audits derived from the codes of the electronics and toy industries, as well as codes governing internal corporate practice, fair trade, supplier responsibilities and the global voluntary guidelines put forward as ISO 26000 (a subject discussed in Chapter 7, *infra*)—among other offerings (regarding compliance with privacy rules in the health fields, for example).

Shamir argues that CSR as practiced and theorized today signals a fundamental rearrangement of public and private authority (including scientific authority) in relation to the regulation of global capitalism, and beyond:

> [T]he discourse of governance essentially gives scientific credibility to the economization of authority, i.e., to the epistemology of conceiving market-like characteristics such as competition, commodity exchange, and utility principles as optimal for the execution of public authority as well. In this sense, the field of CSR may tell us something important about the relationship between latter-day global capitalism and law. This relationship, inasmuch as it manifests itself through schemes of governance, brings about the privatization of law in the deepest sense of the term: The decentralization of the sources of law and the transformation of rules into multiple instruments indicate the ability of latter-day capitalism not only to constantly revolutionize the means and relations of production but also to fundamentally transform the means and relations of political authority.[20]

CSR may be understood as part of a global "audit culture"—a "culture on the make" around an extensive rearrangement of "the financial and the moral" that relies on assessment measures as the primary evidence of authority, efficacy and social

17. Shamir, *supra* note 12, at 531.

18. Lim & Tsutsui, *supra* note 12, at 5. *See* also Ronen Shamir, *The Age of Responsibilization: On Market-Embedded Morality*, 37 Econ. Soc. 1 (2008).

19. Lim & Tsutsui, *supra* note 12, at 4.

20. Shamir, *supra* note 12, at 546.

value.[21] Extending well beyond businesses, the global audit culture of today penetrates a wide range of institutions that rely on and promote indicators—quantitative measures that are the infrastructure of a performance-based legitimacy, as noted in the following overview by Kevin Davis:

> Rule of law indicators. Governance indicators. Indicators of public service performance. What many of these indicators have in common is that they purport to measure some aspect of the performance of a legal system. In other words, they are legal indicators.
>
> Proponents celebrate legal indicators as means of drawing attention to social problems, tools for rigorous analysis of the causes or consequences of policy interventions, and valuable inputs in decision making about matters ranging from allocation of foreign aid to selection of locations for foreign direct investment. The most prominent indicators are cited frequently in both academic literature and the media. Transparency International's Corruption Perceptions Index has been credited with contributing to "the formation of a global movement and widespread consensus against corruption."
>
> Literature produced by the World Bank, the IMF, and other international financial institutions frequently refers to indicators such as the Doing Business indicators and the Worldwide Governance Indicators. At the International Development Association, the African Development Bank, and the Asian Development Bank, internally generated indicators from the Country Policy and Institutional Assessment (CPIA) figure prominently in the algorithms used to allocate aid across countries. Similarly, the Millennium Challenge Corporation (MCC), a US aid agency, uses indicators of whether a country is "ruling justly" and "encouraging economic freedom," along with indicators of "investing in people," to determine eligibility for grants. Case studies have uncovered several examples of reforms motivated by the objective of raising countries' rankings according to the Corruption Perceptions Index and the Doing Business indicators. Finally, indicators can even beget more indicators. A CIA-sponsored effort—the State Failure Task Force (1994–2000)—to identify the determinants of state failure and instability not only produced data and analytical techniques for the CIA and other users but also mobilized a group of scholars who have gone on to become involved in the production of other indicators of state failure.
>
> Critics, either of particular legal indicators or of indicators in general, complain that the metrics are misleading oversimplifications of complex social phenomena that secretly reflect the unstated biases of their creators. The Doing Business indicators in particular have been a lightning rod for

21. Marilyn Strathern, *Introduction* to AUDIT CULTURES: ANTHROPOLOGICAL STUDIES IN ACCOUNTABILITY, ETHICS AND THE ACADEMY 1 (Marilyn Strathern ed. Routledge 2000).

> criticism. A wide range of nongovernmental organizations, as well as states such as Brazil and China, have complained that the Doing Business indicators, and especially the indicators concerning employment, are biased in favor of neoliberal approaches to labor market regulation.
>
> The divergent perspectives on legal indicators reflect radically different views about two issues: (a) Do legal indicators provide sound foundations for beliefs about the phenomena they purport to measure? (b) Do legal indicators have a legitimate role to play in governance? The issues are interrelated. How legal indicators are used may depend on their quality—the demand for obviously flawed indicators is, or at least ought to be, limited—and the quality of indicators that are produced may depend on how they are expected to be used.[22]

CSR is just one of a proliferating array of domains in which indicators are an important tool of governance across the political spectrum, as indicators "jumped" domains from business to human rights and CSR.[23] Their strategic relevance to legal mobilization and reform movements imports controversy into the status of indicators themselves as a technology of knowledge. For proponents, they are a new form of knowledge production that advances accountability, while for critics, they make a pretense of objectivity that masks underlying interests. These perspectives are not incompatible once one considers indicators as part of a political process.[24] Indicators—what and how they measure—have been extensively studied by anthropologist Sally Merry.[25] She notes that their power is not only in the techniques of measurement, but also in how indicators "announce" what they measure—bringing into being new categories of assessment even as the assessment unfolds:

> One of the critical ways an indicator produces knowledge is by announcing what it measures, such as "rule of law" or "poverty." Neither of these categories is self-evident. When sponsoring organizations name their indicators, they interpret what the numbers mean. . . . Labels do not necessarily accurately reflect the data that produce the indicators, however. How indicators are named and who decides what they represent are fundamental to the way an indicator produces knowledge.[26]

As we shall see in the case studies below, private transnational contracting involves extensive problems of knowledge, including but not limited to what indicators may measure.

---

22. Kevin E. Davis, *Legal Indicators: The Power of Quantitative Measures of Law*, 10 Ann. Rev. Law & Soc. Sci., 37, 38 (2014).

23. Sally Engle Merry, *Measuring the World: Indicators, Human Rights, and Global Governance*, 52 Current Anthropololgy S83 (2011).

24. "CSR is inherently political." Aseem Prakash, *Conclusion: Corporate Social Responsibility as Social Regulation*, *in* Corporate Social Responsibility in a Globalizing World 455, 457 (Kiyoteru Tsutsui & Alwyn Lim, eds., 2015).

25. Merry, *supra* note 23.

26. *Id.* at S84.

III. Apple in China

A. China, Congress and the WTO

In the 1990s, the United States agreed to an arrangement that made China's agreement to WTO principles contingent on the U.S. granting China permanent most favored nation status. This agreement led to a bitter congressional debate over normalizing trade with China in 2000. China and the Clinton Administration, supported by big business lobbies, including high-tech manufacturers, pressed Congress hard.[27]

U.S. labor unions were strongly opposed to the bill, on grounds that normalizing trade would accelerate the flight of manufacturing jobs overseas. Both of the presidential candidates in that election year (Albert Gore and George W. Bush) endorsed the trade agreement, but trade with China became a sharply partisan issue in Congress. Democrats were largely opposed on grounds of protecting domestic jobs and on the basis of China's record on human rights—the state's violent suppression of political protest in Tiananmen Square then a recent memory. But China's economy was booming—with an annual growth rate of ten percent and GDP twelve times higher than it was in 1978, when economic reform began.[28] Republicans were largely supportive on grounds of China's potential as a market for U.S. exports and more generally on the basis of a commitment to the prospects of advancing global democracy and peace through trade. The bill became law in October, 2000, and China acceded to the WTO on December 11, 2001.

The bill passed both houses of Congress in a vote that was sharply partisan in the House, but that proved to be a wedge issue in the Senate, resulting in bipartisan passage. The negotiations within the Congress pressed opponents of the trade bill to register criticisms of China as a trading partner on grounds of human rights abuses, piracy and currency manipulation; however, at the same time, opponents tied their own votes to "pork" or concessions for their local constituencies.[29] Anticipating the vote in the House of Representatives, the New York Times refered to the

27. Robert Dreyfuss, *The New China Lobby*, AMERICAN PROSPECT, Jan.–Feb. 1997, http://www.prospect.org/article/new-china-lobby; *see also* Lizette Alvarez, *The China Trade Wrangle: The Silicon Lobby; High-Tech Companies Making Their First Big Push in Congress on a Trade Bill*, N.Y. TIMES, May 18, 2000, http://www.nytimes.com/2000/05/18/world/china-trade-wrangle-silicon-lobby-high-tech-companies-making-their-first-big.html?emc=eta1&pagewanted=print.

28. Yang Yao, *The End of the Beijing Consensus? Can China's Model of Authoritarian Growth Survive?*, FOREIGN AFF., Feb. 2010, https://www.foreignaffairs.com/articles/china/2010-02-02/end-beijing-consensus.

29. On labor protests: Steven Greenhouse & Richard W. Stevenson, *Unions March in Washington, Urging Congress to Defeat Trade Agreement With China*, N.Y. TIMES, April 13, 2000, at A8. On "pork barrel" negotiations: Joseph Kahn, *Horse-Trading (and Pork) on Trade Bill*, N.Y. TIMES, May 11, 2000, at A6.

debate as involving "nearly every aspect of international relations" and far-reaching implications for domestic affairs, as well.[30]

In some respects, the WTO and the key roles played by the executive and legislative branches in authorizing the terms of global trade "look" very much like the scenario in Chapter 2, in which we saw the Montreal Protocol produced out of an extensive collaboration among policy makers, lawmakers and scientists; together, they produced a multi-stakeholder agreement, in effect, sustaining the multi-country protocol. Indeed, there is a strong vertical dimension to global trade—not only in organizations such as the WTO and its functions through GATT, GATS and TRIPS, but also in the informal processes by which corporations and states calibrate their own forms of parity (e.g., corporate CEOs being the "equivalent" of ministers[31]) and mutual interests.

China's economic policies relied, in part, on foreign direct investment to sustain growth, and foreign manufacturers moved quickly to take advantage of China's massive workforce—a workforce described by one analyst as "cheap" and "compliant," and largely young and female.[32] In these opening sections, we consider one employer, known by its trade name Foxconn, the mega-firm that by the end of the new century's first decade was the principal contractor for the assembly of Apple's iPhones and iPads in China. At the time, Apple was the most profitable company in the world. We provide excerpts from China's labor law as well as relevant excerpts from Apple's supplier code of conduct and parallel industry standards for workers' rights, among other international standards. Codes and standards are taken up in more detail in the final sections of the chapter.

B. Social and legal infrastructures

1. Labor Migration Within China

Supply chain contracts contribute significantly to the interlegalities affecting the lives of workers and their families, and, in different ways, the rural or urban communities where factories and workshops are located.[33] In China, rural-urban migration—including to the massive factories in the special economic zones—features prominently

30. Joseph Kahn, *The China Trade Wrangle: Small Print; Furor Over Bill Obscures Crucial Emigration Issue*, N.Y. Times, May 24, 2000. Available at http://www.nytimes.com/2000/05/24/world/china-trade-wrangle-small-print-furor-over-bill-obscures-crucial-emigration.html.

31. *The Gentle Art of Lobbying in China*, Economist, Feb. 15, 2001, http://www.economist.com/node/505497.

32. These characterizations refer specifically to migrant workers in electronics and garment manufacturing in Shenzhen. Pun Ngai, *Women Workers and Precarious Employment in Shenzhen Special Economic Zone, China*, 12 Gender and Dev. 29 (2004).

33. On the social impacts and implications of supply chain contracts in the context of urbanism, see Saskia Sassen, *Global Inter-City Networks and Commodity Chains: Any Intersections?*, 10 Global Networks 1 (2010).

in anthropological accounts of China since Mao. As China entered world markets, it also introduced domestic market reforms. Land reforms since the 1980s privatized (decollectivized) rural communes in favor of individual title, resulting in impoverishment and massive displacement of rural workers—particularly young unmarried women—as they sought livelihoods elsewhere.[34] Such accounts are consistent in attributing rural-urban migration to privatization.[35] They are also consistent in remarking the overwhelmingly young, female presence in the migrant workforce; one analyst—writing about Shenzhen Special Economic Zone—notes that over ninety percent of the workers in the electronics and garment sectors there are women under the age of twenty-five.[36]

Such disparities in displacement point to the profound impact of migration on women's personal futures. These same sources are consistent in their accounts of the precarity of women's lives in the city—whether in the disappointments of domestic work for wealthy families[37] or in the dangers of living and working in the "dormitory labor regime" of the giant factories in the Special Economic Zones.[38] In her study of Shenzhen workers, Professor Ngai finds that all rural workers are classified as "peasants"—and as such are ineligible for permanent residence in the city. In such circumstances, she finds, workers are without basic government services and, despite the explosive growth of Shenzhen (from about 300,000 in 1980 to over four

---

34. Yan estimates that 100 million free laborers were decollectivized in the post-Mao period, and that of the 160 million people who were working as rural laborers in 2012, thirty to fifty percent were young unmarried women. Hairong Yan, *Spectralization of the Rural: Reinterpreting the Labor Mobility of Rural Young Women in Post-Mao China*, 30 AMERICAN ETHNOLOGIST 578 (2003). Most rural migrants sought work in Chinese cities, *id.*, but some sought opportunity in transnational moves, e.g., Korean Chinese migrants who moved to South Korea in what became known as the "Korean Wind," or in offshore firms in India or elsewhere in Asia. On the Korean Wind: June Hee Kwon, *The Work of Waiting: Love and Money in Korean Chinese Transnational Migration*, 30 CULTURAL ANTHROPOLOGY 477 (2015). On offshore migration (in the IT field): Biao Xiang, *The Making of Mobile Subjects: How Institution Reform and Outmigration Intersect in Northeast China*, 50 DEV. 69 (2007).

35. In addition to sources cited in note 34, *supra*, see also Jonathan Bach, *"They Come in Peasants and Leave Citizens": Urban Villages and the Making of Shenzhen, China*, 25 CULTURAL ANTHROPOLOGY 421 (2010); Ngai, *supra* note 32; Pun Ngai, *Subsumption or Consumption? The Phantom of Consumer Revolution in 'Globalizing' China*, 18 CULTURAL ANTHROPOLOGY 469 (2003); Li Zhang, *Migration and Privatization of Space and Power in Late Socialist China*, 28 AMERICAN ETHNOLOGIST 179 (2001). But not all urban migrants are from rural areas; migration is also prompted by industrial layoffs. *See* Mun Young Cho, *"Dividing the Poor": State Governance of Differential Impoverishment in Northeast China*, 39 AMERICAN ETHNOLOGIST 187, 188 (2012).

36. Ngai, *supra* note 32, at 30; *see also* ARIANNE M. GAETANO, OUT TO WORK: MIGRATION, GENDER, AND THE CHANGING LIVES OF RURAL WOMEN IN CONTEMPORARY CHINA (University of Hawai'i Press 2015); WANNING SUN, SUBALTERN CHINA: RURAL MIGRANTS, MEDIA, AND CULTURAL PRACTICES, (Rowman and Littlefield 2014); Yan, *supra* note 34; HAIRONG YAN, NEW MASTERS, NEW SERVANTS: MIGRATION, DEVELOPMENT AND WOMEN WORKERS IN CHINA (Duke University Presss 2008).

37. YAN, *supra* note 36.

38. Ngai, *supra* note 32, at 30.

million in 2000), there is no long-term planning on the part of the government to provide for them in the expansion of the city.[39] In these circumstances, residents rely on networks of brokers—"quasi-informal" and "quasi-legal" bureaucrats who mediate between citizens and the state.[40] In other cities, too, a class of brokers has emerged since privatization, exerting strong powers over access to housing, employment, and other basic needs.[41] Shenzhen is of particular interest since it is the location of the largest Foxconn/Apple assembly plant in China.[42] We shall return to Shenzhen and other aspects of Foxconn's relationship with its labor force below.

Anthropologists studying the situation of workers in migration and in urban economic zones point to the social effects of economic liberalization to caution against confusing China's extensive marketization with the fact or prospect of democratization.[43] Indeed, economist Yukon Huang, analyzing the contemporary situation, finds the emergence of a gap between economic and political reform since the early days of economic reform after Mao.[44] Huang attributes the collapse of initial popular optimism and rising expectations to the effects of ongoing state economic policies that have contributed to income inequality (between individuals and across regions), which are in turn related to pervasive disputes over land rights and (again in turn) to massive rural-urban migration. Land is owned by the state, and—in the face of insufficient credit from banks—local governments selectively privatize, selling off land rights to raise revenue. This situation widens the gaps between richer and poorer regions and has precipitated conflicts over land rights—evident in growing political unrest[45] as well as in the displacement of millions of people from the land.[46] This is the context for Professor Huang's analysis of the situation of rural-urban migrants:

Yukon Huang, *China's Conflict Between Economic and Political Liberalization*

32 SAIS Rev. Int'l Aff. 51, 52 (2012)

No segment of society feels these social pressures more than the 250 million migrant workers who now account for a large share of the urban laborforce, especially

39. *Id.* at 29–30 (providing the basis for demographic data and this assessment).

40. Bach, *supra* note 35, at 477 (referring to Shenzhen).

41. Zhang, *supra* note 35; *see also* You-tien Hsing, *Brokering Power and Property in China's Townships*, 19 Pac. Rev. 103 (2006).

42. Jason Dean, *The Forbidden City of Terry Gou*, Wall Street J., Aug. 11, 2007, www.wsj.com/articles/SB118677584137994489.

43. *See* Ngai, *supra* note 35 at 469–471; Yan, *supra* note 36; Zhang, *supra* note 35.

44. Yukon Huang, *China's Conflict Between Economic and Political Liberalization*, 32 SAIS REV. Int'l Aff. 51, 52 (2012).

45. *Id.* at 61, n. 2 (on official and unofficial reports of unrest).

46. Displacement does not mean that migration does not yield benefits to the migrants, their families, and their home communities, particularly if migrant workers are able to return remittances to their families at home. Nong Zhu & Xubei Luo, *The Impact of Migration on Rural Poverty and Inequality: A Case Study in China*, 41 Agric. Econ. 191, 191–204 (2010).

along the coast. In the early years of reform, the vast majority of potential migrants were eager to leave their hinterland for jobs that paid multiples of what they were formerly eking out. But without formal residency rights (hukou), their dependents often were not eligible to enroll in local schools; nor could they qualify for health insurance or apply for jobs restricted to established residents. Despite the emergence of a private property market, migrants were also more limited in their housing options.

Initially these deprivations did not seem important since the work was seen as temporary and the savings provided security for dependents left behind. Over time, however, with the growing regional divergence in the quality of social services and wage differentials shaped by locality and residency status, arrangements that were intended to be temporary have become permanent.

Periodic campaigns to repatriate migrant workers have only contributed to their sense of being second-class citizens. With the maturation of a younger generation that lacks knowledge of the poverty their parents knew before reform, the inferior status of migrant workers no longer matches aspirations in a modernizing China. Thus even with surging wages in recent years, increasing numbers of migrants have increased their demands for compensation and more rights—contributing to acts of civil disobedience—or returned to their provinces to seek other opportunities.

Policymakers continue to be reluctant to liberalize the hukou system for fear that China's major cities would become unmanageable. Established urban residents also worry that increased labor inflows will depress their wages. And without more revenues, these cities would not have the resources to meet the service needs of such a large contingent.

These restrictive migration policies have created distortions in population settlement patterns. Those who remained trapped in rural areas cannot easily leave to seek better positions elsewhere. Thus, although China's urbanization rate is now slightly over 50 percent, compared to 20 percent three decades ago, it should be much higher. And more importantly, China's restrictive labor migration policy is a major reason why income disparities are so high compared with other countries.

Some analysts see an ambiguous picture for the future in this scenario. Economist Yang Yao anticipates the consequences of a challenge to China's "performance based legitimacy" if the capacity for continued growth on the basis of privatization and FDI proves to be limited:

> Beijing has been extremely cautious in maintaining a balanced budget and keeping inflation down. Purely redistributive programs have been kept to a minimum, and central government transfers have been primarily limited to infrastructure spending. The overall tax burden (measured by the ratio of tax revenue to GDP) is in the range of 20 to 25 percent. The country is the world's second-largest recipient of foreign direct investment, and

> domestically, more than 80 percent of its state-owned enterprises have been released to private hands or transformed into publicly listed companies. Since the Chinese Communist Party (CCP) lacks legitimacy in the classic democratic sense, it has been forced to seek performance-based legitimacy instead, by continuously improving the living standards of Chinese citizens. So far, this strategy has succeeded, but there are signs that it will not last because of the growing income inequality and the internal and external imbalances it has created.[47]

Anthropologists, too, look to the combined effects of new forms of inequality and class consciousness as they consider the implications of the rapid expansion of China's urban middle class since Mao and the cultural dimensions of the political impasses referenced above.[48]

2. China's Labor Law

Law reform in China has, in some respects, tracked economic reform, particularly in relation to the WTO, commercial arbitration and other areas of law associated with foreign investment—a rule of law that functions within the ambit of the state's control regimes.[49] Labor law has also been an object of contention and experimental reforms, particularly as labor protests have erupted in the special economic zones in the Pearl River Delta region in recent years (including Shenzhen, mentioned above).[50] Analysts debate the prospective efficacy of labor law reform with respect to workers' rights, but there seems to be general agreement as to the limited efficacy of current labor rights and worker protections.[51]

---

47. Yang Yao, *The End of the Beijing Consensus*, FOREIGN AFF., Feb. 2, 2010, https://www.foreignaffairs.com/articles/china/2010-02-02/end-beijing-consensus.

48. On China's new middle classes and the loss of class consciousness, see Ann Anagnost, *From 'Class' to 'Social Strata'" Grasping the Social Totality in Reform-Era China*, 29 THIRD WORLD Q. 497 (2008); Yingjie Guo, *Classes With Class Consciousness and Class Consciousness Without Classes: The Meaning of Class in the People's Republic of China*, 21 J. CONTEMP. CHINA 723 (2012).

49. Randall Peerenboom, *A Government of Laws: Democracy, Rule of Law and Administrative Law Reform in the PRC*, 12 J. CONTEMP. CHINA 45 (2003); Scott Wilson, *Law Guanxi: MNC's, State Actors, and Legal Reform in China*, 17 J. CONTEMP. CHINA 25 (2009).

50. Alex Jingwei He & Genghu Huang, *Fighting for Migrant Labor Rights in the World's Factory: Legitimacy, Resource Constraints and Strategies of Grassroots Migrant Labor NGOs in South China*, 24 J. CONTEMP. CHINA 471 (2015). Labor protests and law reform efforts are not limited to the foreign investment sectors or the special economic zones; current protests also press for a larger role for collective representation and bargaining. Cynthia L. Estlund & Seth Gurgel, *Will Labour Unrest Lead to More Democratic Trade Unions in China*? (N.Y. University Pub. Law & Legal Theory Working Papers, Working Paper No. 444 2013), http://lsr.nellco.org/nyu_plltwp/444, Cynthia Estlund, *Will Workers Have a Voice in China's "Socialist Market Economy"? The Curious Revival of the Workers Congress System*, 36 COMP. LAB. L. & POL'Y J. 69 (2014); *see also* CYNTHIA ESTLUND, A NEW DEAL FOR CHINA'S WORKERS? (Harvard University Press 2013).

51. *See, e.g.*, He & Huang, *supra* note 50 (analyzing the importance of NGOs as mediators between the law on the books and in its application to migrant workers in the Pearl River Delta region); Pan Yijia, *The Failure of Labor Dispatch Regulation and its Remedy*, 37 SOC. SCI. CHINA 191 (2016) (on the practical factors that make some labor law reform efforts counter-productive);

Labor law in this sense represents an interlegality in itself—designed in part to meet the needs of foreign investors and the millions of workers employed in the "factory of the world" (as He and Huang put it). In this context, it is difficult to draw a clear line between state law and private governance. In this section and the two following, we present excerpts from China's labor law to show its parallels and divergences with Apple's code of supplier responsibility and the Electronics Industry Code. They are most parallel in their respective statements of employer responsibility for worker safety and well-being, including regular monitoring of compliance with standards. They are most different in relation to issues of worker grievances and enforcement, in that the labor contract law assures workers of access to tribunals and courts, whereas the codes provide for management accountability for compliance, as well as for assuring appropriate monitoring and reporting. Some members of Congress crafted a resolution specifically in support of the law's worker rights protections, while it was still in draft, alleging the opposition of "some United States corporations."[52]

In drawing selections from China's labor law, we focus on the provisions involving working hours and dispute resolution—elements that are relevant to the labor unrest at Foxconn, discussed below.

Labour Contract Law of the People's Republic of China (promulgated by Ministry of Commerce, March 20, 2007)[53]

Chapter 4 Working Hours, Rests, and Leaves

Article 36 The State shall practise a working hour system wherein labourers shall work for no more than eight hours a day and no more than 44 hours a week on the average.

Article 37 In case of labourers working on the basis of piecework, the employer shall rationally fix quotas of work and standards of piecework remuneration in accordance with the working hour system stipulated in Article 36 of this Law.

Article 38 The employer shall guarantee that its labourers have at least one day off a week.

Yunqiu Zhang, *Law and Labor in Post-Mao China*, 14 J. Contemp. China 525 (2005) (arguing that notwithstanding obstacles to access to law, law is an effective tool for workers able to mobilize claims).

52. A resolution supporting the law while it was in draft form was introduced into the U.S. House of Representatives; it was referred to the House Committee on International Relations but was not returned to the floor for a vote. The preamble of the resolution points to the underlying debate over the draft labor law's protections of worker rights and wages: "Expressing the sense of the House of Representatives that the President should express public support for the workers' rights and protection provisions of China's 'Draft Labor Contract Law' and repudiate efforts by some United States corporations and their representatives in China to diminish such rights and protection provisions." H.R. Res. 1110, 109th Cong. (2006).

53. Available at http://english.mofcom.gov.cn/aarticle/policyrelease/internationalpolicy/200703/20070304475283.html.

Article 39 If an enterprise can not follow the stipulations in Article 36 and Article 38 of this Law due to special characteristics of its production, it may follow other rules on work and rest with the approval by labour administrative departments.

* * *

Article 41 The employer can prolong work hours due to needs of production or businesses after consultation with its trade union and labourers. The work hours to be prolonged, in general, shall be no longer than one hour a day, or no more than three hours a day if such prolonging is called for due to special reasons and under the condition that the physical health of labourers is guaranteed. The work time to be prolonged shall not exceed, however, 36 hours a month.

Article 42 The prolonging of work hours shall not be subject to restrictions of stipulations of Article 41 of this Law in any one of the following cases:

(1) Need for emergency treatment during occurrence of natural disasters, accidents or other reasons that threaten the life, health or property safety of labourers;

(2) Need for timely rush-repair of production equipment, transportation lines or public facilities that have gone out of order and as a result affect production and public interests;

(3) Other cases stipulated in laws and administrative decrees.

* * *

Article 44 The employer shall pay labourers more wage remunerations than those for normal work according to the following standards in any one of the following cases:

(1) Wage payments to labourers no less than 150 per cent of their wages if the labourers are asked to work longer hours;

(2) Wage payments to labourers no less than 200 per cent of their wages if no rest can be arranged afterwards for the labourers asked to work on days of rest;

(3) Wage payments to labourers no less than 300 per cent of their wages if the labourers are asked to work on legal holidays.

* * *

Chapter 10 Labour Disputes

Article 77 In case of labour disputes between the employer and labourers, the parties concerned can apply for mediation or arbitration, bring the case to courts, or settle them through consultation.

The principle of mediation is applicable to arbitration and court procedures.

* * *

Article 79 Once a labour dispute occurs, the parties involved can apply to the labour dispute mediation committee of their unit for mediation; if it can not be settled through mediation and one of the parties asks for arbitration, application can be filed to a labour dispute arbitration committee for arbitration. Any one of the parties involved in the case can also apply to a labour dispute arbitration committee for arbitration. The party that has objections to the ruling of the labour arbitration committee can bring the case to a people's court.

Article 80 A labour dispute mediation committee can be set up inside the employer. This committee shall be composed of workers' representatives, the representatives of the employer, and trade union representatives. The chairmanship of this committee shall be held by a trade union representative.

Agreements reached on labour disputes through mediations shall be implemented by the parties involved.

* * *

Article 82 The party that asks for arbitration shall file a written application to a labour dispute arbitration committee within 60 days starting from the date of the occurrance of a labour dispute. Generally speaking, the arbitration committee shall produce a ruling within 60 days after receiving the application. The parties involved shall implement arbitration rulings if they do not have any objections to these rulings.

Article 83 If any of the parties involved in a labour dispute has objections to an arbitration ruling, it can raise a lawsuit with a people's court within 15 days after receiving the ruling. If one of the parties involved neither raises a lawsuit nor implements the arbitration ruling within the legal period of time, the other party can apply to a people's court for forced implementation.

Article 84 Cases of disputes resulted from the conclusion of collective contracts shall be handled through consultation by all the parties concerned brought together by the labour administrative department of a local people's government if these cases can not be handled through consultation between the parties involved. Cases of disputes resulted from the implementation of collective contracts shall be brought to a labour dispute arbitration committee for arbitration if these cases can not be solved through consultation between the parties involved. The party that has objections to a ruling can raise a lawsuit with a people's court within 15 days after receiving the ruling.

Notes and Questions

1. On June 29, 2007, the Standing Committee of the National People's Congress (SCNPC) passed the Labor Contract Law. The new law reaffirmed and supplemented China's 1995 Labor Act, requiring all employers to execute written labor contracts with their employees so as to establish the "rights, interests, and obligations of each party."[54] The new Labor Law, implemented in 2008, established additional rights for workers including limits on the maximum hours employees can work in any given week (forty-four hours per week, on average, plus a maximum of thirty-six hours of

54. *Id.*

overtime per month, under normal circumstances).[55] China's labor laws impose duties on all its private employers to carry out its directives, and it provides for dispute resolution by mediation, arbitration and in "people's courts."

2. In 2012, the legislature in China amended its Labor Contract Law. These amendments primarily focused on stronger protection for "labor dispatch" workers, or temporary employees, and stricter regulation for labor dispatch enterprises. Despite the limited scope of the amendments, the move demonstrated China's desire to "close implementation gaps" within its labor law infrastructure. For further reading, see Virginia Harper Ho & Huang Qiaoyan, *The Recursivity of Reform: China's Amended Labor Contract Law*, 37 Fordham Int'l L.J. 973 (2014). *See also* Pan Yijia, *The Failure of Labor Dispatch Regulation and Its Remedy*, 37 Social Sciences in China 191 (2016).

3. Apple Supplier Code and Social Responsibility Standards

Apple's supplier code of responsibility is shaped on the one side by its alignment with China's labor law, and on the other by the principles and terms it shares with the electronics industry standards. As above, we have selected provisions that are most relevant to the situation at Foxconn, affecting Apple's assembly operations.

The Apple Supplier Code of Conduct (version 4.2 excerpted below) formalizes the company's commitment to humane working conditions, limitations on working hours, and other protections. Apple first enacted its supplier code of conduct in 2005. It requires that suppliers "provide safe working conditions, treat workers with dignity and respect, act fairly and ethically, and use environmentally responsible practices wherever they make products or perform services for Apple."[56] The Code is itself an interlegal document—referencing multiple codes and standards at the end of the text, including the Electronic Industry Code of Conduct, the Ethical Trading Initiative, and the International Labor Organization, among other standards (see text, *infra*).

Apple Supplier Code of Conduct

Effective January 1, 2016[57]

Apple is committed to the highest standards of social and environmental responsibility and ethical conduct. Apple's suppliers are required to provide safe working conditions, treat workers with dignity and respect, act fairly and ethically, and use environmentally responsible practices wherever they make products or perform services for Apple.

Apple requires its suppliers to operate in accordance with the principles in this Apple Supplier Code of Conduct ("Code") and in full compliance with all applicable

---

55. *See Id.* at Ch. 4, Art. 36, 39, 41–42.

56. *See* Apple Supplier Code of Conduct, effective January 1, 2016, https://www.apple.com/supplier-responsibility/pdf/supplier_code_of_conduct.pdf. The Code is updated annually.

57. Available at https://www.apple.com/supplier-responsibility/pdf/supplier_code_of_conduct.pdf. Reprinted courtesy of Apple Inc.

laws and regulations. This Code goes beyond mere compliance with the law by drawing upon internationally recognized standards to advance social and environmental responsibility. When differences arise between standards and legal requirements, the stricter standard shall apply, in compliance with applicable law. This Code outlines Apple's expectations for Supplier conduct regarding labor and human rights, health and safety, environmental protection, ethics, and management practices.

Apple will assess its suppliers' compliance with this Code, and any violations of this Code may jeopardize the supplier's business relationship with Apple, up to and including termination. This Code applies to Apple suppliers and their subsidiaries, affiliates, and subcontractors (each a "Supplier") providing goods or services to Apple, or for use in or with Apple products.

Additionally, Apple maintains detailed standards that explicitly define our expectations for compliance with this Code.

Labor and Human Rights

Apple believes all workers in our supply chain deserve a fair and ethical workplace. Workers must be treated with the utmost dignity and respect, and suppliers shall uphold the highest standards of human rights.

* * *

Prevention of Involuntary Labor and Human Trafficking

Supplier shall ensure that all work is voluntary. Supplier shall not traffic persons or use any form of slave, forced, bonded, indentured, or prison labor. Involuntary labor includes the transportation, harboring, recruitment, transfer, receipt, or employment of persons by means of threat, force, coercion, abduction, fraud, or payments to any person having control over another person for the purpose of exploitation.

Supplier shall not withhold workers' original government-issued identification and travel documents. Supplier shall ensure that workers' contracts clearly convey the conditions of employment in a language understood by the workers. Supplier shall not impose unreasonable restrictions on movement within the workplace or upon entering or exiting company-provided facilities.

Supplier shall ensure that the third-party recruitment agencies it uses are compliant with the provisions of this Code and the law. Suppliers recruiting foreign contract workers either directly or through third party agencies shall be responsible for payment of all recruitment-related fees and expenses.

Prevention of Underage Labor

Supplier shall employ only workers who are at least 15 years of age or the applicable minimum legal age, whichever is higher. Supplier may provide legitimate workplace apprenticeship programs for educational benefit that are consistent with Article 6 of ILO Minimum Age Convention No. 138 or light work consistent with Article 7 of ILO Minimum Age Convention No. 138.

* * *

Working Hours[58]

A workweek shall be restricted to 60 hours, including overtime, and workers shall take at least one day off every seven days except in emergencies or unusual situations. Regular work week shall not exceed 48 hours. Supplier shall follow all applicable laws and regulations with respect to working hours and days of rest, and all overtime must be voluntary.

Wages and Benefits

Supplier shall ensure that all workers receive at least the legally mandated minimum wages and benefits. Supplier shall offer vacation time, leave periods, and time off for legally recognized holidays.

Supplier shall compensate workers for overtime hours at the legal premium rate. Supplier shall communicate pay structure and pay periods to all workers. Supplier shall pay accurate wages in a timely manner, and wage deductions shall not be used as a disciplinary measure. All use of temporary and outsourced labor will be within the limits of the local law.

Freedom of Association and Collective Bargaining[59]

Supplier shall freely allow workers to associate with others, form, and join (or refrain from joining) organizations of their choice, and bargain collectively, without interference, discrimination, retaliation, or harassment. In the absence of formal representation, Supplier shall ensure that workers have a mechanism to report grievances and that facilitates open communication between management and workers.

Health and Safety

Worker health, safety, and well-being is important to Apple. Supplier shall provide and maintain a safe work environment and integrate sound health and safety management practices into its business. Workers shall have the right to refuse unsafe work and to report unhealthy working conditions.

* * *

Incident Management

Supplier shall have a system for workers to report health and safety incidents and near-misses, as well as a system to investigate, track, and manage such reports. Supplier shall implement corrective action plans to mitigate risks, provide necessary medical treatment, and facilitate workers' return to work.

---

58. [Authors' note: Note the reference to "all applicable law and regulations." In the case of Chinese workers, Apple's code is parallel to China's labor law, with the exception of a slight difference in the definition of the regular work week (not to exceed 48 hours for Apple suppliers and averaging 44 hours under China's labor law).]

59. [Authors' note: See discussion of Chinese workers' efforts to expand collective bargaining, *infra*.]

Ergonomics

Supplier shall identify, evaluate, and control worker exposure to tasks that pose ergonomic risk such as excessive force, improper lifting positions, or repetitiveness. Supplier shall integrate this process into the qualification of all new or modified production lines, equipment, tools, and workstations.

Working and Living Conditions

Supplier shall provide workers with reasonably accessible and clean toilet facilities and potable water. Supplier-provided dining, food preparation, and storage facilities shall be sanitary. Worker dormitories provided by Supplier or a third-party shall be clean and safe and provide reasonable living space.

Health and Safety Communication

Supplier shall provide workers with appropriate workplace health and safety training in their primary language. Health and safety related information shall be clearly posted in the facility.

Worker Health and Safety Committees

Supplier is encouraged to initiate and support worker health and safety committees to enhance ongoing health and safety education and to encourage worker input on, and participation in, health and safety issues in the workplace.

* * *

Whistleblower Protection and Anonymous Complaints

Supplier shall provide an anonymous complaint mechanism for managers and workers to report workplace grievances. Supplier shall protect whistleblower confidentiality and prohibit retaliation.

* * *

Management Commitment

Apple believes that sound management systems and commitment are key to enriching the social and environmental well-being of our supply chain. Apple holds its suppliers accountable to this Code and all of its standards. Supplier shall implement or maintain, as applicable, a management system that facilitates compliance with this Code and the law, identifies and mitigates related operational risks, and facilitates continuous improvement.

Company Statement

Supplier shall develop a company statement affirming its commitment to high standards of social and environmental responsibility, ethical conduct, and continuous improvement. Supplier shall post this statement in the primary local language at all of its facilities.

Management Accountability and Responsibility

Supplier shall identify company representatives responsible for ensuring implementation and periodic review of its management systems. Supplier shall have a Corporate Social Responsibility (CSR) or Sustainability representative that reports directly to executive management and has the responsibility and authority to manage social and environmental compliance requirements for the business.

Risk Assessment and Management

Supplier shall develop and maintain a process to identify labor and human rights, health and safety, environmental, business ethics, and legal compliance risks associated with its operations; determine the relative significance of each risk; and implement appropriate procedures and controls to control the identified risks.

Performance Objectives with Implementation Plans and Measures

Supplier shall have written standards, performance objectives, targets, and implementation plans, including periodic assessments of the performance against those objectives.

Audits and Assessments

Supplier shall perform periodic evaluations of its facilities and operations, and the facilities and operations of its subcontractors and next-tier suppliers to ensure compliance with this Code and the law.

Supplier will permit Apple and/or a third party designated by Apple to periodically evaluate Supplier's facilities and operations, and those of its subcontractors and next-tier suppliers, to the extent they are providing goods or services to Apple, for Apple's benefit, or for use in Apple products.

* * *

Corrective Action Process

Supplier shall have a process for timely correction of any deficiencies or violations identified by an internal or external audit, assessment, inspection, investigation, or review.

This Code references internationally accepted principles such as the Electronic Industry Code of Conduct, Ethical Trading Initiative, International Labor Organization's (ILO) International Labor Standards, Social Accountability International, SA 8000, ILO Code of Practice in Safety and Health, National Fire Protection Association, OECD Guidelines for Multinational Enterprises, and OHSAS 18001.

As you will see when you read the next excerpt, the Apple and industry codes are parallel in key provisions; again, we have selected provisions most relevant to the discussion *infra*. Note their attention to the conditions of labor recruitment and, in that context, to distinguishing between recruitment and coercion, and to the definition of a child, under the rubrics of "freely chosen employment" and "young workers"—issues centrally relevant (though in a different industry) to the discussion of the Bridgestone case, in the next chapter.

4. Electronics Industry Code of Conduct

Electronics Industry Citizenship Coalition (EICC) Code of Conduct (2016)[60]

A. LABOR

Participants are committed to uphold the human rights of workers, and to treat them with dignity and respect as understood by the international community. This applies to all workers including temporary, migrant, student, contract, direct employees, and any other type of worker. The recognized standards, as set out in the annex, were used as references in preparing the Code and may be a useful source of additional information. The labor standards are:

1) Freely Chosen Employment

Forced, bonded (including debt bondage) or indentured labor, involuntary prison labor, slavery or trafficking of persons shall not be used. This includes transporting, harboring, recruiting, transferring or receiving persons by means of threat, force, coercion, abduction or fraud for labor or services. There shall be no unreasonable restrictions on workers' freedom of movement in the facility in addition to unreasonable restrictions on entering or exiting company-provided facilities. As part of the hiring process, workers must be provided with a written employment agreement in their native language that contains a description of terms and conditions of employment prior to the worker departing from his or her country of origin. All work must be voluntary and workers shall be free to leave work at any time or terminate their employment. Employers and agents may not hold or otherwise destroy, conceal, confiscate or deny access by employees to their identity or immigration documents, such as government-issued identification, passports or work permits, unless such holdings are required by law. Workers shall not be required to pay employers' or agents' recruitment fees or other related fees for their employment. If any such fees are found to have been paid by workers, such fees shall be repaid to the worker.

2) Young Workers

Child labor is not to be used in any stage of manufacturing. The term "child" refers to any person under the age of 15, or under the age for completing compulsory education, or under the minimum age for employment in the country, whichever is greatest. The use of legitimate workplace learning programs, which comply with all laws and regulations, is supported. Workers under the age of 18 (Young Workers) shall not perform work that is likely to jeopardize their health or safety, including night shifts and overtime. Participant shall ensure proper management of student workers through proper

60. Available at http://www.eiccoalition.org/media/docs/EICCCodeofConduct5_1_English.pdf. The EICC Code of Conduct is periodically updated following an extensive consultation process with members and stakeholders. The next revision process will take place in 2017. The most recent version of the Code can be found on the EICC's website: www.eiccoalition.org.

maintenance of student records, rigorous due diligence of educational partners, and protection of students' rights in accordance with applicable law and regulations. Participant shall provide appropriate support and training to all student workers. In the absence of local law, the wage rate for student workers, interns and apprentices shall be at least the same wage rate as other entry-level workers performing equal or similar tasks.

3) Working Hours

Studies of business practices clearly link worker strain to reduced productivity, increased turnover and increased injury and illness. Workweeks are not to exceed the maximum set by local law. Further, a workweek should not be more than 60 hours per week, including overtime, except in emergency or unusual situations. Workers shall be allowed at least one day off every seven days.

4) Wages and Benefits

Compensation paid to workers shall comply with all applicable wage laws, including those relating to minimum wages, overtime hours and legally mandated benefits. In compliance with local laws, workers shall be compensated for overtime at pay rates greater than regular hourly rates. Deductions from wages as a disciplinary measure shall not be permitted. For each pay period, workers shall be provided with a timely and understandable wage statement that includes sufficient information to verify accurate compensation for work performed. All use of temporary, dispatch and outsourced labor will be within the limits of the local law.

5) Humane Treatment

There is to be no harsh and inhumane treatment including any sexual harassment, sexual abuse, corporal punishment, mental or physical coercion or verbal abuse of workers; nor is there to be the threat of any such treatment. Disciplinary policies and procedures in support of these requirements shall be clearly defined and communicated to workers.

* * *

E. MANAGEMENT SYSTEM

Participants shall adopt or establish a management system whose scope is related to the content of this Code. The management system shall be designed to ensure: (a) compliance with applicable laws, regulations and customer requirements related to the participant's operations and products; (b) conformance with this Code; and (c) identification and mitigation of operational risks related to this Code. It should also facilitate continual improvement.

The management system should contain the following elements:

1) Company Commitment

A corporate social and environmental responsibility policy statements affirming Participant's commitment to compliance and continual improvement, endorsed by executive management and posted in the facility in the local language.

2) Management Accountability and Responsibility

The Participant clearly identiies senior executive and company representative[s] responsible for ensuring implementation of the management systems an associated programs. Senior management reviews the status of the management system on a regular basis.

3) Legal and Customer Requirements

A process to identify, monitor and understand applicable laws, regulations and customer requirements, including the requirements of this Code.

4) Risk Assessment and Risk Management

A process to identify the legal compliance, environmental, health and safety and labor practice and ethics risks associated with Participant's operations. Determination of the relative significance for each risk and implementation of appropriate procedural and physical controls to control the identified risks and ensure regulatory compliance.

* * *

8) Worker Feedback and Participation

Ongoing processes to assess employees' understanding of and obtain feedback on practices and conditions covered by this Code and to foster continuous improvement.

9) Audits and Assessments

Periodic self-evaluations to ensure conformity to legal and regulatory requirements, the content of the Code and customer contractual requirements related to social and environmental responsibility.

10) Corrective Action Process

A process for timely correction of deficiencies identified by internal or external assessments, inspections, investigations and reviews.

11) Documentation and Records

Creation and maintenance of documents and records to ensure regulatory compliance and conformity to company requirements along with appropriate confidentiality to protect privacy.

12) Supplier Responsibility

A process to communicate Code requirements to suppliers and to monitor supplier compliance to the Code.

Notes and Questions

1. Consider the interlegalities at play within the realm of corporate codes of conduct and corporate social responsibility. For example, how do legal systems interact and conflict in the following relationships:

a. The World Trade Organization and the United States

b. The White House and Congress

c. Within Congress itself

d. China, the United States, and U.S. corporations

e. The electronics industry standards and Apple's CSR code

f. Apple and its suppliers worldwide

2. China's Labor Contract Law, the Electronics Industry Citizenship Coalition Code of Conduct, and Apple's Supplier Code of Conduct all address similar issues, including working hours, dispute settlement, and corrective measures. How do they conflict? How are they similar? If you were a manufacturer in China, how would you structure your policies to be in full compliance?

3. Could domestic private law be used to enforce corporate social responsibility codes? If so, would that be an effective form of regulation? Consider how CSR codes and other forms of self-regulation could be enforced in (a) domestic courts and (b) international arbitral tribunals. For further reading, see Anna Beckers, *Legalization under the Premises of Globalization: Why and Where to Enforce Corporate Social Responsibility Codes*, 24 IND. J. GLOBAL LEG. STUD. (forthcoming 2016).

4. Should corporations be bound to certain human rights obligations, or is self-regulation through voluntary CSR codes sufficient? How would a legally binding human rights treaty be enforced against corporations? A recent initiative within the UN Human Rights Council (UNHRC) aims at creating such a treaty on business and human rights, but there is skepticism of its effectiveness. *See* Pierre Thielbörger & Tobias Ackermann, *A Treaty on Enforcing Human Rights Against Business: Closing the Loophole or Getting Stuck in a Loop?*, 24 IND. J. GLOBAL LEG. STUD. (forthcoming 2016).

C. Apple and Foxconn Technology

Apple's supply chain consists of about 700,000 workers employed by companies contracting with Apple to manufacture its products.[61] The scale of electronics manufacturing factories in China, in combination with the ready availability of a labor force, has led Apple executives to locate most of its production in China. One of Apple's primary suppliers, Foxconn Technology, manufactures around forty percent of the world's electronics.[62] Kindle, iPad, and Dell computers all have component parts supplied by Foxconn. With 1.2 million workers at some fourteen plants around the world, Foxconn is China's largest private employer.[63]

---

61. Charles Duhigg & Keith Bradsher, *How the U.S. Lost Out on iPhone Work*, N.Y. TIMES, Jan. 22, 2012, at A1, http://nyti.ms/1DK4hZd.

62. Keith Bradsher & Charles Duhigg, *Signs of Changes Taking Hold in Electronics Factories in China*, N.Y. TIMES, Dec. 26, 2012, http://www.nytimes.com/2012/12/27/business/signs-of-changes-taking-hold-in-electronics-factories-in-china.html.

63. Charles Duhigg & David Barboza, *In China, Human Costs are Built into an iPad*, N.Y. TIMES, Jan. 25, 2012, http://www.nytimes.com/2012/01/26/business/ieconomy-apples-ipad-and-the-human-costs-for-workers-in-china.html?_r=0; *see also* Shai Oster, *Behind the Scenes at Apple's Controversial iPhone Factory*, CHI. TRIB., April 26, 2016, www.chicagotribune.com/business/it-behind-the-scenes-apple-China-iphone-factory-20160426-story.html.

Apple turned to Foxconn to take advantage of the manufacturer's experience with flexible management:

> Apple executives say that going overseas, at this point, is their only option. One former executive described how the company relied upon a Chinese factory to revamp iPhone manufacturing just weeks before the device was due on shelves. Apple had redesigned the iPhone's screen at the last minute, forcing an assembly line overhaul. New screens began arriving at the plant near midnight. A foreman immediately roused 8,000 workers inside the company's dormitories, according to the executive. Each employee was given a biscuit and a cup of tea, guided to a workstation and within half an hour started a 12-hour shift fitting glass screens into beveled frames. Within 96 hours, the plant was producing over 10,000 iPhones a day.[64]

An Apple contract promises significant returns for its major suppliers; however, the constant innovations of function and design are also a source of some precarity, even—or especially—for its main suppliers.[65]

Foxconn came into the news when it won its supplier contract with Apple, and soon thereafter when a wave of worker suicides[66] brought negative attention to working and living conditions at the Foxconn campuses (at Shenzhen and elsewhere in China, as discussed *supra* in Section III.B.1). By the end of 2012, Apple responded with reforms following the critical reports of the Fair Labor Association (adding to the complaints other monitoring groups) and worker protests at Foxconn plants, augmenting its corporate social responsibility staff, reviewing its working arrangements with contractors, taking steps to curb overtime, and "reach[ing] out to advocacy groups it had once rebuffed."[67] Foxconn, too, instituted reforms—while also relocating some of their manufacturing campuses inland and exploring replacing workers with robot labor.[68]

Following worker protests at Foxconn plants (including the suicides at Shenzhen and elsewhere, referenced above[69]) and a New York Times investigation, Apple joined the Fair Labor Association, an independent monitoring organization—the first technology company to do so. FLA, founded in 1999, is a consortium of monitoring groups; its mission statement reads:

> The FLA combines the efforts of socially responsible companies, civil society organizations and colleges and universities to protect workers' rights and

64. *Id.*

65. Adam Satariano & Peter Burrows, *There's a Downside to Making Parts for Apple*, BLOOMBERG, Sept. 18, 2014, http://bloom.bg/1mzjICJ.

66. Lei Guo et al., *A Case Study of the Foxconn Suicides: An International Perspective to Framing the Sweatshop Issue*, 74 INT'L COMM. GAZETTE 484 (2012).

67. Keith Bradsher & Charles Duhigg, *Signs of Changes Taking Hold in Electronics Factories in China*, N.Y. TIMES Dec. 26, 2012, available at http://www.nytimes.com/2012/12/27/business/signs-of-changes-taking-hold-in-electronics-factories-in-china.html.

68. *See id.*

69. Guo, *supra*, note 66.

> improve working conditions worldwide by promoting adherence to international labor standards. The FLA conducts independent monitoring and verification to ensure that the FLA's Workplace Standards are upheld where FLA company products are produced. Through public reporting, the FLA provides consumers with credible information to make responsible buying decisions.[70]

In February, 2012, FLA launched an investigation of the conditions at Foxconn plants, including 35,000 anonymous surveys administered to workers.[71] Eighteen months later, FLA issued its final report, confirming progress except in the area of overtime work, which exceeded limits set by China's contract labor law. Worker protests have continued at the plants, as recent newspaper reports confirm.[72]

IV. The Apparel Industry in Bangladesh

In the case of Apple, the supply contract with Foxconn took advantage of a large labor force—for the most part young women displaced from their rural communities by changes in China's land law. In this section, we turn to the apparel industry in Bangladesh involving a different relation between suppliers and buyers.[73] The urban factories produce garments for resale under numerous brand labels based in Europe and the United States. Second, following two devastating accidents that brought worldwide attention to conditions in the factories, the branding pluralism (so to speak) became the infrastructure of coalitions for the purpose of supporting safe and fair labor conditions. In Europe, an accord stipulated monitoring and enforcement mechanisms; in the United States, a group of major brands (including Walmart, Gap, L.L. Bean, and others) produced an alliance formed around

70. Fair Labor Association, *Apple Joins FLA*, Jan. 13, 2012, www.fairlabor.org/affiliate/apple?page=1. The FLA has its own code of conduct available at http://www.fairlabor.org/our-work/labor-standards.

71. For a detailed account of the investigation, including subsequent monitoring of compliance, see *id.* The final report on Foxconn's implementation of 360 recommendations was completed in November, 2013, confirming compliance in 356 of the 360. All references to the FLA's investigation of Apple refer to this electronic dossier.

72. *See* Oster, *supra* note 63.

73. A conceptual distinction between supplier- and buyer-driven global supply chains is proposed by Rahim: "The GSC [Global Supply Chain] is a quasi-hierarchical relationship between buyers and suppliers, in which the two parties are not joined by ownership, but are engaged in a long-term relationship. This relationship generally includes two types of chains: buyer-driven and supplier-driven chains. Buyer-driven chains are characteristic of labour intensive industries such as the footwear, clothing and toy industries in developing countries. Supplier-driven chains refer to those industries that produce semi-final products such as machineries, petroleum products, electronic parts. It is therefore important that both buyers and suppliers engage in procedures that support socially responsible business practices." Mia Mahmudur Rahim, *Improving Social Responsibility in RMG with a New Governance Approach*, 138 J. Bus. Ethics 1, 2–3 (2013). The codes and quasi-voluntary monitoring and enforcement mechanisms discussed in this chapter are aimed at equalizing the responsibilities of buyers and suppliers.

standards and compliance incentives. The agreements known respectively as "the accord" and "the alliance" are discussed below.

We begin with a summary of the labor situation in Bangladesh's garment sector, authored by the majority staff of the United States Senate Committee on Foreign Relations. As you read, consider the various factors that might have prompted the Committee's interest in overseas garment workers.

A. Ready-made garment manufacture in Bangladesh

Majority Staff of Comm. on Foreign Rel., 113th Cong., Worker Safety and Labor Rights in Bangladesh's Garment Sector

(Comm. Print 2013)[74]

Tazreen, Rana Plaza, and the Need for Organized Labor

On November 24, 2012, a fire started on the ground floor of the Tazreen Fashions factory in Bangladesh, where managers had illegally stored large mounds of fabric and yarn. Fire alarms went off on the factory's 8 floors, alerting the 1,150 workers inside of the mortal danger below. Yet managers on some floors, thinking it was a false alarm and worried about meeting production quotas, ordered workers to ignore the alarms and continue working. Workers who tried to escape down stairwells found them locked or choked with toxic smoke and impassable. Those workers could not demand safe working conditions from their employers because they had no voice, they had no union representation, and 112 lost their lives.

Five months later and less than ten miles away, the workers of Rana Plaza refused to enter the building that housed their factories because they feared it would collapse. Managers threatened to withhold their pay and the workers, desperate for their meager average monthly income of $74 and lacking union representation and a unified voice, reluctantly entered the building. The building collapsed later that day, killing 1,131 and injuring hundreds. Simply put, had the workers of Tazreen Fashions or Rana Plaza belonged to strong, independent unions, they would not have perished in such tragic circumstances.

Since Rana Plaza, just 7 months ago, at least 27 garment workers have been killed and nearly 760 injured in factory fires across Bangladesh.

As a result of the Tazreen Fashions factory fire and the collapse of Rana Plaza, several important initiatives are now underway in Bangladesh to address fire and building safety in garment factories. But Bangladesh's garment workers will never have truly safe, healthy and decent working conditions until they have the ability to speak with a unified voice that is respected by their employers. Greater worker

74. Available at http://www.foreign.senate.gov/imo/media/doc/85633.pdf.

representation, in the form of labor unions, will give Bangladesh's garment workers the power to enforce their rights under the law. Unfortunately, many barriers still exist to greater worker representation in Bangladesh.

Chiefly, garment factory owners and managers have serious misperceptions regarding the role of organized labor and the potential of constructive labor relations. For their part, workers are largely uninformed about their rights to associate, organize, and bargain collectively. A sustained effort to educate employers and workers about these rights will be required before Bangladesh's garment factories can enjoy the benefits of an empowered workforce.

This report is based on a trip to Dhaka made by committee staff in late August 2013, where staff toured garment factories and met with workers, owners, Bangladeshi government officials, union organizers, labor activists, civil society groups, aid workers, brand representatives and U.S. diplomats. Committee staff also held many meetings in Washington, D.C. with retail bodies, labor groups and international organizations, among others. Senator Menendez also chaired a hearing on Bangladeshi labor issues on June 6, 2013. This report will briefly review the development and future potential of Bangladesh's ready-made garment (RMG) sector, evaluate current initiatives underway to improve fire and building safety in RMG factories, and assess efforts and barriers to enhancing workers' rights in the RMG industry.

The Past, Present, and Future of Bangladesh's RMG Industry

Bangladesh's thriving RMG industry has grown from $12,000 in exports in 1978 to $21.5 billion in 2012–13, and now accounts for about 80 percent of total exports. The Multifiber Arrangement (MFA), which started in 1974 and set quotas on garment exports to developed countries, spurred early growth in Bangladesh's RMG industry by providing competitive access to foreign markets. Bangladesh's low cost of labor and high capacity fueled growth when the quota system expired. The industry now directly employs some 4 million Bangladeshis, 80 percent of whom are women, mostly from poor rural households. The sector is estimated to support an additional 8 million tertiary jobs.

With factories concentrated in and around the capital city of Dhaka, the RMG sector has been a major driver of urbanization in Bangladesh. But such rapid growth created serious hazards: the demand for more capacity has led to garment factories sprouting up in apartment buildings and other multi-use structures not built to safely handle large numbers of workers and machines. While fire and building safety standards may have existed on the books, Bangladesh's government had neither the capacity nor the political will to enforce them.

The major factor behind the lack of political will is the enormous political clout wielded by RMG factory owners in Bangladesh. According to one Bangladesh government official, nearly every Member of Parliament has close ties to factory owners and many are direct owners themselves. Many of Bangladesh's RMG factory owners are members of the elite, controlling significant media interests and exerting political influence. Some are satisfied with the status quo, but others recognize the need for change: following the two recent tragedies, factory owners are reportedly now questioned by friends at social gatherings about their factory's level of safety compliance. Second- and third-generation factory owners are reportedly much more focused on compliance than first-generation entrepreneurs, but they only make up about 10–15 percent of owners.

The garment sector is dominated by the Bangladesh Garment Manufacturers and Exporters Association (BGMEA), an industry group that was founded in 1983 and helped the government manage the administrative aspects of the quota system. The BGMEA now enjoys tremendous regulatory powers and in some cases holds more sway over factory owners than the government: a factory owner recently refused orders by the Ministry of Labor to reinstate workers he had fired for union organizing and he rehired them only after the BGMEA threatened to revoke his ability to export. As an association of factory owners, the BGMEA has historically opposed reforms that would give workers more rights. And while BGMEA leaders have said they are welcoming of unions in garment factories, they have yet to show a serious commitment respecting Bangladeshi laws as they relate to the right to bargain collectively and form unions.

The global outrage provoked by the tragedies of Tazreen and Rana Plaza did not appear to have any negative impact on the growth rate of Bangladesh's RMG exports, which saw a 24 percent year-on-year increase in the third quarter of 2013. McKinsey & Company predicts that between the years 2010 and 2015 the sector will double, and then triple by 2020. While recognizing the advantages of its cheap labor and high capacity, the same McKinsey report also identifies several challenges facing the industry, including compliance problems with labor and environmental standards, poor transportation and energy infrastructure, and political instability and labor unrest due to oppressive work environments. Despite these issues, a large plurality of surveyed buyers identified Bangladesh as the future of RMG sourcing for their brands. In addition, a majority of buyers hope to expand into more sophisticated items like formal wear, requiring more skilled workers (there is currently a 25 percent shortage) and moving suppliers up the value chain, where there is less competition and higher profits.

Continued growth of the RMG sector is critical for Bangladesh's development. Between the late 1970s and today, Bangladesh's poverty rate went from 70 percent to less than 40 percent and the average Bangladeshi went from living on $1 a day to more than $5 a day. It is no coincidence that the improvement of those numbers coincides with the rise of the RMG industry. RMG exports will continue to drive Bangladesh's GDP growth and provide jobs for rural poor, especially women, who are moving to the cities. Moving forward, the RMG sector promises to significantly boost economic development in Bangladesh and move it up the industrial value chain, just as it has for other economies around the globe, including Japan, South Korea and, more recently, China.

That is good news for the United States, for which Bangladesh is a country of strategic interest. Geographically, Bangladesh sits at the crossroads of South Asia and Southeast Asia, and it has extensive relations with both India and China. It has the world's seventh largest population and is the third-largest Muslim-majority nation. The United States shares many common strategic interests with Bangladesh, including global peace and security (Bangladesh is a top contributor of UN peacekeepers), counterterrorism, regional stability and global food security. Clearly, the sustained and responsible growth of Bangladesh's RMG sector is in the interests of the United States and the broader international community. But that growth is in danger if working conditions fail to improve. Consumers will reject clothing they believe is stained with the blood of Bangladeshi workers and global brands, anxious to protect their reputations, will be compelled to abandon the "Made in Bangladesh" label. This outcome can and must be avoided.

Fire and Building Safety in Bangladesh's RMG Industry

When the Tazreen Fashions factory burned down, it was the worst garment factory accident in Bangladesh's history. When Rana Plaza collapsed, it was the worst garment factory accident in world history. These tragedies spurred Bangladesh's government, global brands, the United States, other foreign governments, and international organizations into action. There are now several safety initiatives underway to ensure that none of the approximately 3,500 operating garment factories in Bangladesh will become another Tazreen or Rana Plaza. Nonetheless, the danger is still very real. A survey of factories released in June 2013 by the Bangladesh University of Engineering and Technology (BUET) found that 60 percent of factories were structurally vulnerable. And again, abuses are widespread, as evident by the 27 garment workers who have died in factory fires since Rana Plaze collapsed.

Bangladesh's National Action Plan

The National Tripartite Plan of Action on Fire Safety and Structural Integrity (NAP), signed in July 2013 after Rana Plaza, updated a previous fire safety plan signed after Tazreen. The plan stipulates a series of commitments for the government of Bangladesh to meet by certain deadlines. For example, the government has upgraded its labor inspection department to a full directorate with a larger budget and is committed to create 800 positions, including 200 inspectors, by the end of 2013. However, by late November 2013 only four new labor inspectors had been hired since Tazreen, bringing the total to just 56. The NAP also calls for inspection of all garment factories by the end of 2014, the creation of a factory information database, and establishment of a worker safety hotline. In addition, the BGMEA committed to creating a "transparent and accountable" system for sub-contracting in the industry.

Unauthorized sub-contracting is a significant challenge in Bangladesh's RMG industry. Factory owners will often take more orders than they have capacity for and send the excess work to subcontractors. This may not be a problem when those subcontractors are known to the brand and have been properly inspected for labor and safety compliance. But owners may also subcontract to unknown factories that operate in the shadows of Bangladesh's RMG industry. These factories are often the most dangerous in terms of worker safety and the most egregious violators of worker rights.

Despite the efforts of the brands to make clear to suppliers that they do not tolerate unauthorized sub-contracting, the practice continues. The situation provides a strong incentive for brands to facilitate the formation and expansion of independent factory-level unions, which would serve as a bulwark against unauthorized subcontracting. In the longer term, the government of Bangladesh also plans to develop a new 535-acre industrial zone for the RMG sector. The zone will feature all-new, up-to-code buildings where factory owners currently operating in vulnerable buildings will supposedly relocate. However, factory locations in the park will be highly coveted and, according to one Bangladeshi government official, may end up going to owners with political connections and money—a very different group from owners that cannot afford to fix their current factories and operate outside the margins of Bangladeshi law.

U.S., EU, ILO Plans

Citing Bangladesh's failure to improve worker safety and labor rights, in June 2013 the United States government (USG) suspended Bangladesh's eligibility for tariff benefits under the Generalized System of Preferences (GSP) program. Since garments do not receive tariff benefits under the GSP program, suspension of GSP did not impact Bangladesh's over $4 billion worth of annual RMG exports to the United States, however it did effect about $40 million worth of imports in ceramics, tobacco, and other products. But garments receive benefits under the EU's GSP program, and suspension of U.S. GSP raised fears in Bangladesh that the EU might follow suit. In July 2013 the USG released its Bangladesh Action Plan 2013, which sets out several safety and labor benchmarks for Bangladesh to achieve before GSP benefits could be reinstated. Many of the benchmarks match those in the NAP, such as vastly increasing the number of inspectors, inspecting all factories, creating an inspection database, and establishing an effective mechanism for worker safety complaints. As of this report's publication, none of those GSP action plan benchmarks had been met. The GSP action plan also includes several measures on labor rights, discussed below.

The ILO, along with the EU and the United States, supported development of another worker safety and rights agreement called the Sustainability Compact, which was signed by the government of Bangladesh in July 2013. It shares many aspects of the NAP and the GSP action plan, and an official review of Bangladesh's progress will occur sometime in 2014. Progress on implementation of the NAP, GSP action plan, and Sustainability Compact is closely monitored. Unauthorized sub-contracting is a significant challenge in Bangladesh's RMG industry. Factory owners will often take more orders than they have capacity for and send the excess work to subcontractors. This may not be a problem when those subcontractors are known to the brand and have been properly inspected for labor and safety compliance. But owners may also subcontract to unknown factories that operate in the shadows of Bangladesh's RMG industry. These factories are often the most dangerous in terms of worker safety and the most egregious violators of worker rights.

To help Bangladesh with inspections and safety improvements in factories, in October 2013 the International Labor Organization (ILO) launched a $24 million, three-and-a-half year initiative called "Improving Working Conditions in the Ready-Made Garment Sector" (RMGP). The program will assist with inspections of approximately half of Bangladesh's garment factories by helping to stand up 30 structural assessment teams. The program will also work to improve the government's inspection mechanisms, build occupational health and safety awareness in factories, and provide compensation and skills training for victims of the Tazreen and Rana Plaza accidents. The compensation mechanism will establish an international trust fund into which retailers, governments, and others can donate. Some 3,900 claimants have already had their biodata collected and bank accounts established in their names, and full compensation of victims will require approximately $40 million from donors.

Full List Of Recommendations

For the United States Government [USG]

- The USG should hold the government of Bangladesh to the highest standards in implementing the GSP action plan, especially provisions pertaining to labor law reform and protecting the freedom of association and the rights to organize and bargain collectively.
- The USG should increase funding for technical assistance programs in Bangladesh, such as those run by the AFL-CIO's Solidarity Center, that improve workers' capacity to organize and engage in collective bargaining.
- The U.S. Department of State should place a full-time labor attaché from the U.S. Department of Labor at its mission in Dhaka.

For Apparel Brands and Retailers

- Apparel brands and retailers should aggressively continue implementing inspection and remediation programs focused on fire and building safety in their suppliers factories in Bangladesh.
- Apparel brands and retailers, especially those with very large operations in Bangladesh like Wal-Mart, Gap, and others in the Alliance for Bangladesh Worker Safety, should, in coordination with the ILO, launch long-term, well-resourced programs to educate their suppliers of their expectation for compliance with laws allowing the right to organize unions and bargain collectively.
- Apparel brands and retailers, in coordination with the ILO and representative unions, should launch a program to educate garment factory workers about their rights and responsibilities with respect to freedom of association, organization, and collective bargaining.
- Apparel brands and retailers should also collectively develop and implement a policy of zero-tolerance for suppliers who consistently engage in anti-union activity.

For the Government of Bangladesh and BGMEA

- The government of Bangladesh and the BGMEA should immediately develop and implement tough and effective sanctions against factory owners who engage in anti-union activity, and advance progress in sanctioning owners who do not comply with required safety standards.
- The government of Bangladesh and the BGMEA, in coordination with the ILO, should undertake a program to educate garment factory owners on the constructive role of labor unions in garment factories and endeavor to ensure that anti-union activity is eradicated.
- The government of Bangladesh and the BGMEA, in coordination with the ILO and representative unions, should sponsor a program to educate garment factory workers about their rights and responsibilities with respect to freedom of association, organization, and collective bargaining.
- The next government of Bangladesh should act quickly to reform existing labor laws, including EPZ [Export Production Zone] labor laws, to bring them into conformity with international labor standards.

B. Legal infrastructure: The Accord and the Alliance

As noted above, the tragedies in Bangladesh garment factories prompted separate collective actions in Europe and the United States. Note their overlaps and differences. They overlap significantly in their commitment to the safe and fair working conditions as principles of manufacturing and trade; they differ primarily in the explicit role the Accord gives to trade unions and collective bargaining—absent from the Alliance agreement. In addition, the Accord is structured explicitly as an interlegal agreement, drawing on international organizations including the International Labor Organization (ILO) and the United Nations (through UNCITRAL), as well as NGOs and the national laws of Bangladesh (notably the National Action Plan on Fire Safety (NAP)) in the composition of its steering committee and in the architecture of the agreement overall. The emphasis of the Accord is on monitoring, transparency and enforcement of both the voluntary agreement and national laws governing factory safety and accountability.

1. Accord on Fire and Building Safety in Bangladesh

Accord on Fire and Building Safety in Bangladesh[75]

Effective May 13, 2013

The undersigned parties are committed to the goal of a safe and sustainable Bangladeshi Ready-Made Garment ("RMG") industry in which no worker needs to fear fires, building collapses, or other accidents that could be prevented with reasonable

75. Available at http://bangladeshaccord.org.

health and safety measures. The signatories to this Agreement agree to establish a fire and building safety program in Bangladesh for a period of five years.

The programme will build on the National Action Plan on Fire Safety (NAP), which expressly welcomes the development and implementation by any stakeholder of any other activities that would constitute a meaningful contribution to improving fire safety in Bangladesh. The signatories commit to align this programme and its activities with the NAP and to ensure a close collaboration, including for example by establishing common programme, liaison and advisory structures. The signatories also welcome a strong role for the International Labour Organization (ILO), through the Bangladesh office as well as through international programmes, to ensure that both the National Action Plan, and the programme foreseen by the signatories of this Agreement, get implemented.The signatories shall develop and agree an Implementation Plan within 45 days of signing this Agreement. The nongovernmental organisations which are signatories to the Joint Memorandum of Understanding on Fire and Building Safety (dated March 15, 2012), having stated their intention to support the implementation of this programme, shall, at their own election, be signed witnesses to this Agreement.

This Agreement commits the signatories to finance and implement a programme that will take cognizance of the Practical Activities described in the NAP involving, at minimum, the following elements:

SCOPE:

The agreement covers all suppliers producing products for the signatory companies. The signatories shall designate these suppliers as falling into the following categories, according to which they shall require these supplier to accept inspections and implement remediation measures in their factories.

GOVERNANCE:

The signatories shall appoint a Steering Committee (SC) with equal representation chosen by the trade union signatories and company signatories (maximum 3 seats each) and a representative from and chosen by the International Labour Organization (ILO) as a neutral chair. The SC shall have responsibility for the selection, contracting, compensation and review of the performance of a Safety Inspector and a Training Coordinator; oversight and approval of the programme budget; oversight of financial reporting and hiring of auditors; and such other management duties as may be required. The SC will strive to reach decision by consensus, but, in the absence of consensus, decisions will be made by majority vote. In order to develop the activity of the SC, a Governance regulation will be developed.

Dispute resolution. Any dispute between the parties to, and arising under, the terms of this Agreement shall first be presented to and decided by the SC, which shall decide the dispute by majority vote of the SC within a maximum of 21 days of a petition being filed by one of the parties. Upon request of either party, the decision of the SC may be appealed to a final and binding arbitration process. Any arbitration award shall be enforceable in a court of law of the domicile of the signatory against whom enforcement is sought and shall be subject to The Convention on the Recognition and Enforcement of Foreign Arbitral Awards (The New York Convention), where applicable. The process for binding arbitration, including, but not limited to, the allocation of costs relating to any arbitration and the process for selection of the Arbitrator, shall be governed by the UNCITRAL Model Law on International Commercial Arbitration 1985 (with amendments as adopted in 2006).

The signatories shall appoint an Advisory Board involving brands and retailers, suppliers, government institutions, trade unions, and NGOs. The advisory board will ensure all stakeholders, local and international, can engage in constructive dialogue with each other and provide feedback and input to the SC, thereby enhancing quality, efficiency, credibility and synergy. The SC will consult the parties to the NAP to determine the feasibility of a shared advisory structure.

Administration and management of the programme will be developed by the SC in consultation with the 'High-Level Tripartite Committee' established to implement and oversee the National Action Plan on Fire Safety, as well as with the Ministry of Labour and Employment of Bangladesh (MoLE), the ILO and the Deutsche Gesellschaft für Internationale Zusammenarbeit GmbH (GIZ), to maximize synergy at operational level; and the SC may make use of the offices of GIZ for administrative coordination and support.

CREDIBLE INSPECTIONS:

A qualified Safety Inspector, with fire and building safety expertise and impeccable credentials, and who is independent of and not concurrently employed by companies, trade unions or factories, shall be appointed by the SC. Providing the Chief Inspector acts in a manner consistent with his or her mandate under the provisions of this Agreement, and unless there is clear evidence of malfeasance or incompetence on his or her part, the SC shall not restrict or otherwise interfere with the Chief Inspector's performance of the duties set forth in the Agreement as he or she sees fit, including the scheduling of inspections and the publishing of reports.

Where a signatory company's inspection programme, in the opinion of the Safety Inspector, meets or exceeds the standards of thorough and credible inspections, as defined by the Safety Inspector, it will be considered an integral part of the programme activities set forth in this Agreement. Signatory companies wishing to have their inspection programme so considered shall provide the Safety Inspector full access to the findings of their inspections and he or she will integrate these into reporting and remediation activities. Notwithstanding this provision, all factories within the scope of this Agreement shall still be subject to all the provisions of this Agreement, including but not limited to a least one safety inspection carried out by personnel acting under the direction of the Safety Inspector.

Written Inspection Reports of all factories inspected under the programme shall be prepared by the Safety Inspector within two (2) weeks of the date of inspection and shared upon completion with factory management, the factory's health and safety committee, worker representatives (where one or more unions are present), signatory companies and the SC. Where, in the opinion of the Safety Inspector, there is not a functioning health and safety committee at the factory, the report will be shared with the unions which are the signatories to this Agreement.

REMEDIATION:

Where corrective actions are identified by the Safety Inspector as necessary to bring a factory into compliance with building, fire and electrical safety standards, the signatory company or companies that have designated that factory as a Tier 1, 2, or 3 supplier, shall require that factory to implement these corrective actions, according to a schedule that is mandatory and time-bound, with sufficient time allotted for all major renovations.

Signatory companies shall require their supplier factories that are inspected under the Program to maintain workers' employment relationship and regular income during any period that a factory (or portion of a factory) is closed for renovations necessary to complete such Corrective Actions for a period of no longer than six months. Failure to do so may trigger a notice, warning and ultimately termination of the business relationship as described in paragraph 21.

Signatory companies shall make reasonable efforts to ensure that any workers whose employment is terminated as a result of any loss of orders at a factory are offered employment with safe suppliers, if necessary by actively working with other suppliers to provide hiring preferences to these workers.

Signatory companies shall require their supplier factories to respect the right of a worker to refuse work that he or she has reasonable justification to believe is unsafe, without suffering discrimination or loss of pay, including the right to refuse to enter or to remain inside a building that he or she has reasonable justification to believe is unsafe for occupation.

TRAINING:

The Training Coordinator appointed by the SC shall establish an extensive fire and building safety training program.

Health and Safety Committees shall be required by the signatory companies in all Bangladesh factories that supply them, which shall function in accordance with Bangladeshi law, and be comprised of workers and managers from the applicable factory. Worker members shall comprise no less than 50% of the committee and shall be chosen by the factory's trade union, if present, and by democratic election among the workers where there is no trade union present.

COMPLAINTS PROCESS:

The Safety Inspector shall establish a worker complaint process and mechanism that ensures that workers from factories supplying signatory companies can raise in a timely fashion concerns about health and safety risks, safely and confidentially, with the Safety Inspector. This should be aligned with the Hotline to be established under the NAP.

TRANSPARENCY AND REPORTING:

The SC shall make publicly available and regularly update information on key aspects of the programme.

The signatories to this Agreement shall work together with other organizations such as ILO and the High-Level Tripartite Committee and the Bangladeshi Government to encourage the establishment of a protocol seeking to ensure that suppliers which participate fully in the inspection and remediation activities of this Agreement shall not be penalised as a result of the transparency provisions of this Agreement. The objectives of the protocol are to (i) support and motivate the employer to take remediation efforts in the interest of the workforce and the sector and (ii) expedite prompt legal action where the supplier refuses to undertake the remedial action required to become compliant with national law.

SUPPLIER INCENTIVES:

Each signatory company shall require that its suppliers in Bangladesh participate fully in the inspection, remediation, health and safety and, where applicable, training activities, as described in the Agreement. If a supplier fails to do so, the signatory will promptly implement a notice and warning process leading to termination of the business relationship if these efforts do not succeed.

Signatory companies to this agreement are committed to maintaining long-term sourcing relationships with Bangladesh, as is demonstrated by their commitment to this five-year programme. Signatory companies shall continue business at order volumes comparable to or greater than those that existed in the year preceding the inception of this Agreement.

FINANCIAL SUPPORT:

In addition to their obligations pursuant to this Agreement, signatory companies shall also assume responsibility for funding the activities of the SC, Safety Inspector and Training Coordinator as set forth in this Agreement, with each company contributing its equitable share of the funding in accordance with a formula to be established in the Implementation Plan. The SC shall be empowered to seek contributions from governmental and other donors to contribute to costs. Each signatory company shall contribute funding for these activities in proportion to the annual volume of each company's garment production in Bangladesh relative to the respective annual volumes of garment production of the other signatory companies, subject to a maximum contribution of $500,000 per year for each year of the term of this Agreement. A sliding scale of minimum contributions based on factors such as revenues and annual volume in Bangladesh will be defined in the Implementation Plan with annual revisions, while ensuring sufficient funding for the adequate implementation of the Accord and the Plan.

The SC shall ensure that there are credible, robust, and transparent procedures for the accounting and oversight of all contributed funds.

2. The Alliance: Bangladesh Worker Safety Initiative

The Alliance for Bangladesh Worker Safety supports worker safety, monitoring, and enforcement of industry standards as well as Bangladesh laws governing safety and accountability.[76] Like the Accord, it is committed to enforcement of the NAP and builds on a variety of international and national institutions and organizations. In contrast to the Accord, its monitoring efforts are explicitly tied to indicators ("metrics"). Further, while the Accord refers to its comprehensive inclusion of "all stakeholders" (see infra), it does not specifically mention trade unions. It does give attention to "worker empowerment" in its discussion of whistle blowing and other complaint mechanisms for individual workers.

Members Agreement, Alliance for Bangladesh Worker Safety[77]

Effective October 1, 2014

ARTICLE ONE

Purpose

The Members Agreement ("Agreement") of THE ALLIANCE FOR BANGLADESH WORKER SAFETY, INC. ("Alliance") is a governing document to accompany the Bylaws and Certificate of Incorporation for the Alliance. The signatories to this Agreement are the members of the Alliance (the "Members").

Membership is open to all business organizations which are involved in the sale or marketing of ready-made garments ("RMG") and wish to support the principles set forth below. Organizations are encouraged to join the Alliance immediately, but as is set forth in the Alliance's Bylaws, at Article Three, may apply for membership at any time.

The Members are committed to the principles set forth in this Agreement referred to collectively as the Bangladesh Worker Safety Initiative ("BWSI"), which recognize that the safety of workers at RMG factories in the Members' supply chains within Bangladesh (the "Factories" or, if singular, "Factory") is paramount. Specifically, the Members commit to:

- Support the implementation of the National Tripartite Plan of Action on Fire Safety for the Ready-Made Garment Sector in Bangladesh (NAP);
- Empower workers to take an active role in their own safety, and to be able to speak out about unsafe conditions without any risk of retaliation;

76. The Alliance maintains a website at http://www.bangladeshworkersafety.org.

77. Available at http://www.bangladeshworkersafety.org/files/Alliance-Member-Agreement-FINAL.pdf.

- Work with factories that ensure a safe working environment, with each Member committing not to source from any Factory that the Member has deemed to be unsafe;
- Rapid implementation that is results-focused and non-bureaucratic;
- Providing safety inspection, and safety and empowerment training for 100% of Factories in the Members respective supply chains;
- A common standard for safety inspections and safety and worker empowerment training;
- Use of transparency to create accountability for all stakeholders involved;
- Sharing of information on training, current and future fire and building safety inspections and remediation actions;
- Strive to end unauthorized subcontracting within their supply chains, and review their internal policies to ensure application of best practices for addressing unauthorized subcontracting;
- Independent monitoring and verification of their work;
- Inclusion of diverse stakeholders in decision making and collaboration in implementation;
- A Bangladeshi focus, with a framework that engages and builds capacity of key stakeholders, including the Government of Bangladesh and Bangladeshi industry; and
- Commitment of substantial financial resources to accomplish these tasks, as well as encouraging and assisting in the establishment of sustainable mechanisms to meet these objectives.

In seeking to achieve these objectives, the Alliance recognizes the importance of building partnerships with the Bangladeshi government, the Bangladesh Garment Manufacturers and Exporters Association ("BGMEA"), the Bangladesh Knitwear Manufacturers and Exporters Association ("BKMEA"), workers' rights organizations, other RMG buyers' groups (including the Accord on Fire and Building Safety in Bangladesh ("the Accord")), and others who support safer work conditions in Bangladesh RMG Factories.

To this end, the Members agree to the financial commitments and the components of the worker safety program described below. The Alliance Members are fully committed to creating conditions for the benefit of workers in the Bangladesh RMG industry that are not only safe but sustainable, with appropriate and careful oversight and regulation by the Bangladeshi government. The Members of the Alliance recognize that their role is to provide meaningful material assistance to reach these goals and to assist in the creation of a self-reliant Bangladesh RMG industry, while recognizing that ultimately the responsibility for and control over the industry and the safety of its workers rests with the sovereign nation of Bangladesh, its government and its people.

ARTICLE TWO

Funding

(a) Members will create a fund, the Worker Safety Fund ("WSF"), to underwrite Factory-based fire and building safety initiatives in Factories from which Members source RMG products.

* * *

(c) A reserve of 10% of the WSF will be established for the support of temporarily displaced workers due to Factory safety remediation activities. . . .

(d) In addition, the Alliance intends to leverage WSF funds to solicit third party resources focused on improving development within Bangladesh. Such third party resources may include, but will not be limited to, resources made available by the United States and Canadian governments, the Government of Bangladesh, BGMEA/ BKMEA, the International Labor Organization ("ILO"), USAID, the International Finance Corporation (member of the World Bank), multilateral organizations or Non-Governmental Organizations ("NGOs"), philanthropic non-profit organizations, other foreign governments and potential independent funders.

(e) The expenditure of WSF funds shall be directly tied to metrics demonstrating improvement in safety conditions in Bangladesh. The Alliance is fully committed to partnering with Bangladeshi government agencies and other funding sources to establish necessary and reasonable government and Factory milestone targets, as well as achievable metrics for fire and building safety, that collectively seek to assure that Alliance funds are effectively targeted, and that they lead to continued and sustained progress on fire and building safety throughout the Bangladeshi RMG industry. These goals will be clearly stated and recognize that responsibility for conditions in Bangladesh ultimately resides with the local Factory owners and people and government of Bangladesh. Accordingly, the extent and breadth of any future Alliance commitments will be based on the responsible parties making measurable progress that lasts well beyond the five-year horizon of this program and which fosters locally driven and self-sustaining programs for the future benefit of the Bangladeshi RMG industry workers. The Board of Directors will review such progress periodically at their discretion, but the first such review must occur no later than two years from the date of this Agreement.

ARTICLE THREE

Empower Factory Workers

3.1. Principles.

Members of the Alliance are keenly aware that effective worker empowerment is a critical element in achieving meaningful fire and building safety in Bangladesh. To that end, no later than September 10, 2013, Members of the Alliance will work in combination with both mobile technology providers and the workers themselves to develop a uniform, effective, and anonymous means for accessing and improving the ability of workers to have their safety concerns heard and acted upon. Alliance

Members will also incorporate a process for validation and accountability to ensure true worker empowerment.

3.2. Program.

Alliance Members will establish an accountability and validation process to ensure that Worker Participation Committees ("WPCs") are established in all Alliance Member Factories for the primary purpose of empowering Factory workers to report fire and building safety risks without risk of retaliation. WPCs shall be comprised solely of workers and managers from each applicable Factory, Factory workers shall comprise not less than fifty per cent (50%) of each committee, and shall be chosen exclusively by the workers themselves in a democratic election, subject to applicable Bangladeshi law.

(a) The Executive Director, in concert with the Board, shall, within ninety (90) days from the date of hire, design and obtain approval by the Board of a baseline survey whereby workers will be empowered to communicate their Factory fire and building safety concerns directly to the Alliance or to an independent third party acting on behalf of the Alliance, through face-to-face interaction, and indirectly, through random sampling.

(b) No later than November 10, 2013, the Alliance will finalize the implementation of a program to incorporate transparency into worker fire and building safety conditions across the Factories, including the following components:

i. The Training Committee or Taskforce/Executive Director will (1) identify potential third-party hotline and/or mobile technology providers; and (2) submit identified third-party hotline and mobile technology providers to the Board for review and selection;

ii. The Executive Director will engage selected third-party hotline and/or mobile technology providers and supervise the implementation of worker training programs designed to utilize the selected hotline/mobile technology; and

iii. The Executive Director will periodically review WPCs and make a determination of mandatory participants, as required by Bangladeshi law.

Factory management will also be empowered to act on concerns expressed by the WPCs, and ensure their timely remediation.

ARTICLE FOUR

Train and Educate Factory Workers, Supervisors, and Management on Fire and Building Safety.

Members of the Alliance recognize the importance of helping to build and instill a culture in which RMG Factory workers, supervisors, and management alike place safety as their first priority, and in which Factory workers are empowered to report and act on safety concerns.

By July 10, 2014, one hundred percent (100%) of RMG Factories in Bangladesh that manufacture for Members will have its workers and management undergo training for fire and building safety and empowerment that is certified against a common standard. The Alliance will develop a uniform fire and building safety educational standard and curriculum, based in part on training materials, compatible protocols and "best practices" from existing fire and building safety programs. The Alliance and its Members will work with qualified third party organizations to implement this training.

ARTICLE FIVE

Develop and Implement a Common Standard for Assessing Fire and Building Safety

Members of the Alliance agree to establish a common standard by which to provide a uniform and effective method for assessing fire and building safety in new and existing Factories. The Alliance will work in combination with fire and building safety experts, Factory owners, the Bangladeshi government, and the workers themselves to develop and implement a common standard for Factory fire and building safety that is consistent with the NAP, based on existing protocols and initiatives, and that meets or exceeds local legal requirements.

ARTICLE SIX

Expand Industry Fire and Building Safety Inspections and Remediation Programs

6.1. Principles.

Members of the Alliance agree that fire and building safety inspections conducted by Members or their representatives are a critical element of Factory safety. Many Members have already begun comprehensive fire and building safety inspections and evaluations of Factories. As set forth in this Agreement, Members agree that inspections will be conducted by independent Qualified Inspectors ("Qualified Inspectors") and in accordance with the Alliance Fire and Building Safety Standards. The ultimate goal is for Members to utilize Factories that comply with the Alliance Fire and Building Safety Standards, as verified by Qualified Inspectors through an inspection process.

6.2. Factory Inspections and Evaluations

(a) A Committee of Experts in fire and building safety approved by the Board of Directors will be convened for the purpose of creating and helping to implement a program for the Alliance Fire and Building Safety Standards and inspection process.

ARTICLE SEVEN

Share Information on Training, Current and Future Fire and Building Safety Inspections and Remediation Actions

7.1. Principles.

Alliance Members recognize the need to create a clear, transparent, and collaborative process among themselves, Factory owners, Factory workers, the Bangladeshi government and other stakeholder organizations with respect to sharing information on training, fire and building safety Factory inspections, and audits.

7.2. Process and Procedures for Sharing Information.

(a) Except as prohibited by law, Members of the Alliance agree to share information on Factories utilized, fire and building safety training programs and curriculum, safety inspection reports, and audit results.

ARTICLE EIGHT

Commitment to the Prohibition of Unauthorized Subcontracting and Shared Best Practices

8.1. Principles.

Unauthorized subcontracting impedes supply chain transparency and inhibits the ability of Members to enforce their supply chain standards. Although Members each maintain comprehensive policies against unauthorized subcontracting that impose predetermined consequences, in order to maintain proper control over their supply chains and monitor compliance on fire and building and worker safety, the practice of placing production in unauthorized Factories has emerged as a common element in industrial accidents that occur in Bangladesh. Members agree to review their internal policies to address unauthorized subcontracting and collaborate with other Members to identify "best practices" that may help reduce the risks of and seek to end unauthorized subcontracting.

8.2. Review of Existing Policies and Best Practices to Prohibit Unauthorized Subcontracting.

(a) For the purposes of this Agreement, the following definitions apply:

i. ***Unauthorized subcontracting*** is defined as the production and related processes carried out in an undisclosed, unapproved, and/or prohibited facility for the purpose of supplementing the primary production facility.

ii. ***Authorized subcontracting*** is defined as the production and related processes carried out in a disclosed and approved facility for the purpose of supplementing the primary production facility.

iii. ***Predetermined consequences*** is defined as reduced production, cancellation of orders, suspended placements, the indemnification of costs associated with the unauthorized subcontracting activity, and/or termination of contractual relationships.

(b) Members agree to each conduct a review of their internal policies and procedures to identify "best practices" and potential modifications to buying practices that could help to reduce the potential of unauthorized subcontracting.

* * *

ARTICLE TEN
Miscellaneous

10.1. Compliance with Laws.

In carrying out its obligations hereunder each of the Members and the Alliance agrees to adhere to all relevant laws, rules and regulations that are applicable to the actions and activities required of them by this Agreement.

10.2. Amendments.

This Agreement can be amended at any time pursuant to an affirmative vote of two-thirds (2/3) of the Members.

10.3. Choice of Law.

This agreement is to be governed by New York law, without reference to conflicts of laws principles.

10.4. No Third Party Beneficiaries Created.

The Members expressly intend that no rights be created in any third parties by virtue of the undertakings to which the Members have committed to each other in this Agreement. The sole rights to enforce any alleged breach of such commitments by a Member are through the processes described in the Bylaws. No Member has any right of action or other claim against another Member arising out of this Agreement, or such Member's participation in the Alliance, all of which are hereby waived and released.

10.5 Force Majeure.

For the purpose of this Agreement, an "Event of Force Majeure" means any circumstance not within the reasonable control of the Party affected, but only if and to the extent that (i) such circumstance, despite the exercise of reasonable diligence cannot be, or be caused to be, prevented, avoided or removed by such Party, and (ii) such circumstance materially and adversely affects the ability of the Party to perform its obligations under this Agreement, and such Party has taken all reasonable precautions, due care and reasonable alternative measures in order to avoid the effect of such event on the Party's ability to perform its obligations under this Agreement and to mitigate the consequences thereof. In the Event of a Force Majeure, the Board in their reasonable discretion is authorized to modify the deadlines contained in this Agreement.

10.6. Binding Provisions.

The covenants and agreements contained herein shall be binding upon, and inure to the benefit of, the heirs, legal representatives, successors and assigns of the respective parties hereto.

10.7. Counterparts.

This Agreement shall be executed by the Alliance and each of the Members, by the execution of a separate signature page and attached hereto. The body of the Agreement and the signature pages so executed shall constitute one agreement binding on all parties hereto, notwithstanding that all the parties have not signed the same signature page. Any signature page signed by the party against whom enforcement of this Agreement is sought shall be admissible into evidence as an original hereof to prove the contents hereof.

10.8. Severability of Provisions.

Each provision of this Agreement shall be considered severable and if for any reason any provision or provisions herein are determined to be invalid and contrary to any existing or future law, such invalidity shall not impair the operation of or affect those portions of this Agreement which are valid.

* * *

10.10. Entire Understanding.

This Agreement, the Bylaws and Certificate of Incorporation of the Alliance constitute the entire understanding among the Members and the Alliance and supersede all prior written or oral agreements among them with respect to the matters contained herein.

Amendment 1

The Members have agreed to amend the Agreement as follows.

ARTICLE THREE

Empower Factory Workers

3.1 Principles

By inserting the following language at the end of Section 3.1: Further, Alliance Members shall require that the Factories they work with respect the right of a worker to refuse work if he/she has a reasonable justification to believe that a safety situation presents an imminent and serious danger to his/her life, and that such worker shall be protected from undue consequences, in accordance with the relevant ILO Conventions and Bangladeshi Law.

3. *Comparison of the Accord and the Alliance member agreement*

The Senate committee report excerpted earlier concludes with a comparison of the Accord and the Alliance:

Majority Staff of Comm. on Foreign Rel., 113th Cong., Worker Safety and Labor Rights in Bangladesh's Garment Sector

(Comm. Print 2013)[78]

Apparel Companies and Worker Safety

Apparel brands launched two major worker safety initiatives after Rana Plaza. Over 100 companies, mostly European but joined by a few American firms such as

78. Available at http://www.foreign.senate.gov/imo/media/doc/85633.pdf.

PVH (parent company of Calvin Klein, Tommy Hilfiger and Izod), American Eagle, and Abercrombie & Fitch, signed on to an initiative called the Accord on Fire and Building Safety in Bangladesh ("the Accord"). Over 20 American retailers, including Wal-Mart, Gap, Target and JC Penny [sic], declined to join the Accord but formed a similar initiative called the Alliance for Bangladesh Worker Safety ("the Alliance"). Together, the apparel brands and retailers in the Accord and the Alliance source from approximately half of the active garment factories in Bangladesh. The firms in the Accord source from about 1,500 factories and the Alliance's members source from nearly 700 factories; the two share about 350 factories.

Some observers are concerned that factory owners may refuse remediation mandated by Alliance or Accord members and source to a less scrupulous buyer. It will be critical for the government of Bangladesh and BGMEA to impose effective sanctions in these situations.

One key difference between the Accord and the Alliance is the assignment of decision-making authority. The Accord centralizes its decision-making authority in its executive while the Alliance leaves most decisions up to individual retailers.... The Accord also gives an oversight role to trade union signatories, who can initiate binding arbitration against another member of the Accord for noncompliance with the terms of the agreement.

In the Alliance, individual members are responsible for hiring Alliance-approved inspectors. Alliance members can choose whether or not to continue doing business with a factory based on inspection results, and only retailers can initiate arbitration against other retailers, which at worst results in expulsion from the Alliance.

While it is too early to tell whether the different approaches being pursued by the Accord and the Alliance will result in different outcomes regarding improvements in fire and building safety at their supplier factories in Bangladesh, other differences in governance structure and worker empowerment are substantial.

Conclusion

The various worker safety programs initiated in the wake of Tazreen and Rana Plaza have the potential to considerably improve the safety of Bangladesh's garment factories in the short term. But these gains may be lost without strong worker oversight in the form of independent unions.

Some progress has been made recently by Bangladesh's fledgling unions, but much more remains to be done. The biggest obstacles to the future development of unions are the current anti-union mindset of factory owners and a fear and lack of awareness among factory workers. These barriers will take some time to overcome. Progress is clearly possible, though, with sustained and genuine efforts by the governments of the United States, Bangladesh, and other countries, as well as apparel brands and retailers.

International pressure is growing against the government of Bangladesh, apparel brands and factory owners in Bangladesh. Bangladesh's garment sector may not be able to withstand another tragedy on the scale of Tazreen and Rana Plaza. The surest way to guarantee the success of the apparel industry is to avoid another disaster by promoting and protecting labor rights now, while the world's attention is on Bangladesh. The present opportunity to improve working conditions in Bangladesh cannot be squandered.

Among the concerns of U.S. companies that rejected the Accord were the liability risks in the Accord's provisions. The Accord allows worker representative organizations to take enforcement actions, and for U.S. companies, this raised the spectre of litigation. For example, if a worker is killed or injured while working in a factory overseas, groups who represent the workers may bring a lawsuit against the U.S. retailer who received products from that factory. (But see discussion of the Ninth Circuit's decision in Wal-Mart, below, in which the Court, in effect, rejected the idea that liability may jump links in the supply chain.) U.S. companies stated that because the United States legal system is more accessible to plaintiffs than Europe's legal systems, the Accord would raise the risk of litigation for U.S. companies more than it would for European retailers. [79]

The binding arbitration clause included in the Accord was another issue of contention for some U.S. companies. The concern about the arbitration clause also relates to the issue of litigation, since the clause calls for legal recognition of the Accord in the domestic courts of each signatory's country. Under the Accord, a U.S. company may be sued in a U.S. court for noncompliance with the provisions of the Accord (if arbitration has not brought noncompliance to an end). U.S. companies again cited the openness of the U.S. legal system and increased risk for litigation as the reasoning behind their rejection of the Accord.

V. Adjudicating supply chain responsibilities for worker safety

The Ninth Circuit's opinion in *Doe v. Wal-Mart* provides a prime example of the limitations of "soft law" in relation to workers in the offshore operations of U.S. firms. The plaintiffs, employees of foreign supply contractors to the retail giant Wal-Mart, alleged myriad violations of workers' and human rights violations, "including excessive hours or days of work, withheld pay, confiscation of withheld pay, overtime without pay, less than minimum-wage pay, denial of overtime pay, less than required rest periods, lack of safety equipment, denial of maternity benefits, discrimination because of union activities, and physical abuse."[80] One plaintiff alleged that her supervisor "slapp[ed] her face so hard that her nose began bleeding simply because"

---

79. *See* Steven Greenhouse, *U.S. Retailers See Big Risk in Safety Plan for Factories*, N.Y. Times, May 23, 2013, at B1.

80. *Doe I v. Wal-Mart Stores, Inc.*, No. CV 05-7307-AG(MANx), 2007 WL 5975664, at *2 (C.D. Cal. Mar. 30, 2007), *aff'd*, 572 F.3d 677 (9th Cir. 2009).

she was unable to meet her work quota.[81] Another alleged that she was forced to continue working while seventh months pregnant and that, when she tried to take a rest break, her supervisor "kicked her hard in the stomach."[82]

Armed with provisions of the supply contract between Wal-Mart and their immediate employers that, on their face, suggested that Wal-Mart committed to ensure safe working conditions and minimum pay, the workers sought relief in federal court. Consider how the court could have resolved the issues in this case differently.

Doe v. Wal-Mart Stores, Inc.

572 F.3d 677 (9th Cir. 2009)

Gould, Circuit Judge:

The appellants were among the plaintiffs in the district court and are employees of foreign companies that sell goods to Wal-Mart Stores, Inc. ("Wal-Mart"). They brought claims against Wal-Mart based on the working conditions in each of their employers' factories. These claims relied primarily on a code of conduct included in Wal-Mart's supply contracts, specifying basic labor standards that suppliers must meet. The district court dismissed the complaint for failure to state a claim under Federal Rule of Civil Procedure 12(b)(6). We have jurisdiction under 28 U.S.C. § 1291, and we affirm.

I

Plaintiffs are employees of Wal-Mart's foreign suppliers in countries including China, Bangladesh, Indonesia, Swaziland, and Nicaragua. Plaintiffs allege the following relevant facts, which we take as true for purposes of this appeal:

In 1992, Wal-Mart developed a code of conduct for its suppliers, entitled "Standards for Suppliers" ("Standards"). These Standards were incorporated into its supply contracts with foreign suppliers. The Standards require foreign suppliers to adhere to local laws and local industry standards regarding working conditions like pay, hours, forced labor, child labor, and discrimination. The Standards also include a paragraph entitled "RIGHT OF INSPECTION":

> To further assure proper implementation of and compliance with the standards set forth herein, Wal-Mart or a third party designated by Wal-Mart will undertake affirmative measures, such as on-site inspection of production facilities, to implement and monitor said standards. Any supplier which fails or refuses to comply with these standards or does not allow inspection of production facilities is subject to immediate cancellation of any and all outstanding orders, refuse [sic] or return [sic] any shipment, and otherwise cease doing business [sic] with Wal-Mart.

81. *Id.* at ¶ 56 (First Amended Class Action Complaint for Injunctive Relief & Damages).
82. *Id.* ¶ 59.

Thus, each supplier must acknowledge that its failure to comply with the Standards could result in cancellation of orders and termination of its business relationship with Wal-Mart.

Wal-Mart represents to the public that it improves the lives of its suppliers' employees and that it does not condone any violation of the Standards. However, Plaintiffs allege that Wal-Mart does not adequately monitor its suppliers and that Wal-Mart knows its suppliers often violate the Standards. Specifically, Plaintiffs claim that in 2004, only eight percent of audits were unannounced, and that workers are often coached on how to respond to auditors. Additionally, Plaintiffs allege that Wal-Mart's inspectors were pressured to produce positive reports of factories that were not in compliance with the Standards. Finally, Plaintiffs allege that the short deadlines and low prices in Wal-Mart's supply contracts force suppliers to violate the Standards in order to satisfy the terms of the contracts.

Plaintiffs filed a class action lawsuit in California Superior Court in 2005 and Wal-Mart removed the case to federal court based on diversity of citizenship. Plaintiffs then filed an amended complaint in federal court, which is the complaint relevant here. Wal-Mart filed a motion to dismiss under Federal Rule of Civil Procedure 12(b)(6) for failure to state a claim. The district court granted the motion in a written order, and judgment was entered on March 27, 2008. Plaintiffs timely appealed.

II

We review a dismissal under Rule 12(b)(6) *de novo*. *Witt v. Dep't of the Air Force*, 527 F.3d 806, 810 (9th Cir. 2008). We take a plaintiff's allegations in the complaint as true, but we are "not required to indulge unwarranted inferences." *Metzler Inv. GMBH v. Corinthian Colls., Inc.*, 540 F.3d 1049, 1064 (9th Cir. 2008).

III

Plaintiffs present four distinct legal theories, all of which aim to establish that the Standards and California common law provide substantive obligations that can be enforced by the foreign workers against Wal-Mart: (1) Plaintiffs are third-party beneficiaries of the Standards contained in Wal-Mart's supply contracts; (2) Wal-Mart is Plaintiffs' joint employer; (3) Wal-Mart negligently breached a duty to monitor the suppliers and protect Plaintiffs from the suppliers' working conditions; (4) Wal-Mart was unjustly enriched by Plaintiffs' mistreatment. Applying California law, we address each claim in turn.

A

We first address Plaintiffs' third-party beneficiary theory. The common law in California and elsewhere establishes that, as recited in the applicable Restatement (Second) of Contracts: "A promise in a contract creates a duty in the promisor to any intended beneficiary to perform the promise, and the intended beneficiary may enforce the duty." Restatement (Second) of Contracts § 304 (1981). However, the Restatement also explains that a beneficiary is only "an intended beneficiary if recognition of a right to performance in the beneficiary is appropriate to effectuate the intention of the parties. . . ." Restatement (Second) of Contracts § 302(1). Contract interpretation is a question of law that we review *de novo. See Milenbach v. Comm'r of Internal Revenue,* 318 F.3d 924, 930 (9th Cir.2003).

Plaintiffs argue that Wal-Mart promised the suppliers that it would monitor the suppliers' compliance with the Standards, and that Plaintiffs are third-party beneficiaries of that promise to monitor. Plaintiffs rely on this language in the Standards: "Wal-Mart will undertake affirmative measures, such as on-site inspection of production facilities, to implement and monitor said standards." We agree with the district court that this language does not create a duty on the part of Wal-Mart to monitor the suppliers, and does not provide Plaintiffs a right of action against Wal-Mart as third-party beneficiaries.

The language and structure of the agreement show that Wal-Mart reserved the right to inspect the suppliers, but did not adopt a duty to inspect them. The language on which Plaintiffs rely is found in a paragraph entitled "Right of Inspection," contained in a two-page section entitled "Standards for Suppliers." And after stating Wal-Mart's intention to enforce the Standards through monitoring, the paragraph elaborates the potential consequences of a supplier's failure to comply with the Standards—Wal-Mart may cancel orders and cease doing business with that supplier—but contains no comparable adverse consequences for Wal-Mart if Wal-Mart does not monitor that supplier. Because, as we view the supply contracts, Wal-Mart made no promise to monitor the suppliers, no such promise flows to Plaintiffs as third-party beneficiaries. *See Marina Tenants Ass'n v. Deauville Marina Dev. Co.,* 181 Cal.App.3d 122, 226 Cal.Rptr. 321, 327 (1986) ("A third party beneficiary cannot assert greater rights than those of the promisee under the contract.").

Plaintiffs alternatively argue that they are third-party beneficiaries of the suppliers' promises to maintain certain working conditions, and that Plaintiffs may therefore sue Wal-Mart. This theory fails because Wal-Mart was the promisee vis-a-vis the suppliers' promises to follow the Standards, and Plaintiffs have not plausibly alleged a contractual duty on the part of Wal-Mart that would extend to Plaintiffs. *See Martinez v. Socoma Cos.,* 11 Cal.3d 394, 113 Cal.Rptr. 585, 521 P.2d 841, 844–45 (1974) (holding a "donee" third-party beneficiary may recover only against the party that undertook a promise under the contract for the benefit of the beneficiary).

Plaintiffs' allegations are insufficient to support the conclusion that Wal-Mart and the suppliers intended for Plaintiffs to have a right of performance against Wal-Mart under the supply contracts. *See* Restatement (Second) of Contracts § 302(1). We therefore conclude that Plaintiffs have not stated a claim against Wal-Mart as third-party beneficiaries of any contractual duty owed by Wal-Mart, and we affirm the district court's dismissal of the third-party beneficiary contract claim.

B

We next address Plaintiffs' theory that Wal-Mart was Plaintiffs' joint employer, such that they can "sue Wal-Mart directly for any breach of contract or violation of labor laws." We conclude, to the contrary, that Wal-Mart cannot be considered Plaintiffs' employer on the facts alleged.

The key factor to consider in analyzing whether an entity is an employer is "the right to control and direct the activities of the person rendering service, or the manner and method in which the work is performed." *Service Employees Int'l Union v. County of L.A.*, 225 Cal.App.3d 761, 275 Cal.Rptr. 508, 513 (1990) (internal quotations and citation omitted). "A finding of the right to control employment requires ... a comprehensive and immediate level of 'day-to-day' authority over employment decisions." *Vernon v. State,* 116 Cal.App.4th 114, 10 Cal.Rptr.3d 121, 132 (2004).

Here, Plaintiffs' allegations do not support the conclusion that Wal-Mart is Plaintiffs' employer. Plaintiffs' general statement that Wal-Mart exercised control over their day-to-day employment is a conclusion, not a factual allegation stated with any specificity. We need not accept Plaintiffs' unwarranted conclusion in reviewing a motion to dismiss. *See Bell Atl. Corp. v. Twombly,* 550 U.S. 544, 555, 127 S.Ct. 1955, 167 L.Ed.2d 929 (2007) (stating that "a plaintiff's obligation to provide the grounds of his entitlement to relief requires more than labels and conclusions, and a formulaic recitation of the elements of a cause of action will not do") (internal quotation marks and alterations omitted); *Ashcroft v. Iqbal,* 556U.S. 662, 129 S.Ct. 1937, 1953, 173 L.Ed.2d 868 (2009) (holding that the pleading requirements stated in *Twombly* apply in all civil cases); *Adams v. Johnson,* 355 F.3d 1179, 1183 (9th Cir.2004) (stating that "conclusory allegations of law and unwarranted inferences are insufficient to defeat a motion to dismiss"). Plaintiffs allege specifically that Wal-Mart contracted with suppliers regarding deadlines, quality of products, materials used, prices, and other common buyer-seller contract terms. Such supply contract terms do not constitute an "immediate level of 'day-to-day'" control over a supplier's employees so as to create an employment relationship between a purchaser and a supplier's employees. *Vernon,* 10 Cal.Rptr.3d at 132.

Plaintiffs also allege that Wal-Mart exercised control over their employment through Wal-Mart's promise to monitor the suppliers and Wal-Mart's system for monitoring. However, we have already concluded that Wal-Mart undertook no duty to monitor the suppliers and the monitoring and inspections by Wal-Mart were performed to determine whether suppliers were meeting their contractual obligations, not to direct the daily work activity of the suppliers' employees.

Plaintiffs have provided no persuasive support for finding a common law employment relationship between a purchaser and its suppliers' employees on the facts of this case. We conclude that the joint employer theory should here be rejected, and we hold that Wal-Mart is not Plaintiffs' employer.

C

We next address Plaintiffs' negligence claims, which Plaintiffs bring under four distinct theories: third-party beneficiary negligence, negligent retention of control, negligent undertaking, and common law negligence. Whichever theory is invoked, however, we conclude that Wal-Mart did not owe Plaintiffs a common-law duty to monitor

Wal-Mart's suppliers or to prevent the alleged intentional mistreatment of Plaintiffs by the suppliers. Without such a duty, Plaintiffs' negligence theories do not state a claim. *See Paz v. State*, 22 Cal.4th 550, 93 Cal.Rptr.2d 703, 994 P.2d 975, 980–81 (2000) ("The threshold element of a cause of action for negligence is the existence of a duty . . .").

Plaintiffs' "third-party beneficiary" negligence theory relies on the assumption that Wal-Mart owes Plaintiffs a duty under Wal-Mart's supply contracts. Because we have already determined that no legal obligation flows from Wal-Mart to Plaintiffs under Wal-Mart's supply contracts, Plaintiffs do not state a claim for third-party beneficiary negligence.

In order to state a claim for "negligent retention of control and supervision," Plaintiffs must allege facts that, if proven, would show that Wal-Mart exercised significant control over Plaintiffs and that "exercise of retained control *affirmatively contributed* to the employee's injuries." *Hooker v. Dep't of Transp.*, 27 Cal.4th 198, 115 Cal.Rptr.2d 853, 38 P.3d 1081, 1083 (2002) (emphasis in original). We have already determined that Wal-Mart is not Plaintiffs' employer because Wal-Mart exercised minimal or no control over the day-to-day work of Plaintiffs in the suppliers' foreign factories. Accordingly, we hold that Wal-Mart did not owe Plaintiffs a special duty to protect Plaintiffs from the suppliers' alleged intentional misconduct.

Plaintiffs' "negligent undertaking" theory relies on the assumption that Wal-Mart undertook to protect Plaintiffs, and therefore Wal-Mart had to exercise reasonable care in monitoring the suppliers. *See Delgado v. Trax Bar & Grill*, 36 Cal.4th 224, 30 Cal.Rptr.3d 145, 113 P.3d 1159, 1175 (2005) (stating that one who "undertakes to provide protective services to another" must exercise a duty of care). This theory fails because, as we have already concluded, Wal-Mart did not undertake any obligation to protect Plaintiffs. "[T]he scope of any duty assumed depends upon the nature of the undertaking," *id.*, and here Wal-Mart merely reserved the right to cancel its supply contracts if inspections revealed contractual breaches by the suppliers. Any inspections actually performed by Wal-Mart were therefore gratuitous, and do not independently impose a duty on Wal-Mart to protect Plaintiffs. *Id.*

Plaintiffs' "common law negligence" claim provides no additional ground for finding a duty on the part of Wal-Mart. Wal-Mart had no duty to monitor the suppliers or to protect Plaintiffs from the intentional acts the suppliers allegedly committed. Thus, Plaintiffs' theories sounding in negligence do not state a claim. *See Paz*, 93 Cal. Rptr.2d 703, 994 P.2d at 980–81.

D

We turn finally to Plaintiffs' claim of unjust enrichment. Plaintiffs allege that Wal-Mart was unjustly enriched at Plaintiffs' expense by profiting from relationships with suppliers that Wal-Mart knew were engaged in substandard labor practices. Unjust enrichment is commonly understood as a theory upon which the remedy of restitution may be granted. *See* 1 George E. Palmer, Law of Restitution § 1.1 (1st ed. 1978 & Supp. 2009); Restatement of Restitution § 1 (1937) ("A person who has been unjustly enriched at the expense of another is required to make restitution to the other."). California's approach to unjust enrichment is consistent with this general understanding: "The fact that one person benefits another is not, by itself, sufficient to require restitution. The person receiving the benefit is required to make restitution only if the circumstances are such that, as between the two individuals, it is *unjust* for the person to retain it." *First Nationwide Sav. v. Perry,* 11 Cal.App.4th 1657, 15 Cal.Rptr.2d 173, 176 (1992) (emphasis in original).

The lack of any prior relationship between Plaintiffs and Wal-Mart precludes the application of an unjust enrichment theory here. *See Smith v. Pac. Props. & Dev. Corp.,* 358 F.3d 1097, 1106 (9th Cir.2004) (noting that a party generally may not seek to disgorge another's profits unless "a prior relationship between the parties subject to and benefiting from disgorgement originally resulted in unjust enrichment"). Plaintiffs essentially seek to disgorge profits allegedly earned by Wal-Mart at Plaintiffs' expense; however, we have already determined that Wal-Mart is not Plaintiffs' employer, and we see no other plausible basis upon which the employee of a manufacturer, without more, may obtain restitution from one who purchases goods from that manufacturer. That is, the connection between Plaintiffs and Wal-Mart here is simply too attenuated to support an unjust enrichment claim. *See, e.g., Sperry v. Crompton Corp.,* 8 N.Y.3d 204, 831 N.Y.S.2d 760, 863 N.E.2d 1012, 1018 (2007) (holding that "the connection between the purchaser of tires and the producers of chemicals used in the rubbermaking process is simply too attenuated to support" the purchaser's claim of unjust enrichment).

IV

In sum, we conclude that Plaintiffs have not stated a claim against Wal-Mart. Wal-Mart had no legal duty under the Standards or common law negligence principles to monitor its suppliers or to protect Plaintiffs from the suppliers' alleged substandard labor practices. Wal-Mart is not Plaintiffs' employer, and the relationship between Wal-Mart and Plaintiffs is too attenuated to support restitution under an unjust enrichment theory.

AFFIRMED.

Notes and Questions

1. Much of the court's decision rests upon its conclusion that "Wal-Mart did not undertake any obligation to protect Plaintiffs."[83] But what was Wal-Mart's contractual code of conduct if not an undertaking to ensure that its suppliers honored their legal obligations to their employees? As one scholar observes, "The decision that there was no undertaking is surprising given that Wal-Mart publicly stated the 'fundamental objective' of its Factory Certification Program, which it uses to implement the Wal-Mart Standards, was to 'encourag[e] implementation of necessary changes that will ultimately result in an improved quality of life for the workers who supply [its] stores.'"[84]

---

83. *Doe I,* 572 F.3d at 684.

84. Madeleine Conway, *A New Duty of Care? Tort Liability from Voluntary Human Rights Due Diligence in Global Supply Chains,* 40 Queen's L.J. 741, 776 (2015) (quoting the Wal-Mart Factory Certification Supplier Manual).

2. The Ninth Circuit denied the international plaintiffs a remedy against Wal-Mart, but couldn't the plaintiffs instead pursue an action against their immediate employers? According to their complaint, "Plaintiffs and their families would be subjected to threats of reprisal, including threats of current and future job loss, and in many cases, threats of physical danger by the supplier companies and/or their home country governments if they were to fully pursue and enforce these claims in their home countries."[85] Without any legal system that could guarantee the plaintiffs protection from these threats, the plaintiffs could not pursue any legal remedy at all. The United States would not hold Wal-Mart (or, presumably, its supply chain) responsible, so no one would.

3. Writing about private governance in the environmental sector, Michael Vandenbergh notes the absence of stakeholder participation among the accountability mechanisms of private contracts and unilateral standard-setting:

> [A] firm can make substantial changes in the standard it actually imposes on a supplier by stating in broad terms that it has adopted a standard without posting the standard itself, by adopting and announcing a collectively or unilaterally set standard with subtle caveats (limiting a certification requirement to situations of commercial feasibility or adopting the standard as a procurement preference rather than a requirement), or by using contract terms (which typically are not publicly disclosed) that do not track the terms of the publicly available standard.
>
> Stakeholder participation in standard setting and enforcement is not a robust accountability mechanism for private environmental contracting. . . . [A]side from the customer or NGO pressure . . . , little or no stakeholder participation occurs in the formation of private unilaterally set standards. Similarly, certification programs in some cases have adopted requirements for certifiers to consult with stakeholders regarding implementation, but stakeholder participation is still often limited.[86]

Would you expect differences across various sectors (e.g., labor and environmental protection) as to the value of stakeholder participation? Would stakeholder participation contribute to alleviating some of the implementation problems discussed by Sarfaty?

4. In the late 1990s, Nike faced an onslaught of negative publicity after allegations that its employees in factories abroad were suffering under poor working conditions.[87] The allegations involved claims that employees in Vietnam were forced to

---

85. Complaint at ¶ 6, *Doe I v. Wal-Mart Stores, Inc.*, No. CV 05-7307-AG(MANx), 2007 WL 5975664, at *2 (C.D. Cal. Mar. 30, 2007).

86. Michael Vandenbergh, *The New Wal-Mart Effect: The Role of Private Contracting in Global Governance*, 54 UCLA L. Rev. 913, 962–963 (2007) (notes omitted).

87. *E.g.*, Steven Greenhouse, *Nike Shoe Plant in Vietnam Is Called Unsafe for Workers*, N.Y. Times, Nov. 8, 1997, at A1. *See generally* Julia Fisher, Note, *Free Speech to Have Sweatshops? How* Kasky v.

work 65 hour weeks, and that 77 percent of the workers suffered from respiratory diseases caused by poor air quality in the factory.[88] In response to the revelations, Nike launched a public relations campaign pointing to the provisions of its code of conduct regarding working conditions and fair wages.[89]

Marc Kasky, a concerned California resident who believed that Nike was making false statements about its labor practices,[90] brought suit on behalf of the public under the state's unfair competition law (UCL), which defined unfair competition as "any unlawful, unfair or fraudulent business act or practice and unfair, deceptive, untrue or misleading advertising."[91] The trial court and court of appeal sustained Nike's demurrers on First Amendment grounds, but the California Supreme Court reversed in *Nike, Inc. v. Kasky*, holding that Nike's speech was "directed by a commercial speaker to a commercial audience . . . for the purpose of promoting sales of its products. . . . [W]hen a business enterprise . . . makes factual representations about its own operations, it must speak truthfully."[92] The Supreme Court initially granted certiorari to review California's interlocutory ruling, but dismissed the writ as improvidently granted.[93]

Further developments related to the Nike controversy are discussed in the excerpt in the next section.

VI. Interlegalities as arenas of mobilization

In this concluding excerpt, Cesar Rodríguez-Garavito, a lawyer and sociolegal scholar, analyzes the strategic potential in interlegalities of hard and soft law for labor activists. The excerpt points to the strong demand for hard law among workers in the international apparel industry, and it is relevant to the discussion in this chapter as well as Chapter 6.[94]

Nike *Might Provide a Useful Tool to Improve Sweatshop Conditions*, 26 B.C. Third World L.J. 267 (2006).

88. Greenhouse, *supra* note 87.

89. *Nike, Inc. v. Kasky* (*Nike II*), 539 U.S. 654, 685 (2003) (per curiam) (Breyer, J., dissenting) (dismissing writ of certiorari as improvidently granted) (reproducing letter from Nike to university presidents and athletic directors stating, *inter alia*, that while "some violations occur," Nike was "proud that in all material respects the code of conduct is complied with"); *Kasky v. Nike, Inc.* (*Nike I*), 45 P.3d 243, 248 (2002); Fisher, *supra* note 87.

90. *Nike I*, 45 P.3d at 247.

91. Cal. Bus. & Prof. Code § 17200 (West 2008).

92. *Nike I*, 45 P.3d at 247.

93. *Nike II*, 539 U.S. 654. The Court's decision drew two opinions and three dissenters, however, who voiced concerns about the underlying First Amendment issues, finality, and standing. *Compare id.* at 656–65 (Stevens, J., concurring), *with id.* at 665–84 (Breyer, J., dissenting).

94. *See also* Rebecca DeWinter-Schmitt, *Human Rights and Self-Regulation in the Apparel Industry*, *in* Private Security, Public Order: The Outsourcing of Public Services and Its Limits 133–155 (Simon Chesterman & Angelina Fisher, eds. 2009); Harry Arthurs, *Private*

Cesar Rodríguez-Garavito, *Nike's Law: The Anti-Sweatshop Movement, Transnational Corporations, and the Struggle over International Labor Rights in the Americas*

in LAW AND GLOBALIZATION FROM BELOW 64–91[95]

3.1 INTRODUCTION

Just as sweatshops have become the symbol of the perverse effects of neoliberal globalization, the transnational anti-sweatshop movement lies at the heart of the struggle for social justice in the global economy. In the global North, the reemergence of sweatshops in such cities as New York and Los Angeles entails the return of the economic and legal realities of the nineteenth century. In the South, the exploitative labor conditions and the unfulfilled promise of employment and growth have turned *maquilas* into an icon of the failure of late twentieth-century neoliberalism. In bridging the North-South divide through highly plural, dynamic, and decentralized transnational advocacy networks (TANs), the anti-sweatshop movement holds out the prospect of a revamped, twenty-first century labor internationalism.

Beyond its political and symbolic importance, the anti-sweatshop movement offers a privileged vantage point to examine the role of law in counter-hegemonic globalization for two reasons. First, in terms of social movement theory, the "framing" of the anti-sweatshop cause has crucially relied on law and legal discourse. Given that abuses committed in global sweatshops—from physical violence to sexual harassment and misery wages—undermine fundamental conditions of human dignity, TANs have framed their struggle as a vindication of basic human rights. This has not only lent a potent moral force to the movement but has also placed the mobilization of human rights rules and discourses at the center of TANs' strategies. Secondly, as I will argue below, the anti-sweatshop movement can be best understood as a component of a broader movement to regulate the operation of transnational corporations (TNCs) in the global economy. A key stake in this global field of confrontation pitting TNCs against TANs—and the myriad governmental and non-governmental organizations siding with each camp, as well as the lawyers, consultants, aod academics providing the legal and intellectual ammunition to each—is the definition of the rules establishing the rights of corporations and workers in the global economy. As Wallerstein has put it, "the creation of these legal structures as well as their real enforcement becomes therefore one of the prime political arenas of conflict in the world-system." Thus, as I set out to show in this chapter,

---

Ordering and Workers' Rights in the Global Economy: Corporate Codes of Conduct as a Regime of Labour Market Regulation, in LABOR LAW IN AN ERA OF GLOBALIZATION: TRANSFORMATIVE PRACTICES AND POSSIBILITIES 471–487 (Joanne Conaghan, Richard Michael Fischl & Karl Klare, eds., 2002).

95. Cesar Rodríguez-Garavito, *Nike's Law: The Anti-Sweatshop Movement, Transnational Corporations, and The Struggle Over International Labor Rights in the Americas, in* LAW AND GLOBALIZATION FROM BELOW: TOWARDS A COSMOPOLITAN LEGALITY 64–91 (Boaventura de Sousa Santos & Cesar Rodríguez-Garavito, eds. Cambridge University Press 2005).

the counter-hegemonic potential of the normative vision and legal strategies of the anti-sweatshop movement can be assessed only if seen in relation to the hegemonic visions and uses of law through which TNCs and their supporters seek to consolidate their dominance in the global economy.

The legal tools available to actors in the confrontation over labor rights are highly heterogeneous and operate at different scales. In the absence of effective institutions of transnational governance, working conditions in global commodity chains are regulated through myriad public and private arrangements that constitute a legal kaleidoscope rather than a legal system. Thus, in terms of sociolegal theory, the struggle for worker rights takes place in a context of legal pluralism in which national labor laws, ILO conventions, corporate codes of conduct, social clauses in bilateral and regional trade agreements, and unilateral sanctions overlap and clash. This legal kaleidoscope involves both "soft law" created by private actors such as TNCs (e.g. codes of conduct) and NGOs (e.g. alternative treaties) as well as "hard law" backed by state apparatuses. Hegemonic and counter-hegemonic actors actively exploit and shape the unequal opportunities created by the tensions and contradictions within this pluralist legal arena.

The use of plural legal fields by social movements is a staple topic of sociolegal research. The existing literature, however, continues to be largely focused on the local and national scales, thus missing the novel forms of legal pluralism and transnational political mobilization associated with globalization. Specifically in the Americas, the area on which this chapter focuses, two different trends have converged to produce this important blind spot in our understanding of contemporary law and social movements. In Latin America, the vibrant tradition of studies on the alternative use of law by popular actors has overwhelmingly focused on local processes of informal law creation within marginalized communities, or the mobilization of national courts by activists. In the US, despite the recognition of legal pluralism, the literature on legal mobilization continues to be dominated by analyses of the use of litigation and domestic courts by social movement organizations. In both scholarly traditions, therefore, the task of inquiring precisely how transnational social movements shape and are shaped by the plural array of rules regulating the world economy remains to be done.

The growing literature on transnational social movements offers some useful clues for this task. Particularly relevant is recent exploratory work on the role of NGOs in the "social construction of law." However, as Rajagopal has noted, social movement research has yet to systematically examine the use of legal institutions and discourses as frames and arenas of contentious political action across borders.

TNCs' and TANs' strategies constantly shift among different scales and types of law, as well as between political and legal strategies. For instance, TANs simultaneously engage in efforts to bolster national states' regulatory capacity, create effective global corporate codes of conduct for labor and promote direct action campaigns to boycott the products of targeted TNCs at the regional level. Similarly, while strategically invoking their abidance with weak national labor laws to fend off attempts at cross-border regulation, TNCs strive to maintain the non-enforceable character of codes of conduct and use the political muscle stemming from their capacity to shift production away from inhospitable regulatory environments.

The TNCs' balancing act consists in nurturing the legal fiction of complete separation vis-á-vis their contractors even as they remain deeply involved in the day-to-day operation of the factories and set the prices that constrain workers' wages. This largely successful endeavor relies on three strategies to which sourcing and "social responsibility" corporate divisions devote considerable resources. Challenging these strategies in order to subject TNCs to labor regulations through a global regulatory system of joint liability is the central goal of the anti-sweatshop movement.

First, transnational retailers and brand merchandisers zealously protect the secrecy of their contracting arrangements. Based on admittedly shaky arguments on the need to protect "trade secrets," TNCs staunchly resist activists' demands to disclose the identity and location of their suppliers, let alone the wages paid to workers. As joint liability crucially depends on information on the links between transnational retailers and manufacturers and their local suppliers, transparency has been one of the key issues of contention between TNCs and TANs. Requirements on the disclosure of the location and identity of con· tractors, for instance, are one of the key differences among systems of code of conduct monitoring in the US. While some systems such as the student-organized Worker Rights Consortium (WRC) demand full disclosure from producers of collegiate apparel and are now seeking to extend transparency to information on wages, other systems such as the Fair Labor Association (FLA), Social Accountability International (SAI), and the Worldwide Responsible Apparel Production Certification Program (WRAP) allow manufacturers to keep this information confidential. Secrecy is the rule also inside the walls of the factories. As interviews with sweatshop workers in Guatemala and Mexico showed, factory managers take pains to conceal labels and information that would reveal the identity of buyers.

Secrecy, however, is a limited strategy. For today's suppliers are usually not small local workshops but world-class factories built with transnational capital and employing hundreds or thousands of workers. Kukdong, for instance, is a high-tech factory with a capital investment of over US$30 million owned by a Korean TNC with headquarters in Seoul and Los Angeles. Sitting on the side of a major highway, its large facilities topped by Korean and Mexican flags flying in the wind are hard to miss. Moreover, local unions and NGOs as well as transnational activists compile and spread information on the location of the factories and the identity of their buyers.

In light of this, TNCs resort to a second strategy to thwart joint liability regulations: the denial of control over (and thus responsibility for) what goes on in their contractors' factories. The baseline corporate position on the matter is illustrated by the answer of Nike's general manager in Indonesia to a question on labor abuses in supplier factories in that country: "I don't know that we need to know." One decade later, after intense anti-sweatshop campaigning, TNCs' public statements had been moderated but their basic position remained unchanged: in the words of Gap's senior vice president for global affairs, "we are not the all-powerful Oz that rules over what happens in every factory . . . Do we have leverage? Yes. Is it as great as our critics believe? Not by a long shot." TANs and academic analysts contest the claim of lack of control.

I have elsewhere offered a critical review of the prolific, multi-faceted governance literature.Important differences among them notwithstanding, the leitmotiv in studies and proposals on the governance model is the potential of non-state-centered forms of coordination to tackle the regulatory dilemmas of the global economy. In contrast to state centered, top down, "hard law" the governance model relies mainly on flexible, "soft law" formulated through collaboration among private actors (firms, secondary associations, and so on) and participatory problem solving.In the domain of labor relations, for instance, the "hard law" approach of labor laws formulated and implemented by the state's bureaucracy and courts contrasts with the "soft law" approach of voluntary codes of conduct and consensual monitoring involving firms, commercial and independent monitors, civil society organizations, and other private "stakeholders."

The terms of the contrast between hard law and soft law vary widely across different contributions to the debate on governance. While the most compelling analyses see an affirmative state and an empowered civil society as complementary and mutually reinforcing, studies focusing on the virtues of private self-regulation tend to view the latter as an alternative to top-down state regulation, thus envisioning "a paradigm shift from a regulatory to a governance model." In a neo-Weberian twist, the latter version is based on the implicit or explicit claim that just as the regulatory model had an elective affinity with Fordist capitalism, the governance model (with its emphasis on flexibility and networks of private actors) is attuned to the realities of a global, post-Fordist world economy.

Empirical examination of the process of construction of global governance in the field of international labor rights calls into question sweeping claims of the shift from regulation to governance, from hard law to soft law. Rather than a spontaneous process of replacement of the new for the old based on structural affinity between economic and legal models, the process at work is one of struggle over the type of labor law applicable to TNCs. In other words, the "hardness" of international labor standards is in and of itself a key object of contention between TNCs and their critics.

Hegemonic and counter-hegemonic actors do not have fixed preferences for hard or soft law across the board. Instead, they pragmatically privilege one or the other depending on the object of regulation and the specific circumstances at hand. TNCs, for instance, strategically shift among calls for strengthening national and global hard law in matters essential to the profitability of their business (e.g. intellectual property rights), proposals for soft law and self-regulation in other areas (e.g. voluntary codes of conduct for labor), and deregulation in yet other domains (e.g. financial markets). Thus, neoliberal globalization relies neither on "disciplinary" regulation nor on corporate self regulation or deregulation associated with the "retreat of the state." Rather, neoliberal global governance consists in a mixture of both: hard law to protect corporate rights and soft law to regulate social rights. This is most evident in the contrast between the strict, top-down, global regulatory framework on intellectual property rights—embodied by the WTO Agreement on Trade-Related Aspects of Intellectual Property Rights (TRIPS) and the detailed rules imposed by the US in its bilateral trade agreements—and the loose and largely voluntary international system of labor regulation.

TANs are equally pragmatic in their use of hard and soft law. On the one hand, they exploit the obvious contradiction within TNCs' strategies of selectively defending and attacking state-backed regulation. They do so by simultaneously calling for the softening of corporate-friendly regulation (e.g. through limitations to intellectual property rights for reasons of public health ...) and for the hardening of social regulations. In the labor rights field, this strategy entails initiatives to improve the regulatory capacity of national states as well as the enforcement capabilities of international organizations, notably the ILO. On the other hand, TANs engage in ongoing struggles to establish and determine the conditions of soft law regimes, namely, code of conduct monitoring systems. Numerous national and global unions, NGOs, and solidarity organizations in the North and the South have strived to tum existing monitoring systems from corporate public relations ploys into transparent and effective mechanisms for enforcing labor rights. In the Americas, this has involved such organizations as the Centro de Apoyo al Trabajador and Factor X in Mexico; the Commission on the Verification of Codes of Conduct, and the Federation of Foodstuffs Workers (Festras) in Guatemala; ILRF, USAS, AFL-CIO, and US/LEAP in the US; the Maquila Solidarity Network in Canada; and the regional office of the International Textile, Garment and Leather Workers Federation (ITGLWF).

3.4 LEGAL PLURALISM AND THE STRUGGLE OVER THE SCALES OF LABOR LAW

Enhancing the complexity of the legal field of hard and soft standards is the coexistence of labor regulations at different scales. Now overlapping, now conflicting, factory and local labor regulations operate alongside national laws and regional agreements as well as global standards embodied in ILO conventions and codes of conduct. Just as the determination of the "hardness" of the applicable law, the privileged scale of regulation in any given case is the object of a struggle involving TNCs, TANs, state authorities, and international organizations. Far from privileging a particular scale, hegemonic and counter-hegemonic actors simultaneously pursue strategies at different scales and exploit the legal and political opportunities offered by the tensions and contradictions within and among local, national, regional, and global regulations.

VII. Discussion

As noted by Gregory Shaffer and Mark Pollack, hard and soft law interact differently—as "alternatives," "complements" or "antagonists"—under different "scope conditions" related to the variation in the level of "distributive conflict" among the players.[96] In this chapter, we have seen elements of all three, as state actors and corporations cooperate to varying degrees and with diverse interests in the formation and implementation of laws, codes and standards. Considered further from the standpoint of legal mobilization on the part of workers (as in the Apple case study) or coalitions of retailers (as in the Bangladesh case study), the relevance of the relation between hard and soft law takes on yet further complexity. In both cases, steep power differentials from the standpoint of workers are mitigated by the interests of foreign investors—less so in China, where mobilization takes the form of labor actions and litigation, and moreso in Bangladesh, where the Accord and Alliance protocols serve as proxies for consumers more prominently than they do for workers.

From this standpoint, the availability of treaties and supplier contracts as frameworks for advancing the interests of investors and workers (or other third party beneficiaries) in concert rather than as contest becomes an especially interesting issues. Adelle Blackett refers to such arrangements as "tripartism" (an expression of participatory democracy that draws on "three-way interaction, advisory, or more, between governments, workers, and employers"[97]) and finds in them a "potential" to expand "cosmopolitan democratic participation."[98] Such potential appears to be bearing fruit—if only (and that, a major consideration) because the global financial crisis of 2008 clarified the mutual relevance of a far wider range of stakeholders than is usually considered.[99] In her article on transnational labor law, Kathleen Claussen finds that in comparison with the success of "the investment community . . . in establishing a regime for international investment, the labour community, while making considerable progress in recent years, has not achieved the same enforcement strength in the dispute resolution sphere for cross-border labour disputes."[100] Still, she finds that "the incorporation of labour chapters, with enforcement provisions [in bilateral agreements], suggests that some states are taking advantage of treaties with traction to strengthen commitments to secondary social matters that would not have led to their own internationally enforceable agreements. Put differently, states are making use of treaties with political purchase to rope in additional protections."[101]

---

96. Gregory C. Shaffer & Mark A. Pollack, *Hard vs. Soft Law: Alternatives, Complements, and Antagonists in International Governance*, 94 MINN. L. REV. 706, 724 (2010).

97. Adelle Blackett, *Global Governance, Legal Pluarliasm and the Decentered State: A Labor Law Critique of Codes of Corporate Conduct*, 8 IND. J. GLOB. LEGAL STUD. 401, 434 (2000–2001).

98. *Id.* at 446.

99. Harry Arthurs, *Making Bricks without Straw: The Creation of a Transnational Labour Regime*, 23 (Osgood CLPE, Research Paper No. 28, 2012), http://digitalcommons.osgoode.yorku.ca/cgi/viewcontent.cgi?article=1023&context=clpe.

100. Kathleen Claussen, *The Use of Arbitration to Decide International Labor Disputes*, *in* RESEARCH HANDBOOK ON TRANSNATIONAL LABOUR LAW, 395–407, 406 (Adelle Blackett & Anne Trebilcock, eds., Cheltenham Edward Elgar 2015).

101. *Id.* at 406.

David Schneiderman concludes his study of resistance to economic globalization with an observation of "the central role of states both in binding governments and citizens to transnational legal strictures and in the unique legal capacity of states to undo those contraints"—adding that the state has the unique "jurisdiction to both knit and to unravel technologies of contemporary global governance."[102] We continue this discussion in the following chapter—where a suit brought by Liberian workers at the Firestone plantation shows the courts "unraveling" Alien Tort Statute jurisprudence from its extraterritorial applications.

102. David Schneiderman, Resisting Economic Globalization: Critical Theory and International Investment Law, 159 (Palgrave Macmillan 2016).

Chapter 6

Interlegalities of Offshore Labor

In the previous chapter, we focused on the normative infrastructure of major business corporations' overseas operations. In the cases discussed (Apple in China and the ready made garment industry in Bangladesh), the components of that infrastructure include: (1) accession to the WTO; (2) most favored nation status in the United States; (3) reconciliation of domestic labor law with the industry's supplier code of conduct; (4) reconciliation of the industry standards and the supplier code; and (5) various monitoring and enforcement strategies involving (among others) independent monitoring agencies, the press, consumer actions, and labor actions on the part of workers. Reporting, grievance procedures, monitoring, and enforcement remain contentious, but in both settings still within the terms of the supply chain contracts, and, as we have seen in the case of the apparel industry, in further agreements between producers and coalitions of brand consumers.

In this chapter, offshore corporate activity remains our focus but with two major differences that add significantly to an analysis of transnational law. Here, the main case study involves plantation agriculture—by definition tethered to the land, in contrast to the manufacturing enterprises discussed earlier, and the availability of a large mobile labor force. As we shall see, the located aspects of agricultural and extractive work make a difference to the ways territoriality matters in this transnational context. A further distinction between this chapter and the earlier discussion is the extent to which this one involves domestic courts. The range of legal arenas includes courts (in two countries), labor unions (in two countries), labor rights NGOs, government agencies, and other actors—in other words, a complex interlegality emerging from a historical context in which territoriality, various forms of transnationalism, and transnational law have long been in question. In the case at the heart of this chapter, we shall see that transnational law entails territory not just as the state's fixed spatial dimension, but also as its highly flexible social expression.

I. *Bridgestone* and Alien Tort Statute jurisprudence

The main case in this chapter involves the labor conditions at the Firestone rubber plantation in Harbel, Liberia—vital to the supply of rubber for Bridgestone Tires as well as to the economy of Liberia. The Bridgestone case provides us with an opportunity to assess both the potential and the limits of domestic courts in such contexts—in particular, with regard to the availability of U.S. law for human rights violations overseas. (We deal with courts more extensively in Chapter 8.) The Bridgestone case is especially interesting since it represents a fulcrum or turning point in U.S. jurisprudence on the liability of U.S. corporations for human rights abuses in the context of their offshore operations. The case shows the struggle of the district court judge to preserve some aspect of the plaintiffs' standing in U.S. courts. His ruling was subsequently reversed, overtaken by circuit court opinions and ultimately a landmark Supreme Court case, *Kiobel v. Dutch Oil* (also discussed below). The Bridgestone case thus gives us an opportunity to consider the ways U.S. jurisprudence with regard to the Alien Tort Statute is in flux, tending to withhold from U.S. courts the availability of human rights law where overseas investments are concerned.

The case is interesting for other reasons as well. At the Firestone plantation, workers are positioned differently vis-à-vis the labor market than in the industrial sectors we have discussed so far. In the previous chapter, Foxconn and the garment manufacturers in Bangladesh worked with labor recruiters in a position to mobilize rural and small town labor for their respective forms of urban employment—in the case of Foxconn, doing so quickly, and on a large scale. In this chapter, the situation is entirely different: the workers at the Firestone plantation are mainly fourth generation rubber tappers who come by their positions by descent—i.e., most adult workers are the children, grandchildren, and greatgrandchildren of rubber tappers, a system that has prevailed since the establishment of the plantation in 1926. In effect, for many Firestone workers, there is no labor market as such; workers come to their jobs by inheritance. More generally, plantation work—like other forms of agricultural and extractive work—is not mobile in the same way that manufacturing can be, given the literal groundedness of the enterprise. Plantation labor, and to a lesser extent, labor in mining and other forms of extraction (oil, for example[1]) are subjects of extensive anthropological accounts. These studies emphasize the extent to which such operations involve steeply asymmetrical relations, structured around racial, ethnic, gender, and class categories that continue the heritage of colonial overrule—even if the colonial status has terminated.[2] But plantations such as we

1. See Chapter 7 for a discussion of the plethora of cases related to Chevron's operations in Ecuador.

2. Examples from anthropological studies of plantations include: On privatization and plantation work in Tanzania: Alison Holt Norris & Eric Worby, *The Sexual Economy of a Sugar Plantation: Privatization and Social Welfare in Northern Tanzania*, 39 Am. Ethnologist 354 (2012). On contemporary plantation labor law in India: Sarah Besky, *Can a Plantation be Fair? Paradoxes and Possibilities in Fair Trade Darjeeling Tea Certification*, 29 Anthropology of Work Rev. 1 (2008). On health disparities in Sri Lanka tea plantations: Ramani Hettiarachchi, *Colonialism and Health Policy Affecting Workers in Sri Lanka's Plantation Sector*, 27 Anthropology of Work Rev. 14 (2006). On a plantation subsidiary of United Fruit Company: Philippe Bourgois, *Conjugated Oppression: Class and Ethnicity Among Guaymi and Kuna Banana* Workers, 15 Am. Ethnologist 328 (1988). On coffee plantations in transnational tourism and gourmet supply markets: Sarah

discuss in this chapter are also modern enterprises of the global economy—as both transnational businesses and social systems embedded within the national states where they operate.

A. *Bridgestone* and *Flomo*: Labor without labor markets

The Firestone plantation in Harbel, Liberia, at issue in the Bridgestone and Flomo cases about to be discussed, is the largest agricultural operation in Liberia, dominating not only the rubber sector but the country's agricultural sector as a whole, in this mainly agricultural country. [3] Underlying the restrictions set on the availability of ATS and human rights law by the courts in Bridgestone and Flomo were the ILO's conventions on coerced labor and worst forms of child labor. In the absence of a fence or other physical restraint making exit impossible, the courts found that labor conditions on the plantation did not meet the standard for forced labor. In his District Court opinion, Judge Hamilton notes the practical difficulties impinging on that freedom—miles of dense forest without roads, the lack of personal resources beyond what the plantation makes available to workers (housing and marginal services), and the stark challenges of the Liberian labor market. He also notes the particular constraints for children, given their dependent status and vulnerability to the physical hazards of rubber tapping (strong chemicals and heavy loads, primarily). ILO Convention 182 (on worst forms of child labor) includes provision for hazardous work, but leaves the standards for defining hazards, monitoring known hazards, and enforcing protective measures to the respective countries within parameters set by the ILO.[4]

Lyon, *Coffee Tourism in Chiapas: Recasting Colonial Narratives for Contemporary Markets*, 35 Culture, Agric., Food & Envt. 125 (2013). On workers' worldviews within a British plantation in Argentina: Gaston Gordillo, *The Breath of the Devils: Memories and Places of an Experience of Terror*, 29 Am. Ethnologist 33 (2002). On labor activism in plantation zones: Yarimar Bonilla, *The Past Is Made By Walking: Labor Activism and Historical Production in Postcolonial Guadeloupe*, 26 Cultural Anthropology 313 (2011). On coal mining and oil drilling: Anthony F.C. Wallace, Saint Clair: A Nineteenth-Century Coal Town's Experience with a Disaster-Prone Industry (1988); Subterranean Estates: Lifeworlds of Oil and Gas (Hannah Appel, Arthur Mason & Michael Watts, eds., 2015.

3. United States Department of Labor, Bureau of International Labor Affairs, Liberia: 2013 Findings on the Worst Forms of Child Labor (2013). *See also* Department of Labor, Bureau of International Labor Affairs, Project to Combat Child Labor in Areas of Liberian Rubber Production: Notice of Availability of Funds and Solicitation for Cooperative Agreement 4–5 (2012) ("The rubber sector is . . . the largest private employer in Liberia."). Recent progress in child labor and worker safety has come about through the Government of Liberia's land lease and concession agreements with some rubber companies, as well as through collective bargaining agreements between companies and unions, barring child labor. In-country advocates are also pressing for legislation in Liberia that would restrict child labor.

4. *Convention 182*, Int'l Labour Org., http://www.ilo.org/ipec/Campaignandadvocacy/Youthinaction/C182-Youth-orientated/C182Youth_Convention/lang—en/index.htm. (last visited Oct. 8, 2016). This convention was the first to be adopted unanimously by ILO countries (in 1999), and was ratified more quickly than any provision in the history of the ILO. On the development of

The courts' and ILO standards are apparently predicated on a default view of work as the consequence of occupational choice in a competitive labor market—as if continued employment in the absence of physical restraint were *prima facie* evidence of the worker's choice or preference. Or, to put this another way, working is—by itself—presumptive evidence of an individual's choice (even if the only alternative is no paid work at all). This premise is questionable, especially where labor markets are weak. The economist Karl Polanyi's celebrated analysis of the history of modern economic life, *The Great Transformation*, suggests that the very idea of a "labor market" presupposes a "market society" in which society and its institutions are imagined to be subordinate to economic relations, and designed accordingly.[5] One aspect of the emergence of the early modern market society in England, he argues, was the commodification of labor, such that labor was treated like any other commercial product and priced according to the market rather than the inherent needs of the worker him/herself.

Polanyi emphasizes the extent to which labor—along with land and money—have become "elements of industry" and marketable as such, in spite of being goods that were not made "for sale."[6] In contexts where employment is not primarily accessible through market means, such as on the Firestone plantation, Polanyi's evocation of labor is particularly apt: "Labor is only another name for a human activity which goes with life itself, which in its turn is not produced for sale but entirely different reasons, nor can that activity be detached from the rest of life, be stored, or mobilized,"[7] leading Polanyi to conclude that "the commodity description of labor, land, and money is entirely fictitious."[8] By this, he means that there is no natural or objective basis on which to decide the value of labor, land and money. Such fictions are core truths of modern times—their alternatives scarcely imaginable until one reflects on familiar pragmatic forms of career-building savvy (networking for job opportunities, for example), or accepts as entirely normal the fact that household work by family members (caring for a partner, children and elders, cleaning and cooking) is unwaged and unsalaried (a labor of love).

Polanyi stresses the anomalous nature of this disembedding of labor relations from social relations of other kinds in comparison to tribal, feudal, and early

---

the Convention on Worst Forms of Child Labor (C182) and its continuum relationship with earlier conventions on Child Labor (Clause 32) and hazardous labor (Recommendation 190), see G.K. Lieten *The ILO Setting the Terms in the Child Labor Debate*, *in* ILO Histories: Essays on the International Labor Organization and Its Impact on the World During the Twentieth Century 443-460 (Jasmien Van Daele, Magaly Rodriguez Garcia, Geert Van Goethem & Marcel van der Linden, eds. 2010). For ILO Recommendation 190, see: http://www.ilo.org/dyn/normlex/en/f?p=NORMLEXPUB:55:0:::55:P55_TYPE,P55_LANG,P55_DOCUMENT,P55_NODE:SUP,en,R190,/Document.

5. Karl Polanyi, The Great Transformation: The Political and Economic Origins of Our Time 74 (Beacon Press 2d ed. 2001) (1944).

6. *Id.* at 71-80.

7. *Id.* at 75.

8. *Id.* at 76.

mercantilist systems.[9] His insight, though historically tied to England, is suggestive with regard to those and other non-market means by which people enter into employment. The relevance of his insight to the Bridgestone/Flomo cases is in the way it highlights the non-market paths by which labor has been recruited to the Firestone plantation since its inception in 1926—initially by armed labor recruiters, and subsequently by descent (by now four generations deep), ethnic ties, and by family relations (parents and their children constituting a work unit). Firestone may not have hired children as employees, but managers set the work requirement for full wages at such a level that single adults could not fulfill the daily quota without calling on the aid of their spouse and children.[10] Anthropological accounts of plantation labor detail various circumstances in which children labor for their kin—cushioning domestic economies against fluctuations in demand, or in return for subsistence.[11] In offering these observations, we leave to one side the situation of the Firestone plantation during the fourteen years of civil war that engulfed Liberia from 1989 to 2003 (as discussed in the excerpt below, the company allowed Charles Taylor's security forces to occupy the plantation in return for guarantees of security). The civil war was the context for the plaintiffs' grievances in at least two respects: first, their wages lost value by over a third when, during the occupation, the plantation was "dollarized" (i.e., converted from Liberian currency to the United States dollar); and second, the pervasive violence throughout the Liberian countryside during the years of war made its own fence, so to speak.

B. Territory as the expression of transnationalism: The Liberia Truth and Reconciliation Commission Reports

The lease arrangement that provided land for Firestone represented an exchange based on a convergence of interests between the United States and Liberia. The value of the land, and the availability of Liberia's territory for U.S. interests, shifted many times as circumstances changed. The question of the significance of territoriality as litigated in Bridgestone is only the most recent iteration of an arrangement that dates back a century and more. The original Firestone lease was arranged between the U.S. State Department and the Government of Liberia. As U.S. strategic interests deepened in Liberia and in relation to Firestone in particular, the plantation became a materialization of privilege within a transnational regime built on steeply asymmetrical social, political, economic, and military relations. That system prevailed until the civil war erupted in 1989, plunging the country into chaos and resulting in massive displacement of the population (internally and externally, including thousands of emigres to the United States), widespread death and

9. *Id.*

10. *ILRF Engages Firestone in Journalistic Crossfile*, INT'L LABOR RIGHTS FORUM (Nov. 14, 2006), http://www.laborrights.org/blog/200611/ilrf-engages-firestone-journalistic-crossfire.

11. *See, e.g.*, Albert Schrauwers. *Negotiating Parentage: The Political Economy of "Kinship" in Central Sulawesi, Indonesia*, 26 AM. ETHNOLOGIST 310, 312–314, 320 (1999).

destruction, and unstable national borders. With the peace agreement in 2003, the transitional government initiated a process of consolidation and rebuilding, eventually including the establishment of a Truth and Reconciliation Commission. The Firestone/Bridgestone lawsuit was first filed in the United States in 2005.

The following excerpts from the Liberia Truth and Reconciliation Commission 2009 report[12] provide a condensed history of Firestone in Liberia, from its inception through the years of civil war to the present, including a brief reference to then ongoing litigation involving Firestone:

Truth and Reconciliation Commission of Liberia, Report—Preliminary Findings (2009)

From the settling of freedmen in Liberia in 1822 to the coup d'etat of 1980 and the outbreak of armed conflict in 1989, systemic inequality and disenfranchisement from the founding of the Republic to the present has created an immature political culture incapable of producing genuine democracy. While this phenomenon can be linked to the policies of the ACS [American Colonization Society], native Liberian independence claims and Americo-Liberian hegemony, it was the warlord politics—the economic and political treasures of war—of the late 1980's and 1990's and its marriage to globalization and transnational corporatist interests that have served as the most critical conflict causes. Doe's brutal ethnical regime coupled with Charles Taylor's warlord politics have seemingly replaced the old settler-native paradigm with a new form of greed politics that relies equally on the vote of the gun.[13]

Truth and Reconciliation Commission of Liberia, Consolidated Final Report, vol. 2

115–116, 119–120, 160, 288, 303–308

The national life of early Liberia was complicated by chronic financial problems. . . . And in the absence of productive industry to generate funds for sustenance of the bureaucracy, an era of foreign loans was initiated. The first loan of 1871 led to others in 1906, 1912 and 1926. As collateral for these loans, many at high interest rates, state revenues (largely from customs tariffs) were conceded and indigenous lands and produce rights were granted. It was this outward-looking economic

---

12. The chair of the Truth and Reconciliation Commission was Jerome Verdier, a Liberian environmental lawyer who brought the original Bridgestone lawsuit in California. The suit was also based on the research of Alfred Lahai Brownell, president and founder of the Association of Environmental Lawyers of Liberia ("Green Advocates"). *See* Int'l Labor Rights Forum Blog, www.laborrights.org/blog/201003. *See also* Haider Rizvi, *LIBERIA: Firestone Sued Over "Slave" Plantation* (Dec. 8, 2005), http://www.laborrights.org/in-the-news/liberia-firestone-sued-over-slave-plantation.

13. Truth and Reconciliation Commission of Liberia, Final Report: Preliminary Findings and Determinations 53 (2009), http://trcofliberia.org/reports/final-report.

policy that led to the era of concession agreements; the most notable being with Firestone in 1926.

But Liberia had hardly overcome international intrigue, including American high-handedness during the negotiations for the Firestone agreement when, in 1929, allegations of government complicity in a "forced labor" scheme were made. While the external component of the allegations related to Liberia's competition for an African contract labor market in which European colonialists held a commanding role, the internal components reflected yet another consequence of policy choice by the Liberian leadership. Public officials and their associates reaping financial rewards from a system akin to slavery and forced labor involving indigenous Liberians was not a pretty sight. The Liberian state was censured internationally for complicity in a system that the League of Nations alleged was "hardly distinguishable from slave-raiding and slave trading." The political fallout from that crisis . . . led to the downfall of the administration of President Charles D.B. King (1920–1930). To Edwin Barclay (1930–1944), his successor, fell the task of unraveling the internal and external complications of that sordid episode. Those European powers in the League that sought to abrogate Liberia's independence by advocating protectorate mandate status were thwarted both because of the contradictions in international relations as well as the determination of the Barclay administration to forestall that possibility.

The forced labor crisis deeply affected Liberia's governance of segments of its indigenous population. Aggrieved indigenous leaders resisted government authority, even at times attempting to make common cause with external foes of the state. The Barclay administration adopted very repressive policies, which in time came to be intolerant of all political dissent. The Liberian state may have consolidated, but at a price that carried implications for national unity.[14]

Prior to 1940, most parts of the Liberian hinterland were completely lacking in infrastructure. There was virtually no public education, piped water, road system or electricity. The American military presence in Liberia gave the Liberian economy a huge boost. . . .

Liberia began this special relationship with the United States by converting its national currency from the British pound sterling to the United States dollar; United States Lend Lease funds were made available to the Liberian Government, to subsidize the construction of Liberia's first port, the Freeport of Monrovia; the first major airport, Roberts Field, was constructed by Pan Am and the U. S. Government; American military engineers began the construction of major roads from Monrovia to the interior of Liberia.

The American military presence also had a stabilizing effect on the social and political relationship between the Liberian state and indigenous Liberians. The artificial boundary drawn between Liberia and its provinces was broken. Thousands of

14. Truth and Reconciliation Commission of Liberia, Consolidated Final Report, vol. 2, 115–116 (2009), http://trcofliberia.org/reports/final-report.

laborers from the interior of Liberia descended on the coastal region, especially to Roberts Field and the Firestone Rubber Plantations, in search of jobs. This massive migration of indigenous Liberians, which the Liberian Government had previously attempted to restrain by legislation (Liberian territory extended for 40 miles in the interior), and through an agreement with Firestone Plantations Company in the 1920s, was subsequently erased.

* * *

The downside to this American military presence were charges that African-American troops murdered, physically abused, and denigrated indigenous people who lived adjacent to the base. Civilians venturing around the military facilities were reportedly shot at and sometimes killed with impunity. The town adjacent to Roberts Field was even named "Smell-no-Taste" by the local people, because they complained that they smelled the American food, and either never tasted it or never had enough of it. It must be pointed out that these are charges that have been made by eyewitnesses over the years, but have never been investigated and substantiated. It is possible that the firing were warning shots, intended to keep out people from sensitive military equipments and supplies.[15]

[As civil war took hold,] [a] strong desire to end the conflict and secure the peace, led the international community to consider arms embargo on Liberia and further sanctions on the export of raw materials; timber and diamond exports from Liberia. Rubber exports, especially by Firestone, continued throughout the conflict period without sanctions. The US Government made representations for the continuation of this trade during the conflict on behalf of Firestone. Firestone resumed full scale operations on January 22, 1992 pursuant to a memorandum of understanding signed January 17, 1992, with Charles Taylor's NPFL [National Patriotic Front of Liberia] awarding the NPFL US$2 million annually in exchange for NPFL's protection. Firestone plantation was the launch pad for NPFL's infamous "Operation Octopus" attack on Monrovia and ECOMOG [Economic Community Cease-Fire Monitoring Group[16]] to unseat IGNU [International Government of National Unity[17]].[18]

Following the launch of the war, Taylor accumulated millions of dollars within months. He was able to exploit existing industries through activities such as levying fees for industry rights and appropriating a portion of the profits, selling off deserted equipment in NPFL territory, and making demands for equipment, foreign currency, electricity, fuel and oil from timber and mining companies. The NPFL took over rubber plantations at various stages of the two civil wars to obtain other commodities, and corporations allegedly collaborated, by paying rebels for protection and providing

15. *Id.* at 119–120.

16. ECOMOG was a military force under the control of ECOWAS (Economic Community of West African States). *See Waging War to Keep the Peace: The ECOMOG Intervention and Human Rights*, Human Rights Watch vol. 5 (1993), https://www.hrw.org/reports/1993/liberia/#1.

17. *Id.*

18. *Id.* at 160.

them with logistical and other assistance. Other rebel groups later emulated this tactic of taking over rubber plantations. When MODEL [Movement for Democracy in Liberia] took over the Liberian Agricultural Company (LAC) plantation, LAC staff offered the rebels money, vehicles and electronics in an effort to deter the rebels from devastating the plantation. In addition to controlling government coffers and engaging in private procurement activities, Taylor exploited natural resources, including diamonds, rubber, timber, and iron ore, to fuel the war.[19]

In the decades since the United States began intervening in the fate of this small West African territory, it has alternately supported, exploited, welcomed, and abandoned Liberia and Liberians. While the relationship over time has been complex, during several key periods the United States' actions and omissions have led to disastrous results for Liberians. A social system patterned after life in the United States—specifically after life in the pre-civil war American south—predominated. This system was paternalistic in nature and was highly stratified based on wealth and skin color. . . .

A significant driver in the relationship between the United States and Liberia has been U.S. commercial interests. In the nineteen-twenties, U.S. demand for rubber was growing in conjunction with the growth of the U.S. auto industry. In order to break British dominance in the global rubber market, the Firestone Tire and Rubber Company ("Firestone") sought, with assistance from the U.S. State Department, a concession from the Liberian government to tap Liberia's significant rubber resources. In exchange for a $5,000,000 loan from Firestone (which Liberia subsequently used to settle its foreign debt), Liberia leased 1,000,000 acres for ninety nine years at a price of six cents per acre. According to some scholars, Firestone never carried out many of its promises to develop Liberia's infrastructure and the loan was designed to keep Liberia permanently indebted. In addition, the Firestone agreement gave the company ownership of any minerals or oil found in the leased area. In the late nineteen-twenties and early nineteen thirties, Firestone, along with other international entities, was implicated in a forced labor scandal that led to a League of Nations investigation. The Liberian government was ultimately found to have used slavery-like practices to supply laborers to Spanish controlled plantations as well as to the Firestone rubber plantation. The Commission found however, that there was "no evidence that Firestone Plantations Company consciously employs any but voluntary labor on its leased rubber plantations."

* * *

Almost a century after the League of Nations inquiry, Firestone is still under scrutiny for unfair labor practices amounting to forced and child labor. Firestone is currently the object of an Alien Tort Claims Act suit in U.S. court. Nevertheless, the U.S. government has continued its support for Firestone. During the conflict period when most industries in Liberia were sanctioned so as to avoid resources fueling the conflict, rubber remained in legal production.

---

19. *Id.* at 288.

While the UN gave some consideration to imposing sanctions on Liberia's rubber industry in October 2001, U.S. lobbying on behalf of Firestone and the potential economic impact prevented the Security Council from taking further action. In addition to rubber, Liberia's natural resources of iron ore and diamonds were mined and brought a steady influx of U.S. dollars into Liberia until the late nineteen-seventies. A U.S. government memo prepared in the late nineteen-seventies estimated U.S. economic interests in Liberia to be in excess of $300 million in assets. One of these significant assets included the Liberian Maritime Registry, which was run by a U.S. based company that remitted profits to the Government of Liberia .... In 1999, the Liberian Government signed an agreement to transfer administration of the maritime registry to LISCR, a U.S. company run by Taylor associates.

This change provided Taylor with the opportunity to divert millions of dollars from the shipping industry. In addition to providing funds to Taylor, LISCR directly or indirectly aided Taylor and the civil war by agreeing to send registry revenue to nongovernmental bank accounts. A UN Panel of Experts found that this money was used for the delivery of weapons.

In 1910, at the request of the Liberian government, the U.S. Navy sent two war ships to the Liberia coast. Their presence assisted the Liberian Frontier Force in warding off attacks from indigenous armies. Later, from 1912 until 1922 the Frontier Force, which later became the AFL [Armed Forces of Liberia], was led by African-American U.S. Military personnel. The two nations maintained a bilateral military relationship, with the United States positioning its strategic interests and assets within Liberia, and Liberia posing a number of requests for military assistance to the United States. Such military agreements began early with a 1942 defense pact between Liberia and the United States. In 1959, the United States and Liberia signed a mutual defense pact, which provided Liberians with a sense of security and the belief that the United States would come to its aid in case of attack. The United States gained significant strategic assets based on its interactions with Liberia. These included use of Roberts International Airport "without restriction to support U.S. policy objectives," a communications station that provided communications for thirty-four U.S. Embassies and Consulates in Africa, the OMEGA Navigational Station; the Voice of America transmitter and receiver facilities, and the right to establish military installations in the Monrovia port, "should they become necessary for the maintenance of international peace and security."

During the latter part of the nineteen-seventies, however, the close relationship between Liberia and the United States began to deteriorate as President Tolbert adopted a more conciliatory policy towards non-aligned countries. Immediately after the 1980 coup, the U.S. Government's actions were driven by the policies of protecting important U.S. assets in Liberia and preventing the spread of socialism. Accordingly, the United States embraced the Doe administration so as to counteract the influence of the Ethiopians, Libyans, and Russians.

After the 1985 fraudulent elections, the United States failed to withdraw their support for Doe and this shocked many Liberians. Despite condemnations from

Congress regarding the conduct of the 1985 elections, the Reagan administration continued to recognize Doe as the legitimate leader of Liberia and continued to provide him with support. Moreover, the United States provided intelligence to Doe warning him of a coup attempt that was being planned by Doe's PRC [People's Redemption Council] co-founder, Thomas Quiwonkpa. When the coup attempt failed, Quiwonkpa was brutally murdered, and Doe unleashed a campaign of revenge attacks across the country.

Although the United States dramatically decreased its provision of aid during the second half of the nineteen-eighties, the United States was still providing more aid per capita to Liberia than to any other West African nation at the time. In the latter half of the nineteen-eighties even Congressional interest waned as "Liberia had been eclipsed . . . by the question of sanctions against South Africa."

During the conflict from 1989–1997, however, White House officials dismissed the notion that the United States had a special relationship with Liberia. National Security Advisor Robert Gates described the historical relationship as, "meaningless; it doesn't govern us anymore; we treat Liberia just like any other country, and we have no real interest there." Although some diplomatic officials in the region made efforts to secure an end to the fighting, their efforts were blocked at a high level. Moreover, the American public's attention was focused elsewhere, on a war in the Persian Gulf. There were some other early attempts by the United States to engage in diplomatic mediation in an effort to persuade Doe to hold early elections, as well as an aborted attempt to facilitate President Doe's departure and exile into Togo. National Security Advisor, General Brent Scowcroft, reportedly explained that the United States' decision not to extract Doe was based on the view that if the United States had facilitated Doe's departure, the United States would be responsible for taking care of Liberia from that point onward. . . .

Despite the behind the scenes support, negotiations and humanitarian assistance, the United States never sent a sustained peacekeeping mission to Liberia.

The United States role can be summarized as follows:

- Support for the authoritarian rule of the ACS and the settlers' hegemony;
- Support by turning a blind eye to over 27 years of Tubman's rule under a virtual police state pursuant to its cold war objective and intent;
- Pursuant also to its cold war interest, it undermined Tolbert and sought regime change in Liberia because of his ultra liberal non-alignment policy;
- Pursuant also to its economic, commercial and cold war interest, the US supported the Doe junta in an unprecedented way that made Doe the highest recipient of US per capita aid ever in sub-Saharan Africa; most aimed at acquiring military hardware which was used to suppress and violate human rights;
- Even though it was clear that the 1985 elections were rigged, the US supported Doe and declared the elections were free and continued to support the

administration until it no longer served the US long-term interest. Then, support was shifted to Charles Taylor;

- Pursuant to a Defense Pact with Liberia, Liberians were disappointed when the US failed to intervene on at least two occasions to stop the war and prevent the carnage;
- The US acted on all occasions and in all instances first and foremost to foster its economic, commercial and political interests in Liberia rather than protecting the rights of the Liberian people and enhancing their development;
- The US role in Liberia's war by its abandonment of the notion of "special and traditional" relationship with Liberia which under current policies has no meaning to the USA.[20]

II. Legal challenges to plantation labor practices in Liberia

The distinctive situation of plantation agriculture around the world gives us an opportunity to consider how contemporary forms of transnationalism map onto older legal forms. Plantation labor conditions also provide a context to reconsider the premises by which labor is legally deemed to be either coerced or (by contrast) oppressed. As we shall see, as global institutions such as the IMF and the World Bank press particular forms of fiscal accountability on poorer countries, and international trade implicates state borders in multiple ways, territoriality itself comes into question in relation to both state sovereignty and international human rights. Both angles are visible in this chapter, since the Bridgestone case—involving the Alien Tort Statute (ATS) as the basis for a human rights claim in Liberia—unfolded in a larger context that involved the ATS, ultimately resulting in a major revision of ATS jurisprudence at the United States Supreme Court. Both sets of issues—the human rights of plantation laborers and ATS—initially converged on the question of corporate liability. Let us turn now to Bridgestone, emphasizing its legal context in ATS jurisprudence.

A. Roe v. Bridgestone Corporation

In *Roe v. Bridgestone*, 492 F. Supp. 2d 988 (S.D. Ind. 2007), a group of Liberian rubber plantation workers, including adults and children, brought an action against Bridgestone Corporation, a multinational corporation, and other defendants.[21] The plaintiffs alleged that defendants were liable for forced labor, forced child labor, poor working conditions, and low wages under the ATS, the Thirteenth Amendment of the United States Constitution, a federal statute authorizing civil

20. *Id.* at 303–08.

21. *Bridgestone*, 92 F. Supp. 2d at 988.

actions for criminal forced labor violations, and California law.[22] The defendants filed motions to dismiss for lack of subject matter jurisdiction and for failure to state a claim.[23]

The court denied defendants' motion to dismiss all claims for lack of subject matter jurisdiction and denied defendants' motion to dismiss for failure to state a claim as it related to the child plaintiffs. However, the court upheld defendants' motion to dismiss for failure to state a claim as it related to the adult plaintiffs. The following excerpt illustrates the court's holding as it pertained to claims filed under the ATS for both the adult and child plaintiffs.

Roe v. Bridgestone Corp.

492 F. Supp. 2d 988 (S.D. Ind. 2007)

* * *

C. The Alien Tort Statute

The ATS was enacted in 1789 by the First Congress, but it was used only rarely before 1980. That is when the Second Circuit held in *Filartiga v. Pena-Irala*, 630 F.2d 876 (2d Cir. 1980), that citizens of Paraguay could use the ATS to sue another citizen of Paraguay in a United States district court for the torture and death of their son in Paraguay as a violation of international law. Since *Filartiga* held that the ATS could reach wrongs committed in other nations, many plaintiffs have used the ATS to pursue a wide variety of international human rights cases in United States federal courts. See Harold Hongju Koh, *Transnational Public Law Litigation*, 100 Yale L.J. 2347, 2366 (1991); Curtis A. Bradley, *The Alien Tort Statute and Article III*, 42 Va. J. Intl L. 587, 588 (2002); Fuks, Sosa v. Alvarez-Machain *and the Future of ATCA Litigation: Examining Bonded Labor Claims and Corporate Liability*, 106 Colum. L. Rev. 112 (2006). In recent years, the ATS has been used to assert many claims against private corporations. . . .

In 2004, the Supreme Court gave its first detailed consideration to the scope of the ATS in *Sosa v. Alvarez-Machain*, 542 U.S. 692 (2004). That decision effectively supersedes many of the earlier circuit and district court opinions on several key issues. *Sosa* requires close attention, beginning with its facts. Plaintiff Alvarez-Machain was a physician and a citizen of Mexico. United States Drug Enforcement Administration officials received information that led them to believe that Dr. Alvarez had been involved in the torture and murder of an American DEA agent in Mexico in 1985. A United States grand jury indicted Dr. Alvarez, and a United States warrant was issued for his arrest. After unsuccessful efforts to use the usual channels for arresting and transporting a suspect from another country, the DEA approved a plan to hire Mexican nationals to seize Dr. Alvarez and bring him to the United States. He was abducted from his house, held overnight in a motel, and then brought to the

---

22. *Id.* at 990–93, 995–96.

23. *Id.* at 991.

United States by private plane, where he was arrested on the United States charges. He was eventually acquitted of the criminal charges in the United States. 54 U.S. at 697–99.

Dr. Alvarez then sued in a United States federal court under the ATS, among other claims, on the theory that his arrest and detention amounted to torts in violation of international law. The district court and Ninth Circuit eventually ruled in favor of Dr. Alvarez under the ATS. The Supreme Court reversed and ordered dismissal.

The Supreme Court unanimously concluded that the ATS "enabled federal courts to hear claims in a very limited category defined by the law of nations and recognized at common law," but that "the limited, implicit sanction to entertain the handful of international law cum common law claims understood in 1789" should not be taken as authority to recognize the right of action asserted by Dr. Alvarez. 542 U.S. at 712. After a detailed review of the history of the ATS, the unanimous portion of the Court's opinion concluded: "The jurisdictional grant is best read as having been enacted on the understanding that the common law would provide a cause of action for the modest number of international law violations with a potential for personal liability at the time." *Id.* at 724. The First Congress probably had in mind only three such wrongs identified by Blackstone in his Commentaries: violations of safe conducts, violations of the rights of ambassadors, and piracy. *Id.*

The *Sosa* Court divided on whether federal courts may recognize additional torts beyond those three. The dissenters said no. The majority decided to leave the judicial door "ajar subject to vigilant door-keeping, and thus open to a narrow class of international norms today." *Id.* at 729. What did the Court mean by vigilant door-keeping? The Court posted many warning signs against judicial innovation under the ATS, and then held that the extra judicial arrest and abduction of Dr. Alvarez did not pass the test. The Court wrote:

> Whatever the ultimate criteria for accepting a cause of action subject to jurisdiction under § 1350, we are persuaded that federal courts should not recognize private claims under federal common law for violations of any international law norm with less definite content and acceptance among civilized nations than the historical paradigms familiar when § 1350 was enacted. . . . And the determination whether a norm is sufficiently definite to support a cause of action should (and, indeed, inevitably must) involve an element of judgment about the practical consequences of making that cause available to litigants in the federal courts.

542 U.S. at 732–33 (citations and footnotes omitted).

The Court wrote that its standard was generally consistent with the Ninth Circuit's earlier formulation that plaintiffs must show a violation of an international norm that is "specific, universal, and obligatory." *Id.* at 732, quoting *In re Estate of Marcos Human Rights Litigation*, 25 F.3d 1467, 1475 (9th Cir. 1994).

Before reaching that conclusion, the Court identified five reasons for "judicial caution" when considering additional claims that might be recognized under the ATS. The first is the change in the concept of the common law since 1789, recognizing that judges do not find or discover the common law, but make it, which calls for discretionary judgment. 542 U.S. at 725–26. The second is the change in the role of federal courts in making common law after *Erie Railroad Co. v. Tompkins*, 304 U.S. 64 (1938). The third is the recent shift in favor of deferring more to legislative judgment in deciding whether to recognize any private right of action under federal law, particularly in light of "the possible collateral consequences of making international rules privately actionable." 542 U.S. at 727. The fourth is the potential implications for the nation's foreign relations, especially in claiming the power to impose limits on the powers of foreign governments over their own citizens and to hold them accountable in the courts of the United States. *Id.* at 727. The fifth is the absence of any express congressional mandate "to seek out and define new and debatable violations of the law of nations," along with indications that Congress does not want to encourage "greater judicial creativity" in this area. *Id.* at 728.

After posting all these caution signs and requiring that any innovation under the ATS would need to be based on norms of international law as specific, universal, and obligatory as Blackstone's three, the Court then turned to Dr. Alvarez's claim. The Court reviewed available sources of international law and determined that there was not an international norm against arbitrary arrest that was as specific and binding as the eighteenth century common law norms against violations of safe conducts, violations of ambassadors' rights, and piracy. *Id.* at 734–37. The Court's analysis provides a framework for lower courts approaching such issues.

First, while the Court recognized the "moral authority" of the Universal Declaration of Human Rights, it found that the document had no legally binding force. 542 U.S. at 734–35. Second, although the United States had ratified the International Covenant on Civil and Political Rights, it did so with the express understanding that the Covenant was not self-executing. Notwithstanding its moral authority, the Covenant therefore did not create obligations enforceable in federal courts. *Id.* at 735.

On the plaintiff's claim that his arrest and detention violated customary international law, the *Sosa* Court was troubled by the broad scope of his theory, that an arrest or detention anywhere in the world that was unauthorized by local law would also violate international law and support a federal case under the ATS. *Id.* at 736–37. Of particular interest for present purposes, the Court noted that Section 702 of the Restatement (Third) of Foreign Relations Law of the United States (1986), said that a "state violates international law if, as a matter of state policy, it practices, encourages, or condones . . . prolonged arbitrary detention." The Court then commented:

> Although the Restatement does not explain its requirements of a "state policy" and of "prolonged" detention, the implication is clear. Any credible invocation of a principle against arbitrary detention that the civilized world accepts as binding customary international law requires a factual basis beyond relatively brief detention in excess of positive authority. Even the

> Restatement's limits are only the beginning of the enquiry, because although it is easy to say that some policies of prolonged arbitrary detentions are so bad that those who enforce them become enemies of the human race, it may be harder to say which policies cross that line with the certainty afforded by Blackstone's three common law offenses. In any event, the label would never fit the reckless policeman who botches his warrant, even though that same officer might pay damages under municipal law. . . .

As shown below, there is a broad international consensus that at least some extreme practices called "forced labor" violate universal and binding international norms. But the adult plaintiffs in this case allege labor practices that lie somewhere on a continuum that ranges from those clear violations of international law (slavery or labor forced at the point of soldiers' bayonets) to more ambiguous situations involving poor working conditions and meager or exploitative wages. The *Sosa* Court ultimately concluded that the plaintiff's claim based on arrest and detention depended on an aspiration in "the present, imperfect world" that exceeded any binding customary rule that was sufficiently specific to reach his case, and so ordered dismissal. *Id.* at 738; accord, *Doe v. Qi*, 349 F. Supp. 2d 1258, 1278 (N.D. Cal. 2004) ("The question of whether a claim under the ATCA lies thus turns on whether the specific facts (not the general characterization of the claim) violate[d] international norms that are 'specific, universal and obligatory.'").

D. Case Law Dealing with Forced Labor

Plaintiffs cite several pre-*Sosa* federal cases holding or stating that "forced labor" violates the law of nations. Those cases show that some forms of forced labor violate the law of nations, but the facts in those cases are so different from the plaintiffs' allegations in this case as to show that the label "forced labor" adds little to the needed analysis.

In *Iwanowa v. Ford Motor Co.*, 67 F. Supp. 2d 424 (D.N.J. 1999), the plaintiff alleged that during World War II, she was literally sold from her home in Russia and transported by Nazi troops to Germany to work for the German subsidiary of Ford under inhuman conditions and without compensation. 67 F. Supp. 2d at 433–34, 440–41. Then 17 years old, the plaintiff was forced to live with 65 other deportees in a wooden hut without heat, running water, or sewage facilities, and they were locked in at night. *Id.* at 433–34. She was required to perform heavy labor drilling holes in engine blocks. Company officials, she alleged, used rubber truncheons to beat workers who failed to meet their quotas. *Id.* at 434. In the course of dismissing all of her claims on other grounds, the court stated that "the case law and statements of the Nuremberg Tribunals unequivocally establish that forced labor violates customary international law." *Id.* at 441.

In *In re World War II Era Japanese Forced Labor Litigation*, 164 F. Supp. 2d 1160, 1179 (N.D. Cal. 2001), the court also dismissed all claims as time-barred but stated it was inclined to agree with the Iwanowa conclusion that forced labor violates the law of nations. The district court opinion did not dwell on the historical details, but the Ninth Circuit opinion affirming the dismissal described the treatment of the civilians subjected to forced labor by the Japanese military: "[T]hey were all subjected to serious mistreatment, including starvation, beatings, physical and mental torture, being transported in unventilated cargo holds of ships, and being forced to make long marches under a tropical sun without water. Some survived, while others were ultimately executed, or died from disease or physical abuse." Deutsch v. Turner Corp., 324 F.3d 692, 705 (9th Cir. 2003).

In *Jane Doe I v. Reddy*, 2003 U.S. Dist. LEXIS 26120, 2003 WL 23893010, at *8–9 (N.D. Cal. Aug. 4, 2003), the court denied a motion to dismiss forced labor claims under the ATS. The plaintiffs were young women who alleged they were fraudulently induced to come to the United States with promises of education and employment, but were then forced to work long hours under arduous conditions at illegally low wages, and that they were sexually abused, physically beaten, and threatened. 2003 U.S. Dist. LEXIS 26120, at *1 and *9. The court found that the allegations stated claims for forced labor, debt bondage, and trafficking actionable under the ATS. In reaching that conclusion, the court relied on the Universal Declaration of Human Rights and the International Covenant on Civil and Political Rights. 2003 U.S. Dist. LEXIS 26120 at *8. (As noted above, the Supreme Court later held in *Sosa* that both documents were insufficient foundations for ATS claims. 542 U.S. at 734–35.)

Plaintiffs also rely on the Burmese forced labor case against Unocal, *Doe v. Unocal Corp.*, 110 F. Supp. 2d 1294 (C.D. Cal. 2000) (granting summary judgment for defendants), aff'd in part, rev'd in part, 395 F.3d 932, 945 (9th Cir. 2002) (stating that forced labor violates law of nations, also relying on Universal Declaration of Human Rights), vacated on rehearing en banc, 395 F.3d 978 (9th Cir. 2003), appeal dismissed, 403 F.3d 708 (9th Cir. 2005). The plaintiffs in the Burmese forced labor case testified that the Burmese military used both force and threats of force to conscript them to work on Unocal's pipeline and supporting infrastructure. 110 F. Supp. 2d at 1298 & n.3. The district court had no difficulty finding that such evidence showed forced labor in violation of the law of nations, *id.* at 1307–08, and the Ninth Circuit panel agreed, 395 F.3d at 945–47, before the appeal was eventually dismissed.

E. International Norms for Forced Labor

The Complaint in this case uses the same powerful label "forced labor." That conclusory label is not decisive. The court need not take at face value the legal conclusions in a complaint. *Bell Atlantic v. Twombly*, 550 U.S. at —, 127 S. Ct. at 1964–65, citing *Papasan v. Allain*, 478 U.S. 265, 286 (1986) (when deciding a motion to dismiss, a court is not "bound to accept as true a legal conclusion couched as a factual allegation"). This case lies at a point on a continuum far from the forced labor of Nazi Germany, Japanese labor camps, or the workers rounded up more recently by the Burmese military. Even if the adult plaintiffs' factual allegations are credited, as the court must, these plaintiffs have not alleged violations of a specific, universal, and obligatory norm of international law.

The adult plaintiffs in this case rely on several international agreements to show that their working conditions violate international law. The first is ILO Forced Labour Convention (No. 29), June 28, 1930, 39 U.N.T.S. 55, available at http://www.ilo.org/ilolex/english/convdispl.htm (last visited June 25, 2007), Docket No. 2-78, Exhibit A (hereinafter "ILO Convention 29"). ILO Convention 29 entered into force on May 1, 1932. Liberia and Japan have ratified ILO Convention 29, but the United States has not. Article 2 of ILO Convention 29 defines forced labor to mean "all work or service which is exacted from any person under the menace of any penalty and for which the said person has not offered himself voluntarily."[24] In ILO Convention 29, the ratifying members of the ILO agreed to end some forms of forced labor and to impose certain minimum standards for working conditions and wages in cases in which forced labor was permitted. Prohibited forms of forced labor include forced labor "for the benefit of private individuals, companies or associations." Art. 4. This prohibition would apply to forced labor for the benefit of private corporations like the defendants in this case, at least if plaintiffs could allege and prove true forced labor and if ILO Convention 29 were deemed to apply in the United States.

Plaintiffs also rely on the ILO Abolition of Forced Labour Convention (No. 105), (June 26, 1957) 320 U.N.T.S. 291, available at http://www.ilo.org/ilolex/english/convdispl.htm (last visited June 25, 2007), Docket No. 2-79 (hereinafter "ILO Convention 105"). Both Liberia and the United States have ratified ILO Convention 105; Japan has not. ILO Convention 105 also did not outlaw all forms of forced labor. Instead, in Article 1, each ratifying member of the ILO agreed to suppress any form of forced labor for certain prohibited purposes, including political and ideological education, economic development, as a means of labor discipline, as punishment for participating in strikes, and as a means for racial, social, national, or religious discrimination.

The question here is what is "forced labor," keeping in mind that international norms are actionable under the ATS only if they are as specific, universal, and obligatory as Blackstone's three 18th century archetypes—piracy, wrongs against ambassadors, and violations of safe conducts.

Plaintiffs have submitted a 2005 report by the Director General of the ILO entitled "A global alliance against forced labour" that reports on the ILO Declaration on Fundamental Principles and Rights at Work. Docket No. 2-80, Baxter Aff., Ex. C, available at http://www.ilo.org/dyn/declaris/DECLARATIONWEB.GLOBALREPORTDETAILS?var_language=EN&svar_PublicationsID=523286var_ReportType=Report (last visited June 25, 2007). The report tackled the problem of definition in terms that help illuminate the parties' arguments in this case:

> Yet the very concept of forced labour, as set out in the ILO standards on the subject, is still not well understood. In many quarters the term continues to

24. Article 2 of ILO Convention 29 then excludes from the definition several categories of compulsory service, including military service, normal civil obligations, work as part of a criminal sentence under official supervision, and emergency services.

> be associated mainly with the forced labour practices of totalitarian regimes: the flagrant abuses of Hitler's Germany, Stalin's Soviet Union or Pol Pot's Cambodia. At the other end of the spectrum, such terms as "modern slavery", "slavery-like practices" and "forced labour" can be used rather loosely to refer to poor or insalubrious working conditions, including very low wages. Indeed, some national legislation has identified the late payment of wages, or remuneration below the legal minimum wage, as at least one element of a forced labour situation.

Ex. C. at 5. The 2005 ILO report relied on the definition from ILO Convention 29, "all work or service which is exacted from any person under the menace of any penalty and for which the said person has not offered himself voluntarily." The report then explained:

> Forced labour cannot be equated simply with low wages or poor working conditions. Nor does it cover situations of pure economic necessity, as when a worker feels unable to leave a job because of the real or perceived absence of employment alternatives. Forced labour represents a severe violation of human rights and restriction of human freedom, as defined in the ILO Conventions on the subject and in other related international instruments on slavery, practices similar to slavery, debt bondage or serfdom.

Id., at 13.

The ILO report includes a list of factors for "identifying forced labour in practice." *Id.* at 6. For identifying the lack of consent prong of the definition from ILO Convention 29, the ILO report lists the following indicators:

—Birth/descent into "slave" or bonded status

—Physical abduction or kidnapping

—Sale of person into the ownership of another

—Physical confinement in the work location—in prison or private detention

—Psychological compulsion, i.e. an order to work, backed up by a credible threat of a penalty for non-compliance

—Induced indebtedness (by falsification of accounts, inflated prices, reduced value of goods or services produced, excessive interest charges, etc.)

—Deception or false promises about types and terms of work

—Withholding and non-payment of wages.

—Retention of identity documents or other valuable personal possessions

Plaintiffs in this case do not allege that any of these indicators of involuntary work apply to the current generation of adult Plantation workers. The plaintiffs allege that their grandparents and great-grandparents were abducted, kidnapped, and/or physically threatened when the Plantation was established in the 1920s, but plaintiffs are not in a position to assert claims for money damages today based on the mistreatment of their ancestors. Plaintiffs allege that they have nothing left after they spend their wages at company stores and other company facilities (such as schools), but they do not allege induced indebtedness. Plaintiffs allege that they are physically isolated at the Plantation, but they do not allege that Firestone keeps them physically confined there. To the extent plaintiffs allege psychological compulsion, they are clearly alleging what the ILO report calls "pure economic necessity, as when a worker feels unable to leave a job because of the real or perceived absence of employment alternatives," which is not forced labor under international law.

As factors indicating the "menace of any penalty" prong of the forced labor definition from ILO Convention 29, the ILO report lists:

Actual presence or credible threat of:

—Physical violence against worker or family or close associates

—Sexual violence

—(Threat of) supernatural retaliation

—Imprisonment or other physical confinement

—Financial penalties

—Denunciation to authorities (police, immigration, etc.) and deportation

—Dismissal from current employment

—Exclusion from future employment

—Exclusion from community and social life

—Removal of rights or privileges

—Deprivation of food, shelter or other necessities

—Shift to even worse working conditions

—Loss of social status

Id. Plaintiffs allege that they have been threatened with dismissal from current employment. Neither the ILO report nor the plaintiffs explain how a threat of dismissal from current employment is a "menace of a penalty" that forces labor in the same job. It would seem that the expressed fear of losing one's current employment is a clear indicator that the current employment is not forced labor. Plaintiffs' allegations about being told they can leave and join the starving unemployed, see Compl. ¶ 49, describe the brutal economic consequences of losing the jobs they complain they are being forced to perform, in a poor and dangerous country with 80 to 85 percent unemployment. At least in terms of international law, those consequences are not comparable to the practices alleged in *Deutsch v. Turner Corp.*, where laborers confined by the Japanese military were starved if they refused to work. See 324 F.3d at 705.

In other words, the plaintiffs do not allege any of the listed indicators of forced labor—other than those indicating that the persons might lose the same jobs they say they are being forced to perform.

In a discussion of labor practices in Africa, the 2005 ILO report offered these observations, which are relevant here because of the Supreme Court's requirement in *Sosa* that international norms be specific:

> A review of recent trends in Africa needs to take account of some particularities of this continent. First, where extreme poverty is the norm, many workers receive little or no financial payment, but are remunerated mainly through substandard food and lodging, or other payment in kind; delayed payment and non-payment of wages are widespread; and wages rarely match any legally defined minimum. *It can be difficult to determine when the generalized breach of labour contracts, together with poor terms and conditions of work, degenerates into actual forced labour.*
>
> * * *
>
> [T]he results of recent studies commissioned by the ILO indicated that the national researchers, as well as their respondents, had great difficulty in understanding the concept [of forced labour], and in distinguishing forced labour situations from extremely exploitative, but nonetheless "freely chosen", work.

Ex. C at 42, ¶¶ 195 & 200 (emphasis added). Even though there are some forms of forced labor (Nazi Germany, for example) that clearly violate international law, these comments signal that the circumstances alleged by the adult plaintiffs in this Complaint do not violate specific, universal, and obligatory norms of international law.

Plaintiffs acknowledge that the United States has not ratified ILO Convention 29 with its definition of forced labor: "all work or service which is exacted from any person under the menace of any penalty and for which the said person has not offered himself voluntarily." Plaintiffs argue that the United States later bound itself to ILO Convention 29 through the ILO Declaration on Fundamental Principles and Rights at Work (June 1998), available at http://www.ilo/org/dyn/declaris/DeclarationWeb.IndexPage (last visited June 25, 2007), Docket No. 31, Collingsworth Aff., Ex. A. In that document, ILO member nations acknowledged that even if they had not ratified all of the specific ILO conventions, they had an obligation to respect, to promote, and to realize the principles concerning the fundamental rights that are the subjects of the conventions, including "the elimination of all forms of forced or compulsory labour" and "the effective abolition of child labour." *Id.*

That Declaration, however, clearly did not impose any new binding legal obligations on the ILO member nations. The Legal Advisor of the ILO advised the members that "the Declaration and its follow-up does not and cannot impose on any member State any obligation pursuant to any Convention which that State has not ratified through its own constitutional or other requisite legal procedure." Report of the Committee on the Declaration of Principles, International Labour Conference, 86th Sess., at ¶ 325 (1998), Docket No. 34, Ex. A. The Legal Advisor added that the Declaration "is recognized by everyone as not being a binding instrument." A number of member nations expressed similar views in the debate. *Id.*, ¶¶ 183, 186, 188, 193, 224, 226. It would be odd indeed if a United States court were to treat as universal and binding in other nations an international convention that the United States government has declined to ratify itself.

F. Application of Forced Labor Standards to This Case

The adult plaintiffs in this case allege that they are "kept on the Plantation by poverty, fear, and ignorance of the outside world, living in a cycle of poverty and raising their children to be the next generation of Firestone Plantation Workers." Compl. ¶ 64. The adult plaintiffs allege that they seek the simple justice of the freedom [to] choose whether to work, the opportunity to work free of coercion, the security of a proper employment relationship, the benefit of wages that do not leave them in malnourished poverty, and the meager benefits provided under the law of Liberia, including rest days and holidays. Most of all, they seek the cessation of conditions that formed the premise of the Firestone Plantation, and that have left them in the same situation as their own fathers, watching their own children join them as tappers with no future other than the misery they have experienced their entire lives. Compl. ¶ 66. Anyone can appreciate these most basic human aspirations, even from the comfortable distance between Liberia and Indiana. The relief plaintiffs seek, however, and the changes that would resolve their complaints, show that the conditions about which they complain are not "forced labor" as that term is used in any specific, universal, and obligatory norm of international law.

During the hearing on the motion to dismiss, the court asked plaintiffs' counsel what would need to change so that plaintiffs' labor would no longer be forced, in plaintiffs' view. The principal answer was to reduce the daily quota for latex production and thus to raise effective wages on the Firestone Plantation. Tr. 49–50. Plaintiffs' counsel also said that the remedy would include providing information to workers about their rights, upgrading equipment, including safety equipment, and changing the security force. Tr. 50–51. Apart from the comment on the security force, discussed below, those are all clearly matters of wages and working conditions that fall outside any specific, universal, and obligatory understanding of the prohibition against forced labor.

Plaintiffs have not alleged that Firestone fails to pay them. They do not allege that Firestone is using physical force to keep them on the job. They do not allege that Firestone is using legal constraints to keep them on the job. Plaintiffs do not allege that they could not freely quit their jobs if they felt they had better opportunities elsewhere in Liberia. Plaintiffs do not allege that they have been held against their will, tortured, jailed, or threatened with physical harm. Plaintiffs do not allege any form of ownership or trafficking in employees.

Plaintiffs allege instead that they are being kept on the job by the effects of "poverty, fear, and ignorance." As powerful as these forces may be, they are qualitatively different from armed troops keeping kidnapped and deported workers in labor camps. Higher wages, rest days and holidays, and the security of a proper employment relationship, better housing, education, and medical care are all understandable desires. But better wages and working conditions are not the remedy for the forced labor condemned by international law. The remedy for truly forced labor should be termination of the employment and the freedom to go elsewhere. *Pollock v. Williams*, 322 U.S. 4, 18 (1944); *Does v. The Gap, Inc.*, 2002 WL 1000068, at *15 (D.N. Mar. I. May 10, 2002) (dismissing claims for involuntary servitude). Yet the adult plaintiffs allege in their Complaint that they are afraid of losing the very jobs they say they are forced to perform. Compl. ¶ 64 (complaining of "the prospect of starvation just one complaint about conditions away"); ¶ 59 (alleging that Firestone improperly treats plaintiffs as "casual labor which can be fired for any reason"); ¶ 49 (alleging that workers are told they will be dismissed even if they wish to take a day off without pay, and that Liberia's extremely high unemployment rate "allows Firestone to say with confidence that anyone who wants to leave can do so and join the ranks of the starving unemployed").

The court does not mean to diminish the plaintiffs' desires or their fears of the future they face if they lose their jobs or leave the Plantation. But the fact that the plaintiffs face worse prospects elsewhere in Liberia cannot be equated with an employer's use of force or coercion to keep workers on the job. Nor can the allegations in the complaint be equated with the use of military power to force labor on behalf of the Nazi regime in Germany as in *Iwanowa*, or the Japanese Empire in World War II as in *Deutsch v. Turner Corp.*, or the Burmese military government in *Doe v. Unocal.*

G. Force and Physical Coercion

Plaintiffs' claims for relief allege that they "were placed in fear for their lives, were deprived of their freedom, and were forced to suffer severe physical and/or mental abuse designed to coerce them into working on the Firestone Plantation . . . ." Compl. ¶ 88; see also ¶¶ 95, 112, 117, 122, 127. In the absence of more specific factual allegations, these conclusory allegations add nothing to the complaint. See *Bell Atlantic v. Twombly*, 550 U.S. at, 127 S. Ct. at 1964–65.

The Complaint does not include any allegations by any of the plaintiffs stating that they or other Plantation workers have been threatened with physical force. Plaintiffs say they are afraid, but that does not mean that defendants are responsible for their fear. Plaintiffs live in a nation that has been torn apart by vicious civil war over the past generation. Between approximately 1980 and 2003, Liberia was one of the most dangerous places on earth.

In the hearing on the motion to dismiss, plaintiffs' counsel stated that plaintiffs had alleged, or could allege, physical coercion. Tr. 43. By that, plaintiffs mean that they live and work in what counsel calls a "climate of fear." Tr. 44. Many circumstances contributed to that climate. The focus here must be on circumstances for which defendants might be deemed legally responsible. The only one identified in the complaint is the allegation that in 1994, Firestone hired General Adolphus Dolo as chief of its security for the Plantation, and that General Dolo had been part of the forces led by Charles Taylor. Compl. ¶ 62. Plaintiffs also allege that Firestone filled other key positions at the Plantation with "Taylor operatives." *Id.*

It is not surprising that a multinational corporation needed to make security arrangements during a vicious civil war. Nor is it surprising that some of the persons willing and able to provide those services had some history with one side or the other in the civil war. Yet the Complaint does not allege a single incident of physical force, physical threat, or intimidation by those security forces directed against these plaintiffs or other Plantation workers. In the absence of such allegations or other indications of forced labor, the court cannot conclude that the presence of the current security force could transform the alleged circumstances at the Plantation into a violation of a specific, universal, and obligatory international norm against forced labor. Recall also that plaintiffs alleged repeatedly that they are afraid of losing the same jobs they say they are forced to work.

Plaintiffs also argue that they are so isolated on the Plantation that they have no realistic prospect of leaving if they want to do so. Plaintiffs argue that there is no transportation available and that they would starve if they left their jobs. The principal problem with the argument is that those circumstances are not the creation of defendants. Defendants are operating a commercial enterprise in a war-torn nation that is one of the poorest and most dangerous on earth. The court is not aware of a basis in international law for stating that an employer must provide transportation or food or other necessities to a worker who wishes to leave his job.

The court assumes that the plaintiffs do not have better choices available to them as a practical matter. But the absence of those better choices is not the legal responsibility of these defendants. Under the standards of international law, Firestone is not responsible for Liberia's poverty, its history of civil war, or the dangers its people face. This basic distinction between harsh conditions for which an employer is or is not responsible is recognized in the ILO definition of forced labor dating back to ILO Convention 29 in 1930. Forced labor is "work or service which is exacted from any person under the menace of any penalty and for which the said person has not offered himself voluntarily."

The phrase "menace of any penalty" does not refer to the harm a person would suffer if he leaves a job and is unable to earn a living elsewhere. The concept of a penalty is a punishment deliberately inflicted (whether justly or not) by some authority or other actor for some perceived wrongdoing, not the consequences of being homeless and penniless in one of the poorest and most dangerous nations on earth. Without that element of deliberately inflicted harm, the definition of forced labor would expand to reach many people who work at poor jobs to support themselves simply because they have no better alternative. The ILO Director General's 2005 report clearly cautions against such a broad definition: forced labor does not cover "situations of pure economic necessity, as when a worker feels unable to leave a job because of the real or perceived absence of employment alternatives." Baxter Decl., Ex. C, at 5, ¶ 13.

The issue here is not whether Firestone's management of the Plantation (as alleged in the Complaint) is enlightened or meets with approval of legal scholars or judges in the industrialized world. The issue is whether the conditions violate a norm of international law that is as specific, universal, and obligatory as were the norms against piracy, violations of safe conducts, or violations of the rights of ambassadors in 1789.

In the absence of allegations of physical coercion, this case would reflect an unprecedented expansion of international law, contrary to all the cautionary warnings the Supreme Court posted in *Sosa*. The Court instructed lower courts, when deciding whether a norm of international law is sufficiently definite to support a claim under the ATS, to consider the practical implications of recognizing additional types of claims under the ATS. 542 U.S. at 732–33. Those considerations in this case are daunting—far more so than they were in *Sosa*. The merits of this case do not depend at all on the American presence in the chain of corporate ownership. If the working conditions for adults on the Firestone Plantation violate international law, then international law would extend without identifiable boundaries to exploitive working conditions and low wages all over the world. Plaintiffs' basic reasoning—with conditions this bad, why would we stay if we could leave?—could apply all over the world to people who face no good alternatives for earning a living.

The court is confident that improvements in those wages and working conditions for many millions of people would make the world a better place. Yet federal courts in the United States must also keep in mind the *Sosa* Court's caution against having American courts decide and enforce limits on the power of foreign governments over their own citizens. 542 U.S. at 727. How much more intrusive would American law be if American courts took it upon themselves to determine the minimum requirements for wages and working conditions throughout the world? And to enforce those requirements here against any international business with property that could be found in the United States? Beyond situations presenting clear violations of specific, universal, and obligatory international law norms, these are matters left to diplomacy, legislation, publicity, and economic pressure from consumers, and not to the instincts of judges who would love to issue a writ to make the world a better place for some of the poorest and least fortunate members of the human family. The adult plaintiffs have pleaded circumstances in their Complaint that show they have no claim in Count One under the ATS for forced labor in violation of specific, universal, and obligatory norms of international law. Defendants' motion to dismiss is granted with respect to Count One, the adult plaintiffs' claims of forced labor under the ATS.

H. International Norms for Child Labor

Count Two also seeks relief under the ATS, asserting that work done by the child plaintiffs on the Plantation violates international law. The Complaint alleges that the Firestone supervisors on the Plantation encourage and even require the adult latex tappers to put their children to work to help meet the production quotas. ¶¶ 48, 55. Plaintiffs allege that children apply fertilizers and pesticides by hand, without protective equipment. ¶ 55. Plaintiffs also allege that children as young as six years old work at the Firestone Plantation. ¶¶ 12–23. The defendants deny these allegations, but the court must accept these factual allegations for purposes of the motion to dismiss under Rule 12(b)(6).

Plaintiffs have submitted for the court's consideration a United Nations report, U.N. Missions in Liberia, "Human Rights in Liberia's Rubber Plantations: Tapping into the Future" (May 2006), filed as Docket No. 14, Ex. A, available at http://unmil.org/documents/human_rights_liberiarubber.pdf (last visited June 25, 2007). United Nations human rights investigators reported that management at the Firestone Plantation and other rubber plantation stated that child labor was prohibited. Yet the investigators spoke with a number of children working on the Firestone Plantation and other rubber plantations who were 10 to 14 years old. *Id.* at 45. The UN investigators also reported that Firestone management told them that management and the Liberian government did not effectively monitor compliance with policies against child labor. *Id.* This report is not admissible evidence at this point, but its filing as part of the opposition to a Rule 12(b)(6) motion enables plaintiffs to show the types of evidence they expect or hope to offer to support their allegations in the Complaint. See *Thomas v. Guardsmark, Inc.*, 381 F.3d 701, 704 (7th Cir. 2004) (recognizing that plaintiffs opposing Rule 12(b)(6) motion may illustrate their allegations with additional submissions that are not yet fully admissible as evidence).

The question is whether Count Two alleges violations of sufficiently specific, universal, and obligatory norms of international law. Plaintiffs quote a report from the United States Department of State in 1997 stating that there is an international consensus that freedom from "child labor" is one of several "core labor standards." See Baxter Decl. Ex. E. at 131; accord, Leary Aff. ¶ 26 (Docket No. 39) (ILO recognizes elimination of child labor as fundamental or core right). Yet whatever one's initial reaction is to the broad phrase "child labor," reflection shows that national and international norms accommodate a host of different situations and balance competing values and policies. See ILO Report of the Committee on the Declaration of Principles (Geneva, June 1998), Docket No. 34, Ex. A, at 224, 226. What are the relevant age limits, for which types of work? How does access to education affect the appropriate policies? What does one say to a parent who insists that a child work so that the family has enough to eat? It is not always easy to state just which practices under the label "child labor" are the subjects of an international consensus.

One can see this in the United States' own Fair Labor Standards Act. The FLSA prohibits not "child labor" but "oppressive child labor." 29 U.S.C. § 212(c). The phrase is defined so that the law allows employment of minors aged 14 and 15 in occupations other than manufacturing and mining if the employment is confined to periods that do not interfere with schooling and under conditions that will not interfere with their health and well-being. 29 U.S.C. § 203(l). Focusing on agricultural work, such as that alleged here, in the United States minors who are 16 and 17 years old may work in any farm job at any time. Minors who are 14 or 15 years old may work a wide variety of agricultural jobs so long as the work is done outside of school hours. 29 U.S.C. § 213(c)(1)(C). Children who are 12 or 13 years old also may work on a farm with the consent of their parents, outside school hours. 29 U.S.C. § 213(c)(1)(B). The FLSA even allows the employment of a child under the age of 12 by his parent on a farm owned by the parent, or employment on another small farm, again outside school hours. 29 U.S.C. § 213(c)(1)(A). In the United States, even children as young as 10 or 11 years old may hand-harvest some crops with a special waiver from the Department of Labor. 29 U.S.C. § 213(c)(4). Liberian law on this subject is not as detailed, but defendants have come forward with evidence that Liberian law allows children under the age of 16 to be employed so long as their work does not interfere with their education. Paegar Decl. ¶¶ 3–4 86 Ex. A (Docket No. 2-31).

Returning to international standards, ILO Convention 138, the Minimum Age Convention of 1973, also shows the need to draw lines that accommodate a variety of policies. ILO Convention 138 sets forth minimum ages for different types of work in different nations at different stages of economic development. Nevertheless, that convention notes that its age limits apply to certain forms of employment, including "plantations and other agricultural undertakings mainly producing for commercial purposes, but excluding family and small-scale holdings producing for local consumption and not regularly employing hired workers." Art. 5(3). In such settings, ILO Convention 138 prescribes a minimum age of 14 for employees. Yet neither the United States nor Liberia has ratified ILO Convention 138, though Japan has ratified it.

The key source of international child labor standards for present purposes is ILO Convention 182, the 1999 Convention Concerning the Prohibition and Immediate Elimination of the Worst Forms of Child Labor, which the United States, Liberia, and Japan have all ratified. The importance of the line-drawing is evident in that very title. ILO Convention 182 does not seek to outlaw child labor as such, but only its "worst forms." Those worst forms include slavery and forced or compulsory labor, prostitution and production of pornography, and drug trafficking. The worst forms also include "work which, by its nature or the circumstances in which it is carried out, is likely to harm the health, safety or morals of children." Art. 3. ILO Convention 182 leaves to member nations the identification of the jobs likely to harm health, safety, or morals. Art. 4.

Giving plaintiffs the benefit of their factual allegations, the Complaint states that defendants are actively encouraging—even tacitly requiring—the employment of six, seven, and ten year old children. Giving plaintiffs the benefit of their factual allegations, the defendants are actively encouraging that these very young children perform back-breaking work that exposes them to dangerous chemicals and tools. The work, plaintiffs allege, also keeps those children out of the Firestone schools. The court understands that defendants deny the allegations, but defendants have chosen to file a motion that requires the court to accept those allegations as true, at least for now.

The circumstances alleged here include at least some practices that could therefore fall within the "worst forms of child labor" addressed in ILO Convention 182. The conditions of work alleged by plaintiffs (and reported by the UN investigators) are likely to harm the health and safety of at least the very youngest of the child plaintiffs in this case.

As noted above, and as Firestone has argued, national child labor laws and international conventions on child labor are often written to allow even very young children to help out on family farms. Those special accommodations for family farms have no application here. Plaintiffs do not challenge labor practices on subsistence farms. They challenge the practices of a huge multinational corporate family that hires the children's parents and then (allegedly) encourages the parents to require their young children to do much of the work. Plaintiffs allege that defendants have set the daily production quotas so high that use of child labor is both necessary and inevitable, and that defendants take advantage of the parents in this situation. Compl. ¶ 55.

The court recognizes that international legal standards for child labor do not always establish bright lines, though there are some. That is also the case with forced labor, as discussed above. Just as some practices that might be described by some as "forced labor" might not violate international law, some practices that could be described as "child labor" also do not violate international law. One must look more closely at the particular circumstances, as shown by the pleadings and later by the evidence.

At least some of the practices alleged with regard to the labor of very young children at the Firestone Plantation in Liberia may violate specific, universal, and obligatory standards of international law, such that Count Two should not be dismissed on the pleadings. In light of ILO Convention 182, the court believes that the allegations of child labor in Count Two meet the Sosa standard for ATS claims. It would not require great "judicial creativity" to find that even paid labor of very young children in these heavy and hazardous jobs would violate international norms. Those international norms are not inconsistent with Liberian law. Those norms also are stated in an international convention that both the United States and Liberia have ratified. On this record, there is no indication that this lawsuit threatens to cause friction with the foreign policy of the United States. See *Sosa*, 542 U.S. at 725–28 (identifying reasons for caution in recognizing new claims under the ATS). Plaintiffs may face other daunting challenges in pursuing their case, and the court will address those issues as they are raised. The court is also cautious about the practical consequences of recognizing child labor claims under the ATS and international law. See *id.* at 732–33. In a sufficiently extreme case, however, such as plaintiffs have alleged here, the court believes that *Sosa* leaves the ATS door open. The allegations that defendants are encouraging and even requiring parents to require their children as young as six, seven, or ten years old to do this heavy and hazardous work may state a claim for relief under the ATS. Defendants' motion to dismiss is denied as to Count Two.

Notes and Questions

1. Notice that the District Court highlights three wrongs that, under *Sosa*, would allow a cause of action for international law violations: violations of safe conducts, violations of rights of ambassadors, and piracy.[25] What constitutes a "violation of safe conduct"? What constitutes as a "violation of rights of an ambassador"? What constitutes "piracy"? For further discussion of common law violations, see Eugene Kontorovich, *Implementing Sosa v. Alvarez-Machain: What Piracy Reveals About the Limits of the Alien Tort Statute*, 80 Notre Dame L. Rev. 111 (2004); Igor Fuks, *Sosa v. Alvarez-Machain and the Future of ATCA Litigation: Examining Bonded Labor Claims and Corporate Liability*, 106 Colum. L. Rev. 112 (2006).

2. As the opinion in *Bridgestone* notes, the *Sosa* Court divided on whether courts may recognize additional torts beyond the three common law causes of action. The dissent argued that allowing other causes of action would invite judges to assume a lawmaking role that the court was "neither authorized nor suited to perform."[26] Yet, the majority held that the judicial door should be left "ajar subject to vigilant door-keeping, and thus open to a narrow class of international norms today."[27] This division among the *Sosa* Court invites consideration of what the Court meant by vigilant door-keeping.[28]

3. A 2005 ILO report, "A Global Alliance Against Forced Labour," contains the following passage in its discussion of Africa:

> 195. A review of recent trends in Africa needs to take account of some particularities of this continent. First, where extreme poverty is the norm, many workers receive little or no financial payment, but are remunerated mainly through substandard food and lodging, or other payment in kind; delayed payment and non-payment of wages are widespread; and wages rarely match any legally defined minimum. It can be difficult to determine when the generalized breach of labour contracts, together with poor terms and conditions of work, degenerates into actual forced labour.
>
> 196. Second, given the importance of kinship and "tradition" in African economic and social relations, these can be invoked to demand unpaid services from extended family members, lower-status community members or even descendants of former slaves. Freedom of choice is again lacking, but the nature of the associated coercion and penalty may be very intangible, to the extent that victims of abuse (and even the perpetrators) may not even recognize forced labour situations as such. They may be considered as "natural" and socially legitimate. Religious beliefs and threats of supernatural retaliation may also be brought to bear.

---

25. *Sosa*, 542 U.S. at 724.

26. *Id.* at 739.

27. *Id.* at 729.

28. This question was put by Judge David Hamilton in *Roe v Bridgestone*, 492 F. Supp. 2d 988, 1009 (S.D. Ind. 2007).

> 197. Third, forced labour in some African countries has occurred in a context of severe political violence. Collapse of governance and the rule of law give rise to conditions in which forced labour abuses can go unchecked.
>
> 198. Fourth, the incidence of child labour in Africa is the highest of all regions, linked to deep and widespread poverty. The normal dependence of young children on adults is dramatically increased when they move away from their home environment, across a "social" or national frontier, making them even more susceptible to coercion at work. In many parts of Africa, there is a strong tradition of children moving away from home. Current evidence suggests that children may represent a higher proportion of forced labourers in Africa than in other regions of the world.
>
> 199. People enter forced labour situations in Africa in a variety of ways. Birth and descent are of obvious importance in determining "slave" status in certain African countries. Victims of forced labour often come from distinct ethnic or religious minority groups. Forced labour can also be imposed by local authorities, including traditional chiefs.
>
> 200. The legacy of the slave trade can make the recognition of contemporary forced labour especially difficult for those in positions of power as well as for the public at large. Indeed, the very concept of forced labour, as well as slavery, conjures up images from the past in a continent where frequent use was made of forced labour until towards the end of the colonial era. Such factors may help explain the dearth of recent research on the topic, and the difficulty of undertaking it. Indeed, the results of recent studies commissioned by the ILO indicated that the national researchers, as well as their respondents, had great difficulty in understanding the concept, and in distinguishing forced labour situations from extremely exploitative, but nonetheless "freely chosen", work. While anthropologists have studied the issue of present-day vestiges of slavery in West Africa quite intensively, and cross-border trafficking of women and children has been high on policy agendas in recent years, other possible manifestations of forced labour have received scant attention. Thus, there remain significant gaps in the understanding of forced labour in Africa, and of how it can be most effectively tackled.[29]

The excerpt from the ILO report characterizes Africa in general. How does the specific situation at Firestone support or challenge the characterizations offered in the report? How does the characterization of Africa affect the availability of remedies to labor abuses, whether or not in African firms?

4. Because the acceptance and specificity of international norms are crucial under the *Sosa* analysis, the International Labor Organization is relevant to the

29. Int'l Labor Org., *A Global Alliance Against Forced Labour*, Geneva, at 42 (2005), http://www.ilo.org/wcmsp5/groups/public/@ed_norm/@declaration/documents/publication/wcms_081882.pdf.

District Court's reasoning in *Bridgestone*. Now that you have read an excerpt from the ILO report (note 3, above) and additional background materials from Liberia, what factors would you add to the list that ILO provides to determine the presence or absence of forced labor?

B. Flomo v. Firestone Natural Rubber Co.

In *Flomo v. Firestone Natural Rubber Co.*, a follow-up to *Roe v. Bridgestone Corp.*,[30] the appellate court reconsidered the child plaintiffs' claims against Firestone Natural Rubber Co. The court considered defendant's motion for summary judgment on the basis that international law did not impose liability on a corporation, and therefore, the child plaintiffs had no cognizable cause of action. The Seventh Circuit eventually overturned the District Court's decision in *Flomo v. Firestone Natural Rubber Co.* (*Flomo II*), 645 F.3d 1013 (7th Cir. 2011). The Seventh Circuit held that corporate liability was possible under the ATS; however, the child plaintiffs were not able to show under the ATS that the defendant and its officers had utilized hazardous child labor on the rubber plantation in Liberia in violation of customary international law.[31] An excerpt from the opinion follows:

Flomo v. Firestone Natural Rubber Co.

643 F.3d 1013 (7th Cir. 2011)

Before Bauer, Posner, and Manion, Circuit Judges

Posner, Circuit Judge:

The principal issues presented by the appeal are whether a corporation or any other entity that is not a natural person (the defendant is a limited liability company rather than a conventional business corporation) can be liable under the Alien Tort Statute, and, if so, whether the evidence presented by the plaintiffs created a triable issue of whether the defendant has violated "customary international law."

And what is "customary international law"? "International law is part of our law, and . . . where there is no treaty, and no controlling executive or legislative act or judicial decision, resort must be had to the customs and usages of civilized nations." *The Paquete Habana*, 175 U.S. 677, 700 (1900).

The Alien Tort Statute was enacted in 1789, when the principal violations of customary international law were piracy, mistreatment of ambassadors, and violation of safe conducts. *Sosa v. Alvarez-Machain*, 542 U.S. 692, 715, (2004); 4 Blackstone, *supra*, at 68 (1769). But in using the broad term "law of nations" Congress allowed the coverage of the statute to change with changes in customary international law. As

30. In November of 2009, Judge Hamilton was elevated to the Seventh Circuit, and the *Bridgestone* case was transferred to District Judge William Lawrence. During the transfer, the case was renamed *Flomo v. Firestone Natural Rubber Company*.

31. *Flomo v. Firestone Natural Rubber Co.*, 643 F.3d 1013 (7th Cir. 2011).

cautiously stated by the Supreme Court, "the door is still ajar [for further independent judicial recognition of actionable international norms] subject to vigilant doorkeeping, and thus open to a narrow class of international norms today." *Sosa v. Alvarez-Machain, supra*, 542 U.S. at 729.

The concept of customary international law is disquieting in two respects. First, there is a problem of notice: a custom cannot be identified with the same confidence as a provision in a legally authoritative text, such as a statute or a treaty. (Modern common law doesn't present that problem; it is a body of judge-created doctrine, not of amorphous custom.) Second, there is a problem of legitimacy—and for democratic countries it is a problem of democratic legitimacy.

Firestone draws on that mood for its arguments against liability. Its first argument is that conduct by a corporation or any other entity that doesn't have a heartbeat (we'll use "corporation" to cover all such entities) can never be a violation of customary international law, no matter how heinous the conduct. So, according to Firestone, a pirate can be sued under the Alien Tort Statute but not a pirate corporation (Pirates of the Indian Ocean, Inc., with its headquarters and principal place of business in Somalia; cf. U.N. Security Council, "Report of the Monitoring Group on Somalia Pursuant to Security Council Resolution 1853 (2008)" 99 (Feb. 26, 2010).) Firestone argues that because corporations, unlike individuals, have never been prosecuted for criminal violations of customary international law, there cannot be a norm, let alone a "universal" one, forbidding them to commit crimes against humanity and other acts that the civilized world abhors.

The issue of corporate liability under the Alien Tort Statute seems to have been left open in an enigmatic footnote in *Sosa*, 542 U.S. at 732 n. 20 (but since it's a Supreme Court footnote, the parties haggle over its meaning, albeit to no avail). All but one of the cases at our level hold or assume (mainly the latter) that corporations can be liable. *Romero v. Drummond Co.*, 552 F.3d 1303, 1315 (11th Cir. 2008); *Herero People's Reparations Corp. v. Deutsche Bank, A.G.*, 370 F.3d 1192, 1193, 1195, 361 U.S. App. D.C. 468 (D.C. Cir. 2004); *Wiwa v. Royal Dutch Petroleum Co.*, 226 F.3d 88, 91–92 (2d Cir. 2000); *Beanal v. Freeport-McMoran, Inc.*, 197 F.3d 161, 163 (5th Cir. 1999); see also *Abdullahi v. Pfizer, Inc.*, 562 F.3d 163, 174 (2d Cir. 2009); *Sarei v. Rio Tinto, PLC*, 550 F.3d 822, 831 (9th Cir. 2008) (en banc). (Our court hasn't addressed the issue.) The outlier is the split decision in *Kiobel v. Royal Dutch Petroleum Co.*, 621 F.3d 111 (2d Cir. 2010), which indeed held that because corporations have never been prosecuted, whether criminally or civilly, for violating customary international law, there can't be said to be a principle of customary international law that binds a corporation.

The factual premise of the majority opinion in the *Kiobel* case is incorrect. At the end of the Second World War the allied powers dissolved German corporations that had assisted the Nazi war effort, along with Nazi government and party organizations—and did so on the authority of customary international law.

And suppose no corporation had ever been punished for violating customary international law. There is always a first time for litigation to enforce a norm; there has to be. There were no multinational prosecutions for aggression and crimes against humanity before the Nuremberg Tribunal was created.

We have to consider why corporations have rarely been prosecuted criminally or civilly for violating customary international law; maybe there's a compelling reason. But it seems not; it seems rather that the paucity of cases reflects a desire to keep liability, whether personal or institutional, for such violations within tight bounds by confining it to abhorrent conduct—the kind of conduct that invites criminal sanctions. It would have seemed tepid to charge the Nazi war criminals with battery, wrongful death, false imprisonment, intentional infliction of emotional distress, fraud, conversion, trespass, medical malpractice, or other torts. And it was natural in light of the perceived effect of the Nuremberg trials on German and international opinion concerning the type of practices in which Hitler's government had engaged that a tradition would develop of punishing violations of customary international law by means of national or international criminal proceedings; it was a way of underscoring the gravity of violating customary international law.

But this has nothing to do with the issue of corporate liability. Sometimes it's in the interest of a corporation's shareholders for management to violate the law, including the criminal law, including norms of customary international law the violation of which is deemed criminal. Criminal punishment of corporations that commit crimes is not anomalous merely because a corporation cannot be imprisoned or executed. It can be fined; and so if a crime at least ostensibly in the corporation's financial interest is committed or condoned at the managerial or board of directors level of the corporation, the corporation itself is criminally liable.

The Alien Tort Statute, moreover, is civil, and corporate tort liability is common around the world. See, e.g., Paula Giliker, Vicarious Liability in Tort: A Comparative Perspective 46–50 (2010). If a corporation complicit in Nazi war crimes could be punished criminally for violating customary international law, as we believe it could be, then a fortiori if the board of directors of a corporation directs the corporation's managers to commit war crimes, engage in piracy, abuse ambassadors, or use slave labor, the corporation can be civilly liable. *Kiobel v. Royal Dutch Petroleum Co., supra*, 621 F.3d at 170 (concurring opinion); see Doug Cassel, "Corporate Aiding and Abetting of Human Rights Violations: Confusion in the Courts," 6 Nw. U. J. Int'l Human Rights 304, 322–23 (2008). The board members would be liable as well, but they might not have the resources to compensate the victims of the corporation's violation of international customary law, let alone pay punitive damages as well.

If a plaintiff had to show that civil liability for such violations was itself a norm of international law, no claims under the Alien Tort Statute could ever be successful, even claims against individuals; only the United States, as far as we know, has a statute that provides a civil remedy for violations of customary international law ....

We grant that rights and remedies can't be divorced so neatly as we may seem to be suggesting. Suppose the treatment of children at Firestone's Liberian plantation does violate customary international law (our next question), and suppose Spain decreed that anyone who buys tires made from the rubber produced at the plantation can be prosecuted as an aider and abettor of a criminal violation of customary international law. That remedy would stretch customary international law too far. The case of corporate liability is less extreme. But in the United States the liability of a corporation for torts committed by its employees in the course of their employment is strict, on the theory that strict liability for employees' torts gives corporations (and other employers) incentives to police their employees that are needed because the employees themselves will usually be judgment proof and hence not responsive to tort sanctions. The theory attenuates when the employees include local residents of Third World countries, such as the Liberian rubber farmers employed on Firestone's plantation. American corporations that have branches in backward or disordered countries may be incapable of preventing abuses of workers in those countries.

But the concern we've just expressed is an objection not to corporate liability for violations of customary international law but to the scope of that liability; and the plaintiffs concede that corporate liability for such violations is limited to cases in which the violations are directed, encouraged, or condoned at the corporate defendant's decisionmaking level. That is analogous to the liability of municipalities under the *Monell* doctrine, where as we noted recently "a person who wants to impose liability on a municipality for a constitutional tort must show that the tort was committed (that is, authorized or directed) at the policymaking level of government—by the city council, for example, rather than by the police officer who made an illegal arrest." *Vodak v. City of Chicago*, 639 F.3d 738, 747 (7th Cir. 2011). We needn't decide how far corporate vicarious liability for violations of customary international law extends; it's enough that we see no objection to corporate civil liability as circumscribed as the plaintiffs concede.

And if precedent for imposing liability for a violation of customary international law by an entity that does not breathe is wanted, we point to in rem judgments against pirate ships. E.g., *The Malek Adhel*, 43 U.S. (2 How.) 210, 233–34 (1844); *The Marianna Flora*, 24 U.S. (11 Wheat.) 1, 40–41 (1825). Of course the burden of confiscation of a pirate ship falls ultimately on the ship's owners, but similarly the burden of a fine imposed on a corporation falls ultimately on the shareholders.

One of the amicus curiae briefs argues, seemingly not tongue in cheek, that corporations shouldn't be liable under the Alien Tort Statute because that would be bad for business. That may seem both irrelevant and obvious; it is irrelevant, but not obvious. Businesses in countries that have and enforce laws against child labor are hurt by competition from businesses that employ child labor in countries in which employing children is condoned.

Having satisfied ourselves that corporate liability is possible under the Alien Tort Statute, we turn to the question whether the treatment of child labor at the Firestone plantation alleged by the plaintiffs during a period of undetermined length preceding the filing of this lawsuit violated customary international law (itself a two-part question: what is the applicable customary international law and did the working conditions at the plantation violate it?), and whether Firestone is liable under the narrow standard for corporate liability proffered by the plaintiffs.

Three international conventions bear on the first question. They supply pretty much the entire ground on which the plaintiffs pitch their argument that the treatment of children on the Liberian plantation has violated customary international law. Two of these conventions—the United Nations Convention on the Rights of the Child and the International Labour Organization Minimum Age Convention—have not been ratified by the United States, though the third has been—the International Labour Organization Worst Forms of Child Labour Convention. It happens to be the one most helpful to the plaintiffs. And anyway conventions that not all nations ratify can still be evidence of customary international law. *Abdullahi v. Pfizer, Inc., supra*, 562 F.3d at 176–77; *Khulumani v. Barclay Nat'l Bank Ltd.*, 504 F.3d 254, 283–84 (2d Cir. 2007) (concurring opinion); see also *Kiobel v. Royal Dutch Petroleum Co., supra*, 621 F.3d at 137–38. Otherwise every nation (or at least every "civilized" nation) would have veto power over customary international law. (It would be as if U.S. states could forbid the enforcement of federal law within their borders.) Moreover, a nation's legislature might refuse to ratify a convention for reasons unrelated to the convention's core principle.

The United States has enacted legislation making violations of customary international law actionable in U.S. courts: it is the Alien Tort Statute. And so the fact that Congress may not have enacted legislation implementing a particular treaty or convention (maybe because the treaty or convention hadn't been ratified) does not make a principle of customary international law evidenced by the treaty or convention unenforceable in U.S. courts.

Article 32(1) of the United Nations Convention on the Rights of the Child (1989) provides that a child has a right not to perform "any work that is likely to be hazardous or to interfere with the child's education, or to be harmful to the child's health or physical, mental, spiritual, moral or social development." That's much too vague and encompassing to create an international legal norm. Millions of middle-class American children are working part-time after school at jobs that confer no intellectual or characterological benefits merely to obtain pin money for buying video games also barren of intellectual or other benefits, the jobs and the games actually functioning to diminish the children educationally, mentally, physically, and spiritually. Shall their parents, and their employers, be hauled before an international tribunal to answer charges of child abuse?

ILO Convention 138: Minimum Age Convention (1973) provides that children should not be allowed to do other than "light work" unless they're at least 14 years old. But the concept of light work is vague, and it must vary a great deal across nations because of variance in social and economic conditions.

More promising for the plaintiffs is the International Labour Organization's Convention 182: The Worst Forms of Child Labour (June 17, 1999), which as we said is the one the United States has ratified. It provides, so far as bears on this case, that the worst forms of child labor include "work which, by its nature or the circumstances in which it is carried out, is likely to harm the health, safety or morals of children." *Id.*, art. 3(d). This is still pretty vague, in part because no threshold of actionable harm is specified, in part because of the inherent vagueness of the words "safety" and "morals." And it is weakened by the further statement that "the types of work referred to under Article 3(d) shall be determined by national laws or regulations or by the competent authority." Art. 4(1). That sounds like forswearing the creation of an international legal norm.

The Convention's Recommendation 190 adds some stiffening detail; it explains that Article 3(d) encompasses "work in an unhealthy environment which may, for example, expose children to hazardous substances, agents or processes, or to temperatures, noise levels, or vibrations damaging to their health," and "work under particularly difficult conditions such as work for long hours." But a "Recommendation" creates no enforceable obligations; according to the International Labour Organization's constitution, "apart from bringing the Recommendation before the . . . competent authority or authorities, no further obligation shall rest upon the Members, except that they shall report to the Director-General of the International Labour Office, at appropriate intervals as requested by the Governing Body, the position of the law and practice in their country in regard to the matters dealt with in the Recommendation, showing the extent to which effect has been given, or is proposed to be given, to the provisions of the Recommendation and such modifications of these provisions as it has been found or may be found necessary to make in adopting or applying them." ILO Constitution, art. 19(6)(d).

Given the diversity of economic conditions in the world, it's impossible to distill a crisp rule from the three conventions. We would like to think that working conditions of children below the age of 13 that significantly reduce longevity or create a high risk (or actuality) of significant permanent physical or psychological impairment would be deemed to violate customary international law, but we cannot be certain even of that. and anyway the working conditions at the Firestone plantation, while bad, are not that bad—more precisely, the plaintiffs haven't presented evidence that would create a triable issue of whether they're that bad.

Although Firestone doesn't employ children, at least directly, it sets high daily production quotas for its employees, who are poor Liberian agricultural workers. It is difficult for an employee to make his daily quota without help, and there is evidence that if he fails to make it he loses his job. These jobs are well paid by Liberian standards—in 2007 the average annual income of tappers (rubber farmers) on the Firestone plantation was $1559, though Liberia's per capita GDP was only $218 (but this figure probably excludes a fair amount of inkind and unreported income)—so the employees have a strong incentive to fulfill their daily quota. They can assure fulfillment by hiring other poor Liberians to help them; and because Firestone's Liberian employees are paid well by local standards, they can hire helpers cheaply. But alternatively they can dragoon their wives or children into helping them, at no monetary cost; and this happens, though how frequently we don't know.

We can't tell from the record whether Firestone has adopted effective measures for keeping children from working on the plantation. The plantation covers 186 square miles, which is roughly the size of Chicago, and thousands of people live there—approximately 6500 employees of Firestone plus the members of their families. We don't know how many supervisors Firestone has deployed on the plantation, and hence whether there are enough of them to prevent employees from using their children to help them. We don't know the supervisors' routines, or how motivated they are to put a stop to any child labor they observe. Firestone claims that it now has a policy of firing employees who use their children as helpers, but it didn't have such a policy prior to 2005. The suit was filed that year (initially in California, but it was transferred to the district court in Indiana the following year, which is why the docket number in the district court has 06 in it), and though it is unclear when Firestone's alleged violation of international law began—because it is unclear when the principle of customary international law invoked (or imagined) by the plaintiffs came into existence—it certainly began before 2005. And there is evidence that some of the supervisors had observed child labor during the period (whatever exactly it is) of alleged liability and done nothing to stop it. There is also evidence that the company's decisionmakers were aware of, and may even have condoned, some child labor on the plantation.

But does this add up to a violation of customary international law? "Agriculture is the sector with the most child labourers. It is also the sector with the most potential for decent work for rural children and young adolescents who have reached the legal minimum age of employment." International Labour Organization, "Children in Hazardous Work: What We Know, What We Need to Do" 21 (2011). But there is agricultural work and agricultural work. Harvesting rubber is hard, and to a degree hazardous, work. It involves cutting the bark of the rubber trees with machetes to expose the latex inside the tree trunk, draining the latex into buckets, carrying the buckets—which are heavy when they are full of latex—long distances, and applying fungicides and other chemicals to the trees. But not only do we not know how many children work on the plantation; we do not know, except for the 23 plaintiff children, whose ages range from six to sixteen and whose claims may differ from those of many other child workers on the plantation (which is why the district court refused to certify the suit as a class action—and the plaintiffs have not challenged that ruling), how much work the average child does, how hard that work is, and how many children work as hard as the plaintiff children attest to having worked.

Remember too that Firestone doesn't employ children; the argument rather is that by imposing tough quotas it induces its employees to enlist their children as helpers. The plaintiffs' basic objection seems therefore to be to the quotas. This implies that courts must in a case such as this determine on an employer-by-employer basis what level of production quotas violates customary international law by encouraging oppressive child labor.

We also—and this is the biggest objection to this lawsuit—don't know the situation of Liberian children who don't live on the Firestone plantation. Conceivably, because the fathers of the children on the plantation are well paid by Liberian standards, even the children who help their fathers with the work are, on balance, better off than the average Liberian child, and would be worse off if their fathers, unable to fill their daily quotas, lost their jobs or had to pay adult helpers, thus reducing the family's income. There is a tradeoff between family income and child labor; children are helped by the former and hurt by the latter; we don't know the net effect on their welfare of working on the plantation. Pranab Bardhan, "Some Up, Some Down," in Can We Put an End to Sweatshops? 49, 50–51 (Joshua Cohen & Joel Rogers eds. 2001); Frederick B. Jonassen, "A Baby-Step to Global Labor Reform: Corporate Codes of Conduct and the Child," 17 Minn. J. Int'l L. 7, 25–26 (2008).

In short, we have not been given an adequate basis for inferring a violation of customary international law, bearing in mind the Supreme Court's insistence on caution in recognizing new norms of customary international law in litigation under the Alien Tort Statute.

So the suit must fail, but for completeness we note two arguments by the defendant against liability that we reject. The first is that plaintiffs must exhaust their legal remedies in the nation in which the alleged violation of customary international law occurred. The implications of the argument border on the ridiculous; imagine having been required to file suit in a court in Nazi Germany complaining about genocide, before being able to sue under the Alien Tort Statute. What is true is that a U.S. court might, as a matter of international comity, stay an Alien Tort suit that had been filed in the U.S. court, in order to give the courts of the nation in which the violation had occurred a chance to remedy it, provided that the nation seemed willing and able to do that. *Sarei v. Rio Tinto, PLC, supra*, 550 F.3d at 831–32. Liberia is not able.

And second, the defendant argues that the statute has no extraterritorial application, except to violations of customary international law that are committed on the high seas. Courts have been applying the statute extraterritorially (and not just to violations at sea) since the beginning; no court to our knowledge has ever held that it doesn't apply extraterritorially; and Sosa was a case of nonmaritime extraterritorial conduct yet no Justice suggested that therefore it couldn't be maintained. Deny extraterritorial application, and the statute would be superfluous, given the ample tort and criminal remedies against, for example, the use of child labor (let alone its worst forms) in this country.

To sum up, although we disagree with the district court's ruling that corporations cannot be held liable for violating the Alien Tort Statute and we reject many of the defendant's arguments, we agree with the judgment.

AFFIRMED.

Notes and Questions

A United Nations report speaks to the question raised by Judge Posner as to the situation of children in Liberia who are *not* working on the Firestone plantation. The section on "early formative years" (ages 6–11) indicates that this age group is the largest compared to other age cohorts among children working in agriculture and related occupations.[32] The report does not address the Firestone situation specifically. The UNICEF report points to agricultural labor in itself as normal for young children but is also clear in its emphasis on parents' concerns for the security of their children. The predominance of young children in agricultural work may be seen as evidence of limited choices in the context of a persistent security crisis, rather than as a cultural tradition that normalizes risks to children at work. The UNICEF report emphasizes the trade-offs parents face in post-war Liberia, as between keeping children safe at home, working by their side, and sending them to school: "Parents currently are forced to make an unacceptable trade-off between child security and educational opportunity, pressured by education regulation and unable to assess the real risks and benefits, particularly for girls. Children become the victims of this service failure."[33]

III. Collective bargaining in the shadow of litigation

Given the extensive legal and practical challenges to foreign plaintiffs attempting to vindicate human rights claims under the ATS in U.S. courts, what are some possible alternatives to litigation?

As noted above, *Bridgestone* was filed in 2005, and in combination with other suits involving Firestone, remained in active litigation until the Seventh Circuit's ruling in 2011. The plaintiffs were supported by the International Labor Rights Forum—a Washington, DC-based coalition of labor rights and human rights groups—through their advocacy wing. In Liberia, the mobilization was the work of the Save My Future Foundation (SAMFU)[34] and the Firestone Agricultural Workers Union of Liberia (FAWUL). Other U.S. based organizations involved in the campaign included organizations of Liberians in diaspora, African affairs advocates, and U.S. labor unions. The Liberian Firestone workers were represented at various points by the U.S. Steelworkers.

As the court proceedings unfolded in the United States in late 2005 and 2006, labor actions unfolded in Liberia. Firestone plantation workers went on strike, incurring casualties, before union elections were ordered and held in July, 2007—observed by international monitors including a representative from the U.S. Steelworkers' Union. It was a contested election, resulting in a lawsuit that was decided in favor of FAWUL by the Supreme Court of Liberia. The following excerpt summarizes those events:

32. UNICEF, *The Situation of Women and Children in Liberia, 2012: From Conflict to Peace*, p. 59, Figure 14, http://www.unicef.org/liberia/SITAN_LBR2012-2017.pdf.

33. *Id.* At 61.

34. *See* SAMFU, http://www.samfufoundation.org (last visited Oct. 8, 2016).

Stop Firestone Coalition Celebrates Victory as Liberian Supreme Court Decision Approves Union Election on Firestone Plantation

(Dec. 21, 2007)[35]

After a lengthy strike by workers on a rubber plantation owned by the Firestone Natural Rubber Company in Liberia, the Supreme Court of Liberia ruled today that recent union elections held in July 2007 on the plantation were indeed legitimate. The first free, fair and independent union elections to take place on the plantation in its 81 year history in Liberia ushered in a new union leadership, but the previous company-controlled union challenged the elections through the legal system. The Supreme Court ruling confirmed that the union elections were in fact legitimate as the international election observers and the Firestone workers have been asserting for over five months.

The Stop Firestone Coalition, which includes both U.S. and Liberia-based human rights, labor, environmental and Africa-focused organizations, welcomed the ruling and called on Firestone management to immediately recognize the newly elected union leaders.

Austin Nantee, the newly elected President of the Firestone Agriculture Workers' Union of Liberia (FAWUL), said, "The Firestone workers are jubilant and are steadfast in their commitment. The workers themselves have realized their power and are looking forward to carving out a new collective bargaining agreement with the company."

Alfred Brownell, President and founder of the environmental law group Green Advocates in Liberia said, "This is a great Christmas gift and we are looking forward to a new day on the plantation. The Supreme Court has shown a large degree of independence and this is a victory not only for the workers, but also Liberia. The international collective action has produced the results today."

Emira Woods, co-director of Foreign Policy in Focus in the U.S. said, "After 81 years of modern day slavery, the Liberian judiciary has done the right thing to recognize this new union leadership and usher in a new day for the workers in Liberia."

Bama Athreya, Executive Director of the International Labor Rights Forum in the U.S. said, "This is a huge victory for the workers. With the coming of the new year, we hope that Firestone management will resolve to negotiate a new collective bargaining agreement in good faith with the new leaders.

FAWUL did enter into a collective bargaining process with Firestone, and for this victory was lauded by the AFL-CIO in 2008 (and, in 2011, by the U.S. Department

35. *Stop Firestone Coalition Celebrates Victory As Liberian Supreme Court Decision Approves Union Election on Firestone Plantation*, INT'L LABOR RIGHTS FORUM (Dec. 21, 2007), http://www.laborrights.org/releases/stop-firestone-coalition-celebrates-victory-liberian-supreme-court-decision-approves-union.

of Labor for its efforts to end child labor[36]). An excerpt from the AFL-CIO's testimonial, awarding FAWUL the 2007 George Meany-Lane Kirkland Human Rights Award follows, narrating events between the union elections in 2007 and the initiation of negotiations with Firestone in 2008:

Firestone Agricultural Workers Union of Liberia Awarded 2007 George Meany-Lane Kirkland Human Rights Award[37]

In recognition of the extraordinary courage, strength and solidarity of Liberian rubber workers at one of the world's largest rubber plantations, we are proud to nominate the Firestone Agricultural Workers Union of Liberia (FAWUL) for the 2007 George Meany-Lane Kirkland Human Rights Award.

On July 7, 2007, for the first time in the company's 82-year existence in Liberia, the more than 4,000 workers at the Firestone Rubber Plantation Company elected union leaders in a free and fair election. International observers, including representatives of the United Steelworkers (USW) and the Solidarity Center, monitored the election at the invitation of an Ad Hoc Election Commission created by the Liberian government. Workers overwhelmingly elected a reform slate of democratic and independent union leaders for FAWUL.

The workers' victory came not without sacrifice. After more than 14 years of civil war, Liberians elected a new democratic government, led by the first woman president in Africa, in October 2005. The workers at Firestone welcomed the new government and saw it as an opportunity for change in their lives at the plantation. Through a series of wildcat strikes, the workers succeeded in getting the government of Liberia to require new elections at the plantation. During the strikes, workers were intimidated and beaten. Tragically, several workers were killed. Workers who managed to survive on pittances were living without pay and rice subsidies. The commitment of the workers to freedom of association and the right to organize was strong, and they remained unified in their actions. . . .

Although the July 2007 elections were certified as free and fair, the plantation management refused to recognize the new union leadership and engage in collective bargaining. FAWUL's new leadership, however, carried on union activities without salaries, as management refused to release the union dues they continued to collect from the workers. The courageous plantation workers continued their solidarity, providing rice and money to their leaders to provide for their families. On Dec. 6, 2007, the rubber workers went on strike to protest Firestone's refusal to recognize their

36. Press Release, Int'l Labor Rights Forum & Inst. for Policy Studies, Labor Rights Advocates Congratulate Bridgestone/Firestone Workers in Liberia on Award from U.S. Dep't of Labor (Feb. 16, 2011), http://www.laborrights.org/releases/labor-rights-advocates-congratulate-bridgestonefirestone-workers-liberia-award-us-dept.

37. Press Realease, Int'l Labor Rights Forum, Firestone Agricultural Workers Union of Liberia Awarded 2007 George Meany-Lane Kirkland Human Rights Award (Mar. 5, 2008), http://www.laborrights.org/releases/firestone-agricultural-workers-union-liberia-awarded-2007-george-meany-lane-kirkland-human.

leaders. Once again, workers were beaten, disciplined and fired. Finally, on Dec. 21, 2007, Liberia's Supreme Court issued a decision recognizing the results of the union elections. This ruling was a landmark victory for democratic and independent unions. Firestone management recognized the new union leadership after the Supreme Court decision, and negotiations for a new collective bargaining agreement have begun.

The collective bargaining process ensued successfully. In August, 2008, Firestone and FAWUL reached an agreement resulting in retroactive restoration of lost wages averaging 24 percent annually, the construction of three high schools on the plantation, and other concessions for the plantation workers.[38]

IV. *Kiobel v. Royal Dutch Petroleum Co.*

While the restrictions on the availability of ATS and human rights law as detailed in *Bridgestone* and *Flomo* might seem to offer U.S. corporations impunity in their overseas operations, U.S. law also provides domestic employers with impressive latitude—e.g., in the employment of children (under the Fair Labor Standards Act), compulsory prison labor and the exemption of prison labor from the FLSA. Moreover, the Civil Rights Act of 1991 exempts U.S. owned businesses overseas from its provisions if such businesses are managed by foreign agents.[39] The liability of U.S. military personnel as well as private contractors in military settings are additional areas of ambiguity in the current milieu. The availability of ATS became a subject of sharp debate, even with the Second Circuit's rejection of corporate liability abroad under international customary law.[40]

The United States Supreme Court subsequently granted certiorari on the Second Circuit's decision in *Kiobel v. Royal Dutch Petroleum Co.*, 133 S. Ct. 1659, affirming the Second Circuit's decision. But the Supreme Court did not rule explicitly on whether corporations could be subject to liability under the ATS. Although the Court originally granted certiorari on that very issue, it ordered reargument on a separate

---

38. Fatoumata Fofana, *Firestone Bows; Agrees to Workers' Incentives*, Liberian Observer (Aug. 5, 2008), http://www.laborrights.org/in-the-news/firestone-bows-agrees-workers-incentives. *See also* Ansu Konneh, *Firestone Plantation in Liberia Signs Wage Accord With Workers*, Bloomberg News (Aug. 7, 2008), http://www.laborrights.org/in-the-news/firestone-plantation-liberia-signs-wage-accord-workers.

39. At this writing, ownership of Firestone/Bridgestone has passed from the United States to Japan.

40. *See, e.g.*, M. Anderson, *Whether Foreigner or Alien: A New Look at the Original Language of the Alien Tort Statute*, 27 Berkeley J. of Int'l. L. 316, 316–322 (2009) (arguing that the original intent of Congress limited the meaning of "alien" to foreign-born residents of the territorial United States); Richard Herz & Lorraine Leete, *An Alien by Any Other Name: Debunking a New Attempt to Re-Write the Original Language of the Alien Tort Statute*, 7 Berkeley J. Int'l. L. 1 (2011) (arguing against Berry's position, on the grounds of—at that time—consistent Supreme Court jurisprudence, including *Rasul*). These debates were important in the run-up to the U.S. Supreme Court's decision in *Kiobel*, which took a strongly territorial approach to the availability of ATS.

question: "Whether and under what circumstances the [ATS] allows courts to recognize a cause of action for violations of the law of nations occurring within the territory of a sovereign other than the United States." *Id.* at 1663.

The Supreme Court heard oral arguments on *Kiobel* on February 28, 2012. The questions presented to the Supreme Court were:

1. Whether the issue of corporate civil tort liability under the Alien Tort Statute, 28 U.S.C. § 1350, is a merits question, as it has been treated by all courts prior to the decision below, or an issue of subject matter jurisdiction, as the court of appeals held for the first time.
2. Whether corporations are immune from tort liability for violations of the law of nations such as torture, extrajudicial executions or genocide, as the court of appeals decisions provides, or if corporations may be sued in the same manner as any other private party defendant under the ATS for such egregious violations, as the Eleventh Circuit has explicitly held.

During the first round of oral arguments, the Court raised questions about the extraterritorial application of the ATS. The Court instructed parties to rebrief and reargue on that issue specifically: does the Alien Tort Statute apply to conduct that occurs in foreign nations? Upon rehearing, the Court held that there was a presumption against the extraterritorial application of the ATS and that the presumption had not been overcome in *Kiobel*.

In short, *Kiobel* resulted in a stark reduction of the availability of ATS as a means of redress for international human rights violations, but *Kiobel* did not question the validity of the ATS itself as a jurisdictional statute.

Kiobel v. Royal Dutch Petroleum Co.

133 S. Ct. 1659 (2013)

Chief Justice Roberts delivered the opinion of the Court.

Petitioners, a group of Nigerian nationals residing in the United States, filed suit in federal court against certain Dutch, British, and Nigerian corporations. Petitioners sued under the Alien Tort Statute, 28 U.S.C. § 1350, alleging that the corporations aided and abetted the Nigerian Government in committing violations of the law of nations in Nigeria. The question presented is whether and under what circumstances courts may recognize a cause of action under the Alien Tort Statute, for violations of the law of nations occurring within the territory of a sovereign other than the United States.

* * *

II

Passed as part of the Judiciary Act of 1789, the ATS was invoked twice in the late 18th century, but then only once more over the next 167 years. The statute provides district courts with jurisdiction to hear certain claims, but does not expressly provide any causes of action. We held in *Sosa v. Alvarez-Machain*, 542 U.S. 692, 714 (2004), however, that the First Congress did not intend the provision to be "stillborn." The grant of jurisdiction is instead "best read as having been enacted on the understanding that the common law would provide a cause of action for [a] modest number of international law violations." We thus held that federal courts may "recognize private claims [for such violations] under federal common law." The Court in *Sosa* rejected the plaintiff's claim in that case for "arbitrary arrest and detention," on the ground that it failed to state a violation of the law of nations with the requisite "definite content and acceptance among civilized nations."

The question here is not whether petitioners have stated a proper claim under the ATS, but whether a claim may reach conduct occurring in the territory of a foreign sovereign. Respondents contend that claims under the ATS do not, relying primarily on a canon of statutory interpretation known as the presumption against extraterritorial application. That canon provides that "[w]hen a statute gives no clear indication of an extraterritorial application, it has none," *Morrison v. National Australia Bank Ltd.*, 561 U.S. 247 (2010), and reflects the "presumption that United States law governs domestically but does not rule the world."

This presumption "serves to protect against unintended clashes between our laws and those of other nations which could result in international discord." . . .

We typically apply the presumption to discern whether an Act of Congress regulating conduct applies abroad. . . . The ATS, on the other hand, is "strictly jurisdictional." It does not directly regulate conduct or afford relief. It instead allows federal courts to recognize certain causes of action based on sufficiently definite norms of international law. But we think the principles underlying the canon of interpretation similarly constrain courts considering causes of action that may be brought under the ATS.

Indeed, the danger of unwarranted judicial interference in the conduct of foreign policy is magnified in the context of the ATS, because the question is not what Congress has done but instead what courts may do. This Court in *Sosa* repeatedly stressed the need for judicial caution in considering which claims could be brought under the ATS, in light of foreign policy concerns.

These concerns are not diminished by the fact that *Sosa* limited federal courts to recognizing causes of action only for alleged violations of international law norms that are "specific, universal, and obligatory." As demonstrated by Congress's enactment of the Torture Victim Protection Act of 1991, 28 U.S.C. § 1350, identifying such a norm is only the beginning of defining a cause of action. See *id.*, § 3 (providing detailed definitions for extrajudicial killing and torture); *id.*, § 2 (specifying who may be liable, creating a rule of exhaustion, and establishing a statute of limitations). Each of these decisions carries with it significant foreign policy implications.

* * *

III

Petitioners contend that even if the presumption applies, the text, history, and purposes of the ATS rebut it for causes of action brought under that statute. It is true that Congress, even in a jurisdictional provision, can indicate that it intends federal law to apply to conduct occurring abroad. See, *e.g.*, 18 U.S.C. § 1091(e) (2006 ed., Supp. V) (providing jurisdiction over the offense of genocide "regardless of where the offense is committed" if the alleged offender is, among other things, "present in the United States"). But to rebut the presumption, the ATS would need to evince a "clear indication of extraterritoriality." *Morrison*. It does not.

To begin, nothing in the text of the statute suggests that Congress intended causes of action recognized under it to have extraterritorial reach. The ATS covers actions by aliens for violations of the law of nations, but that does not imply extraterritorial reach—such violations affecting aliens can occur either within or outside the United States.

* * *

Petitioners make much of the fact that the ATS provides jurisdiction over civil actions for "torts" in violation of the law of nations.

The reference to "tort" does not demonstrate that the First Congress "necessarily meant" for those causes of action to reach conduct in the territory of a foreign sovereign. In the end, nothing in the text of the ATS evinces the requisite clear indication of extraterritoriality.

Nor does the historical background against which the ATS was enacted overcome the presumption against application to conduct in the territory of another sovereign.... We explained in *Sosa* that when Congress passed the ATS, "three principal offenses against the law of nations" had been identified by Blackstone: violation of safe conducts, infringement of the rights of ambassadors, and piracy. 542 U.S., at 723, 724, 124 S.Ct. 2739; see 4 W. Blackstone, Commentaries on the Laws of England 68 (1769). The first two offenses have no necessary extraterritorial application. Indeed, Blackstone—in describing them—did so in terms of conduct occurring within the forum nation.

* * *

The third example of a violation of the law of nations familiar to the Congress that enacted the ATS was piracy. Piracy typically occurs on the high seas, beyond the territorial jurisdiction of the United States or any other country. This Court has generally treated the high seas the same as foreign soil for purposes of the presumption against extraterritorial application.

* * *

Petitioners contend that because Congress surely intended the ATS to provide jurisdiction for actions against pirates, it necessarily anticipated the statute would apply to conduct occurring abroad.

Applying U.S. law to pirates, however, does not typically impose the sovereign will of the United States onto conduct occurring within the territorial jurisdiction of another sovereign, and therefore carries less direct foreign policy consequences. Pirates were fair game wherever found, by any nation, because they generally did not operate within any jurisdiction. We do not think that the existence of a cause of action against them is a sufficient basis for concluding that other causes of action under the ATS reach conduct that does occur within the territory of another sovereign; pirates may well be a category unto themselves.

* * *

Finally, there is no indication that the ATS was passed to make the United States a uniquely hospitable forum for the enforcement of international norms.

* * *

We therefore conclude that the presumption against extraterritoriality applies to claims under the ATS, and that nothing in the statute rebuts that presumption. "[T]here is no clear indication of extraterritoriality here," *Morrison,* and petitioners' case seeking relief for violations of the law of nations occurring outside the United States is barred.

IV

On these facts, all the relevant conduct took place outside the United States. And even where the claims touch and concern the territory of the United States, they must do so with sufficient force to displace the presumption against extraterritorial application. Corporations are often present in many countries, and it would reach too far to say that mere corporate presence suffices. If Congress were to determine otherwise, a statute more specific than the ATS would be required.

The judgment of the Court of Appeals is affirmed.

JUSTICE KENNEDY, concurring.

The opinion for the Court is careful to leave open a number of significant questions regarding the reach and interpretation of the Alien Tort Statute. In my view that is a proper disposition. Many serious concerns with respect to human rights abuses committed abroad have been addressed by Congress in statutes such as the Torture Victim Protection Act of 1991 (TVPA), 28 U.S.C. § 1350, and that class of cases will be determined in the future according to the detailed statutory scheme Congress has enacted. Other cases may arise with allegations of serious violations of international law principles protecting persons, cases covered neither by the TVPA nor by the reasoning and holding of today's case; and in those disputes the proper implementation of the presumption against extraterritorial application may require some further elaboration and explanation.

JUSTICE ALITO, with whom JUSTICE THOMAS joins, concurring.

I concur in the judgment and join the opinion of the Court as far as it goes. Specifically, I agree that when Alien Tort Statute (ATS) "claims touch and concern the territory of the United States, they must do so with sufficient force to displace the presumption against extraterritorial application." This formulation obviously leaves much unanswered, and perhaps there is wisdom in the Court's preference for this narrow approach. I write separately to set out the broader standard that leads me to the conclusion that this case falls within the scope of the presumption.

* * *

[O]nly conduct that satisfies *Sosa*'s requirements of definiteness and acceptance among civilized nations can be said to have been "the 'focus' of congressional concern," *Morrison*, when Congress enacted the ATS. As a result, a putative ATS cause of action will fall within the scope of the presumption against extraterritoriality—and will therefore be barred—unless the domestic conduct is sufficient to violate an international law norm that satisfies *Sosa*'s requirements of definiteness and acceptance among civilized nations.

Justice Breyer, with whom Justice Ginsburg, Justice Sotomayor and Justice Kagan join, concurring in the judgment.

Unlike the Court, I would not invoke the presumption against extraterritoriality. Rather, guided in part by principles and practices of foreign relations law, I would find jurisdiction under this statute where (1) the alleged tort occurs on American soil, (2) the defendant is an American national, or (3) the defendant's conduct substantially and adversely affects an important American national interest, and that includes a distinct interest in preventing the United States from becoming a safe harbor (free of civil as well as criminal liability) for a torturer or other common enemy of mankind. See *Sosa v. Alvarez-Machain*, 542 U.S. 692, 732 (2004) ("[F]or purposes of civil liability, the torturer has become—like the pirate and slave trader before him—*hostis humani generis*, an enemy of all mankind."). In this case, however, the parties and relevant conduct lack sufficient ties to the United States for the ATS to provide jurisdiction.

In sum, *Bridgestone/Flomo* and *Kiobel* span a crossroads in ATS jurisprudence, as the Court resists being drawn into a judgment that would have wide implications for the law of war as well as for labor in other contexts overseas where U.S. courts might offer stronger protections than formal or informal remedies available on site. Indeed, in these cases (and, as we shall see in Chapters 7 and 8, other cases as well), the Court functions as a mediator or "traffic cop" as litigants invoke different renderings of territoriality in their efforts to defend their interests abroad.

Notes and Questions

1. *Kiobel*'s reasoning and language are broad. Yet, the Court's rationale gives priority to an idea of the territorial national state as the primary actor on the international scene. Consider this proposition in relation to the various formulations of territoriality considered in Chapters 5 and 6. We will consider further developments

related to the role of courts in extraterritoriality in Chapter 8, in the contexts of trade, securities, and anti-trust laws.

2. *Flomo* and *Kiobel* rely in part on published characterizations of Africa as a whole and the situation of laborers, including children, in general. Can you imagine alternative framings? In particular, should it matter (as Judge Posner suggests it should) how Firestone workers fare compared to workers in other working environments? Do you agree that generally poor working conditions should trump a specific plea for relief in a particular instance?

3. As noted in Chapter 1, territoriality is not the same as geography on a map; it is subject to many formulations. The following excerpt from the Civil Rights Act of 1991 includes provisions that show Congress wrestling with the implications of the relationship between ownership, management, employer, and employee with respect to national territory.

Regarding U.S.-owned firms, the Civil Rights Act of 1991 includes the following provisions on extraterritorial employment:

Civil Rights Act of 1991[41]

SEC. 109. PROTECTION OF EXTRATERRITORIAL EMPLOYMENT.

(a) DEFINITION OF EMPLOYEE—Section 701(f) of the Civil Rights Act of 1964 (42 U.S.C. 2000e(f)) and section 101(4) of the Americans with Disabilities Act of 1990 (42 U.S.C. 12111(4)) are each amended by adding at the end the following: "With respect to employment in a foreign country, such term includes an individual who is a citizen of the United States.".

(b) EXEMPTION—

(1) Civil rights act of 1964. Section 702 of the Civil Rights Act of 1964 (42 U.S.C. 2000e-1) is amended—

* * *

(B) by adding at the end the following:

"(b) It shall not be unlawful under section 703 or 704 for an employer (or a corporation controlled by an employer), labor organization, employment agency, or joint labor-management committee controlling apprenticeship or other training or retraining (including on-the-job training programs) to take any action otherwise prohibited by such section, with respect to an employee in a workplace in a foreign country if compliance with such section would cause such employer (or such corporation), such organization, such agency, or such committee to violate the law of the foreign country in which such workplace is located.

"(c)(1) If an employer controls a corporation whose place of incorporation is a foreign country, any practice prohibited by section 703 or 704 engaged in by such corporation shall be presumed to be engaged in by such employer.

41. Civil Rights Act of 1991, Pub. L. No 102-166, 105 Stat. 1071 (1991).

"(2) Sections 703 and 704 shall not apply with respect to the foreign operations of an employer that is a foreign person not controlled by an American employer.

"(3) For purposes of this subsection, the determination of whether an employer controls a corporation shall be based on—

"(A) the interrelation of operations;
"(B) the common management;
"(C) the centralized control of labor relations; and
"(D) the common ownership or financial control,
"of the employer and the corporation."

(2) Americans with disabilities act of 1990. Section 102 of the Americans with Disabilities Act of 1990 (42 U.S.C. 12112) is amended

* * *

(B) by inserting after subsection (b) the following new subsection:

"(c) COVERED ENTITIES IN FOREIGN COUNTRIES—

"(1) IN GENERAL—It shall not be unlawful under this section for a covered entity to take any action that constitutes discrimination under this section with respect to an employee in a workplace in a foreign country if compliance with this section would cause such covered entity to violate the law of the foreign country in which such workplace is located.

"(2) CONTROL OF CORPORATION—

"(A) PRESUMPTION—If an employer controls a corporation whose place of incorporation is a foreign country, any practice that constitutes discrimination under this section and is engaged in by such corporation shall be presumed to be engaged in by such employer.

"(B) EXCEPTION—This section shall not apply with respect to the foreign operations of an employer that is a foreign person not controlled by an American employer.

"(C) DETERMINATION- For purposes of this paragraph, the determination of whether an employer controls a corporation shall be based on—

"(i) the interrelation of operations;

"(ii) the common management;

"(iii) the centralized control of labor relations; and

(iv) the common ownership or financial control, "of the employer and the corporation."

How do the terms and definitions involving the territorial identity of employers and employees in this Act affect the availability of U.S. law to workers in offshore businesses and other overseas operations of U.S. interests?

V. Discussion

The image of the world as a global legal order is predicated on an abstract view of law that upon closer examination is narrowly limited to law's regulatory functions in economic affairs, such that state regulation and private regulation, including self-regulation, might seem to be on the same plane, so to speak, as a continuum. But as the chapters in Part Two have demonstrated, the details of such an abstraction are "elusive,"[42] in part because the abstraction flattens real time, and with it, important empirical, conceptual and strategic considerations. Viewed from the standpoint of the needs of ordinary people—for example, workers in the transnational corporate environments discussed in Chapters 5 and 6—the picture is less one of continuity than it is of disjuncture, as multinational firms may enjoy borderless protections as investors that their own workers overseas (for example) do not, as jurisdiction over human rights questions involves separate agreements, tribunals and, in the United States, territorial constraints. Indeed, as we have seen in Part II, the debate over the extraterritorial availability of U.S. courts in relation to the claims of *Bridgestone* petitioners or *Wal-Mart*'s petitioners under the Alien Tort Statute, underscores the extent to which the concept of territoriality is itself constituted in the tensions between public and private forms of lawmaking where human rights are concerned. We continue that discussion in Part III. For now, we note the disjunction these rights cases flag as between the territoriality of U.S. domestic courts and the relatively borderless operations of multinational firms and investors. In that space, as we have also seen, where territory and transnationalism are both running in the background, firms and investors form their own legal arrangements through the private sector, through contracts and CSR codes. These are sometimes enforceable in domestic courts, and in that sense, public and private law remain indelibly bound to one another as dynamic interlegalities.

The image of globalization as a "world order"[43] is in this sense marked with an investor perspective, just as domestic law is marked with a state perspective. Reinstating the differences and connections between public and private law *in use* is thus crucial. In the next chapter, we begin with a discussion of some of the distinctive institutions of the transnational private sector. Beyond contracts, the private

---

42. Emilie Becault, Matthias Lievens, Jan Wouters & Antoon Braeckman, *Introduction: Global Governance and Democracy: Invitation to a Multidisciplinary Dialogue*, *in* Global Governance and Democracy: A Multidisciplinary Analysis 1–12, at 1 (Jan Wouters, Antoon Braeckman, Matthias Lievens & Emilie Becault eds., 2015).

43. The phrase in this context is Anne-Marie Slaughter's, referring to transnationally networked structures and processes of cooperation. Anne-Marie Slaughter, The New World Order 15–18 (2004).

"side" of transnational law is furnished with institutions responsible for creating international standards for industry, settling investor arbitration disputes, monitoring complex international supply chains, and managing corporate social responsibility protocols (as well as the relevant indicators). Without gainsaying the merits of a view that treats these institutions for their continuities of effect in relation to domestic law, we have emphasized the *dis*continuities between public and private domains, to bring out the contexts in which territoriality becomes a question of *intra*governmental power. As we shall see throughout Part III, intragovernmental tensions are critical to the interlegalities of governance more broadly.

Part Three

Governance through Government

Chapter 7

Interlegalities Between Public and Private Sectors

I. Introduction

For many commentators interested in "global governance," or the "new governance" (i.e., social and economic integration through the transnational private sector),[1] the apparent continuity of public and private law sustains an image of transnational law as global in its scope, applicability and eventual reach. The literature on globalization and global governance is far too vast to review here; suffice it to say that every social science discipline, in addition to law, offers points of entry. The first generation of post-Cold War scholars for whom global governance seemed to be a plausible future set the contours of that image in their evocations of the simultaneous relevance of multiple legal orders, global "flows" of people and ideas, and the promise and perils of managing legal pluralism on a global scale.[2] This image has become central to the meaning of the term "globalization" as a reference to an "emergent" worldwide order that is both the means and ends of global society produced out of the transnational infrastructures of capitalism.[3] For critics of the global governance thesis, the image of a global order offers a point of departure for critique, yet for the

1. This usage is indebted to Kenneth A. Armstrong. KENNETH A. ARMSTRONG, NEW GOVERNANCE AND THE EUROPEAN UNION: AN EMPIRICAL AND CONCEPTUAL CRITIQUE 249 (2013). *See also* Emilie Becault, Matthias Lievens, Jan Wouters & Antoon Braeckman, *Introduction: Global Governance and Democracy: Invitation to a Multidisciplinary Dialogue, in* GLOBAL GOVERNANCE AND DEMOCRACY: A MULTIDISCIPLINARY ANALYSIS 1–12 (Jan Wouters, Antoon Braeckman, Matthias Lievens & Emilie Becault eds., 2015).

2. For further reading on global governance, see UNITED NATIONS COMMISSION ON GLOBAL GOVERNANCE, OUR GLOBAL NEIGHBORHOOD: THE REPORT OF THE COMMISSION ON GLOBAL GOVERNANCE (1995); JAMES N. ROSENAU. ALONG THE DOMESTIC-FOREIGN FRONTIER: EXPLORING GOVERNANCE IN A TURBULENT WORLD (1997); James N. Rosenau, *Governance, Order, and Change in World Politics, in* JAMES N. ROSENAU & ERNST-OTTO CZEMPIEL, GOVERNANCE WITHOUT GOVERNMENT: ORDER AND CHANGE IN WORLD POLITICS 1–12 (1992). Fur further reading on multiplicity and management of legal pluralism, see Paul Schiff Berman, *Global Legal Pluralism*, 80 S. CALIF. L. REV. 1155 (2007); PAUL SCHIFF BERMAN, GLOBAL LEGAL PLURALISM: A JURISPRUDENCE OF LAW BEYOND BORDERS (2014). For further reading on global flows, see ARJUN APPADURAI, MODERNITY AT LARGE: CULTURAL DIMENSIONS OF GLOBALIZATION (1996).

3. Benedict Kingsbury, Nico Krisch, & Richard B. Stewart, *The Emergence of Global Administrative Law*, 68 L. & CONTEMPORARY PROBLEMS 15 (Summer/Autumn 2005); Colin Scott, *Regulating in Global Regimes* (University College Dublin Working Papers in Law, Criminology and Socio-Legal Studies, Research Paper No. 25/2010), http://papers.ssrn.com/sol3/papers.cfm?abstract_id=1598262.

most part without challenging the idea of there being some overarching global system awaiting attention to its moving parts and disparate effects. In this chapter and throughout Part III, we argue for a different starting point—taking as our theme the tensions between public and private forms of authority, their synergistic effects within government and their implications for stakeholders whether or not they are participants in a legal process.

As political sociologist Saskia Sassen writes, globalization involves a "repositioning of the state in a broader field of power and a reconfiguring of the work of states."[4] Drawing on the insights of Sassen and others who question the assumption that globalization weakens state power,[5] we observe that public and private powers in some situations vie against each other, tapping different forms of authority, and different interests. Understanding how public and private law pull against each other (even as they pull together in some contexts) is crucial to appreciating how transnational law surfaces as separation of powers questions—and, relatedly, how it is that state power may decrease in some areas (such as regulation of industries) while increasing in others (such as security).

Addressing this paradox calls on an understanding of territoriality and extraterritoriality as questions of authority—not merely lines on a map. Deference to Congress is both the means and ends of territoriality; issues involving executive power across borders (such as involving immigration or drones) quickly become flashpoints for fundamental political contests over U.S. interests in the world scene. In the U.S., domestic courts are thus central to the territorial aspects of transnational law and global capitalism—functioning as "traffic cops" as questions are routed this way or that through the branches of government, or around them.

This chapter sets the theme of Part III by focusing on public and private powers as offering different interlegalities in the transnational space from the standpoint of its diverse territorial implications and stakes. Courts are then taken up in Chapter 8; the "transnational executive" is the theme of Chapter 9. Overall, Part III reprises the idea of "interlegality" introduced in Part I as a reference to the characteristic tensions produced by the interplay of legal authorities. Public and private powers form interlegal junctures in precisely this sense—an observation that returns us to Boaventura de Sousa Santos's distinction between interlegality and legal pluralism introduced in Chapter 1. Legal pluralism refers to the organization of simultaneously relevant legal authorities. As such, the phrase may refer to a diversity of legal authorities without saying anything about their distinct foundations, interests, normative repertoires and especially their potential for contradiction and persistent tension. As Kenneth Armstrong suggests, a pluralist or sociological approach (an

---

4. Saskia Sassen, Territory, Authority, Rights: From Medieval to Global Assemblages 222–72 (2004) (describing "denationalized state agendas and privatized norm-making"). *See also* Public Governance in the Age of Globalization 51–70 (Karl-Heinz Ladeur ed., 2004).

5. Karl-Heinz Ladeur, *Globalization and Pubic Governance—A Contradiction?*, *in* Public Governance in the Age of Globalization 51–70 (Karl-Heinz Ladeur ed., 2004).

"empirical mapping") is not automatically a critical approach; to accomplish a critical understanding of the current terrain, he argues, governance must be understood not as "delegalisation" but as "an intensification and differentiation in the forms and locations of legal instrumentalism."[6] As noted in Chapter 1, Santos introduces the term *interlegality* to refer to the conceptual problems associated with that roiling legal landscape. In our usage, *interlegality* refers to such processes of intensification and differentiation as political work both internal and external to law. We do not claim that public and private law making are always in competition (they clearly are not[7]); rather, our claim is that the tensions between them illuminate transnational law as a complexly interconnected human endeavor. As Marc Amstutz has noted, "interlegality . . . is a reality", not "a silly whim of legal anthropologists."[8]

In this chapter, we reprise issues from the first two parts of the book, involving states and non-state entities in a range of governing and governance roles. Here, we examine government and governance as interlegalities—i.e., focusing on the confluences (and sometimes confrontations) of the different powers associated with public and private authority—as contexts for particular forms of legal and political work. These contexts offer both opportunities and constraints for a range of actors—courts, lawmakers, consumers, labor, citizens, and indigenous people, to name just a few of the affected stakeholder groups. In the combinations of public and private powers reviewed here, the connecting thread is the extent to which states take secondary roles in relation to the legal regimes developed by the transnational private sector, i.e., as agent, client or contracting party.

The main examples in this chapter involve states in these supporting roles. We start by looking at privately-created international standards and dispute settlement mechanisms, which though created with minimal public participation, sometimes function as quasi-legislative and quasi-judicial institutions. We then look to public authority through the lens of privatization to consider situations in which states are contractors and/or clients for essential resources (such as land) and services (such as welfare administration). Finally, we take up a concluding case study that combines transnational litigation and arbitration—so as to consider in more detail how powers combine and collide, creating tensions (interlegalities) that must be worked out politically, socially, and/or legally. Throughout, we consider these interlegalities from the standpoints of their principal parties and stakeholders. It is in the diverse engagements of such institutions with the challenges of "multidimensional governance"

6. Kenneth A. Armstrong, *New Governance and European Union: An Empirical and Conceptual Critique*, *in* CRITICAL LEGAL PERSPECTIVES ON GLOBAL GOVERNANCE: LIBER AMICORUM DAVID M. TRUBEK 249–71 (Grainne De Burca, Claire Kilpatrick, & Joanne Scott eds., 2014).

7. On the complexity of state and non-state regulation, see David LeviFaur, *The Global Diffusion of Regulatory Capitalism*, 598 THE ANNALS OF THE AMERICAN ACADEMY OF POLITICAL & SOCIAL SCIENCE 12 (2005). On the complexities of global regulation and accountability, see contributions to THE POLITICS OF GLOBAL REGULATION (Walter Mattli & Ngaire Woods eds., 2009).

8. Marc Amstutz, *In-Between Worlds:* Marleasing *and the Emergence of Interlegality in Legal Reasoning*, 11 EUROPEAN L.J. 766, 766 (2005).

that their democratic import is most visible,[9] and the study of globalization moved most productively from a preoccupation with scale and multiplicity—i.e., optics from a distance—to concrete problems of human relations.[10]

II. Standards as interlegalities: International Organization for Standardization (ISO)

We begin with the International Organization for Standardization (ISO), since many scholars regard standards, brought about by consensus of private parties in voluntary associations, as filling gaps in state and international regulation.[11] "While the state traditionally has been viewed as the appropriate overseer of domestic business activity, the scale and structure of contemporary global production challenge the capacity of even highly developed states to regulate activities that extend beyond their borders."[12] Into this void have stepped "standards bodies" that have promulgated voluntary norms to address issues including technical coordination, social and environmental impact, monitoring, and even enforcement.[13] This view of a global order awaiting completion rests in part on assumptions about the nature of power as networked, commensurate, cooperative, convergent, cumulative and (therefore) assured of dominance.

But power tells many stories, and formal integration does not always depend on substantive consensus.[14] Social science and humanities scholars have developed "bottom-up" approaches around issues of diversity, incommensurability, and the intricacy of power flows (with metaphors such as capillaries, rhizomes, and micro-physics).[15] As we will see in this section, standards also create gaps by the nature of

9. Alfred C. Aman, Jr., The Democracy Deficit: Taming Globalization Through Law Reform (2004); Becault et al., *supra* note 1, at 3. "Multidimensional governance" challenges and their democratic implications are the subject of Hari M. Osofsky, *Multidimensional Governance and the BP* Deepwater Horizon *Oil Spill*, 63 Fla. L. Rev 1077 (2011).

10. On the conceptual limitations of scale in relation to globalization studies, see Eric Sheppard, *The Spaces and Times of Globalization: Place, Scale, Networks, and Positionality*, 78 Economic Geography 307 (2002); Neil Brenner, *Beyond State-Centrism? Space, Territoriality, and Geographical Scale in Globalization Studies*, 28 Theory & Soc'y 39 (1999).

11. Kenneth W. Abbott & Duncan Snidal, *The Governance Triangle: Regulatory Standards Institutions and the Shadow of the State*, *in* The Politics of Global Regulation 44, 45 (Walter Mattli & Ngaire Woods eds,. 2009).

12. *Id.* at 44.

13. *Id.*; David A. Wirth, *The International Organization for Standardization: Private Voluntary Standards as Swords and Shields*, 36 B.C. Envtl. Aff. L. Rev. 79, 88 (2009) (noting that voluntary standards are usually implemented "through a private third-party auditing process").

14. For an ethnographic analysis of strategies for managing dissensus in a quasi-legal drafting process, see Annelise Riles, *Infinity Within the Brackets*, 25 Am. Ethnologist 378 (1998).

15. On the capillary nature of power, see Michel Foucault, History of Sexuality, Volume 1: An Introduction (Robert Hurley trans., 1990) (1976). On rhizomes, see Gilles DeLeuze & Felix Guattari, A Thousand Plateaus: Capitalism and Schizophrenia (Brian Massumi trans., 1987). On micro-physics of power, see Jonathan Metzger, Linda Soneryd, & Katrina Tamm Hallstrom, *"Power" Is That Which Remains to Be Explained: Dispelling the Ominous Dark Matter of Critical Planning Studies*, 16 Planning Theory 203 (2017).

their participatory rules (including restrictions on non-member participation) and the inherent fragility of multistakeholder processes.[16] An entire industry may adopt voluntary standards and employ its own enforcement mechanisms (formal or informal) to ensure adherence. Standards may also be incorporated by reference by national or international regulators, giving what began as voluntary standards the force of law. In the space between public and private authority—a classic interlegal zone—standards function in diverse ways: building up the capacity for cooperation and harmonization, but also (from other angles) reducing transparency, restricting public participation and access,[17] reserving significant authority to external private parties, and unsettling canons of democratic legitimacy.[18] International standards are central to global governance, but among scholars, there remains persistent debate as to whether they represent (in the words of Alejandro Pena) an "overarching rationality" or "the coexistence of multiple ones."[19] Such debates underscore both the unevenness of the political landscape around the world, and the extent to which standards (perhaps counterintuitively) represent a highly dynamic and improvisatory process.[20]

A. Purpose and structure of the ISO

The International Organization for Standardization (ISO), founded in 1946, is comprised of standardizing bodies from 165 countries.[21] ISO is not an intergovernmental organization, and its members are not states; rather, ISO provides "a forum for coordinating standardizing efforts by private business," and its member representatives are almost all private standardizing bodies.[22] Originally formed with the goal of standardizing machine and other technical components, the ISO has recently expanded its scope, reaching into social domains with its guidance on corporate social responsibility guidance (ISO 26000). Some ISO statutes are intended to set managerial standards and/or a basis for certification. Others—including ISO

---

16. Magnus Bostrom & Katrina Tamm Hallstrom, *Global Multi-Stakeholder Standard Setters: How Fragile Are They?*, 9 J. GLOBAL ETHICS 93 (2015).

17. Peter L. Strauss, *Private Standards Organizations and Public Law*, 22 WM. & MARY BILL RTS. J. 497 (2013).

18. On unsettling legitimacy, see Ruedinger Hahn & Christian Weidtmann, *Transnational Governance, Deliberative Democracy, and the Legitimacy of IS0 26000: Analyzing the Case of a Global Multistakeholder Process*, 55 BUSINESS & SOC'Y 90 (2012).

19. Alejandro M. Pena, *Governing Differentiation: On Standardization as Political Steering*, 21 EUR. J. INT'L REL. 52, 56 (2015). Reviewing the development of international standards as a topic of scholarship across several disciplines, Pena argues for a systems theory approach that would look to standardization as a political process—an articulation of multiple rationalities. *Id.*

20. On uneven political landscape, see *id.* On dynamism of standardization, see Nils Brunsson, Andreas Rasche & David Seidl, *The Dynamics of Standardization: Three Perspectives on Standards in Organization Studies*, 33 ORG. STUD. 613 (2012). *See also* Jan van den Ende, Geerten van de Kaa, Simo den Uijl & Henk J. deVries, *The Paradox of Standard Flexibility: The Effects of Co-evolution Between Standard and Interorganizational Network*, 33 ORG. STUD. 705 (2012).

21. Wirth, *supra* note 13, at 80; *About Us*, ISO.ORG, http://www.iso.org/iso/home/about.htm.

22. Wirth, *supra* note 13, at 80–81.

26000 on social responsibility—are explicitly intended as guidance rather than as a basis for certifications or legalization. ISO 26000 has nonetheless had a robust and controversial afterlife in various regional and national efforts to develop legal standards for Corporate Social Responsibility.[23] The controversies are strong evidence that the fundamental character of global governance—as integrative or differentiating, as legal or political (among other interpretive possibilities)—remains unresolved, eluding any general solution. This observation brings us to reiterate this chapter's theme: the extent to which public and private authorities are constituted as interlegalities—zones of contention—rather than as automatically complementary domains. We begin with the ISO statutes and a brief discussion of the ISO's institutional development, then turn to the domestic legal implications of ISO standards (including ISO 26000) to consider some of the challenges of merging public and private authority conceptually and pragmatically.

Consider the following excerpts from ISO foundational documents and promotional materials. Who has a voice in ISO standard promulgation? To whom is ISO accountable? How does ISO reach conclusions about what standards to promulgate? What are ISO's goals and how have they changed from ISO's founding? Do these statutes apply equally well to technical and social questions?

ISO Statutes
International Organization for Standardization (2013)

* * *

Article 2: Object

2.1 The object of the Organization shall be to promote the development of standardization and related activities in the world with a view to facilitating international exchange of goods and services and to developing cooperation in the spheres of intellectual, scientific, technological and economic activity.

2.2 As means to these ends, *inter alia*, the Organization may:

> **2.2.1** Take action to facilitate worldwide harmonization of standards and related activities;
>
> **2.2.2** Develop and issue International Standards, and take action for their worldwide implementation;
>
> **2.2.3** Arrange for exchange of information regarding work of its members and of its technical committees;

---

23. On the controversies over ISO 26000 in the EU, see Isabelle Schömann, *ISO 26000: The new face of corporate social responsibility?* European Trade Union Institute Policy Brief number 1/2012 (2012). As one example involving standardization of CSR (based in part on ISO 26000) in Québec, including First Nations participants, see Luc Bres, *The Visible Hand of Consultants in the Construction of the Markets for Virtue: Translating Issues, Negotiating Boundaries and Enacting Responsive Regulations*, 67 Human Rel. 1347, 1368 (2014).

2.2.4 Cooperate with other international organizations interested in related matters, particularly by undertaking studies relating to standardization projects at their request.

* * *

Article 10: Technical committees

10.1 A request for undertaking standards development work in a technical field may be initiated by one or more member bodies, by a technical committee or a policy development committee established by the Council, by the Secretary-General or by an organization outside the Organization.

10.2 Technical committees shall be established by the Technical Management Board and shall work under its authority.

10.3 Each member body interested in a subject for which a technical committee has been authorized shall have the right to be represented on that committee.

* * *

Article 16: Relations with other international organizations

16.1 The Organization may cooperate with other international organizations interested partially or wholly in standardization or related activities. The conditions of cooperation shall be established by the Council.

* * *

Article 17: Finance

17.1 The funds of the Organization shall be derived from the dues and contributions of the members, and from the sale of publications. The acceptance of funds from other sources (gifts, etc.) shall be at the discretion of the Council.

B. ISO's evolution and goals

Consider the following excerpts from the ISO's website chronicling its evolution, present form, and strategy moving forward:

Friendship Among Equals: Recollections From ISO's First Fifty Years International Organization for Standardization (1997)[24]

To begin with, the standardization fields addressed by ISO concerned basic mechanics: screw threads, rolling bearings, pipe sizes, shafts, couplings and power transmission. This work was rooted in the accomplishments of the ISA committees before the Second World War. In fact, the first ISO Recommendation, published in 1951 and titled: "Standard reference temperature for industrial length measurement", would have helped settle a debate at the founding conference of the ISA in

24. Available at http://www.iso.org/iso/2012_friendship_among_equals.pdf.

1926. Delegates were in dispute as to whether the length of a metre varied with the temperature in which a measurement was made, or whether the metre, as a unit of measurement, was exactly the same regardless of the temperature. A representative of the National Bureau of Standards in Washington was called in to settle the impasse. Without reservation, he declared that the latter statement was correct.

* * *

There was a general shift in the 1960s away from producing international standards covering basic test methods and terminologies towards producing standards related to the performance, safety and health aspects of particular products. This trend was reinforced by the 1980 GATT Standards code which called on parties to: "play a full part in the preparation by appropriate international standardizing bodies of international standards for products" and added that: "wherever appropriate, Parties shall specify technical regulations in terms of performance."

Benefits of International Standards[25]

International Standards bring technological, economic and societal benefits. They help to harmonize technical specifications of products and services making industry more efficient and breaking down barriers to international trade. Conformity to International Standards helps reassure consumers that products are safe, efficient and good for the environment.

For Business

International Standards are strategic tools and guidelines to help companies tackle some of the most demanding challenges of modern business. They ensure that business operations are as efficient as possible, increase productivity and help companies access new markets.

Benefits include:

- **Cost savings**—International Standards help optimise operations and therefore improve the bottom line
- **Enhanced customer satisfaction**—International Standards help improve quality, enhance customer satisfaction and increase sales
- **Access to new markets**—International Standards help prevent trade barriers and open up global markets
- **Increased market share**—International Standards help increase productivity and competitive advantage
- **Environmental benefits**—International Standards help reduce negative impacts on the environment

For Society

ISO has over 19,500 standards touching almost all aspects of daily life.

25. Available at http://www.iso.org/iso/home/standards/benefitsofstandards.htm.

When products and services conform to International Standards consumers can have confidence that they are safe, reliable and of good quality. For example, ISO's standards on road safety, toy safety and secure medical packaging are just a selection of those that help make the world a safer place.

To make sure that the benefits of ISO International Standards are as broad as possible, ISO supports the involvement of consumers in standard development work with its Committee on consumer policy (COPOLCO).

International Standards on air, water and soil quality, on emissions of gases and radiation and environmental aspects of products contribute to efforts to preserve the environment and the health of citizens.

For Government

ISO standards draw on international expertise and experience and are therefore a vital resource for governments when developing public policy.

National governments can use ISO standards to support public policy, for example, by referencing ISO standards in regulations. This has a number of benefits, including:

- **Expert opinion**—ISO standards are developed by experts. By integrating an ISO standard into national regulation, governments can benefit from the opinion of experts without having to call on their services directly.
- **Opening up world trade**—ISO standards are international and adopted by many governments. By integrating ISO standards into national regulation, governments help to ensure that requirements for imports and exports are the same the world over, therefore facilitating the movement of goods, services and technologies from country to country.

ISO Strategy: 2016–2020[26]

Through [ISO's] members, it brings together experts to share knowledge and develop voluntary, consensus-based, market-relevant International Standards that support innovation and provide solutions to global challenges. ISO will make every effort to be attractive and responsive to the needs of industry, as well as those of regulators, consumers and other stakeholders.

A leader in its field and supported by a broad member base, ISO enjoys a strong governance, code of ethics and standards development process. The ISO Strategy 2016–2020 builds on this solid foundation and will guide the organization in its decisions over the next five years.

In particular, the Strategy will help the organization respond to a future where:

- Technological, economic, legal, environmental, social and political challenges will require examination and continual improvement of the ISO system

26. Available at http://www.iso.org/iso/iso_strategy_2016-2020_en_-_lr.pdf.

- Stakeholder engagement and the challenges to ISO's intellectual property will continue to be both a key opportunity and risk for ISO

* * *

ISO standards used everywhere

ISO's goal is to produce globally relevant International Standards that are used everywhere. For the period 2016–2020, "ISO standards used everywhere" means:

- Ensuring a coherent and credible collection of standards that are used effectively by industry and bring recognized benefits to economies
- Producing International Standards in a clear, understandable language, that are easy to read and user friendly
- Enabling ISO members to successfully reach their markets, promote the use of ISO standards, and deliver ISO content to their customers
- Increasing the uptake of standards as business performance tools

Identifying and meeting the changing needs of customers, with a focus on how they would like to use and access ISO standards

- Developing supporting information that complements International Standards, which members can provide to their customers as and when needed
- Providing a suite of international conformity assessment standards applicable to all sectors and all types of conformity assessment that help ensure stakeholders have confidence in the implementation of standards
- Implementing intellectual property protection policies that are well understood and respected by developers and customers

---

ISO is an industry-founded organization promulgating industry-focused standards to solve industry issues. From the time of ISO's founding until the 1980s, when ISO standards were "limited and eminently technical,"[27] public bodies perhaps would have been justified in not questioning the transparency of the standardization process:

> To the extent that ISO processes are directed at selecting among essentially arbitrary choices of little societal impact but of great practical utility to industry, such as standardizing film speeds, the Organization's institutional structure has been of little concern from the point of view of public policy. The specifications chosen for film speeds do not really matter so long as they are compatible with all cameras around the world.[28]

---

27. Naomi Roht-Arriaza, *Shifting the Point of Regulation: The International Organization for Standardization and Global Lawmaking on Trade and the Environment*, 22 Ecology L.Q. 479, 490 (1995).

28. Wirth, *supra* note 13, at 87.

Since then, however, ISO has promulgated environmental standards and, by doing so "have entered an arena of public policy" of eminent importance to national and international lawmaking bodies.[29] As we will discuss in detail in the next section, questions of transparency and process warrant even greater scrutiny as lawmaking bodies and treaty organizations have essentially codified ISO and other once-voluntary standards into regulations and international trade agreements.

As a result of increased scrutiny, standards setting organizations have adopted mechanisms "to improve access to rule-making deliberations through provision for greater participation and transparency," for example, by adopting notice-and-comment procedures.[30] This does not mean, however, that such procedures have suddenly provided for open and public deliberation over the propriety of their standards. First, these procedures have generally not covered the "implementation and enforcement functions of these organizations," leaving these critical areas open to capture by narrow economic interests.[31] Second, "[t]he price of 'activating' institutional due process mechanisms . . . is often too high to generate wide societal demand," in part because "international processes of regulation are further removed from public gaze than national ones."[32] Professors Mattli and Woods emphasize the inequitable consequences of this high cost: "In short, . . . if only a few have access to information and the capacity to use it, the resulting demand for regulatory change will favor the 'haves' at the expense of the 'have-nots'—regardless of whether the institutional supply of due process mechanisms is extensive or limited."[33]

C. From voluntary to mandatory (and in between)

The World Trade Organization Agreement on Technical Barriers to Trade (known as the TBT Agreement) was established with three guiding principles: "(1) avoidance of unnecessary obstacles to trade, (2) harmonization of standards, and (3) transparency of regulations."[34] The TBT Agreement also expressly incorporates international standards, including those developed by ISO, and grants government standards that conform to such standards a "rebuttable presumption of validity."[35] WTO members must use these standards except upon a showing that the standard is "an ineffective or inappropriate means for the fulfilment of the legitimate objectives pursued."[36] WTO and other organizations such as NAFTA have adopted private standards as a

29. *Id.*

30. Walter Mattli & Ngaire Woods, *In Whose Benefit? Explaining Regulatory Change in Global Politics*, *in* The Politics of Global Regulation, *supra* note 7, at 1, 18.

31. *Id.*

32. *Id.* at 21.

33. *Id.*

34. Norbert L. W. Wilson, *Clarifying the Alphabet Soup of the TBT and the SPS in the WTO*, 8 Drake J. Agric. L. 703, 710 (2003).

35. Wirth, *supra* note 13, at 95.

36. Agreement on Technical Barriers to Trade, Jan. 1, 1995, 1868 U.N.T.S. 120, https://www.wto.org/english/docs_e/legal_e/17-tbt.pdf art. 2.4.

default, requiring "*public* authorities to justify departures, especially those tending in the direction of more rigorous requirements .... This situation in effect bootstraps a nongovernmental standard into one with binding significance for governmentally established regulatory requirements ... ."[37]

In short, even in technical domains, ISO standards carry implications for domestic regulation. Professor David Wirth illustrates how these standards can be used as both a sword and a shield to frustrate domestic regulators. For example, eco-label schemes such as the Energy Star logo for energy efficient computers or nutritional information labels are governed by ISO standards incorporated into the TBT Agreement. ISO standards provide that these labels must be "accurate, verifiable, relevant, not misleading," and "based on scientific methodology that is sufficiently thorough and comprehensive to support the claim."[38] Each requirement imposes a negative test upon the regulatory body. The ISO standard may, therefore, be used as a sword by a state to challenge another state's regulation in an international trade dispute forum if a regulation permits labels that are not, for example, "relevant."[39] Wirth notes that these concerns are heightened in more complex areas of regulation, "such as the evaluation of policy-relevant science that by definition involve[s] a measure of judgment."[40]

ISO standards can also be used as a shield. For example, California's Low-Carbon Fuel Standard,[41] designed to reduce total carbon emissions per unit of fuel consumed, requires application of a life cycle analysis to take into account emissions from all stages of fuels usage: combustion, production, and transport. Such a requirement can run up against most-favored nation components of trade agreements, which generally mandate nondiscriminatory "treatment among products on the basis of their national origin." [42] However, California could utilize ISO's "remarkably malleable" life cycle analysis methodology, which requires a systematic analysis of "the environmental aspects and impacts of product systems, from raw material acquisition to final disposal, in accordance with the stated goal and scope" and allows consideration of the "acquisition of raw materials; ... distribution/transportation; [and] disposal of process wastes and products."[43] If California were to go this route and adopt the ISO standard, incorporated into the WTO TBT Agreement, then the standard would act as a shield to protect California's Low-Carbon Fuel standard from a trade-based challenge.

All of this raises normative questions of how much influence an industry-dominated private organization should have over domestic regulations with the force of law. Wirth warns that, as ISO and other standards bodies continue to

37. Wirth, *supra* note 13, at 96.

38. *Id.* at 98 (quoting ISO 14020).

39. *Id.*

40. *Id.* at 99.

41. California Alternative and Renewable Fuel, Vehicle Technology, Clean Air, and Carbon Reduction Act of 2007, CAL. HEALTH & SAFETY CODE §§ 44270–44274.5 (West Supp. 2008).

42. Wirth, *supra* note 13, at 100.

43. *Id.* (quoting ISO 14040).

promulgate standards that affect political and social judgments, "we the public may discover only too late that important public policies are affected in a forum that receives little public scrutiny, that is largely inaccessible except to the business community, and that does not necessarily reflect the public interest."[44]

These issues are especially clear in ISO 26000, on social responsibility, issued as guidance rather than as a standard subject to audit and certification. A full discussion of ISO 26000 would take into account its context in other ISO initiatives related to sustainable development, as well as related projects on corporate social responsibility in the European Union, the United Nations, and the ILO, among other transnational efforts. The following excerpt summarizes the history of the ISO 26000 drafting process:[45]

Isabelle Schömann, *ISO 26000: The New Face of Corporate Social Responsibility?*

European Trade Union Institute Policy Brief No. 1 (2012)

The process was initiated in 2001 by the ISO Committee on Consumer Policy, handing over the initiative of consumer organisations so as to confront the impact of multinational practices on populations' living and working conditions, and taken up in 2002 by a multi-party group mandated by the ISO. Work on ISO 26000 began in effect in 2004 with the formation of the social responsibility working group, headed up by the Swedish and Brazilian national standardisation agencies. They were tasked with drawing up the future ISO 26000 standard, following the basic SAG recommendations and a multi-step process based on a stakeholder agreement concerning the content of the working documents.

It should be noted that ISO 26000 emerged from a derogatory procedure in two stages, in that on the one hand it relies on 'stakeholders' rather than on national experts. These stakeholders belonged as individuals to national delegations and not, therefore, to their respective national bodies. Those bodies comprised six categories of participants: government, consumers, employers, workers, NGOs and others. Secondly, ISO 26000 envisages participation with observer status (no voting rights) of 35 contact institutions consisting of trade unions (TUAC, ITUC) and employers' organisations (IOE), as well as private international bodies (CSR Network). The participation of international public institutions such as the ILO, OECD and United Nations was ensured in a rather odd fashion: at the ISO's invitation, the UN's Global Compact bureau signed a memorandum in 2006, and the OECD another one in 2008, in order to be able to attend the ISO meetings so as to draw up ISO 26000: even though the ILO had signed a cooperation agreement in 2005 giving itself the right of veto, specifically so as to ensure that ISO 26000 did not encroach on its spheres of competence.

44. *Id.* at 101.

45. For a detailed account of the drafting process, see Michaela A. Balzarova & Pavel Castka, *Stakeholders' Influence and Contribution to Social Standards Development: The Case of Multiple Stakeholder Approach To ISO 26000 Development*, 111 J. Bus. Ethics 265 (2012).

After eight international meetings, the standard was adopted by a majority of 2/3 of the ISO membership in September 2010 and published in November 2010. Out of the 71 ISO members involved in drafting the ISO 26000 standard, 66 voted in favour including the in extremis vote cast by China, even though it had opposed the draft ever since the start of negotiations and up until 2009, for fear that the standard might one day become a parameter to be taken into account in a world trade context. Once the voluntary implementation of the standard had been made crystal clear, China went along with the consensus even though the US, India, Turkey, Luxembourg and Cuba all voted against. This, then, was the culmination of an international consensus around a universally applicable standard on the concept of Guidance on Social Responsibility (GSR) making it applicable to every organisation.

The introduction to the ISO text below specifically disavows any direct connection between the guidance and an effort to apply it as a management protocol, certification standard, or in some other way that would be mandatory. The guidance articulates seven principles of social responsibility: accountability, transparency, ethical behavior, respect for stakeholder interests, respect for the rules of law, respect for international norms of behavior, and respect for human rights. As you read the following excerpt, consider the basis of its claims that the guidance (i) represents a consensus among a comprehensive range of relevant stakeholder groups, and (ii) is relevant to all forms of organization. In light of these claims, what is the significance of the text's insistence on the voluntary character of its principles?

Introduction, ISO 26000, Guidance on Social Responsibility (2010)[46]

Organizations around the world, and their stakeholders, are becoming increasingly aware of the need for and benefits of socially responsible behaviour. The objective of social responsibility is to contribute to sustainable development.

An organization's performance in relation to the society in which it operates and to its impact on the environment has become a critical part of measuring its overall performance and its ability to continue operating effectively. This is, in part, a reflection of the growing recognition of the need to ensure healthy ecosystems, social equity and good organizational governance. In the long run, all organizations' activities depend on the health of the world's ecosystems. Organizations are subject to greater scrutiny by their various stakeholders. The perception and reality of an organization's performance on social responsibility can influence, among other things:

—its competitive advantage;

—its reputation;

—its ability to attract and retain workers or members, customers, clients or users;

46. Available at https://www.iso.org/obp/ui/#iso:std:iso:26000:ed-1:v1:en.

—the maintenance of employees' morale, commitment and productivity;

—the view of investors, owners, donors, sponsors and the financial community; and

—its relationship with companies, governments, the media, suppliers, peers, customers and the community in which it operates.

This International Standard provides guidance on the underlying principles of social responsibility, recognizing social responsibility and engaging stakeholders, the core subjects and issues pertaining to social responsibility (see Table 2 [omitted]) and on ways to integrate socially responsible behaviour into the organization (see Figure 1 [omitted]). This International Standard emphasizes the importance of results and improvements in performance on social responsibility.

This International Standard is intended to be useful to all types of organizations in the private, public and non-profit sectors, whether large or small, and whether operating in developed or developing countries. While not all parts of this International Standard will be of equal use to all types of organizations, all core subjects are relevant to every organization. All core subjects comprise a number of issues, and it is an individual organization's responsibility to identify which issues are relevant and significant for the organization to address, through its own considerations and through dialogue with stakeholders.

Governmental organizations, like any other organization, may wish to use this International Standard. However, it is not intended to replace, alter or in any way change the obligations of the state.

Every organization is encouraged to become more socially responsible by using this International Standard.

Recognizing that organizations are at various stages of understanding and integrating social responsibility, this International Standard is intended for use by those beginning to address social responsibility, as well as those more experienced with its implementation. The beginner may find it useful to read and apply this International Standard as a primer on social responsibility, while the experienced user may wish to use it to improve existing practices and to further integrate social responsibility into the organization. Although this International Standard is meant to be read and used as a whole, readers looking for specific types of information on social responsibility may find the outline in Table 1 useful [omitted]. Box 1 [omitted] provides summary information to assist users of this International Standard.

This International Standard provides guidance to users and is neither intended nor appropriate for certification purposes. Any offer to certify to ISO 26000 or any claim to be certified to ISO 26000 would be a misrepresentation of the intent and purpose of this International Standard.

Reference to any voluntary initiative or tool in Annex A [omitted] of this International Standard does not imply that ISO endorses or gives special status to that initiative or tool.

Notes and Questions

1. As alluded to above, standards drafted by private organizations (such as ISO) and incorporated by reference into law (through, for example, regulation) are not readily accessible to the public because the published standards are not usually freely available:

> Federal agencies currently "incorporate by reference" thousands of outside standards into binding federal regulations. Free public access to the text is reliably provided only in the Office of the Federal Register's reading room in Washington, D.C. Otherwise a reader may be required to pay substantial access fees set by drafting organizations, significantly obstructing public access, particularly by individuals and small businesses. The right to comment on an agency's proposed "incorporation by reference" of such standards into federal regulations is also impeded by the lack of public access to the text.[47]

The practical barriers to access troubled the ABA Section of Administrative Law and Regulatory Practice enough to urge the ABA to adopt a resolution on the issue:

> RESOLVED, That the American Bar Association urges Congress to amend 5 U.S.C. §552(a)(1) of the Freedom of Information Act (FOIA) to require that when a standard drafted by a private organization is exempted from Federal Register publication because it has been "incorporated by reference" (IBR) into a substantive rule of general applicability, the rulemaking agency must ensure meaningful free public availability of the incorporated text, such as through online access in a centralized online location or access in all government depository libraries.
>
> FURTHER RESOLVED, That the American Bar Association urges Congress to amend 5 U.S.C. §553, the Administrative Procedure Act's rulemaking provisions, to require meaningful free public availability of a proposed IBR standard's text during the public comment period.
>
> FURTHER RESOLVED, That the American Bar Association urges Congress to ensure that private organizations, where appropriate, have access to compensation for financial losses attributable to making their standards publicly available.

The provision for compensation would allow Congress to compensate standards-setting organizations for their time, expertise, and work product. This resolution was withdrawn.[48] Would adoption of the legislation such as that proposed in the ABA Section's resolution have struck an appropriate balance among the varied interests?

---

47. A.B.A. SECTION OF ADMINISTRATIVE LAW AND REGULATORY PRACTICE, REPORT TO THE HOUSE OF DELEGATES, RESOLUTION 106A EXECUTIVE SUMMARY (2016).

48. *See 106A*, AMERICAN BAR ASSOCIATION (2016), http://www.americanbar.org/news/reporter_resources/midyear-meeting-2016/house-of-delegates-resolutions/106a.html.

2. As noted earlier in this section, ISO 26000 sparked a range of efforts to translate its principles into legal requirements. Noting the generally positive reception of ISO 26000 among stakeholder groups in Europe as compared with earlier formulations of corporate social responsibility (particularly with respect to human rights norms), Isabelle Schömann summarizes controversies within the European Union related to the exclusion of trade unions from the drafting process:

Isabelle Schömann, *ISO 26000: The New Face of Corporate Social Responsibility?*

European Trade Union Institute, Policy Brief No. 1 (2012)

Given the European trade unions' long-standing—and unfulfilled—demand to put CSR on a legal footing in Europe, it is interesting but disturbing to see that the global initiative comes from consumer groups, and that it was taken up systematically and thoroughly by the ISO, even though it touches on hitherto unknown areas, namely human rights, decent work and labour practices. Although the procedure was adapted to the new mission invented by the ISO, and although this new-type standardisation is what has emerged from a worldwide consensus (still absent in Europe), it is interesting but worrying to note the low-level representation of workers at the negotiations. After all, if ISO 26000 sets out to try and encourage organisations to contribute to sustainable development on this earth, why would it deprive itself of the resources at its disposal to ensure more effective implementation of the standard? Is it not a delusion to believe that organisations will make better use of the standard because of their involvement in its preparation, even where it appears that the participation of certain groups was connected with the desire to diminish the requirements of the standard, to try and rule themselves out of it by focusing attention on other groups? Groups whose unstated but real goal had been to put forward a private, non-binding alternative to the social calls for global regulation of the activities of transnational companies?

If the most optimistic people see the ISO 26000 standard as a potential extension of private international law into areas that are inaccessible to it (above all organisations) as well as a reference list (added to an already long list) which 'raises the demands that a society imposes on itself', the doctrine remains cautious about developments likely to be associated with ISO 26000, particularly on account of the confusion introduced between law and standardisation. In addition, the ISO 26000 standard takes on board the traditional, authoritative ISO standards with which it is now merged, and which are assimilated into regulations, conferring a presumption of conformity with conduct which will not be submitted to certification. The already porous nature of public standards and private standards will be worsened, in the sense of an erosion of law to the profit of voluntary private regulation. And in an equally political debate, on the role of organisations in contributing to sustainable development, 'Governments can assist organisations in their efforts to operate in a socially responsible manner in many ways. However, promoting the social responsibility of organizations is not and cannot be a substitute for the effective exercise of state duties and responsibilities'.

How does Schömann's account of the trade unionists' critique inform an understanding of the relevance of positionality or standpoint in relation to global governance? How did the exclusion of the unionists from the drafting process allow certain compromises to go forward? How would you expect the absence of unionists to affect the range of compromises available to future efforts to implement the guidance? ISO 26000 has been termed "protolaw" and "a new form of global custom."[49] What would you want to know before agreeing or disagreeing with this terminology in this context?

III. Interlegalities in the world market for land

As we have seen, the ISO's guidance on social responsibility was intended as a resource for sustainable development. As such, its context included other international and multistakeholder agreements that, since the 1990s, have been put in place to support sustainable development as a global project. One landmark among such early post-Cold War efforts was the United Nations' "Agenda 21"—setting forth principles for a program of world trade as means to ends that would take the form of economic and social harmonization. The published agenda represented the collaboration of state governments that came together in Rio de Janeiro in 1992. The conference report sets the context in an assessment of the global economy of the 1980s, as a time when "the developing countries [were] weighted down by external indebtedness, . . . development finance [was] inadequate, . . . barriers restrict[ed] access to markets and . . . commodity prices and the terms of trade of developing countries [were] depressed." The essence of Agenda 21 was a proposal to "reverse" those trends through world trade: "The policies and measures needed to create an international environment that is strongly supportive of national development efforts are thus vital. International cooperation in this area should be designed to complement and support—not to diminish or subsume—sound domestic economic policies, in both developed and developing countries, if global progress towards sustainable development is to be achieved."[50]

For readers of this volume, perhaps it useful to note that the Agenda 21 commitment to global access to markets on equal terms was essentially simultaneous with the negotiations that led to NAFTA. It combined the participatory structure of international treaty-making (such as the Montreal Protocol) with the objectives of a multilateral trade agreement. Subsequent efforts (such as the ISO, as we have seen)

---

49. These terms are drawn from Kernaghan Webb, *ISO 26000 Social Responsibility Standard as 'Proto Law' and a New Form of Global Custom: Positioning ISO 26000 in the Emerging Transnational Regulatory Governance Rule Instrument Architecture*, 6 TRANSNATIONAL LEGAL THEORY 466 (2015).

50. Agenda 21, U.N. Conference on Environment and Development, U.N. Doc. A/CONF.151/26 (1992), https://sustainabledevelopment.un.org/content/documents/Agenda21.pdf.

broadened participation in such global projects to a wider range of stakeholders, including non-state actors. Specifically, subsequent United Nations efforts in support of global trade also involved broader participation. In this section, we take up one such effort—the Food and Agriculture Organization's (FAO) Voluntary Guidelines on the Responsible Governance of Tenure of Land, Fisheries and Forests in the Context of National Food Security. Based on years of intergovernmental negotiation and consultation with governmental and non-governmental actors with relevant expertise, under the auspices of the FAO and the Committee on World Food Security (CFS), the guidelines were passed unanimously by the FAO in 2012, and announced as the "first-ever global land tenure guidelines."[51]

The overall objectives of the initiative entail improvements to governance of land tenure through recognition of rights, regularization of title, transparency in land transfers, respect for the property and human rights of land owners, and respect for law, including indigenous and customary norms. The preliminary section of the document outlines the general objectives:

Food and Agriculture Organization of the United Nations Voluntary Guidelines on the Responsible Governance of Tenure of Land, Fisheries and Forests in the Context of National Food Security (2012)[52]

1. Objectives

1.1 These Voluntary Guidelines seek to improve governance of tenure of land*, fisheries and forests. They seek to do so for the benefit of all, with an emphasis on vulnerable and marginalized people, with the goals of food security and progressive realization of the right to adequate food, poverty eradication, sustainable livelihoods, social stability, housing security, rural development, environmental protection and sustainable social and economic development. All programmes, policies and technical assistance to improve governance of tenure through the implementation of these Guidelines should be consistent with States' existing obligations under international law, including the Universal Declaration of Human Rights and other international human rights instruments.

1.2 These Guidelines seek to:

- improve tenure governance by providing guidance and information on internationally accepted practices for systems that deal with the rights to use, manage and control land, fisheries and forests.
- contribute to the improvement and development of the policy, legal and organizational frameworks regulating the range of tenure rights that exist over these resources.

51. *New UN-backed guidelines aim to protect rights to land, fisheries and forests*, UN News Centre (May 11, 2012) www.un.org/apps/news/story.asp?NewsID=41973#.V4DdmlaQods.

52. Available at http://www.fao.org/docrep/016/i2801e/i2801e.pdf.

- enhance the transparency and improve the functioning of tenure systems.
- strengthen the capacities and operations of implementing agencies; judicial authorities; local governments; organizations of farmers and small-scale producers, of fishers, and of forest users; pastoralists; indigenous peoples and other communities; civil society; private sector; academia; and all persons concerned with tenure governance as well as to promote the cooperation between the actors mentioned.

[The implementation guidelines combine diverse strategies for regularizing tenure within national legal systems.—Authors]

3. Guiding principles of responsible tenure governance

3.A. General principles

> 3.2 Non-state actors including business enterprises have a responsibility to respect human rights and legitimate tenure rights. Business enterprises should act with due diligence to avoid infringing on the human rights and legitimate tenure rights of others. They should include appropriate risk management systems to prevent and address adverse impacts on human rights and legitimate tenure rights. Business enterprises should provide for and cooperate in non-judicial mechanisms to provide remedy, including effective operational-level grievance mechanisms, where appropriate, where they have caused or contributed to adverse impacts on human rights and legitimate tenure rights. Business enterprises should identify and assess any actual or potential impacts on human rights and legitimate tenure rights in which they may be involved. States, in accordance with their international obligations, should provide access to effective judicial remedies for negative impacts on human rights and legitimate tenure rights by business enterprises. Where transnational corporations are involved, their home States have roles to play in assisting both those corporations and host States to ensure that businesses are not involved in abuse of human rights and legitimate tenure rights. States should take additional steps to protect against abuses of human rights and legitimate tenure rights by business enterprises that are owned or controlled by the State, or that receive substantial support and service from State agencies.

3.B. Principles of implementation

These principles of implementation are essential to contribute to responsible governance of tenure of land, fisheries and forests.

1. **Human dignity:** recognizing the inherent dignity and the equal and inalienable human rights of all individuals.
2. **Non-discrimination:** no one should be subject to discrimination under law and policies as well as in practice.
3. **Equity and justice:** recognizing that equality between individuals may require acknowledging differences between individuals, and taking positive

action, including empowerment, in order to promote equitable tenure rights and access to land, fisheries and forests, for all, women and men, youth and vulnerable and traditionally marginalized people, within the national context.

4. **Gender equality:** Ensure the equal right of women and men to the enjoyment of all human rights, while acknowledging differences between women and men and taking specific measures aimed at accelerating de facto equality when necessary. States should ensure that women and girls have equal tenure rights and access to land, fisheries and forests independent of their civil and marital status.
5. **Holistic and sustainable approach:** recognizing that natural resources and their uses are interconnected, and adopting an integrated and sustainable approach to their administration.
6. **Consultation and participation:** engaging with and seeking the support of those who, having legitimate tenure rights, could be affected by decisions, prior to decisions being taken, and responding to their contributions; taking into consideration existing power imbalances between different parties and ensuring active, free, effective, meaningful and informed participation of individuals and groups in associated decision-making processes.
7. **Rule of law:** adopting a rules-based approach through laws that are widely publicized in applicable languages, applicable to all, equally enforced and independently adjudicated, and that are consistent with their existing obligations under national and international law, and with due regard to voluntary commitments under applicable regional and international instruments.
8. **Transparency:** clearly defining and widely publicizing policies, laws and procedures in applicable languages, and widely publicizing decisions in applicable languages and in formats accessible to all.
9. **Accountability:** holding individuals, public agencies and non-state actors responsible for their actions and decisions according to the principles of the rule of law.
10. **Continuous improvement:** States should improve mechanisms for monitoring and analysis of tenure governance in order to develop evidence-based programmes and secure on-going improvements.

Principle 3.2 specifies the obligations of non-state actors, including business enterprises, to observe tenure rights and human rights of farmers—a key provision set up to counter what by then had become a pervasive practice of forced evictions, state-backed pressures to sell, and other tactics of alienation known as "land grabbing."

Land grabbing is not a new practice in itself, but in the current context, the term refers to the period since 2006, when a spike in food prices led relatively richer countries (Saudi Arabia, South Korea, and China) to turn to relatively poorer countries (Madagascar, Ethiopia and elsewhere in sub-Sahara Africa, and Latin America) for access to land by long term lease or sale for purposes of reinforcing their national food supply. The practice is now widespread, still targeting poorer countries but also poorer regions within richer countries.[53] Social scientist Saskia Sassen estimates that over 200 million hectares of land were acquired by foreign governments and firms between 2006 and 2011.[54] It was food insecurity that put land grabbing into the portfolio of the FAO, since one result of land grabs in the poorer countries is hunger, as small farmers are displaced from the land or priced out of the market. The voluntary guidelines approach land grabbing as a form of market disequilibrium, offering various principles in support of uniform conditions for a world market in land. Sassen's projected future of land grabbing has now come about:

> [Foreign land acquisition] requires and in turn stimulates, the making of a vast global market for land. It entails the development of an also vast specialized servicing infrastructure to enable sales and acquisitions, secure property or leasing rights, develop appropriate legal instruments, and even push for the making of new law to accommodate such purchases in a sovereign country. . . . This increasingly sophisticated specialized service sector invents new types of contracts and forms of ownership . . . . As it develops, this specialized sector, in turn, depends on further acquisitions of foreign land as a source of profits. We see the beginnings of a large-scale commodification of land, which may in turn lead to the financializing of the commodity we still call, simply, land.[55]

Today, land grabs reach not only for food, but also for ethanol crops (or multi-purpose crops such as corn or soy), and for non-food resources such as plantation forestry, various forms of extraction, conservation, carbon offsets and—as anticipated by Sassen—as collateral.[56]

Critics of the Voluntary Guidelines point to their focus on the terms of market exchange rather than on the parties to the transfer arrangements—specifically small farmers—as well as to their scope, limited to larger scale transfers. The Transnational Institute (TNI), a Dutch NGO and non-profit research foundation, is critical of the Guidelines' framing around food insecurity, arguing that it is trade liberalization that has made the investments of small farmers "invisible" as the food market has been globalized under terms set by the WTO (and as we saw in the discussion of NAFTA, in Chapter 3). The following excerpt from TNI's "primer" on land grabbing develops an alternative approach.

---

53. Transnational Institute (TNI), The Global Land Grab: A Primer (2013), www.tni.org/files/download/landgrabbingprimer_feb2013.pdf.

54. Saskia Sassen, Expulsions: Brutality and Complexity in the Global Economy 80 (2014).

55. *Id.*, at 81.

56. TNI, *supra* note 53.

Transnational Institute (TNI), The Global Land Grab: A Primer (2013)

Neither the formulation nor implementation of laws and policies takes place in a vacuum, and very often the results of both kinds of processes are mixed. While some laws and policies can be passed to respond to land grabbing, they do not self-interpret nor self-implement. Even the best laws and policies are not automatically implemented in favour of those who should be prioritised from a social justice perspective. Experience shows that good results require enough social pressure from below to shift the balance of power in their favour—and just how much social pressure from below will be enough depends on many situational factors. There is no 'one-size-fits-all' solution to the scourge of land grabbing. It is the context-specific political interactions of various state and non-state actors that will ultimately shape how any law or policy, including guidelines—whether voluntary or not—will eventually be interpreted and implemented, from one setting to another.

Much has been made of the need for more accountability to address land grabbing, yet most advocates of 'responsible' land investment fail to critically analyse the nature of local power relations among social actors in general, and the extremely long and difficult challenge of rural democratisation in particular. Instead, and often out of a real sense of urgency, there is a tendency to call for accountability mechanisms in a short-term and reactive way, but usually in response to land grabbing already underway. If this is the only space given to questions of accountability, then the result is most likely the facilitation of land grabbing and a consolidation of the state-capital alliance that initiated it to begin with.

Effective accountability would rather start by addressing challenges of democratising the decision-making around rural development issues *before* projects hit the ground. This involves supporting the long and difficult struggle to build and maintain autonomous social organisations capable of democratically representing the interests of rural working poor classes, and of demanding state accountability. These conditions and processes cannot be simply manufactured suddenly, once a large-scale land grab hits the ground. They are struggled for and built over time by real people embedded in complex power structures, and in relation to many issues, including land issues.

In the absence or weakness of such organisations capable of demanding accountability from the state, the focus on making land grabs more transparent is unlikely to produce anything more than just more transparent land grabs at least in the short-run. Although the deals may become more transparent, they will not necessarily or automatically become more legitimate in the eyes of those who lose their land and livelihoods—and they may even become more *illegitimate* once those most adversely affected learn the real score. And even legitimate deals will need mobilisation by strong and autonomous social organizations to ensure that affected peoples' land and human rights are guaranteed at every point. Here, there are important insights and lessons to be gathered from past land conflicts and struggles since, after all, land grabbing is indeed not new.

Moving beyond the limitations of 'one-size-fits-all' solutions means taking stock that real state accountability should begin long before land grabs ever come onto the scene, by addressing the rural working poor classes and how can their already existing, meaningful investments in the land be augmented and sustained in order to ensure truly pro-poor outcomes.

Land grabbing is an expression of the dominant development model based on sustained, increased and unequal consumption of both finite and 'renewable' natural resources. The social and ecological limitations of this development path, as well as its extreme inequalities, are widely known and experienced daily, especially by the most vulnerable populations. Dealing with this underlying, multi-faceted and structural problem requires going beyond narrow and partial regulatory takes, in order to address the politico-economic structures where land-grabbing dynamics are rooted, i.e., the existing industrial pattern of agro-commodities (flex crops and flex trees) and energy production and consumption controlled by Transnational Corporations under a world trade and investment system where financial capital reigns.

In the current global debate over land grabbing, investment tends to be equated with corporate investment that is skewed towards large scale, petrol-based and capital intensive/labor expelling ventures. As neoliberal policies were implemented worldwide, state-driven investments in agriculture dried up, while investments by small-scale farmers were made invisible. Orthodox trade liberalisation schemes have wiped out millions of small-scale farming ventures without resulting in increased levels of food security, i.e, through the foreseen augmented capabilities to buy food in the market claimed by free trade promoters.

A fundamental starting point when talking about systemic change to end land grabbing are these two other types of investment, namely public investment and investments by small-scale farmers. The urgent task is to revive state investment while making investments by small-scale farmers visible. It is the combination of state and small farmers' investments that make any systemic change to end land grabbing possible. Additionally, it is urgent to decouple food (and agriculture in general) from dominant corporate-orchestrated trade systems at multilateral (WTO) and regional scales (Free Trade Agreements), as La Vía Campesina has widely called for.

The food sovereignty paradigm encompasses this alternative view. As the *Forum for Food Sovereignty*, held in Mali in 2007, argued: food sovereignty entails 'the right of peoples to healthy and culturally appropriate food produced through ecologically sound and sustainable methods, and their right to define their own food and agriculture systems. It puts the aspirations and needs of those who produce, distribute and consume food at the heart of food systems and policies rather than the demands of markets and corporations' (Declaration of Nyéléni 2007). The food sovereignty paradigm links strategically with the call for land sovereignty in the realms of peoples' land and natural resources access and control rights.

Underpinning this alternative view on food and land sovereignty, agro-ecology captures the need for social equity and ecological sustainability in the previously mentioned joint investment framework. As the High Level Panel of Experts from the FAO-based World Committee on Food Security recommends 'governments should prioritize investment in the small farm sector and in alternative food systems that are socially inclusive and just as well as environmentally sustainable, using agro-ecological principles.'

Notes and Questions

Saskia Sassen reminds us that "[n]ational territory is not merely vacant land." Sassen argues that these transactions potentially devalue citizenship and degrade territorial sovereignty:

> Lands acquired by foreigners include vast stretches of national territory populated and shaped by villages, smallholder agriculture, rural manufacturing districts, and the actors that make these economies and reproduce them . . . . Much of this politico-structural complexity is today being erased from its home territory as a result of these acquisitions. At the extreme, we might ask what citizenship is worth when national territory is downgraded to foreign-owned land for plantations, leading to the eviction of everything else—flora, fauna, villages, smallholders, and the traditional rules that organized land ownership or use.
>
> [These actions] produce a partial denationalization deep inside nation-states, a structural hole in the tissue of national sovereign territory. . . . The contracts developed for these acquisitions become capabilities of an organizing logic that is disarticulated from the national state even as these acquisitions operate deep inside its territory. Further, in so doing, these contracts often go against the interests not only of much of a country's people but also of local capital . . . . [57]

Anthropological literature abundantly confirms the impact of displacement from the land among rural communities and, in particular, small farmers reliant on local markets. Anthropologists working in such communities detail the social significance of land beyond its essential role in subsistence or its marketable form as property—e.g., as ancestral or sacred land.[58] But even if we limit our attention to land as a commodity, such accounts convey the immediacy and material concreteness of national development schemes, as farmers are pressed into dispossession or induced to cash out by (for example) state agents or elites among their own neighbors who stand to gain by bundling properties for eventual resale or long term leasing. The anthropological accounts also detail the legal means at the disposal of developers (such as

57. Sassen, *supra* note 54, at 115–16.

58. *See, e.g.*, Piergiorgio di Giminiani, *The Becoming of Ancestral Land: Place and Property in Mapuche Land Claims*, 42 AMERICAN ETHNOLOGIST 490 (2015); Scott Matter, *Clashing Claims: Neopatrimonial Governance, Land Tenure Transformation, and Violence at Enoosupukia, Kenya*, 33 POLITICAL & LEGAL ANTHROPOLOGY REV. 67 (2010).

eminent domain or, in some contexts, old colonial laws),[59] as peasants are removed from the land to make way for special economic zones, tourism, urban growth, or other purposes.[60] Ethnographic accounts also track the diversity of the means and ends of peasants' strategies of resistance—including local mobilizations, demonstrations of protest, local and national political opposition,[61] litigation,[62] and transnational mobilizations such as the food sovereignty movement.[63] The local responses are as diverse as other elements in their situation, but across these accounts two themes emerge: first, they show vividly the extent to which global "soft law" efforts to eradicate poverty through liberalization push political controversy "down" to the local communities where their contradictions are most visible and deeply felt, and second, in the face of such dilemmas, these communities are not passive victims, but—on the contrary—key players in globalization, even if not always with full information or timely inclusion in multistakeholder negotiations.

Such accounts underscore the many-layered social thickness of the interlegalities on the land, and the tensions these entail, particularly when farmers themselves are effectively written out of the schemes designed to improve their lot. We do not suggest that these are the only reasons global improvement initiatives do not succeed as planned.[64] But our emphasis on interlegality (rather than on pluralism or nested "scales" of law and society) is precisely to underscore the significance of such contests as central to transnational law in practice, since it is in these misleadingly called

---

59. On the modern use of colonial land law in India, see Preeti Sampat, *Special Economic Zones in India: Reconfiguring Displacement in a Neoliberal Order?*, 22 City & Society 166 (2010).

60. *See, e.g.*, Gayatri Thampy, *Loci of Greed in a Caribbean Paradise: Land Conflict in Bocas del Toro, Panama*, 1 Econ. Anthropology 139 (2014); Jeremy M. Campbell, *The Land Question in Amazonia: Cadastral Knowledge and Ignorance in Brazil's Tenure Regularization Program*, 38 Political & Legal Anthropology Rev. 147 (2015).

61. *See* Sampat, *supra* note 59; Keri Vacanti Brondo, Land Grab: Green Neoliberalism, Gender and Garifuna Resistance in Honduras (2013).

62. *See, e.g.*, Sassen, *supra*, note 54; Daniel Fitzpatrick, *Disputes and Pluralism in Modern Indonesian Land Law*, 22 Yale J. Int'l L. 171 (1997).

63. Tom Biolsi, *Imagined Geographies: Sovereignty, Indigenous Space and American Indian Struggle*, 32 Am. Ethnologist 239 (2005); Jessica R. Cattelino, *The Double Bind of American Need-Based Sovereignty*, 25 Cultural Anthropology 235 (2010); Donna L. Chollett, *The Native American Organic Garden: Using Service Learning as a Site of Resistance*, 36 Culture, Agric., Food & Envt. 93 (2014); Nicholas Copeland, *Mayan Imaginaries of Democracy: Interactive Sovereignties and Political Affect in Postrevolutionary Guatemala*, 41 Am Ethnologist 305 (2014); Marc Edelman, *Bringing The Moral Economy Back in to the Study of 21st Century Transnational Peasant Movements*, 107 Am. Anthropologist 331 (2005); David Fazzino & Philip A Loring, *From Crisis to Cumulative Effects: Food Security Challenges in Alaska*, 32 NAPA Bulletin 152 (2009); Ralph A. Litzinger, *Contested Sovereignties and the Critical Ecosystem Partnership Fund*, 29 Political & Legal Anthropology Rev. 66 (2006); Kathleen M. Sullivan, *(Re)Landscaping Sovereignty in British Columbia, Canada*, 29 Political & Legal Anthropology Rev. 44 (2006).

64. Tamar Gutner, *When "Doing Good" Does Not: The IMF and the Millennium Development Goals*, *in* Who Governs the Globe? 266 (Deborah Avant, Martha Finnemore & Susan Sell eds., 2010) (describing organization factors internal to the IMF that limited the viability of the Millennium Development Goals devise to contribute to the eradication of poverty).

"margins" that the globalization of agro-business, petrochemical extraction, and export industries (among other developments) has in fact taken place.

IV. Interlegalities in the globalization of essential services

In this section, we turn our attention from state as agent in global development schemes to state as client in relation to the out-sourcing of government services. Here, the states are dealing not in access to land but in competitive bidding for contracts to provide services to or on behalf of the government. Public-private arrangements designed to carry out the public's business, especially in contexts which we call human-service contracts, invariably involve important political judgments directly affecting the welfare of human beings. Human-service contracts are applied to the needs of vulnerable populations—prisoners, the poor, immigrants, and others who lack political power and who are underrepresented or ignored by most of the processes involved. Typical outsourcing processes exacerbate their political marginalization. These processes seldom involve an opportunity to participate directly in the fundamental decision to use private providers in the first place, and they usually exclude vulnerable human stakeholders from weighing in on the ways these contracts are then created and implemented. By delegating policy issues to the private sector, the chances for participation by those directly affected as well as the ability to contest decisions made on their behalf is often greatly reduced.

A. Privatization and neoliberalization

The following excerpt reviews some of the history of the mainstreaming of neoliberal ideas in the United States, relating the neoliberalization of government to the wider context of the liberalization of global capital and global governance.

Alfred C. Aman, Jr. & Carol J. Greenhouse, *Prison Privatization and Inmate Labor in the Global Economy*

42 Fordham Urb. L.J. 355, 366–75 (2014)

In the United States, privatization should be understood as both a driving and principal effect of globalization. The increasing reliance on marketized forms of administration and corporate self-regulation in lieu of regulation by government is commonly referred to as "the new governance." The new governance is indicative of recent transformations in the relationship between the market and the state itself—transformations that are inseparable from global economic competition and other forms of interdependence between state and non-state actors, domestically and transnationally, as these have developed in recent decades.

Neoliberalization of government in the United States puts a political premium on the financialization of public administration, government services, and other government functions, in turn lending rhetorical heft to two principal distinctions: between the public and private sectors, and, correspondingly, between law and markets as regulatory tools. The realities of financing government are far more complex than these rhetorical distinctions imply. Whereas the rhetoric implies complementarity (more private sector equals less government, for example), the diverse complexity of the state's roles in privatization, as well as the variety of businesses and business models involved, defy neat boundaries. To the extent that maximizing the financialization of government through privatization entails deregulation or outsourcing, one should keep in mind the fact that these tools for minimizing government (as the rhetoric implicitly claims) actually extend government into new areas of the private sector, through contracts, monitoring, and other means. . . .

Privatization by contract became politically popular in the United States as an approach to the governmental provision of social services, especially for the poor, for immigrants, and for prisoners—i.e., dependent populations whose situations expose them extensively to managed care of various kinds.

* * *

Federal and state commitments to privatization are integral to the neoliberalization of global capital, even when the relevant activities are located entirely within the domestic territory of the United States. Understanding domestic privatization in global terms clarifies the scope for law in relation to privatization—though we do not suggest that law alone (for example, in the form of legislation or contracts) will offer solutions to all the problems that currently encumber the systems of corrections in the United States. It also introduces fresh perspectives on the situation of imprisoned people beyond their status as inmates (e.g., as wage earners, family members, citizens, and so forth). Moreover, it highlights a potentially significant role for political engagement involving diverse stakeholder communities—including inmates' families and communities.

The advantage of understanding globalization's "domestic face"—i.e., its embeddedness in the local—is the light shed on the major roles local actors and institutions can potentially play when it comes to creating a more humane conception of globalization and its practices. This in turn draws attention to the role of contracts in the privatization process, and their potential for introducing more specificity, transparency, and accountability into what is otherwise treated as atypical government contracts dealing, for example, with bridge or road construction. . . .

* * *

In the United States, privatization usually means some form of outsourcing, that is, the contracting out of some or all of an administrative agency's regulatory responsibilities to a private firm. The primary governance tool in privatization is the contract. The management of prisons has been increasingly outsourced to the private sector at both the federal and state levels since its inception in the late 1980s and 1990s.

* * *

Privatization is one of the primary mechanisms governments have for aligning the financialization of government with neoliberalization of the global economy. In this section, we explain in broad terms how that alignment works.

When privatization takes the form of outsourcing, it is also a form of deregulation. Deregulation in the form of outsourcing is one of the predominant modes of domestic regulatory reform today, such that private firms now provide many services once provided by governments. Privatization and its close cousin, deregulation, are the hallmarks of U.S. regulation, in what author Alfred Aman has called the era of globalization.

Early signs of the global era were the attempts to substitute market-oriented rules for New Deal-like regulatory regimes that began as early as the Carter Administration and accelerated greatly under the Reagan and Bush Administrations in the 1980s. The nature of this process is perhaps best exemplified by the reforms that occurred at the Federal Communications Commission (FCC) at that time. Throughout the 1980s, the FCC recalibrated its regulatory approaches to replace New Deal regulatory actions with more market-oriented rules. For the most part, courts allowed this, recognizing that the broad public interest language of New Deal statutes such as the Communications Act of 1934 allowed the agency the flexibility to substitute a new conception of what the public's interest required, especially in light of changes in the structure and competitive capacity of the industries involved.

Environmental regulation reform followed a somewhat similar regulatory reform path, as market regulatory approaches gradually replaced so-called command and control rules. Once again, though the statutes involved were not as open-ended as New Deal legislation, there was enough interpretive room in many cases to introduce market means toward regulatory ends. There were limits to this approach, but for the most part agencies themselves did most of the deregulating involved. The New Deal regulation of markets in the public interest left as part of its legacy a discourse in which deregulation in today's different economic circumstances is now similarly justified by some as if it were a corrective swing of the regulatory pendulum. However, the image of the swinging pendulum understates the differences between the Depression era and the current economic environment.

A major difference between those earlier regulatory eras and our own is that natural monopolies and the tragedy of the commons involved market *failures*, in which the government sought to protect the public's interest by intervening in particular market sectors. In the global era, the focal point of regulation is not market failure per se, but competitiveness on a global scale, resulting in a comprehensive transformation of the rationales for government itself. The neoliberalization of government means reformulating the government as a market actor suited to competition on a global scale—one appropriations budget, one agency, one entitlement at a time (to choose just some examples). Such transformations are responsive to political pressures—including strong populist pressures—to maximize the circulation of wealth by eliminating, to the extent possible, the fixed costs of government.

Among the reasons for the popularity of privatized approaches to the provision of government services is a basic, often untested, assumption that efficiencies will result from competition attainable only in the private sector. We call this "the efficiency story." The efficiency story rests on three premises: first, that government services are characteristically unduly encumbered with unnecessary costs and so-called red tape; second, that market competition produces a sort of Darwinian effect of favoring the fittest; and third, that competition is consistently a feature of private sector markets.

None of these premises is valid in relation to the prison sector. With respect to the relativity of public and private efficiency, a popular assumption promoted by the industry is that private prisons are more cost-efficient than public prisons. However, more neutral studies, for example, a 2001 report under the auspices of the Bureau of Justice Assistance (BJA), indicate that the cost differential between private and public prisons is minimal. With regard to market competition: the prison market consists of few private sector providers and only very limited competition (in prison privatization, two main firms among approximately a score of others). These providers are a subset of the larger and more rapidly growing private security industry. With regard to competition: the major public-private partnerships in the corrections field have long histories of multi-sided relationships. But competitiveness is not a fixed notion, nor is it automatically limited to strictly economic issues.

Privatization advocates have framed their appeals largely in terms of benefits to national, state, and local economies, while remaining relatively silent on the global context that today defines the very terms of economic competitiveness.... [A] global context is subsumed within the idea of competitiveness itself.

B. Private Welfare Services

Let us turn to one state's experience with the privatization of welfare, specifically Indiana's outsourcing of the administration of welfare services to IBM.[65]

The following opinion by Chief Judge Vaidik of the intermediate Indiana Court of Appeals, one of many generated by the ensuing litigation, illuminates some of the tensions that may inhere in private administration of essential public services. Consider: Are these tensions insurmountable, or could such a program have succeeded in other circumstances? Who was most affected by the privatization project's shortcomings? Did those most affected have any effective recourse, or remedy for their injuries?

65. *See* Alfred C. Aman, Jr., *Globalization and the Privatization of Welfare Administration in Indiana*, 20 Ind. J. Global Leg. Stud. 377 (2013); *see also* Alfred C. Aman, Jr. and Joseph C. Dugan, *The Human Side of Public-Private Partnerships: From New Deal Regulation to Administrative Law Management*, 102 Iowa L. Rev. 102 (2017).

State ex rel. Indiana Family & Social Services Admin. v. International Business Machines Corp.

4 N.E.3d 696 (Ind. Ct. App. 2014)

VAIDIK, Chief Judge

Case Summary

Indiana's poorest residents live hand-to-mouth trusting that they will receive food stamps to eat and Medicare or other state health insurance in order to receive basic medical care. These citizens do not have the luxury of being able to wait to eat or go to a doctor while a phone goes unanswered, an appointment cannot be scheduled, or an application sits on a desk. The needs of the poor are immediate.

Indiana entered into an arrangement with the federal government to distribute federal funds to those in greatest need. Part of the State's responsibility was to make certain that only the poorest received aid and to help welfare recipients find work. If the State failed to comply with federal guidelines, then it would be penalized by the federal government, resulting in less federal aid for our citizens.

By all accounts, the State was failing in performing its duties. As a result, in December 2006, the State, on behalf of its agency the Indiana Family and Social Services Administration (FSSA), entered into a ten-year, $1.3 billion contract with International Business Machines Corporation (IBM) to modernize and improve the State's welfare system. IBM agreed to the State's proposal, although it argues that the system design was doomed to fail. Nonetheless, IBM received $437 million while assuring the State that it was up to the task. Less than three years into the ten-year contract, the State terminated the contract citing IBM performance issues, and the parties sued each other for breach of contract on the same day in Marion Superior Court. The State sought over $170 million in damages, and IBM sought almost $100 million. The trial court granted IBM summary judgment for $40 million in assignment fees and, after a six-week bench trial in 2012, found no material breach on IBM's part and awarded IBM an additional $9,510,795 in Equipment fees, $2,570,621 in Early Termination Close Out Payments, and $10,632,333 in prejudgment interest, totaling $62,713,749.

While IBM's software, computers, and employee training aided in delivering welfare services, the primary focus of the contract was to provide food and medical care to our poorest citizens in a timely, efficient, and reliable manner within federal guidelines, to discourage fraud, and to increase work-participation rates. In the most basic aspect of this contract—providing timely services to the poor—IBM failed. We therefore reverse the trial court's finding that there was no material breach.

Despite finding a material breach on IBM's part, we affirm the trial court's award of $40 million in assignment fees and $9,510,795 in Equipment fees to IBM. We do so because the State and IBM agreed under the terms of the contract that the State would pay these fees. Further, the State would be unjustly enriched if it were to keep

IBM's equipment and to assume IBM's subcontracts without paying IBM. We further affirm the trial court's denial of Deferred Fees to IBM, reverse the trial court's award of $2,570,621 in Early Termination Close Out Payments and $10,632,333 in prejudgment interest to IBM, and remand the case to the trial court to determine the amount of fees IBM is entitled to for Change Orders 119 and 133. Finally, we remand the case to the trial court to determine the State's damages for IBM's material breach of the contract and to offset any damages awarded to IBM. We therefore affirm in part, reverse in part, and remand the case to the trial court.

Facts and Procedural History

The facts in this case are largely undisputed. During Governor Mitch Daniels's first term as governor, he declared Indiana's welfare system "broken." It was "plagued by high error rates, fraud, wasted dollars, poor conditions for its employees, and very poor service to its clients." Indiana's welfare-to-work record was the worst in the country. Consequently, Governor Daniels dubbed Indiana's welfare system "America's worst welfare system."

Shortly after Governor Daniels was elected in November 2004, he and senior officials—including former Indianapolis Mayor Stephen Goldsmith and FSSA Secretary Mitch Roob—set out to modernize and improve Indiana's welfare system. The new system was modeled after the system in Texas. Under the new model, Indiana citizens would apply for benefits "via web and call center" without the need for a face-to-face meeting with a case worker, and eligibility determinations would be made on a centralized, statewide basis rather than in the local county welfare offices. One of the State's requirements for the new system was to "reduce the number of mandatory visits to local offices" by "giving clients more avenues to interact with the agency," such as "the Internet, an automated and interactive phone system, and local organizations in the community." Analysts had found that citizens most in need of FSSA's help were forced to make more than two million unnecessary trips a year.

[The search for a vendor began in October, 2005, and concluded in May, 2006, when Indiana announced that IBM would receive the contract. Further negotiations lasted until December, 2006, the culmination of which was a "ten-year, $1.3 billion Master Services Agreement ('MSA')" that extended over "160 pages, plus 10 exhibits, 24 schedules, and 10 appendices." Critical Indiana stakeholders—including IBM, the Indiana Economic Development Corporation, Purdue University, and Indiana University—further executed a Memorandum of Understanding on the same day, wherein IBM agreed to stimulate local economic activity and create 1000 new full time jobs.]

[MSA § 1.1(1) and (5) set out specific "Policy Objectives":]

> (1) The overarching policy objectives of the Modernization Project and this Agreement are (i) to provide efficient, accurate and timely eligibility determinations for individuals and families who qualify for public assistance, (ii) to improve the availability, quality and reliability of the services being provided to Clients by expanding access to such services, decreasing

> inconvenience and improving response times, among other improvements, (iii) to assist and support Clients through programs that foster personal responsibility, independence and social and economic self-sufficiency, (iv) to assure compliance with all relevant Laws, (v) to assure the protection and integrity of Personal Information gathered in connection with eligibility determination, and (vi) to foster the development of policies and procedures that underscore the importance of accuracy in eligibility determinations, caseload integrity across all areas of public assistance and work and work-related experience for Clients in the Programs.
>
> * * *
>
> (5) Vendor recognizes that (i) the Services to be performed under this Agreement are vital to the State and its citizens who currently are and in the future will be legally eligible for and reliant upon the assistance available under the Programs and must be continued without interruption and (ii) upon Termination, a Successor must be able to continue to provide the Services in as seamless a transition from Vendor as possible.

In addition, MSA § 1.4, entitled Construction and Interpretation, provided that the agreement "shall be" construed in a manner consistent with the Policy Objectives:

> (5) . . . In all events, the provisions and terms of this Agreement shall be interpreted with a view toward achieving those objectives. Notwithstanding the foregoing, in no event shall the Policy Objectives change or expand Vendor's obligations hereunder unless expressly agreed to by the Parties pursuant to a Change.

[The MSA provided for a gradual rollout. First, IBM would assist Indiana in processing applications under the old procedures. Eventually, the new system would be rolled out across all 92 counties, establishing a new steady state.]

In any event, according to the MSA, the State retained operational control throughout the project, including "general authority and responsibility for operational, technical, financial, and general management and oversight of the Services provided under the Agreement." The State also retained all policy-making authority over the project. Finally, the State made final eligibility determinations for the public-assistance programs. . . .

Under Article 16 of the MSA, the State could terminate the agreement (1) for convenience or (2) for cause. The termination-for-cause section provided that the State could terminate the agreement in three ways[, including a breach by Vendor which could not be reasonably cured within 30 days of Termination Notice; a breach by Vendor which is material, could reasonably be cured by Vendor within the Notice period but which has not been cured within a 60-day period pursuant to a Corrective Action Plan; or a series of breaches following three-months-notice of termination.]

Under the termination-for-convenience provision, the State could terminate the agreement, in whole or in part, "for any reason" that the State determined was "in its best interest."

[Termination payments varied depending on whether the termination was for convenience or for cause. Indiana had the further option to assume IBM's subcontracts in the event of termination. Rollout began in March, 2007, with an information campaign and the shifting of 1500 state employees to IBM subcontractors.]

During this pilot phase, the State's Modernization Project team evaluated the IBM Coalition's performance, including the readiness of the Service Centers, document-processing center, general infrastructure, and application processing. The team, including Secretary Roob, regularly met with the IBM team during the Pilot Phase and throughout the Modernization Project. The parties "saw implementation issues immediately," including unanswered calls and the untimely processing of applications. *See also* June 2007 email from Secretary Roob to IBM Vice President of State and Local Government Brian Whitfield ("tens of thousands of calls unanswered, honestly perhaps the worst performance I have ever seen in a call center.").

The trial court found that two background factors contributed to these initial difficulties. First, by December 2007, which was two months after rollout of the pilot region, the State and the country began to feel the effects of the "Great Recession." Benefit applications skyrocketed, and over the next two years, the State's unemployment rate more than doubled.

Second, in 2008, Indiana was hit by a series of natural disasters that cost the State nearly $2 billion in economic damage. All but ten of Indiana's counties were declared Presidential Disaster Areas. These disasters affected the rollout of the project, which was eventually suspended by mutual agreement of the parties in September 2008 in Change Order 69 in order to accommodate disaster-relief efforts. The State directed the reassignment of approximately one-third of the State and IBM Coalition workforce to help process tens of thousands of emergency food-stamp applications and thousands of FEMA applications.

[Nonetheless, IBM received approval to roll out the new services to a further 47 counties, reaching (at its peak) 59 of the state's 92 counties.]

During the rollout, the State conducted a series of project assessments. In May 2008, FSSA Secretary Roob reported to the Indiana General Assembly that although they "still ha[d] more work to do," modernization had allowed the State to serve "more people statewide and in a timelier manner than we ever have before." In August 2008, FSSA reported to federal authorities that although the start and finish dates of several key milestones had to be adjusted, the Modernization Project had "already made substantial progress toward its goals and objectives." In October 2008, the director of the FSSA's Division of Family Resources gave IBM primarily 9s and 10s (out of a possible 10) in IBM's annual customer satisfaction survey. And in a December 2008 interview, which was nine months before the State terminated the MSA, Governor

Daniels said that the new system was "a work in progress" and "far from perfect" but "far better than what preceded it," noting that critics wanted to "go back to a system where you had to beg for an appointment face to face," which was "atrocious."

The State expanded the scope of IBM's work numerous times during the course of the project, which added $178 million to the contract price. . . . For example, the State significantly increased the scope of the project in 2007 with Change Order 23 in order to include the Healthy Indiana Plan (HIP), which provides health insurance to uninsured Indiana residents who fall below a certain income level. When the HIP launched, the number of applications regularly exceeded the State's predictions, which caused IBM to fall behind on application processing, thereby placing additional strain on the modernized system.

But, as even the trial court found, these accolades and expansions did not mean that the project did not have problems. In November 2008, the IBM Coalition met with Secretary Roob to propose changes to the project because of problems including inconsistent feedback, document acceptance and processing, case-processing timeliness, quality, and higher volumes. Secretary Roob approved many of IBM's proposed reforms. Shortly after Secretary Roob approved the IBM Coalition's proposed reforms, Governor Daniels appointed Roob as Indiana's Secretary of Commerce and CEO of the Indiana Economic Development Corporation; Anne Murphy replaced Roob as FSSA Secretary.

In March 2009, Secretary Murphy sent the IBM Coalition a letter drafted by the State's outside counsel requesting a Corrective Action Plan. [Letter] ("The State of Indiana has raised with IBM multiple issues with the Modernization Project that need to be addressed immediately and believes that it is in the best interest of the State and IBM to enter into a Corrective Action Plan . . . ."). The letter identified thirty-six "issues" that the State wanted the IBM Coalition to address, including excessive wait times at local offices, incorrectly categorized imaged documents, high turnover of staff, scheduling problems, inaccurate and incomplete data gathering, clients not receiving mailed correspondence, poor communication to all staff, unresolved help-desk tickets, untimely expedited food-stamp processing, excessive wait times for applicant appointments, and failure to process Food Stamp, TANF, and Medicaid applications in a timely manner. [IBM largely disputed the need for a corrective action plan.] This implied to the State that:

> IBM has not fully appreciated the depth of the State's concerns about the status of the Modernization Project and the Coalition's failure to achieve expected performance objectives in the modernized regions, ongoing failures in the As-Is regions and failure to make satisfactory progress on the overall implementation of the Modernization Project. These concerns have been expressed as well by many key constituencies, including State legislators, federal agencies, client advocates and other stakeholders.

[On July 2, 2009 IBM and Indiana agreed on a plan.] But in late July 2009, the federal agency overseeing Medicaid programs—Centers for Medicare and Medicaid Services (CMS)—found that Indiana was "consistently not meeting Federal eligibility processing requirements." CMS noted that since the Modernization Project's rollout, it was "plagued" "by ongoing issues and complaints that consumers are losing Medicaid benefits or being denied benefits inappropriately." The problems included extended wait times for processing enrollment applications and in receiving responses to Call Center inquiries, lack of responses to enrollment applications, and inappropriate disenrollments. CMS noted that these problems, which had garnered media attention, "indicate a serious situation in Indiana that is negatively impacting consumers' access to Medicaid." Finding that the State was not in compliance with several provisions of the United States Code and the Code of Federal Regulations, CMS ordered the State to provide its own "Corrective Action Plan (CAP) for ensuring that the Federal eligibility requirements are met."

The trial court found that by mid-October 2009, the IBM Coalition had made "substantial progress" on the Corrective Action Plan entered into between the State and IBM. As support for this finding, the trial court relied on statements made by an attorney general in a September 2009 hearing in *Thornton v. Anne Murphy* in the United States District Court for the Southern District of Indiana. [In a September, 2009, hearing for a federal case over the length of time it was taking to process welfare applications, the attorney general stated:]

> We looked at what were the causes. We tried to identify the causes; and we've initiated a number of activities to correct those causes, many of which—they call it Quick Win[s], but we have made substantial progress in a very short period of time.

The trial court also cited a late September 2009 email which contained public statements from Secretary Murphy that "a team of vendors led by IBM Corp. has already made improvements in technology and added more staff under a corrective action plan submitted in July"; however, Secretary Murphy added that "the timeliness of processing applications for food stamps, Medicaid and other benefits has not improved."

Nevertheless, in September 2009, two months after the State and IBM signed the Corrective Action Plan, the State decided to change course and adopt a hybrid approach to welfare modernization, which the State and IBM referred to as "Plan B." Most notably, Plan B abandoned the centralized Call Center, moving the eligibility determinations to the local office where clients would experience face-to-face interactions with FSSA staff handling their cases. The State noted that "'[t]he largest difference between the Hybrid System and the modernized system will be an increased focus on the face-to-face contact.'" The State approached IBM about implementing the hybrid plan, but an agreement was never reached between the parties because the State could not afford the price that IBM was charging for the plan. Even after the parties failed to agree on an IBM-led rollout of the hybrid plan, the State encouraged IBM to continue as the technology vendor.

On October 15, 2009—less than three years into the ten-year contract—Secretary Murphy delivered a letter to IBM explaining that the State was terminating the MSA "in whole" "for cause" effective December 14, 2009. The State alleged that IBM's breaches included "numerous and repeated quality and timeliness failures." In addition, the State alleged that pursuant to Section 16.3.1(1)(A) of the MSA, IBM's breaches were material ....

[On the same day, Governor Daniels held a press conference to announce the termination and switch to a "hybrid" system. According to the press release, this hybrid system would "incorporate successful elements of the old welfare delivery system and what is known as the modernized system" and "include more face-to-face contact and more localized team-based case management." The press release stated that Indiana terminated the contract because IBM made insufficient progress in welfare services:]

> "The fraud appears to have been stopped and we're still on track to save taxpayers hundreds of millions of dollars, but the intended service improvements have not been delivered, and that's not acceptable," said Daniels. "Those who raised concerns about service quality were correct and we appreciate their efforts. We'll now take the best parts of the old and new and move ahead with a hybrid system in what amounts to a major mid-course correction."

The press release stated that the IBM system suffered from two fundamental flaws in concept: (1) the system tried to remove the burden of required face-to-face meetings and (2) it used a task-based approach rather than a case-based approach to process applications.

In total, the State paid IBM approximately $437 million under the MSA.

[A subsequent Disengagement Plan required Indiana to pay IBM about $4 million for disengagement services. The State also elected to keep almost $10 million in computers and furniture, though it never paid this sum. In May 2010, Indiana filed suit seeking $170 million in damages. Indiana alleged five material breaches: (1) failure to roll out the Modernized system statewide by the agreed date; (2) failure to achieve promised improvements in timeliness, accuracy, client satisfaction, and other established measures; (3) in Modernized counties, performance standards fell below non-Modernized counties, below performance before Modernization, and below federal and state guidelines; (4) failure to satisfy the agreed-upon Corrective Action Plan; and (5) failure to cure deficient performance.

IBM filed suit against Indiana on the same day, seeking deferred fees of over $40 million and the $10 million for the equipment Indiana kept. The litigation produced 12 motions for summary judgment and an emergency transfer over whether Governor Daniels had to sit for a deposition. *See State v. Int'l Bus. Machs. Corp.*, 964 N.E.2d 206 (Ind. 2012). This all built up to a six-week bench trial, involving eight attorneys for Indiana, 11 attorneys for IBM, 92 witnesses, and 7500 exhibits.

On July 18, 2012, the trial court issued a 65-page order, concluding in part that IBM substantially performed and did not materially breach the MSA; that Indiana owed IBM $40 million in assignment fees after Indiana assumed the prime-contractor role to allow the subcontractors to continue; and that Indiana owed IBM $10 million for the equipment it retained.]

Discussion and Decision

This case involves the interpretation of a $1.3 billion contract entered into by two sophisticated parties—the State of Indiana—represented by both outside counsel and the Attorney General's Office—and IBM—a multinational technology and consulting company—represented by multiple attorneys. Both parties alleged breach of this more than 160-page contract.

The ultimate goal of any contract interpretation is to determine the intent of the parties when they made the agreement. We begin with the plain language of the contract, reading it in context and, whenever possible, construing it so as to render each word, phrase, and term meaningful, unambiguous, and harmonious with the whole....

I. Material Breach

[Material breach was the central issue in the case. If IBM materially breached the MSA, it would not be entitled to $44 million in deferred fees and the State would not have to pay other early termination payments.]

According to MSA § 16.3.1(1)(A), in order to terminate the MSA for cause, the State had to prove a breach by IBM that was "material considering this Agreement as a whole[.]" A material breach is one that goes to the heart of the contract.... In determining whether any breach went to the heart of the contract, we find that the core of the contract is identified in the following "Policy Objectives" in the MSA [set out in full on page 2 of the opinion in MSA § 1.1(1)].

In other words, the essence of the Modernization Project was to provide and expand access to services for welfare recipients in a timely, reliable, and efficient manner within federal guidelines, to discourage fraud, and to increase work-participation rates—all of which were problems that plagued the earlier system. Contrary to the trial court's implication in Conclusion No. 100, whether IBM materially breached the contract does not require balancing the number of benefits the State received versus the number of performance standards that IBM failed. Rather, the issue is whether any breach went to the essence of the contract—to provide and expand access to services for welfare recipients in a timely, reliable, and efficient manner within federal guidelines, to discourage fraud, and to increase work-participation rates.

A. The State's Arguments

The State's Dissatisfaction with IBM's Performance. Although the evidence showed that the State was not satisfied with IBM's performance, the trial court concluded that the State's dissatisfaction with IBM's performance did not support a claim of breach (much less a claim of material breach); instead, it was merely one of eight enumerated ways in which IBM's performance was to be judged.

According to MSA § 3.8.2, satisfactory performance of the Agreement by IBM "will be measured by" eight standards, including "Determination by the State of (i) Vendor's satisfactory performance of the Services and the Delegated Activities." The State presented evidence at trial from several people establishing that the State was not satisfied with IBM's performance, including Brian Whitfield, IBM Vice President of State and Local Government when the MSA was executed. Whitfield testified that the "project didn't perform at a level that I would have found to be satisfactory" and conceded that the State was not satisfied with IBM's performance in 2009 and had a reasonable basis to be dissatisfied. Steve Zaudtke, IBM on-site project executive, similarly testified that there were problems in 2009 with IBM's performance and that overall the State was not satisfied. And John Lyons, IBM's trial representative, conceded that over the course of the six-week trial he never heard any of the witnesses say that IBM's performance was good in 2009. . . .

A party to a contract involving requirements of commercial quality, operative fitness, or mechanical utility may condition its obligation to pay upon that party's satisfaction that the other party's performance meets the applicable standard. A party's evaluation of the other party's performance under these criteria will be judged against a reasonable-person standard, and dissatisfaction may not be claimed arbitrarily, capriciously, or unreasonably. A party should be satisfied with another party's performance if a reasonable person in the same circumstances would be satisfied.

The State argues that under this standard, it had a reasonable basis to be dissatisfied with IBM's performance and that IBM's unsatisfactory performance is not "immaterial." Although the State's determination of whether IBM's performance of Services was satisfactory was just one standard to be considered, IBM witnesses admitted that the State was and had a reasonable basis to be dissatisfied with its performance. The State's dissatisfaction should have been considered by the trial court in determining whether there was a material breach.

Failing Performance Standards. [Reversing the trial court's holding to the contrary, the court concluded that the liquidated damages clause did not deprive the State of termination rights, including for-cause termination.]

IBM's Failure to Satisfy Legal Standards. The State argues that the trial court's conclusion that IBM's breaches were not material "ignored other MSA provisions and uncontradicted evidence, including that IBM's performance failed to meet Federal legal standards." The MSA's first-listed Policy Objective was "to provide efficient, accurate and timely eligibility determinations for individuals and families who qualify for public assistance." Notably, the trial court found that "[Key Performance Indicator] metrics for timeliness were consistently missing the mark." In other words, the IBM Coalition was failing on the very issues that the Policy Objectives deemed to be vital. Accordingly, in determining whether there was a material breach, the trial court should have considered the IBM Coalition's breach of performance obligations on the very matters that the MSA stated were its overarching policy objectives.

In addition, ensuring "compliance with all relevant Laws" was another explicit Policy Objective. The State cites evidence that in late July 2009, which was less than two months before the State terminated the MSA for quality and timeliness issues, CMS—the federal agency overseeing Medicaid programs—found that Indiana was "consistently not meeting Federal eligibility processing requirements." CMS noted that since the Modernization Project's rollout, it was "plagued" "by ongoing issues and complaints that consumers are losing Medicaid benefits or being denied benefits inappropriately." The problems included extended wait times for processing enrollment applications and in receiving responses to Call Center inquiries, lack of responses to enrollment applications, and inappropriate disenrollments. CMS noted that these problems, which had garnered media attention, "indicate a serious situation in Indiana that is negatively impacting consumers' access to Medicaid." Finding that the State was not in compliance with several provisions of the United States Code and the Code of Federal Regulations, CMS ordered the State to provide its own "Corrective Action Plan (CAP) for ensuring that the Federal eligibility requirements are met." . . .

Accordingly, the trial court should have considered IBM's failures to meet Federal Program Targets in determining whether to terminate the contract for cause. . . .

Economic Downturn and Flooding. The State argues that the trial court improperly considered the economic downturn and flooding as reasons to excuse IBM's performance. We start with the economic recession. Specifically, the court found that two months after the rollout of the pilot region, "the State and the country began to feel the effects of what has been termed the 'Great Recession.'" The court observed that almost immediately, benefit applications increased 21% and the number of processed applications increased 41% compared to the previous year. The court dubbed the recession, "the most severe crisis since the Great Depression." In addition, the court noted that Indiana's unemployment rate had more than doubled since the MSA was executed and was higher than the national average. The court noted that in response to the economic crisis, in February 2009 Congress passed stimulus legislation, which, among other things, increased the benefits to food-stamp recipients.

The State argues that the trial court wrongly relied on these events because the MSA provided IBM an appropriate remedy "if recession and legislative responses threatened its performance—the Change Order Process" [under the MSA].

The MSA provided for "Material Assumptions," one of which was that there woud be no "material economic downturn in Indiana." The SA provided that IBM could make a request under the Change Order Process if such an assumption proved erroneous, but "[n]o such request was made here."

As for flooding, the trial court found:

> Compounding the challenges presented by the economic downturn and the Project's expansion to HIP, Indiana was hit by a series of natural disasters

> during 2008, which displaced thousands of Hoosiers from their homes and caused nearly $2 billion in economic damages. As described by the State, "[t]he 2008 disasters in Indiana have been among the worst in our state's history." Eighty-two of Indiana's 92 counties were declared Presidential Disaster Areas during 2008.

The trial court also found that "[t]he State directed the reassignment of approximately one third of the State and IBM Coalition workforce 'from every available post,' 'modernized or as-is,' to assist with the processing of tens of thousands of emergency food statement applications" and "thousands of FEMA Individual Assistance applications[.]"

[Again, the MSA provided that in the event of a "Force Majeure Event" (which included "flood"), IBM was to "provide notice ot the State as soon as practicable and shall use Commericially Reasonable Efforts to resume performance of the Services to the extent practicable, despite the Force Majeure Event." IBM failed to give notice as required by the MSA.]

The State again argues that "the parties anticipated and accounted for the implications of unpredictable weather" in the MSA. Specifically, MSA § 21.22 provided:

> In the event that because of [a] Force Majeure Event, Vendor is unable to perform any of its obligations under this Agreement or such performance is rendered impractical, Vendor shall provide notice to the State as soon as practicable and shall use Commercially Reasonable Efforts to resume performance of the Services to the extent practicable, despite the Force Majeure Event.

The MSA's definition of "Force Majeure Event" included "flood." IBM did not give the State notice pursuant to MSA § 21.22.

As for both the economic downturn and flooding, the State also argues that the trial court ignored its pretrial rulings. That is, the State filed a motion for summary judgment relating to the impact of the economic downturn and flooding on IBM's performance. The trial court entered summary judgment in favor of the State . . . .

In response to this argument, IBM argues that the trial court considered these circumstances "not to excuse IBM's performance, but to conduct the required analysis under the Restatement [(Second) of Contracts] as to whether the timeliness failures amounted to a material breach." We find that this difference does not matter. Because the MSA provided IBM with a remedy in the event of an economic downturn or flooding, the trial court should not have considered the economic downturn and flooding as reasons to excuse IBM's performance.

Surge in Applications from the HIP. The State argues that the trial court improperly considered any surge in applications from the HIP as a reason for IBM's performance issues. Specifically, the trial court found that the "HIP significantly increased the scope and cost of the Modernization Project by adding design, development, implementation, continuing services, and reporting requirements." The court also found that the "HIP application volume regularly exceeded the State's predictions.... The State described this as a significant challenge for the modernized system."

However, the MSA specified procedures for seeking service and fee changes when IBM thought that it was warranted....

As the State points out, the record shows that IBM "obtained numerous change orders, yielding $177 million in increased fees." Moreover, the State notes that when the trial court explained that the HIP "significantly increased the scope and cost of the Modernization Project," the court cited an actual change order ....

The State's Motives for Terminating the MSA. The State argues that the trial court improperly considered that the State might have had other motives for terminating the MSA. In its findings, the trial court noted that on the same day that the State delivered the MSA termination letter to IBM, Governor Daniels held a press conference in which he commended IBM for its work, citing a number of benefits that IBM had conferred on the State. In addition, Governor Daniels acknowledged, "They [IBM] did try hard. If resources would have fixed the problem, we wouldn't be making this announcement .... It wasn't resources. It wasn't effort. It was a flawed concept that simply did not work out in practice." In essence, IBM argues that the State did not terminate the MSA for "performance issues," as they have maintained in this litigation.

But as the State points out, a party's motives or reasons for making contract decisions are generally regarded as irrelevant.

Moreover, Justice Sullivan applied these principles in the earlier decision in this case that vacated the trial court's order to depose Governor Daniels. In his concurring-in-result opinion, Justice Sullivan found it unnecessary to discuss the gubernatorial privilege because—contrary to IBM's contentions—any such testimony was irrelevant: "Neither the Governor's 'assessment of IBM's performance' nor his 'state of mind' bear in any way on whether or not IBM breached the contract or the State owes IBM fees or reimbursement." In determining whether the breach was material, the trial court should not have considered that the State might have had other motives or reasons for terminating the MSA.

B. IBM's Arguments

IBM, on the other hand, argues that "[o]verwhelming factual findings support the court's finding of no material breach. The vast majority are not even mentioned in the State's brief, much less challenged." We address each of them.

IBM's first argument is essentially the trial court's balancing test—because the State received an array of benefits, there was no material breach. IBM points to the following benefits that the State received: (1) dramatic improvement in work-participation rates as part of the welfare-to-work program; (2) reduction in fraud; (3) programmatic and administrative cost savings totaling approximately $40 million per year; (4) modern electronic access to the eligibility system, including the online filing of applications; (5) the electronic "paperless" system, which was preferred over boxes;

(6) the Work Flow Management System (WFMS), which the State carried over to the hybrid system; (7) the HIP, which state officials described as "an unqualified success"; (8) the valuable contribution that the IBM Coalition members made in responding to the 2008 natural disasters; and (9) economic development, which, as Governor Daniels explained during his 2009 press conference, brought 1000 new private-sector jobs to Daleville and Anderson.

IBM argues that on top of these benefits, the trial court found that IBM's work provided the foundation for the successful hybrid system. As the trial court explained, "Modernization is the foundation on which the State Hybrid system now stands. For better or worse, and through much transition difficulty, the contract, including IBM's efforts, conferred the overall aggregate benefit sought by the State: a new welfare system that works better."

However, as we explained above and as the State points out, IBM misses the point by highlighting the benefits the State received. The State readily concedes that it received benefits under the MSA, "under [which] it paid IBM over $437,000,000." As the State says, "one would hope the State got something for its $437 million." . . .

IBM next argues that the breach was not material because the State asked IBM to implement the hybrid system; in other words, if the State was truly dissatisfied with IBM's services, it would not have asked IBM to continue providing services. . . . In addition, after the parties failed to come to an agreement on an IBM-led roll out of the hybrid system, the State urged IBM to continue as the technology vendor.

However, it is not far-fetched that the State would ask IBM, a multinational technology and consulting company, to lead the roll-out of the hybrid system given the time both parties had invested in this venture and the fact that IBM was intimately familiar with both the State's old system and the Modernization Project. And when the parties could not come to an agreement, it is just as reasonable that the State wanted IBM to continue in a lesser role as the technology vendor.

IBM next argues that the trial court found that the State's principal complaint about the Modernization Project resulted from a key feature of the system that the State itself designed and required—reduction of face-to-face interactions.

The trial court found that Governor Daniels "sought to change one of the key requirements that the State had developed, that he had previously approved, and which was specified in the MSA—the move away from face-to-face meetings and greater reliance on multiple points of access to the system." Accordingly, IBM argues that it "cannot be faulted, much less held in material breach, for following the design requirements the State developed and the MSA required." However, even though the State may have developed a system that resulted in a reduction of face-to-face meetings, IBM nevertheless agreed to implement this design. If IBM did not think that it could carry out this concept, then it presumably would not have executed the MSA. In addition, IBM agreed "to improve the availability, quality and reliability of the services being provided to Clients by expanding access to such services, decreasing inconvenience and improving response times, among other improvements."

IBM also argues that the trial court found that the State's breach allegations revolved around failure to meet Key Performance Indicators for timely processing of applications, but the Key Performance Indicators were not originally intended to apply during the transition period. . . .

We first note that although the trial court concluded that IBM's failure was "apparently" in the process of being cured at the time of termination, this is just one of five factors to consider in determining whether the breach is material. In addition, we note that the findings that the trial court used to support this conclusion are not persuasive. As support for this finding, the trial court relied on statements from an attorney general in a September 2009 hearing in *Thornton v. Anne Murphy* in the United States District Court for the Southern District of Indiana. The litigation concerned how long it took the State to process applications. Not surprisingly, the attorney general, speaking for the defendant, told the judge:

> We looked at what were the causes. We tried to identify the causes; and we've initiated a number of activities to correct those causes, many of which—they call it Quick Win, but we have made substantial progress in a very short period of time.

The trial court also cited a late September 2009 email which contained public statements from Secretary Murphy that "a team of vendors led by IBM Corp. has already made improvements in technology and added more staff under a corrective action plan submitted in July"; however, Secretary Murphy added that "the timeliness of processing applications for food stamps, Medicaid and other benefits has not improved." This is not persuasive evidence that IBM's performance was steadily improving in 2009.

C. Conclusion

Although the Modernization Project reduced fraud and provided important benefits to the State, the record also shows that the system had problems from the very beginning, including unanswered calls and the untimely processing of applications. . . . [T]he question before the trial court was not the number of benefits the State received but whether the heart of this contract was breached by IBM. We find that the heart of this contract was to provide services to the poor in a way that complied with federal law. In this respect IBM's performance, as the trial court explained, "consistently missed the mark." This substandard performance by IBM, $437 million and 36 months later, went to the essence of this contract.

Yet the trial court excused IBM's substandard performance for a number of inappropriate reasons. In particular, the trial court took into account that the Great Recession and an inordinate amount of flooding occurred in Indiana during the course of the contract. While that is all true, this multinational company under the terms of the contract had the ability to request more money from the State through Change Orders to account for these disasters, but it did not. Strikingly, the trial court excused IBM's performance in part because of the increase in the HIP applications, although IBM was paid extra to handle the increase in the HIP applications.

At the same time, the trial court discounted that the State and frankly IBM were both dissatisfied with IBM's performance, that IBM consistently missed the mark on Key Performance Indicators, and that the federal government imposed penalties on the State for IBM's failings.

We find that the failings of IBM went to the heart of the contract—to provide welfare services to our poorest in a timely, efficient, and reliable manner within federal guidelines—and that this constituted a material breach of the contract. Accordingly, we remand this case to the trial court to determine the State's damages and offset any damages awarded to IBM.

[In the remainder of the opinion, the court affirmed the trial court's award of $40 million in assignment fees and $10 million in equipment fees. The assignment fees were owed because the State elected to assume valuable contracts; as the court said regarding the equipment fees, "The State cannot expect to keep millions of dollars in expensive Equipment for free." Additionally, the court held that the State could still owe fees to IBM for Change Orders based upon changes in the law occurring after the MSA was executed. Finally, the court held that Indiana's limited contractual waiver of sovereign immunity extended to "post-judgment interest but not prejudgment interest."]

Conclusion

We affirm the trial court's award of $40 million in assignment fees and $9,510,795 in Equipment fees to IBM, affirm the trial court's denial of Deferred Fees to IBM, reverse the trial court's award of $2,570,621 in Early Termination Close Out Payments and $10,632,333 in prejudgment interest to IBM, and remand the case to the trial court to determine the amount of fees IBM is entitled to for Change Orders 119 and 133 and to determine the State's damages and offset any damages awarded to IBM as a result of IBM's material breach of the contract.

Affirmed in part, reversed in part, and remanded.

Baker, J., concurs.

[The concurrence and dissent of Judge Friedlander are omitted.]

Notes and Questions

1. The trial court's opinion, which was largely rejected on appeal, began with an evocative introduction:

> Neither party deserves to win this case. This story represents a "perfect storm" of misguided government policy and overzealous corporate ambition. Overall, both parties are to blame and Indiana's taxpayers are left as apparent losers.
>
> The largely undisputed evidence shows that the Governor, the Family and Social Services Administration and various State of Indiana officials set out to fix Indiana's poorly-performing welfare system by inserting an untested theoretical experiment, and substitute personal caseworkers with

> computers and phone calls. This is now admitted to be an error, and there is nothing in this case, or the Court's power, that can be done to correct it, or remedy the lost taxpayer money or personal suffering of needy Hoosiers. All that can be done in this case is to take the first step at setting the final numbers among so many millions already spent.
>
> This case is about nothing but the intent of the parties, performance of the parties, and whether there was a "material breach" of the contract as a whole. Breach of public trust is not included here, consideration of private greed is not included here, nor is any measure of public injury. It is just about the money between the parties, much of which is already spent by the State.
>
> Accordingly, the Court makes its determination fairly and diligently. The good faith of the parties cannot reasonably be questioned, especially the hard-working employees of the State and IBM. But the competence of the parties in this project is sometimes open to question. The short ill-fated life of this super-sized contract will remain an enigma.[66]

What do you make of the trial court's assessment of the *IBM* case? Do you agree that "breach of public trust," "consideration of private greed," and "any measure of public injury" were not at issue in this case?

In contrast, how did Judge Vaidik and the Court of Appeals frame the central issues? The Court of Appeals found that the "core of the contract," as expressed through the "'Policy Objectives' in the MSA," included "provid[ing] efficient, accurate and timely eligibility determinations for individuals and families who qualify for public assistance" and "assist[ing] and support[ing] Clients through programs that foster personal responsibility, independence and social and economic self-sufficiency." Can issues such as "public trust" and "public injury" ever truly not be at issue in cases involving private contracts to administer public services?

2. Aftermath. In October 2014, the Indiana Supreme Court heard oral arguments in the *IBM* case and suggested that the parties mediate. Predictably, these efforts failed. Finally, in March 2016—seven years after the cancellation of IBM's contract—the Supreme Court unanimously affirmed the Court of Appeals, though holding that the materiality of IBM's breach should have been determined solely on the basis of the contractual performance metrics (which referenced the MSA's Performance Objectives) and not by reference to the common-law "heart of the contract" test.[67]

The litigation to determine Indiana's damages from the breach continues.

3. In a 2013 article, Professor Aman reflected upon the process by which Indiana decided to outsource its welfare administration and the impact the decision had upon those reliant upon welfare services:

---

66. Findings of Fact, Conclusions of Law, and Judgment for IBM, State v. IBM, No. 49D10-1005-PL-021451 (Marion Super. Ct., July 18, 2012).

67. State v. IBM, 51 N.E.3d 150 (Ind. 2016).

> The question of whether to outsource these modernizing tasks to a private provider was never aired publicly. Whether new technologies could, in effect, be insourced to the government rather than contracted out to the private sector was a question that could have benefitted from public discussion before the decision to outsource was made. Nor was the question of whether these types of reforms were worth pursuing, given the complexity and diverse nature of the makeup of the welfare applicant pool. The question of under what contractual terms the outsourcing project should proceed, however, was subject to additional consideration and public consultation of a sort. Before the contract to outsource welfare eligibility to IBM was signed, the governor appointed an Interagency Review Committee chaired by his own chief of staff and consisting of the heads of six state agencies. The committee worked for seven months and made further modifications before approving the overall concept and design of the system as outlined in that contract. The changes were based on the experiences of other states and the committee's analysis of what it thought some of the risks might be. There were, however, no public hearings on the contract terms ultimately crafted by this committee. The public representative character of this committee consisted of the fact that the members were all a part of the government, appointed by the governor, and serving as heads of their respective administrative agencies. The representation on this committee could have been considerably broader and included actual welfare recipients or their public interest advocates.[68]

4. Professor Aman argues that one overlooked aspect of the program's failure was its neglect to provide for a legal voice for the actual welfare recipients.

> Indiana law recognizes third-party beneficiaries when (1) the parties to the contract intend to benefit a third party, (2) the contract imposes a duty on one of the parties in favor of the third party, and (3) the performance of the terms of the contract directly benefits the third party. However, courts will not interpret a contract so as to render any clauses, phrases, or words in a contract meaningless. Therefore, contracts that include "no third-beneficiary clauses" unambiguously state the parties' intent to not create third-party beneficiaries. The MSA discussed above had such a clause. The Indiana legislature could therefore enact legislation that would make the state's agreement to such a clause in a contract with vendors for the privatization of government services a violation of public policy. Moreover, the legislature could also require language in the contract explicitly making welfare recipients third-party beneficiaries.[69]

Should welfare recipients have been considered third party beneficiaries of the contract between IBM and the State of Indiana? More generally, when government

68. Alfred C. Aman, Jr., *Globalization and the Privatization of Welfare Administration in Indiana*, 20 Ind. J. Global Leg. Stud. 377, 400–01, 409–12 (2013).

69. *Id.* at 419–20.

functions are outsourced to private providers, how should the beneficiaries and stakeholders be defined?

V. Interlegalities across transnational arbitration and litigation

In the context of the neoliberalization of government services—as in the Indiana case, *supra*—introducing so-called efficiencies in the form of delegating the administration of eligibility to a non-state business firm forms an interlegal juncture. At that juncture, the actual processes of awarding contracts and deciding on welfare recipients' eligibility pull agencies in several directions at once. In the Indiana case, for example, the pool of potential recipients was expanding while the contractual obligation committed IBM to narrowing the pool. Welfare applicants and recipients were not represented in the contract process—neither as principals nor as third party beneficiaries. At best, they represented an audit measure. More broadly, as we reflect back on the previous sections, we see that to the extent that efficiency is a value associated with the competitive demands of the global economy, a priority on efficiency may have the effect of displacing certain classes of beneficiaries from participation in setting the terms of a contract, even when it affects them directly. In such contexts, the exclusion of crucial stakeholder groups highlights the potential for contradiction in the interlegalities of privatized government services.

The interlegalities of contracts, and the disjunctions between contractual rights and citizens' rights (or human rights more broadly), come to the fore in different ways in this section, as we turn to the investor-state regime and the tensions between domestic adjudication and international arbitration.

A. International Arbitration: UNCITRAL and ICSID

With the proliferation of Bilateral Investment Treaties (BITs), arbitration has become central to transnational commerce and investment. In the domestic context in the United States, mediation and arbitration are mainstays of the Alternative Dispute Resolution (ADR) movement.[70] In the international context, commercial arbitration has been a growing professional sector since its inception as a small elite area of the bar.[71] It has grown in importance with the proliferation of regional and bilateral trade and investment agreements, as an arbitration clause is standard in such contracts. Professor Gary Born points to the differences between domestic

70. On alternative dispute resolution in the United States and its salience to social science research agendas, see especially LAURA NADER, NO ACCESS TO LAW: ALTERNATIVES TO THE AMERICAN JUDICIAL SYSTEM (1980).

71. On the evolution of international commercial arbitration, see YVES DEZALAY & BRYANT GARTH, DEALING IN VIRTUE: INTERNATIONAL COMMERCIAL ARBITRATION AND THE CONSTRUCTION OF A TRANSNATIONAL LEGAL ORDER (1996).

and international arbitration from the standpoint of the transnational efficacy of the latter:

> International commercial arbitration is similar in important respects to domestic arbitration. As in domestic matters, international arbitration is a consensual means of dispute-resolution, by a non-governmental decision-maker, that produces a legally binding and enforceable ruling. . . . [But there are also differences.] [I]nternational arbitration is frequently regarded as a means of mitigating the peculiar uncertainties of transnational litigation—which can include protracted jurisdictional disputes and expensive parallel proceedings—by designating a single, exclusive dispute resolution mechanism for the parties' disagreements. Moreover, international arbitration is often seen as a means of obtaining an award that is enforceable in diverse jurisdictions.[72]

Provision for arbitration is standard in BITs, but this does not preclude litigation over implementation or enforcement in domestic courts. Courts are generally reluctant to reverse the decisions of arbitration panels, but still, as noted by Professor Choi, "arbitration cannot be divorced completely from national courts."[73]

Arbitration generally takes place through ICSID (International Center for the Settlement of Investment Disputes—an arm of the International Bank for Reconstruction and Development, an organ of the World Bank), or under the rules of UNCITRAL (United Nations Commission on International Trade Law). Differences between UNCITRAL and ICSID Rules may be significant. In general, UNCITRAL is the more flexible system, in that it is *ad hoc* and more fully within the discretion of the parties.[74]

The UNCITRAL Rules, established by the United Nations General Assembly,[75] were initially created for purposes of commercial arbitrations between two private parties.[76] In that context, they governed the Iran-U.S. Claims Tribunal proceedings (see Chapter 1, *supra*). Since that time, they have been invoked with increasing

---

72. Gary B. Born, International Commercial Arbitration In the United States, 2 (1994).

73. Susan Choi, *Judicial Enforcement of Arbitration Awards Under the ICSID and New York Conventions*, 28 N.Y.U. J. Int'l L. & Pol. 175, 175–76 (1996).

74. UNCITRAL art. 3. The major differences between UNCITRAL and ICSID Rules are further enumerated by UNCTAD. *See* UNCTAD, Investor-State Dispute Settlement: UNCTAD Series on Issues in International Investment Agreements II, at 70–78. UNCTAD/DIAE/IA/2013/2 (2014). Available at: http://unctad.org/en/PublicationsLibrary/diaeia2013d2_en.pdf.

75. David A. Gantz, *Investor-State Arbitration Under ICSID, the ICSID Additional Facility and the UNCTAD Arbitral Rules*, U.S.-Vietnam Trade Council (Aug. 17, 2004), http://www.usvtc.org/trade/other/Gantz/Gantz_ICSID.pdf.

76. *See UNCITRAL Arbitration Rules*, UNCITRAL, http://www.uncitral.org/uncitral/en/uncitral_texts/arbitration/2010Arbitration_rules.html.

frequency[77] in the investor-state arbitration context.[78] Their procedural framework is non-institutional, i.e., the rules do not create a secretariat or specify a particular institution for the arbitration. UNCITRAL arbitration proceedings can be (and often are) administered, or assisted, by the Permanent Court of Arbitration (PCA) in The Hague, or by ICSID. The new rules promulgated in 2013 include a new paragraph on transparency[79]—a further contrast with ICSID rules, in which settlement proceedings are secret.[80]

Under UNCITRAL rules, the venue of arbitration may establish that country's legal system as a source of complementary rules governing procedure.[81] The recognition and enforcement of such awards is principally governed by the New York Convention.[82]

The World Bank established the International Centre for Settlement of Investment Disputes (ICSID) in 1966 to "further the Bank's objective of promoting international investment" as an "independent, depoliticized and effective dispute-settlement institution. Its availability to investors and States helps to promote international investment by providing confidence in the dispute resolution process."[83] The significant features of agreements which subject a state to the jurisdiction of adjudicative bodies such as ICSID "is that they delocalize and denationalize the investment relationship by providing investing corporations and individuals the legal rights to sue the host state directly in binding arbitration proceedings conducted by arbitrators selected by the disputing parties outside the legal institutions of the host state." These agreements "add a public international law dimension even to contract-based investment suits."[84]

---

77. *See* Katharina Diel-Gligor, *Competing Regimes in International Investment Arbitration: Choice Between the ICSID and Alternative Arbitral Systems*, 22 Am. Rev. Int'l Arb. 677, 678–79 (2011). When a dispute arises, States typically have no influence on the choice of the arbitral forum/rules since their advance consent to all of the forums/rules included in the applicable IIA was given in advance—the forum is typically chosen by the claimant alone. *See* UNCTAD, Investor-State Dispute Settlement: UNCTAD Series on Issues in International Investment Agreements II, *supra* note 76 at 64. At the end of 2012, a total of 514 known IIA-based claims were in existence. *See* UNCTAD, *IIA Issues Note: Recent Developments in Investor-State Dispute Settlement* 3 (2013), http://unctad.org/en/PublicationsLibrary/webdiaepcb2013d3_en.pdf. Of the 514 claims, 314 of these were filed at ICSID (including its additional facility), and 131 were filed under UNCITRAL rules. *See id.*

78. *See* UNCTAD, Investor-State Dispute Settlement: UNCTAD Series on Issues in International Investment Agreements II, at 68.

79. UNCITRAL Arbitration Rules. Available at http://www.uncitral.org/pdf/english/texts/arbitration/arb-rules-2013/UNCITRAL-Arbitration-Rules-2013-e.pdf.

80. International Centre for the Settlement of Investment Disputes, ICSID Conventions, Regulations and Rules 110 (2006).

81. *See* Piero Bernadini, *ICSID Versus Non-ICSID Investment Treaty Arbitration*, *in* Liber Amicorum Bernardo Cremades 159 (Arias & Ballesteros eds., 2010).

82. *See id.*

83. *About ICSID*, https://icsid.worldbank.org/apps/ICSIDWEB/about/Pages/default.aspx.

84. Andrea K. Bjorklund, *The Emerging Civilization of Investment Arbitration*, 113 Penn St. L. Rev. 1269, 1271 (2009).

The president of the World Bank serves as chair of ICSID's administrative council. Membership in ICSID is open to member states of IBRD—each of which is represented by one delegate to the administrative council, and each of which may nominate panelists to serve as members of the secretariat. ICSID's secretariat supports two panels—the panel of arbitrators and the panel of conciliators—members of which serve for six year terms, and may or may not be nationals of the nominating member states. Currently, 153 contracting states have ratified the ICSID Convention. Cases are heard at World Bank offices, but there is provision for other venues; expenses of the panels are underwritten by a combination of fees and assessments based on the member states' subscription share in the IBRD. ICSID's Convention gives strong powers to its panels, conferring arbitrators with ultimate authority in the cases heard. Parties agree in advance to abide by the panel's decisions, and to relinquish the right to file subsequent claims before other bodies on the same dispute.[85]

In his analysis of modern arbitral powers over national courts, Michael Goldhaber finds in ICSID a significant departure from longstanding traditions of antisuit injunction—particularly in cases in which arbitrators conduct a final (rather than temporary) review:

> World Bank arbitrators have issued at least eleven antisuit injunctions against states this millennium, and have not provoked a general outcry. But in fact, when it migrated from commercial litigation to investment arbitration, the practice was significantly transformed. For when an antisuit injunction is directed at a state, it imposes obligation not only on the executive acting as litigant, but—as *Chevron* [discussed *infra*] makes explicit—on the state's judiciary. It may be said in this scenario that an antisuit injunction amounts to an arbitral suspension of judicial proceedings.[86]

Referring especially to cases such as *Chevron* (see Section VI, *infra*) in which Chevron has sought a final ruling from arbitrators, Goldhaber continues:

> The urge to control rogue judges has a long tradition in international law under the denial of justice doctrine. But the guarantee by states that foreign investors will not be denied justice has undergone a transformation in recent years. Although denial of justice has not bloomed, as famously predicted by Jan Paulsson, the impulse to restore justice has flowered in different forms—expropriation, effective means, and unfair treatment more generally—which might collectively be called arbitral review of judicial action. While each illustrative case has drawn attention, their family resemblance to each other and denial of justice has gone unnoticed [by commentators].... Recent

85. Convention on the Settlement of Investment Disputes Between States and Nationals of Other States, 575 U.N.T.S. 159 (1966).

86. Michael D. Goldhaber, *The Rise of Arbitral Power Over Domestic Courts*, 1 Stan. J. Complex Litig. 373, 376 (2013).

> arbitration decisions have opened up the possibility of using expropriation and effective means clauses as checks on domestic courts.[87]

Goldhaber notes that between 2000 and 2010, stays of litigation were sought in fifteen ICSID cases, and granted in ten—"with all ten granted in favor of investors."[88] In such cases, arbitrators "may choose to step into the shoes of the first-instance decisionmaker, . . . function[ing] not only as an appellate body, but a highly intrusive one."[89] While granting the merits of providing "a shield against state courts favoring local parties in local disputes,"[90] Goldhaber expresses concern that panels with judicial functions themselves be held to a professional judicial standard, and avoid wherever possible the preemption of domestic judiciaries.[91] Political scientist Claire Cutler expresses related but broader concerns, in voicing "pessimism" in the face of her "deep suspicion of the distinctions between public and private international law, and between economics and politics that work to depoliticize the entire realm of international commercial and economic activity and legality, and to immobilize national political authorities."[92]

As we turn to illustrative case studies of the structural tensions incurred when arbitral power in the investor context (with its borderless authority) and domestic judicial power mix. Such asymmetries are not restricted to structural questions of forum, nor to investor disputes. As we have seen, particularly in the Bridgestone case detailed in Chapter 6, U.S. courts are favored arenas for some tort claims originating abroad (see further discussion in Chapter 8, *infra*)—a trend to "forum shopping" that U.S. courts are increasingly reluctant to accept.[93]

B. International investment agreements, state sovereignty and human rights

The investor-state regime was designed to overcome the barriers to suits against states by private actors under international law, by establishing bilateral agreements:

> The investor-state regime basically provides for investment security by protecting foreign investors from the expropriation of their assets without due compensation and from other measures that might impair their investment. The regime also provides for dispute resolution in delocalized settings to avoid potential interference from national policymakers and courts of law.

87. *Id.* at 377.
88. *Id.* at 381.
89. *Id.* at 393.
90. *Id.* at 397
91. *Id.* at 409, 417.
92. A. Claire Cutler, *Transformations in Statehood, the Investor-State Regime, and the New Constitutionalism*, 23 IND. J. GLOBAL LEGAL STUD. 95, 96 (2016).
93. Alan Sykes, *Transnational Forum Shopping as a Trade and Investment Issue* (John M. Olin Program in Law and Economics, Stanford Law School, Working Paper No. 331, 2007), http://ssrn.com/abstract=956668.

> The regime thus removes significant dimensions of the foreign investment relationship from local or national political and legal contestation, control, and review. This "denationalizing" and "delocalizing" of the investment relationship is precisely what the regime is designed to do.[94]

Through Bilateral Investment Treaties, states in effect contractually revise their statehood by acceding rights to foreign investors, and investors in turn derive benefit from human rights doctrine—a "paradox" noted by Professor Cutler:

> The investor-state regime has . . . made a profound impact on statehood by according significant rights to foreign investors *vis-à-vis* states, but has simultaneously limited the ability of host states to regulate their domestic societies in ways that might impair foreign investment. Paradoxically, foreign investors have utilized these one-way agreements to develop and expand the rights provided them under guaranteed standards of "fair and equitable treatment," "full protection and security," "national treatment," "most-favored nation treatment," and "treatment in accordance with international law." While there are several ways that human rights have entered into the investor-state regime, an interesting dialectic is emerging in the impact that international human rights are having on the investment regime and statehood. In some cases international human rights are being raised by foreign investors in defense of their property and market-based rights under the investment regime. In such cases, human rights are used to shore up and even expand the private property rights protected by investment agreements.[95]

But host states, too, invoke human rights doctrine to contest investors' claims:

> [H]uman rights are used to contest the foundations of the investment regime and to reassert statehood and the protection of rights other than market-based rights. By far the most active reliance on human rights doctrines has been that of foreign investors advancing their right to standards of treatment provided for in the investment agreement or BIT. Indeed, corporations have greatly expanded the scope of corporate rights in the development of arbitral decisions clarifying the nature and scope of treaty-based rights . . . [But] human rights have [also] been relied on to contest the operations of the investor-state regime. . . . Many of these cases concern disputed public utility investments, often prompting the host state's defense that it was protecting a variety of human rights.[96]

Referring to Argentina's privatizations since 1989, legal scholar Christian Courtis writes:

> [It was] a dramatic shift in the longstanding Welfare State arrangements that characterised the local balance between State, market and society more than

94. Cutler, *supra* note 92, at 110.

95. *Id.*

96. Cutler, *supra* note 92, at 111 (notes and paragraphing omitted).

> 50 years. In a very brief period of time, most of the public services and enterprises that were owned or run by the State or under State control since the '40s and '50s, were privatised, deregulated or decentralised. It took less than three years for the then ruling administration to privatise or transfer to the private sector electricity, gas, telephone, post, road, railway, port and airport services . . . and other companies. . . . Paradoxically, this trend took place simultaneously with a growing recognition of the normative value of international human rights law.[97]

Argentina has made such claims in "numerous such cases" but so far without success.[98] For example, in 2005, in *CMS Gas Transmission Company v. Argentine Republic*, Argentina contested the investor's claim (challenging various emergency measures intended to address Argentina's economic crisis) on the grounds of the priority of its constitutional requirement of citizen protection. The tribunal concluded that, while citizen protections are "legitimate" as objectives, they should be "viewed as future aspirations rather than enforceable rights similar to fundamental constitutional rights." [99] The tribunal also rejected Argentina's necessity defense in this case, on the grounds that there was no threat to human rights. [100] Following the tribunal's decision, Argentina filed a Request for Annulment with the ICSID Secretary-General. The annulment committee denied Argentina's request. Blue Ridge Investments, which had purchased CMS Gas Transportation's interest in the ICSID award, brought suit in the Southern District of New York to enforce the arbitration decision. [101] The district court, affirmed by the Second Circuit, held that Argentina waived sovereign immunity by becoming a party to the ICSID convention. The parties reached a settlement in *CMS Gas Transport* and several other investor-state disputes in October, 2013.[102]

In 2010, in *Suez v. Argentine Republic*, several private corporations challenged Argentina's tariff rates and eventual termination of its thirty-year contract to manage a water and sewage concession,[103] granted in part in hopes of improving the

---

97. Christian Courtis, *Social Rights and Privatisation: Lessons from the Argentine Experience, in* Privatisation and Human Rights in the Age of Globalisation 175, 175 (Koen De Feyter & Felipe Gómez Isa eds., 2005).

98. *Id.*

99. Víctor R. Salgado, Comment, *The Case Against Adopting BIT Law in the FTAA Framework*, 2006 Wis. L. Rev. 1025, 1058 (quoting *CMS Gas Transmission* ¶ 88).

100. Cutler, *supra* note 92, at 112.

101. Blue Ridge Investments, LLC v. Republic of Argentina, 902 F. Supp. 2d 367 (S.D.N.Y. 2012) *aff'd* Blue Ridge Investments, L.L.C. v. Republic of Argentina, 735 F.3d 72 (2d Cir. 2013). *See generally Second Circuit Rejects Argentina's Immunity Claim in Action to Confirm ICSID Award*, 107 Am. J. Int'l L. 914 (2013).

102. *Argentina Settles Five Investment Treaty Awards*, Allen & Overy (Nov. 7, 2013), http://www.allenovery.com/publications/en-gb/Pages/Argentina-settles-five-investment-treaty-awards.aspx.

103. Cutler, *supra* note 92, at 112, citing *Suez, Sociedad General de Aguas de Barcelona S. A.*, ICSID Case No. ARB/03/19, Decision on Liability, (July 30, 2010).

overall efficiency of service delivery.[104] Argentina raised the human right to water in its necessity defense for terminating the water concession, supported by the first ever *amici curiae* briefs filed in ICSID history.[105] The tribunal gave only a cursory analysis to the critical water rights issue in addressing whether providing water was an "essential interest" for the purpose of a necessity defense.[106] Similar to *CMS Gas Transmission*, it rejected the necessity defense, in this case on the grounds that there was no inherent trade-off between its treaty and human rights obligations.[107] ICSID made a "loss valuation of US$133.2 million" and determined that that was the compensation owed to the claimant "because Argentina's measures in violation of the BITs were not the only means to satisfy its essential interests and because Argentina itself contributed to the emergency situation that it was facing in 2001–2003."[108]

The NAFTA arbitral tribunal, conducted under UNCITRAL rules, first recognized its authority to accept *amicus* briefs in investment arbitrations in 2001 in *Methanex Corporation v. United States.*[109] In *Methanex*, a methanol manufacturer sought compensation after California banned the use of MTBE, a gasoline additive of which one component is methanol.[110] This innovation drew a critical response from critics who saw *amicus* participation as "a sort of legal 'backdoor.' "[111] To this, the NAFTA tribunal responded that "the rights of the Disputing Parties . . . both procedural and substantive, remain juridically exactly the same before and after receipt of such submissions; and the third person acquires no rights at all."[112]

The NAFTA tribunal emphasized the importance of transparency in cases involving a broad public interest:

> There is an undoubtedly public interest in this arbitration. The substantive issues extend far beyond those raised by the usual transnational arbitration . . . . This is not merely because one of the Disputing Parties is a State . . . . The public interest in this arbitration arises from its subject matter.[113]

---

104. Antenor Gijs Hallo de Wolf, Reconciling Privatization with Human Rights, 620 (Dec. 20, 2011) (unpublished Ph.D. dissertation, Maastricht University), http://digitalarchive.maastrichtuniversity.nl /fedora/get/guid:b46987a8-1ecc-4d8b-84eb-2b74674dd72b/ASSET1.

105. Cutler, *supra* note 92, at 112.

106. *Id.*

107. *Id.*

108. Cutler, *supra* note 92, quoting *Suez.*

109. Decision on Petitions from Third Persons to Intervene as "Amici Curiae," ¶ 25 (NAFTA Arb. 2001).

110. Cutler, *supra* note 92, at 117, quoting Methanex Corp. v. United States, 44 I.L.M. 1345, ¶ 1 (NAFTA Arb. 2005).

111. Katia Fach Gómez, *Rethinking the Role of Amicus Curiae in International Investment Arbitration: How to Draw the Line Favorably for the Public Interest*, 35 Fordham Int'l L.J. 510, 535 (2012) (quoting Barton Legum, *Introductory Note to* Methanex Corporation v. United States of America, 44 Int'l Legal Materials 1343, 1343, (2005)).

112. Gómez, *supra* note 111, at 535–36 (quoting Methanex Corp v. United States, 44 I. L. M. 1345 ¶ 1 (NAFTA Arb. 2005)).

113. Methanex Corp v. United States, 44 I. L. M. 1345 ¶ 49 (NAFTA Arb. 2005).

The NAFTA tribunal was also the first investment treaty tribunal to open its main hearings to the public.[114]

ICSID has been slower to allow non-party participation in its proceedings. In *Aguas del Tunari v. Bolivia*, an American company operated the water and sewage system for a city in Bolivia pursuant to a privatization scheme and, within weeks of beginning operation, hiked up water rates "so much that families living on the minimum wage were being billed up to 25 percent of their monthly income." [115] Several NGOs sought party status or, in the alternative, leave to file *amicus* briefs on behalf of the public to opine on the human right to water. [116] In support, the NGOs cited the right to a fair trial under the *International Covenant on Civil and Political Rights.* ICSID demurred on the grounds that the governing BIT did not give it (ICSID) the power to receive briefs from outside parties without the consent of the parties. [117]

1. Amicus Curiae *and Transparency under ICSID and UNCITRAL Rules*

While some BITs implemented more transparent procedures, such as the U.S. Model BIT (which provides for public hearings, document availability, and an *amicus* procedure [118]) ICSID itself made some adjustments in 2006. In part responding to the NAFTA developments,[119] ICSID amended its rules to include the following in Rule 37(2):

> After consulting both parties, the Tribunal may allow a person or entity that is not a party to the dispute (in this Rule called the "non-disputing party") to file a written submission with the Tribunal regarding a matter within the scope of the dispute. In determining whether to allow such a filing, the Tribunal shall consider, among other things, the extent to which:
>
> (a) the non-disputing party submission would assist the Tribunal in the determination of a factual or legal issue related to the proceeding by bringing a perspective, particular knowledge or insight that is different from that of the disputing parties;
>
> (b) the non-disputing party submission would address a matter within the scope of the dispute;
>
> (c) the non-disputing party has a significant interest in the proceeding.

---

114. *Id.*

115. Cutler, *supra* note 92, at 116.

116. Gómez, *supra* note 111, at 537. *See generally* https://icsid.worldbank.org/ICSID/FrontServlet?requestType=CasesRH&actionVal=showDoc&docId=DC629_En&caseId=C210.

117. Gómez, *supra* note 111, at 537.

118. Gómez, *supra* note 111, at 529.

119. *Id.* at 534.

> The Tribunal shall ensure that the non-disputing party submission does not disrupt the proceeding or unduly burden or unfairly prejudice either party, and that both parties are given an opportunity to present their observations on the non-disputing party submission.[120]

Publication of the award and attendance of non-parties at the hearings are allowed only by consent of parties or through a BIT,[121] though now ICSID rules call for publication of "excerpts of the legal reasoning of the Tribunal."[122]

2. *Human Rights in BIT Formation*

Human rights obligations, among other responsibilities, may be specified in individual trade and investment agreements.[123] The United Nations Human Rights Council issued Guiding Principles in 2011, designed in part to assist states with some of the tensions inherent in the investor-state regime:[124]

> States should maintain adequate domestic policy space to meet their human rights obligations when pursuing business-related policy objectives with other States or business enterprises, for instance through investment treaties or contracts. Economic agreements concluded by States, either with other States or with business enterprises—such as bilateral investment treaties, free-trade agreements or contracts for investment projects—create economic opportunities for States. But they can also affect the domestic policy space of Governments. For example, the terms of international investment agreements may constrain States from fully implementing new human rights legislation, or put them at risk of binding arbitration if they do so. Therefore, States should ensure that they retain adequate policy and regulatory ability to protect human rights under the terms of such agreements, while providing the necessary investor protection.[125]

Consider, for example, the provisions of Article 12 and 13 of the 2012 U.S. Model BIT, which emphasize the predominance of international and domestic obligations in two critical human rights areas: environmental law and labor law.

---

120. ICSID RULES OF PROCEDURE FOR ARBITRATION PROCEEDINGS, p. 117. Available at https://icsid.worldbank.org/ICSID/StaticFiles/basicdoc/partF-chap04.htm [hereinafter ICSID Rules].

121. *See* ICSID Rules 15 (pg. 110), 32(2) (pg. 115) and 48(4) (pg. 122); Gómez, *supra* note 111, at 532–33.

122. ICSID Rule 48(4), pg. 122.

123. *But see* Cutler, *supra* note 92 (on the scarcity of substantive human rights provisions in most BITs).

124. U.N. Special Representative of the Secretary-General, *Guiding Principles on Business and Human Rights: Implementing the United Nations "Protect, Respect and Remedy" Framework: Rep. of the Special Representative of the Secretary-General*, U.N. Doc. A/HRC/17/31 (Mar. 21, 2011).

125. *Id.* at 12.

2012 U.S. Model Bilateral Investment Treaty

Article 12: Investment and Environment

1. The Parties recognize that their respective environmental laws and policies, and multilateral environmental agreements to which they are both party, play an important role in protecting the environment.

2. The Parties recognize that it is inappropriate to encourage investment by weakening or reducing the protections afforded in domestic environmental laws. Accordingly, each Party shall ensure that it does not waive or otherwise derogate from or offer to waive or otherwise derogate from its environmental laws in a manner that weakens or reduces the protections afforded in those laws, or fail to effectively enforce those laws through a sustained or recurring course of action or inaction, as an encouragement for the establishment, acquisition, expansion, or retention of an investment in its territory.

3. The Parties recognize that each Party retains the right to exercise discretion with respect to regulatory, compliance, investigatory, and prosecutorial matters, and to make decisions regarding the allocation of resources to enforcement with respect to other environmental matters determined to have higher priorities. Accordingly, the Parties understand that a Party is in compliance with paragraph where a course of action or inaction reflects a reasonable exercise of such discretion, or results from a bona fide decision regarding the allocation of resources.

4. For purposes of this Article, "environmental law" means each Party's statutes or regulations, or provisions thereof, the primary purpose of which is the protection of the environment, or the prevention of a danger to human, animal, or plant life or health, through the:

(a) prevention, abatement, or control of the release, discharge, or emission of pollutants or environmental contaminants;

(b) control of environmentally hazardous or toxic chemicals, substances, materials, and wastes, and the dissemination of information related thereto; or

(c) protection or conservation of wild flora or fauna, including endangered species, their habitat, and specially protected natural areas, in the Party's territory, but does not include any statute or regulation, or provision thereof, directly related to worker safety or health.

5. Nothing in this Treaty shall be construed to prevent a Party from adopting, maintaining, or enforcing any measure otherwise consistent with this Treaty that it considers appropriate to ensure that investment activity in its territory is undertaken in a manner sensitive to environmental concerns.

* * *

Article 13: Investment and Labor

1. The Parties reaffirm their respective obligations as members of the International Labor Organization ("ILO") and their commitments under the ILO Declaration on Fundamental Principles and Rights at Work and its Follow-Up.

2. The Parties recognize that it is inappropriate to encourage investment by weakening or reducing the protections afforded in domestic labor laws. Accordingly, each Party shall ensure that it does not waive or otherwise derogate from or offer to waive or otherwise derogate from its labor laws where the waiver or derogation would be inconsistent with the labor rights referred to in subparagraphs (a) through (e) of paragraph 3, or fail to effectively enforce its labor laws through a sustained or recurring course of action or inaction, as an encouragement for the establishment, acquisition, expansion, or retention of an investment in its territory.

3. For purposes of this Article, "labor laws" means each Party's statutes or regulations, or provisions thereof, that are directly related to the following:

(a) freedom of association;

(b) the effective recognition of the right to collective bargaining;

(c) the elimination of all forms of forced or compulsory labor;

(d) the effective abolition of child labor and a prohibition on the worst forms of child labor;

(e) the elimination of discrimination in respect of employment and occupation; and

(f) acceptable conditions of work with respect to minimum wages, hours of work, and occupational safety and health.[126]

Investor-state arbitration tribunals are limited in their capacity to allow a state to prioritize human rights when such obligations are not specified in the investor agreement: "The ICSID is . . . not a human rights tribunal. It is arguably not the most adequate forum for venting human rights concerns in spite of the fact that a number of prominent international law experts with ample human rights experience have frequently been appointed as arbitrators in investment disputes . . . ."[127] As we said at the beginning of this Section, the investor-state regime is concerned with just that—the contractual relationships between investors and states. For this reason, as Professor Cutler observes, "the advancement of human rights claims against corporations may be more successful outside the investor-state regime."[128]

Notes and Questions

1. Tribunals have an important role in establishing priorities and distributing responsibilities as between states and investors. What are the implications of allowing a contract to have the final say on such priorities? On what basis can one distinguish between the responsibilities of a tribunal and a legislature?

---

126. http://www.state.gov/documents/organization/188371.pdf.

127. Wolf, *supra* note 104, at 633.

128. Cutler, *supra* note 92, at 119.

2. Why does it matter to the tribunal that Argentina could have addressed its human rights deficits by means other than rescission of the concession? Should it matter?

3. Compare Indiana's contract dispute with IBM with the Argentine cases summarized in this section. What difference did it make that the Argentine cases are framed by BITs, and the Indiana case is framed by domestic contract law? What other differences or similarities do you see between these two types of cases involving citizens' rights under privatization?

VI. Chevron: A complex mix of transnational adjudication and arbitration

A. Chevron — An overview of an on-going lawsuit

This concluding section continues the theme of interlegalities between domestic and arbitral legal regimes, emphasizing the difficulties created by recent complexities of present-day transnational litigation. By this, we refer to its tendency to "encompass several legal issues, [and] require the application of the laws of more than one jurisdiction or legal system"—and, as a formal dispute resolution process that crosses boundaries, where "the number of parties and other stakeholders tends to be higher than in most ordinary disputes."[129] The changes in transnational litigation over the past ten to fifteen years reflect significant interlegal challenges, and in some cases—including *Chevron*—new participants. Anthropologists have given extensive attention to the Lago Agrio community at the core of the litigation, and its on-going mobilization around their suit for damages in the loss of health and livelihood due to dumping of toxic waste from Chevron's extraction operations in the area.[130]

The Chevron litigation provides an instructive example of the difficulties of transnational litigation as interlegal dimensions multiply, intensify and harden. This (still) on-going dispute stems, as noted above, from the environmental damage resulting from oil drilling operations of the multinational company Texaco (now Chevron) in Ecuador's Amazon region.

Ecuadorean nationals, citing harms to health and loss of livelihood that resulted from twenty-eight years of oil drilling and wastewater dumping (concluded in 1992), sought to hold the oil company accountable. The litigation begun by the Lago

---

129. Manuel A. Gómez, *A Sour Battle in Lago Agrio and Beyond: The Metamorphosis of Transnational Litigation and the Protection of Collective Rights in Ecuador*, 46 U. Miami Inter-American L. Rev. 153 (2015).

130. Suzana Sawyer, Crude Chronicles: Indigenous Politics, Multinational Oil, and Neoliberalism in Ecuador (2004); Lindsay Ofrias, *The Fight for Justice in Ecuador's Amazon Continues*, Upside Down World (2015), http://upsidedownworld.org/main/ecuador-archives-49/5291-the-fight-for-justice-for-ecuadors-amazon-continues.

Agrio plaintiffs has crossed U.S./Ecuadorian jurisdictions several times, and has proliferated into multiple suits—including the UNCITRAL arbitration noted earlier in this chapter.

In October 2000, when Texaco was acquired by Chevron, the lawsuit passed to the latter, which continued to resist judgment across several fora. We detail below a chronological slice, a small selection of cases spanning the breadth of the Chevron litigation: first, *Aguinda v. Texaco*, which in many ways serves as the origins of the litigation saga in 1996; second, *Chevron v. Donziger*, where the same district court from *Aguinda* granted Chevron a Temporary Restraining Order barring enforcement of the judgment in Ecuador's *Lago Agrio* class action suit; third, *Chevron Corp. v. Naranjo*, where the Second Circuit ultimately lifted the district court's injunction; and fourth, *Chevron v. Ecuador*, where the D.C. Circuit rejected Ecuador's appeal to withdraw from arbitration.

The following excerpts represent only a very small sample of the litigated suits that were filed worldwide. Moreover, the excerpts are drawn only from U.S. litigation—not from Ecuador's courts or the arbitration tribunal.

1. Aguinda v. Texaco, Inc., *945 F. Supp. 625 (S.D.N.Y. 1996)*

Residents of the Oriente region of Ecuador have twice brought class actions against Texaco in the courts of the United States, seeking extensive relief for vast devastation to that region caused by the decades of oil exploration and extraction activities of a consortium over which both Texaco and Ecuador's state-owned oil company, Petroecuador, have at various times exercised substantial control. The first such action, filed in Harris County, Texas in late August, 1993 and promptly removed to the United States District Court for the Southern District of Texas, was dismissed fewer than five months later on grounds of international comity and forum non conveniens. *Sequihua v. Texaco, Inc.*, 847 F.Supp. 61 (S.D. Tex. 1994). By contrast, when the instant action was filed in the Southern District of New York in early November, 1993, the late Judge Broderick accorded plaintiffs unusual leeway, through discovery and otherwise, to try to prove that this seemingly Ecuadoran-centered lawsuit properly belonged here.... [T]he case was then reassigned in 1996 to this Court, to which the parties presented still further written submissions as well as several hours of oral argument.

In hindsight, such solicitude may have been improvident, for the overwhelming obstacles to the Court's jurisdiction that were already apparent to the court in *Sequihua* have become increasingly obvious to this Court as well. Indeed, after a full review of the underlying record, the Court finds itself obliged to dismiss this action on the same grounds of international comity and forum non conveniens so well stated in *Sequihua*, to which this Court can add little. While it is true that, in contrast to the situation in *Sequihua*, defendant Texaco is headquartered in this judicial district and the Complaint alleges that decisions made by its executives in New York were important to the allegedly unlawful activities undertaken by the consortium in Ecuador, these differences are, in the Court's view, insufficient to overcome the balance of other factors that weigh so heavily against retaining jurisdiction, as outlined in *Sequihua.* As for the submissions offered here by the Congress of Ecuador asking this Court to disregard the submissions of the Government of Ecuador objecting to this Court's retention of jurisdiction, the litany of conflicting submissions from these representatives and officials further evidences the need for this Court to resist intruding on matters that are already the subject of intense political debate in the affected foreign country.

Beyond the grounds specified in *Sequihua,* this Court further concludes that there is another independently-sufficient reason why this action must be dismissed: plaintiffs' failure to join indispensable parties, namely, Petroecuador and the Republic of Ecuador. The extensive equitable relief sought by the plaintiffs—ranging from total environmental "clean-up" of the affected lands in Ecuador to a major alteration of the consortium's Trans-Ecuador pipeline to the direct monitoring of the affected lands for years to come—cannot possibly be undertaken in the absence of Petroecuador, which has owned 100% of the consortium since 1992 and 100% of the pipeline since 1986, or the Republic of Ecuador, which has helped supervise the consortium's activities from the outset and which owns much, if not all, of the affected lands. Petroecuador and the Republic of Ecuador thus are necessary "persons to be joined if feasible" under . . . Fed. R. Civ. P. 19(a).

* * *

Even if this were not so, the factors for determining indispensability set forth in Fed. R. Civ. Proc. 19(b) strongly favor dismissal in these circumstances. In the absence of Petroecuador and the Republic of Ecuador, any order of this Court granting any material part of the Ecuador-directed equitable relief demanded by plaintiffs would be unenforceable on its face, prejudicial to both present and absent parties, and an open invitation to an international political debacle. While the parties dispute whether the courts of Ecuador can provide them with an adequate remedy, it is patently clear that the courts of the United States cannot.

In short, plaintiffs' imaginative view of this Court's power must face the reality that United States district courts are courts of limited jurisdiction. While their power within those limits is substantial, it does not include a general writ to right the world's wrongs.

Accordingly, Texaco's motion to dismiss is granted, and the Clerk is directed to enter judgment on behalf of the defendant.

* * *

SO ORDERED.

2. Chevron v. Donziger, *768 F. Supp. 2d 581 (S.D.N.Y. 2011)*[131]

This claim originated in the United States. Three American lawyers began the original litigation in this Court many years ago. After the New York suit was dismissed

131. Vacated sub nom. Chevron Corp. v. Naranjo, No. 11-1150-CV L, 2011 WL 4375022 (2d Cir. Sept. 19, 2011), rev'd and remanded, 667 F.3d 232 (2d Cir. 2012)

in 2001 on *forum non conveniens* grounds, they brought a successor lawsuit on a different legal theory (the "Lago Agrio" case) in Ecuador. The judgment at issue here was entered in that case.

The LAPs' [the "Lago Agrio Plaintiffs" or "LAPs"] attorneys and other representatives have stated that they intend to seek to collect on that judgment in multiple jurisdictions around the world, including by ex parte attachments, asset seizures, and other means, as promptly as possible, starting before completion of the Ecuadorian appellate process. The purpose of such multiplicitous and burdensome proceedings against a company like Chevron, which would be good for the money if the judgment ultimately stands up, is plain. By their own admissions, it is to exert pressure on Chevron by means of this litigation strategy to force a quick and richer settlement.

Chevron contends that the judgment is not enforceable outside Ecuador because (1) the Ecuadorian legal system does not provide impartial tribunals or procedures compatible with the requirements of due process of law, and (2) it was obtained by fraud led in major degree by a New York City lawyer, Steven Donziger, substantial parts of which were conducted in the United States. It brought this case for, among other relief, a declaration that the judgment is not entitled to recognition or enforcement. It now seeks a preliminary injunction principally to bar the enforcement of the judgment outside Ecuador pending the resolution of this case on the merits or, at least, the resolution of its prayer for a declaratory judgment.

This is an extraordinary case. The amount involved is large. Chevron challenges the fairness and integrity of the judicial system of Ecuador and thus implicates considerations of international comity. There are issues concerning the reach of U.S. law and questions pertaining to the conduct of the New York lawyer and others. There are other concerns.

The Court is mindful of the seriousness of each of them and does not act lightly. In the midst of the many "trees" in this vast record, however, sight should not be lost of the forest. Several points must be borne clearly in mind from the outset.

* * *

Second, the submissions made by Donziger and the two LAPs who have appeared by counsel (the "LAP Representatives")—the rest have defaulted—are replete with complaints that there is no hurry here, that the judgment cannot now be enforced under Ecuadorian law, that Donziger should have been given more time to respond to the motion, that the argument of the motion should have been delayed, and the like. As will appear, none of these contentions has merit even considered in isolation. But the details of each of these points should not obscure this overriding fact.

When it heard the preliminary injunction motion, this Court noted that any urgency could be eliminated if the defendants agreed to a temporary order that they maintain the status quo—that is, that no effort would be made to enforce the judgment—for a period sufficient to permit submission of additional papers and deliberation by the Court. The LAP Representatives refused.

* * *

Third, it must be borne in mind that this is a preliminary injunction motion. As the Supreme Court has said:

> "The purpose of a preliminary injunction is merely to preserve the relative position of the parties until a trial on the merits can be held. Given this limited purpose, and given the haste that is often necessary if those positions are to be preserved, a preliminary injunction is customarily granted on the basis of procedures that are less formal and evidence that is less complete than in a trial on the merits."

Moreover, where, as here, the district court concludes that the risk of harm warrants a TRO to maintain the status quo to permit appropriate consideration of whether to issue a preliminary injunction, "Rule 65," in the eloquent words of the late Judge Friendly, "demands such but only such thoroughness as a burdened federal judiciary can reasonably be expected to attain within" the limited period during which the TRO may remain in effect.

Fourth, there has been a great deal of posturing on both sides. Chevron, for example, complains of the Ecuadorian legal system and judiciary while the LAPs attempt to make much of the fact that Texaco, years ago, successfully obtained a forum non conveniens dismissal of the first of these cases, arguing among other things that the courts of Ecuador would be an adequate forum. Fair enough. But before rising to the bait on either side, however, it is well to bear in mind that the positions of both sides have changed 180 degrees since the predecessor litigation in New York. Chevron then touted the adequacy of the Ecuadorian judiciary, while the plaintiffs—in briefs bearing Donziger's name as counsel—argued that Ecuador could not provide an adequate forum and that its judiciary was corrupt. Similarly, the LAP Representatives argue that the LAPs are poor, indigenous people of the rain forest who cannot properly be sued in New York. In doing so, however, they utterly ignore the fact that they previously have sued both Texaco and Chevron here, voluntarily participated in still other cases in this Court, are voluntarily litigating in other federal courts around the country, and for years used Donziger and his New York office to mount public relations, political and fund raising efforts in support of their Ecuadorian efforts. So a good deal of the rhetoric and argument in this case on these and other issues must be viewed with a critical eye.

The parties here have submitted a large evidentiary record. The facts are essentially undisputed although the same perhaps cannot be said of each of the inferences to be drawn from certain of them. The Court has considered the matter carefully. This is its decision on the motion together with its findings of fact and conclusions of law.

I. Background

* * *

In 1964, Texaco Petroleum Company ("TexPet"), a fourth-tier subsidiary of Texaco, began oil exploration and drilling in the Oriente region of eastern Ecuador. In the following year, TexPet started operating a petroleum concession for a consortium owned in equal shares by TexPet and Gulf Oil Corporation (the "Consortium"). In 1974, the Republic of Ecuador ("ROE") acquired Gulf's interest through its state-owned oil company, Petroecuador. Petroecuador and the ROE became the majority owner of the Consortium in 1976.

* * *

While the *Aguinda* litigation was pending in New York, TexPet in 1994 entered into a Memorandum of Understanding and, in 1995, signed a settlement agreement with the ROE and Petroecuador (the "Settlement"). TexPet agreed to perform specified remedial environmental work in exchange for a release of claims by the ROE. The release, which covered TexPet, Texaco, and related companies, encompassed "all the Government's and Petroecuador's claims against the Releasees for Environmental Impact arising from the Operations of the Consortium, except for those related to the obligations contracted" under the Settlement, which were to be "released as the Environmental Remedial Work is performed to the satisfaction of the Government and Petroecuador." Moreover, the GOE represented that all of the claims asserted in the *Aguinda* action "belong[ed] to the government of the Republic of Ecuador under the Constitution and laws of Ecuador and under international law." Thus, the release by Ecuador seems to have been intended to put an end to any claims or litigation concerning Texaco's alleged pollution.

Three years later, the ROE entered into an agreement with TexPet (the "Final Release") in which the ROE agreed that the Settlement had been "fully performed and concluded" and "proceede[ed] to release, absolve, and discharge" TexPet and related companies, including its successors, "from any liability and claims . . . for items related to the obligations assumed by TexPet" in the Settlement.

* * *

As spelled out in the formal agreement, dated November 20, 1996, between the plaintiffs [in this case] and the Ecuadorian government, the *Aguinda* plaintiffs and their lawyers waived any rights to (1) make any claims against Ecuador, Petroecuador, and affiliates thereof, and (2) to collect from Texaco any amount arising from an award by this Court to Texaco of contribution against Ecuador, Petroecuador or affiliates. In other words, they effectively agreed to reduce the amount of any judgment they might obtain against Texaco by the amount of any award of contribution Texaco might obtain against Ecuador, Petroecuador or affiliates.

* * *

The Lago Agrio Litigation—2003–2008

The Complaint

As noted, the Court of Appeals affirmed the dismissal of the *Aguinda* case in 2002. In 2003, a group of Ecuadorians, including many of the *Aguinda* plaintiffs, sued Chevron and Texaco in Lago Agrio, Ecuador. The complaint, brought on behalf of the [Lago Agrio Plaintiffs (LAPs)], alleges environmental contamination by TexPet,

Texaco's subsidiary, and Texaco in the years up to 1992. It states that Texaco was responsible for the activities of TexPet because it directed and controlled TexPet's operations and capitalized it in a manner designed to limit liability for any complaint derived from its activities. The complaint went on to allege in conclusory terms that Texaco and Chevron on October 9, 2001 merged into a "new company . . . replacing the previously mentioned [Texaco and Chevron] with regard to all obligations and rights" and maintains that Chevron therefore is subject to Texaco and TexPet liabilities. Consistent with [Ecuador's Environmental Management Act of 1999], the complaint sought remediation of alleged pollution said to remain in the region inhabited by the plaintiffs, demanded judgment requiring that the necessary work be done, and sought health improvement and medical monitoring of the inhabitants be done, at the expense of "the defendant."

The Lago Agrio litigation, though it was brought on behalf of similar and, in many cases, the same individuals, was a fundamentally different lawsuit than *Aguinda*. *Aguinda* sought predominantly damages for the plaintiffs and class members for injuries to person or property that each allegedly had suffered. The LAPs, however, sued in something akin to a *parens patriae* capacity to require the defendants to perform, or to pay the cost of performing, environmental and other remediation methods.

* * *

[Chevron meanwhile filed a challenge to the Republic of Ecuador under the terms of the BIT governing U.S.-Ecuador investment.[132] The court reviews the UNCITRAL Arbitration Tribunal's decision, which found a basis for issuing an order to the Republic of Ecuador to "take all measures at its disposal to suspend or cause to be suspended the enforcement or recognition within and without Ecuador of any judgment against [Chevron] in the Lago Agrio case."[133]

This Case

The Complaint

Parties

Chevron filed this action on February 1. The complaint asserts claims against 56 defendants who fall into four groups.

The first group is Donziger and his firm, the Law Offices of Steven R. Donziger.

[The second group is a consulting firm and two of its employees.]

The third group comprises four Ecuadorian individuals and entities who, in various overlapping ways, have participated in the LAPs' representation in the Lago Agrio litigation. . . .

The fourth group of defendants is the LAPs.

132. Investment Treaty with the Republic of Ecuador, August 27, 1993, S. Treaty Doc. No. 103–15.

133. 768 F. Supp. 2d 625 (citing Hendricks Dec. II E 486, at 3).

Additionally, the complaint alleges culpable conduct on the part of a number of nonparties including, *inter alia,* Joe Kohn, who in large part financed the Lago Agrio litigation, the Amazon Watch League, and certain American lawyers and law firms who have represented the LAPs in various U.S. proceedings.

Claims

The complaint asserts nine claims seeking, under a number of theories, damages and an injunction against enforcement of the Lago Agrio judgment.

Counts 1 and 2 assert substantive and conspiracy claims under the Racketeering Influenced and Corrupt Organizations Act ("RICO") against all defendants except the LAPs. These claims allege that the pertinent defendants and a number of non-party co-conspirators engaged in a criminal enterprise to obtain a settlement from or judgment against Chevron through unlawful means including fraud and extortion.

Counts 3 through 5 assert against all defendants state tort claims relating to the allegedly unlawful scheme described above: fraud, tortious interference with contract, and trespass to chattels.

Count 6 asserts against all defendants a claim for unjust enrichment on the ground that any recovery on the Lago Agrio judgment would be inequitable.

Count 7 asserts a state claim for civil conspiracy against all defendants, alleging that they conspired to commit the substantive violations described above.

Count 8 asserts against Donziger and his law firm violations of the New York Judiciary Law governing the conduct of lawyers.

Count 9 seeks a declaratory judgment, pursuant to the federal Declaratory Judgment Act, that the Lago Agrio judgment is not entitled to recognition or enforcement in the United States or anywhere else.

Proceedings to Date

This action was commenced on February 1, 2011. Chevron moved by order to show cause for a temporary restraining order ("TRO") and a preliminary injunction restraining enforcement of the Ecuadorian judgment outside Ecuador on February 3, 2011. The Court issued the TRO after argument on February 8, 2011 and heard argument on the preliminary injunction motion on February 18, 2011. It then closed the record subject to the limited submissions on two specific questions pertaining to appellate practice in Ecuador.

[The decision's legal analysis, covered in detail throughout the opinion, is omitted, but held in relation to the injunction that a) Chevron was threatened with immediate and irreparable injury; b) the balance of hardships tipped toward Chevron; and c) any issue regarding the action's success on the merits (procedural or substantive) did not bar the injunction.]

Conclusion

For the foregoing reasons, Chevron's motion for a preliminary injunction is granted.

* * *

All defendants [other than a few] are enjoined and restrained, pending the final determination of this action, from directly or indirectly funding, commencing, prosecuting, advancing in any way, or receiving benefit from any action or proceeding, outside the Republic of Ecuador, for recognition or enforcement of the judgment previously rendered in *Maria Aguinda y Otros v. Chevron Corporation,* No. 002-2003, in the Provincial Court of Justice of Sucumbios, Ecuador (hereinafter the "*Lago Agrio Case*"), or any other judgment that hereafter may be rendered in the *Lago Agrio Case* by that court or by any other court in Ecuador in or by reason of the *Lago Agrio Case* (collectively, a "Judgment"), or for prejudgment seizure or attachment of assets, outside the Republic of Ecuador, based upon a Judgment.

This Preliminary Injunction takes effect immediately.[134]

3. Chevron Corp. v. Naranjo, *667 F.3d 232 (2d Cir. 2012)*

Lynch, Circuit Judge:

This appeal represents the latest chapter in the ongoing litigation between plaintiff-appellee Chevron Corp. ("Chevron") and the defendants-appellants, elsewhere known as the Lago Agrio Plaintiffs ("LAPs" or "Ecuadorians") and their American attorney Steven Donziger. Chevron brought the present action in part under New York's Uniform Foreign Country Money-Judgments Recognition Act ("the Recognition Act"), N.Y. C.P.L.R. §§ 5301–5309, which allows judgment-creditors to enforce foreign judgments in New York courts, subject to several exceptions. Chevron, a potential judgment-debtor, sought a global anti-enforcement injunction against the LAPs and Donziger prohibiting the latter from attempting to enforce an allegedly fraudulent judgment entered by an Ecuadorian court against Chevron.

On March 7, 2011, the Southern District of New York (Kaplan, J.) granted the global injunction, which the defendants-appellants now challenge. *Chevron Corp. v. Donziger,* 768 F. Supp. 2d 581 (S.D.N.Y.2011) ("*Donziger*"). In an earlier order, we vacated that injunction and stayed the district court's proceedings pending the present opinion. *Chevron Corp. v. Naranjo,* No. 11-1150-cv(L), 2011 WL 4375022 (2d Cir. Sept. 19, 2011). We conclude that the district court erred in construing the Recognition Act to grant putative judgment-debtors a cause of action to challenge foreign judgments before enforcement of those judgments is sought. Judgment-debtors can challenge a foreign judgment's validity under the Recognition Act only defensively, in response to an attempted enforcement—an effort that the defendants-appellees have not yet undertaken anywhere, and might never undertake in New York. Consistent with our earlier order, we therefore reverse the district court's decision, vacate

134. On August 8, 2016, the Court of Appeals for the Second Circuit upheld the District Court's judgment. Chevron Corp. v. Donziger, Docket Nos. 14-0826(L), 14-0832(C).

the injunction, and remand to the district court with instructions to dismiss Chevron's declaratory judgment claim in its entirety.

4. Chevron v. Ecuador, *795 F.3d 200 (D.C. Cir. 2015)*

WILKINS, Circuit Judge:

* * *

I.

In 1973, Chevron and Ecuador signed an agreement allowing Chevron to develop Ecuadorian oil fields in exchange for providing below-market oil to the Ecuadorian government for domestic use. The deal was set to expire in 1992, and the parties were unable to agree to an extension. As the expiration date approached, Chevron filed several breach of contract suits against Ecuador. In 1995, Chevron and Ecuador signed a settlement agreement conclusively terminating all rights and obligations between the parties. The agreement provided for the continuation of the pending lawsuits.

In 1993, the United States and Ecuador signed a Bilateral Investment Treaty ("BIT")—formally known as the Treaty Between the Government of the United States of America and the Government of the Republic of Ecuador for the Encouragement and Reciprocal Protection of Investment—which took effect in 1997. Under this treaty, Ecuador made a standing offer to American investors to arbitrate disputes involving investments that existed on or after the treaty's effective date. For purposes of the BIT, the definition of "investment" included "a claim to money or a claim to performance having economic value, and associated with an investment."

In 2006, Chevron commenced an international arbitration action before a three-member tribunal based out of The Hague, claiming that Ecuador had violated the BIT by failing to resolve its lawsuits in a timely fashion. Ecuador objected to the tribunal's jurisdiction, arguing that it had never agreed to arbitrate with Chevron. The basis of this objection was Ecuador's contention that Chevron's investments in Ecuador had terminated no later than 1995, two years prior to the entry into force of the BIT. The tribunal rejected the jurisdictional challenge, finding that Chevron's lawsuits were "investments" within the meaning of the BIT, and, after determining that Ecuador had delayed disposition of the lawsuits, ultimately decided against Ecuador on the majority of the breach of contract claims, awarding Chevron approximately $96 million. Ecuador challenged the award in the Dutch court system; the challenge was rejected by the District Court of The Hague, The Hague Court of Appeal, and the Dutch Supreme Court.

On July 27, 2012, Chevron petitioned the District Court to confirm the arbitral award under the Convention on the Recognition and Enforcement of Foreign Arbitral Awards ("New York Convention"), which has been incorporated into the Federal Arbitration Act....

[The district court "found that the parties had 'clearly and unmistakably agreed' that the tribunal would resolve" questions on arbitrability. "Having made this finding, the District Court engaged in a deferential review of the tribunal's arbitrability decision and determined that it was clearly supported by the text of the BIT." The district court also rejected Ecuador's argument that the order was against public policy.] We affirm.

II.

As a general matter, the [Foreign Sovereign Immunities Act (FSIA)] grants foreign states immunity from the jurisdiction of the courts of the United States. 28 U.S.C. § 1604. . . . At issue in this case is the arbitration exception, which provides for federal court jurisdiction "in any case . . . in which the action is brought, either to enforce an [arbitration] agreement made by the foreign state with or for the benefit of a private party . . . or to confirm an award made pursuant to such an agreement to arbitrate, if . . . the agreement or award is or may be governed by a treaty . . . in force for the United States calling for the recognition and enforcement of arbitral awards." 28 U.S.C. § 1605(a)(6).

[The district court found that foreign sovereign immunity did not preclude enforcement because the proceeding was pursuant to a BIT.]

A.

. . . Ecuador argues that the § 1605(a)(6) exception requires the District Court to make three findings: "(1) a foreign state has agreed to arbitrate; (2) there is an award based on that agreement; and (3) the award is governed by a treaty signed by the United States calling for the recognition and enforcement of arbitral awards." Chevron argues that the exception allows jurisdiction any time a plaintiff asserts a non-frivolous claim involving an arbitration award.

For the most part, Ecuador has the better argument, and has identified the relevant jurisdictional facts. . . .

As the plaintiff, Chevron bears the initial burden of supporting its claim that the FSIA exception applies. "[T]his is only a burden of production; the burden of persuasion rests with the foreign sovereign claiming immunity, which must establish the absence of the factual basis by a preponderance of the evidence." Chevron has met its burden of production by producing the BIT, Chevron's notice of arbitration against Ecuador, and the tribunal's arbitration decision.

Ecuador argues that the FSIA required the District Court to make a *de novo* determination of whether Ecuador's offer to arbitrate in the BIT encompassed Chevron's breach of contract claims. . . .

Ecuador conflates the jurisdictional standard of the FSIA with the standard for review under the New York Convention. For FSIA purposes, Chevron made a prima facie showing that there was an arbitration agreement by producing the BIT and the notice of arbitration. Once Chevron made this showing, the burden shifted to Ecuador to demonstrate by a preponderance of the evidence that the BIT and the notice to arbitrate did not constitute a valid arbitration agreement between the parties. The jurisdictional task before the District Court was to determine whether Ecuador had sufficiently rebutted the presumption that the BIT and Chevron's notice of arbitration constituted an agreement to arbitrate.

The Supreme Court's recent decision in *BG Group, PLC v. Republic of Argentina*, 134 S. Ct. 1198 (2014), is instructive on this point. In *BG Group*, Argentina's primary argument was similar to Ecuador's in the present case. By its terms, the Bilateral Investment Treaty between the United Kingdom and Argentina required an investor to litigate its claims in the local court system before submitting the claims to arbitration. BG Group submitted a claim to arbitration without observing this process. The arbitration panel concluded that Argentina had waived the local litigation requirement and found in BG Group's favor on the merits.

* * *

The Court "treat[ed] the document . . . as if it were an ordinary contract between private parties"—Argentina and BG Group—and concluded that the parties had intended to allow the arbitrator to determine whether the local litigation requirement had been satisfied. *BG Group*, 134 S. Ct. at 1206 (majority op.). In doing so, the Court implicitly rejected Argentina's contention that its offer to arbitrate only applied to investors who complied with the local litigation requirement. As the Chief Justice noted in his dissent, "[t]he majority opinion nowhere explains when and how Argentina agreed *with BG Group* to submit to arbitration. Instead, the majority seems to assume that, in agreeing with the United Kingdom to adopt [the arbitration provision] along with the rest of the treaty, Argentina thereby formed an agreement with all potential U.K. investors . . . to submit all investment-related disputes to arbitration." *BG Group*, 134 S. Ct. at 1216 (Roberts, C.J., dissenting).

While we are mindful of the Chief Justice's concerns, we agree with his interpretation of the Court's opinion. The BIT includes a standing offer to all potential U.S. investors to arbitrate investment disputes, which Chevron accepted in the manner required by the treaty. The FSIA therefore allows federal courts to exercise jurisdiction over Ecuador in order to consider an action to confirm or enforce the award. The dispute over whether the lawsuits were "investments" for purposes of the treaty is properly considered as part of review.

* * *

C.

Even were we to conclude that the FSIA required a *de novo* determination of arbitrability, however, we would still find that the District Court had jurisdiction. In order to prevail on its jurisdictional argument, Ecuador would have to demonstrate by a preponderance of the evidence that Chevron's suits were not "investments" within the meaning of the BIT. This Ecuador has failed to do.

For purposes of the BIT, " 'investment' means every kind of investment in the territory of one Party owned or controlled directly or indirectly by nationals or companies of the other Party . . . and includes . . . a claim to money or a claim to performance having economic value, and associated with an investment." Ecuador argues that the final phrase—"and associated with an investment"—means that a lawsuit must be associated with an investment that existed within the effective period of the BIT in order to qualify as an investment under the BIT. This is a misreading of the treaty terms for two reasons.

First, Article I.3 provides that "[a]ny alteration of the form in which assets are invested or reinvested shall not affect their character as investment."

* * *

Second, Article XII limits the application of the BIT "to investments existing at the time of entry into force as well as to investments made or acquired thereafter."

* * *

The District Court correctly determined that the BIT and Chevron's notice to arbitrate satisfied the jurisdictional requirements of the FSIA. Even if the FSIA required the *de novo* review of arbitrability suggested by Ecuador, however, the District Court would still have properly exercised jurisdiction because Ecuador failed to demonstrate by a preponderance of the evidence that Chevron's lawsuits were not protected by the BIT.

* * *

As recognized by the court below, "the [New York Convention] affords the district court little discretion in refusing or deferring enforcement of foreign arbitral awards."

* * *

Contrary to Ecuador's protestations, enforcement of the arbitral award is fully consistent with the public policy of the United States, most notably the "emphatic federal policy in favor of arbitral dispute resolution," *Mitsubishi Motors Corp. v. Soler Chrysler-Plymouth, Inc.*, 473 U.S. 614, 631 (1985). By signing the BIT, Ecuador agreed to allow independent and neutral arbitrators to determine whether an investor company could take advantage of the substantive and procedural protections in the BIT. Chevron followed the proper procedure to request arbitration under the BIT, and the arbitrator determined that it had jurisdiction. Four courts have also considered and rejected Ecuador's argument that Chevron did not have the right to avail itself of the BIT's arbitration clause. Ecuador has given us no reason to conclude that these many authorities ruled in error.

* * *

Notes and Questions

1. What are the different ways in which jurisdiction features in the series of causes and cases excerpted here? What is the strategic significance of territory to plaintiffs and defendants as they parry back and forth over the decades, and as the case morphs from a toxic tort to a contract dispute over a BIT?

2. How does forum shopping differ (if it does) from forum proliferation? Does the multiplicity of forums available to prospective investor claimants clarify or confound the issue(s) at hand? *See* INVESTOR-STATE DISPUTES ARISING FROM INVESTMENT TREATIES: A REVIEW, at 17–18, UNCTAD/ITE/IIT/2005/4 (2005).

3. In June 2016, the Supreme Court denied the petition for writ of certiorari to review the D.C. Circuit's decision, bringing a close to at least one thread of the Chevron saga.[135]

B. Chevron and transnational litigation: Two perspectives

Theodore J. Boutrous, Jr., *Ten Lessons from the Chevron Litigation: The Defense Perspective*

1 STAN. J. COMPLEX LITIG. 219 (2013)

Of the many thorny issues raised by transnational litigation against U.S. companies, the lawsuit that Chevron Corporation is fighting in Ecuador touches on them all: legal ethics, weak and corrupt foreign judiciaries, litigation fraud, judgment enforcement, third-party litigation financing, cross-border discovery, and international arbitration, to name just a few. In fact, one of the attorneys representing the Ecuadorian plaintiffs recently described the case as a "model" for future transnational litigation, a template for forcing U.S. companies to foot the bill for all manner of alleged injuries abroad.

If the Chevron litigation is to serve as a roadmap for future transnational lawsuits, however, then plaintiffs' lawyers seeking to bring claims in foreign jurisdictions, especially those with troubled judiciaries that lack independence and basic due process protections, had better understand exactly where that map will lead them—and make sure they are comfortable going there. American lawyers are bound by ethical rules that follow them beyond the courthouse door and, indeed, beyond this Nation's borders. Practitioners who view the weaknesses of certain foreign judicial systems as a business opportunity ripe for exploitation would be well-advised to avoid the path that other plaintiffs' attorneys, including those in the Chevron litigation and a prior series of cases against Dole Food Company, Inc., have blazed. And companies forced to defend against exploitative and unscrupulous litigation behavior overseas should understand the tools at their disposal to protect against the injustice of corrupt foreign judgments.

... These lessons are important not just for the legal profession and our legal system, but also for our global marketplace and society.

... One of the most disturbing patterns in transnational litigation matters is that U.S. lawyers, when they traverse the globe and bring tort claims in countries with weak or corrupt judicial systems, sometimes act as though the usual rules of truth

135. Republic of Ecuador v. Chevron Corp., 136 S. Ct. 2410 (2016).

and accuracy do not apply. Perhaps it is because they are far from home or because they think that American-style discovery and adversarial truth seeking will not apply. Whatever the reason, making false statements inside and outside the courthouse becomes a major feature of the plaintiffs' litigation strategy.

... As Chevron has laid out in the complaint, motions, exhibits, and other court documents submitted in support of the Racketeer Influenced and Corrupt Organizations Act ("RICO") case it filed in the Southern District of New York against the Ecuadorian plaintiffs' attorneys, Messrs. Donziger and Fajardo and their collaborators used false statements about the conditions in Ecuador and about Chevron to create a fictional narrative of environmental harm and disruption of indigenous communities that has superficial but powerful appeal. Their internal files, which Chevron has obtained in U.S.-based discovery proceedings, reveal that this was in fact a major part of their strategy: to smear Chevron in the press and before U.S. and foreign government bodies with a false story to try to bludgeon the company into settling the case for huge sums that have no basis in fact or law.

To be sure, not every case being litigated in a foreign country is fraudulent. This same strategy, however, was at work when Dole was defending a series of cases emanating from Nicaragua, which were litigated both in Nicaragua and the United States. In an order dismissing some of those actions on grounds of fraud, the Los Angeles Superior Court found: "These Plaintiffs, and their counsel were part of a broader conspiracy that permeates all [related] litigation arising from Nicaragua.... The purpose of this conspiracy was to manufacture evidence and improperly influence the outcome of [the] cases pending in Nicaragua and the United States to obtain millions of dollars in judgments that would then be enforced in the U.S. and possibly elsewhere." Lies have a way of unraveling no matter how many times they are repeated, and a strategy built on lies is bound to backfire sooner or later.

... Courts in the United States refuse to enforce a foreign judgment that is the product of a judicial system lacking unbiased tribunals or due process, or a system that otherwise fosters fraud. As has been well documented in both legal opinions and the press, Chevron has amassed a mountain of evidence that the $19 billion Ecuadorian judgment issued in February 2011 by Ecuadorian Judge Zambrano is the product of a fraud. As Judge Kaplan found, "there is probable cause ... to suspect that [the plaintiffs'] lawyers and other representatives later bribed Judge Zambrano to obtain the result they wanted and, pursuant to the arrangement they struck with him, actually wrote the decision to which he signed his name." Moreover, it is basically undisputed that the Cabrera report—the report of the supposedly neutral, court-appointed expert—was ghostwritten from start to finish by the plaintiffs' lawyers and their consultants....

At least 8 federal courts around the country have similarly found that the Ecuadorian proceedings were tainted by the plaintiffs' team's fraud....

Judith Kimerling, *Lessons from the Chevron Ecuador Litigation: The Proposed Intervenors' Perspective*

1 Stan. J. Complex Litig. 241, 241–48 (2013)

The consortium led by Texaco extracted nearly 1.5 billion barrels of Amazon crude over a period of twenty-eight years (1964–1992). During its tenure as operator, Texaco's wholly-owned subsidiary, Texaco Petroleum, drilled 339 wells in an area that now spans more than one million acres. It built a 498-kilometer Trans-Ecuadorian pipeline system to transport oil from the remote Amazon region across the Andes Mountains to the Pacific coast, in addition to some 1,000 kilometers of secondary pipelines and flow lines in the rainforest and more than six hundred kilometers of unpaved roads. Among other sources of pollution, Texaco regularly sprayed roads with crude oil for maintenance and dust control, and deliberately dumped tons of toxic drilling and maintenance wastes, in addition to an estimated 19.3 billion gallons of oil field brine (also known as produced water), into the environment—contaminating countless rivers and streams that served as rich fisheries and freshwater resources for local communities.

In addition to routine, willful discharges and emissions, accidental spills were common. During the time that Texaco operated the Trans-Ecuadorian pipeline, that line alone spilled more than 19 million gallons of crude oil into the environment, mostly in the Amazon basin. By comparison, the Exxon Valdez spilled an estimated 10.8 million gallons into the Prince William Sound. Spills from secondary pipelines, flow lines, production tanks, and other facilities were also frequent and continue to this day. In contrast to the oil industry's typically energetic response to spills in the United States, Texaco's response in Ecuador was limited to shutting off the flow of petroleum into the damaged portion of the pipeline, and allowing the oil already in the line to spill into the environment before making the necessary repairs. No cleanup activities were undertaken, and damages were not compensated.

In 2002, after nine years of litigation, the *Aguinda v. Texaco* lawsuit was dismissed on the ground of forum non conveniens, in favor of litigation in Ecuador. Forum non conveniens is a doctrine that allows a court to dismiss a case that could be litigated in a different court. In May 2003, Ecuadorian lawyers contracted by the *Aguinda v. Texaco* plaintiffs' lawyers filed a new lawsuit against ChevronTexaco (now Chevron) in Lago Agrio, Ecuador, the boom town that sprang up around Texaco's first commercial field. After another nine years of litigation, the Ecuadorian court found Chevron liable for more than $19 billion in total damages, the largest amount ever awarded in an environmental lawsuit.

Chevron, however, is contesting the validity of the judgment in two other fora: an arbitration proceeding against Ecuador at The Hague ("the BIT Arbitration"), and a lawsuit against the Lago Agrio plaintiffs and their lead lawyers and associates in federal court in New York (*Chevron v. Donziger*). Both cases are based on allegations of fraud and other misconduct by the Lago Agrio plaintiffs' legal team, allegations of improper collusion between representatives of the plaintiffs and Ecuadorian government officials, and allegations of systemic failures in the administration of justice in Ecuador.

* * *

I. Application of the Forum Non Conveniens Doctrine by the *Aguinda v. Texaco* Court

* * *

[T]his Article will cut to the chase: The application of the forum non conveniens doctrine to dismiss *Aguinda v. Texaco* was colored by a series of detailed, but questionable, factual assumptions.

When a federal court applies the forum non conveniens doctrine, it first determines whether there is an alternative forum, and then balances private and public interest factors to determine whether they overcome the ordinarily strong presumption in favor of the plaintiffs' chosen forum. In *Aguinda*, the district court ruled that Texaco had demonstrated that (1) Ecuador's courts provide an alternative forum and (2) the balance of private and public interest factors "tips overwhelmingly in favor of dismissal." Despite the fact that Texaco's headquarters was just a few miles from the courthouse where the lawsuit had been filed, the judge, Jed Rakoff, concluded that the case has "everything to do with Ecuador and nothing to do with the United States."

Some of the facts used by the Court to support its legal analysis were uncontested. For example, there were no allegations of injury in the United States; Texaco's wholly-owned subsidiary, Texaco Petroleum, built and operated the facilities; and after operations began, Ecuador acquired majority ownership of the assets and continued to operate them after Texaco Petroleum's contract expired. Other facts, however, were in dispute. One area that was especially germane relates to control of the operations. While not determinative, by itself, of the legal questions, the factual issue of where decisions were made about the technology and practices that caused the pollution, and who made them, was a material element of the analysis of both private and public interest factors, and clearly colored the decision to dismiss.

The proposition—advocated by Texaco and accepted by the Court without live testimony—that Ecuadorians controlled the relevant decisions, that no one from Texaco or anyone else operating out of the United States made any material decisions or was involved in designing, directing, guiding or assisting the activities that caused the pollution, and that environmental practices were heavily regulated by Ecuador, was a recurring theme. The Court also distinguished Texaco from Texaco Petroleum, the subsidiary that operated in Ecuador. That distinction, and the portrait of Texaco Petroleum as essentially an Ecuadorian company whose operations were far removed from the parent, is dramatically different from the image of "Texaco" in Ecuador and the impression there that the government had contracted with the U.S. company, Texaco. It is also at odds with the portrait cultivated by Texaco before it was sued, of a multinational industry leader that transferred world class technology to Ecuador. Altogether, the *Aguinda* Court's depiction of Texaco's role in the operations is clearly incongruous with reality of oil development in Ecuador, including the environmental law vacuum and culture of impunity in the oil frontier, the experience of Amazonian peoples and other Ecuadorians with the company, and the portrait that Texaco cultivated during its tenure in Ecuador.

Ecuador relied on Texaco, as the operator of the first commercial oil fields in the Amazon region, to transfer hydrocarbon extraction technology. Ecuadorian officials saw Texaco as a prestigious international company with vast experience and access to "world class" technology and capital. They relied on Texaco to design, procure, install, and operate the infrastructure that turned Ecuador into an oil exporter. In its contract with the State, Texaco agreed to use "modern and efficient" equipment, hire a minimum percentage of Ecuadorian workers, train Ecuadorian students, and turn over the field operations and equipment to Petroecuador "in good condition" when the contract ended in 1992.

* * *

III. The Lago Agrio Lawsuit and Related Litigation

The complaint in the Lago Agrio lawsuit asserts claims on behalf of the Huaorani and other so-called "Afectados," local residents who have been harmed by Chevron's operations. The Afectados include four indigenous peoples (the Huaorani, Cofan, Secoya and Siona), members of the Kichwa people, and colonists (settlers, known locally as "colonos"). However, the Huaorani were not consulted about the litigation or included among the plaintiffs, and no relief was requested directly for the affected communities and community members (or even for the plaintiffs). Instead, the complaint seeks a judicial determination of the costs of a comprehensive environmental remediation and an order directing Chevron to pay the full amount to a local nongovernmental organization (NGO), Amazon Defense Front (Frente de Defensa de la Amazonia), which would then "apply" the funds to the ends determined in the judgment. The complaint also claims a ten percent share of the remedial monies for the plaintiffs, but requests that those funds also be paid to Amazon Defense Front.

Amazon Defense Front was founded in 1994 by a group of colonists in Lago Agrio who heard about the *Aguinda v. Texaco* lawsuit on the radio and decided to establish a local institution to administer monies that they expected to be forthcoming from the case. The group has developed close ties with the plaintiffs' lawyers and some external NGOs, but is controlled by colonists and is not regarded by the affected Indigenous peoples as their legitimate representative. Moreover, its efforts to claim a monopoly of representation of all people affected by Texaco and manage local politics in an undemocratic fashion have alienated many people in the affected communities. In addition to issues related to representation, another recurring concern involves possible remedies. Efforts by local residents, at different junctures over the years, to demand "clarity and transparency in the process," obtain information from Amazon Defense Front and its lawyers, and engage them in a dialogue about remedial plans—in the event of a victory in court or out-of-court settlement—have been rebuffed. The decision to designate Amazon Defense Front, which is not a plaintiff, as the trustee in charge of administering any judgment was evidently made by the plaintiffs' lawyers and Amazon Defense Front without consulting or informing the affected communities.

In February 2011, the court in Lago Agrio ruled that Chevron is responsible for widespread pollution that has harmed, and continues to threaten, the environment, public health, and Indigenous cultures. In a 188-page opinion, the court ordered Chevron to pay $8,646,160,000 for remedial measures, and another $8,646,160,000 in punitive damages if the company did not apologize to the affected communities within fifteen days. The court also awarded an additional ten percent of the "amount sentenced" to Amazon Defense Front. Chevron has not apologized (and has publicly vowed not to apologize), so the award to Amazon Defense Front is now worth $1.729232 billion and the total value of the judgment is more than $19 billion. The Lago Agrio judgment further directs the parties to set up a trust fund to administer the remedial monies, and provides that the sole beneficiary of the trust, and its board of directors, shall be Amazon Defense Front or the person or persons it designates.

The purpose of the remedial measures is "to return things to their natural state" and restore natural resources and environmental conditions to the way they were before Chevron caused the damage that gave rise to the litigation. The court recognized, however, that it will be impossible to achieve that objective in many cases and, for that reason, included three types of remedies in the judgment: "principal" measures to remediate contaminated soils and ground waters; "complementary" measures to compensate for the inability to fully restore natural resources; and "mitigation" measures to address the impacts on human health and Indigenous cultures that cannot be reversed or fully repaired. The objective of the punitive damages is to compensate the affected communities for their pain and suffering, and punish Chevron for unreasonable and malicious conduct in the litigation which prolonged the suffering of the victims.

The Lago Agrio judgment has been affirmed in all material respects by the appellate division of the Lago Agrio court (the "Sole Division," or plenary of that court), and is now enforceable under Ecuadorian law. The appellate division also ordered Chevron to pay an additional 0.1 percent of the value of the judgment as legal fees and directed the parties to establish a second trust fund to administer the punitive damages monies, to be managed by the same board of directors as the trust with the environmental remediation, compensation, and mitigation monies.

Chevron appealed the judgment to Ecuador's National Court of Justice, and that appeal is pending. However, Chevron evidently does not expect to prevail in Ecuador's courts—at least while the current President, Rafael Correa, is in power—and the company has limited assets in Ecuador. Consequently, Chevron has been preparing to defend itself against possible enforcement actions in the United States and around the world by challenging the legitimacy of the judgment in the BIT

Arbitration, discussed above, and the *Chevron v. Donziger* lawsuit. Both cases are based on allegations of fraud and other misconduct by the Lago Agrio plaintiffs' legal team, improper collusion with Ecuador's government, and systemic failures in the administration of justice. In an effort to reconcile its current allegations with Texaco's spirited defense of Ecuador's legal and judicial system in the *Aguinda v. Texaco* litigation, Chevron contends that the rule of law has deteriorated in Ecuador since the U.S. lawsuit was dismissed, and that in view of current judicial reforms and the public support expressed by President Correa for the Lago Agrio plaintiffs, the "judiciary now lacks the necessary independence and institutional stability to adequately adjudicate highly politicized cases."

* * *

The bottom line [to the Chevron Litigation], however, is that after nearly two decades of litigation, there is a judgment in favor of the plaintiffs but the viability of that judgment is in question. Litigation is now under way in six countries on three continents, with no end in sight. There is considerable uncertainty about how decisions by those different legal regimes will intersect, and there is no single, controlling supranational authority to adjudicate those potential disputes. Moreover, even if the Lago Agrio judgment is upheld on appeal, and the plaintiffs' lawyers succeed in collecting it (or portions of it)—or if the parties decide to settle the case instead of litigating in courtrooms around the world—the impact of *Aguinda* on the Huaorani and other Afectados will still be uncertain.

For now, sadly, this new chapter in the litigation appears to be shifting the focus of the legal and political contest from allegations about Texaco's misconduct to allegations of misconduct by the lawyers and activists who manage the Lago Agrio case, and from concern about the rights of the affected communities to the rights of Chevron. The alleged misconduct has prolonged the litigation, and Chevron is using it to try to also taint the credibility of the victims' claims and jeopardize their rights to remedies. Those developments have eclipsed the situation on the ground—where environmental conditions continue to deteriorate, people's rights are still being violated, and no one is accepting responsibility.

Notes and Questions

1. The Chevron Ecuador litigation is a quintessential example of the challenges that plaintiffs, defendants, and domestic courts must navigate when attempting to resolve a complex issue with transnational dimensions. The Lago Agrio chapter of the saga, which concluded in a judgment against Chevron, has been described as "by all measures the largest and most complex award rendered against a multinational oil company in Ecuador, and perhaps in the entire region."[136] Consider the following summary of the Chevron litigation:

136. Manuel A. Gómez, *The Global Chase: Seeking the Recognition and Enforcement of the Lago Agrio Judgment Outside of Ecuador*, 1 Stan. J. Complex Litig. 429, 433 (2014).

> [W]e have on the playing field: (i) a judgment from an international arbitral tribunal against Ecuador awarding Chevron $100 million; (ii) an award in Ecuadorian courts against Chevron awarding the Lago Agrio plaintiffs over $18 billion; (iii) two pending matters—one before an international arbitral tribunal and another before the U.S. courts—in which Chevron has alleged that the Lago Agrio litigation was conducted in violation of both domestic and international law; and (iv) a petition filed by the Lago Agrio plaintiffs against Ecuador before a human rights commission, which was subsequently withdrawn. Evidence has shown that with regard to the two pending proceedings, both U.S. domestic courts and the international arbitral tribunals are willing to recognize the acts of the other. Only time will tell whether . . . we will be forced to deal with conflicting decisions and next determine how they can be resolved, if ever.[137]

Chevron's litigation costs have been estimated at more than $2 billion overall since the original litigation regarding the incident began over a quarter of a century ago. It remains on-going, amounting to what has been called a "litigation catastrophe."[138]

2. Some commentators argue that the Chevron Ecuador litigation shows that transnational litigation has become excessively diffuse. Consider the following analysis:

> [T]ransnational litigation is increasingly multipolar. . . . First, U.S. courts are no longer as attractive to litigants as they supposedly once were. Meanwhile, other countries are increasingly drawing litigants to their courts through a combination of ex ante forum selection agreements, and ex post forum shopping. Lord Denning famously quipped that "[a]s a moth is drawn to the light, so is a litigant drawn to the United States." However, both empirical trends and anecdotal evidence from practitioners of transnational litigation suggest that the light may not be burning as brightly as it once did . . . [T]he Supreme Court has reinvigorated the forum non conveniens doctrine as an anti-forum-shopping device, restricted personal jurisdiction in transnational suits, limited the extraterritorial application of U.S. statutes, and imposed stricter pleading standards, making it more difficult for plaintiffs to gain access to one of the major attractions of the U.S. legal system: liberal discovery.[139]

Applying this analysis to Chevron, would you characterize the Chevron litigation as "multipolar"?

---

137. Charles N. Brower & Diane Brown, *From Pinochet in the House of Lords to the Chevron/Ecuador Lago Agrio Dispute: The Hottest Topics in International Dispute Resolution*, 26 Pac. McGeorge Global Bus. & Dev. L.J. 1, 2 (2013).

138. Amazon Defense Coalition, *In 2016, Chevron Faces Potential "Litigation Catastrophe" Over Ecuador Pollution Liability*, CSRwire (Jan. 4, 2016), http://www.csrwire.com/press_releases/38590-In-2016-Chevron-Faces-Potential-Litigation-Catastrophe-Over-Ecuador-Pollution-Liability.

139. Christopher A. Whytock, *Some Cautionary Notes on the "Chevronization" of Transnational Litigation*, 1 Stan. J. Complex Litig. 467, 469 (2013).

3. Michael Goldhaber offers a comparative analysis of the arbitral and judicial aspects of the suite of *Chevron* cases, arguing for arbitration rules that more closely mirror those of judicial proceedings. In relation to *Chevron v. Ecuador*, he writes:

> It has often been remarked that confidentiality is more appropriate in a purely commercial arbitration than in the semi-public or public context of a standard investor-state arbitration, which implicates the interests of taxpayers, and often calls upon arbirtators to balance competing visions of the public interest. Transparency is *a fortiori* demanded if the public is asked to entrust the aritrators with the suspension or review of public court proceedings.
>
> The case for transparency, as well as broad participation rights, is at its maximum when—as in *Chevron v. Ecuador*—an investor-state tribunal is asked to suspend and then review a national court trial where the plaintiffs were a third party not before the tribunal, and where groups representing civil society may justly claim to have interests implicated in both proceedings.[140]

On what basis would you agree or disagree with Goldhaber's assessment of the importance of transparency in relation to the public interest in an investor case? What is it about transparency that constitutes its value in such contexts?

VII. Discussion

In this chapter, we have considered cases in which the interlegal aspect highlights crucial aspects of transnational law, as the concept of "the global" finds expression in particular institutional forms. As the pragmatics of those institutions yield new forms of legality and power, characteristic tensions surface around issues of sovereignty and contract, and between the rights of citizens and investors. These are not automatically or inevitably in tension; however, the normal operations of BITs have produced these effects. We make this observation as an empirical point, indicative of the potential range of mobilization and advocacy as the demand for law, and the availability of law, continue to evolve with the infrastructures of global capitalism. We began with global standards, emphasizing ISO 26000, to show how the shift from technical to social issues accentuates questions of stakeholder participation (as trade unions were excluded from the consultations over ISO 26000). We next turned to the FAO's voluntary guidelines on land tenure, again yielding questions of stakeholder participation—this time in relation to small farmers. The creation of terms for a global land market drives politics "down" to national, subnational, and community groups—and "out" to transnational peasant and food sovereignty movements. In cases such as those sections discussed, states have traditional roles as parties to a treaty-like international agreement; however, they also have the role

140. Michael D. Goldhaber, *The Rise of Arbitral Power Over Domestic Courts*, 1 Stan. J. Complex Litig. 373, 407 (2013).

of agent, as they accept by reference the ISO standards, and enter into bilateral investor treaties that invite direct foreign investment involving land use.

The contract framework led us to two further examples. In the section on the Indiana contract with IBM, we found critical dilemmas arising from the exclusion of welfare recipients from the contract both in its creation and in its definition of beneficiaries. In the section on arbitration, we saw that ICSID and UNCITRAL attain highly flexible powers that may supersede domestic judicial powers. The discussion of the Chevron case reprises each of these elements, as the litigation broadened across several types of forum in several countries over a span of many years—leaving the communities most affected by the firm's wastewater operations without redress.

Our emphasis on the challenges of interlegalities is intended to highlight the ways global capitalism creates new forms of power through law—new forms of power that are not limited to the "global" level, as if that were some continuous legal space. As we see repeatedly in this chapter, efforts to enhance the global by filling in its gaps (for example, with standards of various kinds) may produce new gaps, or rather, make visible the intensified pressures on domestic politicians and courts to reinsert excluded stakeholders and/or resist certain forms of marketization. Such counter-movements are often referred to as "anti-globalization" (see Chapter 4, *supra*), but this greatly understates their complexity—including the extent to which counter-movements may themselves involve transnational mobilizations whose purposes are not withdrawal, but rather fuller participation or different aspirations for the world. As capitalism continues to evolve alongside the new political forms borne of cross-cutting demands for law, interlegalities of the sort described in this chapter will offer scholars and advocates new intellectual problems across disciplines and new spaces for advocacy.

For now, we reiterate once more the major themes of this chapter. First, the concept of interlegalities is more comprehensive than legal pluralism, in pointing not just to the empirical fact of diversely interrelated legal arenas, but also to their disjunctures and pragmatic and conceptual tensions. Second, taking up those tensions, we have emphasized that global initiatives such as "soft law" governance potentially drive domestic political debate, particularly where they involve stakeholders without including them as participants, even when they are directly and materially affected. Third, given the extent to which this is the case, we should not imagine that the relevance of such political contestation is merely reactive or oppositional to globalization, but rather constitutes a fundamental challenge to the idea of "globalization" as a top-down and inevitably worldwide arrangement.

As we carry this line of discussion forward in the rest of Part III, we turn back to the pressures on domestic government occasioned by interlegalities as these emerge as tensions between investor interests and domestic concerns with human rights and democratic participation. In this, the United States is no exception. The next chapters deal with pressures on U.S. courts and the executive branch. As we have seen, transnational law concerned with trade and especially investors' rights can be made in effect borderless; however, law concerned with transnational harms in the form of torts and human rights violations is highly (though not exclusively) territorial. Powers created in one area of the law become available for other domains—e.g., the foreign affairs powers of the executive travel across trade and security, and back again. In the following chapters, these interlegal dilemmas take the form of separation of powers issues and other questions arising from the contemporary transnational legal space.

Chapter 8

Transnational Law, Courts and Judicial Review

I. The proliferation of international courts

As we saw in Chapter 7, investor arbitration is a flexible procedure, making it readily adaptable to diverse circumstances. Most of the history of investor arbitration involves unequal parties, i.e., parties with asymmetrical incentives to maintain the relationship and unequal, too, in their access to alternatives should the agreement fail. To put this differently, investor arbitration has a long history in general, but a relatively short one as a process involving equals. Legal scholars Cory Adkins and David Singh Grewal summarize the context:

> A cousin of "diplomatic protection," [investor arbitration] was first used to protect colonial investments in the eighteenth and nineteenth centuries. After the decolonization of the twentieth century, investment arbitration became a tool of economic development for the newly christened "developing world" . . . [in] areas subject to ongoing economic and political uncertainty. Bilateral investment treaties . . . sought to establish minimally fair and equitable treatment for investments in countries where self-dealing autocrats might seize all of a foreign investor's property or ruling nationalist parties might view investment from abroad with hostility in the context of recently concluded anticolonial struggles.[1]

As they observe, the expansion of bilateral treaties and the development of standardized arbitration regimes through ICSID and UNCITRAL (discussed in Chapter 7, *supra*) in recent decades has greatly expanded the field of investor-state arbitration,[2] resulting in a revision of that asymmetrical profile. Today, investor arbitrations increasingly involve complaints against "developed democracies." In this new context, Adkins and Grewal note "collisions between arbitral regimes and the modern regulatory state" develop as arbitration moves beyond expropriations "to [include] regulatory actions that negatively impact the profits of foreign investors."[3] They find that "investment arbitration [is now] at an impasse" as it

1. Cory Adkins & David Singh Grewal, *Democracy and Legitimacy in Investor-State Arbitration*, 126 Yale L. J. Forum 65, 66 (June 1, 2016) (footnotes omitted), http://www.yalelawjournal.org/forum/democracy-and-legitimacy-in-investor-state-arbitration.

2. *Id.* at 66, n.7 (reporting 457 bilateral treaties in 1990, growing to 2,926 in 2016).

3. *Id.* at 65.

acquires "an expanded role in which it becomes a forum for the recognition of foreign interests in the review of domestic laws."[4]

Courts find themselves in the middle of the current historical chapter anticipated by Adkins and Grewal. Reflecting on the transnational role of U.S. courts in a related context, Austen Parrish finds a conceptual break in the U.S. Supreme Court's recent shift away from its former acceptance of domestic litigation as a means of addressing "the international system's enforcement gap."[5] Now, he writes, the Court "has stalled efforts to broaden U.S. extraterritorial judicial power"[6]—in particular "scal[ing] back on the ability of plaintiffs to litigate foreign claims against foreign defendants in the United States."[7] In Chapter 6, we saw the Court's retreat from a long tradition that in certain circumstances had made the Alien Tort Statute available extraterritorially—a development that would seem to confirm a widespread view (as noted by Parrish) that the Court has become anti-internationalist.[8] In Chapter 7, we saw courts not so much retreating from transnationalism as implicitly marking an *interlegal* space between global capitalism and domestic law as their own to define, to the extent that circumstances leave that question open.

In this chapter, we argue that domestic courts—in their very resistance to extraterritorial applications of domestic law under some circumstances—are integral to the production of globalization, particularly in perpetuating, as if a natural duality, the borderless world of capital investment and the bordered world of nations. Or, to put this differently, it shows domestic courts to be key to the contemporary *political* significance of territoriality.

Courts at all levels now play a significant role in shaping law and global norms. The focus of this chapter will be primarily on transnational law as made and applied by U.S. domestic courts; but we begin with international courts, since their recent proliferation (along with arbitration tribunals and other fora) is part of a larger context of legal transformation in the international sphere.[9] International law scholar Martti Koskenniemi regards specialization as the driver behind the development of those new

4. *Id.* at 68–69 (discussing investment arbitration in the context of their analysis of *Clayton v. Canada*).

5. Austen Parrish, *Fading Extraterritoriality and Isolationism? Developments in the United States*, 24 IND. J. GLOBAL LEGAL STUD. (forthcoming Feb. 2017).

6. *Id.* at 116.

7. *Id.* at 102.

8. The use of foreign law by Supreme Court Justices as an aid to domestic constitutional interpretation has stirred vigorous debates among the Justices and among legal scholars. The late Justice Scalia and Justice Thomas were the Court's most outspoken critics of the use of foreign law in domestic opinions. For an analysis of U.S. legal exceptionalism, see Francisco J. Rivera Juaristi, *U.S. Exceptionalism and the Strengthening Process of the Inter-American Rights System*, 20 HUM. RTS. BRIEF 19, 19 (2013).

9. On the proliferation of international courts and quasi-judicial tribunals, see Candice Whyte, Book Note, 12 U. MIAMI INT'L & COMP. L. REV. 231 (2004) (reviewing YUVAL SHANY, THE COMPETING JURISDICTIONS OF INTERNATIONAL COURTS AND TRIBUNALS (Phillipe Sands et al. eds., 2003)).

courts and quasi-judicial bodies—noting, in particular, the consequent importance of specialized expertise as the new courts "reversed established legal hierarchies":

> [T]he new developments in the [public international] law did not point to unity. The more powerfully they dealt with international problems—problems of economics, development, human rights, environment, criminality, security—the more they began to challenge old principles and institutions. Specializations such as 'trade law', 'human rights law', 'environmental law', 'criminal law', 'security law', 'European law' and so on started to reverse established legal hierarchies in favour of the structural bias in the relevant functional expertise. Even though this process was often organized through intergovernmental organisations, the governmental delegations were often composed of technical (economic, environmental, legal) experts in a way that transposed the functional differentiation at the national level onto the international plane. Moreover, the resulting regimes have often been formulated in an open-ended manner, leaving power to decide—above all, to decide on how scarce resources should be distributed—to the legal and technical experts appointed to the supervisory organs. It is this change to which international lawyers have reacted by speculating on the 'dangers' of incoherence, forum shopping and, perhaps characteristically, 'loss of overall control'.[10]

Lawyers' unease, he argues, is expressed in their preoccupation with jurisdictional control—amounting (in Koskenniemi's view) to a new politics of law, as interests become increasingly tightly wound through the very structure of the court system:

> Recent debates of global governance and especially international law's fragmentation have well demonstrated the emergence and operation of structural bias. Through specialization—that is to say, through the creation of special regimes of knowledge and expertise in areas such as 'trade law', 'human rights law', 'environmental law', 'security law', 'international criminal law', 'European law ', and so on—the world of legal practice is being sliced up in institutional projects that cater for special audiences with special interests and special ethos. The point of creating such specialized institutions is precisely to affect the outcomes that are being produced in the international world. Very little is fully random out there, as practising lawyers know very well, directing their affairs to those institutions where they can expect to receive the most sympathetic hearing. This is why much about the search for political direction today takes the form of jurisdictional conflict, struggle between competing expert vocabularies, each equipped with a specific bias. If such regimes are bold in ambition, and able to rely on the support of some powerful sector of the political world, then they may succeed in changing the general bias in the law. For example, the rise of the bilateral

---

10. Martti Koskenniemi, The Politics of International Law 334 (2011).

investment treaty has certainly transformed the relationship between the private investor and host state from what it was 20 years ago.[11]

In this new context, Professor Koskiennemi points to the political question inherent in jurisdiction: "The point of the emergence of something like 'international criminal law' or 'international human rights law' (or any other special law) is precisely to institutionalise the new priorities carried within such fields. As a result, political conflict will often take the form of conflict of jurisdictions. Who shall decide?"[12]

In contrast, international law scholar Anne-Marie Slaughter sees the emergence of "a global community of law":

Anne-Marie Slaughter, *Judicial Globalization*

40 Va. J. Int'l L. 1103–04 (2000)[13]

"Globalization" summons images more of corporations than courts. The compression of distance and the dissolution of borders that drives globalization has proved far more efficient at producing global markets than global justice. Computers may transcend culture and a new generation of migrants may weave together a global society, but law—particularly the law handed down by judges—still seems inherently national. Yet, notwithstanding this perception, judges are globalizing as well, in ways that have important implications for foreign, comparative, and international law.

The existing literature on the role of national courts in an emerging global legal system typically focuses on the ways in which these relationships enhance the salience and impact of international law. National courts are the vehicles through which international treaties and customary law that have not been independently incorporated into domestic statutes enter domestic legal systems. As such, they have long been a source of hope for international lawyers: a 1993 resolution by the French Institute of International Law calls upon national courts to become independent actors in the international arena, and to apply international norms impartially, without deferring to their governments.

Judicial globalization, by contrast, describes a much more diverse and messy process of judicial interaction across, above and below borders, exchanging ideas and cooperating in cases involving national as much as international law. This essay sets forth five different categories of judicial interaction: relations between national courts and the European Court of Justice (ECJ) in the European Union (EU); interactions between the European Court of Human Rights and national courts; the emergence of "judicial comity" in transnational litigation; constitutional cross-fertilization; and face-to-face meetings among judges around the world. The contexts are very different, involving both "vertical" relations between national and international tribunals and "horizontal" relations across national borders. The factors driving these forms of

11. Martti Koskenniemi, *The Politics of International Law—20 Years Later*, 20 Eur. J. Int'l L. 7, 9 (2009).

12. Koskenniemi, *supra* note 10, at 335.

13. Available at https://www.princeton.edu/~slaughtr/Articles/VJIL.pdf.

interaction also vary widely, including a structural provision in an international treaty, the globalization of commerce, and the need for judicial training in many fledgling democracies. The activities of the many different types of courts involved in this process do not conform to a template of an emerging global legal system in which national and international tribunals play defined and coordinated roles. But all are examples of judges looking, talking, and sometimes acting beyond the confines of national legal systems, responding to the myriad forces of globalization. All are also contingent on a deep sense of participation in a common global enterprise of judging, an awareness that provides a foundation for a global community of law.[14]

The cases and problems considered in this volume so far capture something of the positions in both of these excerpts, as they point to different conceptions of transnational law in relation to globalization—as an aggregation of nations that is potentially unifiable (for Professor Slaughter) or as a fluid political repertoire that offers strategic advantage in the proliferation of specialized legalities (for Professor Koskenniemi). We begin with two cases that—along substantially different pathways—show U.S. courts actively involved in drawing the line between national and international courts.

II. Resisting international law: Two case studies

To explore these issues, we begin with two case studies in which we find the U.S. Supreme Court explicitly resisting the relevance of international law. The first case dates from the 1980s, as Haitian immigrants brought suit to halt U.S. interdiction of migrants at sea; in that case, the U.S. refused to comply with the decision of the Inter-American Commission. In the second case, dating from 2008, the Court acknowledged the obligations of international law but rejected the enforceability of those obligations with respect to a Mexican national convicted of murder and sentenced to death in Texas.

A. Haitian immigrants and the Inter-American Commission[15]

In 1971, Jean-Claude Duvalier assumed power in Haiti—an oppressive regime that resulted in the arrests and imprisonment of hundreds of journalists, political

14. *Id.* at 1104.

15. The Inter-American Court (and Commission) on Human Rights is the closest tribunal to the United States geographically. The Court, which is given legal authority through a treaty, is tasked with safeguarding "the essential rights of man in the American continent." It has "competence to observe human rights violations," but only when the states involved have ratified the treaty. The United States has not. There are other tribunals of note. The International Criminal Court tries individuals that are accused of the most serious of international crimes, including genocide and war crimes. The ICC's jurisdiction is limited to the 122 states which have joined the treaty providing the Court's legal authority. Needless to say, many human rights violations are beyond the ICC's reach in

leaders, and human rights activists.[16] Haitians began fleeing the country, many of them heading for the United States by sea.[17] The United States government responded to this sudden influx with a strict enforcement program that resulted in Coast Guard vessels interdicting large numbers of Haitian refugees. President Ronald Reagan issued an executive order directing the U.S. State Department to work with foreign governments for the purpose of preventing migration to the United States. The order also directed the Coast Guard to "enforce the suspension of the entry of undocumented aliens" and interdict "any defined vessel carrying such aliens."[18] The Coast Guard was instructed:

> To return the vessel and its passengers to the country from which it came, when there is reason to believe that an offense is being committed against the United States immigration laws, or appropriate laws of a foreign country with which we have an arrangement to assist; provided, however, that no person who is a refugee will be returned without his consent.[19]

Once a vessel was boarded, the Coast Guard conducted interviews with the passengers. If the interviewer found an indication that the passenger might qualify for refugee status, an additional interview was held. If the second interview revealed that the passenger had a bona fide claim to refugee status, then the Coast Guard would be required to transport the person to the United States to present the claim.[20] Individuals who established that bona fide claim would then enter United States territorial waters and U.S. territory.

From 1981 to 1987, the Coast Guard interdicted over seventy-eight vessels carrying over 1800 Haitian refugees.[21] Of those 1800 refugees, the government found none to have a bona fide claim to refugee status. All were returned to Haiti. The Reagan administration defended the results of its policy, characterizing the Haitian boat evacuees as economic refugees (i.e., not political refugees).[22]

The repatriated Haitian citizens were specifically subjected to arrest, torture, and execution upon their return to Haiti.

---

both legal and realpolitik terms. The European Court of Human Rights was created by a treaty in 1959. The tribunal has issued well over 10,000 decisions with the intent to secure fundamental human rights for not only European citizens, but all individuals living within the Court's jurisdiction. Additionally, temporary tribunals are occasionally established to deal with specific issues.

16. Alex Stepick, *Haitian Boat People: A Study in Conflicting Forces Shaping U.S. Immigration Policy*, 45 U.S. Immigration Pol'y 163, 165 (1982), http://scholarship.law.duke.edu/cgi/viewcontent.cgi?article=3657&context=lcp.

17. *Id.* at 163.

18. Exec. Order No. 12324, 46 Fed. Reg. 48109 (Sept. 29, 1981).

19. *Id.*

20. Haitian Refugee Ctr. v. Gracey, 809 F.2d 794, 797 (D.C. Cir. 1987).

21. *Id.*

22. Peter A. Schey & Todd Howland, *Perspective on Haitian Refugees: No Haven for the Poor and Black: Terror is Driving Thousands to Risk Their Lives at Sea; Our Government's Response is Unlawful and Inhumane*, L.A. Times, Dec. 1, 1991, http://articles.latimes.com/1991-12-01/opinion/op-1083_1_haitian-refugees.

In 1985, several plaintiffs, including the U.S.-based Haitian Refugee Center (the "Center"), brought suit in U.S. federal district court in Washington, D.C.[23] The complaint alleged several causes of action. First, the Center alleged that the interdiction program violated two federal laws, the Refugee Act of 1980 and the Immigration and Nationality Act. The second count alleged that the interdictions violated the Fifth Amendment's due process guarantees. The third count alleged violations of "the 'nonrefoulement obligation' imposed by the United Nations Protocol and Universal Declaration of Human Rights by creating a substantial risk that political refugees will be forcibly returned to face persecution."[24] Plaintiffs also alleged that the policy violated prohibitions on racial and other discrimination under the United Nations Convention. Finally, the fourth count alleged violations of the federal extradition statute and extradition treaty between the United States and Haiti.

The district court dismissed the case. Although the court found that the plaintiffs had standing to sue, Judge Richey held that they had failed to state a claim. First, the court held that the statutes relied upon in the first count applied only to refugees that actually reached the United States. Because the interdictions here occurred on the open seas, the statutes were inapplicable. The court also rejected the Fifth Amendment claims, explaining that "[a]liens have no constitutional rights to enter the United States."[25] Rather, aliens seeking admission to the United States are requesting a privilege and must accept whatever statutory rights and privileges Congress provides. The court further rejected the third cause of action, holding that the United Nations protocol was not self-executing and therefore did not create a private cause of action on its own.[26] The court also rejected appeals to the Universal Declaration of Human Rights, characterizing it as "merely a nonbinding resolution, not a treaty."[27] Finally, the court dismissed the fourth count, holding that the extradition statute and treaty applied only to Haitians in the United States, not those on the high seas.

On appeal, the D.C. Circuit affirmed the dismissal for lack of standing, bringing to an end the plaintiffs' attempt to gain redress through the United States judiciary.

With U.S. remedies unproductive, the plaintiffs turned to the Inter-American Commission on Human Rights. In their petition to the Commission, the plaintiffs asked for the interdiction program to be suspended and for a declaration that the program had violated international human rights obligations.[28]

---

23. Haitian Refugee Ctr., Inc. v. Gracey, 600 F. Supp. 1396 (D.D.C. 1985), *aff'd sub nom.* Haitian Refugee Ctr. v. Gracey, 809 F.2d 794 (D.C. Cir. 1987).

24. *Id.* at 1401.

25. *Id.* at 1405.

26. For more on treaty adoption mechanisms and their legal statuses, see *supra* Chapter 1.

27. Haitian Refugee Ctr., Inc. v. Gracey, 600 F. Supp. 1396, 1406 (D.D.C. 1985), *aff'd sub nom.* Haitian Refugee Ctr. v. Gracey, 809 F.2d 794 (D.C. Cir. 1987).

28. The Haitian Centre for Human Rights et al. v. United States. Inter-American Commission on Human Rights, Case 10.675, Inter-Am. Comm'n H.R., Report No. 51/96, OEA/Ser.L/V/II.95, doc. 7 rev. ¶ 11 (1997).

The United States, a member of the Organization of American States, defended the program before the Commission:

> The United States submits that this program is consistent with the human rights standards of the American Declaration of the Rights and Duties of Man and is a proper exercise of the United States' sovereign right to prevent illegal immigration to the United States. Since no other country in the region has been willing to accept significant numbers of Haitians departing by sea, the only relevant options are return or admission to the United States. There is no legal duty, however, on the United States or any other nation to accept fleeing Haitians, including those with legitimate refugee claims. In light of the firm belief that bringing all interdicted Haitians to the United States would likely precipitate a massive and dangerous outflow, the United States has chosen to return Haitians to Haiti. Nonetheless, the United States has undertaken extensive efforts to afford Haitian nationals the opportunity to pursue refugee claims in a safe alternative to boat departures, through the incountry refugee processing program.[29]
>
> Far from constituting a violation of the rights of Haitian nationals, the United States' actions on behalf of Haitians through the interdiction program and incountry refugee processing have saved many Haitian lives, have established secure and regular migration channels for qualified Haitians to come to the United States without risking their lives at sea, have enforced United States immigration law, and have avoided the potential humanitarian tragedy of a massive seaborne surge from Haiti. Presuming that the Commission does not enter into this question with prejudgments, the United States believes that it has presented a compelling case that the United States has upheld the humanitarian efforts to restore democracy to Haiti and to ensure respect for the human rights of all Haitian citizens.[30]

The Petitioners replied:

> Petitioners have never objected to any efforts which the United States Government may undertake to save and rescue people at sea. This petition has nothing to do with saving and rescuing people at sea. It instead challenges the United States Government's policy of forcibly returning people to a country where serious human rights violations are widespread without providing fair, full and nondiscriminatory asylum interviews in compliance with international law.
>
> A government cannot avoid Commission review of an illegal policy by simply changing the policy every few months. While it stopped providing any interviews to interdicted Haitians in April 1992, a change in policy is also challenged by petitioners in several submissions and hearings before the

29. *Id.* at ¶ 51.
30. *Id.* at ¶ 80.

> Commission, as repeatedly stated by President Clinton and other high United States Government officials, its policy is constantly under review and changing. The question remains whether the United States Government's policies challenged in this petition have been lawful. In fact, its policy for the moment is to again provide brief interviews on vessels on the high seas, forcibly return the vast majority of Haitians, refuse to admit any interdicted Haitians into the United States, refuse to provide legal counsel to assist Haitians before their interviews, and refuse to provide judicial review of any aspect of the process or decisions reached.
>
> The United States Government argues that there is no legal duty on the United States to accept fleeing Haitians, including those with legitimate refugee claims. For the reasons expressed in our previous submissions and stated in the Interim Measure resolution issued by the Commission in February 1993, we respectfully disagree. The interdiction of Haitian nationals and their forced return to Haiti without a full and fair opportunity to have their refugee claims considered violates the various Articles of the Declaration, American Convention, the other international human rights instruments and customary international law. Contrary to the position of the United States Government, the American Declaration has acquired legally binding force by virtue of U.S. membership in the OAS and ratification of the Charter of the OAS.
>
> Customary international law in this case has been violated because there has been extensive and virtually uniform adoption of the policy of nonrefoulement throughout the world. The policy of interdicting Haitians based on their national origin (while, coincidentally, liberally admitting others, such as Cuban nationals), and forcibly returning them to Haiti without asylum interviews of any sort, clearly violated the principle of nonrefoulement.

A primary issue in the dispute involved the interpretation of the language of the American Declaration of the Rights and Duties of Man.[31] Although several articles in the Declaration were implicated in the case, Article XXVII is especially relevant: "Every person has the right, in case of pursuit not resulting from ordinary crimes, to seek and receive asylum in foreign territory, in accordance with the laws of each country and with international agreements."

---

31. The American Declaration of the Rights and Duties of Man predates the Universal Declaration of Human Rights by less than a year and, like the Universal Declaration, "was never intended to be a legally binding instrument." The IACHR "has maintained that the American Declaration acquired legally binding force because it was the only human rights document in existence in 1967, when the Charter of the Organization of American States was amended and elevated the Inter-American Commission to the status of a 'principal organ' of the regional body." Christina M. Cerna, *Reflections on the Normative Status of the American Declaration of the Rights and Duties of Man*, 30 U. PA. J. INT'L L. 1211 at 2011, 2012 (2009). Professor Cerna was Principal Specialist at the General Secretariat of the Organization of American States' Secretariat for the Inter-American Commission on Human Rights.

The Commission ruled against the United States. First, the Commission found that the American Declaration had been violated:

> It is convenient to begin with an analysis of Article XXVII of the American Declaration. Article XXVII of the American Declaration is entitled "Right of Asylum." This Article outlines two criteria which are cumulative and both of which must be satisfied in order for the right to exist. The first criterion is that the right to seek and receive asylum on foreign territory must be in "accordance with the laws of each country," that is the country in which asylum is sought. The second criterion is that the right to seek asylum in foreign territory must be "in accordance with international agreements."
>
> The Commission finds that the United States summarily interdicted and repatriated Haitian refugees to Haiti without making an adequate determination of their status, and without granting them a hearing to ascertain whether they qualified as "refugees." The Commission also finds that the dual criteria test of the right to "seek" and "receive" asylum as provided by Articles XXVII in "foreign territory" (in accordance with the laws of each country and with international agreements) of the American Declaration has been satisfied. Therefore, the Commission finds that the United States breached Article XXVII of the American Declaration when it summarily interdicted, and repatriated Jeanette Gedeon, Dukens Luma, Fito Jean, and unnamed Haitians to Haiti, and prevented them from exercising their right to seek and receive asylum in foreign territory as provided by the American Declaration.[32]

The Commission also found that the 1951 Convention Relating to the Status of Refugees, to which the United States is a party, was violated:

> An important provision of the 1951 Convention is Article 33(1) which provides that: "No Contracting State shall expel or return ('refouler') a refugee in any manner whatsoever to the frontiers of territories where his life or freedom would be threatened on account of his race, religion, nationality, membership of a particular social group or political opinion." The Supreme Court of the United States . . . construed this provision as not being applicable in a situation where a person is returned from the high seas to the territory from which he or she fled. Specifically, the Supreme Court held that the principle of nonrefoulement in Article 33 did not apply to the Haitians interdicted on the high seas and not in the United States' territory.
>
> The Commission does not agree with this finding. The Commission shares the view advanced by the United Nations High Commissioner for Refugees in its Amicus Curiae brief in its argument before the Supreme Court, that Article 33 had no geographical limitations.[33]

---

32. *The Haitian Centre for Human Rights et al.*, Case 10.675, Report No. 51/96, OEA/Ser.L/V/II.95, at ¶ 151, 163.

33. *Id.* at ¶ 156–57.

The Commission ruled that the United States should provide adequate compensation for the plaintiffs. After coming to a decision on the merits, the Commission sent a written copy of its opinion to the United States government. The United States sent the following letter in reply:

> The United States Government has long been one of the strongest supporters of the Commission. We are also a strong supporter of democracy and human rights in Haiti, and a leading contributor to UN and OAS operations in Haiti designed to foster peace, stability and the protection of human rights.
>
> We must respectfully disagree with the conclusions reached by the Commission in this case. I will not here repeat the response of the United States to each allegation made in this case. Our views were set forth in detail in our lengthy submissions to the Commission, and, we believe, demonstrated why the actions of the United States did not contravene any human rights standards contained in the American Declaration of the Rights and Duties of Man. In particular, our submissions demonstrated that there is no basis for interpreting those human rights standards to require the U.S. to admit fleeing Haitians into the United States. Nor do those standards preclude the United States from repatriating the migrants to Haiti.
>
> My government also believes that the Commission's analysis is legally flawed. For example, it was error to hold that the 1967 Protocol to the UN Convention on the Status of Refugees applies to Haitian migrants interdicted on the high seas. It was also error to interpret the nonrefoulement obligation to require high seas interdictees to receive the same hearing on their asylum claims as they would receive if they were present within the territory of the interdicting state and to hold that one group of intending immigrants is entitled to receive the more preferential treatment given another group. Moreover, there is no basis in law to hold the U.S. liable for acts and omissions of another government with respect to that government's own citizens.
>
> The United States Government has been and remains deeply committed to restoring democracy in Haiti, to saving human lives and to the fair treatment of genuine refugees. We believe that our actions were consistent with those goals and violated no human rights obligations. However, for the reasons explained here and detailed in our previous submissions to the Commission, we can find no basis on which to agree with the Commission's decision and thus will not comply with its demand to pay compensation.[34]

Notes and Questions

1. Why did the plaintiffs originally bring suit in United States courts? After that suit failed, why did they sue in the Inter-American Commission on Human Rights?

---

34. *Id.* at ¶ 182.

If the United States was determined to refuse to honor the Commission's ruling, why did the United States bother to defend the suit at all? Why invest the time, resources, and attorneys to argue before the tribunal?

2. Is there a consistent theory underlying the United States position? Is it as simple as "my land, my rules"?

3. Might there have been a different result if the aggrieved parties first brought suit in an international forum followed by an enforcement action in the United States? The distinction between obligation and enforcement is at issue in the next case study.

B. Medellín v. Texas

Writing in 2006, in the context of an intensified politicization of the issue of international law in domestic courts (driven in part by controversies over the U.S. role in the war in Iraq), Professor Harold Hongju Koh distinguished between "transnationalist" and "nationalist" perspectives on the U.S. Supreme Court:

> [T]he Supreme Court has now divided into transnationalist and nationalist factions, which hold sharply divergent attitudes toward transnational law.[15] The transnationalist faction—which includes Justices Breyer, Souter, Stevens, Ginsburg, and at times, Justice Kennedy—tends to follow an approach suggested by Justice Blackmun in the late 1980s: that U.S. courts must look beyond national interest to the "mutual interests of all nations in a smoothly functioning international legal regime" and must "consider if there is a course that furthers, rather than impedes, the development of an ordered international system." In contrast, another group of Justices, which includes the new Chief Justice John Roberts and Justices Scalia, Thomas, and Alito, seems committed to a more nationalist course.[35]

In Professor Koh's view, the transnationalist/nationalist divide represents a fundamental worldview schism with wide-ranging implications extending to fundamental questions of the powers of the three branches of government, and in particular presidential power in relation to foreign affairs:

> Generally speaking, the transnationalists tend to emphasize the interdependence between the United States and the rest of the world, while the nationalists tend instead to focus more on preserving American autonomy. The transnationalists believe in and promote the blending of international and domestic law; while nationalists continue to maintain a rigid separation of domestic from foreign law. The transnationalists view domestic courts as having a critical role to play in domesticating international law into U.S. law, while nationalists argue instead that only the political branches can internalize international law. The transnationalists believe that U.S. courts can

35. Harold Hongju Koh, *Why Transnational Law Matters*, 24 Penn St. Int'l L. Rev. 745, 748 (2006).

> and should use their interpretive powers to promote the development of a global legal system, while the nationalists tend to claim that U.S. courts should limit their attention to the development of a national system. Finally, the transnationalists urge that the power of the executive branch should be constrained by judicial review and the concept of international comity, while the nationalists tend to believe that federal courts should give extraordinarily broad deference to executive power in foreign affairs.[36]

As you read the following case from the same period as Professor Koh's analysis, consider how the Court obviates the choice between the nationalist and transnationalist positions he outlines, by framing the ruling as an issue of federalism—in the process, resisting deference to international law but without adopting a rendering of executive power that would make it the automatic expression of national autonomy.

Medellín v. Texas

552 U.S. 491 (2008)

Chief Justice Roberts delivered the opinion of the Court.

The International Court of Justice (ICJ), located in the Hague, is a tribunal established pursuant to the United Nations Charter to adjudicate disputes between member states. In the *Case Concerning Avena and Other Mexican Nationals (Mex. v. U.S.)*, 2004 I.C.J. 12 (Judgment of Mar. 31) (*Avena*), that tribunal considered a claim brought by Mexico against the United States. The ICJ held that, based on violations of the Vienna Convention, 51 named Mexican nationals were entitled to review and reconsideration of their state-court convictions and sentences in the United States. This was so regardless of any forfeiture of the right to raise Vienna Convention claims because of a failure to comply with generally applicable state rules governing challenges to criminal convictions.

In *Sanchez-Llamas v. Oregon*, 548 U.S. 331 (2006)—issued after *Avena* but involving individuals who were not named in the *Avena* judgment—we held that, contrary to the ICJ's determination, the Vienna Convention did not preclude the application of state default rules. After the *Avena* decision, President George W. Bush determined, through a Memorandum for the Attorney General, that the United States would "discharge its international obligations" under *Avena* "by having State courts give effect to the decision."

Petitioner José Ernesto Medellín, who had been convicted and sentenced in Texas state court for murder, is one of the 51 Mexican nationals named in the *Avena* decision. Relying on the ICJ's decision and the President's Memorandum, Medellín filed an application for a writ of habeas corpus in state court. The Texas Court of Criminal Appeals dismissed Medellín's application as an abuse of the writ under state law, given Medellín's failure to raise his Vienna Convention claim in a timely manner

---

36. *Id.* at 749–50; *see* Alicia J. Surdyk, *John Roberts: Nationalism, Conservatism, and the Shifting Trends on the Contemporary Supreme Court*, 13 Touro Int'l L. Rev. 165 (2010).

under state law. We granted certiorari to decide two questions. First, is the ICJ's judgment in *Avena* directly enforceable as domestic law in a state court in the United States? Second, does the President's Memorandum independently require the States to provide review and reconsideration of the claims of the 51 Mexican nationals named in *Avena* without regard to state procedural default rules? We conclude that neither *Avena* nor the President's Memorandum constitutes directly enforceable federal law that pre-empts state limitations on the filing of successive habeas petitions. We therefore affirm the decision below.

I

B

Petitioner José Ernesto Medellín, a Mexican national, has lived in the United States since preschool. A member of the "Black and Whites" gang, Medellín was convicted of capital murder and sentenced to death in Texas for the gang rape and brutal murders of two Houston teenagers.

Medellín first raised his Vienna Convention claim in his first application for state postconviction relief. The state trial court held that the claim was procedurally defaulted because Medellín had failed to raise it at trial or on direct review. The trial court also rejected the Vienna Convention claim on the merits, finding that Medellín had "fail[ed] to show that any non-notification of the Mexican authorities impacted on the validity of his conviction or punishment."[37] The Texas Court of Criminal Appeals affirmed.

Medellín then filed a habeas petition in Federal District Court. The District Court denied relief, holding that Medellín's Vienna Convention claim was procedurally defaulted and that Medellín had failed to show prejudice arising from the Vienna Convention violation.

While Medellín's application for a certificate of appealability was pending in the Fifth Circuit, the ICJ issued its decision in Avena. The ICJ held that the United States had violated Article 36(1)(b) of the Vienna Convention by failing to inform the 51 named Mexican nationals, including Medellín, of their Vienna Convention rights. In the ICJ's determination, the United States was obligated "to provide, by means of its own choosing, review and reconsideration of the convictions and sentences of the [affected] Mexican nationals." The ICJ indicated that such review was required without regard to state procedural default rules.

The Fifth Circuit denied a certificate of appealability. The court concluded that the Vienna Convention did not confer individually enforceable rights. The court further ruled that it was in any event bound by this Court's decision in *Breard v. Greene*, 523 U.S. 371, 375 (1998) (per curiam), which held that Vienna Convention

37. [1] The requirement of Article 36(1)(b) of the Vienna Convention that the detaining state notify the detainee's consulate "without delay" is satisfied, according to the ICJ, where notice is provided within three working days. Here, Medellín confessed within three hours of his arrest—before there could be a violation of his Vienna Convention right to consulate notification.

claims are subject to procedural default rules, rather than by the ICJ's contrary decision in *Avena*.

This Court granted certiorari. Before we heard oral argument, however, President George W. Bush issued his Memorandum for the United States Attorney General, providing:

> "I have determined, pursuant to the authority vested in me as President by the Constitution and the laws of the United States of America, that the United States will discharge its international obligations under the decision of the International Court of Justice in [*Avena*], by having State courts give effect to the decision in accordance with general principles of comity in cases filed by the 51 Mexican nationals addressed in that decision."

Medellín, relying on the President's Memorandum and the ICJ's decision in *Avena*, filed a second application for habeas relief in state court.

II

Medellín first contends that the ICJ's judgment in *Avena* constitutes a "binding" obligation on the state and federal courts of the United States. He argues that "by virtue of the Supremacy Clause, the treaties requiring compliance with the Avena judgment are already the 'Law of the Land' by which all state and federal courts in this country are 'bound.'" Accordingly, Medellín argues, *Avena* is a binding federal rule of decision that pre-empts contrary state limitations on successive habeas petitions.

No one disputes that the *Avena* decision—a decision that flows from the treaties through which the United States submitted to ICJ jurisdiction with respect to Vienna Convention disputes—constitutes an international law obligation on the part of the United States. But not all international law obligations automatically constitute binding federal law enforceable in United States courts. The question we confront here is whether the Avena judgment has automatic domestic legal effect such that the judgment of its own force applies in state and federal courts.

[W]hile treaties "may comprise international commitments . . . they are not domestic law unless Congress has either enacted implementing statutes or the treaty itself conveys an intention that it be 'self-executing' and is ratified on these terms." *Igartua-De La Rosa v. United States*, 417 F.3d 145, 150 (C.A.1 2005) (en banc) (Boudin, C.J.).

Medellín and his amici nonetheless contend that the Optional Protocol, United Nations Charter, and ICJ Statute supply the "relevant obligation" to give the *Avena* judgment binding effect in the domestic courts of the United States. Because none of these treaty sources creates binding federal law in the absence of implementing legislation, and because it is uncontested that no such legislation exists, we conclude that the *Avena* judgment is not automatically binding domestic law.

A

The obligation on the part of signatory nations to comply with ICJ judgments derives . . . from Article 94 of the United Nations Charter—the provision that specifically addresses the effect of ICJ decisions. Article 94(1) provides that "[e]ach Member of the United Nations *undertakes to comply* with the decision of the [ICJ] in any case to which it is a party." 59 Stat. 1051 (emphasis added). The Executive Branch contends that the phrase "undertakes to comply" is not "an acknowledgement that an ICJ decision will have immediate legal effect in the courts of U.N. members," but rather "a *commitment* on the part of U.N. members to take future action through their political branches to comply with an ICJ decision."

We agree with this construction of Article 94. . . . [T]he U.N. Charter reads like "a compact between independent nations" that "depends for the enforcement of its provisions on the interest and the honor of the governments which are parties to it." *Head Money Cases*, 112 U.S. 580, 598 (1884).[38]

The remainder of Article 94 confirms that the U.N. Charter does not contemplate the automatic enforceability of ICJ decisions in domestic courts. Article 94(2)—the enforcement provision—provides the sole remedy for noncompliance: referral to the United Nations Security Council by an aggrieved state.

The U.N. Charter's provision of an express diplomatic—that is, nonjudicial—remedy is itself evidence that ICJ judgments were not meant to be enforceable in domestic courts. And even this "quintessentially international remed[y]," *id.*, at 355, 126 S.Ct. 2669, is not absolute. First, the Security Council must "dee[m] necessary" the issuance of a recommendation or measure to effectuate the judgment. Art. 94(2), 59 Stat. 1051. Second, as the President and Senate were undoubtedly aware in subscribing to the U.N. Charter and Optional Protocol, the United States retained the unqualified right to exercise its veto of any Security Council resolution.

If ICJ judgments were instead regarded as automatically enforceable domestic law, they would be immediately and directly binding on state and federal courts pursuant to the Supremacy Clause. Mexico or the ICJ would have no need to proceed to the Security Council to enforce the judgment in this case. Noncompliance with an ICJ judgment through exercise of the Security Council veto—always regarded as an option by the Executive and ratifying Senate during and after consideration of the U.N. Charter, Optional Protocol, and ICJ Statute—would no longer be a viable alternative. There would be nothing to veto. In light of the U.N. Charter's remedial scheme, there is no reason to believe that the President and Senate signed up for such a result.

Medellín argues that because the *Avena* case involves him, it is clear that he—and the 50 other Mexican nationals named in the *Avena* decision—should be regarded as parties to the *Avena* judgment. But cases before the ICJ are often precipitated by disputes involving particular persons or entities, disputes that a nation elects to take up as its own.

---

38. [5] We do not read "undertakes" to mean that "[t]he United States . . . shall be at liberty to make respecting th[e] matter, such laws as they think proper." *Post* (Breyer, J., dissenting). Whether or not the United States "undertakes" to comply with a treaty says nothing about what laws it may enact. The United States is always "at liberty to make . . . such laws as [it] think[s] proper." Indeed, a later-in-time federal statute supersedes inconsistent treaty provisions. . . .

That has never been understood to alter the express and established rules that only nation-states may be parties before the ICJ, Art. 34, and—contrary to the position of the dissent, post—that ICJ judgments are binding only between those parties, Art. 59.

C

Our conclusion that *Avena* does not by itself constitute binding federal law is confirmed by the "postratification understanding" of signatory nations. There are currently 47 nations that are parties to the Optional Protocol and 171 nations that are parties to the Vienna Convention. Yet neither Medellín nor his amici have identified a single nation that treats ICJ judgments as binding in domestic courts. In determining that the Vienna Convention did not require certain relief in United States courts in *Sanchez-Llamas*, we found it pertinent that the requested relief would not be available under the treaty in any other signatory country. See 548 U.S., at 343–344, and n. 3. So too here the lack of any basis for supposing that any other country would treat ICJ judgments as directly enforceable as a matter of their domestic law strongly suggests that the treaty should not be so viewed in our courts.

Moreover, the consequences of Medellín's argument give pause. An ICJ judgment, the argument goes, is not only binding domestic law but is also unassailable. As a result, neither Texas nor this Court may look behind a judgment and quarrel with its reasoning or result. (We already know, from *Sanchez-Llamas*, that this Court disagrees with both the reasoning and result in *Avena*.) Medellín's interpretation would allow ICJ judgments to override otherwise binding state law; there is nothing in his logic that would exempt contrary federal law from the same fate. And there is nothing to prevent the ICJ from ordering state courts to annul criminal convictions and sentences, for any reason deemed sufficient by the ICJ. Indeed, that is precisely the relief Mexico requested.

Even the dissent flinches at reading the relevant treaties to give rise to self-executing ICJ judgments in all cases. It admits that "Congress is unlikely to authorize automatic judicial enforceability of all ICJ judgments, for that could include some politically sensitive judgments and others better suited for enforcement by other branches." Our point precisely. But the lesson to draw from that insight is hardly that the judiciary should decide which judgments are politically sensitive and which are not.

D

Our holding does not call into question the ordinary enforcement of foreign judgments or international arbitral agreements. Indeed, we agree with Medellín that, as a general matter, "an agreement to abide by the result" of an international adjudication—or what he really means, an agreement to give the result of such adjudication domestic legal effect—can be a treaty obligation like any other, so long as the agreement is consistent with the Constitution. The point is that the particular treaty obligations on which Medellín relies do not of their own force create domestic law.

III

Medellín next argues that the ICJ's judgment in *Avena* is binding on state courts by virtue of the President's February 28, 2005 Memorandum. The United States contends that while the *Avena* judgment does not of its own force require domestic courts to set aside ordinary rules of procedural default, that judgment became the law of the land with precisely that effect pursuant to the President's Memorandum and his power "to establish binding rules of decision that preempt contrary state law." Accordingly, we must decide whether the President's declaration alters our conclusion that the *Avena* judgment is not a rule of domestic law binding in state and federal courts.

The United States maintains that the President's constitutional role "uniquely qualifies" him to resolve the sensitive foreign policy decisions that bear on compliance with an ICJ decision and "to do so expeditiously." We do not question these propositions . . . . In this case, the President seeks to vindicate United States interests in ensuring the reciprocal observance of the Vienna Convention, protecting relations with foreign governments, and demonstrating commitment to the role of international law. These interests are plainly compelling.

Such considerations, however, do not allow us to set aside first principles. The President's authority to act, as with the exercise of any governmental power, "must stem either from an act of Congress or from the Constitution itself." *Youngstown Sheet & Tube Co. v. Sawyer*, 343 U.S. 579, 585 (1952).

Justice Jackson's familiar tripartite scheme provides the accepted framework for evaluating executive action in this area.

B

1

The President has an array of political and diplomatic means available to enforce international obligations, but unilaterally converting a non-self-executing treaty into a self-executing one is not among them. The responsibility for transforming an international obligation arising from a non-self-executing treaty into domestic law falls to Congress. As this Court has explained, when treaty stipulations are "not self-executing they can only be enforced pursuant to legislation to carry them into effect." Moreover, "[u]ntil such act shall be passed, the Court is not at liberty to disregard the existing laws on the subject."

A non-self-executing treaty, by definition, is one that was ratified with the understanding that it is not to have domestic effect of its own force. That understanding precludes the assertion that Congress has implicitly authorized the President—acting on his own—to achieve precisely the same result. We therefore conclude, given the absence of congressional legislation, that the non-self-executing treaties at issue here did not "express[ly] or implied[ly]" vest the President with the unilateral authority to make them self-executing. *See Youngstown*, at 635 (Jackson, J., concurring). Accordingly, the President's Memorandum does not fall within the first category of the *Youngstown* framework.

None of this is to say, however, that the combination of a non-self-executing treaty and the lack of implementing legislation precludes the President from acting to comply with an international treaty obligation. It is only to say that the Executive cannot unilaterally execute a non-self-executing treaty by giving it domestic effect. That is, the non-self-executing character of a treaty constrains the President's ability to comply with treaty commitments by unilaterally making the treaty binding on domestic courts. The President may comply with the treaty's obligations by some other means, so long as they are consistent with the Constitution. But he may not rely upon a non-self-executing treaty to "establish binding rules of decision that preempt contrary state law."

3

Medellín argues that the President's Memorandum is a valid exercise of his "take Care" power. The United States, however, does not rely upon the President's responsibility to "take Care that the Laws be faithfully executed." U.S. Const., Art. II, § 3. We think this a wise concession. This authority allows the President to execute the laws, not make them. For the reasons we have stated, the *Avena* judgment is not domestic law; accordingly, the President cannot rely on his Take Care powers here.

The judgment of the Texas Court of Criminal Appeals is affirmed.

Justice Stevens, concurring in the judgment.

There is a great deal of wisdom in Justice Breyer's dissent. I agree that the text and history of the Supremacy Clause, as well as this Court's treaty-related cases, do not support a presumption against self-execution. I also endorse the proposition that the Vienna Convention on Consular Relations, Apr. 24, 1963, [1970] 21 U.S.T. 77, T.I.A.S. No. 6820, "is itself self-executing and judicially enforceable." Moreover, I think this case presents a closer question than the Court's opinion allows. In the end, however, I am persuaded that the relevant treaties do not authorize this Court to enforce the judgment of the International Court of Justice in *Avena*.

The source of the United States' obligation to comply with judgments of the ICJ is found in Article 94(1) of the United Nations Charter, which was ratified in 1945. Article 94(1) provides that "[e]ach Member of the United Nations *undertakes to comply* with the decision of the [ICJ] in any case to which it is a party." 59 Stat. 1051, T.S. No. 993 (emphasis added). In my view, the words "undertakes to comply"—while not the model of either a self-executing or a non-self-executing commitment—are most naturally read as a promise to take additional steps to enforce ICJ judgments.

Even though the ICJ's judgment in *Avena* is not "the supreme Law of the Land," U.S. Const., Art. VI, cl. 2, no one disputes that it constitutes an international law obligation on the part of the United States, *ante*, at 1356. By issuing a memorandum declaring that state courts should give effect to the judgment in *Avena*, the President made a commendable attempt to induce the States to discharge the Nation's obligation. I agree with the Texas judges and the majority of this Court that the President's memorandum is not binding law. Nonetheless, the fact that the President cannot legislate unilaterally does not absolve the United States from its promise to take action necessary to comply with the ICJ's judgment.

Under the express terms of the Supremacy Clause, the United States' obligation to "undertak[e] to comply" with the ICJ's decision falls on each of the States as well as the Federal Government. One consequence of our form of government is that sometimes States must shoulder the primary responsibility for protecting the honor and integrity of the Nation. Texas' duty in this respect is all the greater since it was Texas that—by failing to provide consular notice in accordance with the Vienna Convention—ensnared the United States in the current controversy. Having already put the Nation in breach of one treaty, it is now up to Texas to prevent the breach of another.

The decision in *Avena* merely obligates the United States "to provide, by means of its own choosing, review and reconsideration of the convictions and sentences of the [affected] Mexican nationals," 2004 I.C.J., at 72, ¶ 153(9), "with a view to ascertaining" whether the failure to provide proper notice to consular officials "caused actual prejudice to the defendant in the process of administration of criminal justice," *id.*, at 60, ¶ 121. The cost to Texas of complying with *Avena* would be minimal, particularly given the remote likelihood that the violation of the Vienna Convention actually prejudiced José Ernesto Medellín. It is a cost that the State of Oklahoma unhesitatingly assumed.

On the other hand, the costs of refusing to respect the ICJ's judgment are significant. The entire Court and the President agree that breach will jeopardize the United States' "plainly compelling" interests in "ensuring the reciprocal observance of the Vienna Convention, protecting relations with foreign governments, and demonstrating commitment to the role of international law." When the honor of the Nation is balanced against the modest cost of compliance, Texas would do well to recognize that more is at stake than whether judgments of the ICJ, and the principled admonitions of the President of the United States, trump state procedural rules in the absence of implementing legislation.

The Court's judgment, which I join, does not foreclose further appropriate action by the State of Texas.

Justice Breyer, with whom Justice Souter and Justice Ginsburg join, dissenting.

The Constitution's Supremacy Clause provides that "all Treaties . . . which shall be made . . . under the Authority of the United States, shall be the supreme Law of the Land; and the Judges in every State shall be bound thereby." Art. VI, cl. 2. The Clause means that the "courts" must regard "a treaty . . . as equivalent to an act of the legislature, whenever it operates of itself without the aid of any legislative provision." *Foster v. Neilson*, 2 Pet. 253, 314 (1829) (majority opinion of Marshall, C. J.).

The United States has signed and ratified a series of treaties obliging it to comply with ICJ judgments in cases in which it has given its consent to the exercise of the ICJ's adjudicatory authority. Specifically, the United States has agreed to submit, in this kind of case, to the ICJ's "compulsory jurisdiction" for purposes of "compulsory settlement." Optional Protocol Concerning the Compulsory Settlement of Disputes (Optional Protocol or Protocol), Art. I, Apr. 24, 1963, [1970] 21 U.S.T. 326,

T.I.A.S. No. 6820. And it agreed that the ICJ's judgments would have "binding force . . . between the parties and in respect of [a] particular case." United Nations Charter, Art. 59, 59 Stat. 1062, T.S. No. 993 (1945). President Bush has determined that domestic courts should enforce this particular ICJ judgment. And Congress has done nothing to suggest the contrary. Under these circumstances, I believe the treaty obligations, and hence the judgment, resting as it does upon the consent of the United States to the ICJ's jurisdiction, bind the courts no less than would "an act of the [federal] legislature."

I

The critical question here is whether the Supremacy Clause requires Texas to follow, i.e., to enforce, this ICJ judgment. The Court says "no." And it reaches its negative answer by interpreting the labyrinth of treaty provisions as creating a legal obligation that binds the United States internationally, but which, for Supremacy Clause purposes, is not automatically enforceable as domestic law. In the majority's view, the Optional Protocol simply sends the dispute to the ICJ; the ICJ Statute says that the ICJ will subsequently reach a judgment; and the U.N. Charter contains no more than a promise to "undertak[e] to comply" with that judgment. Such a promise, the majority says, does not as a domestic-law matter (in Chief Justice Marshall's words) "operat[e] of itself without the aid of any legislative provision." Rather, here (and presumably in any other ICJ judgment rendered pursuant to any of the approximately 70 U.S. treaties in force that contain similar provisions for submitting treaty-based disputes to the ICJ for decisions that bind the parties) Congress must enact specific legislation before ICJ judgments entered pursuant to our consent to compulsory ICJ jurisdiction can become domestic law.

In my view, the President has correctly determined that Congress need not enact additional legislation. The majority places too much weight upon treaty language that says little about the matter. The words "undertak[e] to comply," for example, do not tell us whether an ICJ judgment rendered pursuant to the parties' consent to compulsory ICJ jurisdiction does, or does not, automatically become part of our domestic law. To answer that question we must look instead to our own domestic law, in particular, to the many treaty-related cases interpreting the Supremacy Clause. Those cases, including some written by Justices well aware of the Founders' original intent, lead to the conclusion that the ICJ judgment before us is enforceable as a matter of domestic law without further legislation.

A

[S]elf-executing treaty provisions are not uncommon or peculiar creatures of our domestic law; that they cover a wide range of subjects; that the Supremacy Clause itself answers the self-execution question by applying many, but not all, treaty provisions directly to the States; and that the Clause answers the self-execution question differently than does the law in many other nations. The cases also provide criteria that help determine which provisions automatically so apply—a matter to which I now turn.

B

1

The case law provides no simple magic answer to the question whether a particular treaty provision is self-executing. But the case law does make clear that, insofar as today's majority looks for language about "self-execution" in the treaty itself and insofar as it erects "clear statement" presumptions designed to help find an answer, it is misguided. See, *e.g., ante*, at 517 (expecting "clea[r] state[ment]" of parties' intent where treaty obligation "may interfere with state procedural rules"); *ante*, at 526 (for treaty to be self-executing, Executive should at drafting "ensur[e] that it contains language plainly providing for domestic enforceability").

The many treaty provisions that this Court has found self-executing contain no textual language on the point. Few, if any, of these provisions are clear. Those that displace state law in respect to such quintessential state matters as, say, property, inheritance, or debt repayment, lack the "clea[r] state[ment]" that the Court today apparently requires. This is also true of those cases that deal with state rules roughly comparable to the sort that the majority suggests require special accommodation....

In a word, for present purposes, the absence or presence of language in a treaty about a provision's self-execution proves nothing at all. At best the Court is hunting the snark. At worst it erects legalistic hurdles that can threaten the application of provisions in many existing commercial and other treaties and make it more difficult to negotiate new ones.

2

The case law also suggests practical, context-specific criteria that this Court has previously used to help determine whether, for Supremacy Clause purposes, a treaty provision is self-executing. The provision's text matters very much. But that is not because it contains language that explicitly refers to self-execution. For reasons I have already explained, one should not expect that kind of textual statement. Drafting history is also relevant. But, again, that is not because it will explicitly address the relevant question. Instead text and history, along with subject matter and related characteristics, will help our courts determine whether, as Chief Justice Marshall put it, the treaty provision "addresses itself to the political ... department[s]" for further action or to "the judicial department" for direct enforcement. *Foster*, 2 Pet., at 314; see also *Ware*, 3 Dall., at 244 (opinion of Chase, J.) ("No one can doubt that a treaty may stipulate, that certain acts shall be done by the Legislature; that other acts shall be done by the Executive; and others by the Judiciary").

In making this determination, this Court has found the provision's subject matter of particular importance. Does the treaty provision declare peace? Does it promise not to engage in hostilities? If so, it addresses itself to the political branches. *See id.*, at 259–262 (opinion of Iredell, J.). Alternatively, does it concern the adjudication of traditional private legal rights such as rights to own property, to conduct a business, or to obtain civil tort recovery? If so, it may well address itself to the judiciary.

Enforcing such rights and setting their boundaries is the bread-and-butter work of the courts.

One might also ask whether the treaty provision confers specific, detailed individual legal rights. Does it set forth definite standards that judges can readily enforce? Other things being equal, where rights are specific and readily enforceable, the treaty provision more likely "addresses" the judiciary.

Alternatively, would direct enforcement require the courts to create a new cause of action? Would such enforcement engender constitutional controversy? Would it create constitutionally undesirable conflict with the other branches? In such circumstances, it is not likely that the provision contemplates direct judicial enforcement.

C

Applying the approach just described, I would find the relevant treaty provisions self-executing as applied to the ICJ judgment before us (giving that judgment domestic legal effect) for the following reasons, taken together.

First, the language of the relevant treaties strongly supports direct judicial enforceability, at least of judgments of the kind at issue here. The Optional Protocol bears the title "Compulsory Settlement of Disputes," thereby emphasizing the mandatory and binding nature of the procedures it sets forth. The body of the Protocol says specifically that "any party" that has consented to the ICJ's "compulsory jurisdiction" may bring a "dispute" before the court against any other such party. And the Protocol contrasts proceedings of the compulsory kind with an alternative "conciliation procedure," the recommendations of which a party may decide "not" to "accep[t]."

True, neither the Protocol nor the Charter explicitly states that the obligation to comply with an ICJ judgment automatically binds a party as a matter of domestic law without further domestic legislation. But how could the language of those documents do otherwise? The treaties are multilateral.

And even if I agreed with Justice Stevens that the language is perfectly ambiguous (which I do not), I could not agree that "the best reading . . . is . . . one that contemplates future action by the political branches." The consequence of such a reading is to place the fate of an international promise made by the United States in the hands of a single State. And that is precisely the situation that the Framers sought to prevent by enacting the Supremacy Clause.

Second, the Optional Protocol here applies to a dispute about the meaning of a Vienna Convention provision that is itself self-executing and judicially enforceable. The Convention provision is about an individual's "rights," namely, his right upon being arrested to be informed of his separate right to contact his nation's consul. The provision language is precise.

This Court has found similar treaty provisions self-executing. . . . It is consequently not surprising that, when Congress ratified the Convention, the State Department reported that the "Convention is considered entirely self-executive and does not require any implementing or complementing legislation." S. Exec. Rep. No. 91-9, p. 5 (1969); see also *id.*, at 18, 7 S.Ct. 385 ("To the extent that there are conflicts with Federal legislation or State laws the Vienna Convention, after ratification, would govern"). And the Executive Branch has said in this Court that other, indistinguishable Vienna Convention provisions are self-executing.

Third, logic suggests that a treaty provision providing for "final" and "binding" judgments that "settl[e]" treaty-based disputes is self-executing insofar as the judgment in question concerns the meaning of an underlying treaty provision that is itself self-executing. Imagine that two parties to a contract agree to binding arbitration about whether a contract provision's word "grain" includes rye. They would expect that, if the arbitrator decides that the word "grain" does include rye, the arbitrator will then simply read the relevant provision as if it said "grain including rye." They would also expect the arbitrator to issue a binding award that embodies whatever relief would be appropriate under that circumstance.

To put the same point differently: What sense would it make (1) to make a self-executing promise and (2) to promise to accept as final an ICJ judgment interpreting that self-executing promise, yet (3) to insist that the judgment itself is not self-executing (i.e., that Congress must enact specific legislation to enforce it)?

Fourth, the majority's very different approach has seriously negative practical implications. The United States has entered into at least 70 treaties that contain provisions for ICJ dispute settlement similar to the Protocol before us. Many of these treaties contain provisions similar to those this Court has previously found self-executing—provisions that involve, for example, property rights, contract and commercial rights, trademarks, civil liability for personal injury, rights of foreign diplomats, taxation, domestic-court jurisdiction, and so forth.... And the consequence is to undermine longstanding efforts in those treaties to create an effective international system for interpreting and applying many, often commercial, self-executing treaty provisions. I thus doubt that the majority is right when it says, "We do not suggest that treaties can never afford binding domestic effect to international tribunal judgments." In respect to the 70 treaties that currently refer disputes to the ICJ's binding adjudicatory authority, some multilateral, some bilateral, that is just what the majority has done.

Seventh, neither the President nor Congress has expressed concern about direct judicial enforcement of the ICJ decision. To the contrary, the President favors enforcement of this judgment. Thus, insofar as foreign policy impact, the interrelation of treaty provisions, or any other matter within the President's special treaty, military, and foreign affairs responsibilities might prove relevant, such factors favor, rather than militate against, enforcement of the judgment before us.

Notes and Questions

1. The majority says that the "dissent's contrary approach would assign to the courts—not the political branches—the primary role in deciding when and how international agreements will be enforced. To read a treaty so that it sometimes has the effect of domestic law and sometimes does not is tantamount to vesting with the judiciary the power not only to interpret but also to create the law."[39] But the executive branch had also chimed in, insisting that *Avena* is binding upon state courts, so the judicial voice would certainly not be the sole branch of government in favor of enforcing the ICJ's judgment. All that is supposedly missing, according to the majority, is Congress's assent. What do you think Congress expected when they ratified the treaty framework described in the opinion? Which of the three opinions in *Medellín* has the better argument about Congress's expectations?

2. Both the majority and dissent emphasize the meaning of the phrase "undertakes to comply." The majority asserts that the phrase imposes only "a commitment on the part of U.N. members to take future action through their political branches to comply with an ICJ decision."[40] The dissent rejoins by pointing to the structure of the treaty, which provides that ICJ decisions between consenting parties have "binding force" and that "undertaking" also indicates "a present obligation to execute."[41] Is this agreement simply about the difference between "recognition" of the ICJ's judgment and "enforcement" of the same judgment?[42] The Court in *Medellín* certainly "recognizes" the ICJ's decision in *Avena* as conclusive as to that particular issue between the particular parties. But it refuses to enforce the remedy ordered by the ICJ.[43] Why and when might a U.S. court recognize but not enforce an international decision? Was there any legitimate reason *not* to enforce *Avena* as President Bush suggested?

3. Justice Stevens in concurrence argues that the (apparently unenforceable) duty to comply with *Avena* falls upon Texas:

> Under the express terms of the Supremacy Clause, the United States' obligation to "undertak[e] to comply" with the ICJ's decision falls on each of the States as well as the Federal Government. One consequence of our form of government is that sometimes States must shoulder the primary responsibility for protecting the honor and integrity of the Nation. Texas' duty in this respect is all the greater since it was Texas that—by failing to provide

---

39. *Medellín*, 552 U.S. at 516.

40. *Id.* at 508 (emphasis and quotation omitted).

41. *Id.* at 553.

42. *See* Baker by Thomas v. Gen. Motors Corp., 522 U.S. 222, 235 (1998) (holding that the equitable decrees of sister states are entitled to *recognition* in all states, but that "[*e*]*nforcement* measures do not travel with the sister state judgment").

43. *See Medellín*, 552 U.S. at 504 ("No one disputes that the *Avena* decision . . . constitutes an international law obligation on the part of the United States. But not all international law obligations automatically constitute binding federal law enforceable in United States courts.").

> consular notice in accordance with the Vienna Convention—ensnared the United States in the current controversy. Having already put the Nation in breach of one treaty, it is now up to Texas to prevent the breach of another.[44]

Is it within the competence of state courts to make this type of foreign-relations-based determination?

4. Justice Stevens states that "the Nation [is] in breach of one treaty." Does he (or the majority) convincingly explain why the Supreme Court is unable to mandate compliance to remedy the United States' breach?

III. Transnational litigation: Domestic courts

Let us turn now to consider cases in which domestic courts accept an extraterritorial role, so as to explore the jurisdictional bases of such roles and their underlying concepts of transnationalism. Jurisdiction is sometimes clear—a statute might be explicit in claiming extraterritorial application, for example—but it is often ambiguous, leaving the court to decide for itself, in effect, what there is to decide. In yet other cases, the law to be applied by domestic courts may have been crafted and interpreted by international bodies. In such cases, domestic courts must decide the extent to which they are bound by these bodies. These are among the issues in the following sections.

A. The presumption against extraterritoriality

In 1991, the Supreme Court decided a case involving the question of whether Title VII of the Civil Rights Act of 1964 protected U.S. citizens working for U.S. employers abroad from sex, race, and religious discrimination. In *E.E.O.C. v. Arabian Am. Oil Co. (Aramco)*,[45] by a six-to-three majority, the Court held that it did not.

Ali Boureslan, a naturalized U.S. citizen from Lebanon, worked for Aramco, a U.S. corporation, in Saudi Arabia after requesting a transfer from Houston. Five years after his transfer, Mr. Boureslan was fired. He brought suit under Title VII, alleging that he was harassed and discharged because of his race, religion, and national origin.

After first recognizing that "Congress has the authority to enforce its laws beyond the territorial boundaries of the United States," Chief Justice Rehnquist articulated his *raison d' être* for the case's disposition: for Title VII to apply to Aramco's conduct, Boureslon would have to identify language that "gives any indication of a congressional purpose to extend its coverage beyond places over which the United

44. *Id.* at 536 (Stevens, J., concurring).
45. 499 U.S. 244 (1991).

States has sovereignty or has some measure of legislative control"—clear expression of "the affirmative intention of the Congress" to regulate conduct abroad.

Boureslan, joined by the EEOC, pointed to two provisions in an effort to satisfy this requirement. First, Boureslan argued that the statutory definitions "employer" and "commerce" encompassed U.S. companies employing Americans abroad. As the Court summarized these matters:

> An employer is subject to Title VII if it has employed 15 or more employees for a specified period and is "engaged in an industry affecting commerce." An industry affecting commerce is "any activity, business, or industry in commerce or in which a labor dispute would hinder or obstruct commerce or the free flow of commerce and includes any activity or industry 'affecting commerce'" .... "Commerce," in turn, is defined as "trade, traffic, commerce, transportation, transmission, or communication among the several States; or between a State and any place outside thereof; or within the District of Columbia, or a possession of the United States; or between points in the same State but through a point outside thereof."

These definitions admitted of two possible interpretations. Boureslan argued that the

> "broad jurisdictional language" reveals Congress' intent to extend the statute's protections to employment discrimination anywhere in the world by a United States employer who affects trade "between a State and any place outside thereof." More precisely, they assert that since Title VII defines "States" to include States, the District of Columbia, and specified territories, the clause "between a State and any place outside thereof" must be referring to areas beyond the territorial limit of the United States.

Aramco responded that the same language only provided the "jurisdictional nexus required to regulate commerce that is not wholly within a single state" to allow for regulating interstate commerce; or that the lack of a reference to "commerce with foreign nations" meant that there was no intent for the statute to apply overseas; or that the omission of terms such as "foreign commerce" or "foreign nations" (which were included in the draft bill) indicated Congress's intent to limit extraterritorial application.

But despite these "plausible" interpretations, the Court declined to

> choose between these competing interpretations as we would be required to do in the absence of the presumption against extraterritorial application .... The language relied upon by petitioners—and it is they who must make the affirmative showing—is ambiguous, and does not speak directly to the question presented here. The intent of Congress as to the extraterritorial application of this statute must be deduced by inference from boilerplate language which can be found in any number of congressional Acts, none of which have ever been held to apply overseas.

Boureslan's second argument, that the "alien-exemption provision" provided the necessary expression to warrant extraterritorial application, fared no better. That provision, 42 U.S.C. § 2000e-1, stated that Title VII "shall not apply to an employer with respect to the employment of aliens outside any State." According to Chief Justice Rehnquist:

> If petitioners are correct that the alien-exemption clause means that the statute applies to employers overseas, we see no way of distinguishing in its application between United States employers and foreign employers. Thus, a French employer of a United States citizen in France would be subject to Title VII—a result at which even petitioners balk. The EEOC assures us that in its view the term "employer" means only "American employer," but there is no such distinction in this statute and no indication that the EEOC in the normal course of its administration had produced a reasoned basis for such a distinction. Without clearer evidence of congressional intent to do so than is contained in the alien-exemption clause, we are unwilling to ascribe to that body a policy which would raise difficult issues of international law by imposing this country's employment-discrimination regime upon foreign corporations operating in foreign commerce.

Justice Marshall (joined by Justices Blackmun and Stevens) rejoined with a thorough canvass of the case law. Justice Marshall concluded: "In the hands of the majority, the presumption against extraterritoriality is transformed from a 'valid approach whereby unexpressed congressional intent may be ascertained,' *Foley Bros.*, 336 U.S., at 285, into a barrier to any genuine inquiry into the sources that reveal Congress' actual intentions."

The majority invited "Congress, should it wish to do so, [to] amend Title VII . . . ." Congress quickly did so in 1991—the same year the Court decided *Aramco.*[46] After *Aramco*, Congress understood the need to be precise about the territorial reach of its statutes; when Congress explicitly affirms the extraterritorial application of a statute, the courts follow that direction. By default, when Congress is silent, the Court's presumption is that Congress's intent was against extraterritorial application.

The Torture Victim Protection Act, passed by Congress in 1992, is one such statute.[47] The statute provides federal jurisdiction for civil suits against individuals who torture another individual, even if the conduct occurred overseas.

In the accompanying Senate Report, the legislature explained its intent in passing the TVPA:

> The purpose of this legislation is to provide a Federal cause of action against any individual who, under actual or apparent authority or under color of

46. Civil Rights Act of 1991, § 109(a), 105 Stat. 1077, codified at 42 U.S.C. § 2000e(f) ("With respect to employment in a foreign country," the term "employee" "includes an individual who is a citizen of the United States.").

47. Torture Victim Protection Act of 1991 , Pub. L. No. 102-256, 106 Stat. 73.

> law of any foreign nation, subjects any individual to torture or extrajudicial killing. This legislation will carry out the intent of the Convention Against Torture and Other Cruel, Inhuman or Degrading Treatment or Punishment, which was ratified by the U.S. Senate on October 27, 1990. The convention obligates state parties to adopt measures to ensure that torturers within their territories are held legally accountable for their acts. This legislation will do precisely that—by making sure that torturers and death squads will no longer have a safe haven in the United States.[48]

The legacy of *Aramco* is less its lasting impact on Title VII, than its strong articulation of the presumption against extraterritoriality. While explicit statutory intent remains the surest method for ensuring extraterritorial application of federal statutes, some statutes that were enacted long before *Aramco*—including ATS (until recently; see Chapter 6, *supra*)—had long been assumed to have an extraterritorial reach. These remain open to revision under the *Aramco* doctrine.

Consider the impact of this presumption on the Supreme Court's reasoning in the next case.

Morrison v. National Australia Bank Ltd.

561 U.S. 247 (2010)

JUSTICE SCALIA delivered the opinion of the Court.

We decide whether § 10(b) of the Securities Exchange Act of 1934 provides a cause of action to foreign plaintiffs suing foreign and American defendants for misconduct in connection with securities traded on foreign exchanges.

I

Respondent National Australia Bank Limited (National) was, during the relevant time, the largest bank in Australia. Its Ordinary Shares—what in America would be called "common stock"—are traded on the Australian Stock Exchange Limited and on other foreign securities exchanges, but not on any exchange in the United States. There are listed on the New York Stock Exchange, however, National's American Depositary Receipts (ADRs), which represent the right to receive a specified number of National's Ordinary Shares.

The complaint alleges the following facts, which we accept as true. In February 1998, National bought respondent HomeSide Lending, Inc., a mortgage servicing company headquartered in Florida. HomeSide's business was to receive fees for servicing mortgages (essentially the administrative tasks associated with collecting mortgage payments). The rights to receive those fees, so-called mortgage-servicing rights, can provide a valuable income stream. How valuable each of the rights is depends, in part, on the likelihood that the mortgage to which it applies will be fully

48. S. REP. No. 102-249, at 3 (1991) (Conf. Rep.).

repaid before it is due, terminating the need for servicing. HomeSide calculated the present value of its mortgage-servicing rights by using valuation models designed to take this likelihood into account. It recorded the value of its assets, and the numbers appeared in National's financial statements.

From 1998 until 2001, National's annual reports and other public documents touted the success of HomeSide's business, and respondents Frank Cicutto (National's managing director and chief executive officer), Kevin Race (HomeSide's chief operating officer), and Hugh Harris (HomeSide's chief executive officer) did the same in public statements. But on July 5, 2001, National announced that it was writing down the value of HomeSide's assets by $450 million; and then again on September 3, by another $1.75 billion. The prices of both Ordinary Shares and ADRs slumped. After downplaying the July write-down, National explained the September write-down as the result of a failure to anticipate the lowering of prevailing interest rates (lower interest rates lead to more refinancings, i.e., more early repayments of mortgages), other mistaken assumptions in the financial models, and the loss of goodwill. According to the complaint, however, HomeSide, Race, Harris, and another HomeSide senior executive who is also a respondent here had manipulated HomeSide's financial models to make the rates of early repayment unrealistically low in order to cause the mortgage-servicing rights to appear more valuable than they really were. The complaint also alleges that National and Cicutto were aware of this deception by July 2000, but did nothing about it.

As relevant here, petitioners Russell Leslie Owen and Brian and Geraldine Silverlock, all Australians, purchased National's Ordinary Shares in 2000 and 2001, before the write-downs.[49] They sued National, HomeSide, Cicutto, and the three HomeSide executives in the United States District Court for the Southern District of New York for alleged violations of §§ 10(b) and 20(a) of the Securities and Exchange Act of 1934, 48 Stat. 891, 15 U.S.C. §§ 78j(b) and 78t(a), and SEC Rule 10b-5, 17 CFR § 240.10b-5 (2009), promulgated pursuant to § 10(b). They sought to represent a class of foreign purchasers of National's Ordinary Shares during a specified period up to the September write-down.

Respondents moved to dismiss for lack of subject-matter jurisdiction under Federal Rule of Civil Procedure 12(b)(1) and for failure to state a claim under Rule 12(b)(6). The District Court granted the motion on the former ground, finding no jurisdiction because the acts in this country were, "at most, a link in the chain of an alleged overall securities fraud scheme that culminated abroad." The Court of Appeals for the Second Circuit affirmed on similar grounds. The acts performed in the United States did not "compris[e] the heart of the alleged fraud." We granted certiorari.

---

49. [1] Robert Morrison, an American investor in National's ADRs, also brought suit, but his claims were dismissed by the district court because he failed to allege damages. Petitioners did not appeal that decision and it is not before us. Inexplicably, Morrison continued to be listed as a petitioner in the court of appeals and here.

II

Before addressing the question presented, we must correct a threshold error in the Second Circuit's analysis. It considered the extraterritorial reach of § 10(b) to raise a question of subject-matter jurisdiction, wherefore it affirmed the District Court's dismissal under Rule 12(b)(1). In this regard it was following Circuit precedent. The Second Circuit is hardly alone in taking this position.

But to ask what conduct § 10(b) reaches is to ask what conduct § 10(b) prohibits, which is a merits question. Subject-matter jurisdiction, by contrast, "refers to a tribunal's power to hear a case." It presents an issue quite separate from the question whether the allegations the plaintiff makes entitle him to relief. The District Court here had jurisdiction under 15 U.S.C. § 78aa to adjudicate the question whether § 10(b) applies to National's conduct.

[W]e proceed to address whether petitioners' allegations state a claim.

III

A

It is a "longstanding principle of American law that legislation of Congress, unless a contrary intent appears, is meant to apply only within the territorial jurisdiction of the United States." *EEOC v. Arabian American Oil Co.*, 499 U. S. 244, 248 (1991) (*Aramco*). This principle represents a canon of construction, or a presumption about a statute's meaning, rather than a limit upon Congress's power to legislate. It rests on the perception that Congress ordinarily legislates with respect to domestic, not foreign matters. Thus, "unless there is the affirmative intention of the Congress clearly expressed" to give a statute extraterritorial effect, "we must presume it is primarily concerned with domestic conditions." *Aramco*, *supra*, at 248. The canon or presumption applies regardless of whether there is a risk of conflict between the American statute and a foreign law. When a statute gives no clear indication of an extraterritorial application, it has none.

Despite this principle of interpretation, long and often recited in our opinions, the Second Circuit believed that, because the Exchange Act is silent as to the extraterritorial application of § 10(b), it was left to the court to "discern" whether Congress would have wanted the statute to apply. This disregard of the presumption against extraterritoriality did not originate with the Court of Appeals panel in this case. It has been repeated over many decades by various courts of appeals in determining the application of the Exchange Act, and § 10(b) in particular, to fraudulent schemes that involve conduct and effects abroad. That has produced a collection of tests for divining what Congress would have wanted, complex in formulation and unpredictable in application.

The Second Circuit had thus established that application of § 10(b) could be premised upon either some effect on American securities markets or investors or significant conduct in the United States. It later formalized these two applications into (1) an "effects test," "whether the wrongful conduct had a substantial effect in the

United States or upon United States citizens," and (2) a "conduct test," "whether the wrongful conduct occurred in the United States." *SEC v. Berger*, 322 F.3d 187, 192–193 (CA2 2003). These became the north star of the Second Circuit's § 10(b) jurisprudence, pointing the way to what Congress would have wished. Indeed, the Second Circuit declined to keep its two tests distinct on the ground that "an admixture or combination of the two often gives a better picture of whether there is sufficient United States involvement to justify the exercise of jurisdiction by an American court." *Itoba Ltd. v. Lep Group PLC*, 54 F.3d 118, 122 (1995). The Second Circuit never put forward a textual or even extra-textual basis for these tests. [I]t confessed that "if we were asked to point to language in the statutes, or even in the legislative history, that compelled these conclusions, we would be unable to respond."

As they developed, these tests were not easy to administer. The conduct test was held to apply differently depending on whether the harmed investors were Americans or foreigners: When the alleged damages consisted of losses to American investors abroad, it was enough that acts "of material importance" performed in the United States "significantly contributed" to that result; whereas those acts must have "directly caused" the result when losses to foreigners abroad were at issue. And "merely preparatory activities in the United States" did not suffice "to trigger application of the securities laws for injury to foreigners located abroad." This required the court to distinguish between mere preparation and using the United States as a "base" for fraudulent activities in other countries. But merely satisfying the conduct test was sometimes insufficient without "some additional factor tipping the scales" in favor of the application of American law.

The results of judicial-speculation-made-law—divining what Congress would have wanted if it had thought of the situation before the court—demonstrate the wisdom of the presumption against extraterritoriality. Rather than guess anew in each case, we apply the presumption in all cases, preserving a stable background against which Congress can legislate with predictable effects.

B

Rule 10b-5, the regulation under which petitioners have brought suit, [fn6] was promulgated under § 10(b), and "does not extend beyond conduct encompassed by § 10(b)'s prohibition." Therefore, if § 10(b) is not extraterritorial, neither is Rule 10b-5.

On its face, § 10(b) contains nothing to suggest it applies abroad:

> "It shall be unlawful for any person, directly or indirectly, by the use of any means or instrumentality of interstate commerce or of the mails, or of any facility of any national securities exchange . . . [t]o use or employ, in connection with the purchase or sale of any security registered on a national securities exchange or any security not so registered, . . . any manipulative or deceptive device or contrivance in contravention of such rules and regulations as the [Securities and Exchange] Commission may prescribe. . . ."
> 15 U.S.C. 78j(b).

Petitioners and the Solicitor General contend, however, that three things indicate that § 10(b) or the Exchange Act in general has at least some extraterritorial application.

First, they point to the definition of "interstate commerce," a term used in § 10(b), which includes "trade, commerce, transportation, or communication . . . between any foreign country and any State." 15 U.S.C. § 78c(a)(17). [10] But "we have repeatedly held that even statutes that contain broad language in their definitions of 'commerce' that expressly refer to 'foreign commerce' do not apply abroad." *Aramco*, 499 U. S., at 251. The general reference to foreign commerce in the definition of "interstate commerce" does not defeat the presumption against extraterritoriality.

Petitioners and the Solicitor General next point out that Congress, in describing the purposes of the Exchange Act, observed that the "prices established and offered in such transactions are generally disseminated and quoted throughout the United States and foreign countries." 15 U.S.C. §78b(2). The antecedent of "such transactions," however, is found in the first sentence of the section, which declares that "transactions in securities as commonly conducted upon securities exchanges and over-the-counter markets are affected with a national public interest." § 78b. Nothing suggests that this national public interest pertains to transactions conducted upon foreign exchanges and markets. The fleeting reference to the dissemination and quotation abroad of the prices of securities traded in domestic exchanges and markets cannot overcome the presumption against extraterritoriality.

Finally, there is § 30(b) of the Exchange Act, 15 U.S.C. § 78dd(b), which does mention the Act's extraterritorial application: "The provisions of [the Exchange Act] or of any rule or regulation thereunder shall not apply to any person insofar as he transacts a business in securities without the jurisdiction of the United States," unless he does so in violation of regulations promulgated by the Securities and Exchange Commission "to prevent . . . evasion of [the Act]." (The parties have pointed us to no regulation promulgated pursuant to § 30(b).) The Solicitor General argues that "[this] exemption would have no function if the Act did not apply in the first instance to securities transactions that occur abroad."

We are not convinced. In the first place, it would be odd for Congress to indicate the extraterritorial application of the whole Exchange Act by means of a provision imposing a condition precedent to its application abroad. And if the whole Act applied abroad, why would the Commission's enabling regulations be limited to those preventing "evasion" of the Act, rather than all those preventing "violation"? The provision seems to us directed at actions abroad that might conceal a domestic violation, or might cause what would otherwise be a domestic violation to escape on a technicality. At most, the Solicitor General's proposed inference is possible; but possible interpretations of statutory language do not override the presumption against extraterritoriality. *See Aramco*, *supra*, at 253.

The Solicitor General also fails to account for § 30(a), which reads in relevant part as follows:

> "It shall be unlawful for any broker or dealer . . . to make use of the mails or of any means or instrumentality of interstate commerce for the purpose of effecting on an exchange not within or subject to the jurisdiction of the United States, any transaction in any security the issuer of which is a resident of, or is organized under the laws of, or has its principal place of business in, a place within or subject to the jurisdiction of the United States, in contravention of such rules and regulations as the Commission may prescribe. . . ." 15 U.S.C. § 78dd(a).

Subsection 30(a) contains what § 10(b) lacks: a clear statement of extraterritorial effect. Its explicit provision for a specific extraterritorial application would be quite superfluous if the rest of the Exchange Act already applied to transactions on foreign exchanges—and its limitation of that application to securities of domestic issuers would be inoperative. Even if that were not true, when a statute provides for some extraterritorial application, the presumption against extraterritoriality operates to limit that provision to its terms. No one claims that § 30(a) applies here.

The concurrence claims we have impermissibly narrowed the inquiry in evaluating whether a statute applies abroad, citing for that point the dissent in *Aramco*. But we do not say, as the concurrence seems to think, that the presumption against extraterritoriality is a "clear statement rule," if by that is meant a requirement that a statute say "this law applies abroad." Assuredly context can be consulted as well. But whatever sources of statutory meaning one consults to give "the most faithful reading" of the text, there is no clear indication of extraterritoriality here. The concurrence does not even try to refute that conclusion, but merely puts forward the same (at best) uncertain indications relied upon by petitioners and the Solicitor General. As the opinion for the Court in *Aramco* (which we prefer to the dissent) shows, those uncertain indications do not suffice.

In short, there is no affirmative indication in the Exchange Act that § 10(b) applies extraterritorially, and we therefore conclude that it does not.

IV

A

Petitioners argue that the conclusion that § 10(b) does not apply extraterritorially does not resolve this case. They contend that they seek no more than domestic application anyway, since Florida is where HomeSide and its senior executives engaged in the deceptive conduct of manipulating HomeSide's financial models; their complaint also alleged that Race and Hughes made misleading public statements there. This is less an answer to the presumption against extraterritorial application than it is an assertion—a quite valid assertion—that that presumption here (as often) is not self-evidently dispositive, but its application requires further analysis. For it is a rare case of prohibited extraterritorial application that lacks all contact with the territory of the United States. But the presumption against extraterritorial application would be a craven watchdog indeed if it retreated to its kennel whenever some domestic activity is involved in the case. The concurrence seems to imagine just such a timid sentinel, but our cases are to the contrary. In *Aramco*, for example, the Title VII plaintiff had been hired in Houston, and was an American citizen. The Court concluded, however, that neither that territorial event nor that relationship was the "focus" of congressional concern, but rather domestic employment.

Applying the same mode of analysis here, we think that the focus of the Exchange Act is not upon the place where the deception originated, but upon purchases and sales of securities in the United States. Section 10(b) does not punish deceptive conduct, but only deceptive conduct "in connection with the purchase or sale of any security registered on a national securities exchange or any security not so registered." 15 U.S.C. §78j(b). Those purchase-and-sale transactions are the objects of the statute's solicitude. It is those transactions that the statute seeks to "regulate;" it is parties or prospective parties to those transactions that the statute seeks to "protect." And it is in our view only transactions in securities listed on domestic exchanges, and domestic transactions in other securities, to which § 10(b) applies.

The primacy of the domestic exchange is suggested by the very prologue of the Exchange Act, which sets forth as its object "[t]o provide for the regulation of securities exchanges . . . operating in interstate and foreign commerce and through the mails, to prevent inequitable and unfair practices on such exchanges. . . ." 48 Stat. 881. We know of no one who thought that the Act was intended to "regulat[e]" foreign securities exchanges—or indeed who even believed that under established principles of international law Congress had the power to do so. The Act's registration requirements apply only to securities listed on national securities exchanges. 15 U.S.C. §78l(a).

With regard to securities not registered on domestic exchanges, the exclusive focus on domestic purchases and sales is strongly confirmed by §30(a) and (b), discussed earlier. The former extends the normal scope of the Exchange Act's prohibitions to acts effecting, in violation of rules prescribed by the Commission, a "transaction" in a United States security "on an exchange not within or subject to the jurisdiction of the United States." §78dd(a). And the latter specifies that the Act does not apply to "any person insofar as he transacts a business in securities without the jurisdiction of the United States," unless he does so in violation of regulations promulgated by the Commission "to prevent evasion [of the Act]." §78dd(b). Under both provisions it is the foreign location of the transaction that establishes (or reflects the presumption of) the Act's inapplicability, absent regulations by the Commission.

The same focus on domestic transactions is evident in the Securities Act of 1933, 48 Stat. 74, enacted by the same Congress as the Exchange Act, and forming part of the same comprehensive regulation of securities trading. See *Central Bank of Denver, N.A. v. First Interstate Bank of Denver, N.A.*, 511 U. S. 164, 170–171 (1994). That legislation makes it unlawful to sell a security, through a prospectus or otherwise, making use of "any means or instruments of transportation or communication in interstate commerce or of the mails," unless a registration statement is in effect.

15 U.S.C. § 77e(a)(1). The Commission has interpreted that requirement "not to include . . . sales that occur outside the United States." 17 CFR § 230.901 (2009).

Finally, we reject the notion that the Exchange Act reaches conduct in this country affecting exchanges or transactions abroad for the same reason that *Aramco* rejected overseas application of Title VII to all domestically concluded employment contracts or all employment contracts with American employers: The probability of incompatibility with the applicable laws of other countries is so obvious that if Congress intended such foreign application "it would have addressed the subject of conflicts with foreign laws and procedures." Like the United States, foreign countries regulate their domestic securities exchanges and securities transactions occurring within their territorial jurisdiction. And the regulation of other countries often differs from ours as to what constitutes fraud, what disclosures must be made, what damages are recoverable, what discovery is available in litigation, what individual actions may be joined in a single suit, what attorney's fees are recoverable, and many other matters. See, *e.g.*, Brief for United Kingdom of Great Britain and Northern Ireland as Amicus Curiae 16–21. The Commonwealth of Australia, the United Kingdom of Great Britain and Northern Ireland, and the Republic of France have filed amicus briefs in this case. So have (separately or jointly) such international and foreign organizations as the International Chamber of Commerce, the Swiss Bankers Association, the Federation of German Industries, the French Business Confederation, the Institute of International Bankers, the European Banking Federation, the Australian Bankers' Association, and the Association Française des Entreprises Privées. They all complain of the interference with foreign securities regulation that application of § 10(b) abroad would produce, and urge the adoption of a clear test that will avoid that consequence. The transactional test we have adopted—whether the purchase or sale is made in the United States, or involves a security listed on a domestic exchange—meets that requirement.

B

The Solicitor General suggests a different test, which petitioners also endorse: "[A] transnational securities fraud violates [§]10(b) when the fraud involves significant conduct in the United States that is material to the fraud's success." Neither the Solicitor General nor petitioners provide any textual support for this test. The Solicitor General sets forth a number of purposes such a test would serve: achieving a high standard of business ethics in the securities industry, ensuring honest securities markets and thereby promoting investor confidence, and preventing the United States from becoming a "Barbary Coast" for malefactors perpetrating frauds in foreign markets. But it provides no textual support for the last of these purposes, or for the first two as applied to the foreign securities industry and securities markets abroad. It is our function to give the statute the effect its language suggests, however modest that may be; not to extend it to admirable purposes it might be used to achieve.

If, moreover, one is to be attracted by the desirable consequences of the "significant and material conduct" test, one should also be repulsed by its adverse consequences. While there is no reason to believe that the United States has become the Barbary Coast for those perpetrating frauds on foreign securities markets, some fear that it has become the Shangri-La of class-action litigation for lawyers representing those allegedly cheated in foreign securities markets. See Buxbaum, Multinational Class Actions Under Federal Securities Law: Managing Jurisdictional Conflict, 46 Colum. J. Transnat'l L. 14, 38–41 (2007).

As case support for the "significant and material conduct" test, the Solicitor General relies primarily on *Pasquantino v. United States*, 544 U.S. 349 (2005). In that case we concluded that the wire-fraud statute, 18 U.S.C. § 1343 (2009 ed., Supp. II), was violated by defendants who ordered liquor over the phone from a store in Maryland with the intent to smuggle it into Canada and deprive the Canadian Government of revenue. Section 1343 prohibits "any scheme or artifice to defraud"—fraud simpliciter, without any requirement that it be "in connection with" any particular transaction or event. The *Pasquantino* Court said that the petitioners' "offense was complete the moment they executed the scheme inside the United States," and that it was "[t]his domestic element of petitioners' conduct [that] the Government is punishing." 544 U.S., at 371. Section 10(b), by contrast, punishes not all acts of deception, but only such acts "in connection with the purchase or sale of any security registered on a national securities exchange or any security not so registered." Not deception alone, but deception with respect to certain purchases or sales is necessary for a violation of the statute.

The Solicitor General points out that the "significant and material conduct" test is in accord with prevailing notions of international comity. If so, that proves that if the United States asserted prescriptive jurisdiction pursuant to the "significant and material conduct" test it would not violate customary international law; but it in no way tends to prove that that is what Congress has done.

Finally, the Solicitor General argues that the Commission has adopted an interpretation similar to the "significant and material conduct" test, and that we should defer to that. In the two adjudications the Solicitor General cites, however, the Commission did not purport to be providing its own interpretation of the statute, but relied on decisions of federal courts—mainly Court of Appeals decisions . . . that we discussed earlier. We need "accept only those agency interpretations that are reasonable in light of the principles of construction courts normally employ." *Aramco*, 499 U.S., at 260 (SCALIA, J., concurring in part and concurring in judgment). Since the Commission's interpretations relied on cases we disapprove, which ignored or discarded the presumption against extraterritoriality, we owe them no deference.

Section 10(b) reaches the use of a manipulative or deceptive device or contrivance only in connection with the purchase or sale of a security listed on an American stock exchange, and the purchase or sale of any other security in the United States. This case involves no securities listed on a domestic exchange, and all aspects of the purchases complained of by those petitioners who still have live claims occurred outside the United States. Petitioners have therefore failed to state a claim on which relief can be granted. We affirm the dismissal of petitioners' complaint on this ground.

It is so ordered.

JUSTICE BREYER, concurring in part and concurring in the judgment.

Section 10(b) of the Securities Exchange Act of 1934 applies to fraud "in connection with" two categories of transactions: (1) "the purchase or sale of any security registered on a national securities exchange" or (2) "the purchase or sale of . . . any security not so registered." 15 U.S.C. § 78j(b). In this case, the purchased securities are listed only on a few foreign exchanges, none of which has registered with the Securities and Exchange Commission as a "national securities exchange." See § 78f. The first category therefore does not apply. Further, the relevant purchases of these unregistered securities took place entirely in Australia and involved only Australian investors. And in accordance with the presumption against extraterritoriality, I do not read the second category to include such transactions. Thus, while state law or other federal fraud statutes, see, *e.g.*, 18 U.S.C. § 1341 (mail fraud), § 1343 (wire fraud), may apply to the fraudulent activity alleged here to have occurred in the United States, I believe that § 10(b) does not. This case does not require us to consider other circumstances.

To the extent the Court's opinion is consistent with these views, I join it.

- JUSTICE STEVENS, with whom JUSTICE GINSBURG joins, concurring in the judgment.

While I agree that petitioners have failed to state a claim on which relief can be granted, my reasoning differs from the Court's. I would adhere to the general approach that has been the law in the Second Circuit, and most of the rest of the country, for nearly four decades.

I

Today the Court announces a new "transactional test" for defining the reach of § 10(b) of the Securities Exchange Act of 1934 (Exchange Act), 15 U.S.C. § 78j(b), and SEC Rule 10b-5: Henceforth, those provisions will extend only to "transactions in securities listed on domestic exchanges . . . and domestic transactions in other securities." If one confines one's gaze to the statutory text, the Court's conclusion is a plausible one. But the federal courts have been construing § 10(b) in a different manner for a long time, and the Court's textual analysis is not nearly so compelling, in my view, as to warrant the abandonment of their doctrine.

The text and history of § 10(b) are famously opaque on the question of when, exactly, transnational securities frauds fall within the statute's compass. As those types of frauds became more common in the latter half of the 20th century, the federal courts were increasingly called upon to wrestle with that question. The Court of Appeals for the Second Circuit, located in the Nation's financial center, led the effort. [Justice Stevens then described the history and operation of the conduct and effects tests, explained in the majority opinion.]

The Second Circuit's test became the "north star" of § 10(b) jurisprudence, not just regionally but nationally as well. . . . Neither Congress nor the Securities Exchange Commission (Commission) acted to change the law. To the contrary, the Commission largely adopted the Second Circuit's position in its own adjudications.

In light of this history, the Court's critique of the decision below for applying "judge-made rules" is quite misplaced. This entire area of law is replete with judge-made rules, which give concrete meaning to Congress' general commands. "When we deal with private actions under Rule 10b-5," then-Justice Rehnquist wrote many years ago, "we deal with a judicial oak which has grown from little more than a legislative acorn." *Blue Chip Stamps v. Manor Drug Stores*, 421 U.S. 723, 737 (1975). The "Mother Court" of securities law tended to that oak. *Id.*, at 762 (Blackmun, J., dissenting) (describing the Second Circuit). One of our greatest jurists—the judge who, "without a doubt, did more to shape the law of securities regulation than any [other] in the country"—was its master arborist.

The development of § 10(b) law was hardly an instance of judicial usurpation. Congress invited an expansive role for judicial elaboration when it crafted such an open-ended statute in 1934. And both Congress and the Commission subsequently affirmed that role when they left intact the relevant statutory and regulatory language, respectively, throughout all the years that followed.

[W]e have unanimously endorsed the Second Circuit's basic interpretive approach to § 10(b)—ridiculed by the Court today—of striving to "divin[e] what Congress would have wanted." "Our task," we have said, is "to attempt to infer how the 1934 Congress would have addressed the issue."

Thus, while the Court devotes a considerable amount of attention to the development of the case law, it draws the wrong conclusions. The Second Circuit refined its test over several decades and dozens of cases, with the tacit approval of Congress and the Commission and with the general assent of its sister Circuits. That history is a reason we should give additional weight to the Second Circuit's "judge-made" doctrine, not a reason to denigrate it. "The longstanding acceptance by the courts, coupled with Congress' failure to reject [its] reasonable interpretation of the wording of § 10(b), . . . argues significantly in favor of acceptance of the [Second Circuit] rule by this Court." *Blue Chip*, 421 U.S., at 733.

II

The Court's other main critique of the Second Circuit's approach—apart from what the Court views as its excessive reliance on functional considerations and reconstructed congressional intent—is that the Second Circuit has "disregard[ed]" the presumption against extraterritoriality. It is the Court, however, that misapplies the presumption, in two main respects.

First, the Court seeks to transform the presumption from a flexible rule of thumb into something more like a clear statement rule. We have been here before. In the case on which the Court primarily relies, *Aramco*, CHIEF JUSTICE REHNQUIST's majority opinion included a sentence that appeared to make the same move.

Yet even *Aramco*—surely the most extreme application of the presumption against extraterritoriality in my time on the Court—contained numerous passages suggesting that the presumption may be overcome without a clear directive. And our cases both before and after *Aramco* make perfectly clear that the Court continues to give effect to "all available evidence about the meaning" of a provision when considering its extraterritorial application, lest we defy Congress' will. Contrary to JUSTICE SCALIA's personal view of statutory interpretation, that evidence legitimately encompasses more than the enacted text. Hence, while the Court's dictum that "[w]hen a statute gives no clear indication of an extraterritorial application, it has none," makes for a nice catchphrase, the point is overstated. The presumption against extraterritoriality can be useful as a theory of congressional purpose, a tool for managing international conflict, a background norm, a tie-breaker. It does not relieve courts of their duty to give statutes the most faithful reading possible.

Second, and more fundamentally, the Court errs in suggesting that the presumption against extraterritoriality is fatal to the Second Circuit's test. For even if the presumption really were a clear statement (or "clear indication") rule, it would have only marginal relevance to this case.

It is true, of course, that "this Court ordinarily construes ambiguous statutes to avoid unreasonable interference with the sovereign authority of other nations," and that, absent contrary evidence, we presume "Congress is primarily concerned with domestic conditions." Accordingly, the presumption against extraterritoriality "provides a sound basis for concluding that Section 10(b) does not apply when a securities fraud with no effects in the United States is hatched and executed entirely outside this country." But that is just about all it provides a sound basis for concluding. And the conclusion is not very illuminating, because no party to the litigation disputes it. No one contends that § 10(b) applies to wholly foreign frauds.

Rather, the real question in this case is how much, and what kinds of, domestic contacts are sufficient to trigger application of § 10(b). In developing its conduct-and-effects test, the Second Circuit endeavored to derive a solution from the Exchange Act's text, structure, history, and purpose. Judge Friendly and his colleagues were well aware that United States courts "cannot and should not expend [their] resources resolving cases that do not affect Americans or involve fraud emanating from America."

The question just stated does not admit of an easy answer. The text of the Exchange Act indicates that § 10(b) extends to at least some activities with an international component, but, again, it is not pellucid as to which ones. The Second Circuit draws the line as follows: § 10(b) extends to transnational frauds "only when substantial acts in furtherance of the fraud were committed within the United States" or when the fraud was "intended to produce" and did produce "detrimental effects within" the United States. This approach is consistent with the understanding shared by most scholars that Congress, in passing the Exchange Act, "expected U. S. securities laws to apply to certain international transactions or conduct." Buxbaum, Multinational Class Actions Under Federal Securities Law: Managing Jurisdictional Conflict, 46 Colum. J. Transnat'l L. 14, 19 (2007). It is also consistent with the traditional understanding, regnant in the 1930's as it is now, that the presumption against extraterritoriality does not apply "when the conduct [at issue] occurs within the United States," and has lesser force when "the failure to extend the scope of the statute to a foreign setting will result in adverse effects within the United States." And it strikes a reasonable balance between the goals of "preventing the export of fraud from America," protecting shareholders, enhancing investor confidence, and deterring corporate misconduct, on the one hand, and conserving United States resources and limiting conflict with foreign law, on the other.

Thus, while § 10(b) may not give any "clear indication" on its face as to how it should apply to transnational securities frauds, it does give strong clues that it should cover at least some of them. And in my view, the Second Circuit has done the best job of discerning what sorts of transnational frauds Congress meant in 1934—and still means today—to regulate. I do not take issue with the Court for beginning its inquiry with the statutory text, rather than the doctrine in the Courts of Appeals. I take issue with the Court for beginning and ending its inquiry with the statutory text, when the text does not speak with geographic precision, and for dismissing the long pedigree of, and the persuasive account of congressional intent embodied in, the Second Circuit's rule.

Repudiating the Second Circuit's approach in its entirety, the Court establishes a novel rule that will foreclose private parties from bringing § 10(b) actions whenever the relevant securities were purchased or sold abroad and are not listed on a domestic exchange. The real motor of the Court's opinion, it seems, is not the presumption against extraterritoriality but rather the Court's belief that transactions on domestic exchanges are "the focus of the Exchange Act" and "the objects of [its] solicitude." In reality, however, it is the "public interest" and "the interests of investors" that are the objects of the statute's solicitude. And while the clarity and simplicity of the Court's test may have some salutary consequences, like all bright-line rules it also has drawbacks.

Imagine, for example, an American investor who buys shares in a company listed only on an overseas exchange. That company has a major American subsidiary with executives based in New York City; and it was in New York City that the executives masterminded and implemented a massive deception which artificially inflated the stock price—and which will, upon its disclosure, cause the price to plummet. Or, imagine that those same executives go knocking on doors in Manhattan and convince an unsophisticated retiree, on the basis of material misrepresentations, to invest her life savings in the company's doomed securities. Both of these investors would, under the Court's new test, be barred from seeking relief under § 10(b).

The oddity of that result should give pause. For in walling off such individuals from §10(b), the Court narrows the provision's reach to a degree that would surprise and alarm generations of American investors—and, I am convinced, the Congress that passed the Exchange Act. Indeed, the Court's rule turns § 10(b) jurisprudence (and the presumption against extraterritoriality) on its head, by withdrawing the statute's application from cases in which there is both substantial wrongful conduct that occurred in the United States and a substantial injurious effect on United States markets and citizens.

III

In my judgment, if petitioners' allegations of fraudulent misconduct that took place in Florida are true, then respondents may have violated § 10(b), and could potentially be held accountable in an enforcement proceeding brought by the Commission. But it does not follow that shareholders who have failed to allege that the bulk or the heart of the fraud occurred in the United States, or that the fraud had an adverse impact on American investors or markets, may maintain a private action to recover damages they suffered abroad. Some cases involving foreign securities transactions have extensive links to, and ramifications for, this country; this case has Australia written all over it. Accordingly, for essentially the reasons stated in the Court of Appeals' opinion, I would affirm its judgment.

The Court instead elects to upend a significant area of securities law based on a plausible, but hardly decisive, construction of the statutory text. In so doing, it pays short shrift to the United States' interest in remedying frauds that transpire on American soil or harm American citizens, as well as to the accumulated wisdom and experience of the lower courts. I happen to agree with the result the Court reaches in this case. But "I respectfully dissent," once again, "from the Court's continuing campaign to render the private cause of action under § 10(b) toothless." *Stoneridge*, 552 U.S., at 175 (STEVENS, J., dissenting).

Notes and Questions

1. What exactly is the "presumption against territoriality" described in *Aramco* and *Morrison*? What purpose does it serve? How, according to the Court, can it be overcome?

2. As noted in the Court's footnote 1 (reprinted as note 49, *supra*), the lone United States investor dropped out of the case relatively early in the proceedings and did not appeal. Only Australian investors remained in the case. Why do you think the Australian investors brought suit in the United States? Could the majority's decision be motivated in part by international forum shopping concerns? If so, why would the Court's rule exclude American plaintiffs who bought their shares nominally "abroad," for example, on an online exchange?

3. After the Court's lengthy discussion of the presumption against territoriality, the Court engages in a much shorter discussion of the purpose of the Exchange Act. After all, not every relevant action occurred abroad; while both parties were from Australia and the transaction took place in Australia, the allegedly fraudulent bookkeeping occurred in the United States. The majority determined that "Section 10(b) does not punish deceptive conduct, but only deceptive conduct 'in connection with the purchase or sale of any security....' Those purchase-and-sale transactions [occurring in the United States] are the objects of the statute's solicitude."[50] Justice Stevens, in concurrence, argued that "it is the 'public interest' and 'the interests of [American] investors' that are the objects of the statute's solicitude," regardless of where the transaction occurs.[51] Which opinion has the better argument?

4. What role (if any) should the advance in technology have played in the Court's decision? The vast majority of securities transactions originating all over the world occur online, accessible from one's couch. Are territorial lines really the best way to deal with these types of commercial transactions? What problems might one have in localizing these transactions? It is easy enough where a transaction is on NYSE or the Australian Stock Exchange Limited, but what about secondary transactions? Does the Court's rule allow foreign companies to structure transactions to unfairly circumvent § 10(b) liability?

5. In the end, all eight participating Justices agreed that the plaintiffs failed to state a claim because, as Justice Stevens observed, "this case has Australia written all over it."[52] Does this make it an easy case? If (as the axiom goes) hard cases make bad law, does it follow that an easy case makes good law?

6. Notice that *both* the majority and principal concurrence cite to Professor Hannah Buxbaum's article, *Multinational Class Actions Under Federal Securities Law.*[53] In the portion to which the majority cited, Professor Buxbaum explains that there was evidence of a rising tide of "foreign cubed" plaintiffs (foreign plaintiffs purchasing foreign securities on foreign exchanges) in securities cases. In the portion to which the concurrence cited, Professor Buxbaum identifies evidence demonstrating that Congress intended the securities laws to have at least some extraterritorial application. Professor Buxbaum ultimately endorses a "transaction-based approach" grounded in subject-matter jurisdiction limits (for example, to allow only for claims based on transactions on U.S. markets) to "add clarity to jurisdictional analysis and ameliorate regulatory conflict with other nations."[54] But Professor Buxbaum adds that this would be

50. *Morrison*, 561 U.S. at 266.

51. *Id.* at 284 (Stevens, J., concurring).

52. *Id.* at 286.

53. Hannah L. Buxbaum, *Multinational Class Actions Under Federal Securities Law: Managing Jurisdictional Conflict*, 46 Colum. J. Transnat'l L. 14 (2007).

54. *Id.* at 69.

> nevertheless a second-best solution. It fails to address the central dynamic of cross-border securities fraud, which multinational class actions present with such particular clarity: the more integrated the securities markets, the more likely it is that wrongdoers can take advantage of that integration in order to reap financial benefit—and the less feasible it is to achieve effective regulation . . . . A better solution, however, will not be achieved through the unilateral application by domestic courts of national regulatory law. It must wait on . . . the increased opportunity for coordination among affected states.[55]

7. Emmanuel Gaillard, author of the French government's amicus brief in *Morrison*, warns that foreign litigants might try to dodge *Morrison* by instead trying to bring a suit in the United States, but based on foreign law.[56] He argues that it is the procedural advantages for plaintiffs—jury civil trials, large damage rewards—that litigants seek, rather than the benefit of substantive U.S. securities law. Gaillard further argues that the only way to prevent this litigation, while also effectively prosecuting securities fraud, is to forge a global convention on the subject.

8. Justice Scalia relied heavily on foreign governments' *amicus* briefs (which argued that extending U.S. jurisdiction would impinge on their own regulatory systems) in his opinion. This, Daniel Schimmel writes, shows "that *amicus* briefs, including briefs of international and European organizations, have an impact on the courts' substantive decision-making process and the issues considered by the court, especially where the *amicus* provides unique information or a different perspective on the specific issues pending before the court."[57]

Is this a form of transnational decision making? Why might adversarial proceedings bring out briefs from international sovereigns, but these same sovereigns cannot make any serious headway toward a treaty?

9. Congress ultimately amended the securities laws in the Dodd-Frank Wall Street Reform and Consumer Protection Act of 2010 to allow for extraterritorial SEC enforcement actions (but not private actions) based upon the "conduct and effects" tests rejected in *Morrison*.

B. Antitrust law

The global reach of U.S. antitrust law is litigated in the next case. U.S. law is attractive to litigants for many reasons, not the least of which is that the Sherman Antitrust Act provides for treble damages as a remedy—far more coercive than legal regimes in other countries' courts, including European courts. Moreover, plaintiffs in U.S. antitrust litigation are not responsible for court costs generally (as they are in Europe,

---

55. *Id.* at 69–70.

56. Emmanuel Gaillard, *After Morrison: The Case for a New Hague Convention on the Law Applicable to Securities Frauds*, 5 Disp. Resol. Int'l 35, 41–43 (2011).

57. Daniel Schimmel, *The Influence of Amicus Briefs and Morrison*, Conflict of Laws.net (July 5, 2010), http://conflictoflaws.net/2010/the-influence-of-amicus-briefs-and-morrison/.

for example). The anticipation of remedies such as those offered by U.S. anti-trust law may be a particular deterrent for cartels with global operations, as damages compound quickly in such circumstances. But in the following case, the Court goes in a different direction, away from the extraterritorial application of U.S. anti-trust law. As you read, track the arguments as to why this is the case, and what it tells us about the role the Court sees for itself in relation to regulating transnational cartels.

Hoffman-La Roche Ltd. v. Empagran S.A.

542 U.S. 155 (2004)

Justice Breyer delivered the opinion of the Court.

The Foreign Trade Antitrust Improvements Act of 1982 (FTAIA) excludes from the Sherman Act's reach much anticompetitive conduct that causes only foreign injury. It does so by setting forth a general rule stating that the Sherman Act "shall not apply to conduct involving trade or commerce . . . with foreign nations." 15 U.S.C. § 6a. It then creates exceptions to the general rule, applicable where (roughly speaking) that conduct significantly harms imports, domestic commerce, or American exporters.

We here focus upon anticompetitive price-fixing activity that is in significant part foreign, that causes some domestic antitrust injury, and that independently causes separate foreign injury. We ask two questions about the price fixing conduct and the foreign injury that it causes. First, does that conduct fall within the FTAIA's general rule excluding the Sherman Act's application? That is to say, does the price-fixing activity constitute "conduct involving trade or commerce . . . with foreign nations"? We conclude that it does.

Second, we ask whether the conduct nonetheless falls within a domestic-injury exception to the general rule, an exception that applies (and makes the Sherman Act nonetheless applicable) where the conduct (1) has a "direct, substantial, and reasonably foreseeable effect" on domestic commerce, and (2) "such effect gives rise to a [Sherman Act] claim." §§ 6a(1)(A), (2). We conclude that the exception does not apply where the plaintiff's claim rests solely on the independent foreign harm.

To clarify: The issue before us concerns (1) significant foreign anticompetitive conduct with (2) an adverse domestic effect and (3) an independent foreign effect giving rise to the claim. In more concrete terms, this case involves vitamin sellers around the world that agreed to fix prices, leading to higher vitamin prices in the United States and independently leading to higher vitamin prices in other countries such as Ecuador. We conclude that, in this scenario, a purchaser in the United States could bring a Sherman Act claim under the FTAIA based on domestic injury, but a purchaser in Ecuador could not bring a Sherman Act claim based on foreign harm.

I

The plaintiffs in this case originally filed a class-action suit on behalf of foreign and domestic purchasers of vitamins under, *inter alia*, § 1 of the Sherman Act, 15

U.S.C. § 1, and §§ 4 and 16 of the Clayton Act, 15 U.S.C. §§ 15, 26. Their complaint alleged that petitioners, foreign and domestic vitamin manufacturers and distributors, had engaged in a price-fixing conspiracy, raising the price of vitamin products to customers in the United States and to customers in foreign countries.

As relevant here, petitioners moved to dismiss the suit as to the foreign purchasers (the respondents here), five foreign vitamin distributors located in Ukraine, Australia, Ecuador, and Panama, each of which bought vitamins from petitioners for delivery outside the United States. Respondents have never asserted that they purchased any vitamins in the United States or in transactions in United States commerce, and the question presented assumes that the relevant "transactions occur[ed] entirely outside U.S. commerce."

We granted certiorari to resolve a split among the Courts of Appeals about the exception's application.

II

The FTAIA seeks to make clear to American exporters (and to firms doing business abroad) that the Sherman Act does not prevent them from entering into business arrangements (say, joint-selling arrangements), however anticompetitive, as long as those arrangements adversely affect only foreign markets. See H.R. Rep. No. 97-686 (1982) (hereinafter House Report). It does so by removing from the Sherman Act's reach, (1) export activities and (2) other commercial activities taking place abroad, unless those activities adversely affect domestic commerce, imports to the United States, or exporting activities of one engaged in such activities within the United States.

The FTAIA says:

> "Sections 1 to 7 of this title [the Sherman Act] shall not apply to conduct involving trade or commerce (other than import trade or import commerce) with foreign nations unless—
>
> "(1) such conduct has a direct, substantial, and reasonably foreseeable effect—
>
> "(A) on trade or commerce which is not trade or commerce with foreign nations [i.e., domestic trade or commerce], or on import trade or import commerce with foreign nations; or
>
> "(B) on export trade or export commerce with foreign nations, of a person engaged in such trade or commerce in the United States [i.e., on an American export competitor]; and
>
> (2) such effect gives rise to a claim under the provisions of sections 1 to 7 of this title, other than this section.
>
> "If sections 1 to 7 of this title apply to such conduct only because of the operation of paragraph (1)(B), then sections 1 to 7 of this title shall apply to such conduct only for injury to export business in the United States." 15 U.S.C. § 6a.

This technical language initially lays down a general rule placing all (non-import) activity involving foreign commerce outside the Sherman Act's reach. It then brings such conduct back within the Sherman Act's reach provided that the conduct both (1) sufficiently affects American commerce, i.e., it has a "direct, substantial, and reasonably foreseeable effect" on American domestic, import, or (certain) export commerce, and (2) has an effect of a kind that antitrust law considers harmful, i.e., the "effect" must "giv[e] rise to a [Sherman Act] claim." §§ 6a(1), (2).

We ask here how this language applies to price-fixing activity that is in significant part foreign, that has the requisite domestic effect, and that also has independent foreign effects giving rise to the plaintiff's claim.

III

Respondents make a threshold argument. They say that the transactions here at issue fall outside the FTAIA because the FTAIA's general exclusionary rule applies only to conduct involving exports. The rule says that the Sherman Act "shall not apply to conduct involving trade or commerce (other than import trade or import commerce) *with* foreign nations." The word "with" means *between* the United States and foreign nations. And, they contend, commerce between the United States and foreign nations that is not import commerce must consist of export commerce—a kind of commerce irrelevant to the case at hand.

The difficulty with respondents' argument is that the FTAIA originated in a bill that initially referred only to "export trade or export commerce." But the House Judiciary Committee subsequently changed that language to "trade or commerce (other than import trade or import commerce)." And it did so deliberately to include commerce that did not involve American exports but which was wholly foreign.

The House Report says in relevant part:

> "The Subcommittee's 'export' commerce limitation appeared to make the amendments inapplicable to transactions that were neither import nor export, i.e., transactions within, between, or among other nations. . . . *Such foreign transactions should, for the purposes of this legislation, be treated in the same manner as export transactions*—that is, there should be no American antitrust jurisdiction absent a direct, substantial and reasonably foreseeable effect on domestic commerce or a domestic competitor. The Committee Amendment therefore deletes references to 'export' trade, and substitutes phrases such as 'other than import' trade. *It is thus clear that wholly foreign transactions as well as export transactions are covered by the amendment*, but that import transactions are not."

For those who find legislative history useful, the House Report's account should end the matter. Others, by considering carefully the amendment itself and the lack of any other plausible purpose, may reach the same conclusion, namely that the FTAIA's general rule applies where the anticompetitive conduct at issue is foreign.

IV

We turn now to the basic question presented, that of the exception's application. Because the underlying antitrust action is complex, potentially raising questions not directly at issue here, we reemphasize that we base our decision upon the following: The price-fixing conduct significantly and adversely affects both customers outside the United States and customers within the United States, but the adverse foreign effect is independent of any adverse domestic effect. In these circumstances, we find that the FTAIA exception does not apply (and thus the Sherman Act does not apply) for two main reasons.

First, this Court ordinarily construes ambiguous statutes to avoid unreasonable interference with the sovereign authority of other nations. This rule of construction reflects principles of customary international law—law that (we must assume) Congress ordinarily seeks to follow.

This rule of statutory construction cautions courts to assume that legislators take account of the legitimate sovereign interests of other nations when they write American laws. It thereby helps the potentially conflicting laws of different nations work together in harmony—a harmony particularly needed in today's highly interdependent commercial world.

No one denies that America's antitrust laws, when applied to foreign conduct, can interfere with a foreign nation's ability independently to regulate its own commercial affairs. But our courts have long held that application of our antitrust laws to foreign anticompetitive conduct is nonetheless reasonable, and hence consistent with principles of prescriptive comity, insofar as they reflect a legislative effort to redress domestic antitrust injury that foreign anticompetitive conduct has caused.

But why is it reasonable to apply those laws to foreign conduct *insofar as that conduct causes independent foreign harm and that foreign harm alone gives rise to the plaintiff's claim?* Like the former case, application of those laws creates a serious risk of interference with a foreign nation's ability independently to regulate its own commercial affairs. But, unlike the former case, the justification for that interference seems insubstantial. Why should American law supplant, for example, Canada's or Great Britain's or Japan's own determination about how best to protect Canadian or British or Japanese customers from anticompetitive conduct engaged in significant part by Canadian or British or Japanese or other foreign companies?

We recognize that principles of comity provide Congress greater leeway when it seeks to control through legislation the actions of American companies; and some of the anticompetitive price-fixing conduct alleged here took place in America. But the higher foreign prices of which the foreign plaintiffs here complain are not the consequence of any domestic anticompetitive conduct that Congress sought to forbid, for Congress did not seek to forbid any such conduct insofar as it is here relevant, i.e., insofar as it is intertwined with foreign conduct that causes independent foreign harm.

Rather Congress sought to release domestic (and foreign) anticompetitive conduct from Sherman Act constraints when that conduct causes foreign harm. Congress, of course, did make an exception where that conduct also causes domestic harm. But any independent domestic harm the foreign conduct causes here has, by definition, little or nothing to do with the matter.

We thus repeat the basic question: Why is it reasonable to apply this law to conduct that is significantly foreign insofar as that conduct causes independent foreign harm and that foreign harm alone gives rise to the plaintiff's claim? We can find no good answer to the question.

The Areeda and Hovenkamp treatise notes that under the Court of Appeals' interpretation of the statute

> "a Malaysian customer could . . . maintain an action under United States law in a United States court against its own Malaysian supplier, another cartel member, simply by noting that unnamed third parties injured [in the United States] by the American [cartel member's] conduct would also have a cause of action. Effectively, the United States courts would provide worldwide subject matter jurisdiction to any foreign suitor wishing to sue its own local supplier, but unhappy with its own sovereign's provisions for private antitrust enforcement, provided that a different plaintiff had a cause of action against a different firm for injuries that were within U.S. [other-than-import] commerce. It does not seem excessively rigid to infer that Congress would not have intended that result."

P. Areeda & H. Hovenkamp, Antitrust Law ¶ 273, pp. 51–52 (Supp. 2003).

We agree with the comment. We can find no convincing justification for the extension of the Sherman Act's scope that it describes. Respondents reply that many nations have adopted antitrust laws similar to our own, to the point where the practical likelihood of interference with the relevant interests of other nations is minimal. Leaving price fixing to the side, however, this Court has found to the contrary. *See, e.g., Hartford Fire*, 509 U.S. at 797–799 (noting that the alleged conduct in the London reinsurance market, while illegal under United States antitrust laws, was assumed to be perfectly consistent with British law and policy).

Regardless, even where nations agree about primary conduct, say price fixing, they disagree dramatically about appropriate remedies. The application, for example, of American private treble-damages remedies to anticompetitive conduct taking place abroad has generated considerable controversy. And several foreign nations have filed briefs here arguing that to apply our remedies would unjustifiably permit their citizens to bypass their own less generous remedial schemes, thereby upsetting a balance of competing considerations that their own domestic antitrust laws embody. *E.g.*, Brief for Federal Republic of Germany et al. as Amici Curiae 2 (setting forth German interest "in seeing that German companies are not subject to the extraterritorial reach of the United States' antitrust laws by private foreign plaintiffs—whose injuries were sustained in transactions entirely outside United States commerce—seeking treble damages in private lawsuits against German companies"); Brief for Government of Canada as Amicus Curiae 14 ("treble damages remedy would supersede" Canada's "national policy decision"); Brief for Government of Japan as Amicus Curiae 10 (finding "particularly troublesome" the potential "interfere[nce] with Japanese governmental regulation of the Japanese market").

These briefs add that a decision permitting independently injured foreign plaintiffs to pursue private treble-damages remedies would undermine foreign nations' own antitrust enforcement policies by diminishing foreign firms' incentive to cooperate with antitrust authorities in return for prosecutorial amnesty. Brief for Federal Republic of Germany et al. as Amici Curiae 28–30; Brief for Government of Canada as Amicus Curiae 11–14. See also Brief for United States as Amicus Curiae 19–21 (arguing the same in respect to American antitrust enforcement).

Respondents alternatively argue that comity does not demand an interpretation of the FTAIA that would exclude independent foreign injury cases across the board. Rather, courts can take (and sometimes have taken) account of comity considerations case by case, abstaining where comity considerations so dictate.

In our view, however, this approach is too complex to prove workable. The Sherman Act covers many different kinds of anticompetitive agreements. Courts would have to examine how foreign law, compared with American law, treats not only price fixing but also, say, information sharing agreements, patent-licensing price conditions, territorial product resale limitations, and various forms of joint venture, in respect to both primary conduct and remedy. The legally and economically technical nature of that enterprise means lengthier proceedings, appeals, and more proceedings—to the point where procedural costs and delays could themselves threaten interference with a foreign nation's ability to maintain the integrity of its own antitrust enforcement system. Even in this relatively simple price-fixing case, for example, competing briefs tell us (1) that potential treble-damage liability would help enforce widespread anti-price-fixing norms (through added deterrence) and (2) the opposite, namely that such liability would hinder antitrust enforcement (by reducing incentives to enter amnesty programs). How could a court seriously interested in resolving so empirical a matter—a matter potentially related to impact on foreign interests—do so simply and expeditiously?

We conclude that principles of prescriptive comity counsel against the Court of Appeals' interpretation of the FTAIA. Where foreign anticompetitive conduct plays a significant role and where foreign injury is independent of domestic effects, Congress might have hoped that America's antitrust laws, so fundamental a component of our own economic system, would commend themselves to other nations as well. But, if America's antitrust policies could not win their own way in the international marketplace for such ideas, Congress, we must assume, would not have tried to impose them, in an act of legal imperialism, through legislative fiat.

Second, the FTAIA's language and history suggest that Congress designed the FTAIA to clarify, perhaps to limit, but not to expand in any significant way, the

Sherman Act's scope as applied to foreign commerce. And we have found no significant indication that at the time Congress wrote this statute courts would have thought the Sherman Act applicable in these circumstances....

Nevertheless, respondents now have called to our attention six cases, three decided by this Court and three decided by lower courts. In the first three cases the defendants included both American companies and foreign companies jointly engaged in anticompetitive behavior having both foreign and domestic effects.

In all three cases, however, the plaintiff was the Government of the United States. A Government plaintiff, unlike a private plaintiff, must seek to obtain the relief necessary to protect the public from further anticompetitive conduct and to redress anticompetitive harm. And a Government plaintiff has legal authority broad enough to allow it to carry out this mission. 15 U.S.C. § 25....

Neither did the Court focus explicitly in its opinions on a claim that the remedies sought to cure only independently caused foreign harm.

The upshot is that no pre-1982 case provides significant authority for application of the Sherman Act in the circumstances we here assume.

Taken together, these two sets of considerations, the one derived from comity and the other reflecting history, convince us that Congress would not have intended the FTAIA's exception to bring independently caused foreign injury within the Sherman Act's reach.

V

Respondents point to several considerations that point the other way. For one thing, the FTAIA's language speaks in terms of the Sherman Act's applicability to certain kinds of conduct. The FTAIA says that the Sherman Act applies to foreign "conduct" with a certain kind of harmful domestic effect. Why isn't that the end of the matter? How can the Sherman Act both apply to the conduct when one person sues but not apply to the same conduct when another person sues? The question of who can or cannot sue is a matter for other statutes (namely, the Clayton Act) to determine.

Moreover, the exception says that it applies if the conduct's domestic effect gives rise to "a claim," not to "*the plaintiff's* claim" or "*the claim* at issue." 15 U.S.C. § 6a(2) (emphasis added). The alleged conduct here did have domestic effects, and those effects were harmful enough to give rise to "a" claim. Respondents concede that this claim is not their own claim; it is someone else's claim. But, linguistically speaking, they say, that is beside the point. Nor did Congress place the relevant words "gives rise to a claim" in the FTAIA to suggest any geographical limitation; rather it did so for a here neutral reason, namely, in order to make clear that the domestic effect must be an *adverse* (as opposed to a beneficial) effect.

Despite their linguistic logic, these arguments are not convincing. Linguistically speaking, a statute can apply and not apply to the same conduct, depending upon other circumstances; and those other circumstances may include the nature of the lawsuit (or of the related underlying harm). It also makes linguistic sense to read the words "a claim" as if they refer to the "plaintiff's claim" or "the claim at issue."

At most, respondents' linguistic arguments might show that respondents' reading is the more natural reading of the statutory language. But those arguments do not show that we must accept that reading. And that is the critical point. The considerations previously mentioned—those of comity and history—make clear that the respondents' reading is not consistent with the FTAIA's basic intent. If the statute's language reasonably permits an interpretation consistent with that intent, we should adopt it. And, for the reasons stated, we believe that the statute's language permits the reading that we give it.

Finally, respondents point to policy considerations that we have previously discussed, namely, that application of the Sherman Act in present circumstances will (through increased deterrence) help protect Americans against foreign-caused anticompetitive injury. As we have explained, however, the plaintiffs and supporting enforcement-agency amici have made important experience-backed arguments (based upon amnesty-seeking incentives) to the contrary. We cannot say whether, on balance, respondents' side of this empirically based argument or the enforcement agencies' side is correct. But we can say that the answer to the dispute is neither clear enough, nor of such likely empirical significance, that it could overcome the considerations we have previously discussed and change our conclusion.

For these reasons, we conclude that petitioners' reading of the statute's language is correct. That reading furthers the statute's basic purposes, it properly reflects considerations of comity, and it is consistent with Sherman Act history.

VI

We have assumed that the anticompetitive conduct here independently caused foreign injury; that is, the conduct's domestic effects did not help to bring about that foreign injury. Respondents argue, in the alternative, that the foreign injury was not independent. Rather, they say, the anticompetitive conduct's domestic effects were linked to that foreign harm. Respondents contend that, because vitamins are fungible and readily transportable, without an adverse domestic effect (i.e., higher prices in the United States), the sellers could not have maintained their international price-fixing arrangement and respondents would not have suffered their foreign injury. They add that this "but for" condition is sufficient to bring the price-fixing conduct within the scope of the FTAIA's exception.

The Court of Appeals, however, did not address this argument, and, for that reason, neither shall we. Respondents remain free to ask the Court of Appeals to consider the claim. The Court of Appeals may determine whether respondents properly preserved the argument, and, if so, it may consider it and decide the related claim.

For these reasons, the judgment of the Court of Appeals is vacated, and the case is remanded for further proceedings consistent with this opinion.

It is so ordered.

JUSTICE SCALIA, with whom JUSTICE THOMAS joins, concurring in the judgment.

I concur in the judgment of the Court because the language of the statute is readily susceptible of the interpretation the Court provides and because only that interpretation is consistent with the principle that statutes should be read in accord with the customary deference to the application of foreign countries' laws within their own territories.

Notes and Questions

1. In today's world, the question of the proper role for domestic courts in the globalized society is inescapable. In the cases we have seen so far, what role does the Supreme Court ascribe to the judiciary in relation to the diverse scenarios of transnationalism? In light of the types of issues we have discussed so far and will be discussing throughout the rest of this chapter, are you persuaded by the Court's reasoning? Does the U.S. Constitution require a definition of territoriality that equates it with—or gives priority to—land? Did *Empagran* improve on *Morrison*? Consider Professor Buxbaum's reflections on such cases in *National Jurisdiction and Global Business Networks*:[58]

> To a significant degree, the problem of regulating business networks has become global in scale. Consider the activities of a price-fixing cartel, in which companies from a number of different countries enter into pricing arrangements that artificially elevate the price of their goods in markets around the world. It is possible, and I will return to this point, to characterize the result simply as an aggregation of many localized harms (overcharges in the United States, overcharges in England, overcharges in each market in which transactions took place).
>
> Yet it is the global aspect of the cartel's strategy that makes it successful. Where the goods in question are fungible, the price-fixing must take place on all markets; otherwise, it could be avoided through arbitrage. It is therefore the networking of the cartel's actions at the global level that enables the scheme, and so, I would argue, it is the networking that a successful regulatory strategy must address.
>
> Consider also the insolvency of a multinational corporate enterprise, with assets, debtors and creditors scattered around the world. It is possible to address that insolvency through an aggregation of local bankruptcy proceedings conducted under national bankruptcy laws one in each country in which assets of that enterprise are located. Yet without a global plan to identify all assets and to ensure that all creditors are treated similarly, no fair distribution can take place—and certainly the reorganization of that enterprise would be difficult. Here, then, the goal of equitable distribution of an insolvent enterprise's assets has shifted up to the global level.

58. 17 IND. J. GLOBAL LEGAL STUD. 165, 168–73 (2010).

What these examples are intended to illustrate is simply that the fact of globalization in the business world enables certain harms and creates certain regulatory challenges that are situated at the global level. This argues for scaling the regulation of such networks up to the global level as well.

The dominant paradigm used to consider the role of domestic courts does not focus on how the activity of those courts relates to the scale of the problems they address. Rather, it focuses on how the activity of national courts as governmental actors relates to the activity of other governmental actors—in other words; it focuses on whether the exercise of jurisdiction by a particular court interferes with the authority of courts or governments in other jurisdictions.

If we consider, as directed by this paradigm, whether U.S. domestic courts are acting within the sphere of their authority, how should we define that sphere? What is the political (governmental) space within which U.S. courts operate? It is bounded, first, by federalism. Constitutional and statutory rules define a certain sphere for federal courts as apart from state courts (in the form partly of their limited subject-matter jurisdiction, in contrast to the unlimited jurisdiction of state courts). They are also very connected to the states in which they sit, because they are required, in many cases, to apply the substantive law of those states. In addition, their space of engagement is bounded by doctrines flowing from the separation of powers. Although judicial authority to decide cases or controversies properly presented is not constitutionally eliminated when those cases touch on foreign relations, the political question doctrine and doctrines of deference to the executive in matters of foreign affairs are tools that are used to limit judicial activity in such cases. Thus, speaking generally, the constitutional separation of powers defines a certain sphere for U.S. courts as set apart from other U.S. actors—other branches of the federal government.

These limitations in sum can be seen as creating the political space of engagement of domestic courts. Even with respect to their engagement with international law, U.S. courts take their frame of reference from the domestic Constitution. U.S. domestic courts do of course act as part of the international legal order—for instance, by interpreting and applying treaty rules—but in the U.S. system international law is seen, as reflected in its positioning within the Restatement of Foreign Relations Law, as part of foreign affairs, which is constructed as a matter of domestic law. For that reason, as to this aspect of their engagement, U.S. courts do not share a common frame of reference with courts of other countries.

I draw two conclusions from this review. First: the international relations paradigm, particularly as it is filtered through U.S. constitutional law, is a very locally directed one. Second, and following from the first, the vision of scale it supports is one in which domestic courts handle only domestic problems, to avoid infringing on the authority of other nations. Thus, presumably, we would need regional courts to address regional problems, and international tribunals to address international problems. However, lacking such institutions to deal with the regulation of global business networks, and despite the construction of the political space of operation for the federal courts, U.S. courts are nevertheless being drawn into a different space of engagement by the various forms of global business that generate litigation. This suggests the need to rethink our conception of the proper role for domestic courts.

2. In *Hartford Fire Insurance Co. v. California*, a 1993 case, U.S. plaintiffs sued defendant insurance companies, some based in the United States and others in Britain, for anti-competitive behavior.[59] Justice Souter held that the Sherman Act may apply to foreign defendants as long as (1) the conduct of the foreign defendant has a substantial effect in the United States, and (2) it is possible for the foreign defendant to comply with both U.S. and home law. In dissent, Justice Scalia argued that the canon of statutory interpretation against violating the "law of nations" without express congressional intent precluded application of the Sherman Act to foreign defendants. Justice Scalia observed that Britain had its own system for the regulation of anti-competitive behavior, with which the suit would interfere.

What role did comity play in the Court's decisions in *Morrison* and *Empagran*? How does the presumption against interfering with foreign regulation differ from the presumption against extraterritoriality?

3. The underlying action in *Empagran* was eventually dismissed after the trial judge held that the foreign anti-competitive effects of the defendant's behavior could be distinguished from its domestic anti-competitive effects. Professor Buxbaum, writing shortly after *Empagran*, argued for an alternative means of regulating transnational litigation: allow foreign litigants to try their cases in U.S. courts where the litigants' country agrees to permit the litigation.[60] This would solve one of the majority's critical concerns: respecting the prerogative of sovereign states to regulate the behavior of their own citizens.

In *Empagran*, however, the litigants' home states did more than simply refuse to permit the litigation—they actively opposed it, submitting *amicus* briefs upon which Justice Breyer relied to conclude that comity did not support allowing the plaintiffs to pursue their case.

4. Professor John Setear argues that Justice Breyer's rule of statutory construction is too vague to be a rule at all. What does it mean to interfere "unreasonably"? Professor Setear says that the rule offers judges no meaningful guideline or test.[61]

59. 509 U.S. 764 (1993).

60. Hannah L. Buxbaum, *Transnational Regulatory Litigation*, 46 VA. J. INT'L L. 269 (2006).

61. John K. Setear, *A Forest With No Trees: The Supreme Court and International Law in the 2003 Term*, 91 VA. L. REV. 579, 606–11 (2005).

Setear's view that Justice Breyer's standard is too vague to be meaningfully applied is shared by several commentators. *See, e.g.*, Sam Foster Halabi, *The "Comity" of Empagran*, 46 HARV. INTL. L.J. 279, 289 (2005) ("The list from which to draw inferences of 'unreasonable' jurisdiction is long and ambiguous."); Christopher Sprigman, *Fix Prices Globally, Get Sued Locally? U.S. Jurisdiction over International Cartels*, 72 U. CHI. L. REV. 265, 279 (2005).

5. In a number of recent cases, including *Kiobel* and *Morrison*, the Supreme Court has adopted in extremely restrictive holdings and rationales when a more liberal interpretation could have opened U.S. courts to claims by foreign parties. Why are the courts so wary of opening the door to such suits?

A similar question involving claims by foreign parties was considered by the Supreme Court in *Piper Aircraft Co. v. Reyno.*[62] The question in *Piper* was whether a case could be dismissed under forum non conveniens principles even if the law of the alternative forum was less favorable for the plaintiff. The Court held that "the possibility of an unfavorable change in law should not, by itself, bar dismissal."

The Court noted:

> Reyno candidly admits that the action against Piper and Hartzell was filed in the United States because its laws regarding liability, capacity to sue, and damages are more favorable to her position than are those of Scotland. Scottish law does not recognize strict liability in tort. Moreover, it permits wrongful-death actions only when brought by a decedent's relatives. The relatives may sue only for "loss of support and society."[63]

The Court stated a number of reasons for upholding the dismissal despite the change in law suffered by the plaintiff. One reason offered by the Court focused on judicial economy:

> Upholding the decision of the Court of Appeals would result in other practical problems. At least where the foreign plaintiff named an American manufacturer as defendant, a court could not dismiss the case on grounds of forum non conveniens where dismissal might lead to an unfavorable change in law. The American courts, which are already extremely attractive to foreign plaintiffs, would become even more attractive. The flow of litigation into the United States would increase and further congest already crowded courts.[64]

6. A trio of recent Supreme Court cases on personal jurisdiction—in short, the constitutional doctrine that limits which defendants may be brought before the U.S. courts—demonstrates how embedded territoriality has become as a limit on judicial authority.

---

62. 454 U.S. 235 (1981).
63. *Id.* at 240.
64. *Id.* at 251–52.

The first of these, a 2011 case captioned *J. McIntyre Machinery, Ltd. v. Nicastro*,[65] concerned the ability of domestic plaintiffs to sue foreign defendants for domestic harms caused by the defendants' commercial activities. *J. McIntyre* involved a products liability case with a foreign manufacturer. The company directed its products—scrap metal processing machines—to be sold into the United States through a separate company and further sold their wares at trade shows around the country. One of the machines was brought into New Jersey, where it severed several fingers off of the plaintiff's hand. The plaintiff sought jurisdiction on the basis of the defendant's sale of the particular machine (called "specific personal jurisdiction").

Justice Kennedy, writing for a three-justice plurality, stated that the defendant company's actions were insufficient to allow for jurisdiction. "The principal inquiry in cases of this sort is whether the defendant's activities manifest an intention to submit to the power of a sovereign," Justice Kennedy wrote. While the foreign company may have intended to ship goods to the United States, its activities failed to manifest the requisite intent to submit to the power of any particular state.

Justice Breyer concurred in the judgment and, joined by Justice Alito, wrote that the problem in this particular case was simply the lack of volume of sales to the particular state. Justice Ginsburg, joined by two others, dissented and argued that the defendant's decision to deal with the United States as a single market was sufficient to subject it to nationwide jurisdiction.

J. McIntyre dealt with jurisdiction arising from a defendant's particular actions. Two other recent cases, both with opinions authored by Justice Ginsburg, dealt with personal jurisdiction arising not from a defendant's particular actions (like the sale of the scap metal machine), but instead from the defendant's general connectedness with the forum state ("general personal jurisdiction"). In *Goodyear Dunlop Tires Operations, S.A. v. Brown*,[66] Justice Ginsburg held that a defendant had to be so connected to the forum as to be "at home" in the jurisdiction to allow for suit under general jurisdiction. In *Goodyear*, foreign plaintiffs allegedly injured by tires manufactured by Goodyear "Europe" brought suit in North Carolina, home of Goodyear USA. The fact that Goodyear Europe's tires were occasionally manufactured in North Carolina was insufficient to render Goodyear Europe "at home" in North Carolina.

In *Daimler AG v. Bauman*, 134 S. Ct. 746 (2014), Argentinian plaintiffs brought sut against Daimler's U.S. affiliate seeking damages for human rights violations allegedly committed by Daimler Germany in collaboration with Argentinian state security forces. Justice Ginsburg held that even when imputing the U.S. affiliate's contacts to the German company, the company's contacts were not sufficiently systematic and continuous so as to be "at home" in the state of California. This was because

65. 564 U.S. 873 (2011).
66. 564 U.S. 915 (2011).

Daimler's California contacts were minimal when compared with its "nationwide and worldwide" activities.

Justice Sotomayor, concurring in the judgment, criticized the majority for injecting a new sort of "proportionality" analysis into the personal jurisdiction assessment. A gargantuan company will almost always have relatively minor contacts in any state when considered alongside the corporation's global business activities. The larger companies would receive greater due process protections than smaller corporations under such a proportionality analysis.

As it stands, general personal jurisdiction for corporations is almost always limited to the state of incorporation and the state of headquarters—both of which frequently bear no relation to a corporation's actual activities, especially since companies may seek the most friendly corporate law schemes available and then operate elsewhere. Personal jurisdiction limits are rooted in the Fourteenth Amendment's Due Process Clause. Do the holdings in these cases sufficiently account for the different stakeholders' interests in fairness? Must due process be inextricably linked with physical, territorial contacts?

7. According to Professor Alan O. Sykes, if U.S. legal rules are applied to some, but not all, foreign companies, the result will be transnational forum shopping that imposes negative externalities on the global economic welfare.

> Professor Sykes argues:
>
> [T]he potential distortion of trade and investment patterns that can result from implicit "discrimination" in the applicability of legal rules to producers or investors of different nationalities. Such distortions are akin to those associated with discriminatory tariff or tax policies. In particular, the application of more stringent U.S. liability standards to some, but not all, firms doing business in a foreign jurisdiction may cause efficient firms subject to suit in the United States to be displaced by inefficient firms that are not subject to suit, or may cause inefficient corporate restructuring to avoid the reach of U.S. law. Global (and national) economic welfare may decline as a result, affording an argument in appropriate cases for limiting foreign tort plaintiffs to the law and forum of the jurisdiction in which their harm arose. This argument can hold even if the substantive or procedural law of the foreign jurisdiction in question is demonstrably inferior to U.S. law from an economic standpoint.[67]

Sykes observes that there are situations where application of U.S. law is economically beneficial:

> When U.S. law is superior and its application to conduct abroad will not divert production to inefficient firms, the application of U.S. law will enhance

67. Alan O. Sykes, *Transnational Forum Shopping as a Trade and Investment Issue*, 37 J. LEGAL STUD. 339, 340 (2008).

> global welfare. Further, if tort liability in a foreign jurisdiction is inadequate but consumer demand for the goods or services of an industry that causes external harm is sufficiently elastic, the substitution of higher cost firms for lower cost firms may cause such a large reduction in output and the attendant tort injuries that a welfare gain can arise. In addition, the application of less stringent foreign tort standards to harms that occur abroad may induce domestic companies to relocate production facilities abroad inefficiently. Finally, when harms are suffered by well-informed parties who stand in a market relationship with the tortfeasor, it is desirable to apply the more efficient law regardless of where the harm occurs.[68]

In short, Sykes concludes that the discriminatory application of U.S. law to extraterritorial conduct would likely yield negative consequences as compared with an outright refusal to extend U.S. law to extraterritorial conduct. Opening U.S. courts only to suits against U.S. companies for their extraterritorial conduct, when their foreign competitors are free from liability under U.S. law, would create what Sykes calls a "tort subsidy" in favor of the foreign firms.

IV. Courts without borders: Extraterritorial jurisdiction in lower courts

One solution to the problem of extraterritoriality for domestic courts is to claim "direct authority over entire transactions including those elements outside the territorial boundaries of the regulating state."[69] As Professor Putnam notes, "[t]he United States has been by far the most assertive state with respect to giving its domestic rules extraterritorial effect, with U.S. courts playing a key role. Since 1945, U.S. courts have considered a growing number of new claims involving extraterritorial conduct."[70] According to Putnam,

> U.S. courts and those in other powerful liberal democracies can and do influence outcomes and processes at the international level. When U.S. courts exercise authority over legal claims with an extraterritorial dimension, they function as international-level actors in a direct sense. Indirectly as well, the activities of domestic courts matter to international political processes. Whether vindicating, extending, or nullifying public policies and privately held rights and entitlements, court decisions have distributional consequences. To the extent that the preferences and strategies of foreign policy

68. *Id.* at 340–41.

69. Tonya L. Putnam, *Courts Without Borders: Domestic Sources of U.S. Extraterritoriality in the Regulatory Sphere*, 63 Int'l Org. 459, 459–60 (2009).

70. *Id.*

> officials are conditioned on domestic interests, who wins and who loses in domestic regulatory battles impacts international affairs.[71]

Putnam advances a theory accounting for U.S. courts' assertions of the extraterritorial reach of domestic rules:

> I argue that U.S. courts can be expected to interpret U.S. rules as reaching extraterritorial conduct in two types of situations. The first is where extraterritorial conduct threatens to undercut the domestic operation of a regulatory rule or regime. Such situations arise when private actors are able to capture domestic benefits of conduct prohibited under U.S. law (for example, forming a cartel, passing information for insider trading) simply by undertaking all or part of a prohibited transaction outside U.S. territory. Where this type of expected private gain outweighs the expected costs of undertaking extraterritorial conduct, it creates predictable incentives for others to follow suit. The foreseeable consequence in the absence of intervention is for rational behavior on the part of private actors to undercut both the rule in question, and the public policy it is meant to serve. Where extraterritorial conduct does not create such incentives, a court may forego regulation without risking harm to the domestic regulatory order—even where it results in some demonstrable costs to U.S.-based entities.
>
> U.S. courts are also likely to find extraterritorial regulation appropriate where conduct is alleged to violate a short list of "basic" rights at the core of U.S. political and legal identity. Rights considered "basic" for these purposes are those receiving strict scrutiny in U.S. constitutional review, and those considered *jus cogens* under international law. This includes rights not to be deprived of life, liberty, or property without due process of law, rights to free speech, and freedom from discrimination on the basis of national origin or membership in a traditionally disadvantaged group, and also the right not to be subjected to torture or other "crimes against humanity." The rationale behind this type of extraterritoriality differs in important respects from the first. Here the regulatory objective involves re-enforcing core norms of the political community. As such, membership in the polity, through citizenship or other forms of close association with the United States, is an especially critical dimension. In addition, the need to demonstrate actual harmful effects from extraterritorial conduct is weaker, as every violation of a core norm by a member of the community is considered harmful per se.

As we have seen above, extending domestic laws and regulations to extraterritorial conduct is not necessarily costless. The challenge, then, is to find an appropriate balance. But often the factors under consideration are not commensurate. For example, how do we assign a value to providing a forum—perhaps the *only* forum—for vindicating human rights as against other considerations such as

71. *Id.* at 461.

profitability or sustainability for a firm? Is this difficulty perhaps part of the reason that some courts prefer to be agnostic with respect to the gravity of a particular cause of action, while others embrace the social effects of a ruling as among its legitimate considerations?

The Supreme Court is clearly reluctant to open U.S. courts to transnational suits. But given their fact-finding responsibilities, lower level courts must often grapple with transnational issues which require an extraterritorial solution. Consider the following case, in which the Third Circuit reviewed a trial court's decision to level sanctions against the Republic of Philippines for witness harassment.

Republic of Philippines v. Westinghouse Elec. Corp.

43 F.3d 65 (3d Cir. 1994)

Lewis, Circuit Judge

This case raises important issues at the intersection of two principles: our deep-seated belief that a district court must be permitted to protect the integrity of its fact-finding process, and the settled considerations which courts in the United States must heed when considering whether to enjoin the executive activities of a foreign sovereign carried out in that sovereign's own territory. The district court found that the Republic of the Philippines was harassing witnesses who had testified against it in a suit it had brought in federal court in New Jersey. Thus, the court enjoined the Republic from continuing this harassment. The court also denied interlocutory certification of an underlying jury verdict so as to enforce its injunction, and ordered that any settlement in the case be conditioned upon acceptance of the court's continuing jurisdiction to enforce its injunctions. Because the district court exceeded its authority, we will reverse.

I

A

In 1988, the Republic of the Philippines (the "Republic") and the National Power Corporation ("NPC") filed a complaint against Westinghouse Electrical Corporation and Westinghouse International Projects Company (collectively "Westinghouse") and Burns and Roe Enterprises, Inc. ("Burns and Roe") concerning the construction of a nuclear power plant in Bagac, Bataan. The fifteen-count complaint alleged breach of contract, fraud, tortious interference with fiduciary duties, negligence, civil conspiracy, violations of state and federal racketeering statutes, and violations of the Robinson-Patman Act and the New Jersey Consumer Fraud Act. The district court determined that all but two of the counts against Westinghouse were subject to international arbitration. Thus, most of the Republic's claims against Westinghouse were referred to arbitration under the Rules of Conciliation and Arbitration of the International Chamber of Commerce. In the remaining two counts, the Republic and NPC alleged that Westinghouse and Burns and Roe had conspired to bribe then-President Ferdinand Marcos in order to win the power plant contract, and had thus tortiously interfered with the fiduciary duties that Marcos had owed the people of the Philippines.

While preparation for the trial on the tortious interference counts proceeded in New Jersey, arbitration implicating the other counts proceeded apace in Geneva. In late 1991, reaching the bribery allegations in the context of the Republic's challenge to the validity of the contract's arbitration clause, the arbitrators found that the Republic had failed to show that Westinghouse had bribed President Marcos. When the arbitrators included this finding in a preliminary award in favor of Westinghouse and Burns and Roe entered in December, 1991, the defendants moved for summary judgment in the district court, claiming the arbitrators' preliminary award collaterally estopped the Republic and NPC from litigating the bribery and tortious interference claims. The district court denied the motion and, when settlement discussions broke down, the case went to trial in March, 1993.

As the district court noted in the opinion supporting the order now before us, "[f]rom all accounts in the Philippine press, [the filing of the suit against Westinghouse and Burns and Roe and the arbitration in Geneva] assumed enormous importance in the eyes of Philippines leaders." The court explained that "[c]onstruction of the power plant had been undertaken to help solve the desperate electrical power shortage in the Philippines. Huge foreign loans were incurred to pay for the project." When Marcos left the Philippines and the Aquino government suspended construction of the power plant, "the Republic found itself with a partially completed plant which was producing no electricity, an ever worsening shortage of electrical power, and a huge foreign debt burden on which, it is said, interest alone amounts to $300,000 each day." Thus, the court surmised that "[i]t appears that the leaders of the Republic looked to a judgment in this case and in the arbitration proceedings as the solution to these staggering problems." The court further surmised that this factual context "may provide some explanation of the untoward events which transpired after the jury rendered a verdict against the Republic."

During the trial, two Filipino Westinghouse workers, Pedro A. Padre, Jr. and Jerry R. Orlina, testified for Westinghouse. In addition, Westinghouse introduced an affidavit from Perfecto V. Fernandez, a professor of law at the government-owned University of the Philippines. The affidavit had been rendered two years prior to the trial, when Westinghouse had moved for summary judgment, and discussed Philippine law relevant to the issues in the case. This testimony, the subsequent actions threatened and taken by the Republic against the witnesses, and the court's responses are the subjects of this appeal.

B

After a lengthy trial, the jury returned a verdict for Westinghouse and Burns and Roe on the bribery and tortious interference counts. Because the other claims were still stayed pending arbitration, the Republic filed a motion for certification pursuant to Fed. R. Civ. P. 54(b) to appeal the issues that had been adjudicated. At a hearing held on June 28, 1993 to consider this motion, the court was inclined to grant certification, stating that "there is no case more appropriate for certification than this one" and that "clearly [the case] should be certified."

However, Westinghouse then advised the court that it had evidence that Padre, Orlina and Fernandez were being harassed and subjected to retaliation by Philippine officials because of their testimony on behalf of Westinghouse. When these allegations were brought to its attention, the court abruptly changed its mind about certification, stating that although the facts needed to be developed,

> if there is a basis to [the allegation of harassment], it is a very, very serious charge, because nobody could come into this Court and then abuse people who come and testify. Some very dramatic, drastic remedies would have to be provided .... It would be destructive of our whole system. No foreign government should be allowed to use our court system and then not play fair with the witnesses in the case. I can't think of anything more destructive of our system, and simply could not permit it.

The court concluded that it must "hold off" on signing the Rule 54(b) certification because it would lose jurisdiction once the notice of appeal was filed.

The court ordered briefing and requested a motion from Westinghouse formally requesting relief from the court. Westinghouse filed a motion requesting that the court (1) enjoin the Republic from further harassing any witnesses, (2) sanction the Republic by barring it from further prosecuting its claims before the district court or appealing the adverse jury verdict, and (3) grant Westinghouse its attorneys' fees incurred on the motion.

On October 4, 1993, the court filed the opinion and order. The court found that, since the jury verdict, Orlina, Padre, and Professor Fernandez had been "the target of vilification in the public press inspired by officials in the Philippines government and each has been the target of actual or threatened government action." The court stated that the "attack[s]" were "spearheaded" by Francisco A. Villa, Overall Deputy Ombudsman of the Republic, a presidential appointee whose duties include initiating investigations and directing "any public official to perform any act required by law and to request assistance from any governmental agency."

The court found that Deputy Ombudsman Villa had threatened on numerous occasions to take legal action for tax fraud against Padre and Orlina as a result of their testimony on behalf of Westinghouse. The court found that both Padre and Orlina had faced public censure and lost business opportunities because of the Republic's actions, and that they would be financially ruined if tax evasion charges were brought against them. In this regard, the court also found it significant that another Filipino who had been involved in the same activities as Padre and Orlina had agreed to testify for the Republic—and was then granted immunity from prosecution for tax evasion.

The court also documented that Villa had initiated disciplinary proceedings against Professor Fernandez for having allegedly violated Philippine law by testifying against the government while under its employ. Although the Republic had known about Fernandez' affidavit when it was submitted to the court in 1991, Villa filed charges relating to the affidavit on May 31, 1993, twelve days after the verdict. Villa charged that, by filing an affidavit on behalf of Westinghouse, Fernandez had violated his duty as a public officer "to be loyal at all times to the Republic and the Filipino people. . . ." The court noted that the administrative complaint concluded by stating that Fernandez, "in a cowardly attempt to escape the clutches of the law, whimpered 'I'm not even a government official. I'm just a lowly college professor.'" The complaint also quoted approvingly from a news columnist who had written that "Professor Fernandez should not only be fired from the State University but should be hanged in public at the courtyard of the Nuclear Plant in Morong, Bataan . . . ." The court additionally found that Villa had called Fernandez a traitor "on a number of occasions, including a television show," and that "this characterization was repeated in the Philippine press." Based on the tone and substance of the administrative complaint, as well as the circumstances surrounding its filing, the court concluded that the charges against Fernandez were "motivated by rage at the jury verdict rather than considered judgment . . . ."

The Republic had submitted an affidavit from Villa purporting to establish that he did not institute proceedings against Fernandez because of the jury verdict, that Padre's and Orlina's fears are unwarranted, and that the Ombudsman's Office has not harassed any witness and had no intention of doing so. However, the court found that Villa lacked credibility. Given the evidence of record, "for [Villa] to state that '[Padre's and Orlina's] fears and apprehensions are unfounded' is poppycock." Furthermore, according to the court, the statements about Fernandez in Villa's affidavit continued to "reflect the Republic's rage at losing the case and its intent to strike out at one of the three persons seized upon as scapegoats for that loss." And the court found that Villa's assertion that the Ombudsman's Office was not guilty of harassment was "simply not true."

Although the evidence of harassment centered on Villa, the court determined that other members of the Philippines government had supported Villa's efforts. The court found ample evidence that Villa "was acting in accordance with the policies of the Office of the Executive, President Ramos." The court also found that the harassment was not confined to the executive branch of government.

The court acknowledged that the Republic had submitted evidence purporting to show that the government did not support any action designed to harass or intimidate witnesses, and that the government specifically did not intend to pursue any charges against Padre, Orlina, or Fernandez. The court noted that the evidence demonstrated "a partial retreat from the retaliatory conduct" the court had documented and indicated that the Republic intends "not to pursue the retaliatory conduct further against Padre and Orlina." However, the court noted that the proceedings against Fernandez "continue[d] unabated."

Because the court found that the Republic's actions "threaten[] both the integrity of a United States District Court and the foundations of our system of justice," it concluded that it must take action. Accordingly, it (1) enjoined the Republic from harassing any witness who had given evidence or will give evidence in this case or the arbitration proceeding; (2) directed the Republic to renounce and abandon its retaliatory actions, and to advise Padre and Orlina officially of its actions and intended actions with respect to their personal income taxes; (3) denied certification under Fed. R. Civ. P. 54(b) until the Republic established that it was in compliance with the injunctive provisions of the court's order and that the proceedings against Fernandez were resolved "in a manner which cures the retaliatory actions"; and (4) directed that any settlement in the case must provide that the parties agree to the court's retention of jurisdiction to enforce the provisions of the order. The Republic appeals this order in its entirety.

II

The Republic's challenge to the district court's order presents three issues: (1) whether the district court exceeded its authority in issuing the injunctive portions of its order; (2) whether the district court erred in refusing Rule 54(b) certification; and (3) whether the district court exceeded its authority in ordering that if the parties settle, they must stipulate to the district court's continuing jurisdiction to enforce its order. We have jurisdiction over the injunctive portions of this order under 28 U.S.C. § 1292(a)(1), and because of our resolution of the Republic's challenge to the injunctions, we find that the Rule 54(b) issue becomes moot.

III

A

The Republic has not adequately presented the issue of whether the district court's factual findings constitute clear error. Nevertheless, it is clear from the briefing that the Republic disputes the district court's factual conclusions, and we reach the Republic's challenge because of the significance of this case not only to a foreign sovereign, but also to our domestic legal system. We believe the evidence supports the district court's conclusion that Deputy Ombudsman Villa, with the support of other members of the Philippines government, pursued a campaign designed to smear Padre, Orlina, and Fernandez as scapegoats for the Republic's failure to achieve victory in the district court.

We further agree with the district court's observation that such behavior had "a doubly subversive effect. First, witnesses, who should have been able to rely upon both the implicit and explicit assurances of th[e district] court that they could testify fully and freely without fear of any retaliatory actions, have been betrayed." Additionally, "witnesses from the Philippines will fear to testify for Westinghouse and against the Republic in the arbitration proceedings and in any future proceedings in th[e district] court, preventing each tribunal from receiving all the facts." We therefore find no error in the district court's conclusion that the Republic's harassment created a "situation that no court can tolerate, and that effective relief must be granted."

Before we turn to the question of whether the district court's chosen relief was an abuse of its discretion, however, we note certain facts of significance. Although the district court found that the Republic's acts were retaliatory, it did not find that they were without foundation. In other words, the district court did not find that Padre and Orlina could not, under normal circumstances, be prosecuted for the activities they admitted to in open court in New Jersey. The court also stated that it accepted for purposes of its order that "under normal circumstances" Villa could file charges against Fernandez for his acceptance of compensation for providing an affidavit in this case.

The court also concluded that by the time it filed its order, the Republic had taken steps to "cure the effects of the retaliatory actions against Padre and Orlina and any additional steps which may be required can be taken readily." The only element of the challenged conduct that remained was the administrative complaint against Fernandez.

Additionally, the court concluded for the purposes of its order that the Ombudsman's Office is independent of the Executive Branch. Thus, it tacitly accepted the argument that the Republic could not compel Villa to withdraw his complaint against Fernandez and for the purposes of this opinion, we make the same assumption.

We also note a subsequent factual development not considered by the district court. During the pendency of this matter before us, we were informed by counsel for the Republic that the administrative proceeding that had been initiated by Villa against Fernandez had been dismissed by the President of the University of the Philippines. Noting that Fernandez had offered his opinion on a matter of public importance, the President of the University wrote that while

> [i]t is conceded that Prof. Fernandez' point of view may appear to be unacceptable to some or more Filipinos[,] . . . the role of academe is to continually engender varying thoughts, positions, theories and postulates on various key issues and concerns affecting the nation. This is not the first time that a dissenting voice has been put forth against the position taken by officials of the Republic and if the University is to remain at all one of the bastions of free thought and speech, it most certainly will not be the last.

With these facts in mind, we now address whether the injunctive portions of the court's order were lawful exercises of the court's discretion.

B

The district court's findings force us to confront fundamental issues involving a federal court's power to control litigants who come before it. As discussed below, a district court's power to sanction or exercise other forms of judicial control over a foreign sovereign is not coterminous with its power to regulate or punish other litigants. Here, in issuing an order which purports to supervise and control the law enforcement activities of a foreign sovereign nation against its own citizens on its own soil, the district court exceeded the boundaries of its lawful discretion.

1

Our legal system will endure only so long as members of society continue to believe that our courts endeavor to provide untainted, unbiased forums in which justice may be found and done. Thus, it is beyond peradventure that district courts have broad authority to preserve and protect their essential functions. To ensure that district courts have tools available to protect their truth-seeking process, the Federal Rules of Civil Procedure allow district courts to sanction parties who fail to meet minimum standards of conduct in many different contexts. Congress has also enacted laws providing additional powers to district courts to police misconduct.

Nor do those formal rules and legislative dictates exhaust district courts' power to control misbehaving litigants. To the contrary, the Supreme Court recently reaffirmed that a district court has *inherent* authority to impose sanctions upon those who would abuse the judicial process. . . . "[I]t has long been understood that certain implied powers must necessarily result to our Courts of justice from the nature of their institution, powers which cannot be dispensed with in a Court, because they are necessary to the exercise of all others." *Chambers v. NASCO, Inc.*, 501 U.S. 32, 43–44 (1991). Such salutary powers, the Court noted, "are governed not by rule or statute but by the control necessarily vested in courts to manage their own affairs so as to achieve the orderly and expeditious disposition of cases." *Id.*

Of course, "[b]ecause of their very potency, inherent powers must be exercised with restraint and discretion." *Id.* "A primary aspect of [a district court's] discretion is the ability to fashion an *appropriate* sanction for conduct which abuses the judicial process." *Id.* Thus, a district court must ensure that there is an adequate factual predicate for flexing its substantial muscle under its inherent powers, and must also ensure that the sanction is tailored to address the harm identified. In exercising its discretion under its inherent powers, the court should be guided by the same considerations that guide it in the imposition of sanctions under the Federal Rules. First, the court must consider the conduct at issue and explain why the conduct warrants sanction. Obviously, a pattern of wrongdoing may require a stiffer sanction than an isolated incident; a grave wrongdoing may compel a more severe sanction than might a minor infraction; and wrongdoing that actually prejudices the wrongdoer's opponent or hinders the administration of justice may demand a stronger response than wrongdoing that, through good fortune or diligence of court or counsel, fails to achieve its untoward object. Furthermore, there may be mitigating factors that must be accounted for in shaping the court's response.

Second, having evaluated the conduct at issue, the district court must specifically consider the range of permissible sanctions and explain why less severe alternatives to the sanction imposed are inadequate or inappropriate. Although the court need not "exhaust all other sanctioning mechanisms prior to resorting to its inherent power," the court must explain why it has chosen any particular sanction from the range of alternatives it has identified.

2

The district court did not explain under what authority it was proceeding in enjoining the Republic. We deduce from the circumstances, and assume for purposes of evaluating the injunctive provisions of the district court's order, that it was acting under its inherent authority. "We review a district court's imposition of sanctions under its inherent power for abuse of discretion", but we have made it clear that "a district court 'would necessarily abuse its discretion if it based its ruling on an erroneous view of the law or on a clearly erroneous assessment of the evidence.'"

At their core, the injunctive portions of the district court's order implicate international comity, that elusive doctrine—something more than mere international manners, but less than obligation—which attempts to mediate the frictions inherent in a community of sovereign states. Comity, in the words of Justice Gray,

> is the recognition which one nation allows within its territory to the legislative, executive, or judicial acts of another nation, having due regard both to international duty and convenience, and to the rights of its own citizens or of other persons who are under the protection of its laws.

Hilton v. Guyot, 159 U.S. 113, 164 (1895). The doctrine "is a nation's expression of understanding which demonstrates due regard both to international duty and convenience and to the rights of persons protected by its own laws." Consequently, "comity serves our international system like the mortar which cements together a brick house. No one would willingly permit the mortar to crumble or be chipped away for fear of compromising the entire structure."

[C]omity must yield to domestic policy: "no nation will suffer the laws of another to interfere with her own to the injury of her citizens . . . ." *Hilton,* 159 U.S. at 164. Thus, "from the earliest times, authorities have recognized that the obligation of comity expires when the strong public policies of the forum are vitiated by the foreign act."

But while it is true that principles of comity cannot compel a domestic court to uphold foreign interests at the expense of the public policies of the forum state, it can—and does—force courts in the United States to tailor their remedies carefully to avoid undue interference with the domestic activities of other sovereign nations. Comity is essentially a version of the golden rule: a "concept of doing to others as you would have them do to you . . . ." Thus, it may be permissible to prescribe and enforce rules of law in a foreign country, but unreasonable to do so in a particular manner because of the intrusiveness of a particular type of sanction. That is the case here: the district court had the power to sanction the Republic for its wrongdoing, but it should not have entered the injunctive provisions at issue here.

The mere fact of sovereignty does not insulate a litigant from sanction for failure to abide by the rules governing litigation in American courts. It would be perverse to allow a foreign sovereign litigant to "take our law free from the claims of justice." *National City Bank of New York v. Republic of China,* 348 U.S. 356, 362 (1955). The

Republic's actions, although taken in a foreign country, undeniably had effects in the United States. Under general principles of international law, a tribunal may prescribe laws with respect to "conduct outside its territory that has or is intended to have substantial effect within its territory." Restatement (Third) of the Foreign Relations Law of the United States § 402(c) (1987).... Thus, because the district court found that the Republic's actions compromised the court's ability to adjudicate fairly the claims before it, the district court had the power to address the retaliatory conduct notwithstanding that it transpired on foreign soil half a world away.

However, any exercise of jurisdiction to prescribe and enforce sanctions based on the effects of foreign activity in a domestic court requires the court to balance the interests it seeks to protect against the interests of any other sovereign that might exercise authority over the same conduct.

This balancing is evident in the principal cases advanced by both the Republic and Westinghouse in support or their respective positions. [The court then summarized several circuit court opinions. It concluded that trial courts could, with evidence of intent to interfere with or circumvent domestic proceedings, enjoin parties from litigating the same issues abroad in some instances.]

[T]he court here did not simply enjoin private litigants from pursuing parallel litigation in foreign jurisdictions. Here, the district court's injunctions purport to place the court in the position of supervising the law enforcement activities of a foreign sovereign nation against its own citizens on its own soil. The injunctive paragraphs of the district court's order provide the following:

> (1) the Republic is "permanently enjoined from taking any action against any witness who has testified or will testify" in this action or the arbitration "where that action is in retaliation for such testimony or has the intent or effect of harassing such a witness for his or her testimony or intimidating such a witness to change or withhold his or her testimony"; and
>
> (2) the Republic is "directed to take appropriate steps to renounce and abandon the retaliatory actions which the court has found to have taken place, which steps shall include officially advising Pedro A. Padre, Jr. and Jerry R. Orlina of the Republic's actions and intended actions with respect to their personal income taxes...."
>
> (3) "Should the parties settle this case, the agreement of settlement and any judgment implementing it shall contain a provision that each party accepts the continuing jurisdiction of th[e district] court to enforce the provisions of this order."

The first two injunctive provisions thrust the district court into the internal affairs of the Republic. The district court acknowledged that the first injunctive paragraph ... could place it in the position of acting, as the Republic's counsel put it to the district court, as "a special master over at least 50 witnesses who have already participated for both sides and are participating today in the arbitration, as well as literally hundreds of potential witnesses...." If any of those Filipinos received a traffic citation, or was involved in a tax fraud investigation, or had any other scrape with the law, the court acknowledged that it could be called upon by the individual to make a finding as to whether the Republic's prosecution was intended to harass or intimidate the witness. And although the court did not go so far as to find that tax charges against Padre and Orlina would be unfounded, the second injunctive paragraph effectively directs the Republic to grant Padre and Orlina immunity from prosecution for past tax law violations.

We are unaware of any court in the United States—or elsewhere—that has ever attempted to inject itself in this manner into the internal law enforcement activities of a foreign sovereign, The unique nature of the district court's injunctions is demonstrated by comparison to background precepts of international relations. Although countries sometimes exercise jurisdiction to prescribe and enforce laws that reach extraterritorial conduct, it is nevertheless widely accepted that each sovereign nation has the sole jurisdiction to prescribe and administer its own laws, in its own country, pertaining to its own citizens, in its *own* discretion. This principle was articulated in by Chief Justice Marshall in *The Schooner Exchange v. M'Faddon,* 11 U.S. (7 Cranch) 116 (1812):

> The jurisdiction of the nation within its own territory is necessarily exclusive and absolute. It is susceptible of no limitation not imposed by itself. Any restriction upon it, deriving validity from an external source, would imply a diminution of its sovereignty to the extent of the restriction, and an investment of that sovereignty to the same extent in that power which could impose such restriction.

Id.

It is fundamental that law enforcement is a core function of government, and a court should be loathe to interfere with a foreign sovereign's exercise of such power if alternatives are available that may achieve the same result with less derogation of sovereignty. As we have made clear, the district court had substantial power at its disposal in this case. It could have imposed monetary sanctions to signal its disapproval of the Republic's conduct and its intolerance of any future harassment or intimidation. It could also have dismissed the case. To have exercised its discretion consistent with its authority, however, the district court should have balanced the interests at stake. This the court did not do, and thus it failed to recognize that the extraordinarily intrusive nature of its injunctive provisions made such relief inappropriate.

Additionally, in this case as in any other, the district court should have noted what alternative sanctions were available, and at the very least should have explained why those options would not have achieved the results desired

The district court's error was compounded by its response when the Republic came forward, before the court's order was formalized, with evidence that it had achieved substantial compliance with paragraphs (1) and (2) of the draft order, at least with respect to Padre and Orlina. At that point, it was particularly inadvisable for the district court to have followed through by entering those portions of its order because there was evidence that they were no longer even necessary.

Consequently, those portions of the court's order must be vacated. Although the district court could sanction the Republic for taking lawful actions for retaliatory reasons, the court could not interpose itself into the Republic's law enforcement functions as it attempted to do in its order. As explained below, we will remand for a redetermination of sanctions.

Because we are vacating the principal injunctive portions of the district court's order, it is also necessary to vacate its third injunctive provision, in which the court required that any settlement include a provision acknowledging the district court's continued jurisdiction to enforce its order. That provision no longer has any purpose once the other injunctions are vacated.

C

[The court declined to "reach the thorny issue of whether—and how—we could assert jurisdiction over a district court's denial of a motion to certify under Rule 54(b)."]

IV

The Republic should be sanctioned for having retaliated against Padre, Orlina, and Fernandez. The district court moved with commendable expedition and firmness to address the trespass on its authority and integrity embodied in the retaliation by the Republic against Padre, Orlina and Fernandez. An American court cannot tolerate litigants' intimidation of witnesses, regardless of whether a litigant happens to be a foreign sovereign. However, for the reasons given, we conclude that the central elements of the district court's order went too far, and, accordingly, that order will be vacated. On remand, the district court shall reassess what sanctions should be imposed upon the Republic consistent with international comity. The district court should take into consideration the status of the Republic's actions regarding Padre, Orlina, and Fernandez, but we do not prejudge what sanctions should be imposed.

Notes and Questions

1. We have discussed the doctrine of comity as applied by the United States Supreme Court in some of the cases above. Lower courts have many other issues with which they must deal, such as issuing and enforcing subpoenas. *See, e.g., F.T.C. v. Compagnie De Saint-Gobain-Pont-à-Mousson*, 636 F.2d 1300 (D.C. Cir. 1980) (involving the intricacies of serving a subpoena on a foreign citizen on foreign soil). Is comity a less powerful doctrine militating against judicial injunctive relief when a lower court is involved? Why or why not?

2. Did the government of the Philippines engage in witness harassment in this case, so far as the appellate court was concerned? If so, what was so intrusive about this injunction that the Third Circuit found it to be inappropriate? Were there core governmental functions involved?

V. Discussion

In this chapter, we have reviewed a selection of cases that highlight several major issues with regard to the transnational role of domestic courts in the United States:

(1) Like other scholars, we note the trends that others have called anti-internationalist or isolationist. Rather than speculate on the Justices' private motives, we have interpreted the court's retreat from its former embrace of a gap-filling role in the enforcement of international law as part of a larger context. In that context, a proliferation of courts and tribunals, and investor-state arbitration, have together emerged as a quasi-judicialization of transnational capitalism in terms that support its autonomy and independence from national state regulation. In this regard, we have noted the efforts of the U.S. Supreme Court to uncouple the international obligations of the U.S. from their domestic enforcement as a means of reconciling nationalist and transnationalist pressures (*Medellín*).

(2) We have provided cases that signaled important turning points in the Court's demonstration of its willingness to resist the rulings of international bodies (*Haitian Refugees* and *Medellín*).

(3) We have also provided cases that show the shift in jurisprudence that now requires an explicit congressional declaration of extraterritorial intent, and, by implication, a default presumption against extraterritoriality (*Aramco*).

(4) Further, we have provided cases that clarify the Court's determined retreat from allowing U.S. courts to be used by foreigners claiming harm at the hands (literally or figuratively) of other foreigners (*Morrison* and *Empagran*, as well as *Kiobel* in Chapter 6).

(5) Were we to examine lower courts more extensively, e.g., in the cases cited in the previous section, we would see that their responsibilities as triers of fact place them squarely in transnational situations, where they must balance considerations of comity against their own procedural traditions and needs.

Taking these major points together, we may consider that the Supreme Court and the lower courts operate in somewhat different worlds, at least under some circumstances—the lower courts in particular faced with the pragmatic immediacy of extraterritoriality in fact situations with which they regularly deal, and the high court with more evident concern for the autonomy of the United States and, in consequence, with foreign affairs as a distinct realm of governing. The Court's presumption against extraterritoriality in the legislative context leaves unaddressed significant extraterritorial affairs—leaving open the possibility of extending the transnational powers of the executive. This, too, is a vexed area, as we shall see in the next chapter, as our account comes full circle to the president's role as a transnational executive.

Chapter 9

The Transnational Executive

The previous parts of this volume have highlighted cases and problems illustrative of areas critical to the development of transnational law today, particularly as these involve interlegalities of governments and corporations in ways that press the jurisdictional significance of territoriality beyond the conventions of cartography. The chapters of Part I described different situations involving treaties and tariff agreements among sovereign states. Among other things, the discussion suggested the extent to which intergovernmental agreements entail complexly diverse political contingencies and impacts, within and across the national states involved. The chapters of Part II provided case studies involving corporate activity abroad, mainly in relation to questions arising from various alignments of labor law, codes of responsibility, and accountability offshore. The overseas operations of U.S. corporations emerged as key nodes in the extraterritorial extensions of particular forms of domestic law (e.g., contracts and labor law), as well as new demands for law (e.g., on the part of worker organizations).

Taken together, Parts I and II showed that the borderless world that has been made for transnational capitalism is not an automatic or autonomous effect of economic activity, but an on-going project in real time and space. Global trade and investment are inseparable from the legalities that open borders and set the terms of those relations—sometimes in tension, sometimes in alignment or even integrally. In Part III, then, we have focused directly on cases and problems arising from the interlegalities of transnational law. In Chapter 7, we considered public/private arrangements from this perspective, focusing in particular on the different ways in which territoriality plays out under different governance regimes. In Chapter 8, we highlighted the courts' role as territorial gate keepers as they decide cases involving the availability of U.S. courts, processes and remedies in specific transnational contexts. That chapter concluded with the observation that the Court's post-*Aramco* deference to Congress in matters of extraterritorial applicability reinforces a theoretical distinction between domestic and foreign affairs. But in practice, as the chapter also showed, that distinction is inconsistent—sometimes aligned with the presumption against extrajurisdictionality in international law, and sometimes not. Legal scholar John Knox points to some of the more pressing areas of unsettlement and contradiction:

> Much of the inconsistency in the Court's jurisprudence results from failure to clarify how the presumption against extraterritoriality relates to another, underlying canon. For most of U.S. history, the Supreme Court determined the reach of federal statutes in the light of international law, specifically, the international law of legislative jurisdiction. In effect, it applied a presumption

> against extrajurisdictionality: that is, a presumption that federal law does not extend beyond the jurisdictional limits set by international law.... In the early twentieth century, the Court adopted the presumption against extraterritoriality as a limited, weaker version of the underlying presumption against extrajurisdictionality, which continued to apply in its own right. The Court [since then] never clarified, however, how the two presumptions mesh.[1]

In short, the question of the scope of executive power in transnational law is inseparable from the question of executive power in domestic law. Executive power is crucial to the connections and distinctions between these domains, yet without being decisive in itself. The indeterminacy of executive power is a familiar issue after *Youngstown*, in which Justice Jackson, in his famous concurrence, referred to the complexities of executive power conceived in terms of "the art of governing":

> The actual art of governing under our Constitution does not and cannot conform to judicial definitions of the power of any of its branches based on isolated clauses or even single Articles torn from context. While the Constitution diffuses power the better to secure liberty, it also contemplates that practice will integrate the dispersed powers into a workable government. It enjoins upon its branches separateness but interdependence, autonomy but reciprocity. Presidential powers are not fixed but fluctuate, depending upon their disjunction or conjunction with those of Congress. We may well begin by a somewhat over-simplified grouping of practical situations in which a President may doubt, or others may challenge, his powers, and by distinguishing roughly the legal consequences of this factor of relativity.
>
> 1. When the President acts pursuant to an express or implied authorization of Congress, his authority is at its maximum, for it includes all that he possesses in his own right plus all that Congress can delegate. In these circumstances, and in these only, may he be said (for what it may be worth) to personify the federal sovereignty. If his act is held unconstitutional under these circumstances, it usually means that the Federal Government as an undivided whole lacks power. A seizure executed by the President pursuant to an Act of Congress would be supported by the strongest of presumptions and the widest latitude of judicial interpretation, and the burden of persuasion would rest heavily upon any who might attack it.
>
> 2. When the President acts in absence of either a congressional grant or denial of authority, he can only rely upon his own independent powers, but there is a zone of twilight in which he and Congress may have concurrent authority, or in which its distribution is uncertain. Therefore, congressional inertia, indifference or quiescence may sometimes, at least as a practical matter, enable, if not invite, measures on independent presidential

1. John H. Knox, *A Presumption Against Interjurisdictionality*, 104 Am. J. Int'l L. 351, 352 (2010) (notes omitted).

responsibility. In this area, any actual test of power is likely to depend on the imperatives of events and contemporary imponderables rather than on abstract theories of law.

3. When the President takes measures incompatible with the expressed or implied will of Congress, his power is at its lowest ebb, for then he can rely only upon his own constitutional powers minus any constitutional powers of Congress over the matter.[2]

In this chapter, we find examples of each of Justice Jackson's three categories as we examine courts' involvements in the formulation of executive power in diverse circumstances. As the chapter unfolds, we shall have abundant reason to note the difficulty with which Congress and the courts struggle over these categories and their contemporary significance. The results are inconsistent, in part because of the difficulty—a difficulty at once conceptual, political and legal—of disentangling separation of powers principles from the issue of territoriality in the modern context. As we saw in Chapter 8, what is territorial or extraterritorial depends in part on how federal powers are construed. In this chapter, where we look directly at executive power, we continue to deal with that same recursive effect, with the result that over recent years the executive has been accorded extensive extraterritorial powers of search and seizure, detention, torture, targeted killing, and metadata sweeps, but has encountered checks in programs related to immigrants within the territory and seeking admission. The contemporary complexities in relation to executive power include the fact that the silences of Congress arise at least as much from its deep political divisions as they do from the sort of tacit acquiescence such as Justice Jackson might have had in mind. The state of war that has existed since 2001 is also a factor in current debates over executive power. Meanwhile, the concluding case in this chapter, *Zivotofsky v. Kerry*, seems to signal yet another formulation that returns the question of executive power to a bright line distinction between domestic and foreign affairs in the diplomatic domain. Whether the bright line in diplomacy will guide future litigation in other domains of transnational executive power remains to be seen.

As we turn to the theme of what we call *the transnational executive*, we are mindful that each of the themes in what follows is the subject of a vast literature. This is true throughout the book, but even more vividly here, as the chapter is meant to highlight particular issues rather than provide a comprehensive account of the executive branch's responsibilities or separation of powers jurisprudence. Separation of powers issues, and the claims to presidential authority in the context of the militarization of the international counterterrorism effort after the attacks on the United States on September 11, 2001, would fill volumes by themselves. Our discussion focuses more selectively on key moments in the recent development of executive power with respect to the status of citizens and other human beings—as the distinctions between foreign and domestic, resident and non-resident, citizen and non-citizen have in recent decades become unsettled or indeterminate, with direct consequences for

2. Youngstown Sheet and Tube Co. v. Sawyer, 343 U.S. 579, 635 (1952).

individuals. In this way, we continue the anthropological thread of our analysis in a different register, as presidential power and the status of the person emerge as deeply and mutually implicated social facts.[3]

To offer one obvious example of this point: the current security crisis—since the attacks of September 11, 2001, widely perceived as a permanent state of war against the determined aggression of non-state actors—has fused jurisdiction to territory through executive power in novel ways.[4] President George W. Bush's Military Order of November 13, 2001, claimed extensive judicial authority for the president with respect to a new category of offender—"enemy combatant." That category does not distinguish between citizens and non-citizens. Similarly, the choice of Guantanamo (located in Cuba) as the site of the detention camp for enemy combatants was supported by some administration supporters as an expedient way of removing the camp from the purview of the federal courts.[5]

But the cases reviewed here do not begin with 2001. They show the modern development of the executive's transnational powers in the zone between international and domestic law largely since the advent of economic globalization in the 1980s—the fluidity of capital presaging the inherent transnationalism that subsequently became essential (if in a different form) to the prosecution of terrorists. The cases show that even before 2001, the executive had substantial extraterritorial and extrajurisdictional powers arising from U.S. military ventures abroad, international policing arising from the so-called "War on Drugs" and other matters. The Bush administration's overreach into the judicial arena was in some respects checked by the courts; however, other elements of the judicialization of war remain in place—such as allow for NSA sweeps of communications metadata and targeted killings (including of U.S. citizens) by drones in overseas fields of operations. We cannot do more than touch on these questions—the main purpose of this discussion being to situate executive power in our analysis of interlegality, and, more specifically, to sustain the connection we have strived to foreground throughout this volume between institutions and actual people through their interrelated responsibilities, aspirations and powers.

Relevant to a fuller discussion of the transnational executive would be the many realms in which national executives work together directly (in contexts such as the G-20) or indirectly through their representatives and agencies; however, we limit our

3. "Once we see that the boundary between the state and civil society is itself an effect of power, then we can begin to conceptualize 'the state' *within* (and not automatically distinct from) other institutional forms through which social relations are lived, such as the family, civil socity, and the economy." Aradhana Sharma & Akhil Gupta, *Introduction: Rethinking Theories of the State in an Age of Globalization*, *in* The Anthropology of the State: A Reader 9 (Sharma & Gupta, eds. 2006).

4. The practical and interpretive problems arising from gaps and ambiguities of international law with respect to the rules of war and nonstate actors are subjects of an extensive legal literature. *See* John B. Bellinger III & Vijay M. Padmanabhan, *Detention Operations in Contemporary Conflict: Four Challenges for the Geneva Convention and Other Existing Law*, 105 Am. J. Int'l L. 201 (2011).

5. For an ethnographic reading of the controversy over the Military Order of November 13, 2001, see Carol J. Greenhouse, *Hegemony and Hidden Transcripts: The Discursive Arts of Neoliberal Legitimation*, 107 Am. Anthropologist 356, 360–65 (2005), http://www.jstor.org/stable/3567021.

discussion to the interlegal spaces (again, here conceived as the uneasy relation of international and domestic law) where the extraterritorial powers of the president have been particularly remarked in relation to citizens and other persons.

In the United States, as will be clear from discussion in previous chapters, the functions of the transnational executive involve accommodations with the other branches of government: for example, in trade, congressional extension of "fast track" powers to the president.[6] The transnational executive also involves intragovernmental pressures that are not readily adapted to a traditional separation of powers approach, given the ways in which a bright line between domestic and foreign affairs is elusive in areas such as national security and immigration (discussed further below). Such situations are a source of persistent tension, especially between the president and the Congress. Some of these tensions are preempted by work-arounds such as executive orders and other presidential directives to executive agencies. Others are absorbed politically. Still others come before the courts.

As we shall see, cases involving the adjudication of the president's extraterritorial powers potentially have significant lateral effects on other aspects of presidential authority. Issues involving extraterritorial jurisdiction are broadly relevant to questions arising from military operations, anti-trust and securities law enforcement, corporate accountability, and human rights law—among other potential extraterritorial applications of domestic law. Executive power is deeply implicated in all of these areas in ways that crosscut many (if not all) domains of domestic law as conventionally taught.

But as we shall also see, the theme of transnational executive power also entails intra-governmental asymmetries of power, as executives may be sensitive to the interests in international partnerships in ways that other branches of government are not—or vice versa. In the United States, congressional opposition to the Obama administration coalesced around international agreements of various kinds, such as the Iranian nuclear weapons agreement[7] and the TPP.[8]

6. Consider, for example, in the context of trade agreements. See Jane M. Smith et al., Cong. Res. Serv., Why Certain Trade Agreements Are Approved as Congressional-Executive Agreements Rather Than Treaties (Apr. 15, 2013), http://fpc.state.gov/documents/organization/207798.pdf.

7. A comprehensive background of the specifics of the deal, as negotiated by the executive, can be found here, *The Iran Nuclear Deal: What You Need to Know About the JCPOA* (July 2015), https://www.whitehouse.gov/sites/default/files/docs/jcpoa_what_you_need_to_know.pdf; *see also The Historic Deal That Will Prevent Iran from Acquiring a Nuclear Weapon*, WhiteHouse.gov, http://www.whitehouse.gov/issues/foreign-policy/iran-deal/ (last visited June 1, 2016). A detailed review of steps taken by the Obama administration, can be found in Bryan R. Gibson, The Long Road to Tehran: The Iran Nuclear Deal in Perspective (2015), http://www.lse.ac.uk/IDEAS/publications/reports/pdf/LSE-IDEAS-Long-Road-to-Tehran.pdf.

8. On the expansion of executive power in the twentieth century, see, for example, Martin Flaherty, *Separation of Powers, the Rule of Law, and Executive "Creativity" in* Hamdan v. Rumsfeld, *in* Separation of Powers: The U.S. Perspective (D. Sujatha ed. 2009); Martin Flaherty, *Surrendering the Rule of Law in Foreign Relations*, 32 Fordham Int'l L.J. 1154 (2009); M. Elizabeth McGill, *Can Process Cure Substance? A Response to Neal Katyal's "Internal Separation of Powers"*, 116

I. Defining national executive power: The paradigm of trade and investment

United States v. Curtiss-Wright Export Corporation, presented below, is generally acknowledged to have set the standard by which the president attains to extraterritorial powers in the domain of foreign affairs. We present it here for that reason, but also to consider how *Curtiss-Wright* featured in the expansion of executive powers domestically. Edward Purcell writes:

> In 1934, President Franklin D. Roosevelt signed a narrowly tailored joint congressional resolution directed at ending the Chaco War between Paraguay and Bolivia. The resolution authorized the president, under certain conditions, to issue a proclamation making it unlawful to sell arms in the United States to either country, and Roosevelt promptly declared the conditions met and issued the requisite proclamation. Subsequently, the government brought a criminal prosecution against the Curtiss-Wright Export Corporation for violating the proclamation by selling fifteen machine guns to Bolivia. The trial court dismissed the indictment on the ground that the resolution constituted "an invalid delegation of legislative power."
>
> [T]he trial court ruled that . . . the resolution lacked "an intelligible principle" to which the executive was required to conform and was, consequently, unconstitutional. On direct appeal to the Supreme Court, the parties concentrated on the delegation issue.[9]

Reflecting on *Curtiss-Wright* in 1986, fifty years after the decision—i.e., in the aftermath of the Vietnam War, the Pentagon Papers, and Watergate—Professors Edgar and Schmidt express their "sense of puzzlement and unease" to find that executive authority over government secrecy has expanded with the endorsement of the Supreme Court, and with silence from Congress:

> In several important decisions, the Supreme Court's choice of techniques for dealing with legal materials, as well as the tone of its opinions, seem to signal the Court's belief that Congress need not participate in the determination of national security secrecy needs. Even though Congress has been quite active in legislating about national security problems generally, the current Supreme Court seems reluctant to abide the slow politics of our

---

Yale L.J. Pocket Part 125 (2006); Keith E. Whittington & Daniel P. Carpenter, *Executive Power in American Institutional Development*, 1 Persp. Pol. 495 (2003).

9. Edward A. Purcell, Jr., *Understanding* Curtiss-Wright, Law & Hist. Rev., Nov. 2013, at 657–59 (notes omitted). *See generally* Kimberley L. Fletcher, *The Court's Decisive Hand Shapes the Executive's Foreign Affairs Policymaking Power*, 73 Md. L. Rev. 247 (2013). Decided at the height of President Franklin D. Roosevelt's "institutionalization of the presidency," comprised of many initiatives including "an extrovert phase in American foreign policy," *Curtiss-Wright* signaled the United States' hegemonic presence on the world stage. *See id.* at 253.

> separation of powers, and appears to believe that only the Executive and the Judiciary are capable of defending the nation's ultimate interests. We believe this message has been heard by lower courts in national security matters, generating a highly fluid and aggressive approach to secrecy problems and espionage prosecutions.
>
> Justice Black's stringent statement of legislative hegemony over domestic lawmaking in his opinion for the Court in *Steel Seizure*, and Justice Sutherland's *Curtiss-Wright* obiter dictum concerning the "very delicate, plenary and exclusive power of the President as the sole organ of the federal government in the field of international affairs," are the opposing judicial statements confronting those who would make sense of separation of powers analysis. Each of these powerful extremes is as simplistic as it is sweeping, and there is ground for skepticism about any straightforward characterization of what these decisions stand for.[10]
>
> Separation of powers problems almost never involve an explicit collision between executive action and statutory mandate; when such collisions arise, no one doubts that the will of Congress prevails. The interesting issue, then, is not which branch has the ultimate law-creating authority, but where to place the burdens of initiative, inertia, and clear statement.[11]

As you read *Curtiss-Wright*, consider how the Court's distinction between foreign and domestic leaves room for a territorial distinction to morph into a jurisdictional distinction. And as you continue with the cases in this chapter, keep Professors Edgar and Schmidt's questions in view. Where are "the burdens of initiative, inertia, and clear statement" placed?

United States v. Curtiss-Wright Export Corp.

299 U.S. 304 (1936)

Justice Sutherland delivered the opinion of the Court.

On January 27, 1936, an indictment was returned in the court below, the count of which charges that appellees, beginning with the 29th day of May, conspired to sell in the United States certain arms of war, namely, fifteen guns, to Bolivia, a country then engaged in armed conflict in the in violation of the Joint Resolution of Congress approved May 28, 1934, the provisions of a proclamation issued on the same day by the President of United States pursuant to authority conferred by section 1 of the resolution.

Whether, if the Joint Resolution had related solely to internal affairs, it be open to the challenge that it constituted an unlawful delegation of legislative power to the

10. Harold Edgar & Benno C. Schmidt, Curtiss-Wright *Comes Home: Executive Power and National Security Secrecy*, 21 Harv. C.R.-C.L. L. Rev. 349, 351–52 (1986) (notes omitted).

11. *Id.* at 353.

Executive, we find it unnecessary to determine. The whole aim of the resolution is to affect a situation entirely external to the United States, and falling within the category of foreign affairs. In other words, assuming (but not deciding) that the challenged delegation, if it were confined to internal affairs, would be invalid, may it nevertheless be sustained on the ground that its exclusive aim is to afford a remedy for a hurtful condition within foreign territory?

It will contribute to the elucidation of the question if we first consider the differences between the powers of the federal government in respect of foreign or external affairs and those in respect of domestic or internal affairs. That there are differences between them, and that these differences are fundamental, may not be doubted.

The two classes of powers are different, both in respect of their origin and their nature. The broad statement that the federal government can exercise no powers except those specifically enumerated in the Constitution, and such implied powers as are necessary and proper to carry into effect the enumerated powers, is categorically true only in respect of our internal affairs. In that field, the primary purpose of the Constitution was to carve from the general mass of legislative powers then possessed by the states such portions as it was thought desirable to vest in the federal government, leaving those not included in the enumeration still in the states. *Carter v. Carter Coal Co.*, 298 U.S. 238, 294 (1936). That this doctrine applies only to powers which the states had is self-evident. And since the states severally never possessed international powers, such powers could not have been carved from the mass of state powers but obviously were transmitted to the United States from some other source. During the Colonial period, those powers were possessed exclusively by and were entirely under the control of the Crown. By the Declaration of Independence, "the Representatives of the United States of America" declared the United (not the several) Colonies to be free and independent states, and as such to have "full Power to levy War, conclude Peace, contract. Alliances, establish Commerce and to do all other Acts and Things which Independent States may of right do."

As a result of the separation from Great Britain by the colonies, acting as a unit, the powers of external sovereignty passed from the Crown not to the colonies severally, but to the colonies in their collective and corporate capacity as the United States of America. Even before the Declaration, the colonies were a unit in foreign affairs, acting through a common agency—namely, the Continental Congress, composed of delegates from the thirteen colonies. That agency exercised the powers of war and peace, raised an army, created a navy, and finally adopted the Declaration of Independence. Rulers come and go; governments end and forms of government change; but sovereignty survives. A political society cannot endure without a supreme will somewhere. Sovereignty is never held in suspense. When, therefore, the external sovereignty of Great Britain in respect of the colonies ceased, it immediately passed to the Union. That fact was given practical application almost at once. The treaty of peace, made on September 3, 1783, was concluded between his Brittanic Majesty and the "United States of America."

The Union existed before the Constitution, which was ordained and established among other things to form "a more perfect Union." Prior to that event, it is clear that the Union, declared by the Articles of Confederation to be "perpetual," was the sole possessor of external sovereignty, and in the Union it remained without change save in so far as the Constitution in express terms its exercise. The Framers' Convention was called and exerted its upon the irrefutable postulate that though the states were several their people in respect of foreign affairs were one.

It results that the investment of the federal government with the powers of sovereignty did not depend upon the affirmative grants of the Constitution. The powers to declare and wage war, to conclude peace, to make to maintain diplomatic relations with other sovereignties, if they had been mentioned in the Constitution, would have vested in the federal government as necessary concomitants of nationality. Neither the Constitution nor the laws passed in pursuance of it have any force in foreign territory unless in respect of our own citizens; and operations of the nation in such must be governed by treaties, international understandings and compacts, and the principles of international law. As a member of the family of nations, the right and power of the United States in that field are equal to the and power of the other members of the international family. Otherwise, United States is not completely sovereign. The power to acquire territory by discovery and occupation, the power to expel undesirable aliens, the power to such international agreements as do not constitute treaties in the constitutional sense, none of which is expressly affirmed by the Constitution, nevertheless exist as inherently inseparable from the conception of nationality.

Not only, as we have shown, is the federal power over external affairs in origin and essential character different from that over internal affairs, but participation in the exercise of the power is significantly limited. In this vast external realm, with its important, complicated, delicate and manifold problems, the President alone has the power to speak or listen as a representative of the nation. He makes treaties with the advice and consent of the Senate; but he alone negotiates. Into the field of negotiation the Senate cannot intrude; and Congress itself is powerless to invade it. As Marshall said in his great argument of March 7, 1800, in the House of Representatives, "The President is the sole organ of the nation in its external relations, and its sole representative with foreign nations." Annals, 6th Cong., col. 613. The Senate Committee on Foreign Relations at a very early day in our history (February 15, 1816), reported to the Senate, among other things, as follows:

> The President is the constitutional representative of the United States with regard to foreign nations. He manages our concerns with foreign nations and must necessarily be most competent to determine when, how, and upon what subjects negotiation may be urged with the greatest prospect of success. For his conduct he is responsible to the Constitution. The committee considers this responsibility the surest pledge for the faithful discharge of his duty. They think the interference of the Senate in the direction of foreign negotiations calculated to diminish that responsibility and thereby to impair the best security for the national safety. The nature of transactions with foreign

> nations, moreover, requires caution and unity of design, and their success frequently depends on secrecy and dispatch.

It is important to bear in mind that we are here dealing not alone with an authority vested in the President by an exertion of legislative power, but with such an authority plus the very delicate, plenary and exclusive power of the President as the sole organ of the federal government in the field of international relations—a power which does not require as a basis for its exercise an act of Congress, but which, of course, like every other governmental power must be exercised in subordination to the applicable provisions of the Constitution. It is quite apparent that if, in the maintenance of our international relations, embarrassment—perhaps serious embarrassment—is to be avoided and success for our aims achieved, congressional legislation which is to be made effective through negotiation and inquiry within the international field must often accord to the President a degree of discretion and freedom from statutory restriction which would not be admissible were domestic affairs alone involved. Moreover, he, not Congress, has the better opportunity of knowing the conditions which prevail in foreign countries, and especially is this true in time of war. He has his confidential sources of information. He has his agents in the form of diplomatic, consular and other officials. Secrecy in respect of information gathered by them may be highly necessary, and the premature disclosure of it productive of harmful results. Indeed, so clearly is this true that the first President refused to accede to a request to lay before the House of Representatives the instructions, correspondence and documents relating to the negotiation of the Jay Treaty—a refusal the wisdom of which was recognized by the House itself and has never since been doubted.

Practically every volume of the United States Statutes contains one or more acts or joint resolutions of Congress authorizing action by the President in respect of subjects affecting foreign relations, which either leave the exercise of the power to his unrestricted judgment, or provide a standard far more general than that which has always been considered requisite with regard to domestic affairs.

The result of holding that the joint resolution here under attack is void and unenforceable as constituting an unlawful delegation of legislative power would be to stamp this multitude of comparable acts and resolutions as likewise invalid. And while this court may not, and should not, hesitate to declare acts of Congress, however many times repeated, to be unconstitutional if beyond all rational doubt it finds them to be so, an impressive array of legislation such as we have just set forth, enacted by nearly every Congress from the beginning of our national existence to the present day, must be given unusual weight in the process of reaching a correct determination of the problem. A legislative practice such as we have here, evidenced not by only occasional instances, but marked by the movement of a steady stream for a century and a half of time, goes a long way in the direction of proving the presence of unassailable ground for the constitutionality of the practice, to be found in the origin and history of the power involved, or in its nature, or in both combined.

The judgment of the court below must be reversed and the cause remanded for further proceedings in accordance with the foregoing opinion.

Notes and Questions

1. *Curtiss-Wright* marks a central breaking point with prior definitions of President's role in foreign affairs—it became a significant constitutional moment where the Court blazed a new path for the development of the branch.[12] Decided at the height of President Franklin D. Roosevelt's "institutionalization of the presidency," comprised of many initiatives including "an extrovert phase in American foreign policy," *Curtiss-Wright* signaled the United States' emergence as a world power.[13]

2. Much of the post-*Curtiss Wright* expansion of the executive branch rests on Justice Sutherland's famous passage in the decision where, contending the role of foreign affairs rested in the hands of the Executive, he invokes then-Congressman John Marshall's reference to the presidency as the "sole organ" of U.S. foreign policy within a speech delivered to the House of Representatives in 1800.[14] This language invited numerous executive branch lawyers to rely on *Curtiss-Wright* to stand for the proposition that Congress was without constitutional authority to determine the substance of any foreign affairs actions—so much so that Harold Koh famously referred to the case as the executive lawyer's "*Curtiss-Wright*, so I'm right."[15]

3. In light of *Curtiss-Wright*, is the fast-track authority that we examined in Chapter 3 (leading to NAFTA) constitutional? As indicated in the excerpt from Ackerman and Golove in Chapter 3, the current answer is yes. Are there contrary arguments to be made?[16] From a separation of powers perspective, should fast-track authority be constitutional?

4. What impact does fast-track authority have on democracy? Legal scholar Chantal Thomas, critical of the assumptions implicit in the view, has argued that trade liberalization results in a general benefit to the majority of Americans. In particular, she argues that the protectionist tendencies of the legislature should not be assumed to be counter-majoritarian, and she challenges the conventional justification for fast-track authority with empirical evidence demonstrating that the theories supporting a reduced role for the legislature are largely unjustified—even if they are widely held.[17]

---

12. *See generally* Fletcher, *supra*, note 9.

13. *See id.* at 253.

14. *See id.* at 258–59.

15. See Marty Lederman, *Thoughts on* Zivotofsky, *Part Seven:* "Curtiss-Wright—*out of Sight,*" *and the Fate of the Argument for an Exclusive Executive Diplomatic Authority*, JustSecurity.org (June 14, 2015, 12:56 PM), http://www.justsecurity.org/23875/thoughts-zivotofsky-part-seven-fate-exclusive-diplomatic-authority-and-sole-organ-argument/.

16. *See* Richard Epstein, *A More Modern Constitution*, N.Y.U. J. Law & Liberty (June 7, 2016), http://lawandlibertyblog.com/nyujll/2016/6/7/a-more-modern-constitution (arguing that fast-track authority stems from "a serious misreading of American constitutional history," to posit that "[c]hanged social circumstances have not rendered the framers' constitutional design obsolete").

17. *See* Chantal Thomas, *Challenges for Democracy and Trade: The Case of the United States*, 41 Harv. J. Leg. 1 (2004).

5. The appeal of fast-track authority is to some extent contingent on one's assessment of the legislative process. For example, in *Relic,* William G. Howell and Terry M. Moe take a very bleak view of the political process—arguing that fast-track authority should be expanded, because otherwise, legislators committed to special interests will always derail potential trade agreements:

> Congress is a boiling cauldron of protectionism, with powerful groups of every imaginable stripe taking aim at each provision of each trade agreement and pressing for changes that would work to their own special advantage, regardless of the impact on the nation. It is the president, not Congress, who insists on trade policies that best promote the national interest—and these are usually policies that expand trade, are not protectionist, and rise above special-interest pressures.[18]

What implicit or explicit assessments of Congress do you find in fast-track debates and other scenarios where executive power is in question?

6. One's assessment of fast-track also depends to some extent on how one formulates "globalization" as open to revision, redirection and, for some, even reversal. Such debates have been most recently witnessed in the U.S. Senate during the latest rounds of Congressional-Executive exchange on the Trans-Pacific Partnership.[19]

7. The cases in this chapter demonstrate in diverse ways how the executive's transnational powers are justified and deployed. While reading, note the diversity of such circumstances and the justifications they entail. Taking note of the standard under *Curtiss-Wright*, consider how constitutional limits to executive power are reasoned and applied in the further contexts explored below.

II. Extraterritoriality in question: Search and surveillance

A. Executive action that contravenes customary international law

The following Department of Justice memorandum details the position of the Office of Legal Counsel supporting extraterritorial criminal arrest by the FBI on the order of the president or attorney general. The memorandum specifically revises an earlier memorandum on this subject, reversing that memo's reading of domestic and international law on key points. We excerpt here the sections of the 1989 memo that deal most directly with the constitutional and customary bases of executive power, and the extent to which the statutory authority of an executive agency may

---

18. William G. Howell & Terry M. Moe, Relic: How Our Constitution Undermines Effective Government 159 (2016).

19. *See* John Nichols, *No Debate Equals No Democracy: The Folly of Fast Track*, Nation (May 21, 2015), http://www.thenation.com/article/no-debate-equals-no-democracy-folly-fast-track.

"travel" extraterritorially. Consider the 1989 memo's reasoning in relation to *Medellín* (discussed in Chapter 8) and the post-9/11 cases involving extraterritorial apprehension and killing discussed later in this chapter.

Authority of the Federal Bureau of Investigation to Override International Law in Extraterritorial Law Enforcement Activities

June 21, 1989

MEMORANDUM OPINION FOR THE ATTORNEY GENERAL

This memorandum responds to the request of the Federal Bureau of Investigation ("FBI") that we reconsider our 1980 opinion that the FBI has no authority under 28 U.S.C. § 533(1) to apprehend and abduct a fugitive residing in a foreign state when those actions would be contrary to customary international law. Extraterritorial Apprehension by the Federal Bureau of Investigation, 4B Op. O.L.C. 543 (1980) (the "1980 Opinion" or "Opinion"). After undertaking a comprehensive review of the applicable law, we conclude that the 1980 Opinion erred in ruling that the FBI does not have legal authority to carry out extraterritorial law enforcement activities that contravene customary international law.

First, we conclude that, with appropriate direction, the FBI may use its broad statutory authority under 28 U.S.C. § 533(1) and 18 U.S.C. § 3052 to investigate and arrest individuals for violations of United States law even if those investigations and arrests are not consistent with international law. Second, we conclude that the President, acting through the Attorney General, has inherent constitutional authority to order the FBI to investigate and arrest individuals in a manner that departs from international law. The international law that may be abridged in this manner includes not only customary international law but also Article 2(4) of the U.N. Charter and other unexecuted treaties or treaty provisions that have not become part of the domestic law of the United States. Finally, we reaffirm the conclusion of the 1980 Opinion that an arrest departing from international law does not violate the Fourth Amendment, and we further conclude that an arrest in violation of foreign law does not abridge the Fourth Amendment.

We caution that this memorandum addresses only whether the FBI has the legal authority to carry out law enforcement operations that contravene international law. It does not address the serious policy considerations that may weigh against carrying out such operations.

The 1980 Opinion

The 1980 Opinion addressed the legal implications of a proposed operation in which FBI agents would forcibly apprehend a fugitive in a foreign country that would not consent to the apprehension. That Opinion acknowledges that 28 U.S.C. § 533(1), the statute authorizing FBI investigations, contains no explicit geographical restrictions. It also refers to a previous opinion issued by this Office that concluded that the statute's general authorization to detect and prosecute crimes against the United States appears broad enough to include such law enforcement activity no matter where it is undertaken. The 1980 Opinion asserts, however, that customary and other international law limits the reach of section 533(1). Under customary international law, as viewed by the 1980 Opinion, it is considered an invasion of sovereignty for one country to carry out law enforcement activities within another country without that country's consent. Thus, the Opinion concludes that section 533(1) authorizes extraterritorial apprehension of a fugitive only where the apprehension is approved by the asylum state.

The Opinion supports this conclusion with "two distinct but related lines of analysis." First, citing *The Schooner Exchange v. McFaddon*, 11 U.S. (7 Cranch) 116, 136 (1812) (Marshall, C.J.), the Opinion concludes that the authority of the United States outside its territory is limited by the sovereignty of other nations. The Opinion does not explain the juridical source of this limitation on the authority of the United States. In *The Schooner Exchange*, however, Chief Justice Marshall relies on customary international law for many of his conclusions, and this part of the 1980 Opinion appears to suggest that customary international law imposes absolute jurisdictional limitations on the United States' lawmaking authority.

Second, the Opinion implicitly relies on the principle of statutory construction that statutes should be construed, when possible, so as to avoid conflict with international law. The Opinion notes that a statute imposing a duty ordinarily is construed to authorize all reasonable and necessary means of executing that duty. The Opinion concludes that although the law enforcement methods at issue may be necessary to carry out the FBI agents' duties under section 533(1), those methods are "unreasonable" and hence, unauthorized, if executed in violation of international law. Thus, the Opinion concludes that without asylum state consent, "the FBI is acting outside the bounds of its statutory authority when it makes an apprehension of the type proposed here—either because § 533 could not contemplate a violation of international law or because the powers of the FBI are delimited by those of the enabling sovereign."

The 1980 Opinion's impact on the ability of the United States to execute necessary law enforcement operations may be significant. The reasoning of the 1980 Opinion would seem to apply to a broad range of law enforcement activities other than forcible apprehension. United States law enforcement agents frequently are required to travel to foreign countries to conduct investigative activities or to meet foreign informants. Formal consent cannot always be obtained from the foreign government, and indeed, in many cases to seek such consent would endanger both the agents and their investigation. Although such activities are less intrusive than forcible apprehension and removal of the fugitive, under the 1980 Opinion they nonetheless may be viewed as encroachments on the asylum state's sovereignty and hence, violations of international law, if not authorized by that state. Thus, the 1980 Opinion has the potential to preclude the United States not only from apprehending fugitives in foreign countries, but also from engaging in a variety of more routine law enforcement activities. The United States is facing increasingly serious threats to its domestic security from both international terrorist groups and narcotics traffickers. While targeting the United States and United States citizens, these criminal organizations frequently operate from foreign sanctuaries.

Unfortunately, some foreign governments have failed to take effective steps to protect the United States from these predations, and some foreign governments actually act in complicity with these groups. Accordingly, the extraterritorial enforcement of United States laws is becoming increasingly important to the nation's ability to protect its own vital national interests.

We believe, consistent with earlier opinions of this Office, that sections 533(1) and 3052 authorize extraterritorial investigations and arrests. Section 533(1) has been described as granting "broad general investigative power." Section 3052 confers an equally broad arrest power. Neither statute by its terms limits the FBI's authority to operations conducted within the United States. Moreover, reading these sections as applying extraterritorially accords with Congress' intent to give certain criminal statutes extraterritorial reach. In many statutes, Congress has extended the United States' substantive criminal jurisdiction extraterritorially. See, e.g., 18 U.S.C. § 844(i) (enacting penalties for destruction of property used in foreign commerce); 18 U.S.C. § 1116(c) (implementing Convention on the Prevention and Punishment of Crimes Against Internationally Protected Persons); 18 U.S.C. § 1203(b)(1) (implementing Hostage Convention); 49 U.S.C. § 1472(1) (enacting penalties for carrying weapons or explosives aboard aircraft). These statutes are enforced principally by the FBI. In order for the FBI to have the authority necessary to execute these statutes, its investigative and arrest authority must have an equivalent extraterritorial scope.

The Effect of Customary International Law on the FBI's Extraterritorial Powers

The 1980 Opinion offers two bases for its conclusion that customary international law limits the FBI's extraterritorial powers. First, the Opinion asserts that the FBI's powers are delimited by those of the enabling sovereign and that the United States itself lacks the legal authority to take actions that contravene customary international law. The implication is that both Congress and the Executive are powerless to authorize actions that impinge on the sovereignty of other countries. Second, the Opinion concludes that the FBI's statutory authority must be read as constricted by the requirements of customary international law. We conclude that both bases for decision are erroneous.

1. Effect on the Sovereign's Power

The 1980 Opinion was clearly wrong in asserting that the United States is legally powerless to carry out actions that violate international law by impinging on the sovereignty of other countries. It is well established that both political branches—the Congress and the Executive—have, within their respective spheres, the authority to override customary international law. Indeed, this inherent sovereign power has been recognized since the earliest days of the Republic.

Chief Justice Marshall unequivocally reaffirmed the validity of [the principle that a sovereign may "claim and exercise jurisdiction" but that "such power [must] be exerted in a manner not to be misunderstood"] in *Brown v. United States*, 12 U.S. 110, in which he stated:

> This usage [the rule of customary international law] is a guide which the sovereign follows or abandons at his will. The rule, like other precepts of morality, of humanity, and even of wisdom, is addressed to the judgment of the sovereign; and although it cannot be disregarded by him without obloquy, yet it may be disregarded.

The understanding that the political branches have the power under the Constitution to exercise the sovereign's right to override international law (including obligations created by treaty) has been repeatedly recognized by the courts. . . . Leading commentators also agree that the United States, acting through its political branches, has the prerogative to take action in disregard of international law.

Indeed, the sovereign's authority to override customary international law necessarily follows from the nature of international law itself. Customary international law is not static: it evolves through a dynamic process of state custom and practice. States ultimately adhere to a norm of practice because they determine that upholding the norm best serves their long-run interests and because violation of the norm may subject the nation to public obloquy or expose it to retaliatory violations. States necessarily must have the authority to contravene international norms, however, for it is the process of changing state practice that allows customary international law to evolve. Thus, the power in the Executive to override international law is a necessary attribute of sovereignty and an integral part of the President's foreign affairs power. Indeed, the absence of such authority in the Executive would profoundly and uniquely disable the United States—rendering the nation a passive bystander, bound to follow practices dictated by other nations, yet powerless to play a role in shaping those practices.

Thus, we think it clear that, contrary to the 1980 Opinion's assertions, customary international law does not impose absolute legal limits on the power of the United States to exercise its law enforcement jurisdiction in foreign countries. Both the Congress and the President, acting within their respective spheres, retain the authority to override any such limitations imposed by customary international law.

2. Effect on the FBI's Statutory Authority

We also believe that the 1980 Opinion erred in concluding that the statutes granting the FBI its investigative and arrest powers must be construed as limited by customary international law. The 1980 Opinion notes that a conventional rule of statutory construction states that where a statute prescribes a duty, by implication it authorizes all reasonable and necessary means to effectuate that duty. The Opinion concludes, based principally on the disapproval expressed in several academic journals, that an extraterritorial apprehension is "unreasonable," and hence, unauthorized, when it violates international law. In substance, though not explicitly, the 1980 Opinion relies on the canon of statutory interpretation that a statute should be construed when possible so as not to conflict with international law. We believe this line of analysis is wholly inapposite.

First, this canon does not apply to the kind of statutes at issue here. Sections 533(1) and 3052 are broad authorizing statutes "carrying into execution" core Executive powers. In creating the FBI and conferring on it broad investigative and arrest authority, Congress has created an agency through which the President carries out his constitutionally assigned law enforcement functions. Such general enabling statutes, in the absence of an explicit restriction, must be read as conferring on the agency a scope of authority commensurate with that of the Executive. Because, as part of his law enforcement powers, the President has the inherent authority to override customary international law, it must be presumed that Congress intended to grant the President's instrumentality the authority to act in contravention of international law when directed to do so. Unless Congress places explicit limitations on the FBI's investigative and arrest powers, it must be presumed that Congress did not intend to derogate from Presidential authority by limiting those statutory powers.

This presumption is all the more compelling where, as here, the President's foreign relations powers are implicated. Courts have long recognized that delegations of discretion involving the President's constitutional powers must be construed broadly, especially in matters involving foreign affairs. *See e.g., Dames & Moore v. Regan*, 453 U.S. 654, 677 (1981) (Hostage Act and International Emergency Economic Powers Act, although not providing specific authorization for the President's actions, are still relevant because they "indicat[e] congressional acceptance of a broad scope for executive action" in settling claims against Iran); *Sardino v. Federal Reserve Bank of New York*, 361 F.2d 106, 111 (2d Cir.), cert. denied, 385 U.S. 898 (1961) (noting that especially with respect to foreign affairs, statutory delegations of power to the President must be read more broadly than other delegations). *See Chicago & Southern Air Lines, Inc. v. Waterman Steamship Corp.*, 333 U.S. 103, 110–14 (1948) (denying availability of judicial review over presidential decisions based on statutory authority involving broad foreign policy matters); *see also United States v. Curtiss-Wright Export Corp.*, 299 U.S. 304, 319 (1936) (upholding broad statutory delegation that implicated President's foreign affairs responsibilities).

In sum, then, we conclude that the FBI has authority under sections 533(1) and 3052 to carry out overseas investigations and arrests that contravene customary international law. Those statutes do not explicitly require the FBI to conform its activities to customary international law, and there is no basis for gratuitously assuming that Congress intended to impose such limitations on the FBI. On the contrary, in view of the President's authority to override customary international law, it must be presumed that Congress granted the FBI commensurate statutory authority.

The President's Constitutional Power to Authorize Actions Inconsistent with Customary International Law

We believe that the 1980 Opinion also erred because it failed to consider the President's inherent constitutional power to authorize law enforcement activities.

Pursuant to the constitutional command to "take Care that the laws be faithfully executed," the President has the power to authorize agents of the executive branch to engage in law enforcement activities in addition to those provided by statute.

This Office also has previously opined that the President, pursuant to his inherent constitutional authority, can authorize enforcement actions independent of any statutory grant of power (the "1970 Opinion"). In that opinion, this Office ruled that the President's inherent constitutional authority permitted Department of Transportation personnel to be deputized as Deputy U.S. Marshals and authorized to carry firearms, to take necessary action to prevent air piracy while an American carrier is in flight anywhere in the world, and to make arrests for violations of United States laws regarding air piracy and related offenses. The opinion recognized that there was no statute expressly authorizing this protection and enforcement action. Relying on *In re Neagle* and *In re Debs*, 158 U.S. 564, 581 (1895), however, it concluded that "since the United States has jurisdiction to punish air piracy and related offenses, it likewise has inherent authority to take reasonable and necessary steps to prevent these offenses." In its analysis, the 1970 Opinion noted that "the exercise of their authority . . . could give rise to conflicts with the countries involved of an international nature. But this would not, in our view, affect the legality of their actions under U.S. domestic law."

Accordingly, we believe that even if sections 533(1) and 3052 are construed as authorizing enforcement action only within the limits imposed by international law, the President retains the constitutional authority to order enforcement actions in addition to those permitted by statute. As discussed supra pp. 168–71, this constitutional authority carries with it the power to override customary international law. Thus, Executive agents, when appropriately directed pursuant to the President's constitutional law enforcement authority, may lawfully carry on investigations and make arrests that contravene customary international law.

The Status of Article 2(4) of the U.N. Charter and Other Unexecuted Treaties or Treaty Provisions

To this point, we have discussed the Executive's power to override customary international law. Another issue is whether Article 2(4) of the U.N. Charter would prohibit the Executive as a matter of domestic law from authorizing forcible abductions absent acquiescence by the foreign government. We do not believe that it does.

The text of Article 2(4) does not prohibit extraterritorial law enforcement activities, and we question whether Article 2(4) should be construed as generally addressing these activities. Nevertheless, even if Article 2(4) were construed as prohibiting certain forcible abductions, we believe that the President has the authority to order such actions in contravention of the Charter. Treaties that are self-executing can provide rules of decision for a United States court, but when a treaty is non-self-executing, it "addresses itself to the political, not the judicial department; and the legislature must execute the [treaty] before it can become a rule for the Court." *Foster v. Neilson*, 27 U.S. 253, 314 (1829) (Marshall, C.J.). Accordingly, the decision whether to act consistently with an unexecuted treaty is a political issue rather than a legal one, and unexecuted treaties, like customary international law, are not legally binding on the political branches. The President, acting within the scope of his constitutional or statutory authority, thus retains full authority to determine whether to pursue action abridging the provisions of unexecuted treaties.

[W]e conclude that as a matter of domestic law, the Executive has the power to authorize actions inconsistent with Article 2(4) of the U.N. Charter.

The President's Ability to Delegate to the Attorney General the Power to Authorize Enforcement Actions Inconsistent with International Law

Even though the Constitution vests the "executive power" in the President, see U.S. Const. art. II, § 1, we do not believe that the President's statutory or constitutionally based Executive power to override customary or other international law can be exercised only by him. Rather, we believe that this Executive power can be exercised by the Attorney General as well, and that this conclusion obtains regardless of whether the authority is viewed as derived from statute or from the President's inherent constitutional authority. Section 533(1) designates the Attorney General as the responsible executive branch official.

Thus, all enforcement action authorized pursuant to this statute, including enforcement action that departs from customary or other international law, may be undertaken by the Attorney General .... The Attorney General also may exercise the President's constitutional power to override customary international law because "[t]he President speaks and acts through the heads of the several departments in relation to subjects which appertain to their respective duties." *Wilcox v. Jackson*, 38 U.S. 498, 513 (1839).

Thus, we believe that the Attorney General has the power to authorize departures from customary or other international law in the course of law enforcement activities and that the President need not personally approve such actions. We would not recommend, however, that the Attorney General delegate the authority to more subordinate officials. Even if he is viewed as exercising statutory authority pursuant to section 533(1) or section 3052, we think that as a prudential matter the Attorney General should, in this case, exercise it personally.

International and Foreign Law and the Fourth Amendment

The 1980 Opinion concluded that an arrest in violation of customary international law did not violate the Fourth Amendment. We agree. The Opinion did not address whether the violation of foreign statutes or other law would create a Fourth Amendment violation. We conclude that it would not.

The central question is whether an arrest that violates international law or foreign statutory law is "unreasonable" within the meaning of the Fourth Amendment's proscription of unreasonable searches and seizures. The Fourth Amendment is an autonomous rule of federal law that represents a judgment by the United States as to the appropriate balance between individual rights and the authority of the government to enforce the law. The Court recently held that state standards for reasonable searches and seizures are irrelevant to determining whether the Fourth Amendment has been violated. *California v. Greenwood*, 486 U.S. 35 (1988). The Court stated:

> We reject respondent['s] . . . alternative argument for affirmance: that his expectation of privacy . . . should be deemed reasonable as a matter of federal constitutional law because the warrantless search and seizure . . . was impermissible as a matter of California law. . . . We have never intimated . . . that whether or not a search is reasonable within the meaning of the Fourth Amendment depends on the law of the particular State in which the search occurs. . . . Respondent's argument is no less than a suggestion that concepts of privacy under the laws of each State are to determine the reach of the Fourth Amendment. We do not accept this submission.

It would be contrary to the Fourth Amendment's purpose to incorporate into it rules of international law or analogous foreign statutes authorizing only local law enforcement officers to investigate and arrest. Such laws would have as their purpose the protection of another country's sovereignty. In contrast, the Fourth Amendment is concerned with the protection of individual rights. As the Fifth Circuit has stated:

> Whether the search and seizure were Fourth-Amendment-unreasonable must be established by showing that the interests to be served by the Fourth Amendment were violated, and not merely by establishing the violation of general principles of international law.

United States v. Cadena, 585 F.2d 1252, 1264 (5th Cir. 1978). We believe that the requirements of the Fourth Amendment are met when officers with authority under United States law arrest with probable cause.

Accordingly, we conclude that an arrest in violation of foreign law does not violate the Fourth Amendment. In addition, based on the analysis in the 1980 Opinion, we reaffirm that an arrest departing from international law does not violate the Fourth Amendment.

Conclusion

This Office concludes that at the direction of the President or the Attorney General the FBI may use its statutory authority under 28 U.S.C. § 533(1) and 18 U.S.C. § 3052 to investigate and arrest individuals for violations of applicable United States law, even if those actions depart from customary international law or unexecuted treaties. Moreover, we conclude that the President, acting through the Attorney General, has inherent constitutional authority to deploy the FBI to investigate and arrest individuals for violations of United States law, even if those actions contravene international law. Finally, we conclude that an arrest that is inconsistent with international or foreign law does not violate the Fourth Amendment.[20]

20. Dep't of Justice, *Authority of the Federal Bureau of Investigation to Override International Law in Extraterritorial Law Enforcement Activities* (June 21, 1989), https://www.justice.gov/olc/opinion/authority-federal-bureau-investigation-override-international-law-extraterritorial-law.

B. Abrogating the Fourth Amendment

The reasoning in the Office of Legal Counsel's memo (excerpted above) appears to find strong parallels in *Verdugo-Urquidez*, in which the Supreme Court held that the Fourth Amendment does not bar the federal government from searching and seizing property owned by a nonresident alien outside of the United States. As the dissents make clear, it also put a question mark over the Fourth Amendment rights of undocumented immigrants within the United States.[21] The context of *Verdugo-Urquidez* at the time of the decision was generally understood to be the War on Drugs (as it was popularly known) and the campaigns to stem undocumented immigration, but its relevance survived to include the War on Terror (again, using the popular phrase for the international counterterrorism operation).[22] The sweeping force of *Verdugo-Urquidez* subsequently met a substantial check in *Boumediene v. Bush*,[23] in which the Supreme Court held that non-residents abroad (in this case Guantanamo detainees) could not be denied constitutional rights on the basis of their detention location outside the United States.[24] But the wider relevance of *Verdugo-Urquidez* remains an open question—for example, with respect to the ambiguity of the Fourth Amendment's reference to "persons."

As you read the excerpt from *Verdugo-Urquidez*, consider the implications of the citizen/person distinction, as well as the taken-for-granted context of transnational law enforcement and military operations, in relation to the authorized use of executive power.

United States v. Verdugo-Urquidez

494 U.S. 259 (1990)

Chief Justice Rehnquist delivered the opinion of the Court.

The question presented by this case is whether the Fourth Amendment applies to the search and seizure by United States agents of property that is owned by a nonresident alien and located in a foreign country. We hold that it does not.

---

21. Victor C. Romero, *Whatever Happened to the Fourth Amendment: Undocumented Immigrants' Rights after* INS v. Lopez-Mendoza *and* United States v. Verguo-Urquidez, 65 S. Cal. L. Rev. 999, 1003 (1992) ("*Verdugo* potentially eliminates Fourth American protections for undocumented immigrants altogether."). *See also* Karen Nelson Moore, *Aliens and the Constitution*, 88 N.Y.U. L. Rev. 801, 835–837 (2013) ("*Verdugo-Urquidez* has spurred disagreement over the territorial reach of the Fourth Amendment, and over whether certain classes of aliens are afforded better Fourth Amendment protection than others.").

22. Anna Su, *Speech Beyond Borders: Extraterritoriality and the First Amendment*, 67 Vand. L. Rev. 1373, 1385 (2014) (referring to the Court's "slippery slope concern that applying the Constitution to aliens extraterritorially would produce deleterious and disruptive consequences for U.S. military and law enforcement operations abroad as they would be besieged by aliens' claims for damages").

23. 128 S. Ct. 2229 (2008).

24. Gerald L. Neuman, *The Extraterritorial Constitution after* Boumediene v. Bush, 82 S. Cal. L. Rev. 259, 268 (2009).

Respondent Rene Martin Verdugo-Urquidez is a citizen and resident of Mexico. He is believed by the United States Drug Enforcement Agency (DEA) to be one of the leaders of a large and violent organization in Mexico that smuggles narcotics into the United States. Based on a complaint charging respondent with various narcotics-related offenses, the Government obtained a warrant for his arrest on August 3, 1985. In January 1986, Mexican police officers, after discussions with United States marshals, apprehended Verdugo-Urquidez in Mexico and transported him to the United States Border Patrol station in Calexico, California. There, United States marshals arrested respondent and eventually moved him to a correctional center in San Diego, California, where he remains incarcerated pending trial.

Following respondent's arrest, Terry Bowen, a DEA agent assigned to the Calexico DEA office, decided to arrange for searches of Verdugo-Urquidez's Mexican residences located in Mexicali and San Felipe. Bowen believed that the searches would reveal evidence related to respondent's alleged narcotics trafficking activities and his involvement in the kidnaping and torture-murder of DEA Special Agent Enrique Camarena Salazar (for which respondent subsequently has been convicted in a separate prosecution). Bowen telephoned Walter White, the Assistant Special Agent in charge of the DEA office in Mexico City, and asked him to seek authorization for the search from the Director General of the Mexican Federal Judicial Police (MFJP). After several attempts to reach high ranking Mexican officials, White eventually contacted the Director General, who authorized the searches and promised the cooperation of Mexican authorities. Thereafter, DEA agents working in concert with officers of the MFJP searched respondent's properties in Mexicali and San Felipe and seized certain documents. In particular, the search of the Mexicali residence uncovered a tally sheet, which the Government believes reflects the quantities of marijuana smuggled by Verdugo-Urquidez into the United States.

The District Court granted respondent's motion to suppress evidence seized during the searches, concluding that the Fourth Amendment applied to the searches and that the DEA agents had failed to justify searching respondent's premises without a warrant. A divided panel of the Court of Appeals for the Ninth Circuit affirmed. [The Fourth Amendment] prohibits "unreasonable searches and seizures" whether or not the evidence is sought to be used in a criminal trial, and a violation of the Amendment is "fully accomplished" at the time of an unreasonable governmental intrusion. For purposes of this case, therefore, if there were a constitutional violation, it occurred solely in Mexico. Whether evidence obtained from respondent's Mexican residences should be excluded at trial in the United States is a remedial question separate from the existence vel non of the constitutional violation. The Fourth Amendment provides:

> The right of the people to be secure in their persons, houses, papers, and effects, against unreasonable searches and seizures, shall not be violated, and no Warrants shall issue, but upon probable cause, supported by Oath or affirmation, and particularly describing the place to be searched, and the persons or things to be seized.

That text, by contrast with the Fifth and Sixth Amendments, extends its reach only to "the people." Contrary to the suggestion of amici curiae that the Framers used this phrase "simply to avoid [an] awkward rhetorical redundancy," "the people" seems to have been a term of art employed in select parts of the Constitution. The Preamble declares that the Constitution is ordained and established by "the People of the United States." The Second Amendment protects "the right of the people to keep and bear Arms," and the Ninth and Tenth Amendments provide that certain rights and powers are retained by and reserved to "the people." While this textual exegesis is by no means conclusive, it suggests that "the people" protected by the Fourth Amendment, and by the First and Second Amendments, and to whom rights and powers are reserved in the Ninth and Tenth Amendments, refers to a class of persons who are part of a national community or who have otherwise developed sufficient connection with this country to be considered part of that community. *See United States* ex rel. *Turner v. Williams*, 194 U.S. 279, 292 (1904) (Excludable alien is not entitled to First Amendment rights, because "[h]e does not become one of the people to whom these things are secured by our Constitution by an attempt to enter forbidden by law"). The language of these Amendments contrasts with the words "person" and " accused" used in the Fifth and Sixth Amendments regulating procedure in criminal cases.

What we know of the history of the drafting of the Fourth Amendment also suggests that its purpose was to restrict searches and seizures which might be conducted by the United States in domestic matters. The Framers originally decided not to include a provision like the Fourth Amendment, because they believed the National Government lacked power to conduct searches and seizures. Many disputed the original view that the Federal Government possessed only narrow delegated powers over domestic affairs, however, and ultimately felt an Amendment prohibiting unreasonable searches and seizures was necessary. Madison, for example, argued that "there is a clause granting to Congress the power to make all laws which shall be necessary and proper for carrying into execution all of the powers vested in the Government of the United States," and that general warrants might be considered "necessary" for the purpose of collecting revenue. The driving force behind the adoption of the Amendment, as suggested by Madison's advocacy, was widespread hostility among the former colonists to the issuance of writs of assistance empowering revenue officers to search suspected places for smuggled goods, and general search warrants permitting the search of private houses, often to uncover papers that might be used to convict persons of libel. The available historical data show, therefore, that the purpose of the Fourth Amendment was to protect the people of the United States against arbitrary action by their own Government; it was never suggested that the provision was intended to restrain the actions of the Federal Government against aliens outside of the United States territory.

There is likewise no indication that the Fourth Amendment was understood by contemporaries of the Framers to apply to activities of the United States directed against aliens in foreign territory or in international waters.

The global view taken by the Court of Appeals of the application of the Constitution is also contrary to this Court's decisions in the *Insular Cases*, which held that not every constitutional provision applies to governmental activity even where the United States has sovereign power. In [*Dorr v. United States*, 195 U.S. 138 (1904)], we declared the general rule that in an unincorporated territory—one not clearly destined for statehood—Congress was not required to adopt "a system of laws which shall include the right of trial by jury, and that the Constitution does not, without legislation and of its own force, carry such right to territory so situated." Only "fundamental" constitutional rights are guaranteed to inhabitants of those territories. If that is true with respect to territories ultimately governed by Congress, respondent's claim that the protections of the Fourth Amendment extend to aliens in foreign nations is even weaker. And certainly, it is not open to us in light of the *Insular Cases* to endorse the view that every constitutional provision applies wherever the United States Government exercises its power.

Indeed, we have rejected the claim that aliens are entitled to Fifth Amendment rights outside the sovereign territory of the United States. In *Johnson v. Eisentrager*, 339 U.S. 763 (1950), the Court held that enemy aliens arrested in China and imprisoned in Germany after World War II could not obtain writs of habeas corpus in our federal courts on the ground that their convictions for war crimes had violated the Fifth Amendment and other constitutional provisions. The *Eisentrager* opinion acknowledged that in some cases constitutional provisions extend beyond the citizenry; "[t]he alien . . . has been accorded a generous and ascending scale of rights as he increases his identity with our society." But our rejection of extraterritorial application of the Fifth Amendment was emphatic:

> Such extraterritorial application of organic law would have been so significant an innovation in the practice of governments that, if intended or apprehended, it could scarcely have failed to excite contemporary comment. Not one word can be cited. No decision of this Court supports such a view. None of the learned commentators on our Constitution has even hinted at it. The practice of every modern government is opposed to it.

If such is true of the Fifth Amendment, which speaks in the relatively universal term of "person," it would seem even more true with respect to the Fourth Amendment, which applies only to "the people."

To support his all-encompassing view of the Fourth Amendment, respondent points to language from the plurality opinion in *Reid v. Covert*, 354 U.S. 1 (1957). *Reid* involved an attempt by Congress to subject the wives of American servicemen to trial by military tribunals without the protection of the Fifth and Sixth Amendments. The Court held that it was unconstitutional to apply the Uniform Code of Military Justice to the trials of the American women for capital crimes. Four Justices "reject[ed] the idea that when the United States acts against citizens abroad it can do so free of the Bill of Rights." The plurality went on to say:

> The United States is entirely a creature of the Constitution. Its power and authority have no other source. It can only act in accordance with all the limitations imposed by the Constitution. When the Government reaches out to punish a citizen who is abroad, the shield which the Bill of Rights and other parts of the Constitution provide to protect his life and liberty should not be stripped away just because he happens to be in another land.

[*Reid*] decided that United States citizens stationed abroad could invoke the protection of the Fifth and Sixth Amendments. The concurrences by Justices Frankfurter and Harlan in Reid resolved the case on much narrower grounds than the plurality and declined even to hold that United States citizens were entitled to the full range of constitutional protections in all overseas criminal prosecutions. Since respondent is not a United States citizen, he can derive no comfort from the *Reid* holding.

Verdugo-Urquidez also relies on a series of cases in which we have held that aliens enjoy certain constitutional rights. These cases, however, establish only that aliens receive constitutional protections when they have come within the territory of the United States and developed substantial connections with this country. Respondent is an alien who has had no previous significant voluntary connection with the United States, so these cases avail him not.

Justice Stevens' concurrence in the judgment takes the view that even though the search took place in Mexico, it is nonetheless governed by the requirements of the Fourth Amendment because respondent was "lawfully present in the United States . . . even though he was brought and held here against his will." But this sort of presence—lawful but involuntary—is not of the sort to indicate any substantial connection with our country. The extent to which respondent might claim the protection of the Fourth Amendment if the duration of his stay in the United States were to be prolonged—by a prison sentence, for example—we need not decide. When the search of his house in Mexico took place, he had been present in the United States for only a matter of days. We do not think the applicability of the Fourth Amendment to the search of premises in Mexico should turn on the fortuitous circumstance of whether the custodian of its nonresident alien owner had or had not transported him to the United States at the time the search was made.

The Court of Appeals found some support for its holding in our decision in *INS v. Lopez-Mendoza*, 468 U.S. 1032 (1984), where a majority of Justices assumed that the Fourth Amendment applied to illegal aliens in the United States. . . . The illegal aliens in *Lopez-Mendoza* were in the United States voluntarily and presumably had accepted some societal obligations; but respondent had no voluntary connection with this country that might place him among "the people" of the United States.

Not only are history and case law against respondent, but as pointed out in *Johnson v. Eisentrager*, 339 U.S. 763 (1950), the result of accepting his claim would have significant and deleterious consequences for the United States in conducting activities beyond its boundaries. The rule adopted by the Court of Appeals would apply not only to law enforcement operations abroad, but also to other foreign policy operations which might result in "searches or seizures." The United States frequently employs Armed Forces outside this country—over 200 times in our history—for the protection of American citizens or national security. Application of the Fourth Amendment to those circumstances could significantly disrupt the ability of the political branches to respond to foreign situations involving our national interest. Were respondent to prevail, aliens with no attachment to this country might well bring actions for damages to remedy claimed violations of the Fourth Amendment in foreign countries or in international waters. Perhaps a *Bivens* action might be unavailable in some or all of these situations due to "'special factors counselling hesitation,'" but the Government would still be faced with case-by-case adjudications concerning the availability of such an action. And even were *Bivens* deemed wholly inapplicable in cases of foreign activity, that would not obviate the problems attending the application of the Fourth Amendment abroad to aliens. The Members of the Executive and Legislative Branches are sworn to uphold the Constitution, and they presumably desire to follow its commands. But the Court of Appeals' global view of its applicability would plunge them into a sea of uncertainty as to what might be reasonable in the way of searches and seizures conducted abroad. Indeed, the Court of Appeals held that absent exigent circumstances, United States agents could not effect a "search or seizure" for law enforcement purposes in a foreign country without first obtaining a warrant—which would be a dead letter outside the United States—from a magistrate in this country. Even if no warrant were required, American agents would have to articulate specific facts giving them probable cause to undertake a search or seizure if they wished to comply with the Fourth Amendment as conceived by the Court of Appeals.

We think that the text of the Fourth Amendment, its history, and our cases discussing the application of the Constitution to aliens and extraterritorially require rejection of respondent's claim. At the time of the search, he was a citizen and resident of Mexico with no voluntary attachment to the United States, and the place searched was located in Mexico. Under these circumstances, the Fourth Amendment has no application.

For better or for worse, we live in a world of nation-states in which our Government must be able to "functio[n] effectively in the company of sovereign nations." Some who violate our laws may live outside our borders under a regime quite different from that which obtains in this country. Situations threatening to important American interests may arise half-way around the globe, situations which in the view of the political branches of our Government require an American response with armed force. If there are to be restrictions on searches and seizures which occur incident to such American action, they must be imposed by the political branches through diplomatic understanding, treaty, or legislation.

The judgment of the Court of Appeals is accordingly Reversed.

[Concurring opinion of Justice Kennedy is omitted.]

JUSTICE STEVENS, concurring in the judgment.

In my opinion aliens who are lawfully present in the United States are among those "people" who are entitled to the protection of the Bill of Rights, including the Fourth Amendment. Respondent is surely such a person even though he was brought and held here against his will. I therefore cannot join the Court's sweeping opinion. I do agree, however, with the Government's submission that the search conducted by the United States agents ... was not "unreasonable" as that term is used in the first clause of the Amendment.

JUSTICE BRENNAN, with whom JUSTICE MARSHALL joins, dissenting.

Today the Court holds that although foreign nationals must abide by our laws even when in their own countries, our Government need not abide by the Fourth Amendment when it investigates them for violations of our laws. I respectfully dissent.

I

Particularly in the past decade, our Government has sought, successfully, to hold foreign nationals criminally liable under federal laws for conduct committed entirely beyond the territorial limits of the United States that nevertheless has effects in this country. Foreign nationals must now take care not to violate our drug laws, our antitrust laws, our securities laws, and a host of other federal criminal statutes. The enormous expansion of federal criminal jurisdiction outside our Nation's boundaries has led one commentator to suggest that our country's three largest exports are now "rock music, blue jeans, and United States law." Grundman, *The New Imperialism: The Extraterritorial Application of United States Law*, 14 Int'l Law. 257, 257 (1980).

The Constitution is the source of Congress' authority to criminalize conduct, whether here or abroad, and of the Executive's authority to investigate and prosecute such conduct. But the same Constitution also prescribes limits on our Government's authority to investigate, prosecute, and punish criminal conduct, whether foreign or domestic. As a plurality of the Court noted in *Reid v. Covert*, 354 U.S. 1, 5–6 (1957): "The United States is entirely a creature of the Constitution. Its power and authority have no other source. It can only act in accordance with all the limitations imposed by the Constitution."

The Court today creates an antilogy: the Constitution authorizes our Government to enforce our criminal laws abroad, but when Government agents exercise this authority, the Fourth Amendment does not travel with them. This cannot be. At the very least, the Fourth Amendment is an unavoidable correlative of the Government's power to enforce the criminal law.

A

The Fourth Amendment guarantees the right of "the people" to be free from unreasonable searches and seizures and provides that a warrant shall issue only upon presentation of an oath or affirmation demonstrating probable cause and particularly describing the place to be searched and the persons or things to be seized. According to the majority, the term "the people" refers to "a class of persons who are part of a national community or who have otherwise developed sufficient connection with this country to be considered part of that community." The Court admits that "the people" extends beyond the citizenry, but leaves the precise contours of its "sufficient connection" test unclear. At one point the majority hints that aliens are protected by the Fourth Amendment only when they come within the United States and develop "substantial connections" with our country. At other junctures, the Court suggests that an alien's presence in the United States must be voluntary and that the alien must have "accepted some societal obligations." At yet other points, the majority implies that respondent would be protected by the Fourth Amendment if the place searched were in the United States.

What the majority ignores, however, is the most obvious connection between Verdugo-Urquidez and the United States: he was investigated and is being prosecuted for violations of United States law and may well spend the rest of his life in a United States prison. The "sufficient connection" is supplied not by Verdugo-Urquidez, but by the Government. Respondent is entitled to the protections of the Fourth Amendment because our Government, by investigating him and attempting to hold him accountable under United States criminal laws, has treated him as a member of our community for purposes of enforcing our laws. He has become, quite literally, one of the governed. Fundamental fairness and the ideals underlying our Bill of Rights compel the conclusion that when we impose "societal obligations," such as the obligation to comply with our criminal laws, on foreign nationals, we in turn are obliged to respect certain correlative rights, among them the Fourth Amendment.

By concluding that respondent is not one of "the people" protected by the Fourth Amendment, the majority disregards basic notions of mutuality. If we expect aliens to obey our laws, aliens should be able to expect that we will obey our Constitution when we investigate, prosecute, and punish them. We have recognized this fundamental principle of mutuality since the time of the Framers. James Madison, universally recognized as the primary architect of the Bill of Rights, emphasized the importance of mutuality when he spoke out against the Alien and Sedition Acts less than a decade after the adoption of the Fourth Amendment:

> [I]t does not follow, because aliens are not parties to the Constitution, as citizens are parties to it, that, whilst they actually conform to it, they have no right to its protection. Aliens are no more parties to the laws than they are parties to the Constitution; yet it will not be disputed that, as they owe, on one hand, a temporary obedience, they are entitled, in return, to their protection and advantage.

Mutuality is essential to ensure the fundamental fairness that underlies our Bill of Rights. Foreign nationals investigated and prosecuted for alleged violations of United States criminal laws are just as vulnerable to oppressive Government behavior as are United States citizens investigated and prosecuted for the same alleged violations. Indeed, in a case such as this where the Government claims the existence of an international criminal conspiracy, citizens and foreign nationals may be codefendants, charged under the same statutes for the same conduct and facing the same penalties if convicted. They may have been investigated by the same agents pursuant to the same enforcement authority. When our Government holds these codefendants to the same standards of conduct, the Fourth Amendment, which protects the citizen from unreasonable searches and seizures, should protect the foreign national as well.

Mutuality also serves to inculcate the values of law and order. By respecting the rights of foreign nationals, we encourage other nations to respect the rights of our citizens. Moreover, as our Nation becomes increasingly concerned about the domestic effects of international crime, we cannot forget that the behavior of our law enforcement agents abroad sends a powerful message about the rule of law to individuals everywhere. As Justice Brandeis warned in *Olmstead v. United States*, 277 U.S. 438 (1928):

> If the Government becomes a lawbreaker, it breeds contempt for law; it invites every man to become a law unto himself; it invites anarchy. To declare that in the administration of the criminal law the end justifies the means . . . would bring terrible retribution. Against that pernicious doctrine, this Court should resolutely set its face.

This principle is no different when the United States applies its rules of conduct to foreign nationals. If we seek respect for law and order, we must observe these principles ourselves. Lawlessness breeds lawlessness.

Finally, when United States agents conduct unreasonable searches, whether at home or abroad, they disregard our Nation's values. For over 200 years, our country has considered itself the world's foremost protector of liberties. The privacy and sanctity of the home have been primary tenets of our moral, philosophical, and judicial beliefs. Our national interest is defined by those values and by the need to preserve our own just institutions. We take pride in our commitment to a Government that cannot, on mere whim, break down doors and invade the most personal of places. We exhort other nations to follow our example. How can we explain to others—and to ourselves—that these long cherished ideals are suddenly of no consequence when the door being broken belongs to a foreigner?

The majority today brushes aside the principles of mutuality and fundamental fairness that are central to our Nation's constitutional conscience. The Court articulates a "sufficient connection" test but then refuses to discuss the underlying principles upon which any interpretation of that test must rest. I believe that by placing respondent among those governed by federal criminal laws and investigating him for violations of those laws, the Government has made him a part of our community for purposes of the Fourth Amendment.

B

In its effort to establish that respondent does not have sufficient connection to the United States to be considered one of "the people" protected by the Fourth Amendment, the Court relies on the text of the Amendment, historical evidence, and cases refusing to apply certain constitutional provisions outside the United States. None of these, however, justifies the majority's cramped interpretation of the Fourth Amendment's applicability.

The majority looks to various constitutional provisions and suggests that "'the people' seems to have been a term of art." But the majority admits that its "textual exegesis is by no means conclusive." One Member of the majority even states that he "cannot place any weight on the reference to 'the people' in the Fourth Amendment as a source of restricting its protections." The majority suggests a restrictive interpretation of those with "sufficient connection" to this country to be considered among "the people," but the term "the people" is better understood as a rhetorical counterpoint to "the Government," such that rights that were reserved to "the people" were to protect all those subject to "the Government." Cf. *New Jersey v. T.L.O.*, 469 U.S. 325, 335 (1985) ("[T]he Court has long spoken of the Fourth Amendment's strictures as restraints imposed upon 'governmental action'"). "The people" are "the governed."

[T]he Framers of the Bill of Rights did not purport to "create" rights. Rather, they designed the Bill of Rights to prohibit our Government from infringing rights and liberties presumed to be pre-existing. The Fourth Amendment, for example, does not create a new right of security against unreasonable searches and seizures. It states that "[t]he right of the people to be secure in their persons, houses, papers, and effects, against unreasonable searches and seizures, shall not be violated." The focus of the Fourth Amendment is on what the Government can and cannot do, and how it may act, not on against whom these actions may be taken. Bestowing rights and delineating protected groups would have been inconsistent with the Drafters' fundamental conception of a Bill of Rights as a limitation on the Government's conduct with respect to all whom it seeks to govern. It is thus extremely unlikely that the Framers intended the narrow construction of the term "the people" presented today by the majority.

The drafting history of the Fourth Amendment also does not support the majority's interpretation of "the people." First, the Drafters chose not to limit the right against unreasonable searches and seizures in more specific ways. They could have limited the right to "citizens," "freemen," "residents," or "the American people." The conventions called to ratify the Constitution in New York and Virginia, for example, each recommended an amendment stating, "That every freeman has a right to be secure from all unreasonable searches and seizures." But the Drafters of the Fourth Amendment rejected this limitation and instead provided broadly for "[t]he right of the people to be secure in their persons, houses, papers, and effects." Second, historical materials contain no evidence that the Drafters intended to limit the availability of the right expressed in the Fourth Amendment. The Amendment was introduced on the floor of Congress, considered by Committee, debated by the House of Representatives and the Senate, and submitted to the 13 States for approval. Throughout that entire process, no speaker or commentator, pro or con, referred to the term "the people" as a limitation.

The Court also relies on a series of cases dealing with the application of criminal procedural protections outside of the United States to conclude that "not every constitutional provision applies to governmental activity even where the United States has sovereign power." None of these cases, however, purports to read the phrase "the people" as limiting the protections of the Fourth Amendment to those with "sufficient connection" to the United States, and thus none gives content to the majority's analysis. The cases shed no light on the question whether respondent—a citizen of a nonenemy nation being tried in a United States federal court—is one of "the people" protected by the Fourth Amendment.

The majority's rejection of respondent's claim to Fourth Amendment protection is apparently motivated by its fear that application of the Amendment to law enforcement searches against foreign nationals overseas "could significantly disrupt the ability of the political branches to respond to foreign situations involving our national interest." The majority's doomsday scenario—that American Armed Forces conducting a mission to protect our national security with no law enforcement objective "would have to articulate specific facts giving them probable cause to undertake a search or seizure"—is fanciful. Verdugo-Urquidez is protected by the Fourth Amendment because our Government, by investigating and prosecuting him, has made him one of "the governed." Accepting respondent as one of "the governed," however, hardly requires the Court to accept enemy aliens in wartime as among "the governed" entitled to invoke the protection of the Fourth Amendment.

Moreover, with respect to non-law-enforcement activities not directed against enemy aliens in wartime but nevertheless implicating national security, doctrinal exceptions to the general requirements of a warrant and probable cause likely would be applicable more frequently abroad, thus lessening the purported tension between the Fourth Amendment's strictures and the Executive's foreign affairs power. Many situations involving sensitive operations abroad likely would involve exigent circumstances such that the warrant requirement would be excused. Cf. *Warden v. Hayden*, 387 U.S. 294, 298 (1967). Therefore, the Government's conduct would be assessed only under the reasonableness standard, the application of which depends on context. See *United States v. Montoya de Hernandez*, 473 U.S. 531, 537 (1985) ("What is reasonable depends upon all of the circumstances surrounding the search or seizure and the nature of the search or seizure itself").

In addition, where the precise contours of a "reasonable" search and seizure are unclear, the Executive Branch will not be "plunge[d] . . . into a sea of uncertainty," that will impair materially its ability to conduct foreign affairs. Doctrines such as official immunity have long protected Government agents from any undue chill on the exercise of lawful discretion. See, *e.g.*, *Butz v. Economou*, 438 U.S. 478 (1978). Similarly, the Court has recognized that there may be certain situations in which the offensive use of constitutional rights should be limited. Cf. *Bivens v. Six Unknown Fed. Narcotics Agents*, 403 U.S. 388, 396 (1971) (precluding suits for damages for violations of the Fourth Amendment where there are "special factors counselling hesitation"). In most cases implicating foreign policy concerns in which the reasonableness of an overseas search or seizure is unclear, application of the Fourth Amendment will not interfere with the Executive's traditional prerogative in foreign affairs because a court will have occasion to decide the constitutionality of such a search only if the Executive decides to bring a criminal prosecution and introduce evidence seized abroad. When the Executive decides to conduct a search as part of an ongoing criminal investigation, fails to get a warrant, and then seeks to introduce the fruits of that search at trial, however, the courts must enforce the Constitution.

II

Because the Fourth Amendment governs the search of respondent's Mexican residences, the District Court properly suppressed the evidence found in that search because the officers conducting the search did not obtain a warrant. I cannot agree with JUSTICE BLACKMUN and JUSTICE STEVENS that the Warrant Clause has no application to searches of noncitizens' homes in foreign jurisdictions because American magistrates lack the power to authorize such searches. The Warrant Clause would serve the same primary functions abroad as it does domestically, and I see no reason to distinguish between foreign and domestic searches.

The primary purpose of the warrant requirement is its assurance of neutrality.... The Warrant Clause cannot be ignored simply because Congress has not given any United States magistrate authority to issue search warrants for foreign searches. Congress cannot define the contours of the Constitution. If the Warrant Clause applies, Congress cannot excise the Clause from the Constitution by failing to provide a means for United States agents to obtain a warrant.

Nor is the Warrant Clause inapplicable merely because a warrant from a United States magistrate could not "authorize" a search in a foreign country. Although this may be true as a matter of international law, it is irrelevant to our interpretation of the Fourth Amendment. As a matter of United States constitutional law, a warrant serves the same primary function overseas as it does domestically: it assures that a neutral magistrate has authorized the search and limited its scope. The need to protect those suspected of criminal activity from the unbridled discretion of investigating officers is no less important abroad than at home.

III

When our Government conducts a law enforcement search against a foreign national outside of the United States and its territories, it must comply with the Fourth Amendment. Absent exigent circumstances or consent, it must obtain a search warrant from a United States court. When we tell the world that we expect all people, wherever they may be, to abide by our laws, we cannot in the same breath tell the world that our law enforcement officers need not do the same. Because we cannot expect others to respect our laws until we respect our Constitution, I respectfully dissent.

Notes and Questions

1. How convincing is the Court's assertion that application of the Fourth Amendment is a burden on the transnational presidency's ability to respond "to foreign situations involving [the] national interest"? Does it necessarily follow that requiring executive agencies, like the DEA, to obtain a warrant to search and seize property of aliens, like Verdugo-Urquidez, will shackle the government branch with "actions for damages to remedy claimed violations of the Fourth Amendment in foreign countries or in international waters"? Or will it, as the dissent suggests, only affect those instances where the executive, in exercising its foreign affairs power, brings forward "a criminal prosecution and introduce[s] evidence seized abroad"?

2. Justice Stevens states that people who, like Verdugo-Urquidez, are "brought and held [in the United States] against his will" are included in those "people" who are entitled to the protection of the nation's constitutional rights. How does the majority respond to this assertion?

3. Is it an "antilogy" (i.e., a logical contradiction in its own terms) that the Constitution can create an executive branch to enforce our criminal laws abroad, but when the branch and its entities act in that manner, the other strictures of the Constitution do not apply?

4. What is to be made of the dissent's emphasis on "mutuality" as a principle of fundamental fairness? Does disregard of this principle by the transnational presidency—i.e., excluding from the panoply of rights of foreign nationals the Fourth Amendment, a domestic constitutional right—amount to "lawlessness" on the part of the executive branch? Or is it a concern of another type—i.e., categorically neither fair nor unfair—for the executive, inundated with the concerns of the effects of international crime on domestic governance, to exclude a particular process right in the interest of having to deal "in the company of sovereign nations"?

5. How do you evaluate the distinction, made by the dissent, that the executive's foreign affairs policy concerns are distinct from its extraterritorial criminal concerns? As a factual matter, do these investigations remain distinct or, as a matter of practice, are they virtually indistinguishable?

6. Considering other discussions that wind throughout earlier chapters, what is your reaction to the majority's intention to permit—even at the expense of uncoupling a constitutional safeguard from its intended target—the executive sufficient flexibility to "function effectively" in a "world of nation states," or "sovereign nations"? Is the majority's perspective in sync with the world of today? Namely, do the Office of the President and any related agencies operate synchronously? Regarding the exterritoriality of the nation's criminal laws, are their actions unified at an interagency-wide level? Are they on the same page, with the entities' interests and motivations always complimentary across the board?

In their influential book, Michael Hardt & Antonio Negri, Empire 1–64 (2000), describe the modern world as now consisting of global networks that are increasingly expansive, yet fluid, frontiers of communication and control that are no longer tethered to national sovereignty. To what extent does *Verdugo-Urquidez* assume that "people" refers to a nation, i.e., a national community?[25]

---

25. *See also* Note, *The Meaning(s) of "the People" in the Constitution*, 126 Harv. L. Rev. 1078 (2013).

III. Citizenship in question

A. Detention without trial

Following the terrorist attacks on the United States on September 11, 2001, the executive branch claimed significantly broadened powers, initially under the terms of President George W. Bush's Military Order of November 13, 2001,[26] and the National Security Strategy of 2002 (see discussion of the latter in Chapter 3, *supra*). Relying in part on Congress's Authorization for Use of Military Force Joint Resolution (Public Law 107-40, 115 Stat. 224), the Military Order claimed specific judicial powers for the president with regard to the detention and trial of "enemy combatants." That was a new category, as we have noted above, that does not distinguish between U.S. citizens and non-citizens. As we have seen, the Court was already grappling with that question in *Verdugo-Urquidez.* But unlike the plaintiff in *Verdugo-Urquidez,* Yaser Eram Hamdi was a U.S. citizen. We offer *Hamdi* as a crucial opening round in the contest (over many years) between the Bush administration and the Court over the administration's position on detainees' due process rights. We have selected *Hamdi* because of its historical importance in that long contest, and for Justice O'Connor's now-famous statement that "a state of war is not a blank check for the President when it comes to the rights of the Nation's citizens." Professor Elgart, writing at the time, sets the stage and the mood:

> According to President George W. Bush, the United States is now engaged in a "war on terror" and the detention of so-called "enemy combatants" falls within the purview of the President's authority. The United States government has detained numerous individuals . . . , calling into question the detainees' due process rights. Last Term, in *Hamdi v. Rumsfeld,* the Supreme Court held that although Congress authorized the detention of enemy combatants in certain circumstances, due process requires that an American citizen held in the United States as an enemy combatant must be given a meaningful opportunity to contest the factual basis for that detention before a neutral decisionmaker. The Court's decision is rightly considered a victory for civil liberties and a defeat of the Bush administration's sweeping position on the power to detain enemy combatants. Nevertheless, the decision left the exact scope of detainees' due process rights undetermined.[27]

As you read *Hamdi,* consider what is and is not settled in the executive's authority in relation to due process in wartime—or any time.

---

26. Military Order of November 13, 2001: Detention, Treatment, and Trial of Certain Non-Citizens in the War Against Terrorism, Presidential Documents, Pages 57831–57836 Federal Register: November 16, 2001 (Volume 66, Number 222).

27. Allison Elgart, Hamdi v. Rumsfeld*: Due Process Requires that Detainees Receive Notice and Opportunity to Contest Basis for Detention,* 40 HARV. C.R.-C.L. L.REV. 239, 239 (2005) (notes omitted).

Hamdi v. Rumsfeld

542 U.S. 507 (2004)

O'Connor, J., announced the judgment of the Court and delivered an opinion, in which Rehnquist, C.J., and Kennedy and Breyer, JJ., joined.

At this difficult time in our Nation's history, we are called upon to consider the legality of the Government's detention of a United States citizen on United States soil as an "enemy combatant" and to address the process that is constitutionally owed to one who seeks to challenge his classification as such. The United States Court of Appeals for the Fourth Circuit held that petitioner's detention was legally authorized and that he was entitled to no further opportunity to challenge his enemy-combatant label. We now vacate and remand. We hold that although Congress authorized the detention of combatants in the narrow circumstances alleged here, due process demands that a citizen held in the United States as an enemy combatant be given a meaningful opportunity to contest the factual basis for that detention before a neutral decision-maker.

I

On September 11, 2001, the al Qaeda terrorist network used hijacked commercial airliners to attack prominent targets in the United States. Approximately 3,000 people were killed in those attacks. One week later, in response to these "acts of treacherous violence," Congress passed a resolution authorizing the President to "use all necessary and appropriate force against those nations, organizations, or persons he determines planned, authorized, committed, or aided the terrorist attacks" or "harbored such organizations or persons, in order to prevent any future acts of international terrorism against the United States by such nations, organizations or persons." Authorization for Use of Military Force ("the AUMF"). Soon thereafter, the President ordered United States Armed Forces to Afghanistan, with a mission to subdue al Qaeda and quell the Taliban regime that was known to support it.

This case arises out of the detention of a man whom the Government alleges took up arms with the Taliban during this conflict. His name is Yaser Esam Hamdi. Born an American citizen in Louisiana in 1980, Hamdi moved with his family to Saudi Arabia as a child. By 2001, the parties agree, he resided in Afghanistan. At some point that year, he was seized by members of the Northern Alliance, a coalition of military groups opposed to the Taliban government, and eventually was turned over to the United States military. The Government asserts that it initially detained and interrogated Hamdi in Afghanistan before transferring him to the United States Naval Base in Guantanamo Bay in January 2002. In April 2002, upon learning that Hamdi is an American citizen, authorities transferred him to a naval brig in Norfolk, Virginia, where he remained until a recent transfer to a brig in Charleston, South Carolina. The Government contends that Hamdi is an "enemy combatant," and that this status justifies holding him in the United States indefinitely—without formal charges or proceedings—unless and until it makes the determination that access to counsel or further process is warranted.

In June 2002, Hamdi's father, Esam Fouad Hamdi, filed the present petition for a writ of habeas corpus under 28 U.S.C. § 2241 in the Eastern District of Virginia, naming as petitioners his son and himself as next friend.... The habeas petition asks that the court, among other things, (1) appoint counsel for Hamdi; (2) order respondents to cease interrogating him; (3) declare that he is being held in violation of the Fifth and Fourteenth Amendments; (4) "[t]o the extent Respondents contest any material factual allegations in this Petition, schedule an evidentiary hearing, at which Petitioners may adduce proof in support of their allegations"; and (5) order that Hamdi be released from his "unlawful custody." Although his habeas petition provides no details with regard to the factual circumstances surrounding his son's capture and detention, Hamdi's father has asserted in documents found elsewhere in the record that his son went to Afghanistan to do "relief work," and that he had been in that country less than two months before September 11, 2001, and could not have received military training. The 20-year-old was traveling on his own for the first time, his father says, and "[b]ecause of his lack of experience, he was trapped in Afghanistan once that military campaign began."

The District Court found that Hamdi's father was a proper next friend, appointed the federal public defender as counsel for the petitioners, and ordered that counsel be given access to Hamdi. The United States Court of Appeals for the Fourth Circuit reversed that order, holding that the District Court had failed to extend appropriate deference to the Government's security and intelligence interests. It directed the District Court to consider "the most cautious procedures first," and to conduct a deferential inquiry into Hamdi's status. It opined that "if Hamdi is indeed an 'enemy combatant' who was captured during hostilities in Afghanistan, the government's present detention of him is a lawful one."

On remand, the Government filed a response and a motion to dismiss the petition. It attached to its response a declaration from one Michael Mobbs (hereinafter "Mobbs Declaration"), who identified himself as Special Advisor to the Under Secretary of Defense for Policy. Mobbs indicated that in this position, he has been "substantially involved with matters related to the detention of enemy combatants in the current war against the al Qaeda terrorists and those who support and harbor them (including the Taliban)." He expressed his "familiar[ity]" with Department of Defense and United States military policies and procedures applicable to the detention, control, and transfer of al Qaeda and Taliban personnel, and declared that "[b]ased upon my review of relevant records and reports, I am also familiar with the facts and circumstances related to the capture of ... Hamdi and his detention by U.S. military forces."

Mobbs then set forth what remains the sole evidentiary support that the Government has provided to the courts for Hamdi's detention. The declaration states that Hamdi "traveled to Afghanistan" in July or August 2001, and that he thereafter "affiliated with a Taliban military unit and received weapons training." It asserts that Hamdi "remained with his Taliban unit following the attacks of September 11" and that, during the time when Northern Alliance forces were "engaged in battle with the Taliban," "Hamdi's Taliban unit surrendered" to those forces, after which he "surrender[ed] his Kalishnikov assault rifle" to them. The Mobbs Declaration also states that, because al Qaeda and the Taliban "were and are hostile forces engaged in armed conflict with the armed forces of the United States," "individuals associated with 'those groups' were and continue to be enemy combatants." Mobbs states that Hamdi was labeled an enemy combatant "[b]ased upon his interviews and in light of his association with the Taliban." According to the declaration, a series of "U.S. military screening team[s]" determined that Hamdi met "the criteria for enemy combatants," and "a subsequent interview of Hamdi has confirmed that he surrendered and gave his firearm to Northern Alliance forces, which supports his classification as an enemy combatant."

The District Court found that the Mobbs Declaration fell "far short" of supporting Hamdi's detention. It criticized the generic and hearsay nature of the affidavit, calling it "little more than the government's 'say-so.'" It ordered the Government to turn over numerous materials for in camera review, including copies of all of Hamdi's statements and the notes taken from interviews with him that related to his reasons for going to Afghanistan and his activities therein; a list of all interrogators who had questioned Hamdi and their names and addresses; statements by members of the Northern Alliance regarding Hamdi's surrender and capture; a list of the dates and locations of his capture and subsequent detentions; and the names and titles of the United States Government officials who made the determinations that Hamdi was an enemy combatant and that he should be moved to a naval brig. The court indicated that all of these materials were necessary for "meaningful judicial review" of whether Hamdi's detention was legally authorized and whether Hamdi had received sufficient process to satisfy the Due Process Clause of the Constitution and relevant treaties or military regulations.

The Government sought to appeal the production order, and the District Court certified the question of whether the Mobbs Declaration, "'standing alone, is sufficient as a matter of law to allow meaningful judicial review of [Hamdi's] classification as an enemy combatant.'" The Fourth Circuit reversed, but did not squarely answer the certified question. It instead stressed that, because it was "undisputed that Hamdi was captured in a zone of active combat in a foreign theater of conflict," no factual inquiry or evidentiary hearing allowing Hamdi to be heard or to rebut the Government's assertions was necessary or proper. Concluding that the factual averments in the Mobbs Declaration, "if accurate," provided a sufficient basis upon which to conclude that the President had constitutionally detained Hamdi pursuant to the President's war powers, it ordered the habeas petition dismissed.

II

The threshold question before us is whether the Executive has the authority to detain citizens who qualify as "enemy combatants." There is some debate as to the proper scope of this term, and the Government has never provided any court with the full criteria that it uses in classifying individuals as such. It has made clear, however, that, for purposes of this case, the "enemy combatant" that it is seeking to detain is an individual who, it alleges, was "'part of or supporting forces hostile to the United States or coalition partners'" in Afghanistan and who "'engaged in an armed conflict against the United States'" there. We therefore answer only the narrow question before us: whether the detention of citizens falling within that definition is authorized.

The Government maintains that no explicit congressional authorization is required, because the Executive possesses plenary authority to detain pursuant to Article II of the Constitution. We do not reach the question whether Article II provides such authority, however, because we agree with the Government's alternative position, that Congress has in fact authorized Hamdi's detention, through the AUMF.

The AUMF authorizes the President to use "all necessary and appropriate force" against "nations, organizations, or persons" associated with the September 11, 2001, terrorist attacks. There can be no doubt that individuals who fought against the United States in Afghanistan as part of the Taliban, an organization known to have supported the al Qaeda terrorist network responsible for those attacks, are individuals Congress sought to target in passing the AUMF. We conclude that detention of individuals falling into the limited category we are considering, for the duration of the particular conflict in which they were captured, is so fundamental and accepted an incident to war as to be an exercise of the "necessary and appropriate force" Congress has authorized the President to use.

III

Even in cases in which the detention of enemy combatants is legally authorized, there remains the question of what process is constitutionally due to a citizen who disputes his enemy-combatant status. Hamdi argues that he is owed a meaningful and timely hearing and that "extra-judicial detention [that] begins and ends with the submission of an affidavit based on third-hand hearsay" does not comport with the Fifth and Fourteenth Amendments. The Government counters that any more process than was provided below would be both unworkable and "constitutionally intolerable." Our resolution of this dispute requires a careful examination both of the writ of habeas corpus, which Hamdi now seeks to employ as a mechanism of judicial review, and of the Due Process Clause, which informs the procedural contours of that mechanism in this instance.

A

Though they reach radically different conclusions on the process that ought to attend the present proceeding, the parties begin on common ground. All agree that, absent suspension, the writ of habeas corpus remains available to every individual detained within the United States. U.S. Const., Art. I, § 9, cl. 2 ("The Privilege of the Writ of Habeas Corpus shall not be suspended, unless when in Cases of Rebellion or Invasion the public Safety may require it"). Only in the rarest of circumstances has Congress seen fit to suspend the writ.... At all other times, it has remained a critical check on the Executive, ensuring that it does not detain individuals except in accordance with law.... All agree suspension of the writ has not occurred here. Thus, it is undisputed that Hamdi was properly before an Article III court to challenge his detention under 28 U.S.C. § 2241 .... Further, all agree that § 2241 and its companion provisions provide at least a skeletal outline of the procedures to be afforded a petitioner in federal habeas review. Most notably, § 2243 provides that "the person detained may, under oath, deny any of the facts set forth in the return or allege any other material facts," and § 2246 allows the taking of evidence in habeas proceedings by deposition, affidavit, or interrogatories. ...

C

[A] tension ... often exists between the autonomy that the Government asserts is necessary in order to pursue effectively a particular goal and the process that a citizen contends he is due before he is deprived of a constitutional right. The ordinary mechanism that we use for balancing such serious competing interests, and for determining the procedures that are necessary to ensure that a citizen is not "deprived of life, liberty, or property, without due process of law" is the test that we articulated in *Mathews v. Eldridge*, 424 U.S. 319 (1976). *Mathews* dictates that the process due in any given instance is determined by weighing "the private interest that will be affected by the official action" against the Government's asserted interest, "including the function involved" and the burdens the Government would face in providing greater process. The Mathews calculus then contemplates a judicious balancing of these concerns, through an analysis of "the risk of an erroneous deprivation" of the private interest if the process were reduced and the "probable value, if any, of additional or substitute safeguards." We take each of these steps in turn.

1

It is beyond question that substantial interests lie on both sides of the scale in this case. Hamdi's "private interest ... affected by the official action," is the most elemental of liberty interests—"the interest in being free from physical detention by one's own government." We have always been careful not to "minimize the importance and fundamental nature" of the individual's right to liberty, and we will not do so today.

Nor is the weight on this side of the *Mathews* scale offset by the circumstances of war or the accusation of treasonous behavior, for "[i]t is clear that commitment for any purpose constitutes a significant deprivation of liberty that requires due process protection," and at this stage in the *Mathews* calculus, we consider the interest of the erroneously detained individual. Indeed, as amicus briefs from media and relief organizations emphasize, the risk of erroneous deprivation of a citizen's liberty in the absence of sufficient process here is very real. Moreover, as critical as the Government's interest may be in detaining those who actually pose an immediate threat to the national security of the United States during ongoing international conflict, history and common sense teach us that an unchecked system of detention carries the potential to become a means for oppression and abuse of others who do not present that sort of threat. Because we live in a society in which "[m]ere public intolerance or animosity cannot constitutionally justify the deprivation of a person's physical liberty," our starting point for the *Mathews v. Eldridge* analysis is unaltered by the allegations surrounding the particular detainee or the organizations with which he is alleged to have associated. We reaffirm today the fundamental nature of a citizen's right to be free from involuntary confinement by his own government without due process of law, and we weigh the opposing governmental interests against the curtailment of liberty that such confinement entails.

2

On the other side of the scale are the weighty and sensitive governmental interests in ensuring that those who have in fact fought with the enemy during a war do not return to battle against the United States. . . . [T]he law of war and the realities of combat may render such detentions both necessary and appropriate, and our due process analysis need not blink at those realities. Without doubt, our Constitution recognizes that core strategic matters of war making belong in the hands of those who are best positioned and most politically accountable for making them.

The Government also argues at some length that its interests in reducing the process available to alleged enemy combatants are heightened by the practical difficulties that would accompany a system of trial-like process. In its view, military officers who are engaged in the serious work of waging battle would be unnecessarily and dangerously distracted by litigation half a world away, and discovery into military operations would both intrude on the sensitive secrets of national defense and result in a futile search for evidence buried under the rubble of war. To the extent that these burdens are triggered by heightened procedures, they are properly taken into account in our due process analysis.

3

Striking the proper constitutional balance here is of great importance to the Nation during this period of ongoing combat. But it is equally vital that our calculus not give short shrift to the values that this country holds dear or to the privilege that is American citizenship. It is during our most challenging and uncertain moments that our Nation's commitment to due process is most severely tested; and it is in those times that we must preserve our commitment at home to the principles for which we fight abroad.

With due recognition of these competing concerns, we believe that neither the process proposed by the Government nor the process apparently envisioned by the District Court below strikes the proper constitutional balance when a United States citizen is detained in the United States as an enemy combatant. That is, "the risk of erroneous deprivation" of a detainee's liberty interest is unacceptably high under the Government's proposed rule, while some of the "additional or substitute procedural safeguards" suggested by the District Court are unwarranted in light of their limited "probable value" and the burdens they may impose on the military in such cases.

We therefore hold that a citizen-detainee seeking to challenge his classification as an enemy combatant must receive notice of the factual basis for his classification, and a fair opportunity to rebut the Government's factual assertions before a neutral decision-maker. For more than a century the central meaning of procedural due process has been clear: "Parties whose rights are to be affected are entitled to be heard; and in order that they may enjoy that right they must first be notified." It is equally fundamental that "the right to notice and an opportunity to be heard 'must be granted at a meaningful time and in a meaningful manner.'" *Fuentes v. Shevin*, 407 U.S. 67 (1972). These essential constitutional promises may not be eroded.

At the same time, the exigencies of the circumstances may demand that, aside from these core elements, enemy combatant proceedings may be tailored to alleviate their uncommon potential to burden the Executive at a time of ongoing military conflict. Hearsay, for example, may need to be accepted as the most reliable available evidence from the Government in such a proceeding. Likewise, the Constitution would not be offended by a presumption in favor of the Government's evidence, so long as that presumption remained a rebuttable one and fair opportunity for rebuttal were provided. Thus, once the Government puts forth credible evidence that the habeas petitioner meets the enemy-combatant criteria, the onus could shift to the petitioner to rebut that evidence with more persuasive evidence that he falls outside the criteria. A burden-shifting scheme of this sort would meet the goal of ensuring that the errant tourist, embedded journalist, or local aid worker has a chance to prove military error while giving due regard to the Executive once it has put forth meaningful support for its conclusion that the detainee is in fact an enemy combatant. In the words of *Mathews*, process of this sort would sufficiently address the "risk of erroneous deprivation" of a detainee's liberty interest while eliminating certain procedures that have questionable additional value in light of the burden on the Government.

We think it unlikely that this basic process will have the dire impact on the central functions of war making that the Government forecasts. The parties agree that initial captures on the battlefield need not receive the process we have discussed here; that process is due only when the determination is made to continue to hold those who have been seized. The Government has made clear in its briefing that documentation regarding battlefield detainees already is kept in the ordinary course of military affairs. Any fact finding imposition created by requiring a knowledgeable affiant to summarize these records to an independent tribunal is a minimal one. Likewise, arguments that military officers ought not have to wage war under the threat of litigation lose much of their steam when factual disputes at enemy-combatant hearings are limited to the alleged combatant's acts. This focus meddles little, if at all, in the strategy or conduct of war, inquiring only into the appropriateness of continuing to detain an individual claimed to have taken up arms against the United States. While we accord the greatest respect and consideration to the judgments of military authorities in matters relating to the actual prosecution of a war, and recognize that the scope of that discretion necessarily is wide, it does not infringe on the core role of the military for the courts to exercise their own time-honored and constitutionally mandated roles of reviewing and resolving claims like those presented here.

In sum, while the full protections that accompany challenges to detentions in other settings may prove unworkable and inappropriate in the enemy combatant setting, the threats to military operations posed by a basic system of independent review are not so weighty as to trump a citizen's core rights to challenge meaningfully the Government's case and to be heard by an impartial adjudicator.

D

In so holding, we necessarily reject the Government's assertion that separation of powers principles mandate a heavily circumscribed role for the courts in such circumstances. Indeed, the position that the courts must forgo any examination of the individual case and focus exclusively on the legality of the broader detention scheme cannot be mandated by any reasonable view of separation of powers, as this approach serves only to condense power into a single branch of government. We have long since made clear that a state of war is not a blank check for the President when it comes to the rights of the Nation's citizens. *Youngstown Sheet & Tube Co. v. Sawyer*, 343 U.S. 579 (1952). Whatever power the United States Constitution envisions for the Executive in its exchanges with other nations or with "enemy organizations in times of conflict, it most assuredly envisions a role for all three branches when individual liberties are at stake...." [U]nless Congress acts to suspend it, the Great Writ of habeas corpus allows the Judicial Branch to play a necessary role in maintaining this delicate balance of governance, serving as an important judicial check on the Executive's discretion in the realm of detentions. Thus, while we do not question that our due process assessment must pay keen attention to the particular burdens faced by the Executive in the context of military action, it would turn our system of checks and balances on its head to suggest that a citizen could not make his way to court with a challenge to the factual basis for his detention by his government, simply because the Executive opposes making available such a challenge. Absent suspension of the writ by Congress, a citizen detained as an enemy combatant is entitled to this process.

Because we conclude that due process demands some system for a citizen detainee to refute his classification, the proposed "some evidence" standard is inadequate. Any process in which the Executive's factual assertions go wholly unchallenged or are simply presumed correct without any opportunity for the alleged combatant to demonstrate otherwise falls constitutionally short. As the Government itself has recognized, we have utilized the "some evidence" standard in the past as a standard of review, not as a standard of proof. That is, it primarily has been employed by courts in examining an administrative record developed after an adversarial proceeding—one with process at least of the sort that we today hold is constitutionally mandated in the citizen enemy—combatant setting. This standard therefore is ill suited to the situation in which a habeas petitioner has received no prior proceedings before any tribunal and had no prior opportunity to rebut the Executive's factual assertions before a neutral decisionmaker.

Today we are faced only with such a case. Aside from unspecified "screening" processes, and military interrogations in which the Government suggests Hamdi could have contested his classification, Hamdi has received no process. An interrogation by one's captor, however effective an intelligence-gathering tool, hardly constitutes a constitutionally adequate fact finding before a neutral decisionmaker .... Plainly, the "process" Hamdi has received is not that to which he is entitled under the Due Process Clause.

There remains the possibility that the standards we have articulated could be met by an appropriately authorized and properly constituted military tribunal. Indeed, it is notable that military regulations already provide for such process in related instances, dictating that tribunals be made available to determine the status of enemy detainees who assert prisoner-of-war status under the Geneva Convention. In the absence of such process, however, a court that receives a petition for a writ of habeas corpus from an alleged enemy combatant must itself ensure that the minimum requirements of due process are achieved. Both courts below recognized as much, focusing their energies on the question of whether Hamdi was due an opportunity to rebut the Government's case against him. The Government, too, proceeded on this assumption, presenting its affidavit and then seeking that it be evaluated under a deferential standard of review based on burdens that it alleged would accompany any greater process. As we have discussed, a habeas court in a case such as this may accept affidavit evidence like that contained in the Mobbs Declaration, so long as it also permits the alleged combatant to present his own factual case to rebut the Government's return. We anticipate that a District Court would proceed with the caution that we have indicated is necessary in this setting, engaging in a fact finding process that is both prudent and incremental. We have no reason to doubt that courts faced with these sensitive matters will pay proper heed both to the matters of national security that might arise in an individual case and to the constitutional limitations safeguarding essential liberties that remain vibrant even in times of security concerns.

IV

Hamdi asks us to hold that the Fourth Circuit also erred by denying him immediate access to counsel upon his detention and by disposing of the case without permitting him to meet with an attorney. Since our grant of certiorari in this case, Hamdi has been appointed counsel, with whom he has met for consultation purposes on several occasions, and with whom he is now being granted unmonitored meetings. He unquestionably has the right to access to counsel in connection with the proceedings on remand. No further consideration of this issue is necessary at this stage of the case.

The judgment of the United States Court of Appeals for the Fourth Circuit is vacated, and the case is remanded for further proceedings.

It is so ordered.

[Justice Scalia dissented, and was joined by Justice Stevens. In his dissent, Justice Scalia criticized the Court for its use of the *Mathews v. Eldridge* test, pointing out that that case involved withdrawal of disability benefits, and the detention here was of a much more serious character. Scalia argued that there were only two options for detaining Hamdi. The U.S. could either bring full criminal proceedings against him, or Congress could suspend the writ of habeas corpus. Justice Scalia pointed out that non-criminal detention of citizens is limited to very narrow and concrete categories, such as temporary quarantine to prevent the spread of infectious diseases, or civil commitment of the dangerously mentally ill. In cases outside of these narrow categories, the criminal process was the only constitutionally acceptable procedure for detention, whether it was intended to punish or to incapacitate.]

Justice Souter, with whom Justice Ginsburg joins, concurring in part, dissenting in part, and concurring in the judgment.

Because I find Hamdi's detention forbidden by § 4001(a) and unauthorized by the Force Resolution, I would not reach any questions of what process he may be due in litigating disputed issues in a proceeding under the habeas statute or prior to the habeas enquiry itself. For me, it suffices that the Government has failed to justify holding him in the absence of a further Act of Congress, criminal charges, a showing that the detention conforms to the laws of war, or a demonstration that § 4001(a) is unconstitutional. I would therefore vacate the judgment of the Court of Appeals and remand for proceedings consistent with this view.

Since this disposition does not command a majority of the Court, however, the need to give practical effect to the conclusions of eight members of the Court rejecting the Government's position calls for me to join with the plurality in ordering remand on terms closest to those I would impose. Although I think litigation of Hamdi's status as an enemy combatant is unnecessary, the terms of the plurality's remand will allow Hamdi to offer evidence that he is not an enemy combatant, and he should at the least have the benefit of that opportunity.

It should go without saying that in joining with the plurality to produce a judgment, I do not adopt the plurality's resolution of constitutional issues that I would not reach. It is not that I could disagree with the plurality's determinations (given the plurality's view of the Force Resolution) that someone in Hamdi's position is entitled at a minimum to notice of the Government's claimed factual basis for holding him, and to a fair chance to rebut it before a neutral decision maker, nor, of course, could I disagree with the plurality's affirmation of Hamdi's right to counsel. On the other hand, I do not mean to imply agreement that the Government could claim an evidentiary presumption casting the burden of rebuttal on Hamdi, or that an opportunity to litigate before a military tribunal might obviate or truncate enquiry by a court on habeas.

Subject to these qualifications, I join with the plurality in a judgment of the Court vacating the Fourth Circuit's judgment and remanding the case.

Notes and Questions

1. Hamdi was one of three "War on Terrorism" cases decided by the Supreme Court in 2004. The other two cases dealt with issues involving the jurisdiction of the federal courts to review the detentions of suspected terrorists. In *Rasul v. Bush*, 542 U.S.

466 (2004), the Court, with Justice Stevens writing the majority opinion, ruled that U.S. courts have jurisdiction under the same habeas corpus statute involved in Hamdi to consider challenges to the legality of the detentions of foreign nationals captured abroad and imprisoned at a U.S. naval base at Guantanamo Bay, Cuba. Three Justices dissented. *Rumsfeld v. Padilla*, 124 S. Ct. 2711 (2004), held that a U.S. citizen seized in the U.S. and held as an enemy combatant had brought his legal challenge in the wrong federal district court. It thus left open the question of whether a U.S. citizen who, unlike Hamdi, was captured in the U.S. and not on a foreign battlefield can bring such a claim.

2. Following the Supreme Court's staunch proclamation that "[i]t is during our most challenging and uncertain moments that our Nation's commitment to due process is most severely tested; and it is in those times that we must preserve our commitment at home to the principles for which we fight abroad," the Bush administration faced a choice: either hold a hearing for Hamdi—risking an embarrassment for the administration—or negotiate with him on an arrangement where he would be removed from the country. In September 2004, a deal was struck: Hamdi was to be released from detention and a U.S. military aircraft would fly him to Saudi Arabia. This agreement came with the extraordinary condition that he relinquish his U.S. citizenship. Additionally, Hamdi was required to renounce terrorism, agree to live in Saudi Arabia for five years and not sue the U.S. government over his captivity.[28]

3. In *In re Guantanamo*, 355 F. Supp. 2d 443 (2005), the U.S. District Court for the District of Columbia applied *Rasul* in the light of *Hamdi*, determining that the detainees are entitled to the protection of the Due Process Clause. Among the court's further determinations was its finding that the definition of "enemy combatant" contained in the Combatant Status Review Tribunal order is overly broad and vague. The order states that an "enemy combatant" shall mean "an individual who was part of or supporting Taliban or al Qaeda forces, or associated forces that are engaged in hostilities against the United States or its coalition partners. This includes any person who has committed a belligerent act nor has directly supported hostilities in aid of enemy armed forces." The court points out that use of the word "includes" suggests that an "enemy combatant" could refer to a person who had neither committed a belligerent act nor directly supported hostilities.

4. As we saw in *Verdugo-Urquidez*, the Court's majority favored legislation as the appropriate forum for clarifying the constitutional rights of non-residents and, under some circumstances, non-citizen residents. Here, referencing recent Guantanamo cases, legal scholar Geoffrey Stone takes a different view, pointing to courts as the most appropriate location for weighing the trade-offs between civil liberties and security. Reflecting on the Supreme Court's rejection of key elements of the

28. *See generally* Peter Nyers, *The Accidental Citizen: Acts of Sovereignty and (Un)Making Citizenship*, 35 ECON. & SOC. 22 (2006); *see also* Lina Nasr El Hag Ali, *Waging War on the Citizen: State Sovereignty, Citizen Death and the War on Terror*, 1 J. INT'L REL., PEACE STUDS. & DEV. (2015).

government's position in then-recent cases involving detainees, he welcomes what he sees as a shift in the Court's approach—from deference to close scrutiny:

> As a practical matter, military and executive officials will invariably overvalue national security concerns at the expense of civil liberties. There may be sound reasons for judges to be cautious when they second-guess military and executive officials, but pragmatism—informed by experience—demands that courts be more rigorous in their exercise of judicial review if we are to avoid more decisions like *Schenck, Korematsu*, and *Dennis*. Of course, the comparative advantage of courts over the executive and legislative branches in interpreting and enforcing individual liberties is familiar. Responsiveness to the electorate may be essential to the day-to-day workings of democracy, but that responsiveness can lead the government too readily to sacrifice the rights of those who are regarded as different, dangerous, or disloyal. Judges with life tenure and a more focused attention on the preservation of civil liberties are more likely to protect our freedoms than the elected branches of government.
>
> Because we know from experience that there is a pattern of excessive restriction of civil liberties in wartime, courts in the twenty-first century must abandon the "logical" presumption of deference to executive and military authority and employ a more rigorous standard of review. In light of experience, we know that the "logical" presumption is counter-productive. The lesson of decisions like *Schenck, Korematsu* and *Dennis* is that courts must closely scrutinize invocation of military necessity and national security as justification for limiting civil liberties.[29]

What do you see as the best reasons to prefer Congress or the courts as the source of answers to the most difficult civil liberties questions as they arise in wartime or other times of crisis? And if war is permanent, does the logic of "wartime" remain valid?

B. Surveillance without warrants

In the wake of September 11, 2001, President George W. Bush authorized the President's Surveillance Program as one component of the international counter-terrorism effort. As part of this initiative, the National Security Agency (NSA) implemented the Terrorist Surveillance Program (TSP) with the purpose of intercepting al Qaeda communications overseas where these involved at least one party who is not a U.S. citizen. In 2005, a *New York Times* article questioned the legal legitimacy of this surveillance program,[30] sparking a widespread controversy over

29. Geoffrey Stone, *National Security v. Civil Liberties*, 95 Cal. L. Rev. 2203, 2209 (2007) (notes omitted).

30. James Risen & Eric Lichtblau, *Bush Lets U.S. Spy on Callers Without Courts*, N.Y. Times (December 16, 2005), http://www.nytimes.com/2005/12/16/politics/bush-lets-us-spy-on-callers-without-courts.html?_r=0.

the president's authority to establish such a program, and the legitimacy of the NSA's surveillance operation. Shortly thereafter, a lawsuit against the NSA was brought by the American Civil Liberties Union on behalf of journalists and others whose contacts led them to believe they may have been among those secretly surveilled.

The Sixth Circuit's opinion is excerpted below:

American Civil Liberties Union v. National Security Agency

493 F.3d 644 (6th Cir. 2007)

Batchelder, Circuit Judge.

The United States National Security Agency ("NSA") appeals from the decision of the District Court for the Eastern District of Michigan that granted summary judgment against the NSA and imposed a permanent injunction. The plaintiffs are a collection of associations and individuals led by the American Civil Liberties Union, and they cross-appeal. Because we cannot find that any of the plaintiffs have standing for any of their claims, we must vacate the district court's order and remand for dismissal of the entire action.

I

Sometime after the September 11, 2001, terrorist attacks, President Bush authorized the NSA to begin a counter-terrorism operation that has come to be known as the Terrorist Surveillance Program ("TSP"). Although the specifics remain undisclosed, it has been publicly acknowledged that the TSP includes the interception (i.e., wiretapping), without warrants, of telephone and email communications where one party to the communication is located outside the United States and the NSA has "a reasonable basis to conclude that one party to the communication is a member of al Qaeda, affiliated with al Qaeda, or a member of an organization affiliated with al Qaeda, or working in support of al Qaeda."

The plaintiffs in this action include journalists, academics, and lawyers who regularly communicate with individuals located overseas, who the plaintiffs believe are the types of people the NSA suspects of being al Qaeda terrorists, affiliates, or supporters, and are therefore likely to be monitored under the TSP. From this suspicion, and the limited factual foundation in this case, the plaintiffs allege that they have a "well founded belief" that their communications are being tapped. According to the plaintiffs, the NSA's operation of the TSP—and the possibility of warrantless surveillance—subjects them to conditions that constitute an irreparable harm.

The plaintiffs filed suit in the Eastern District of Michigan, seeking a permanent injunction against the NSA's continuation of the TSP and a declaration that two particular aspects of the TSP—warrantless wiretapping and data mining—violate the First and Fourth Amendments, the Separation of Powers Doctrine, the Administrative Procedures Act ("APA"), Title III of the Omnibus Crime Control and Safe Streets Act ("Title III"), and the Foreign Intelligence Surveillance Act ("FISA"). Both sides moved for summary judgment. The district court dismissed the data mining aspect of the plaintiffs' claim, but granted judgment to the plaintiffs regarding the warrantless wiretapping. See *ACLU v. NSA*, 438 F.Supp.2d 754, 782 (E.D.Mich.2006).

The NSA had invoked the State Secrets Doctrine to bar the discovery or admission of evidence that would "expose [confidential] matters which, in the interest of national security, should not be divulged." See *United States v. Reynolds*, 345 U.S. 1, 10 (1953). The NSA argued that, without the privileged information, none of the named plaintiffs could establish standing. The district court applied the state secrets privilege, but rejected the NSA's argument, holding instead that three publicly acknowledged facts about the TSP—(1) it eavesdrops, (2) without warrants, (3) on international telephone and email communications in which at least one of the parties is a suspected al Qaeda affiliate—were sufficient to establish standing. Moreover, the district court found these three facts sufficient to grant summary judgment to the plaintiffs on the merits of their claims, resulting in a declaratory judgment and the imposition of an injunction. These three facts constitute all the evidence in the record relating to the NSA's conduct under the TSP.

In deciding the merits, the district court construed the Fourth Amendment as an absolute rule that "requires prior warrants for any reasonable search," and announced that "searches conducted without prior approval by a judge or magistrate were per se unreasonable." Having found that the NSA was operating without warrants, the district court concluded without further explanation that President Bush had "undisputedly violated the Fourth [Amendment] . . . and accordingly ha[d] violated the First Amendment Rights of these Plaintiffs as well." Proceeding from this conclusion, the court deemed the TSP unconstitutional and issued an order enjoining its further operation entirely:

> IT IS HEREBY ORDERED that Defendants [i.e., NSA], its agents, employees, representatives, and any other persons or entities in active concert or participation with Defendants, are permanently enjoined from directly or indirectly utilizing the Terrorist Surveillance Program (hereinafter "TSP") in any way, including, but not limited to, conducting warrantless wiretaps of telephone and internet communications, in contravention of the Foreign Intelligence Surveillance Act (hereinafter "FISA") and Title III;
>
> IT IS FURTHER ORDERED AND DECLARED that the TSP violates the Separation of Powers doctrine, the Administrative Procedures Act, the First and Fourth Amendments to the United States Constitution, the FISA and Title III[.]

The NSA moved for a stay of the injunction pending appeal, which the district court denied. Meanwhile, the NSA appealed, arguing that the plaintiffs lacked standing and that the State Secrets Doctrine prevented adjudication on the merits. This court stayed the injunction pending the outcome of this appeal. See *ACLU v. NSA*, 467 F.3d 590, 591 (6th Cir.2006).

Standing to litigate this claim requires a showing of three elements: (1) injury in fact, (2) causation, and (3) redressability.

Injury in Fact

[T]o allege a sufficient injury under the First Amendment, a plaintiff must establish that he or she is regulated, constrained, or compelled directly by the government's actions, instead of by his or her own subjective chill. The D.C. Circuit's decision in *Presbyterian Church v. Reagan*, 738 F.2d 1375, at 1380, involved a plaintiff's First Amendment challenge to alleged government surveillance. The *Reagan* court clarified why mere subjective chill deriving from government surveillance is insufficient to establish a concrete injury, stating:

> The harm of "chilling effect" is to be distinguished from the immediate threat of concrete, harmful action. The former consists of present deterrence [of the plaintiff, by the government,] from First Amendment conduct because of the difficulty [that plaintiff has in] determining the application of a [government practice] to that conduct, and will not by itself support standing.

"'Chilling effect' is cited as the reason why the governmental imposition is invalid [under the First Amendment] rather than as the harm which entitles the plaintiffs to challenge it." In an attempt to establish harm, the *Reagan* plaintiffs claimed that they were "especially likely to be targets of the unlawful [surveillance] authorized by the order," but the court explained:

> Even if it were conceded that . . . the plaintiffs [were] at greater risk than the public at large, that would still fall far short of the "genuine threat" required to support this theory of standing, as opposed to mere "speculative" harm. It must be borne in mind that this order does not direct intelligence-gathering activities against all persons who could conceivably come within its scope, but merely authorizes them.

The *Reagan* court therefore held that the plaintiffs failed to satisfy the injury-in-fact requirement because they did not allege that "any direct governmental constraint" was "threatened or even contemplated against them." The present case is no different.

Causation

In the present case, the "putatively illegal action" is the NSA's interception of overseas communications without warrants (specifically FISA warrants), and the "threatened or actual injury" is the added cost of in-person communication with the overseas contacts (or correspondingly, the diminished performance resulting from the inability to communicate). Therefore, to show causation, the plaintiffs must show that, but for the lack of warrants (or FISA compliance), they would not incur this added cost. There are two causal pathways based on the two types of alleged injury. In the first: (1) the NSA's warrantless wiretapping, (2) creates in the plaintiffs a "well founded belief" that their overseas telephone and email communications are being intercepted, which (3) requires the plaintiffs to refrain from these communications (i.e., chills communication), and (4) compels the plaintiffs to travel overseas to meet personally with these contacts in order to satisfy their professional responsibilities, thereby (5) causing the plaintiffs to incur additional costs. In the second: (1) the NSA's warrantless wiretapping (2) causes the "well founded belief," which (3) compels the overseas contacts to refuse to communicate by telephone or email (i.e., chills communication), thereby (4) requiring in-person communication, with its (5) associated additional costs. The district court attempted to articulate this relationship: "All of the Plaintiffs contend that the TSP has caused clients, witnesses and sources to discontinue their communications with plaintiffs out of fear that their communications will be intercepted." From this, the district court theorized: "Plaintiffs would be able to continue using the telephone and email in the execution of their professional responsibilities if the Defendants were not undisputedly and admittedly conducting warrantless wiretaps of conversations." In considering these causal pathways, I question the second step (whether the "well founded belief" is actually founded on the warrantless wiretapping) and refute the third step (whether the unwillingness to communicate is actually caused by the warrantless character of the wiretaps).

Redressability

In the present case, the plaintiffs requested a declaratory judgment and an injunction. They theorize that their injury (i.e., deficient professional performance or the additional cost of in-person communication) will be redressed by a declaration that the NSA's practice of warrantless wiretapping is unlawful, because it naturally follows that the unlawful conduct will be prohibited. The declaratory judgment thus forms the basis for an injunction prohibiting interception of communications without FISA compliance. The district court agreed, declaring the NSA's conduct illegal and imposing an injunction, on the belief that its injunction would redress the plaintiffs' injury by assuring them "that they could freely engage in conversations and correspond via email without concern, at least without notice, that such communications were being monitored." This theory of redressability rests on the premise that the NSA's compliance with FISA's warrant requirements will entice the plaintiffs and their contacts to "freely engage in conversations and correspond via email without concern." The likelihood of this outcome, however, "can, at best, be termed only speculative"; it is just as likely (if not more likely) that, even with the imposition of a warrant requirement, the plaintiffs' current situation will not change—their fears will not be abated.

For the foregoing reasons, the plaintiffs in the present action have no standing to pursue their First Amendment claim. Even if they could demonstrate injury, they cannot establish causation, and their alleged injury is not redressable by the remedy they seek....

VI

We hold that the plaintiffs do not have standing to assert their claims in federal court. Accordingly, we VACATE the order of the district court and REMAND this case to the district court with instructions to DISMISS for lack of jurisdiction.

Notes

1. In *American Civil Liberties Union v. National Security Agency*, the U.S. Court of Appeals for the Sixth Circuit refused to rule on the legality of the program after

finding that plaintiffs for the case did not have standing to bring the lawsuit, because they could not prove that they had been targets of the program. They could not, in part, because the program itself, as well as its targets, were secret. This "catch-22" aspect of the argument was widely criticized, as were the court's reliance on a view of executive power in the context of state secrets and its reading of the Fourth Amendment—leaving the plaintiffs with no recourse.

2. In 2008, the U.S. Supreme Court turned down an appeal from the ACLU to pursue the lawsuit against the NSA. The case illustrates the legal obstacles facing plaintiffs who wish to bring a claim against the NSA. This early controversy marked the beginning of a long debate regarding the powers of the executive in enacting surveillance programs. The following case note argues for the merits of granting standing as a contribution to a more robust check on executive power:

> [T]he influence of the state secrets privilege is operating as an artificial bar to standing in *ACLU v. NSA*. That is, there is no real question that there is an Article III "case or controversy" here, or that some people have an injury that is "actual or imminent, not 'conjectural' or 'hypothetical' and that was caused by government action. Thus there are good reasons for courts to err on the side of limiting the distorting effect of the state secrets privilege on the judicial system when it is possible to do so without endangering national security. Recognizing standing for TSP plaintiffs with a low level of probabilityof injury is one opportunity to do so. All this is not to say that finding standing for the plaintiffs willnecessarily result in an injunction against the government. Courts may find that the President has inherent authority to conduct warrantlesssurveillance in the foreign intelligence sphere, or that there isnot enough information available about the program to find that it violated FISA or the Fourth Amendment, or that the controversy ismoot because the President has suggested that TSP is no longer in operation,or that this type of dispute is best left to the political branches or to the electorate. There may, in short, be good reasons to ultimately deny TSP plaintiffs relief. But it is inappropriate to do so through the rote application of traditionally restrictive Fourth Amendment injury standards.[31]

In 2013, the ACLU again attempted to challenge the NSA's actions. The lawsuit came after Edward Snowden's disclosures provided evidence of NSA's surveillance operations. Edward Snowden, a former employee of an NSA contractee, leaked documents acquired in the course of his employment. He sought asylum in Russia where (at this writing) he remains.

In a separate development, the British newspaper, The Guardian, revealed that the U.S. Foreign Intelligence Surveillance Court—established by FISA to review applications for warrants related to national security regulations—had ordered Verizon

---

31. *Federal Courts—Standing—Sixth Circuit Denies Standing To Challenge Terrorist Surveillance Program.*—ACLU v. NSA, *493 F.3d 644 (6th Cir. 2007)*, 121 Harv. L. Rev. 922, 929 (2008) (notes omitted).

to provide the NSA with data about citizens' telephone calls over a three-month period without requiring NSA to obtain a warrant. Under the terms of the USA PATRIOT Act, the data sought by NSA, classified as "metadata," does not require a warrant. The ACLU challenged warrantless collection of metadata as a violation of the First and Fourth Amendment rights of U.S. citizens, seeking a permanent injunction. The government's motion for dismissal was granted by the district court but remanded on appeal by the Second Circuit. Meanwhile, the section of the USA PATRIOT Act authorizing metadata collection expired, and Congress revised that provision when it passed the successor legislation known as the USA FREEDOM Act.[32] The new provision barred metadata sweeps of the kind at issue in the suit, but allowed a continuation for a transition period of 180 days. The ACLU sought an injunction before the Second Circuit, and this was denied on the grounds of the court's reluctance to "disturb the decision by Congress to provide for a 180-day transition to put an orderly end to the telephone metadata program."[33]

C. Extraterritorial targeted killing

Drones, including remotely piloted vehicles and unmanned aerial vehicles (UAVs), have long been part of the U.S. military's arsenal, and are now a key component in the fight against terrorism. The United States has increasingly conducted drone programs since the mid-2000s, most recently in Afghanistan, Iraq, Libya, and Syria,[34] to target enemy combatants overseas, including U.S. citizens.[35]

> Although the drone program remains officially classified, a mix of on-the-ground reporting, eye-witness accounts, and leaked information allow [for] tentative assessments of the legality of signature drone strike protocol, both in theory and as it has been executed. The head of the Central Intelligence Agency ("CIA") developed "signature strikes," and the CIA made critical decisions about the development and use of the drone program [that] target individuals due solely to their observed pattern of behavior, or "signature."[36]

---

32. American Civil Liberties Union v. Clapper, 804 F.3d 617 (2d Cir. 2015).

33. *Id.* at 618.

34. *See* Oren Gross, *The New Way of War: Is There a Duty to Use Drones?*, 67 Fla. L. Rev. 1, 2–3 (2015).

35. Letter from Eric H. Holder, U.S. Attorney Gen., to Senator Patrick J. Leahy, Chairman, Comm. on the Judiciary 1–5 (May 22, 2013), http://i2.cdn.turner.com/cnn/2013/images/05/22/holder-letter-5-22-13.pdf; *see also* Gross, *supra* note 34, at 4 ("The Obama '[A]dministration has enthusiastically embraced the . . . drone program, an ambitious and historically unusual war campaign by American spies,' [with] Leon Panetta, the former director of the CIA, famously proclaimed that drones were 'the only game in town in terms of confronting and trying to disrupt the al-Qa[e]da leadership.'").

36. Kristina Benson, *"Kill 'em and Sort it Out Later:" Signature Drone Strikes and International Humanitarian Law*, 27 Glob. Bus. & Dev. L.J. 17 (2014).

It is an understatement to say that the drone attacks are controversial as extraterritorial killings, especially when these involve U.S. citizens as targets.[37]

In February 2013, an unsigned Justice Department White Paper was released outlining the Department's legal justification for the lawful use of lethal force against American citizens abroad, acting as leaders of terrorist organizations such as Al-Qa'ida as a senior operational leader of Al-Qa'ida or a similar organization.[38] The White Paper acknowledges the extraterritorial applicability of the Fourth and Fifth Amendments, but not a shield granting immunity to Americans who commit harms against the United States in the service of a hostile force. The White Paper outlines three conditions that must be met to carry out such an operation: at "(1) an informed, high-level official of the U.S. government has determined that the targeted individual poses an imminent threat of violent attack against the United States, (2) capture is infeasible, and the United States continues to monitor whether capture becomes feasible; and (3) the operation would be conducted in a manner consistent with the applicable law of war principles." Each reflects the principles of necessity, distinction, proportionality, and humanity.

The White Paper additionally addresses the due process concerns of citizens abroad, relying on *Hamdi,* excerpted *supra*, to provide the legal framework for lawful, lethal operations. The memo recites the simple balancing test from *Mathews v. Eldredge*[39]—that the Government's interest must outweigh an individual's private interest before a deprivation of life, liberty, or property—to analyze whether an American citizen's Fifth Amendment rights are violated by a U.S. overseas operation aimed at killing American Al-Qa'ida operatives abroad. In weighing these interests, the government must, among other things, show that the alleged Al-Qa'ida operative "poses an imminent threat of violent attack against the United States."[40] This, however, does not require the United States to have clear evidence that a specific attack on U.S. persons and interests will take place in the immediate future.[41]

International law scholar Professor Mary Ellen O'Connell responded to the White Paper in a New York Times op ed, criticizing the White Paper's "sweeping claims of executive power" that exceed constitutional and prudential boundaries: "The paper

37. *See generally* Alberto R. Gonzales, *Drones: The Power to Kill*, 82 GEO. WASH. L. REV. 1 (2013); Gross, *supra* note 34 at 1.

38. The Department of Justice memo was authored and marked classified in 2010; under pressure from Congress and the press, the White House authorized the release of a 16-page White Paper outlining the legal arguments in justification of targeting U.S. citizens in drone attacks. Department of Justice White Paper, *Lawfulness of a Lethal Operation Directed Against a U.S. Citizen who is a Senior Operational Leader of Al-Qa'ida or an Associated Force*, http://msnbcmedia.msn.com/i/msnbc/sections/news/020413_DOJ_White_Paper.pdf. *See also* Letter of Attorney General Holder to Senator Leahy (May 22, 2013), https://www.justice.gov/slideshow/AG-letter-5-22-13.pdf.

39. 548 U.S. 557, 628–31 (2006).

40. White Paper, *supra* note 38, at 1.

41. *Id.* at 7.

denies Congress and the federal courts a role in authorizing the killings—or even reviewing them afterward."[42]

Professor O'Connell argues that the United States is involved in a true armed conflict only in Afghanistan. Yet drone attacks have been carried out in Yemen, Somalia and Pakistan and may soon begin in Libya, Mali and Nigeria. None of these countries have attacked America, so no right of self-defense can be invoked under the United Nations Charter, as the white paper asserts.

The White Paper rejected this line of argument as lacking "authoritative precedent." Instead, citing *Hamdan v. Rumsfeld*, the Justice Department asserted that the armed conflict with Al-Qa'ida is not an "international" conflict given that the enemy "is a transnational non-state actor"—a crucial distinction for our purposes.

O'Connell's essay contributed to the public's concern with regard to bystander deaths in drone attacks. In July 2016, the Obama administration took the unprecedented step of releasing statistics of counterterrorism strikes.[43] From January 20, 2009, until the end of 2015, the United States conducted 473 "strikes against terrorist targets outside areas of active hostilities."[44] According to the government, these efforts resulted in between 2372 and 2581 combatant deaths, and between 64 and 116 noncombatant deaths, including "deaths for which there is an insufficient basis for assessing that the deceased is a combatant."[45] Independent studies find higher numbers of bystander casualties.[46]

Notes and Questions

1. Drones continue to be at the center of legal and political debates. See, for example, Rosa Brooks—referring to the drones and secret operations against extraterritorial terrorism as a "secret war":

> This secret war . . . has gotten us very far away from anything Congress contemplated in the 2001 Authorization to Use Military Force (AUMF). Go back and look at the language of the AUMF: It states that the President may "[U]se all necessary and appropriate force against those nations, organizations, or persons he determines planned, authorized, committed, or aided the terrorist attacks that occurred on September 11, 2001, or harbored such organizations or persons, in order to prevent any future acts of international terrorism against the United States by such nations, organizations or persons."

---

42. Mary Ellen O'Connell, *The Questions Brennan Can't Dodge*, N.Y. Times, Feb. 7, 2011, at A27.

43. Charlie Savage & Scott Shane, *U.S. Makes Public the Death Toll From Airstrikes*, N.Y. Times, July 2, 2016, at A1; Scott Shane, *Drone Strike Data Reveals Limits of Fighting Terrorists From Sky*, N.Y. Times, July 4, 2016 at A1.

44. https://assets.documentcloud.org/documents/2938258/Airstrike-Death-Toll.pdf.

45. *Id.*

46. "The Long War Journal, whose estimates are lowest, counted 207 civilian deaths in Pakistan and Yemen alone. The security policy group New America in Washington estimated a minimum of 216 in those two countries, and the London-based Bureau of Investigative Journalism estimated the civilian toll under Mr. Obama between 380 and 801." Shane, *supra* note 43.

> Note that although this language gives the executive branch authorization to use force, it does not authorize the use of force against anyone, anywhere, anytime. Rather, it authorizes the use of force specifically and solely against those organizations and states that planned, authorized, committed, or aided the September 11 attacks, or who harbored those who did.[47]

Brooks' comment highlights what may be at stake in different analyses of executive power as between structural accounts (e.g., residing in separation of powers, or categories of foreign versus domestic) and situational accounts (e.g., security crises). She argues that the AUMF was situationally specific, and that its extension to the current "secret war" gives it (in effect) an unwarranted structural legitimacy. How do you respond to this critique—whether in agreement, disagreement, or something in between—given the flexibility of executive power in other areas of transnational law?

2. Note the Justice Department assertion that armed conflict against Al-Qa'ida is not an "international" conflict, given that the enemy is a "transnational non-state actor"?[48] To what extent does this usage of *transnational* correspond to transnationalism in other contexts, such as investor-state agreements? Do executive transnational powers follow or lead the transnationalism of capital investment, or is there no necessary connection?

D. Torture

In contrast to the examples above where American citizens were enemy combatants, the following case, *Vance v. Rumsfeld*, reflects the differences in two major perspectives concerning ordinary citizens whose Fourth Amendment rights may have been violated abroad. We excerpt the first judgment reached in the case by Seventh Circuit Judge David Hamilton, rejecting the government's claims to immunity. We then excerpt the Seventh Circuit's ruling upon rehearing the case *en banc*, affirming the breadth of executive power in the circumstances involved in the case.

1. Panel Opinion

In *Vance v. Rumsfeld*,[49] two American contractors working in Iraq during the Iraq War, brought suit against then-Secretary of Defense Donald Rumsfeld and the United States, alleging that they were detained indefinitely at a U.S. military prison and tortured by U.S. military personnel. Donald Vance and Nathan Ertel's complaint

---

47. Rosa Brooks, *Cross-Border Targeted Killings:"Lawful but Awful"?*, 2 HARV. J.L. & PUB. POL'Y: FEDERALIST ED. 233, 235 (notes and paragraphing omitted).

48. *Compare* Andrew C. Orr, Note, *Unmanned, Unprecedented, and Unresolved: The Status of American Drone Strikes in Pakistan Under International Law*, 44 CORNELL INT'L L. J. 729 (2011) (making the case that the campaign as a whole is permissible under international law), *with* Kristina Benson, *"Kill 'em and Sort it Out Later:" Signature Drone Strikes and International Humanitarian Law*, 27 GLOB. BUS. & DEV. L.J. (2014); Frédéric Mégret, *The Humanitarian Problem with Drones*, 2013 UTAH L. REV. 1283 (2013); Milena Sterio, *The United States' Use of Drones in the War on Terror: The (Il)legality of Targeted Killings under International Law*, 45 CASE W. RES. J. INT'L L. 197 (2012).

49. 701 F.3d 193 (7th Cir. 2012) (en banc), *rev'g*, 701 F.3d 193 (7th Cir. 2012) (notes omitted).

alleged that they suffered through a horrific ordeal, despite their continual efforts to follow the military's commands: After reporting to the U.S. government the suspicious and illegal activity they saw while working for a private Iraqi security services firm, Shield Group Security ("SGS"), SGS became suspicious of the plaintiffs and confiscated the men's credentials to access the secure "Green Zone." This left the plaintiffs trapped in SGS's compound in the insecure "Red Zone." The U.S. government told the men to follow hostage situation protocol and that they would be rescued by U.S. government forces.

U.S. forces extracted the men from the SGS compound and took the men to the U.S. Embassy in Baghdad. There, military personnel seized the plaintiffs' belongings. After a few hours of sleep, they were arrested, blindfolded, and moved to Camp Prosperity, a U.S. military compound in Baghdad. There, the plaintiffs were jailed, strip-searched, threatened, and held in solitary confinement without access to lawyers.

Two days later, the plaintiffs were moved to another military installation in Baghdad, Camp Cropper. There, civilian and military officials subjected the plaintiffs to physical and psychological torture for the remainder of their stays in Iraq; Ertel was held for six weeks, while Vance was held for three months. Their treatment included solitary confinement in dirty jail cells which were kept lighted at all times; air-conditioning to excessively cold temperatures; "intolerably-loud volumes" of music; and withholding food, water, and medical care. Outside the cells, during interrogation sessions, the plaintiffs were allegedly "hooded" and slammed into walls while being led about blindfolded. At all times, the plaintiffs were threatened with "excessive force" should they not comply with the military's demands.

Despite all of this, the plaintiffs were never charged with any crime or even designated as security threats. Both men were eventually released and dropped off at the Baghdad International Airport to find their own ways home.

The plaintiffs filed a *Bivens* action, charging the government, Rumsfeld, and other unknown defendants with Fourth Amendment violations. In particular, the plaintiffs alleged that Secretary Rumsfeld had personal knowledge of the government's constitutional violations. The government moved to dismiss the plaintiffs' claims under Federal Rule of Civil Procedure 12(b)(6), and the trial court denied the motion.

The defendants appealed to the Seventh Circuit. In his opinion for the panel, Judge David Hamilton first found that the plaintiffs adequately alleged Secretary Rumsfeld's personal responsibility for their mistreatment in Iraq in their complaint (as is required in a *Bivens* claim), finding that the plaintiffs "pled facts showing that it is plausible, and not merely speculative, that Secretary Rumsfeld was personally responsible for creating the policies that caused the alleged unconstitutional torture." In particular, it was Secretary Rumsfeld who personally approved the use of techniques such as isolation, loud music, and extreme temperatures in Iraq.

Second, Judge Hamilton rejected Secretary Rumsfeld's qualified immunity defense, based on a theory that a government employee could have reasonably believed the treatment was not unconstitutional. Judge Hamilton found the alleged abuse to violate the plaintiffs' clearly-established constitutional rights and that a person in Secretary Rumsfeld's position should reasonably have known that American citizens have the right to be free from government torture.

Finally—and by far most critically—Judge Hamilton held that U.S. civilians are entitled to a constitutional remedy under *Bivens* against military officials, even if the conduct occurred in a war zone. As Judge Hamilton explained:

> The unprecedented breadth of defendants' argument should not be overlooked. The defendants contend that a *Bivens* remedy should not be available to U.S. citizens for any constitutional wrong, including torture and even cold-blooded murder, if the wrong occurs in a war zone. The defendants' theory would apply to any soldier or federal official, from the very top of the chain of command to the very bottom.
>
> In fact, Congress has acted to provide civil remedies to *aliens* who are tortured by *their* governments. It would be extraordinary to find that there is no such remedy for *U.S. citizens* tortured by *their own government.*
>
> If we were to accept the defendants' invitation to recognize the broad and unprecedented immunity they seek, then the judicial branch—which is charged with enforcing constitutional rights—would be leaving our citizens defenseless to serious abuse or worse by another branch of their own government. We recognize that wrongdoers in the military would still be subject to criminal prosecution within the military itself. Relying solely on the military to police its own treatment of civilians, however, would amount to an extraordinary abdication of our government's checks and balances that preserve Americans' liberty. The district court correctly allowed plaintiffs to proceed with their *Bivens* claims for torture.

The Seventh Circuit panel opinion was groundbreaking. In effect, it established limits on the immunities conferred upon high-ranking officials, and could have potentially left those officials liable for their roles in creating and enforcing policies that permitted torture, even on enemy lands surrounded by the rage of war.

2. En banc opinion

Six months after Judge Hamilton's opinion was issued, the eleven active judges of the Seventh Circuit gathered to rehear the government's arguments en banc. The rehearing produced five different opinions, with Chief Judge Easterbrook authoring the opinion for the court that reversed the panel's opinion across the board.[50]

First, the court declined to recognize a *Bivens*[51] or other implied cause of action:

50. Vance v. Rumsfeld, 701 F.3d 190 (7th Cir. 2012) (en banc).

51. The reference is to *Bivens v. Six Unknown Fed. Narcotics Agents*, 403 U.S. 388 (1971). In *Bivens*, the court found "a federal cause of action under the Fourth Amendment for which damages are recoverable upon proof of injuries resulting from the federal agents' violation of that Amendment." A *Bivens* action allows damages arising from a federal agent's violation of the petitioner's constitutional rights under color of federal authority.

When considering whether to create an extra-statutory right of action for damages against military personnel who mistreat detainees, we assume that at least some of the conditions to which plaintiffs were subjected violated their rights. Although the Constitution's application to interrogation outside the United States is not settled, Rumsfeld concedes (for current purposes at least) that it governs. The conduct alleged in the complaint appears to violate the Detainee Treatment Act, 10 U.S.C. § 801 note and 42 U.S.C. §§ 2000dd to 2000dd-1, and may violate one or more treaties. The source of the substantive right does not matter for the analysis that follows.

Unless there is a right of action against soldiers and their immediate commanders, however, there cannot be a right of action for damages against remote superiors such as former Secretary Rumsfeld. . . . Plaintiffs therefore ask us to create a right of action under federal common law [*Bivens*].

What plaintiffs want is an award of damages premised on a view that the military command structure should be different—that, for example, the Secretary of Defense must do more (or do something different) to control misconduct by interrogators and other personnel on the scene in foreign nations. They want a judicial order that would make the Secretary of Defense care less about the Secretary's view of the best military policy, and more about the Secretary's regard for his own finances. Plaintiffs believe that giving the Secretary of Defense a financial stake in the conduct of interrogators would lead the Secretary to hold the rights of detainees in higher regard—which surely is true, but that change would come at an uncertain cost in national security.

If the judiciary never erred, damages awards against soldiers and their civilian supervisors would be all gain and no loss. But judges make mistakes: They may lack vital knowledge, may accept claims that should be rejected on the facts or the law, or may award excessive damages on justified claims or create supervisory liability when they shouldn't. Accounting for human fallibility is an important part of the design of a legal system. Military prosecutors (or civilian prosecutors acting under the President's direction) can consider the needs of effective military action when exercising prosecutorial discretion. Judges lack information that executive officials possess, and in civil litigation there is no source of discretion comparable to a prosecutor's. The Justices concluded in [previous cases] that Congress and the Commander-in-Chief (the President), rather than civilian judges, ought to make the essential tradeoffs, not only because the constitutional authority to do so rests with the political branches of government but also because that's where the expertise lies. That is as true here as it was in [those cases].

The Detainee Treatment Act can be—and has been—enforced by criminal prosecutions. The Department of Defense has procedures for reporting claims of abuse; these procedures require all reports to be investigated and require prosecution to follow substantiated reports. Failure by military personnel to follow these procedures is a court-martial offense. . . . But

> Congress has not authorized awards of damages against soldiers and their superiors, and creating a right of action in common-law fashion would intrude inappropriately into the military command structure.
>
> A *Bivens*-like remedy could cause other problems, including diverting Cabinet officers' time from management of public affairs to the defense of their bank accounts. Then there are problems with evidence. When the state-secrets privilege did not block the claim, a court would find it challenging to prevent the disclosure of secret information. Anyone, whether or not a *bona fide* victim of military misconduct, could sue and then use graymail (the threat of disclosing secrets) to extract an undeserved settlement. That's not a problem under the Military Claims Act and the Foreign Claims Act, which allow proceedings to be conducted in confidence.

Second, the court held that even if a cause of action did exist for torture by military personnel in a war zone, Rumsfeld would not have been liable:

> Plaintiffs' theme is that Secretary Rumsfeld, having authorized harsh interrogation tactics for enemy combatants in 2002 and 2003, should have intervened after receiving reports that non-combatants were being subjected to these tactics and that interrogators had not properly implemented the Detainee Treatment Act of 2005. Yet the standard form of intervention would have been criminal prosecution (in the civilian courts or by court-martial). The Department of Defense did prosecute some soldiers through courts-martial, and the Department of Justice filed some criminal prosecutions. Plaintiffs think that they should have done more, but no one can demand that someone else be prosecuted. A court cannot say that, if there are too few prosecutions (or other enforcement), and thus too much crime, then the Attorney General or the Secretary of Defense is personally liable to victims of (preventable) crime. Yet that's what plaintiffs' approach entails.
>
> Although Vance and Ertel contend that their injuries can be traced (remotely) to Secretary Rumsfeld's policies of 2002 and 2003, as well as to the misconduct of personnel in Iraq, they do not contend that the policies authorized harsh interrogation of security detainees, as opposed to enemy combatants. It is therefore unnecessary to decide when, if ever, a Cabinet officer could be personally liable for damages caused by the proper application of an unlawful policy or regulation .... The extent to which untenable directives, policies, and regulations may support awards of damages can safely be postponed to another day.

Thus, the court concluded,

> [b]ecause we have held that a common-law right of action for damages should not be created—and that plaintiffs' complaint would fail to state a claim against former Secretary Rumsfeld even if such a right of action were to be created—it is unnecessary to decide whether Rumsfeld violated plaintiffs' clearly established rights.

Judge Hamilton dissented, joined by Judges Rovner and Williams:

> All members of this court agree that plaintiffs Vance and Ertel have alleged that members of the United States military tortured them in violation of the United States Constitution, and that in reviewing a denial of a motion to dismiss under Rule 12(b)(6), we must accept those allegations as true. Our disagreement is about whether plaintiffs have a civil remedy available to them under *Bivens*, which allows a victim of a constitutional violation to sue a responsible federal officer or employee for damages.
>
> If a victim of torture by the Syrian military can find his torturer in the United States, U.S. law provides a civil remedy against the torturer. Torture Victim Protection Act of 1991, 28 U.S.C. § 1350 note. If the victim is killed, the same U.S. law provides his survivors a civil remedy. The same could be said for victims of torture by any other government in the world—any other, that is, except one. Under the majority's decision, civilian U.S. citizens who are tortured or worse by our own military have no such remedy. That disparity attributes to our government and to our legal system a degree of hypocrisy that is breathtaking.
>
> The majority's result is not required or justified by Supreme Court precedent, and it fails to carry out the judiciary's responsibility under Supreme Court precedents to protect individual rights under the Constitution, including a right so basic as not to be tortured by our government. Although the majority opinion is written in terms of whether to "create" a cause of action under *Bivens*, the majority in effect creates a new absolute immunity from *Bivens* liability for all members of the U.S. military. This new absolute immunity applies not only to former Secretary Rumsfeld but to all members of the military, including those who were literally hands-on in torturing these plaintiffs. It applies to military mistreatment of civilians not only in Iraq but also in Illinois, Wisconsin, and Indiana.

Judge Hamilton further argued that the allegations of Rumsfeld's personal approval of the policies under which plaintiffs were tortured was sufficient involvement to establish *Bivens* liability—regardless of the difficulty of proving such allegations. From this perspective, the majority's concern with the challenges of proving liability up the chain of command was not germane. Further, since the plaintiffs learned the identities of their captors (formerly designated as "Does") between issuance of the panel opinion and rehearing en banc, they could still have had a cause of action against their immediate abusers. But the court's rejection of any cause of action under the circumstances—against anyone—meant that no one would be held civilly liable:

> Our courts have a long history of providing damages remedies for those whose rights are violated by our government, including our military. In *Little v. Barreme*, 6 U.S. (2 Cranch) 170, 178–79 (1804), the Supreme Court held that the commander of a warship was liable to the

owner of a neutral vessel seized pursuant to orders from the President but in violation of a statute.

The majority's grant of absolute civil immunity to the U.S. military for violations of civilian citizens' constitutional rights departs from that long heritage. We leave citizens legally defenseless to serious abuse or worse by their own government. I recognize that wrongdoers in the military are still subject to criminal prosecution within the military itself. Relying solely on the military to police its own treatment of civilians fails to use the government's checks and balances that preserve Americans' liberty. The legal foundations for the claims before us are strong and in keeping with the Supreme Court's decisions and the best traditions of American liberty and governance. We should affirm the district court's decision to allow plaintiffs to try to prove their claims for torture.

Judges Williams and Rovner (joined in each instance by the other two dissenters) filed additional dissenting opinions. Judge Wood concurred in the judgment.

Consider Judge Easterbrook's argument in the *en banc* opinion. With our distinction between structure and situation in mind (see previous section, Note 1), do you agree with his assessment that the plaintiffs' suit was "premised on a view that the military command structure should be different—that, for example, the Secretary of Defense must do more (or do something different) to control misconduct . . . in foreign nations"? Or does plaintiffs' suit involve a different premise—keyed to the situation of their mistreatment and its personal aftermath? From that perspective, the suit did not reach the question of the structure of military authority, but only of the federal government's responsibility for injuries arising from the circumstances of allegedly unconstitutional harms to U.S. citizens. Furthermore, as Judge Hamilton pointed out, the decision not to recognize *any* cause of action—as opposed to limiting a cause of action to certain actors—meant that the discussion of Secretary Rumsfeld's personal responsibility was dicta. The outcome was that Vance and Ertel could recover damages from *no one*, including those individuals known to be directly responsible for their injuries.

IV. Borders in question: Immigration

A long legal tradition in the United States, with roots in English common law, gives the president broad powers over immigration. Even as the breadth of those powers is widely recognized, recent political controversy over immigration has called into question the extent of those powers. In November, 2014, the Obama administration announced two programs allowing temporary status to two classes of undocumented immigrants—non-citizen children of immigrant parents (Deferred Action for Childhood Arrivals, DACA) and non-citizen parents of citizen children (Deferred Action for Parents of Americans and Lawful Permanent Residents, DAPA). Professor Cade sets the context for DACA and DAPA in recent trends arising from Congress's failure to achieve legislation addressing undocumented immigration:

Jason A. Cade, *Enforcing Immigration Equity*

84 Fordham L. Rev. 661 (2015)

DAPA and DACA [are] part of a significant and ongoing transition in immigration law. These programs, though important in themselves, are best seen as one component of the broad relocation of equitable authority within the American deportation system from back-end adjudicators to frontline enforcement officials. . . . [A]mendments to the immigration code heralded the rise of criminal history, very broadly defined, as the primary marker of undesirability, while squeezing consideration of humanitarian or fairness concerns almost completely out of the adjudicative stages of deportation or criminal proceedings. As a result of this statutory shift, considerations of equity enter the deportation system (if at all) primarily through the discretionary decisions of enforcement actors at both federal and state levels.

Any normatively justifiable deportation system requires equity. . . . Equity mitigates the effect of overly broad, punitive, and inflexible statutes in ways that help ensure the law is fair and proportional in its application to individual human beings. This principle is well recognized in criminal law, where the extensive proliferation of penal laws to regulate behavior that is not clearly blameworthy, the establishment of mandatory minimum sentences, and the general inability of formal law to predict and accommodate all possible mitigating circumstances create the potential for injustice in many cases. . . .

The removal system similarly imposes dire penalties on the basis of a broad range of civil infractions. . . . President Obama's Administration clearly recognizes that the breadth and severity of modern immigration rules, along with the scale of the removable noncitizen population, have created a system that consolidates tremendous power over the equitable implementation of immigration law in enforcement actors.

Importantly, the use of the DACA and DAPA mechanisms depart from the typical invocation of prosecutorial discretion in that they assign equitable assessments to a special unit within a separate DHS agency. This institutional design for discretionary consideration offers the possibility of significant gains in transparency and consistency, not least because of the crushing workloads currently facing ICE prosecutors in deportation court. On the other hand, this division of agency functions has led some observers to argue that these programs involve the affirmative grant of benefits as opposed to discretionary forbearance with regard to removal. Indeed, on February 16, 2015, a federal district court preliminarily enjoined the rollout of DAPA along with the expanded version of DACA announced by President Obama in late 2014.[52]

Although some critics of President Obama's enforcement policies argue he is "soft" on immigration, the on-the-ground reality is more complex. The immigration enforcement agencies have taken an increasingly hard line against all noncitizens defined as "criminal aliens." This designation all but guarantees removal, regardless

52. Authors' Note: This injunction led to *Texas v. United States*, 809 F.3d 134 (5th Cir. 2015), discussed *infra*.

of the seriousness of the underlying offense, the passage of time, the permanent resident status of the noncitizen, the degree of hardship that deportation would cause the noncitizen's family, or other mitigating factors.... [E]quity through enforcement discretion has fallen short when it comes to noncitizens who encounter the criminal justice system.

This situation cries out for redress. Instead of continuing to rely on prosecutorial discretion to ensure fairness in the deportation system, Congress should enact legislation that both scales back the breadth of removal provisions and restores opportunities for adjudicators to balance equities in a wider swath of individual cases. Likewise, Congress should consider legalization programs that would allow undocumented persons with significant equities to become lawfully present, thus easing the burden on enforcement officials to sort out which of the eleven million removable noncitizens would not justifiably be deported. These reforms are critical if we want a removal system that consistently avoids disproportionate deportations.[53]

As Professor Cade notes in the excerpt above, deferred action is a long-standing tool of prosecutorial discretion in the immigration contex,[54] but these programs were immediately controversial.[55] A suit challenging the programs was filed by a coalition of states and governors. The Fifth Circuit upheld the challenge, as we will see in the case below.

As the government's briefs explained, immigration is exclusively within the province of the federal government—and particularly the federal political branches—to regulate and execute. In 1885, the Supreme Court explained:

> The power of congress to exclude aliens altogether from the United States, or to prescribe the terms and conditions upon which they may come to this country, and to have its declared policy in that regard enforced exclusively through executive officers, without judicial intervention, is settled by our previous adjudications.[56]

53. Jason A. Cade, *Enforcing Immigration Equity*, 84 Fordham L. Rev. 661, 662–69 (2015).

54. Jill E. Family, *DAPA and the Future of Immigration Law as Adinistrative Law*, 55 Washburn L.J. 89, 91–92 (2015).

55. Criticism was not limited to conservative state governors with anti-immigrant constituencies and their attorneys general. Some immigration advocates were concerned with the risk of personal vulnerabilities for undocumented immigrants who registered through DAPA/DACA, given the possibility of future revisions of the policy and other uses of that list. The situations of undocumented migrants at the border, as asylum seekers, and in U.S. communities are subjects of extensive anthropological literatures. For discussion of the dynamic swings in U.S. immigration policy and laws affecting asylum, and their personal effects on immigrants in the United States, see Susan Bibler Coutin, Legalizing Moves: Salvadoran Immigrants Struggle for Residency (2002), see also Susan Bibler Coutin, Nations of Emigrants: Shifting Boundaries of Citizenship in El Salvador and the United States (2007).

56. Lem Moon Sing v. United States, 158 U.S. 538, 547 (1895).

Furthermore, the authority to prioritize enforcement is integral to federal powers in immigration, as the Court explained in *Reno v. American-Arab Anti-Discrimination Committee*:

> Even in the criminal-law field, a selective prosecution claim is a *rara avis.* Because such claims invade a special province of the Executive—its prosecutorial discretion—we have emphasized that the standard for proving them is particularly demanding, requiring a criminal defendant to introduce "clear evidence" displacing the presumption that a prosecutor has acted lawfully. *United States v. Armstrong,* 517 U.S. 456, 463–465 (1996). We have said:
>
>> "This broad discretion [afforded the Executive] rests largely on the recognition that the decision to prosecute is particularly ill-suited to judicial review. Such factors as the strength of the case, the prosecution's general deterrence value, the Government's enforcement priorities, and the case's relationship to the Government's overall enforcement plan are not readily susceptible to the kind of analysis the courts are competent to undertake. Judicial supervision in this area, moreover, entails systemic costs of particular concern. Examining the basis of a prosecution delays the criminal proceeding, threatens to chill law enforcement by subjecting the prosecutor's motives and decisionmaking to outside inquiry, and may undermine prosecutorial effectiveness by revealing the Government's enforcement policy. All of these are substantial concerns that make the courts properly hesitant to examine the decision whether to prosecute." *Wayte v. United States,* 470 U.S. 598, 607–608, 105 S.Ct. 1524, 84 L.Ed.2d 547 (1985). These concerns are greatly magnified in the deportation context.[57]

In this context, Professor Shoba Sivaprasad Wadhia emphasizes the transnational implications of the federal government's authority over immigration:

> DHS and DOJ are but two of the plethora of agencies within the Executive Branch responsible for administering and enforcing the immigration laws. The Executive Branch's role in enforcing immigration laws is breathtaking and has affected both domestic populations and countries of the world. Moreover, the Supreme Court has interpreted the various portions of the United States Constitution to give the "political branches" the plenary power to regulate immigration. The plenary power doctrine has been applied to exclude and deport noncitizens without a check from the judiciary.
>
> The ultimate source for the exercise of prosecutorial discretion in the Federal Government is the power of the President. Under Article II, Section 1 of the Constitution, the executive power is vested in the President. Article

57. 525 U.S. 471, 489–90 (1999).

II, Section 3, states that the President "shall take care that the laws be faithfully executed."[58]

With this background in mind, consider the Fifth Circuit's treatment of several states' challenge to the Obama Administration's Deferred Action for Parents of Americans and Lawful Permanent Residents program.

Texas v. United States

809 F.3d 134 (5th Cir. 2015)

SMITH, CIRCUIT JUDGE:

The United States appeals a preliminary injunction, pending trial, forbidding implementation of the Deferred Action for Parents of Americans and Lawful Permanent Residents program ("DAPA"). Twenty-six states challenged DAPA under the Administrative Procedure Act ("APA") and the Take Care Clause of the Constitution; the district court enjoined the program on the ground that the states are likely to succeed on their claim that DAPA is subject to the APA's procedural requirements. Reviewing the district court's order for abuse of discretion, we affirm the preliminary injunction.

I.A.

In June 2012, the Department of Homeland Security ("DHS") implemented the Deferred Action for Childhood Arrivals program ("DACA"). In the DACA Memo to agency heads, the DHS Secretary "set[] forth how, in the exercise of . . . prosecutorial discretion, [DHS] should enforce the Nation's immigration laws against certain young people" and listed five "criteria [that] should be satisfied before an individual is considered for an exercise of prosecutorial discretion." The Secretary further instructed that "[n]o individual should receive deferred action . . . unless they [*sic*] first pass a background check and requests for relief . . . are to be decided on a case by case basis." Although stating that "[f]or individuals who are granted deferred action . . . , [U.S. Citizenship and Immigration Services ('USCIS')] shall accept applications to determine whether these individuals qualify for work authorization," the DACA Memo purported to "confer[] no substantive right, immigration status or pathway to citizenship." At least 1.2 million persons qualify for DACA, and approximately 636,000 applications were approved through 2014.

In November 2014, by what is termed the "DAPA Memo," DHS expanded DACA by making millions more persons eligible for the program. The Secretary also "direct[ed] USCIS to establish a process, similar to DACA," known as DAPA, which applies to "individuals who . . . have, [as of November 20, 2014], a son or daughter who is a U.S. citizen or lawful permanent resident" and meet five additional criteria. The Secretary stated that, although "[d]eferred action does not confer any form of legal status in this country, much less citizenship[,] it [does] mean[] that, for a

---

58. Shoba Sivaprasad Wadhia, *In Defense of DACA, Deferred Action, and the Dream Act*, 91 TEX. L. REV. 59, 61–62, 64 (2013).

specified period of time, an individual is permitted to be *lawfully present* in the United States." Of the approximately 11.3 million illegal aliens in the United States, 4.3 million would be eligible for lawful presence pursuant to DAPA.

"Lawful presence" is not an enforceable right to remain in the United States and can be revoked at any time, but that classification nevertheless has significant legal consequences. [A]s the government admits in its opening brief, persons granted lawful presence pursuant to DAPA are no longer "bar[red] . . . from receiving social security retirement benefits, social security disability benefits, or health insurance under Part A of the Medicare program." [This is because] the exclusion of benefits in § 1611(a) "shall not apply to any benefit[s] payable . . . to an alien who is *lawfully present* in the United States as determined by the Attorney General. . . ." (emphasis added). A lawfully present alien is still required to satisfy independent qualification criteria before receiving those benefits, but the grant of lawful presence removes the categorical bar and thereby makes otherwise ineligible persons eligible to qualify.

"Each person who applies for deferred action pursuant to the [DAPA] criteria . . . shall also be eligible to apply for work authorization for the [renewable three-year] period of deferred action." The United States concedes that "[a]n alien with work authorization may obtain a Social Security Number," "accrue quarters of covered employment," and "correct wage records to add prior covered employment within approximately three years of the year in which the wages were earned or in limited circumstances thereafter." The district court determined—and the government does not dispute—"that DAPA recipients would be eligible for earned income tax credits once they received a Social Security number."

As for state benefits, although "[a] State may provide that an alien who is *not lawfully present* in the United States is eligible for any State or local public benefit for which such alien would otherwise be ineligible under subsection (a)," Texas has chosen not to issue driver's licenses to unlawfully present aliens. Texas maintains that documentation confirming lawful presence pursuant to DAPA would allow otherwise ineligible aliens to become eligible for state-subsidized driver's licenses. Likewise, certain unemployment compensation "[b]enefits are not payable based on services performed by an alien unless the alien . . . was *lawfully present* for purposes of performing the services . . . ." Texas contends that DAPA recipients would also become eligible for unemployment insurance.

B.

The states sued to prevent DAPA's implementation. On appeal, the United States maintains that the states do not have standing or a right to judicial review and, alternatively, that DAPA is exempt from the notice-and-comment requirements. The government also contends that the injunction, including its nationwide scope, is improper as a matter of law.

II.

We review a preliminary injunction for abuse of discretion. A preliminary injunction should issue only if the states, as movants, establish (1) a substantial likelihood of success on the merits, (2) a substantial threat of irreparable injury if the injunction is not issued, (3) that the threatened injury if the injunction is denied outweighs any harm that will result if the injunction is granted, and (4) that the grant of an injunction will not disserve the public interest. As to each element of the district court's preliminary-injunction analysis . . . findings of fact are subject to a clearly-erroneous standard of review, while conclusions of law are subject to broad review and will be reversed if incorrect.

III.

The government claims the states lack standing to challenge DAPA. As we will analyze, however, their standing is plain, based on the driver's-license rationale.

A.

We begin by considering whether the states are entitled to "special solicitude" in our standing inquiry under *Massachusetts v. EPA*. They are.

[The Court briefly recapped the holding in *Massachusetts v. EPA*, excerpted in Chapter 2, *supra*.]

Like Massachusetts, the instant plaintiffs—the states—"are not normal litigants for the purposes of invoking federal jurisdiction." In enacting the APA, Congress intended for those "suffering legal wrong because of agency action" to have judicial recourse, and the states fall well within that definition. Because the states here challenge DHS's decision to act, rather than its decision to remain inactive, a procedural right similar to that created by the Clean Air Act is not necessary to support standing.

As we will show, DAPA would have a major effect on the states' fiscs, causing millions of dollars of losses in Texas alone, and at least in Texas, the causal chain is especially direct: DAPA would enable beneficiaries to apply for driver's licenses, and many would do so, resulting in Texas's injury.

Second, DAPA affects the states' "quasi-sovereign" interests by imposing substantial pressure on them to change their laws, which provide for issuing driver's licenses to some aliens and subsidizing those licenses.

Moreover, these plaintiff states' interests are like Massachusetts's in ways that implicate the same sovereignty concerns. When the states joined the union, they surrendered some of their sovereign prerogatives over immigration. . . . Both these plaintiff states and Massachusetts now rely on the federal government to protect their interests.

We stress that our decision is limited to these facts. In particular, the direct, substantial pressure directed at the states and the fact that they have surrendered some of their control over immigration to the federal government mean this case is sufficiently similar to *Massachusetts v. EPA*, but pressure to change state law may not be enough—by itself—in other situations.

B.

Instead of disputing those figures, the United States claims that the costs would be offset by other benefits to the state. It theorizes that, because DAPA beneficiaries would be eligible for licenses, they would register their vehicles, generating income for the state, and buy auto insurance, reducing the expenses associated with uninsured motorists. The government suggests employment authorization would lead to increased tax revenue and decreased reliance on social services.

Even if the government is correct, that does not negate Texas's injury, because we consider only those offsetting benefits that are of the same type and arise from the same transaction as the costs.

Here, none of the benefits the government identifies is sufficiently connected to the costs to qualify as an offset. The only benefits that are conceivably relevant are the increase in vehicle registration and the decrease in uninsured motorists, but even those are based on the independent decisions of DAPA beneficiaries and are not a direct result of the issuance of licenses. . . .

In the instant case, the states have alleged an injury, and the government predicts that the later decisions of DAPA beneficiaries would produce offsetting benefits. Weighing those costs and benefits is precisely the type of "accounting exercise" in which we cannot engage. Texas has shown injury.

C.

Texas has satisfied the second standing requirement by establishing that its injury is "fairly traceable" to DAPA. It is undisputed that DAPA would enable beneficiaries to apply for driver's licenses, and there is little doubt that many would do so because driving is a practical necessity in most of the state.

The United States urges that Texas's injury is not cognizable, because the state could avoid injury by not issuing licenses to illegal aliens or by not subsidizing its licenses. The United States maintains that Texas's injury is self-inflicted because the state voluntarily chose to base its driver's license policies on federal immigration law. In *Pennsylvania v. New Jersey*, the Court held that several states lacked standing to contest other states' laws taxing a portion of nonresidents' incomes. 426 U.S. 660, 664, 666 (1976). The Court flatly rejected that theory of standing. Nothing required Maine, Massachusetts, and Vermont to extend a tax credit to their residents for income taxes paid to New Hampshire, and nothing prevents Pennsylvania from withdrawing that credit for taxes paid to New Jersey. No State can be heard to complain about damage inflicted by its own hand.

The more recent decision in *Wyoming v. Oklahoma*, 502 U.S. 437 (1992), also informs our analysis. There, the Court held that Wyoming had standing to challenge an Oklahoma law requiring some Oklahoma power plants to burn at least 10% Oklahoma-mined coal. The Court explained that Wyoming taxed the extraction of coal in the state and that Oklahoma's law reduced demand for that coal and Wyoming's corresponding revenue. The Court emphasized that the case involved an "undisputed" "direct injury in the form of a loss of specific tax revenues." . . . The Court did not cite *Pennsylvania v. New Jersey* or discuss the theory that Wyoming's injury was self-inflicted.

Both the *Pennsylvania v. New Jersey* plaintiffs and Wyoming structured their laws in ways that meant their finances would have been affected by changes in other states' laws. *Wyoming v. Oklahoma* directs our decision. The plaintiffs in *Pennsylvania v. New Jersey* could have achieved their policy goal in myriad ways, such as basing their tax credits on residents' out-of-state incomes instead of on taxes actually paid to other states. The fact that Texas had no similar option means its injury is not self-inflicted.

The legislature enacted the law one year before DACA and three years before DAPA was announced, and there is no hint that the state anticipated a change in immigration policy—much less a change as sweeping and dramatic as DAPA. Despite the dissent's bold suggestion that Texas's license-plate-cost injury "is entirely manufactured by Plaintiffs for this case," the injury is not self-inflicted.

In addition to its notion that Texas could avoid injury, the government theorizes that Texas's injury is not fairly traceable to DAPA because it is merely an incidental and attenuated consequence of the program. But *Massachusetts v. EPA* establishes that the causal connection is adequate.

DAPA beneficiaries have strong incentives to obtain driver's licenses, and it is hardly speculative that many would do so if they became eligible. Without the program, there would be little risk of a dramatic increase in the costs of the driver's-license program. Texas's injury is fairly traceable to DAPA . . . .

E.

The United States submits that Texas's theory of standing is flawed because it has no principled limit. In the government's view, if Texas can challenge DAPA, it could also sue to block a grant of asylum to a single alien or any federal policy that adversely affects the state.

The flaw in the government's reasoning is that *Massachusetts v. EPA* entailed similar risks, but the Court still held that Massachusetts had standing. After *Massachusetts v. EPA,* the answer to those criticisms is that there are other ways to cabin policy disagreements masquerading as legal claims. First, a state that has standing still must have a cause of action. . . .

V.B.

The government urges that this case is not justiciable even though " 'a federal court's 'obligation' to hear and decide cases within its jurisdiction is 'virtually unflagging.' " We decline to depart from that well-established principle. And in invoking our jurisdiction, the states do not demand that the federal government "control immigration and . . . pay for the consequences of federal immigration policy" or "prevent illegal immigration."

Neither the preliminary injunction nor compliance with the APA requires the Secretary to enforce the immigration laws or change his priorities for removal, which have expressly not been challenged. Nor have the states "merely invited us to substitute our judgment for that of Congress in deciding which aliens shall be eligible to participate in [a benefits program]." DAPA was enjoined because the states seek an opportunity to be heard through notice and comment, not to have the judiciary formulate or rewrite immigration policy. "Consultation between federal and state officials is an important feature of the immigration system," and the notice-and-comment process, which "is designed to ensure that affected parties have an opportunity to participate in and influence agency decision making," facilitates that communication.

At its core, this case is about the Secretary's decision to change the immigration classification of millions of illegal aliens on a class-wide basis. The states properly maintain that DAPA's grant of lawful presence and accompanying eligibility for benefits is a substantive rule that must go through notice and comment, before it imposes substantial costs on them, and that DAPA is substantively contrary to law. The federal courts are fully capable of adjudicating those disputes.

VI.

Because the interests that Texas seeks to protect are within the INA's zone of interests, and judicial review is available, we address whether Texas has established a substantial likelihood of success on its claim that DAPA must be submitted for notice and comment. The United States urges that DAPA is exempt as an "interpretative rule, general statement of policy, or rule of agency organization, procedure, or practice." 5 U.S.C. § 553(b)(A). "In contrast, if a rule is 'substantive,' the exemption is inapplicable" . . . .

A.

The government advances the notion that DAPA is exempt from notice and comment as a policy statement. We evaluate two criteria to distinguish policy statements from substantive rules: whether the rule (1) "impose[s] any rights and obligations" and (2) "genuinely leaves the agency and its decision-makers free to exercise discretion."

Although the DAPA Memo facially purports to confer discretion, the district court determined that "[n]othing about DAPA '*genuinely* leaves the agency and its [employees] free to exercise discretion,'" a factual finding that we review for clear error. That finding was partly informed by analysis of the implementation of DACA, the precursor to DAPA.

Like the DAPA Memo, the DACA Memo instructed agencies to review applications on a case-by-case basis and exercise discretion, but the district court found that those statements were "merely pretext" [for a variety of reasons.]

The DACA and DAPA Memos purport to grant discretion, but a rule can be binding if it is "applied by the agency in a way that indicates it is binding," and there was evidence from DACA's implementation that DAPA's discretionary language was pretextual. [D]espite the differences [between DACA and DAPA], there are important similarities: The Secretary "direct[ed] USCIS to *establish a process, similar to DACA,* for exercising prosecutorial discretion," and there was evidence that the DACA application process *itself* did not allow for discretion, regardless of the rates of approval and denial.

Reviewing for clear error, we conclude that the states have established a substantial likelihood that DAPA would not genuinely leave the agency and its employees free to exercise discretion.

VII.

A "reviewing court shall . . . hold unlawful and set aside agency action . . . found to be—(A) arbitrary, capricious, an abuse of discretion, or otherwise not in accordance with law . . . [or] (C) in excess of statutory jurisdiction, authority, or limitations, or short of statutory right." 5 U.S.C. § 706(2). [A]s an alternate and additional ground for affirming the injunction, we address this substantive issue, which was fully briefed in the district court.

In specific and detailed provisions, the [Immigration and Nationalization Act ("INA")] expressly and carefully provides legal designations allowing defined classes of aliens to be lawfully present and confers eligibility for "discretionary relief allowing [aliens in deportation proceedings] to remain in the country." Congress has also identified narrow classes of aliens eligible for deferred action . . . . Entirely absent from those specific classes is the group of 4.3 million illegal aliens who would be eligible for lawful presence under DAPA were it not enjoined.

[The Court's detailed description of the INA's structure is omitted.]

The INA's careful employment-authorization scheme "protect[s] against the displacement of workers in the United States," and a "primary purpose in restricting immigration is to preserve jobs for American workers." DAPA would dramatically increase the number of aliens eligible for work authorization, thereby undermining Congress's stated goal of closely guarding access to work authorization and preserving jobs for those lawfully in the country.

DAPA would make 4.3 million otherwise removable aliens eligible for lawful presence, employment authorization, and associated benefits, and "we must be guided to a degree by common sense as to the manner in which Congress is likely to delegate a policy decision of such economic and political magnitude to an administrative agency." DAPA undoubtedly implicates "question[s] of deep 'economic and political significance' that [are] central to this statutory scheme; had Congress wished to assign that decision to an agency, it surely would have done so expressly."

Presumably because DAPA is not authorized by statute, the United States posits that its authority is grounded in historical practice, but that "does not, by itself, create power," and in any event, previous deferred-action programs are not analogous to DAPA. "[M]ost . . . discretionary deferrals have been done on a country-specific basis, usually in response to war, civil unrest, or natural disasters," but DAPA is not such a program. Likewise, many of the previous programs were bridges from one legal status to another, whereas DAPA awards lawful presence to persons who have never had a legal status and may never receive one.

DAPA is far from interstitial [to a statutory legalization scheme]: Congress has repeatedly declined to enact the Development, Relief, and Education for Alien Minors Act ("DREAM Act"), features of which closely resemble DACA and DAPA.

Historical practice that is so far afield from the challenged program sheds no light on the Secretary's authority to implement DAPA. Indeed, as the district court recognized, the President explicitly stated that "it was the failure of Congress to enact such a program that prompted him . . . to 'change the law.'" At oral argument, and despite being given several opportunities, the attorney for the United States was unable to reconcile that remark with the position that the government now takes. And the dissent attempts to avoid the impact of the President's statement by accusing the district court and this panel majority of "relying . . . on selected excerpts of the President's public statements."

As we have indicated, the INA prescribes how parents may derive an immigration classification on the basis of their child's status and which classes of aliens can achieve deferred action and eligibility for work authorization. DAPA is foreclosed by Congress's careful plan; the program is "manifestly contrary to the statute" and therefore was properly enjoined.

VIII.

The states have alleged a concrete threatened injury in the form of millions of dollars of losses. The harms the United States has identified are less substantial. It claims that the injunction "obstructs a core Executive prerogative" and offends separation-of-powers and federalism principles. Those alleged harms are vague, and the principles the government cites are more likely to be affected by the resolution of the case on the merits than by the injunction.

Separately, the United States postulates that the injunction prevents DHS from effectively prioritizing illegal aliens for removal. But the injunction "does not enjoin or impair the Secretary's ability to marshal his assets or deploy the resources of the DHS [or] to set priorities," including selecting whom to remove first, and any inefficiency is outweighed by the major financial losses the states face.

The government also complains that the injunction imposes administrative burdens because DHS has already leased office space and begun hiring employees to implement DAPA. Such inconveniences are common incidental effects of injunctions, and the government could have avoided them by delaying preparatory work until the litigation was resolved. Finally, the government reasonably speculates that the injunction burdens DAPA beneficiaries and their families and discourages them from cooperating with law-enforcement officers and paying taxes. But those are burdens that Congress knowingly created, and it is not our place to second-guess those decisions.

Although the United States cites the public interest in maintaining separation of powers and federalism by avoiding judicial and state interference with a legitimate executive function, there is an obvious difference: The interest the government has identified can be effectively vindicated after a trial on the merits. The interest the states have identified cannot be, given the difficulty of restoring the *status quo ante* if DAPA were to be implemented. The public interest easily favors an injunction.

IX.

The government claims that the nationwide scope of the injunction is an abuse of discretion and requests that it be confined to Texas or the plaintiff states. But the Constitution requires "an *uniform* Rule of Naturalization"; Congress has instructed that "the immigration laws of the United States should be enforced vigorously and *uniformly*"; and the Supreme Court has described immigration policy as "a comprehensive and *unified* system."

Furthermore, the Constitution vests the District Court with "the judicial Power of the United States." That power is not limited to the district wherein the court sits but extends across the country. It is not beyond the power of a court, in appropriate circumstances, to issue a nationwide injunction.

The district court did not err and most assuredly did not abuse its discretion. The order granting the preliminary injunction is AFFIRMED.

King, Circuit Judge, dissenting:

Although there are approximately 11.3 million removable aliens in this country today, for the last several years Congress has provided the Department of Homeland Security (DHS) with only enough resources to remove approximately 400,000 of those aliens per year. Recognizing DHS's congressionally granted prosecutorial discretion to set removal enforcement priorities, Congress has exhorted DHS to use those resources to "mak[e] our country safer." In response, DHS has focused on removing "those who represent threats to national security, public safety, and border security." The DAPA Memorandum at issue here focuses on a subset of removable aliens who are unlikely to be removed unless and until more resources are made available by Congress: those who are the parents of United States citizens or legal permanent residents, who have resided in the United States for at least the last five years, who lack a criminal record, and who are not otherwise removal priorities as determined by DHS. The DAPA Memorandum has three primary objectives for these aliens: (1) to permit them to be lawfully employed and thereby enhance their ability to be self-sufficient, a goal of United States immigration law since this country's earliest immigration statutes; (2) to encourage them to come out of the shadows and to identify themselves and where they live, DHS's prime law enforcement objective; and (3) to maintain flexibility so that if Congress is able to make more resources for removal available, DHS will be able to respond.

Plaintiffs do not challenge DHS's ability to allow the aliens subject to the DAPA Memorandum—up to 4.3 million, some estimate—to remain in this country indefinitely. Indeed, Plaintiffs admit that such removal decisions are well within DHS's prosecutorial discretion. Rather, Plaintiffs complain of the consequences of DHS's decision to use its decades-long practice of granting "deferred action" to these individuals, specifically that these "illegal aliens" may temporarily work lawfully for a living and may also eventually become eligible for some public benefits. Deferred action decisions, such as those contemplated by the DAPA Memorandum, are quintessential exercises of prosecutorial discretion. As the Supreme Court put it sixteen years ago, "[a]t each stage [of the removal process] the Executive has discretion to abandon the endeavor, [including by] engaging in a regular practice (which had come to be known as 'deferred action') of exercising that discretion for humanitarian reasons or simply for its own convenience."

The DAPA Memorandum

[T]he agency is faced with important prioritization decisions as to which aliens should be the subject of removal proceedings. Congress has made clear that those decisions are to be made by DHS, not by Congress itself—and certainly not by the courts. Indeed, Congress has delegated to the Secretary of Homeland Security the authority to "[e]stablish[] national immigration enforcement policies and priorities," 6 U.S.C. § 202(5), and to "establish such regulations; . . . issue such instructions; and perform such other acts as he deems necessary for carrying out" his responsibilities, 809 F.3d 134.

Justiciability

Plaintiffs concede that if the DAPA Memorandum is only an exercise in enforcement discretion—without granting any "additional benefits"—it is unreviewable under 5 U.S.C. § 701(a). . . . In other words, deferred action itself is merely a brand of "presumptively unreviewable" prosecutorial discretion. Notably, such prosecutorial discretion is heightened in the immigration context.

Because the DAPA Memorandum contains only guidelines for the exercise of prosecutorial discretion and does not itself confer any benefits to DAPA recipients, I would deem this case non-justiciable. The policy decisions at issue in this case are best resolved not by judicial fiat, but via the political process.

APA Procedural Claim

Our precedent is clear: "As long as the agency remains free to consider the individual facts in the various cases that arise, then the agency action in question has not established a binding norm," and thus need not go through the procedures of notice-and-comment. . . . As the majority admits, the Memorandum "facially purports to confer discretion." But the district court ignored this clear language, concluding that agency officials implementing DAPA will defy the Memorandum and simply rubberstamp applications.

Conclusion

There can be little doubt that Congress's choices as to the level of funding for immigration enforcement have left DHS with difficult prioritization decisions. But those decisions, which are embodied in the DAPA Memorandum, have been delegated to the Secretary by Congress. Because federal courts should not inject themselves into such matters of prosecutorial discretion, I would dismiss this case as non-justiciable.

Furthermore, the evidence in the record (the importance of which should not be overlooked) makes clear that the injunction cannot stand. A determination of "pretext" on the part of DHS *must* have a basis in concrete evidence. Based on the record as it currently stands, the district court's conclusion that DAPA applications will not be reviewed on a discretionary, case-by-case basis cannot withstand even the most deferential scrutiny. I have a firm and definite conviction that a mistake has been made. That mistake has been exacerbated by the extended delay that has occurred in deciding this "expedited" appeal. There is no justification for that delay. I dissent.

Notes and Questions

1. Is DAPA/DACA evidence of the *limits* of executive power, or its *excesses*? Professor Cade's critical analysis underscores the extent to which DAPA and DACA are evidence of the *limited* powers of the executive—i.e., limited to law enforcement where Congress has failed to provide for equity through legislative reform. The plaintiffs in *Texas v. U.S.*, on the other hand, argue that President Obama has *exceeded* his authority, preempting the authority of the Congress in a matter of domestic policy. Might this very debate suggest that under some circumstances, partisan divisions within Congress broaden the scope for expanded executive authority, particularly when partisanship becomes an impasse to legislation?

2. Deferred action can be described as a means of exercising prosecutorial discretion, as the various materials explain. Under DAPA/DACA, specific categories of undocumented immigrants would be eligible for deferred action. On what grounds does Texas claim a basis for forcing the federal government to take a different approach to enforcement? Are you convinced? In another context, the Supreme Court has held that the federal government cannot "commandeer" state law enforcement agencies by requiring them to conduct background checks on handgun purchasers.[59] In *Texas v. U.S.*, is the Fifth Circuit allowing the states to commandeer the federal government to implement the *states'* preferred immigration policy, even though immigration policy generally is solely power of the federal government?

3. All decisions not to prosecute may be seen as "conferring benefits" (to borrow the majority's words) upon the nonprosecuted individual. From this standpoint, are you persuaded that the situation underlying *Texas v. U.S.* is unique? Or that it calls for unique attention in some way?

4. On appeal, the case went to the Supreme Court—where (following the death of Justice Scalia) it resulted in a 4–4 tie, therefore affirming the decision of the court below.[60] The Department of Justice has filed for a rehearing.[61]

V. Foreign affairs reconsidered

As we have seen, the line between domestic and foreign has been blurred or fragmented such that, in key contexts, the difference between foreign and domestic affairs is a difference without a distinction, or at least without a clear distinction. In this context, legal scholars Sataraman and Wuerth find a trend toward "normalization" of executive power in foreign affairs.

> [T]ogether the Court's decisions over the last quarter century on political questions, standing, federalism, preemption, statutory interpretation, and

59. Printz v. United States, 521 U.S. 898, 902 (1997).

60. 136 S. Ct. 2271 (2016).

61. The petition can be found here: http://immigrationimpact.com/wp-content/uploads/2016/07/united_states_v_texas_rehearing_petition.pdf.

> executive power form an unmistakable pattern of normalization across the most important debates in foreign relations law over the last century. This normalization trend is particularly significant because it continued even in the midst of war, when one would expect exceptionalist arguments to be at their zenith.
>
> [N]ormalization is in many ways a counter-revolution because it is eliminating exceptionalist reasoning from foreign relations law. Where the rise of exceptionalism meant nonjusticiability, normalization increases the courts' involvement in adjudicating disputes. Where the rise of exceptionalism meant federal power trumped the states, normalization requires courts to follow routine preemption and federalism analyses. And where the rise of exceptionalism meant expansive deference to the executive, normalization means the executive cannot count on vague claims of foreign policy expertise to win.[62]

The trend toward normalization was pulled sharply into question with the Supreme Court's decision in the cases known as *Zivotofsky I* and *II* (addressing issues of justiciability and the merits, respectively; discussed further below). Anticipating what follows, we note the importance of the debate over the ruling in *Zivotofsky II*, over the significance of the Court's reasoning with respect to *Curtiss-Wright* (*supra*) and *Youngstown*, as well as its likely future impact on domestic and foreign affairs law. Professor Goldsmith anticipates sweeping consequences for *Zivotofsky*:

> *Zivotofsky II* is the most important Supreme Court decision ever on the sources and scope of the President's independent and exclusive powers to conduct foreign relations—powers that fall in Justice Jackson's *Youngstown* Categories Two and Three, respectively. The Court provided novel guidance on these issues in the course of upholding for the first time "a President's direct defiance of an Act of Congress in the field of foreign affairs," as the Chief Justice said in dissent. Its analysis made a mess of Justice Jackson's third category in *Youngstown*, revived a functional approach to exclusive presidential power that many scholars thought was dead, and left Congress's legislative power related to diplomacy and foreign affairs in an uncertain but probably shrunken position. These and other elements of the analytically promiscuous decision will influence separation-of-powers disputes far beyond the recognition context.[63]

Professor Wuerth similarly finds a signal of revision and a certain lack of clarity in the rulings, but, referring to her analysis of the trend toward normalization in foreign affairs law (quoted above[64]), is more measured in her assessment of the wider significance of the case as evidence of a shift to exceptionalism:

---

62. Ganesh Sitaraman & Ingrid Wuerth, *The Normalization of Foreign Affairs Law,* 128 Harv. L. Rev. 1897 (2015).

63. Jack Goldsmith, Zivotofsky II *as Precedent in the Executive Branch*, 129 Harv. L. Rev. 112, 114 (2015).

64. Sitaraman &Wuerth, *supra* note 62.

> The significance of *Zivotofsky II* for normalization is less clear.... The Court's functional reasoning in *Zivotofsky II* is more narrowly tailored to recognition and to the facts of this case than the Court's broad dicta in *Curtiss-Wright*. Thus, the Court focuses on the nation's need to speak with "one voice" specifically on the topic of recognition, not with respect to foreign relations generally. The Court uses functional reasoning in non-foreign relations cases, too, so narrowly tailored functional analysis is a move toward normalization. Future litigants and political actors will certainly use the functional analysis from *Zivotofsky* outside the narrow context of recognition—but whether they will be successful is an issue for another day and another case.[65]

As you read, consider how Justice Kennedy employs the president's express constitutional powers (under the Reception and Treaty Clauses and his ability to send ambassadors to foreign nations) in order to reach a more expansive and comprehensive recognition of presidential power.

Zivotofsky v. Kerry

135 S. Ct. 2076 (2015)

[Menachem Zivotofsky was born in Jerusalem in 2002. Shortly thereafter, Zivotofsky's parents applied for a passport for their infant son, requesting that Israel be designated as Menachem's place of birth in accordance with Section 214(d) of the Foreign Relations Authorization Act. This section allows an individual born in Jerusalem or their legal guardian to request Israel to be listed as the place of birth on a passport. The State Department denied the family's request, explaining that in spite of the 2002 law, the United States government has not recognized any country as having sovereignty over the city of Jerusalem since the choice by the Truman administration to accord Jerusalem "special and separate treatment" from the rest of Israel. The Zivotofskys challenged this decision. In *Zivotofsky I*, the Court held that the political question doctrine did not bar judicial review of Zivotofsky's claim. 132 S. Ct. 1421. On remand, the Court of Appeals held that the statute was unconstitutional, because it contradicted an exercise of lawful executive power. In *Zivotosfky II*, after nearly thirteen years of litigation, the Court settled the interbranch dispute with the following opinion.]

Justice Kennedy delivered the opinion of the Court.

A delicate subject lies in the background of this case. That subject is Jerusalem. Questions touching upon the history of the ancient city and its present legal and international status are among the most difficult and complex in international affairs. In our constitutional system these matters are committed to the Legislature and the Executive, not the Judiciary. As a result, in this opinion the Court does no more, and must do no more, than note the existence of international debate and tensions respecting Jerusalem. Those matters are for Congress and the President to discuss and consider as they seek to shape the Nation's foreign policies.

---

65. Ingrid B. Weurth, Zivotofsky ex rel. Zivotofsky v. Kerry, 109 Am. J. Int'l Law 636, 640–641 (2015).

The Court addresses two questions to resolve the interbranch dispute now before it. First, it must determine whether the President has the exclusive power to grant formal recognition to a foreign sovereign. Second, if he has that power, the Court must determine whether Congress can command the President and his Secretary of State to issue a formal statement that contradicts the earlier recognition. The statement in question here is a congressional mandate that allows a United States citizen born in Jerusalem to direct the President and Secretary of State, when issuing his passport, to state that his place of birth is "Israel."

I.A.

Jerusalem's political standing has long been, and remains, one of the most sensitive issues in American foreign policy, and indeed it is one of the most delicate issues in current international affairs. In 1948, President Truman formally recognized Israel in a signed statement of "recognition." That statement did not recognize Israeli sovereignty over Jerusalem. Over the last 60 years, various actors have sought to assert full or partial sovereignty over the city, including Israel, Jordan, and the Palestinians. Yet, in contrast to a consistent policy of formal recognition of Israel, neither President Truman nor any later United States President has issued an official statement or declaration acknowledging any country's sovereignty over Jerusalem. Instead, the Executive Branch has maintained that "'the status of Jerusalem ... should be decided not unilaterally but in consultation with all concerned.'"

The President's position on Jerusalem is reflected in State Department policy regarding passports and consular reports of birth abroad. Understanding that passports will be construed as reflections of American policy, the State Department's Foreign Affairs Manual instructs its employees, in general, to record the place of birth on a passport as the "country [having] present sovereignty over the actual area of birth." Dept. of State, 7 Foreign Affairs Manual (FAM) § 1383.4 (1987). If a citizen objects to the country listed as sovereign by the State Department, he or she may list the city or town of birth rather than the country. The FAM, however, does not allow citizens to list a sovereign that conflicts with Executive Branch policy. Because the United States does not recognize any country as having sovereignty over Jerusalem, the FAM instructs employees to record the place of birth for citizens born there as "Jerusalem."

In 2002, Congress passed the Act at issue here, the Foreign Relations Authorization Act, Fiscal Year 2003, 116 Stat. 1350. Section 214 of the Act is titled "United States Policy with Respect to Jerusalem as the Capital of Israel." The subsection that lies at the heart of this case, § 214(d), addresses passports. That subsection seeks to override the FAM by allowing citizens born in Jerusalem to list their place of birth as "Israel." Titled "Record of Place of Birth as Israel for Passport Purposes," § 214(d) states "[f]or purposes of the registration of birth, certification of nationality, or issuance of a passport of a United States citizen born in the city of Jerusalem, the Secretary shall, upon the request of the citizen or the citizen's legal guardian, record the place of birth as Israel."

When he signed the Act into law, President George W. Bush issued a statement declaring his position that § 214 would, "if construed as mandatory rather than advisory, impermissibly interfere with the President's constitutional authority to formulate the position of the United States, speak for the Nation in international affairs, and determine the terms on which recognition is given to foreign states." The President concluded, "U.S. policy regarding Jerusalem has not changed." *Ibid.*

II

In considering claims of Presidential power this Court refers to Justice Jackson's familiar tripartite framework from *Youngstown Sheet & Tube Co. v. Sawyer*, 343 U.S. 579, 635–638, (1952) (concurring opinion). The framework divides exercises of Presidential power into three categories: First, when "the President acts pursuant to an express or implied authorization of Congress, his authority is at its maximum, for it includes all that he possesses in his own right plus all that Congress can delegate." Second, "in absence of either a congressional grant or denial of authority" there is a "zone of twilight in which he and Congress may have concurrent authority," and where "congressional inertia, indifference or quiescence may" invite the exercise of executive power. Finally, when "the President takes measures incompatible with the expressed or implied will of Congress . . . he can rely only upon his own constitutional powers minus any constitutional powers of Congress over the matter." *Ibid.* To succeed in this third category, the President's asserted power must be both "exclusive" and "conclusive" on the issue.

In this case the Secretary contends that § 214(d) infringes on the President's exclusive recognition power by "requiring the President to contradict his recognition position regarding Jerusalem in official communications with foreign sovereigns." Brief for Respondent 48. In so doing the Secretary acknowledges the President's power is "at its lowest ebb." Because the President's refusal to implement § 214(d) falls into Justice Jackson's third category, his claim must be "scrutinized with caution," and he may rely solely on powers the Constitution grants to him alone.

A

Recognition is a "formal acknowledgement" that a particular "entity possesses the qualifications for statehood" or "that a particular regime is the effective government of a state." Restatement (Third) of Foreign Relations Law of the United States § 203, Comment a, p. 84 (1986). It may also involve the determination of a state's territorial bounds. Recognition is often effected by an express "written or oral declaration." It may also be implied—for example, by concluding a bilateral treaty or by sending or receiving diplomatic agents.

Legal consequences follow formal recognition. Recognized sovereigns may sue in United States courts and may benefit from sovereign immunity when they are sued. The actions of a recognized sovereign committed within its own territory also receive deference in domestic courts under the act of state doctrine. Recognition at international law, furthermore, is a precondition of regular diplomatic relations. Recognition is thus "useful, even necessary," to the existence of a state.

Despite the importance of the recognition power in foreign relations, the Constitution does not use the term "recognition," either in Article II or elsewhere. The Secretary asserts that the President exercises the recognition power based on the Reception Clause, which directs that the President "shall receive Ambassadors and other public Ministers." Art. II, § 3. As Zivotofsky notes, the Reception Clause received little attention at the Constitutional Convention. In fact, during the ratification debates, Alexander Hamilton claimed that the power to receive ambassadors was "more a matter of dignity than of authority," a ministerial duty largely "without consequence."

At the time of the founding, however, prominent international scholars suggested that receiving an ambassador was tantamount to recognizing the sovereignty of the sending state. It is a logical and proper inference, then, that a Clause directing the President alone to receive ambassadors would be understood to acknowledge his power to recognize other nations.

The inference that the President exercises the recognition power is further supported by his additional Article II powers. It is for the President, "by and with the Advice and Consent of the Senate," to "make Treaties, provided two thirds of the Senators present concur." Art. II, § 2, cl. 2. In addition, "he shall nominate, and by and with the Advice and Consent of the Senate, shall appoint Ambassadors" as well as "other public Ministers and Consuls." *Ibid.*

As a matter of constitutional structure, these additional powers give the President control over recognition decisions. At international law, recognition may be effected by different means, but each means is dependent upon Presidential power. In addition to receiving an ambassador, recognition may occur on "the conclusion of a bilateral treaty," or the "formal initiation of diplomatic relations," including the dispatch of an ambassador. The President has the sole power to negotiate treaties, and the Senate may not conclude or ratify a treaty without Presidential action. The President, too, nominates the Nation's ambassadors and dispatches other diplomatic agents. Congress may not send an ambassador without his involvement. Beyond that, the President himself has the power to open diplomatic channels simply by engaging in direct diplomacy with foreign heads of state and their ministers. The Constitution thus assigns the President means to effect recognition on his own initiative. Congress, by contrast, has no constitutional power that would enable it to initiate diplomatic relations with a foreign nation. Because these specific Clauses confer the recognition power on the President, the Court need not consider whether or to what extent the Vesting Clause, which provides that the "executive Power" shall be vested in the President, provides further support for the President's action here. Art. II, § 1, cl. 1.

Recognition is a topic on which the Nation must " 'speak . . . with one voice.' " That voice must be the President's. Between the two political branches, only the Executive has the characteristic of unity at all times. And with unity comes the ability to exercise, to a greater degree, "[d]ecision, activity, secrecy, and dispatch." The Federalist No. 70, p. 424 (A. Hamilton). The President is capable, in ways Congress is not, of engaging in the delicate and often secret diplomatic contacts that may lead to a decision on recognition. He is also better positioned to take the decisive, unequivocal action necessary to recognize other states at international law. These qualities explain why the Framers listed the traditional avenues of recognition—receiving ambassadors, making treaties, and sending ambassadors—as among the President's Article II powers.

It remains true, of course, that many decisions affecting foreign relations—including decisions that may determine the course of our relations with recognized countries—require congressional action. Congress may "regulate Commerce with foreign Nations," "establish an uniform Rule of Naturalization," "define and punish Piracies and Felonies committed on the high Seas, and Offences against the Law of Nations," "declare War," "grant Letters of Marque and Reprisal," and "make Rules for the Government and Regulation of the land and naval Forces." U.S. Const., Art. I, § 8. In addition, the President cannot make a treaty or appoint an ambassador without the approval of the Senate. Art. II, § 2, cl. 2. The President, furthermore, could not build an American Embassy abroad without congressional appropriation of the necessary funds. Art. I, § 8, cl. 1. Under basic separation-of-powers principles, it is for the Congress to enact the laws, including "all Laws which shall be necessary and proper for carrying into Execution" the powers of the Federal Government. § 8, cl. 18. . . .

A clear rule that the formal power to recognize a foreign government subsists in the President therefore serves a necessary purpose in diplomatic relations. All this, of course, underscores that Congress has an important role in other aspects of foreign policy, and the President may be bound by any number of laws Congress enacts. In this way ambition counters ambition, ensuring that the democratic will of the people is observed and respected in foreign affairs as in the domestic realm. See The Federalist No. 51, p. 322 (J. Madison).

B

No single precedent resolves the question whether the President has exclusive recognition authority and, if so, how far that power extends. In part that is because, until today, the political branches have resolved their disputes over questions of recognition. The relevant cases, though providing important instruction, address the division of recognition power between the Federal Government and the States or between the courts and the political branches—not between the President and Congress. As the parties acknowledge, some isolated statements in those cases lend support to the position that Congress has a role in the recognition process. In the end, however, a fair reading of the cases shows that the President's role in the recognition process is both central and exclusive.

The Secretary now urges the Court to define the executive power over foreign relations in even broader terms. He contends that under the Court's precedent the President has "exclusive authority to conduct diplomatic relations," along with "the bulk of foreign-affairs powers." In support of his submission that the President has broad, undefined powers over foreign affairs, the Secretary quotes *United States v. Curtiss-Wright Export Corp.*, which described the President as "the sole organ of the federal government in the field of international relations." This Court declines to acknowledge that unbounded power. A formulation broader than the rule that the President alone determines what nations to formally recognize as legitimate—and that he consequently controls his statements on matters of recognition—presents different issues and is unnecessary to the resolution of this case.

In a world that is ever more compressed and interdependent, it is essential the congressional role in foreign affairs be understood and respected. For it is Congress that makes laws, and in countless ways its laws will and should shape the Nation's course. The Executive is not free from the ordinary controls and checks of Congress merely because foreign affairs are at issue. It is not for the President alone to determine the whole content of the Nation's foreign policy.

That said, judicial precedent and historical practice teach that it is for the President alone to make the specific decision of what foreign power he will recognize as legitimate, both for the Nation as a whole and for the purpose of making his own position clear within the context of recognition in discussions and negotiations with foreign nations. Recognition is an act with immediate and powerful significance for international relations, so the President's position must be clear. Congress cannot require him to contradict his own statement regarding a determination of formal recognition.

III

As the power to recognize foreign states resides in the President alone, the question becomes whether § 214(d) infringes on the Executive's consistent decision to withhold recognition with respect to Jerusalem.

Section 214(d) requires that, in a passport or consular report of birth abroad, "the Secretary shall, upon the request of the citizen or the citizen's legal guardian, record the place of birth as Israel" for a "United States citizen born in the city of Jerusalem." That is, § 214(d) requires the President, through the Secretary, to identify citizens born in Jerusalem who so request as being born in Israel. But according to the President, those citizens were not born in Israel. As a matter of United States policy, neither Israel nor any other country is acknowledged as having sovereignty over Jerusalem. In this way, § 214(d) "directly contradicts" the "carefully calibrated and longstanding Executive branch policy of neutrality toward Jerusalem."

If the power over recognition is to mean anything, it must mean that the President not only makes the initial, formal recognition determination but also that he may maintain that determination in his and his agent's statements. This conclusion is a matter of both common sense and necessity. If Congress could command the President to state a recognition position inconsistent with his own, Congress could override the President's recognition determination. Under international law, recognition may be effected by "written or oral declaration of the recognizing state." 1 Moore § 27, at 73. In addition an act of recognition must "leave no doubt as to the intention to grant it." 1 Oppenheim's International Law § 50, at 169. Thus, if Congress could alter the President's statements on matters of recognition or force him to contradict them, Congress in effect would exercise the recognition power.

If Congress may not pass a law, speaking in its own voice, that effects formal recognition, then it follows that it may not force the President himself to contradict his earlier statement. That congressional command would not only prevent the Nation from speaking with one voice but also prevent the Executive itself from doing so in conducting foreign relations.

Although the statement required by § 214(d) would not itself constitute a formal act of recognition, it is a mandate that the Executive contradict his prior recognition determination in an official document issued by the Secretary of State. See *Urtetiqui v. D'Arcy*, 9 Pet. 692, 699 (1835) (a passport "from its nature and object, is addressed to foreign powers" and "is to be considered . . . in the character of a political document"). As a result, it is unconstitutional. This is all the more clear in light of the longstanding treatment of a passport's place-of-birth section as an official executive statement implicating recognition. The Secretary's position on this point has been consistent: He will not place information in the place-of-birth section of a passport that contradicts the President's recognition policy. If a citizen objects to the country listed as sovereign over his place of birth, then the Secretary will accommodate him by listing the city or town of birth rather than the country. But the Secretary will not list a sovereign that contradicts the President's recognition policy in a passport. Thus, the Secretary will not list "Israel" in a passport as the country containing Jerusalem.

The flaw in § 214(d) is further underscored by the undoubted fact that the purpose of the statute was to infringe on the recognition power—a power the Court now holds is the sole prerogative of the President. The statute is titled "United States Policy with Respect to Jerusalem as the Capital of Israel." The House Conference Report proclaimed that § 214 "contains four provisions related to the recognition of Jerusalem as Israel's capital." And, indeed, observers interpreted § 214 as altering United States policy regarding Jerusalem—which led to protests across the region. From the face of § 214, from the legislative history, and from its reception, it is clear that Congress wanted to express its displeasure with the President's policy by, among other things, commanding the Executive to contradict his own, earlier stated position on Jerusalem. This Congress may not do.

It is true, as Zivotofsky notes, that Congress has substantial authority over passports. The Court does not question the power of Congress to enact passport legislation of wide scope. In *Kent v. Dulles*, 357 U.S. 116 (1958), for example, the Court held that if a person's " 'liberty' " to travel "is to be regulated" through a passport, "it must be pursuant to the law-making functions of the Congress." See *id.*, at 129. Later cases . . . also proceeded on the assumption that Congress must authorize the grounds on which passports may be approved or denied. This is consistent with the extensive lawmaking power the Constitution vests in Congress over the Nation's foreign affairs.

The problem with § 214(d), however, lies in how Congress exercised its authority over passports. It was an improper act for Congress to "aggrandiz[e] its power at the expense of another branch" by requiring the President to contradict an earlier recognition determination in an official document issued by the Executive Branch. To allow Congress to control the President's communication in the context of a formal recognition determination is to allow Congress to exercise that exclusive power itself. As a result, the statute is unconstitutional.

In holding § 214(d) invalid the Court does not question the substantial powers of Congress over foreign affairs in general or passports in particular. This case is confined solely to the exclusive power of the President to control recognition determinations, including formal statements by the Executive Branch acknowledging the legitimacy of a state or government and its territorial bounds. Congress cannot command the President to contradict an earlier recognition determination in the issuance of passports.

The judgment of the Court of Appeals for the District of Columbia Circuit is Affirmed.

JUSTICE BREYER, concurring.

I continue to believe that this case presents a political question inappropriate for judicial resolution. But because precedent precludes resolving this case on political question grounds, I join the Court's opinion.

JUSTICE THOMAS, concurring in the judgment in part and dissenting in part.

Our Constitution allocates the powers of the Federal Government over foreign affairs in two ways. First, it expressly identifies certain foreign affairs powers and vests them in particular branches, either individually or jointly. Second, it vests the residual foreign affairs powers of the Federal Government—i.e., those not specifically enumerated in the Constitution—in the President by way of Article II's Vesting Clause.

Section 214(d) of the Foreign Relations Authorization Act, Fiscal Year 2003, ignores that constitutional allocation of power insofar as it directs the President, contrary to his wishes, to list "Israel" as the place of birth of Jerusalem-born citizens on their passports. The President has long regulated passports under his residual foreign affairs power, and this portion of § 214(d) does not fall within any of Congress' enumerated powers.

By contrast, § 214(d) poses no such problem insofar as it regulates consular reports of birth abroad. Unlike passports, these reports were developed to effectuate the naturalization laws, and they continue to serve the role of identifying persons who need not be naturalized to obtain U.S. citizenship. The regulation of these reports does not fall within the President's foreign affairs powers, but within Congress' enumerated powers under the Naturalization and Necessary and Proper Clauses.

Rather than adhere to the Constitution's division of powers, the Court relies on a distortion of the President's recognition power to hold both of these parts of § 214(d) unconstitutional. Because I cannot join this faulty analysis, I concur only in the portion of the Court's judgment holding § 214(d) unconstitutional as applied to passports. I respectfully dissent from the remainder of the Court's judgment.

[The remainder of Justice Thomas's dissent is omitted.]

CHIEF JUSTICE ROBERTS, with whom JUSTICE ALITO joins, dissenting [omitted].

JUSTICE SCALIA, with whom THE CHIEF JUSTICE and JUSTICE ALITO join, dissenting.

Before this country declared independence, the law of England entrusted the King with the exclusive care of his kingdom's foreign affairs. The royal prerogative included the "sole power of sending ambassadors to foreign states, and receiving them at home," the sole authority to "make treaties, leagues, and alliances with foreign states and princes," "the sole prerogative of making war and peace," and the "sole power of raising and regulating fleets and armies." The People of the United States had other ideas when they organized our Government. They considered a sound structure of balanced powers essential to the preservation of just government, and international relations formed no exception to that principle.

The People therefore adopted a Constitution that divides responsibility for the Nation's foreign concerns between the legislative and executive departments. . . . This case arises out of a dispute between the Executive and Legislative Branches about whether the United States should treat Jerusalem as a part of Israel. The Constitution contemplates that the political branches will make policy about the territorial claims of foreign nations the same way they make policy about other international matters: The President will exercise his powers on the basis of his views, Congress its powers on the basis of its views. That is just what has happened here.

II

The Court frames this case as a debate about recognition. Recognition is a sovereign's official acceptance of a status under international law. A sovereign might recognize a foreign entity as a state, a regime as the other state's government, a place as part of the other state's territory, rebel forces in the other state as a belligerent power, and so on. President Truman recognized Israel as a state in 1948, but Presidents have consistently declined to recognize Jerusalem as a part of Israel's (or any other state's) sovereign territory.

The Court holds that the Constitution makes the President alone responsible for recognition and that § 214(d) invades this exclusive power. I agree that the Constitution empowers the President to extend recognition on behalf of the United States, but I find it a much harder question whether it makes that power exclusive.

Recognition is more than an announcement of a policy. Like the ratification of an international agreement or the termination of a treaty, it is a formal legal act with effects under international law. It signifies acceptance of an international status, and it makes a commitment to continued acceptance of that status and respect for any attendant rights. "Its legal effect is to create an estoppel. By granting recognition, [states] debar themselves from challenging in future whatever they have previously acknowledged. In order to extend recognition, a state must perform an act that unequivocally manifests that intention. That act can consist of an express conferral of recognition, or one of a handful of acts that by international custom imply recognition—chiefly, entering into a bilateral treaty, and sending or receiving an ambassador.

To know all this is to realize at once that § 214(d) has nothing to do with recognition. Section 214(d) does not require the Secretary to make a formal declaration about Israel's sovereignty over Jerusalem. And nobody suggests that international custom infers acceptance of sovereignty from the birthplace designation on a passport or birth report, as it does from bilateral treaties or exchanges of ambassadors. Recognition would preclude the United States (as a matter of international law) from later contesting Israeli sovereignty over Jerusalem. But making a notation in a passport or birth report does not encumber the Republic with any international obligations.

Section 214(d) performs a more prosaic function than extending recognition. Just as foreign countries care about what our Government has to say about their borders, so too American citizens often care about what our Government has to say about their identities. The State Department does not grant or deny recognition in order to accommodate these individuals, but it does make exceptions to its rules about how it records birthplaces. Although normal protocol requires specifying the bearer's country of birth in his passport, the State Department will, if the bearer protests, specify the city of birth instead—so that an Irish nationalist may have his birthplace recorded as "Belfast" rather than "United Kingdom." And although normal protocol requires specifying the country with present sovereignty over the bearer's place of birth, a special exception allows a bearer born before 1948 in what was then Palestine to have his birthplace listed as "Palestine." Section 214(d) requires the State Department to make a further accommodation. Even though the Department normally refuses to specify a country that lacks recognized sovereignty over the bearer's birthplace, it must suspend that policy upon the request of an American citizen born in Jerusalem. Granting a request to specify "Israel" rather than "Jerusalem" does not recognize Israel's sovereignty over Jerusalem, just as granting a request to specify "Belfast" rather than "United Kingdom" does not derecognize the United Kingdom's sovereignty over Northern Ireland.

The best indication that § 214(d) does not concern recognition comes from the State Department's policies concerning Taiwan. According to the Solicitor General, the United States "acknowledges the Chinese position" that Taiwan is a part of China, but "does not take a position" of its own on that issue. Even so, the State Department has for a long time recorded the birthplace of a citizen born in Taiwan as "China." It indeed insisted on doing so until Congress passed a law (on which § 214(d) was modeled) giving citizens the option to have their birthplaces recorded as "Taiwan." The Solicitor General explains that the designation "China" "involves a geographic description, not an assertion that Taiwan is . . . part of sovereign China." Quite so. Section 214(d) likewise calls for nothing beyond a "geographic description"; it does not require the Executive even to assert, never mind formally recognize, that Jerusalem is a part of sovereign Israel. Since birthplace specifications in citizenship documents are matters within Congress's control, Congress may treat Jerusalem as a part of Israel when regulating the recording of birthplaces, even if the President does not do so when extending recognition. Section 214(d), by the way, expressly directs the Secretary to "*record* the place of birth as Israel" "[f]or purposes of the registration of birth, certification of nationality, or issuance of a passport." (Emphasis added.) And the law bears the caption, "*Record* of Place of Birth as Israel for Passport Purposes." (Emphasis added.) Finding recognition in this provision is rather like finding admission to the Union in a provision that treats American Samoa as a State for purposes of a federal highway safety program, 23 U.S.C. § 401.

III

The Court complains that § 214(d) requires the Secretary of State to issue official documents implying that Jerusalem is a part of Israel; that it appears in a section of the statute bearing the title "United States Policy with Respect to Jerusalem as the Capital of Israel"; and that foreign "observers interpreted [it] as altering United States policy regarding Jerusalem." But these features do not show that § 214(d) recognizes Israel's sovereignty over Jerusalem. They show only that the law displays symbolic support for Israel's territorial claim. That symbolism may have tremendous significance as a matter of international diplomacy, but it makes no difference as a matter of constitutional law.

Even if the Constitution gives the President sole power to extend recognition, it does not give him sole power to make all decisions relating to foreign disputes over sovereignty. To the contrary, a fair reading of Article I allows Congress to decide for itself how its laws should handle these controversies. Read naturally, power to "regulate Commerce with foreign Nations," § 8, cl. 3, includes power to regulate imports from Gibraltar as British goods or as Spanish goods. Read naturally, power to "regulate the Value . . . of foreign Coin," § 8, cl. 5, includes power to honor (or not) currency issued by Taiwan. And so on for the other enumerated powers. These are not airy hypotheticals. A trade statute from 1800, for example, provided that "the whole of the island of Hispaniola"—whose status was then in controversy—"shall for purposes of [the] act be considered as a dependency of the French Republic." In 1938, Congress allowed admission of the Vatican City's public records in federal courts, decades before the United States extended formal recognition. The Taiwan Relations Act of 1979 grants Taiwan capacity to sue and be sued, even though the United States does not recognize it as a state. 22 U.S.C. § 3303(b)(7). Section 214(d) continues in the same tradition.

The Constitution likewise does not give the President exclusive power to determine which claims to statehood and territory "are legitimate in the eyes of the United States." Congress may express its own views about these matters by declaring war, restricting trade, denying foreign aid, and much else besides. To take just one example, in 1991, Congress responded to Iraq's invasion of Kuwait by enacting a resolution authorizing use of military force. No doubt the resolution reflected Congress's views about the legitimacy of Iraq's territorial claim. The preamble referred to Iraq's "illegal occupation" and stated that "the international community has demanded . . . that Kuwait's independence and legitimate government be restored." These statements are far more categorical than the caption "United States Policy with Respect to Jerusalem as the Capital of Israel." Does it follow that the authorization of the use of military force invaded the President's exclusive powers? Or that it would have done so had the President recognized Iraqi sovereignty over Kuwait?

In the final analysis, the Constitution may well deny Congress power to recognize—the power to make an international commitment accepting a foreign entity as a state, a regime as its government, a place as a part of its territory, and so on. But whatever else § 214(d) may do, it plainly does not make (or require the President to make) a commitment accepting Israel's sovereignty over Jerusalem.

International disputes about statehood and territory are neither rare nor obscure. Leading foreign debates during the 19th century concerned how the United States should respond to revolutions in Latin America, Texas, Mexico, Hawaii, Cuba. During the 20th century, attitudes toward Communist governments in Russia and China became conspicuous subjects of agitation. Disagreements about Taiwan, Kashmir, and Crimea remain prominent today. A President empowered to decide all questions relating to these matters, immune from laws embodying congressional disagreement with his position, would have uncontrolled mastery of a vast share of the Nation's foreign affairs.

That is not the chief magistrate under which the American People agreed to live when they adopted the national charter. They believed that "[t]he accumulation of all powers, legislative, executive, and judiciary, in the same hands, . . . may justly be pronounced the very definition of tyranny." The Federalist No. 47, p. 301 (Madison). For this reason, they did not entrust either the President or Congress with sole power to adopt uncontradictable policies about any subject—foreign-sovereignty disputes included. They instead gave each political department its own powers, and with that the freedom to contradict the other's policies. Under the Constitution they approved, Congress may require Zivotofsky's passport and birth report to record his birthplace as Israel, even if that requirement clashes with the President's preference for neutrality about the status of Jerusalem.

I dissent.

Notes and Questions

1. Consider the different perspectives of Professors Goldsmith and Wuerth, cited above. Now that you have read the case, how do you assess its significance with respect to the future of executive power? To what extent does the decision of the majority facilitate the extension of presidential power abroad? Or, conversely, to what extent does it fuse presidential power abroad to his or her domestic powers?

2. *Zivotofsky II* sets executive power over that of Congress in at least a narrow area of foreign affairs. Challenging questions involving the relation of executive and Congressional power also arise from inverse circumstances. Consider Section 1036 of the National Defense Authorization Act For Fiscal Year 2016, which states:

> PROHIBITION ON USE OF FUNDS.—No amounts authorized to be appropriated or otherwise made available for the Department of Defense for fiscal year 2016 may be used—(1) to close or abandon United States Naval

> Station, Guantanamo Bay, Cuba; (2) to relinquish control of Guantanamo Bay to the Republic of Cuba; or (3) to implement a material modification to the Treaty Between the United States of America and Cuba signed at Washington, D.C. on May 29, 1934 that constructively closes United States Naval Station, Guantanamo Bay.[66]

The bill passed the Senate 91-to-3 and the House 370 to 58, reflecting overwhelming bicameral and bipartisan support. David M. Herszenhorn, *Bill Making it Harder to Close Guantánamo Is Approved by Senate*, N.Y. Times, November 11, 2015, at A21. Does this Senate bill circumvent the Supreme Court's admonition in *United States v. Lovett*, 328 U.S. 303 (1946), that Congress cannot use its appropriations power to achieve goals otherwise beyond its constitutional authority? Consider the argument of Former White House counsel Gregory Craig, and Cliff Sloan, President Obama's Special Envoy for Guantanamo Closure in the U.S. State Department in 2013 and 2014:

> The determination on where to hold detainees is a tactical judgment at the very core of the president's role as commander in chief, equivalent to decisions on the disposition of troops and the use of equipment. The question here is not whether the president can unilaterally take the nation to war or hold detainees without congressional authorization. The question is whether Congress can tell the president where military detainees must be held.[67]

Or do you agree with Congresman Jim Sensenbrenner (R-Wisconsin) who, in a response, argues that Craig and Sloan mischaracterize the issue? Congressman Sensenbrenner emphasizes that:

> Congress has not required that any individual detainee be held in a specific facility. Rather, it prohibited the use of federal funds to move detainees from Guantanamo to the United States. This is not a de facto mandate that the president maintain the detention facility at Guantanamo Bay .... It is a legitimate exercise of congressional power to prevent the president from housing some of the world's most dangerous terrorists on U.S. soil. This, emphatically, Congress can do.[68]

How does this debate align with the reasoning in *Zivotofsky II*? Does the executive power authorized by that decision justify the president's decision to act in the face of congressional legislation?[69]

---

66. Section 1036 of the National Defense Authorization Act For Fiscal Year 2016, Pub. L. No. 114-92 (2015).

67. Gregory B. Craig & Cliff Sloan, *The President Can Close Guantanamo*, Washington Post, November 8, 2015, at A17.

68. Jim Sensenbrenner, *Congress Can't Be Ignored on Guantanamo*, Washington Post, November 22, 2015, at A29.

69. *See* Dan de Luce, *To Close Guantánamo, Obama Will Have to Test the Limits of Presidential Power*, Foreign Policy, Nov. 12, 2015, http://foreignpolicy.com/2015/11/12/to-close-guantanamo-obama-will-have-to-test-the-limits-of-presidential-power/. *Cf.* Jack Goldsmith, *Why Obama Hasn't Closed Guantanamo Bay—and Probably Never Will*, Time, Jan. 13, 2016, http://time.com/4178779/obama-close-guantanamo-bay/. Regarding the on-going controversy surrounding the

3. Note that the historical context of this case involves several previous junctures at which the distance between Congress and the executive is palpable: first, in the essentially unilateral decision of President Truman to bracket Jerusalem for purposes of registering the birthplace of Americans born there, and second, in President George W. Bush's signing statement at the time he signed the legislation at issue in *Zivotofsky*, indicating his position that there would be no change in U.S. policy with respect to registering place of birth, in spite of Congress's intention otherwise. These circumstances are detailed in Goldsmith (*supra*). As we have seen in his dissent in *Zivotofsky*, Justice Scalia argued for another such elision of intent, in making the case that a passport notation would "not encumber the Republic with any international obligations."[70]

VI. Discussion

In this chapter, we have focused on key issues defining contemporary executive authority that especially illuminate its transnational character beyond the settings of government and governance discussed in Parts I and II: (1) separation of powers in the conduct of international affairs; (2) extraterritorial search and surveillance; (3) extraterritorial killing; (4) detention; and (5) immigration. As such, this chapter introduced interlegality in a further sense, less as a contingency of legal pluralism or the cross-currents of transnational capitalism and national states (as in the previous chapters) than as a function of intragovernmental and partisan political tension over the powers of the federal government—in particular the powers of the president. Readers whose memories do not reach back to the 1980s and 1990s may be surprised to find the extraterritorial powers of the executive already so broadly established at that time—i.e., before "9/11" and the "war on terror." And readers who came of age in the Obama era may be too young to remember when partisan opposition routinely stopped short of obstruction. With the exception of the classic separation of powers case, *Curtiss-Wright*, the cases in this chapter span roughly three decades punctuated midway by the terrorist attacks on the United States in 2001, and the U.S.-led war in the Middle East. It is beyond the scope of this account to analyze what difference the war has made to executive power, beyond noting what is by now the thorough imbrication of war powers with powers of other kinds.

While our discussion has focused on cases (and a small selection at that) more than their historical context and social effects, we note once more that these are legal areas steeped in implications for the status of the individual person—reminding us yet again that legal authority entails diverse effects that sometimes bring the highest levels of government directly to bear on individuals (citizens and non-citizens alike). To provide the constitutional separations of powers background involved in these

proposed Guantanamo closure, see Charles Levinson, *Exclusive: Justice Department opposes new Obama proposal on Guantanamo*, REUTERS, June 21, 2016, http://www.reuters.com/article/us-usa-gitmo-justice-exclusive-idUSKCN0Z719D.

70. Zivotofsky v. Kerry, 135 S. Ct. 2076, 2119 (2015) (J. Scalia, dissent).

areas of executive power, we began and ended with separation of powers cases: opening with *Curtiss-Wright*, which set the standard for proper exercise of executive power, until *Zivotofsky* revised it with what is arguably a significant expansion of executive power.

Readers who are more accustomed to starting the question of transnational law with the distinction between domestic and foreign states, or between public and private actors, or among the three branches of government, may be surprised by our location of these questions at the *end* of this book, rather than at the beginning. But in our analyses of cases and problems involving contestation over these very concepts, we hope to have shown something of both the nature of contemporary transnationalism, and the potential openings for "taming globalization through law reform."[71]

While the nature of this volume does not call for conclusions as such, it may be useful to reprise the main through-lines of the volume, if only to distill our own orientation as readers reach their own conclusions.

Throughout the work, we have found a productive point of departure in the fact that transnational law involves powers of diverse kinds. This accounts for our emphasis on the dynamic interrelations, contradictions and disjunctions across legal domains, and on interlegality as essential to an understanding of transnational law and its effects on domestic law—including the prospects for legal change, and for improving people's lives through law.

Given its myriad legal, political, economic and social locations, transnational law is irreducibly complex. "Globalization" in this context is inevitably clumsy shorthand, but we use the term since it is also a keyword in contemporary debates about transnational law and its relation to other spheres of experience. In recent years, it has also become a potent political keyword, and our discussion has touched on some of those debates.

Throughout, we emphasize the interrelation of domestic and transnational law, and have drawn our law cases primarily from U.S. courts, even as the case studies and discussion overall range more widely. We give primary attention to U.S. law in part because we anticipate that most readers of the book will be students in U.S. classrooms. But, more fundamentally, it is to demonstrate at close range how the connections between transnational and domestic law present compelling problems of jurisprudence and social justice.

We do not assume that U.S. law somehow dominates or otherwise represents or embodies transnational law—or should. Our attention to the U.S. is specific; however, our relational approach to interlegality and our emphasis on the relevance of interdisciplinary analysis potentially travels beyond the U.S. context.

71. Alfred C. Aman, Jr., The Democracy Deficit: Taming Globalization through Law Reform (2004).

Relatedly, and more generally, our analysis treats states as relevant to transnational law in multiple ways, but not as unitary wholes. States themselves are not actors as unified wholes (even when they are parties to an international agreement). We have treated states from the standpoint of their internal diversity, and the complexity of intragovernmental interests. In other words, we have approached states through their specific agencies and effects, in legal, political, economic and social contexts that are not necessarily (and certainly not automatically) effectively coordinated. We have found this specificity analytically productive as we considered the cross-currents that shape the various chapters, and in our thinking about transnational law as open to political and legal challenges, and to change.

Indeed, transnational law is not fixed. Domestic law remains a potent resource for those who seek alternative globalizations and reforms that would reduce income inequality and remove barriers to improved life conditions, or achieve other improvements. Access to law does not guarantee an optimum result (whatever that might be for the parties involved), but still, as the chapters show, law provides more direct and independent fora for certain forms of contestation than multinational corporations, particularly for workers. A further point along these lines is the relevance of unions and collective bargaining to transnational law; several of the case studies show this in various ways (especially in Chapters 3, 5 and 6).

For our purposes, *interlegality* represents a conceptual improvement over more structural accounts of law, e.g., approaches that present transnational law as a layer or level in a nested set of institutions. Our account has emphasized dynamic interlegalities—i.e., situations in place and in time where the tensions or elisions across legal regimes become ground for improvisation as people imagine ways of maximizing opportunities or navigating constraints of specific kinds. Interlegality in our usage refers to the experience of legal pluralism—a complex register of human experience, rather than some abstract space "between" systems, as if everywhere and nowhere.

Finally, our interest in transnational law arises in part from our interest as academics and as citizens in contemporary dilemmas of responsibility as problems of knowledge. Responsibility is thinkable only where alternatives are brought into being as thinkable and achievable. Responsibility and creativity in this sense walk hand in hand, and that has been the spirit behind this interdisciplinary endeavor. We hope that that spirit will encourage readers to find their own answers to the questions presented in this book, and to develop questions of their own.

Index